In Mixed Company

Communicating in Small Groups and Teams

Ninth Edition

J. Dan Rothwell

Cabrillo College

CENGAGE
Learning®

Australia • Brazil • Japan • Korea • Mexico • Singapore • Spain • United Kingdom • United States

CENGAGE
Learning®

In Mixed Company: Communicating in Small Groups and Teams, Ninth Edition
J. Dan Rothwell

Product Director: Monica Eckman

Product Manager: Nicole Morinon

Senior Content Developer:
Kathy Sands-Boehmer

Associate Content Developer:
Karolina Kiwak

Product Assistant: Colin Solan

Media Developer: Jessica Badiner

Marketing Manager: Kristin Davis

Senior Content Project Manager:
Corinna Dibble

Senior Art Director: Linda May

Manufacturing Planner: Doug Bertke

IP Analyst: Ann Hoffman

IP Project Manager: Farah Fard

Production Service and Compositor:
Integra Software Services

Text and Cover Designer: Chris Miller

Cover Image: JOHN VIZCAINO/Reuters/
Landov

For product information and technology assistance,
contact us at **Cengage Learning
Customer & Sales Support, 1-800-354-9706**

For permission to use material from this text or product,
submit all requests online at **www.cengage.com/permissions.**
Further permissions questions can be emailed to
permissionrequest@cengage.com.

Library of Congress Control Number: 2014952830

ISBN: 978-1-285-44460-4

Cengage Learning
20 Channel Center Street
Boston, MA 02210
USA

Cengage Learning is a leading provider of customized learning solutions with office locations around the globe, including Singapore, the United Kingdom, Australia, Mexico, Brazil, and Japan. Locate your local office at **www.cengage.com/global.**

Cengage Learning products are represented in Canada by Nelson Education, Ltd.

To learn more about Cengage Learning Solutions, visit **www.cengage.com.**

Purchase any of our products at your local college store or at our preferred online store **www.cengagebrain.com.**

Printed in the United States of America
Print Number: 02   Print Year: 2016

Brief Contents

In Mixed Company is the number one selling small group communication textbook. Almost 300,000 students at hundreds of colleges and universities have used it. I am profoundly grateful to all who have helped make *In Mixed Company* such a great success. The eight most recent professional reviews of *In Mixed Company* were exceedingly complimentary. I sincerely thank all reviewers for their helpful insights and suggestions.

For this ninth edition, I have preserved the essence of previous versions. The central unifying theme, that cooperation in small groups is usually superior to competition, has been maintained. The communication competence model continues to guide discussions of key small group concepts and processes. The model is one of the communication discipline's unique contributions to understanding and improving human behavior. It is thoroughly integrated throughout the text. Systems theory also remains as a key theoretical component of the text, providing a conceptual framework for analysis and insights. Finally, the unique focus on power in groups remains. As Dacher Keltner (2007) notes, "To be human is to be immersed in power dynamics." Power is a central underlying element in small group conflict, teamwork, decision making, problem solving, normative behavior, roles, and leadership. I strongly believe that it deserves careful analysis, not simply obligatory mention or cursory coverage.

In addition, I continue to place great emphasis on readability. Textbooks are not meant to read like spy thrillers, but neither should they induce a coma by reading like instructions for filling out your income tax forms. Unlike calculus, which I have no idea how to make interesting, group communication, because of its relevance to your lives, should stir your interest. I have made a concerted effort to stimulate, not sedate you. The risk in telling you this, obviously, is that you may respond, "And that's the best you could do?" Alas, yes. Whatever the shortcomings of this work, I was ever mindful of my audience. I have searched in obvious and not-so-obvious places for the precise example, the poignant instance, and the dramatic case to enhance your reading enjoyment. I have employed a more *narrative or storytelling style* than is usual in textbook writing. I try to tell a story, not merely provide seemingly endless laundry lists of do's and don'ts. Chapter 6, for example, lists several perspectives on effective leadership, but I try to connect these perspectives to the story of how each evolved one from the other. This permits you to see the logical progression of theory and research on leadership. When I do provide lists of do's and don'ts, I try to make at least some of them more interesting to read than a cookbook recipe (see, for example, the "thou shalt nots" of leader emergence; steps for dealing with difficult group members, six steps of the Standard Agenda, guidelines for brainstorming, guidelines for effective meetings). The Closer Look boxes, vivid examples, and personal experiences are also narrative in nature, included to illustrate ideas and concepts and trigger reader interest. Research confirms that the narrative style not only adds interest but also increases comprehension and recall of information (Fernald, 1987).

I also have attempted to enliven and personalize the writing style by incorporating colorful language and lively metaphors that bring interesting images to mind, and to depart from standard academic practice by employing the "perpendicular pronoun" I. Occasional use of first-person singular speaks more directly and personably to readers than the more impersonal style of writing commonly used in textbooks (such as "in this author's view"). Although it has been suggested that I employ the "editorial we" instead of the first-person singular, I tend to agree with Mark Twain, who said that "people with tapeworms have the right to use the editorial 'we'," but others should avoid it. I could use the passive voice and avoid the first-person singular, but that makes copyeditors twitch.

Finally, I am a great believer in the potential of humor to gain and maintain the attention of my readers. I love to laugh and it gives me great satisfaction to see my students laugh in class, even if it is at my expense because of some goofy mistake I have made (not uncommon). Humor can often cross generational divides and spark interest in scholarly subjects that can seem distant and abstract until a humorous example, quip, or story enlivens the reading and ignites interest, even understanding. There is humor to be found in every chapter. Some chapters have more humor than others, but I have attempted to infuse some amusement for your entertainment and interest whenever possible.

Significant Substantive Changes

There is often the suspicion, not always without merit, that a new edition of a textbook offers mostly cosmetic changes (a few new photos or an occasional new example or reference). This is emphatically not the case for *In Mixed Company*. **Numerous substantive changes have been made for this edition, some obvious and many not so obvious.** They are:

1. The "Roles and Leadership" chapter has been split into two separate chapters. *Discussion of group roles has about doubled in size.* Chapter material has been significantly reorganized. Types of informal group roles have been vastly expanded from a mere table with cursory descriptions to more comprehensive explanations of task, maintenance, and disruptive roles. A section on how these informal roles are actively transacted has been included. Treatment of the newcomer role has

been moved from Chapter 2 to the final section of the roles chapter. The Closer Look box on hazing has been moved from Chapter 3 to the roles chapter to add insight regarding how groups often treat newcomers and why hazing occurs.

The leadership chapter has been pruned in some places and expanded in others. Charismatic leadership has received more extensive treatment as has the traits perspectives on effective leadership. A new section on psychopathic leaders (horrible bosses) has been added.

2. Careful editing has condensed chapters. Some chapters have been significantly reduced in size, especially Chapter 8 that, ironically, previously included a too lengthy discussion of information overload.

3. Research and theory have been thoroughly updated in every chapter. Almost 200 recent references have been added that incorporate the most current research and theory on small group communication, and more than a hundred older references have been expunged. In all subject areas I have searched energetically for the very latest research and insights. In many cases, the newer research has strengthened support for claims made in previous editions. In other instances, recent research has required important modifications.

4. New, sharper examples have replaced shopworn illustrations. *New business-oriented and workplace examples, surveys, and studies appear throughout the text.* I have also included numerous recent events to illustrate key points and to give the text a contemporary feel.

5. Discussion of technology and its influence on small group communication also has been expanded considerably. In addition to updated coverage of technology in Chapter 12, I have included substantial new material on virtual groups and social media throughout the text.

Continued and Expanded Pedagogical Features

Several acclaimed features of previous editions have been maintained and expanded.

1. Closer Look segments have been updated and carefully edited. See especially "Gender and Communication Competence"; "Gender and Ethnic Bias in Leadership Emergence"; "Dealing with Difficult Group Members"; "Different Criteria Produce Different Outcomes"; and "Murphy's Law."

2. Tables, each called Second Look, act as succinct summaries of complicated or detailed material. These can be useful when studying for exams. Each Second Look has been reviewed and in some cases revised.

3. Self-Assessment Instruments in the eighth edition were well received. Some of these instruments have been slightly revised. Self-assessments remain an important part of engaging student learning.

4. The very popular Video Case Studies segment appearing at the end of every chapter has been expanded and includes many recent examples. Some reviewers have requested a DVD with all of the video case studies provided as a free ancillary. As advantageous as this would obviously be to any instructor using the video case studies suggested, the cost of gaining permission to use copyright-protected videos for such a DVD would be astronomical, inevitably sending the cost of producing this new edition into the stratosphere. In this period of hypersensitivity to textbook pricing, such an option is unfortunately not feasible.

5. A glossary of key terms for quick reference appears at the end of the text. Terms that are boldfaced in each chapter are included in the glossary. Many new terms have been added for this edition. A digital glossary is available. See the instructions below to access additional course materials online.

6. Practice quizzes for each chapter appear on the *In Mixed Company* MindTap. These quizzes help prepare students for graded exams. Students frequently mention to me how helpful these practice quizzes have been to them. See the instructions below to access additional course materials online.

7. An already substantial "visual package"—photos, cartoons, and graphics—has been improved. Considerable resources have been expended to make *In Mixed Company* the most visually interesting small group communication textbook on the market. The new, striking cover and the chapter opening photos of Cirque du Soleil should make this improvement immediately obvious.

8. To engage readers, encourage active learning and the development of critical thinking skills, and help students prepare for exams, several photo and cartoon interactive captions offer quiz questions.

9. MindTap Speech, available for the first time with *In Mixed Company*, is a fully online, highly personalized learning experience that enhances learner engagement and improves outcomes while reducing instructor workload. By combining readings, multimedia, activities, and assessments into a singular Learning Path, MindTap guides students through their course with ease and engagement. Instructors personalize the Learning Path by customizing Cengage Learning resources and adding their own content via apps that integrate into the MindTap framework seamlessly with any Learning Management System.

10. PowerPoint slides have been prepared for classroom presentation of material. The new PowerPoint package has been vastly improved!

11. The comprehensive *Instructor's Resource Manual* has been revised. The test bank of exam questions for each chapter has been expanded with more than one version of each question (single answer or multiple answers) available. Both the extensive activities and the test bank included in the manual have been extremely well received.

12. A video entitled, "Working Together," has been shot in documentary style, which illustrates several key classroom activities (e.g., "Building Blocks" and "Power Carnival"). This video can serve either as a substitute for having students do the activities or as a visual guide on how to conduct these very successful innovative exercises in class. The video is available as an ancillary to the text. No longer available from the publisher, interested parties may contact the author and request a DVD copy.

To access additional course materials online, please visit www.cengagebrain.com. At the CengageBrain.com home page, search for the ISBN of your title (from the back cover of your book) using the search box at the top of the page. This will take you to the product page where these resources can be found.

All *In Mixed Company*'s companion resources are available to qualified adopters, and ordering options for student supplements are flexible. Instructors, please consult your local Cengage Learning sales representative for more information, to evaluate examination copies of any of the student or instructor resources, or to request product demonstrations.

Text Organization

Although there is no ideal organizational pattern, my schema for the sequence of chapters is quite simple. A theoretical foundation is discussed first (Chapters 1 and 2), followed by how groups are formed and developed (Chapter 3). Then a discussion of how to establish the proper climate for the group to work effectively is presented (Chapter 4). This is followed by an explanation and analysis of what roles group members are likely to play (Chapter 5 and 6). Then, how to build teams and instill effective teamwork in groups is addressed (Chapter 7). This is followed by a discussion of decision making/problem solving—the primary work to be performed by most groups–with special focus on critical thinking (Chapters 8 and 9). The close connection between power and conflict is then explored (Chapters 10 and 11). Finally, virtual groups and technology are addressed (Chapter 12). I can see other ways of organizing this same material, but the order I have chosen works well for me, students seem satisfied with the sequence of topics, and reviewers have praised the organization.

Acknowledgments

My sincere thanks are extended to all those who reviewed this edition of *In Mixed Company*. They are Derek Bolen, Angelo State University; Lori Britt, James Madison University; Alexis Davidson, Sacramento State University; Sandy Hanson, University of North Carolina, Charlotte; Cheryl Hebert, Estrella Mountain Community College; Rozanne Leppington, James Madison University; Paul Mabrey, James Madison University; Jan McKissick, Butte-Glenn Community College; Robert Sidelinger, Oakland University; Karen Swett, California State University, Northridge; and Megan Tucker, George Mason University. I also wish to extend a sincere thanks to all those who reviewed previous editions of *In Mixed Company*, now too numerous to include their names here. My considerable gratitude is extended to the Product Manager, Nicole Morinon. I especially want to thank the Content Developer, Kathy Sands-Boehmer, whose stewardship of this project was stellar from start to finish. To the entire Cengage Learning team, I express my deep appreciation for a job well done. It is a pleasure to work with such capable and pleasant professionals.

I also express my heartfelt gratitude to my colleagues in the communication studies department at Cabrillo College. You are a continuing source of inspiration for me, and you demonstrate daily that cooperation and teamwork can be practical realities, not merely wishful thinking. Finally, to my amazing wife, Marcy, a special thanks for being so understanding and loving when I spent hundreds of hours isolated in my home office working on three textbooks. I remained sane in no small part because of you. The fact that you are such an accomplished and respected professional in your own right is for me a source of great pride and admiration. You have many extraordinary gifts and talents, but I love you just for being the person that you are.

About the Author

J. Dan Rothwell is chair of the Communication Studies Department at Cabrillo College. He has a B.A. in American History from the University of Portland (Oregon), an M.A. in Rhetoric and Public Address, and a Ph.D. in Communication Theory and Social Influence. His M.A. and Ph.D. are both from the University of Oregon. He is the author of four other books: *In the Company of Others: An Introduction to Communication, Telling It Like It Isn't: Language Misuse and Malpractice, Interpersonal Communication: Influences and Alternatives* (with James Costigan), and *Practically Speaking.*

During his extensive teaching career, Dr. Rothwell has received almost two dozen teaching awards, including the *2010 Ernest L. Boyer International Award for Excellence in Teaching, Learning, and Technology* conferred by the Center for the Advancement of Teaching and Learning, Florida State College, and the National Council of Instructional Administrators; the *2010 Cabrillo College "Innovative Teacher of the Year"* award; the 2011 National Communication Association *"Community College Educator of the Year"* award; a 2012 official resolution by the California State Senate acknowledging Dr. Rothwell's excellence in teaching, and the 2014 *"Master Teacher"* award from the Western States Communication Association.

Professor Rothwell encourages feedback and correspondence from both students and instructors regarding *In Mixed Company.* Anyone so inclined may communicate with him by email at darothwe@cabrillo.edu. Dr. Rothwell may also be reached by phone at 1-831-479-6511.

To my family: Marcy, Hilary, Geoff, Barrett, and Clare

1

Communication Competence in Groups

A. Myths about Communication
1. Myth 1: Communication Is a Cure-All
2. Myth 2: Communication Can Break Down
3. Myth 3: Effective Communication Is Merely Skill Building
4. Myth 4: Effective Communication Is Just Common Sense

B. Communication Defined
1. Communication as Transactional: The Four-Legged Perspective
2. Communication as a Process: The Continuous Flow
3. Communication as Sharing Meaning: Making Sense
   a. *Verbal Communication: Telling It Like It Isn't*
   b. *Nonverbal Communication: Wordless Meaning*
   c. *Verbal and Nonverbal Interconnectedness: Joined at the Hip*
   d. *Context: The Communication Environment*

C. Communication Competence
1. Effectiveness: Achieving Goals
   a. *A Matter of Degree: From Deficiency to Proficiency*
   b. *We (Not Me) Oriented: Primacy of Groups*
Focus on Culture: Individualism versus Collectivism: A Basic Cultural Difference
2. Appropriateness: Following the Rules

D. Achieving Communication Competence
1. Knowledge: Learning the Rules
2. Skills: Showing, Not Just Knowing
3. Sensitivity: Receptive Accuracy
4. Commitment: A Passion for Excellence
5. Ethics: The Right and Wrong of Communication
Focus on Gender: Gender and Communication Competence

E. Definition of a Group
1. Groups: More than People Standing at a Bus Stop
2. Interpersonal Communication and Public Speaking: Ungroups

If you want to find out what people think about groups, ask them. I have. Periodically, I pass out a questionnaire in some of my small group communication classes. The results are quite revealing. Many students seem to view working in groups with the same fondness they have for wisdom tooth removal. Comments include: "If God had ordered a committee to create the world, it would still be discussing proposals." "Working in groups is like eating tofu. I'm told it's good for me, but it makes me gag." "I've had the swine flu and I've had to work in groups. I prefer the flu." "I hate groups. I hate group assignments. I hate teachers who require group assignments. Take the hint." One study found that 58% of students surveyed responded that they did not like group work, and 83% of the same sample, if given a choice, did not prefer to work in groups for a variety of reasons (Gurrie, 2013). Additional surveys of students reveal similar negative views on working in groups (Karau & Elsaid, 2009; Myers & Goodboy, 2005). Sorensen (1981) coined the term **grouphate** to describe how troublesome the group experience is for many people.

There are several reasons for the prevalence of grouphate. First, individuals often believe they have contributed far more to group endeavors than other group members. A whopping 97% of students surveyed by Gurrie (2013) responded that they have experienced being "stuck with all of the work" when doing group tasks. This sole-contributor belief produces a low opinion of groups (Caruso et al., 2006; Epley et al., 2006). Second, there are those group members, called *social loafers*, who underperform (Hoigaard et al., 2006). Their lackluster effort can become contagious because

MindTap

Start with a quick warm-up activity.

other group members want to avoid being taken advantage of, so they reduce their own effort, thereby contributing to group ineffectiveness and a dislike of group work (Hoigaard & Ommundsen, 2007). Third, group work can be time-consuming and unproductive. Executives spend approximately a third of their time trapped in group meetings, and they consider about half of these meetings to be a brain-deadening waste of time (Lippincott, 1999; Schell, 2010). Even more intrusive is the number of separate meetings individuals must attend daily. Employees feel fatigued and overworked when meetings are frequent, and this can put everyone in a surly frame of mind (Kauffeld & Lehmann-Willenbrock, 2012; Luong & Rogelberg, 2005).

Despite these negative views of groups, almost everyone can point to positive group experiences, including some that are profoundly rewarding (Rains & Young, 2009). The rewards include a feeling of belonging and affection gained from **primary groups** (family and friends) and **social networks** (Facebook, LinkedIn, and Twitter); and social support in difficult times acquired from self-help and **support groups** (Alcoholics Anonymous, cancer survivors groups). Also, you gain satisfaction from solving challenging problems by working in **project groups** (task forces, self-managing work teams), you enhance your knowledge from participating in **learning groups** (class study groups, college seminar groups, Bible study groups, mock trial teams), you experience thrills and entertainment from participating in **activities groups** (chess club, sports teams), and you gain a sense of community from joining **neighborhood groups** (homeowners associations). Finally, you can acquire an identity and achieve pleasure from helping others through **social and service groups** (fraternities, sororities, Rotary, Lions, and Kiwanis clubs), and you may find a creative outlet in **music and artistic groups** (bands, choirs, quilting circles). Of course, a single group may provide many of these benefits.

The most successful groups are composed of members who love working in groups and who experience the rewards. The least successful groups are composed of members who dislike working in groups and who see primarily the disadvantages (Karau & Elsaid, 2009). Participating in successful groups—those that achieve desirable goals and reap valued rewards—improves one's attitude about groups (Isaksen, 1988). Because communication plays such a central role in achieving this group success and producing rewarding experiences, **competent communication is a principal means of counteracting grouphate** (Sorensen, 1981). For example, negative attitudes about group meetings are neutralized when meetings are conducted competently (Rogelberg et al., 2006). Those individuals with the most instruction in competent group communication have the most positive attitude about working in groups. Unfortunately, most people do not receive the requisite communication training to be effective in groups, so grouphate flourishes.

Whatever the degree of your satisfaction or dissatisfaction with groups, there is no escaping them, unless you plan to live your life alone in a cave as an out-of-touch survivalist. Reliance on groups will increase, not diminish, in the future. The American

Association for the Advancement of Science, the National Council of Teachers of English, the National Council of Teachers of Mathematics, and the National Communication Association all recommend frequent group activity in the college classroom. Four-fifths of both Fortune 1000 companies and manufacturing organizations use self-managing work teams (MacDonald, 2014). This is a worldwide phenomenon (Wright & Drewery, 2006). Advances in computers and electronic technology have boosted the reliance on **virtual teams**—groups whose members are connected by electronic technology. One large study reported that 80% of employees participate in virtual teams (Solomon, 2010). The same study concluded that "virtual teams are an ever-growing component of global business" (Solomon, 2010; see also "Managing Virtual Teams," 2009). The "virtual classroom" is also an increasingly popular distance learning option at colleges and universities around the world. In the United States, more than 6.7 million students, a record number, enrolled in online degree programs and courses by the start of 2013 (Sheehy, 2013). Most of these courses require online group discussions and activities, and team projects.

Maximizing the benefits of our unavoidable group experiences seems like a worthy goal. **The central purpose of this textbook, then, is to teach you how to be a competent communicator in small groups and teams.** This purpose presupposes, of course, that there is much for you to learn. Because we all have participated in many groups, it may be tempting to conclude that these experiences leave relatively little for you to learn. Experience, however, isn't always an effective teacher. Sometimes experience teaches us bad habits and misinformation (note the myths discussed in the next section). I will not presume to tell you what you know and don't know about small group communication. That is for you to assess, perhaps with the help of your instructor.

When making this initial self-assessment, however, please consider this: **Most Americans have a common tendency to overestimate their communication proficiency in groups.** A long-term study of 600 teams and 6,000 team members in a wide variety of organizations found that assessments of leaders by team members were a whopping *50% lower* than the leaders' self-assessments (LaFasto & Larson, 2001). These same team members also noted the serious communication deficiencies of teams as a whole. Ironically, it is the poorest communicators who inflate their self-assessments the most (Dunning, 2003).

No one is a perfect communicator, so everyone has room to improve his or her communication skills in groups. **The primary purpose of this chapter is to establish the theoretical groundwork for a communication competence approach to small groups and teams.** There are four chapter objectives:

1. To correct some common misconceptions regarding the human communication process,

2. To explain what communication is and isn't,

3. To identify broadly what constitutes competent communication,

4. To discuss general ways to achieve communication competence.

Myths about Communication

Before tackling the question "What is communication?" and then, more specifically, "What is competent communication?" let's sweep out some of the musty misconceptions many people have stored in their intellectual attics regarding the communication process. As American humorist Will Rogers reputedly remarked, "It isn't what we don't know that gives us trouble, it's what we know that ain't so" (Fitzhenry, 1993, p. 243). Foolishness springs from holding firmly to indefensible myths. Consider four of them.

▶ Myth 1: Communication Is a Cure-all

Communication is not the magical answer to all your woes. Sometimes more communication aggravates differences between people and exposes qualities in others you may find unappealing. Active listening may reveal truths that make it impossible for you to remain in a group. Sometimes groups dismantle, not because the communication is poor, but because members have personalities or values that severely clash or because they have contradictory visions for the group. Also, perhaps you'd rather be slow-roasted over a bed of hot coals than address the tedious, trivial task your team must tackle. Pitch-perfect communication won't likely improve the task or your motivation.

Communication is a tool that, in the possession of someone knowledgeable and skillful, can be used to help solve most problems that arise in groups. **Communication, however, is not an end in itself but merely a means to an end.** You will not solve every conceivable problem in groups by learning to communicate more effectively, because not all group problems are communication based.

▶ Myth 2: Communication Can Break Down

Communication does not break down. Machines break down; they quit, and if they belong to me they do so with amazing regularity. Human beings continue to communicate even when they may wish not to do so. Behaviors such as not showing up for a group meeting, remaining silent during group discussions, or walking out in the middle of a group discussion without saying a word don't stop communication. Group members infer messages from these nonverbal acts—perhaps incorrect messages, but potentially important ones nonetheless.

The view that communication can break down comes partly from the recognition that we do not always achieve our goals through communication; the group may disband in failure. But failure to achieve group goals may occur even when communication between the parties in conflict is exemplary. So where's the breakdown?

▶ Myth 3: Effective Communication Is Merely Skill Building

The skills orientation to communication assumes that if you learn a few key communication skills, you will become a much better communicator. **Without understanding the complexities of the communication process, no amount of skills training will be meaningful, and it may be harmful.** Merely teaching the skill of assertiveness to a battered woman, for example, without addressing the volatile and often unpredictable circumstances of abusive relationships in families, could prove fatal for the abused woman and her children (O'Leary et al., 1985). Assertiveness with your boss or team leader may get you fired or demoted to a position equivalent to cleaning up after parading elephants. One skill doesn't fit all circumstances.

Teaching communication skills without knowledge, without a well-researched theoretical map guiding our behavior, is like constructing a house without a carefully developed set of blueprints. The blueprint offered later in this chapter to help you succeed in groups is the communication competence model.

▶ Myth 4: Effective Communication Is Just Common Sense

Consider **hindsight bias**—the "I-knew-it-already" tendency (Roese & Vohs, 2012). We tend to overestimate our prior knowledge once we have been told the correct answers. Anything can seem like mere common sense when you've been given the correct answers, or as psychologist David Myers (2002) observes, "How easy it is to seem wise when drawing the bull's-eye after the arrow has struck" (p. 89). Everybody knows that opposites attract, right? When told this by Myers, most students find this conclusion unsurprising. But wait! When college students are told the *opposite* ("Birds of a feather flock together"), most also find this result unsurprising and merely common sense.

The hindsight bias may influence us to view competent communication as mere common sense once we have received communication training. If, however, it is just common sense, why does miscommunication occur so often? For example, most teams in organizations fail to achieve their goals (Ellis et al., 2005), and between 80% and 90% of teams have significant difficulty performing well (Buzaglo & Wheelan, 1999; see also Coutu, 2009). A principal reason most teams struggle is lack of communication training in how to make teams work effectively (Ellis et al., 2005).

The simple way to test whether competent communication in groups is merely common sense and you knew it all along is to pose questions before training is received. I often quiz my students at the beginning of a term on general knowledge of group communication (see Box 1.1). I do not ask technical questions or definitions of concepts (making this the least challenging test of the term). Typical questions include: True or False? "Competition motivates higher achievement and performance in groups

BOX 1.1 HINDSIGHT TEST

True-False

Write T or F.

1. _____ Groups should never close off communication, because remaining open to others is a key principle of competent communication.

2. _____ Compromising should be the ultimate and most desired goal when we try to resolve difficult conflicts in groups.

3. _____ Venting your anger, not holding it in, is a constructive and productive way to manage your anger because it allows you to "blow off steam" before it builds to an explosive point.

4. _____ Reward systems that stress individual achievement, such as merit pay plans where the highest-performing group members receive bonuses or pay increases, work well to boost motivation and performance of the vast majority of group members.

5. _____ Competition builds character and teaches most group members how to accept defeat gracefully.

6. _____ If you are highly intelligent, have excellent speaking skills, and are physically attractive, you are highly likely to be an effective group leader.

7. _____ A group can never have too much information when trying to make high-quality decisions on complex problems.

8. _____ The greater the harmony within a group, the better will be the decisions made by the group.

9. _____ Achieving a consensus (unanimity) is always possible in groups if members try hard enough and are skillful in their communication.

10. _____ Some group members can be completely powerless.

11. _____ In general, leaders are born with certain leadership traits. Discovering which member of a group possesses these traits is the best way to determine who will likely be the most effective member to be the group leader.

12. _____ As the size of a group increases, this is almost always constructive because the group's resources increase.

13. _____ To conduct an effective group meeting in an orderly fashion, parliamentary procedure (a detailed, specific set of rules) should be followed in groups large and small.

14. _____ Intergroup (between groups) competition often increases intragroup (within each group) cohesiveness (bonding among members).

15. _____ Groups need to keep conflict at infrequent levels or even nonexistent if possible to be truly effective.

Answers are given at the end of the chapter.

for most people" and "There is a strong relationship between intelligence and effective group leadership." Consistently, students do very poorly on this quiz (most flunk). Such results are not surprising or cause for ridicule. I would be foolish to expect my students to do well on this exam before they've taken the class.

Learning requires a degree of humility, a willingness to recognize and address our shortcomings. To paraphrase Alfred Korzybski, no one knows everything about anything. Everyone has more to learn. You are invited to approach this text, not with an attitude of contentment with your knowledge and skills (whatever their level), but with a strong desire to learn more and to improve your communication in groups. This improvement comes not just from knowing the right answers on tests of your knowledge of group communication, but also from demonstrating an ability to put this knowledge into skillful practice in a wide variety of challenging group situations.

Communication Defined

Thus far, I have indicated what communication is not, but not what it is. What communication is can be ascertained clearly by first considering several fundamental principles.

Focus Questions

1. How are the content and the relationship dimensions of messages different from each other?

2. "Communication is a process." What does this mean?

▶ Communication as Transactional: The Four-Legged Perspective

Wendall Johnson once defined human communication as a process with four legs. Merely sending a message does not constitute communication; there also has to be a receiver. But communication is more than a mere transmission of information from sender to receiver and back again, like Ping-Pong balls batted to and fro. Communication is a **transaction**. This means essentially two things. First, **each person communicating is both a sender and a receiver simultaneously, not merely a sender or a receiver.** As you speak, you receive *feedback* (responses), mostly nonverbal, from listeners; this, in turn, influences the messages that you continue to send. Skillful communicators read feedback accurately and adjust their ensuing message appropriately.

Second, **communication as a transaction also means that all parties influence each other.** You don't communicate in quite the same manner with your parents as you do with a group of close friends. Your team leader may have his Donald Trump act in high gear, exhibiting an imperious, scowling demeanor that is intimidating. If so, your communication is probably more measured and stiff than it would be with a different leader who manifests a more relaxed, less fearsome style.

You can see this mutual-influence process clearly by examining the two dimensions of a message—content and relationship (Watzlawick et al., 1967). The **content dimension** refers to the information transmitted. The **relationship dimension** refers to how messages define or redefine the relationship among group members.

Consider the following transactional dialogue:

Anne: We should meet to prepare our group presentation.

Benny: I can't meet until Wednesday night after 6:30. I work.

Charise: Wednesday, say about 7:00, works fine for me. How about the rest of you?

David: No can do! I'm busy.

Eduardo: Well, get unbusy because our project is due in a week and we're way behind schedule.

David: Hey, Satan's spawn, come up with another time. Wednesday night doesn't work for me.

Benny: Come on, everybody, let's chill. No need to get ugly.

Anne: Exactly how busy are you on Wednesday night, David? Can't you change your plans?

David: I'm busy! Let's leave it at that.

Eduardo: Well, because you're causing the problem, why don't you come up with a time that works with your "busy" schedule?

Charise: How about next Monday evening?

Anne: Now I've got a schedule conflict.

The content of this group transaction is the need to schedule a group meeting and the schedule conflicts that exist. The relationship dimension, however, is far more complex. Group members are not merely identifying scheduling difficulties; they're maneuvering for power positions in the group. Who gets to tell whom what to do is a subtext (the meaning is derived not from a literal interpretation of the words, but from how the words are used). How messages are spoken (sarcastically or as a request) influences group members' responses. Whether group members are being cooperative or competitive with each other is a concern affecting the discussion.

When you are in a group, every utterance, choice, and action continually defines and redefines who you are in relation to other group members and who they are in relation to you. This is ongoing and unavoidable. Individuals affect the group and the group influences the individual. Communication in groups is a continuous series of transactions.

▶ Communication as a Process: The Continuous Flow

Identifying communication as a process recognizes that nothing stands still, or as the bumper sticker proclaims, "Change is inevitable—except from a vending machine." Communication reveals the dynamic nature of relationships and events.

Communication is a process because changes in events and relationships are part of a continuous flow. You can't understand the ocean by freezing a single wave on film. The ocean is understood only in its dynamism—its tides, currents, waves in motion, plant and animal life interacting symbiotically, and so forth. Similarly, communication makes sense not by isolating a word, sentence, gesture, facial expression, or exclamation, but by looking at currents of thought and feelings expressed verbally and nonverbally as a whole.

As a student, for instance, you affect the quality of instruction by your attitude and degree of interest in the subject matter. Great lectures may fall flat with students who don't care or have an antagonistic relationship with the instructor. Conversely, mediocre presentations by instructors can be made more dynamic by the enthusiastic participation of students. Students may be bored one minute and attentive the next. Relationships between teachers and students may change in the short span of a single class period or in the flash of an ill-chosen phrase, especially when controversial material is presented.

We cannot freeze relationships in time. Every conversation is a point of departure for an ensuing conversation. Every communication experience is the result of the accumulation of experiences preceding the present one. Each new experience affects future transactions. Human communication is a process.

▶ Communication as Sharing Meaning: Making Sense

Our world becomes meaningful through communication with others. You do not establish meaning in social isolation. Sharing ideas, feelings, ruminations, and experiences with others is part of the process of constructing meaning, of determining connections and patterns in our minds, of making sense of our world.

Verbal Communication: Telling It Like It Isn't We share meaning verbally with language. **Language** is a structured system of symbols for sharing meaning. **Symbols** are representations of *referents*—whatever the symbol refers to. Because symbols represent referents but are not the objects, ideas, events, or relationships represented, symbols have no meaning apart from us. The story of a psychiatrist giving a Rorschach inkblot test to a client demonstrates this point. When asked to identify the meaning of each inkblot, the client responds to the first, "a couple making love," to the second, "a nude woman silhouetted behind a shower curtain," and to the third, "a couple walking naked hand in hand." The psychiatrist pauses, then remarks, "Mr. Smith, you seem obsessed with sex." Mr. Smith indignantly retorts, "What do you mean? You're the one showing me the dirty pictures." Meaning is in the mind of the beholder. There is no inherent meaning in any inkblot any more than there is inherent meaning in any word. Words are symbols, so meaning is not contained in words. We aren't "telling it like it is" (identifying objective reality); we're telling others with words what our subjective view of the world is. Meaning is derived from the associations or connections each of us makes when we interpret these words.

Comedian Steven Wright asks, "Why is it that when you transport something by car it's called a shipment but when you transport something by ship it's called cargo?" and "Why are they called apartments when they are all stuck together?" Similarly, linguist Richard Lederer (1990) asks why our feet can smell and our noses can run. The simple answer is that the **meaning and usage of words depend on common agreement.** As a speech community, English speakers tacitly agree to certain meanings and appropriate usages for words.

This common agreement, however, doesn't always avoid misunderstandings because words can be ambiguous; they can have double or multiple common meanings. A *booty call* could be an invitation to a treasure hunt or a search for something quite different. Actual newspaper headlines reported by the *Columbia Journalism Review* illustrate this ambiguity: "Prostitutes Appeal to Pope," "Schools Can Expect More Students Than Thought," and "Kids Make Nutritious Snacks." A study of "problematic communication" among crew members and in pilot–air traffic controller interactions concludes that "it is almost certain that communication has played a central role in a significant proportion of aviation accidents" (Howard, 2008, p. 371). "Multiple meanings of words and phrases" was listed as one of the principal problems.

Verbal misunderstandings are further complicated by culture. Electrolux, a Scandinavian vacuum cleaner manufacturer, once used the sales slogan in the United States, "Nothing sucks like an Electrolux." The slogan was quickly pulled once the misunderstanding was revealed. In preparation for the 2008 Summer Olympics in Beijing, China, a retired army colonel named David Tool, who resided in the capital city, was hired to correct notoriously poor translations featured on English signs. "Beijing Anus Hospital" was changed to "Beijing Proctology Hospital," and "Deformed Man Toilet" thankfully was changed to "Disabled Person Toilet" (Boudreau, 2007).

The increasing globalization of business makes the choice of language to communicate within and among multicultural groups and organizations an important consideration. "Those who share a mother tongue have a linguistic bond that differs from those who speak the same language as a second language" (Victor, 2007, p. 3). If English is chosen as the preferred language of business, this can create an in-group/out-group dynamic between those who speak it easily and those who do not. The choice of language to conduct business can directly affect teamwork and long-term business relationships for good or ill (Chen et al., 2006; Swift & Huang, 2004). When a group speaks a language not well understood by all its members, as can occur in our increasingly multicultural workplaces, those left out of the conversation because of difficulties fully understanding the language spoken may feel socially ostracized and angry. This *linguistic divide* can reduce group productivity (Dotan-Eliaz et al., 2009).

The emergence of global virtual teams has also created an international linguistic challenge. Increasingly, virtual teams (especially in the realm of international business) are composed of members from various cultures, many of whom speak English as a second language (Solomon, 2010). English is the dominant language of the Internet ("Internet World Users by Language," 2014). Inevitably, the nuances and complexities of mastering a language such as English lead to problems of interpretation and even translation, especially for global virtual teams (Rad & Levin, 2003). A study of virtual teams showed that 64% of respondents found language difficulties challenging (Solomon, 2010). Consider, for example, whether the email from your team leader saying that the team project "is fine" should be interpreted as damning (with faint praise) or as giving a genuine thumbs-up for a job well done. In addition, "maybe" to an American means possibly yes, but to a Japanese, "maybe" means a polite no (Kameda, 2003).

When you assume that everyone in your group has the same meaning for a word, it is called **bypassing**. You counteract bypassing by clearly defining key words that may cause misunderstandings. Nevertheless, some misunderstandings will occur because language can be complex and ambiguous even with the best effort to avoid bypassing.

Nonverbal Communication: Wordless Meaning We share meaning nonverbally as well as verbally. **Nonverbal communication** is sharing meaning with others without using words. Our facial expressions, eye contact, personal appearance, tone of voice, gestures, posture, touch, and use of space and time all have the potential to communicate messages to group members (Manusov & Patterson, 2006). When we compete with group members, for example, we tend to sit across from each other or increase distance between each other, but when we cooperate, we tend to sit side by side or corner to corner at a table (Forsyth, 1990). Cooperating group members tend to mirror (copy) posture, whereas competing members tend to exhibit the opposite posture pattern (Ketrow, 1999). Seating patterns and posture can signal whether group members are focused on competing or cooperating. Business meetings in U.S. culture are expected to begin on time. Even small delays of 5 to 10 minutes can be offensive and irritating, but most Latin American, southern European, African, and Middle Eastern cultures are not nearly as time sensitive. Delays of 15 minutes or even as long as a day are viewed as acceptable and inoffensive (Martin & Nakayama, 2008; Trompenaars, 1994).

Nonverbal communication, like verbal communication, is often ambiguous. When group members look down for several minutes while you are speaking, does it mean they are bored, uncomfortable with your message, not listening, carefully

Language can be ambiguous, creating confusion, even amusement.

considering your message, or devising a plan to exit the meeting early? When a group member frowns, is he or she showing confusion, taking offense at something said, or contemplating something unrelated to the discussion? Jury consultant Howard Varinsky notes that attempting to decipher a jury's verdict by observing whether jurors look at or avoid eye contact with the defendant before the pronouncement of guilt or innocence is silly. "Who they look at when they come into the courtroom—you can interpret looks 50 different ways." Rich Matthews, a jury consultant with Decision Analysis in San Francisco, also states that it is "practically impossible and it's just dangerous to interpret facial expressions and gestures and reactions" during a trial (quoted in Sulek, 2004a, p. 9A; see also "Jurors' Body Language," 2013).

Even though nonverbal communication can be ambiguous and difficult to read accurately, it can nevertheless have a big impact on our impressions of others (Giles & LePoire, 2006). In 2004, Scott Peterson was found guilty of murdering his pregnant wife and unborn child. Jurors revealed after the trial that they chose the death penalty as his punishment partly because, as juror Richelle Nice put it, "For me, a big part of it was at the end—the verdict—no emotion. No anything. That spoke a thousand words—loud and clear. Today—the giggle at the table. Loud and clear." Jury foreman Steve Cardosi echoed this reaction: "He lost his wife and his child and it didn't seem to faze him" (quoted in Sulek, 2004b, p. 16A). Similarly, one study of jurors' reactions to nonverbal communication by judges during mock trials showed particular sensitivity and a negative reaction to a judge's perceived lack of involvement (e.g., pen tapping, paper shuffling) and apparent bias (e.g., scornful facial expressions) (Burnett & Badzinski, 2005).

This cartoon illustrates (more than one answer may be correct):

1. Nonverbal communication is less ambiguous than verbal communication.
2. Nonverbal communication can be highly ambiguous.
3. A single nonverbal expression, such as a wink, has only a single meaning.
4. A single nonverbal expression may have multiple meanings.

Answers are given at the end of the chapter.

NICK UT/AFP/Getty Images

Is Robert Noel, who was on trial for involuntary manslaughter in a famous dog mauling case, communicating "nothing" to you, or do you form an impression from his facial expression?

Verbal and Nonverbal Interconnectedness: Joined at the Hip Although we commonly discuss them as though they were completely separate, verbal and nonverbal communication are interconnected. Nonverbal cues that accompany language can be as important as the words spoken, or more so. For example, an interesting verbal message can be made boring by a glacially slow speaking pattern, monotonous voice, poor eye contact, expressionless face, and frequent hesitations.

Mixed messages also show the connection between verbal and nonverbal communication. A **mixed message** occurs when there is positive verbal and negative nonverbal communication, or vice versa. A group member may verbally endorse the group's decision but nonverbally exhibit disagreement, even contempt. It is easier to hide our real feelings verbally than it is nonverbally. Attempting to wipe an opinion off your face is a real challenge.

One of the difficulties with communicating in virtual groups is the absence of nonverbal cues, in whole or in part, that accompany verbal, face-to-face messages (Wallace, 1999). The emotional tone of an online written message can easily be misinterpreted as hostile, impersonal, or disagreeable because vocal tone, facial expressions, posture, gestures, and the normal array of nonverbal cues are missing unless video is available for virtual meetings (Johnson et al., 2009). One study of virtual teams revealed that "inability to read nonverbal cues" was identified by 94% of respondents as a significant problem (Solomon, 2010). Emoticons—typed icons or combinations of punctuation marks meant to indicate emotional tone—help but are still limited, and using them often can interrupt the flow of messages. Individuals may also be hesitant to use emoticons in business communication for fear of appearing too informal and unprofessional.

Context: The Communication Environment Every communication transaction has a context, or an environment in which meaning emerges. **Context** consists of *who* (sender) communicates *what* (message) to *whom* (receiver), *why* (purpose) the communicator does it, *where* (setting), *when* (time), and *how* (way) it is done. **Context is a central element of verbal communication.** Little notice may be given to obscene words and phrases used unthinkingly when talking with a group of friends. If used during a job interview, however, they would probably be highly objectionable and cause for rejection of an applicant by an interview panel.

Context is also central to nonverbal communication. For instance, in 1997 a Newton, Massachusetts, jury found Louise Woodward, a British teenager employed as a nanny by an American couple, guilty of second degree murder for the death of the couple's infant. Why did the jury not believe Woodward's testimony that the infant's death was an accident, and would a British jury have made the same verdict? Jonathon Raban (1997), a British author living in the United States and present at the trial, concluded, "My English eyes saw one thing; my American-resident eyes saw something else altogether" (p. 53). Raban's "English eyes" saw a Louise Woodward with "shoulders hunched submissively forward, eyes lowered, voice a humble whisper. Ms. Woodward made a good impression as an English church mouse. Her posture announced that she knew her place, that she acknowledged the superior authority of the court, that she was a nobody." He concluded, "I thought she was telling the truth." Raban's "American-resident eyes," however, saw something quite different. "My second pair of eyes saw Ms. Woodward as sullen, masked, affectless, dissembling. Her evasive body language clearly bespoke the fact that she was keeping something of major importance hidden from the court." He concluded, "I thought she was telling lies" (p. 55). Raban's dual-culture perspective emphasizes the ambiguity of nonverbal communication and the influence of context (e.g., American or British culture) on interpreting nonverbal messages. This trial was watched with great interest in Britain, where, according to CNN, most believed Woodward was innocent.

I have thus far discussed what communication is not and, conversely, what communication is. To summarize by way of definition, **communication** is a transactional process of sharing meaning with others. The intricacies of sharing meaning with others in group situations will become more apparent when I discuss what constitutes competent communication, the next topic for consideration.

Communication Competence

Knowing what constitutes human communication does not tell you how to engage in the process in a competent manner. To accomplish this goal, it helps to understand what it means to communicate competently. **Communication competence** is engaging in communication with others that is both effective and appropriate within a given context (Spitzberg, 2000). This definition requires brief elaboration.

Focus Questions
1. How do you determine communication competence?
2. Does appropriate communication require unswerving conformity to group rules and standards?
3. Does being a competent communicator mean never engaging in poor communication practices?

▶ Effectiveness: Achieving Goals

Communication competence is predicated on results. Consequently, **effectiveness** is defined as how well we have progressed toward the achievement of goals. Someone who knows the changes in communication behavior that need to be made, and who wants to make these changes but never does, can hardly be deemed a competent communicator.

A Matter of Degree: From Deficiency to Proficiency Communication effectiveness is a relative concept—a matter of degree (Spitzberg & Cupach, 1989). We speak of communicators along a continuum, from highly proficient in achieving goals to woefully deficient, with designations in between such as ordinary and average. All of us have our communication strengths and weaknesses in certain situations and circumstances. Some individuals are at ease in social situations such as parties or gatherings of strangers, but they would rather be dipped in molasses and strapped to an anthill than confront conflict in their own group. We can be highly proficient in one circumstance but minimally skillful or depressingly ineffective in another situation. Therefore, the label "competent communicator" is a judgment of an individual's degree of proficiency in achieving goals in a particular context, not an inherent characteristic of any individual.

We (Not Me) Oriented: Primacy of Groups In groups, our primary attention is on the group (we), not the individual (me). Zander (1982) even goes so far as to claim, "A body of people is not a group if the members are primarily interested in individual accomplishment" (p. 2). This, however, is not the same as saying that groups should always supersede individual interests. Nevertheless, trying to achieve your individual goals at the expense of the group's goals usually produces unsatisfactory outcomes for both you and the group. As former NBA coach Pat Riley (1994) notes in his book *The Winner Within,* some group members develop the "disease of me." He describes it this way: "They develop an overpowering belief in their own importance. Their actions virtually shout the claim, 'I'm the one'" (p. 41). Riley concludes that the "disease of me" inevitably produces "the defeat of us" (p. 52).

There are potential dividends when group members assume a We-orientation. Teams win championships, businesses innovate, and students earn better grades. A We-orientation requires concern for others, not merely concern for self. Consequently, communication competence in groups necessitates behavior that is both effective and appropriate.

▶ Appropriateness: Following the Rules

The appropriateness of a person's communication is determined by examining the context. Thus, **appropriateness** means complying with rules and their accompanying expectations (Spitzberg & Cupach, 1989). A **rule** is a prescription that indicates what you should or shouldn't do in specific contexts (Shimanoff, 1980).

Consider two examples. First, a study of student-to-teacher email and text messaging showed that students often send overly casual messages to teachers. Messages such as, "R U Able to Meat Me," incline an instructor "to like the student less, view them as less credible, have a lesser opinion of the message quality, and make them less willing to comply with students' simple email requests" (Stephens et al., 2009, p. 318). Text abbreviations ("R U" instead of "are you") are particularly disliked by teachers,

68/George Doyle/Ocean/Corbis

In an individualistic country such as the United States, you are on your own when interviewing for a job. In collectivist cultures, typically, it is more who you know than how well you have sold yourself to a panel.

and misspellings and apparent lack of proofreading ("meat" instead of "meet") clearly diminish the sender's credibility. Standard implicit rules for teacher–student communication dictate that students communicate thoughtfully and respectfully with teachers. If your study group or project team needs to email or text message your instructor, show care and respect by avoiding overly casual, inappropriate messaging, especially when your instructor is not very familiar with group members (early in the term).

Second, a survey of 2,201 "hiring managers and human resource professionals" conducted by Harris Interactive for Career Builder, a web-based employment organization,

Focus on Culture

Individualism versus Collectivism: A Basic Cultural Difference

A poll of 131 businesspeople, scholars, government officials, and professionals in eight East Asian countries and the United States showed glaring differences in the value placed on order and personal rights and freedoms (as cited in Simons & Zielenziger, 1996). For the question, "Which of the following are critically important to your people?" the results were as follows:

	Asians	Americans
An orderly society	70%	11%
Personal freedom	32%	82%
Individual rights	29%	73%

All cultures vary in the degree of emphasis they place on individuals exploring their uniqueness and independence versus maintaining their conformity and interdependence. This individualism–collectivism dimension is thought by some scholars to be the most important, deep-seated value that distinguishes one culture from another (Hui & Triandis, 1986). It has provoked voluminous research (Schimmack et al., 2005). The individualism–collectivism dimension is at the center of the communication competence model's We-orientation perspective.

The autonomy of the individual is of paramount importance in individualist cultures, hence the emphasis placed on self-actualization and personal growth. Words such as *independence, self, privacy,* and *rights* imbue cultural conversations. Individualist cultures have an "I" consciousness. Competition, not cooperation, is encouraged. Decision making is predicated on what benefits the individual, even if this jeopardizes the group welfare. Individual achievement and initiative are stressed. Self-promotion is expected, even encouraged (Hofstede & Hofstede, 2010).

In collectivist cultures, by contrast, commitment to the group is paramount. Words such as *loyalty, responsibility* (to the group welfare), and *community* imbue collectivist cultural conversations. Collectivist cultures have a "We" consciousness. Cooperation within valued groups (family, friends, coworkers) is strongly emphasized, although transactions with groups perceived as outsiders (foreigners, strangers) can become competitive (a threat to a valued group) (Yu, 1998). Individuals often downplay personal goals in favor of advancing the goals of a valued

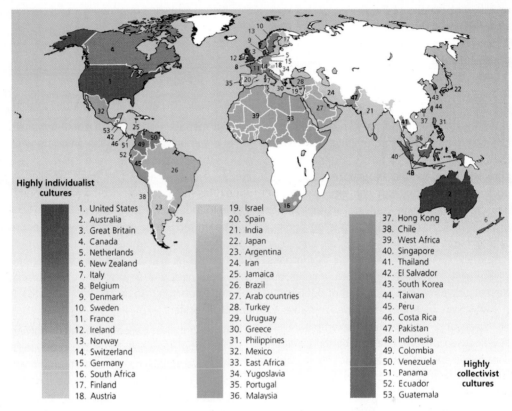

FIGURE 1.1

Map of individualist and collectivist cultures.

From In the Company of Others, Fourth Edition, by J. Dan Rothwell. 2013, Oxford University Press. Reprinted with permission of Geert Hofstede.

group. Self-promotion is discouraged (Hofstede & Hofstede, 2010).

All cultures have both individualist and collectivist influences, but one tends to predominate over the other. A worldwide study of 50 countries and three geographic areas ranks the United States as the number-one individualistic country (Hofstede & Hofstede, 2010). The United States is followed by other Western countries such as Australia, Great Britain, Canada, the Netherlands, and New Zealand, in that order. Latin American, Asian, and West and East African countries rank high on collectivism. Guatemala is the most collectivist. Ecuador,

Panama, Venezuela, Colombia, Indonesia, Taiwan, and Singapore are also among the most collectivist (see Figure 1.1). Most of the world's population live in collectivist cultures (Hofstede & Hofstede, 2010).

Despite strong cultural pressure, no population uniformly accepts its culture's values (see Box 1.2 to check your degree of individualism or collectivism). A review of 35 studies involving thousands of participants showed that African Americans are significantly more individualistic than European Americans (white respondents), but both are substantially more individualistic than are Asian Americans (Oyserman et al., 2002).

(Continued)

Even different regions of the United States vary. Individualism is strongest in the Mountain West and Great Plains states, but collectivism is quite strong in the Deep South (Vandello & Cohen, 1999).

In the United States, the preoccupation with individualism has drawn fire (Derber, 2009; "Excessive Individualism," 2009). Sociologist Charles Derber (1996) claims, "As individualism intensifies, the balance of commitment can tilt so far toward the self that the family and other building blocks of society decompose" (p. 111).

Excessive individualism can be faulted, but excessive collectivism has its dangers too. The perils of group pressure and blind conformity to groups, issues that will be discussed at length later in this book, remind us of the risks involved with excessive loyalty to any group. Collectivist cultures require a level of conformity and restrictive rules that are unacceptable to most Americans. Singapore, for example, levies heavy fines on anyone littering, spitting, smoking in public places, or failing to flush public toilets—actions that are monitored by government employees (Aglionby, 2002; En-Lai, 2003). Requiring students to take drug tests is a routine practice, and groups of five individuals or more cannot meet on the street without police permission. Video cameras are set up at busy intersections to monitor compliance with traffic laws; heavy censorship of printed material, music, and motion pictures is widespread; only the police can own guns; and political opposition to the government is a risky undertaking, often resulting in fines and imprisonment for dissidents (Mydans, 2008).

Individualist and collectivist cultures exhibit glaring differences in their perceptions of the world and how people should behave. Individualist and collectivist values, however, do not always conflict (Schwartz, 1990). When an individual learns conflict management skills or improves interpersonal communication skills, the group benefits as well as the group member. Nevertheless, if groups are to succeed, individual goals and agendas should be of secondary, not primary, importance (LaFasto & Larson, 2001).

The United States does not have to become a collectivist culture where the group is supreme, but teamwork and putting the group ahead of individual needs and goals are often appropriate and important. As Larson and LaFasto (1989) pointedly state:

> The potential for collective problem-solving is so often unrealized and the promise of collective achievement so often unfulfilled, that we exhibit what seems to be a developmental disability in the area of social competence....
>
> Clearly, if we are to solve the enormous problems facing our society, we need to learn how to collaborate more effectively. We need to set aside individual agendas (pp. 13–14).

Emphasizing team building and collaborative effort can prove beneficial to both individuals and society.

QUESTIONS FOR THOUGHT

1. Do you agree that the United States has become excessively Me-oriented? Explain.
2. Singapore has low crime, safe cities, low unemployment, and few homeless citizens. The United States has the opposite. Should we strive to become collectivist and emulate the Singaporeans?
3. Could the United States ever become a collectivist nation, given our individualist history?

listed "appearing disinterested, dressing inappropriately, and answering a cell phone or texting during the interview" as the most common mistakes made by job applicants (Grasz, 2014). An interviewing panel expects appropriate behavior from applicants. Interrupting an interview to answer a cell phone or to send a text message communicates less interest in the job and more interest in immediate communication with others. Dressing too casually for a formal interview sends the message, "I don't take this interview seriously." Know the rules and meet expectations accordingly or you'll flub the interview.

The appropriateness of your communication cannot be determined by merely examining a message that is isolated from the rich complexity of context. For instance, you may self-disclose intimate information about yourself to members of some groups but not others. If you attend a therapy group on marriage, self-disclosing will be expected and encouraged because it is compatible with the group's purpose. If, however, you are talking to a meeting of the Student Senate or the Dormitory Advisory Committee, intimate self-disclosure will likely make members squirm in their chairs and wish for an earthquake.

BOX 1.2

Be Ye Individualist or Collectivist?

How closely do you personally reflect individualist or collectivist values of your culture or co-culture? Consider the following statements and, using a scale from 1 (strongly disagree) to 9 (strongly agree), indicate your degree of agreement or disagreement with each statement.*

1. I prefer to be direct and forthright when I talk with people.
2. I would do what would please my family, even if I detested that activity.
3. I enjoy being unique and different from others in many ways.
4. I usually sacrifice my self-interest for the benefit of my group.
5. I like my privacy.
6. Children should be taught to place duty before pleasure.
7. I like to demonstrate my abilities to others.
8. I hate to disagree with others in my group.
9. When I succeed, it is usually because of my abilities.
10. Before taking a major trip, I consult with most members of my family and many friends.

Total your score for all odd-numbered statements (1, 3, etc.), then total your score for even-numbered statements (2, 4, etc.). All odd-numbered statements reflect individualism and all even-numbered statements reflect collectivism. Which are you? Overall, do you agree more with individualist statements (higher score on odd-numbered statements) than with collectivist statements (lower score on even-numbered statements)? If so, you reflect the prevailing individualist values of American culture.

*For the entire 63-statement measuring instrument, see Triandis (1995).

The purpose of these groups is not therapeutic, so the expectations regarding what constitutes appropriate communication in these contexts are different from expectations found at meetings of Alcoholics Anonymous or Marriage Encounter.

Communication becomes inappropriate if it violates rules of the group when such violations could have been avoided, without sacrificing a goal, by choosing different communication behaviors (Getter & Nowinski, 1981). In short, inappropriateness is usually the result of being clueless or clumsy.

Achieving Communication Competence

Defining communication competence identifies what it is, but not how to achieve it. **There are five general ways to improve your effectiveness and appropriateness in groups:** You can acquire knowledge, hone communication skills, improve your sensitivity, redouble your commitment, and apply ethical standards to your communication choices (see Figure 1.2).

▶ Knowledge: Learning the Rules

I have already noted the centrality of appropriateness and effectiveness to the definition of communication competence. Both require knowledge. **Knowledge** means

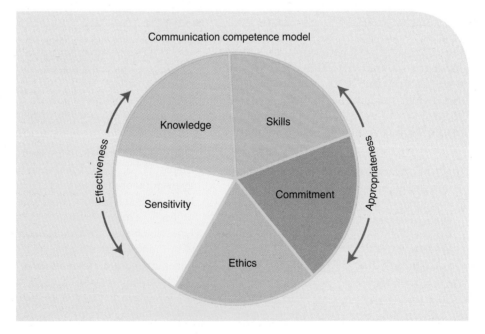

FIGURE 1.2
Communication competence model.

learning the rules and understanding what is required to be appropriate and effective in your communication.

Communication may be appropriate but not effective, and vice versa. Knowledge of the context tells you which is most likely. Consider the following example:

> Brian Holtz is a U.S. businessperson assigned by his company to manage its office in Thailand. Mr. Thani, a valued assistant manager in the Bangkok office, has recently been arriving late for work. Holtz has to decide what to do about this problem. After carefully thinking about his options, he decides there are four possible strategies: (1) Go privately to Mr. Thani, ask him why he has been arriving late, and tell him that he needs to come to work on time. (2) Ignore the problem. (3) Publicly reprimand Mr. Thani the next time he is late. (4) In a private discussion, suggest seeking Mr. Thani's assistance in dealing with employees in the company who regularly arrive late for work, and solicit his suggestions about what should be done (Lustig & Koester, 2010, p. 73).

What choice would you make? The first option is often the way Americans would handle this type of situation. It is direct, and it probably would be effective in getting Mr. Thani to arrive at work on time. Nevertheless, considering the Thai culture (context), where one person does not directly criticize another person (Knutson et al., 2003), this choice would be very inappropriate, even disastrous (Knutson & Posirisuk, 2006). Conversely, the second choice would be appropriate but hardly effective, because Mr. Thani would likely persist in his tardiness. The third choice would be neither appropriate nor effective. Public humiliation would likely induce Mr. Thani, a valuable employee, to resign in shame. Thus, the fourth choice is best because it is both appropriate and effective (Lustig & Koester, 2010). Mr. Thani would receive the message indirectly that he must arrive at work on time, yet he could save face. He can respond affirmatively to the indirect request that he change his behavior from tardiness to punctuality, without suffering public humiliation.

Knowledge in any communication situation is critical, whether the context is yours or another culture's. **We cannot determine what is appropriate and effective without knowing the rules operating in a given situation.**

We don't always make the wisest communication choices, but we are likely to make a fair number of foolish ones if our limited knowledge shields us from appropriate alternatives. In communicative matters, a little knowledge is like the dim flicker of a candle flame in a dark mine shaft. There's just enough illumination to see choices, but not enough light to provide effective direction. If you are uncertain what is expected or required in a given situation, you should seek knowledge from those who are likely to know and who can enhance your understanding.

▶ Skills: Showing, Not Just Knowing

Communication competence encompasses the ability to apply your knowledge in actual situations. **To be effective, you have to combine knowledge with skill.** Despite the increasing popularity of teams in organizations, researchers have discovered that teams are often unsuccessful because members lack teamwork knowledge *and* skill (Hollenbeck et al., 2004; Marks et al., 2002). They may know what to do but not how to do it skillfully.

A **communication skill** is "the successful performance of a communication behavior... [and] the ability to repeat such a behavior" (Spitzberg & Hecht, 1984, p. 577). Practice, of course, is essential to the mastery of any communication skill. Group members who are trained and practice together acquire skills and improve group performance (Ellis et al., 2005).

There is abundant evidence that links communication skills with success or failure in the workplace. For example, an annual survey of more than 400 employers conducted by the National Association of Colleges and Employers ranked communication skills (*for the thirteenth year in a row*) as the most important qualification a candidate for employment can possess, and it ranked teamwork skills as third most desirable ("Top 10 Skills for Job Candidates," 2013). A survey of 2,115 managers and executives by the American Management Association agreed with these results, but added that communication and teamwork skills will become even more important in the future ("AMA 2010 Critical Skills Survey," 2010). This study also noted that employees are generally deficient in such skills. "Successful communication is critical in business" (Hansen & Hansen, 2005). Employers want to hire skillful communicators who can work in teams and make effective decisions in groups.

Communication competence, of course, is not simply a matter of learning a single skill or even a set of skills. As indicated earlier, skills without knowledge of when and how to use them are mostly useless, even harmful. **The key is learning many skills and using them flexibly, with the proper knowledge of what's appropriate for a given context** (Riggio, 2006).

▶ Sensitivity: Receptive Accuracy

Having the knowledge to determine what constitutes appropriate communication in a specific context and having the skills to be effective are great, but what if you don't have your antenna extended to pick up signals that indicate inappropriateness? What if you aren't attentive to signals from group members that indicate hostility, tension, anger, irritation, disgust, or uneasiness? In addition to knowledge and skills, the competent communicator needs sensitivity. **Sensitivity** is receptive accuracy whereby you can detect, decode, and comprehend signals and emotional cues sent within groups (Bernieri, 2001). Dr. Louisa Parks of the Brain Health Center at California Pacific

Medical Center notes that people are spending so much time on social networking devices that "the ability to recognize things like sarcasm, humor, or even the emotions on a human face" are on the wane (quoted in Brown, 2013, p. A16). Mediated communication increasingly substitutes for face-to-face interactions. A frowny emoticon is more recognizable to many than an actual frowning human face (Brown, 2013).

Failure to attend to and comprehend signals can severely affect your relationships with group members (Hall & Bernieri, 2001). The more group members exhibit the ability to identify accurately the feelings of others, the greater the likelihood that groups will cooperate and solve problems effectively. This ability is even more important than the general intelligence of group members. Women exhibit a greater facility for such sensitivity, so including women in task-oriented groups is highly advisable (Woolley et al., 2010).

Problems that lie just below the surface go unattended by groups and magnify difficulties unless members are sensitive to the nuances and subtleties of communication transactions between members. Fortunately, sensitivity can be learned (Hall & Bernieri, 2001). One of the functions of this text is to assist you in developing greater sensitivity by identifying patterns of communication that pose problems in group transactions and by providing solutions for these dysfunctional patterns.

► Commitment: A Passion for Excellence

Effectiveness requires commitment. **Commitment** is persistent effort to achieve goals and produce excellence. Little that is worthwhile comes without commitment. Do you want a romantic relationship to last? Commitment is essential (Epstein, 2010). Do you want to be a great athlete? Then you must commit yourself to the hard work necessary to achieve greatness. Do you want to receive an academic scholarship, earn good grades, finish a degree, and get a great job? It won't happen by listless attention in class and lackluster attendance. You have to want it, work for it, have a passion to achieve it—you must be committed.

The predominant motivation of the competent communicator is the desire to avoid previous mistakes and to find better ways of communicating with group members. Someone who makes the same mistakes repeatedly and shows little interest in altering his or her behavior is a nuisance, or worse, a deadweight who can sink a group. Such anemic commitment is a frequent source of frustration in groups, and it can fester into grouphate. It is easily the most frequent complaint I hear from my group communication students each term. Who wants to deal with a lethargic social loafer who can't be counted on to produce and doesn't seem to care? In sports, they are booted off the team; in business, they are fired; in politics, they are voted out of office; in college, they are invited to leave.

Commitment to improving your communication effectiveness requires self-monitoring. When you interact in groups you have to be a **participant-observer**. You assume a detached view of yourself. You analyze your communication behavior, looking for areas to improve, while noting successes. Ultimately, the competent communicator considers it a personal responsibility to make the necessary effort to interact with group members as effectively and productively as possible.

▶ Ethics: The Right and Wrong of Communication

Why should anyone care about ethics in communication? Because as humans we contemplate the moral correctness of our behavior. It's one of the characteristics that distinguishes us from a banana slug. The very definition of communication competence requires it. **Appropriateness and the We-orientation make ethics important.** Competent communicators concern themselves with more than what works for them personally. A group member taking vastly greater credit for the success of a group project than what he or she deserves is self-centered, and it diminishes the important contributions of other group members. This violates standards of ethics.

Ethics is a system for judging the moral correctness of human behavior by weighing that behavior against an agreed upon set of standards of what constitutes right and wrong. Five essential values, based on the Credo for Ethical Communication adopted by the National Communication Association (*www.natcom.org*), constitute the set of standards for judging the moral correctness of our communication behavior. They are as follows:

1. *Honesty.* "There is no more fundamental ethical value than honesty" (Josephson, 2002). The American culture presumes that honesty is valued and dishonesty is wrong (Bok, 1978). Accuse a person of lying and immediately they become defensive. All ethical systems condemn lying (Jaksa & Pritchard, 1994). Imagine trying to keep a family together when everyone lies regularly and no one can be trusted.

2. *Respect.* Relationships in groups fall apart, and groups can't function effectively when members show disrespect for each other (Gastil et al., 2008). One survey by the Josephson Institute of Ethics reported that 99% of respondents rated respect as "very important" or "essential" to them, and treating others with respect received a similar rating (Jarc, 2012). From an ethical viewpoint, respect is right and disrespect is wrong even if showing respect to others works against a group goal (such as defeating a team). Show respect to others as you would want them to show respect to you (the golden rule). "Some form of the golden rule is embraced by virtually all of the major religious and moral systems" (Jaksa & Pritchard, 1994, p. 101).

3. *Fairness.* Prejudice treats people unfairly. Bigots want different rules for themselves than those applied to a disfavored group. Bigotry should have no place in the communication arena. Students recognize immediately how unfair it would be if an instructor gave an advantage to some students in class and penalized

others based on their sex, ethnicity, age, or lifestyle. One study of community college students reported a mean score on the importance of fairness fell between "very important" and "extremely important" (Kidder et al., 2002).

4. ***Choice***. Freedom to choose for oneself without threat of force or intimidation is a basic ethical value (Jaksa & Pritchard, 1994). It is why most nations have outlawed torture. Coercion prevents choice. There is no real option presented. Choice goes hand in hand with honesty. If you fear reprisals for telling the truth, then your freedom to choose truthfulness instead of deceit is compromised.

5. ***Responsibility***. Ethical communication is We-oriented. Every group member and the group as a whole have a responsibility, a duty, to be concerned about more than merely what works to achieve personal or even group goals. How goals are achieved is also a vital consideration. The study of community college students previously cited reported the highest score among a list of choices was for the importance of responsibility as a "moral value" (Kidder et al., 2002).

These general ethical values serve as guidelines for appropriate communication behavior. For example, undermining other group members by spreading malicious gossip about them to enhance one's own status and position in the group is dishonest and disrespectful. Promising your group that you will conduct research and provide the group with important information when you have no intention of coming through is irresponsible and dishonest. Resisting leadership from a group member merely because she is a woman is unfair and disrespectful.

Focus on Gender

Gender and Communication Competence

Although men and women mostly communicate in similar ways (Dindia, 2006; Hyde, 2005), research does show large and significant gender differences in some areas, especially in mixed-sex group interactions (Anderson, 2006; Wood, 2015). Despite the stereotype that women are far more talkative than men, a review of 63 studies revealed that men speak far more than women in committee meetings, classroom discussions, problem-solving groups, and other public settings (Crawford & Kaufman, 2006; Leaper & Ayres, 2007). This difference is especially pronounced when men outnumber women in a group. Women speak 75% less than men in such a situation (Karpowitz et al., 2012). Men interrupt far more to seize the floor during group discussions, while women interrupt group discussions typically to indicate interest, ask for clarification of points made, and to make supportive comments (Anderson & Leaper, 1998; Wood, 2015). Why do these and other gender differences occur? Some scholars argue that men and women exhibit *different communication styles* that are a product of

(Continued)

gender role expectations (Bruess & Pearson, 1996; Wood, 2007). Deborah Tannen (1990) popularized this perspective. She explains that for most women, talk is primarily a means to "establish connections and negotiate relationships"; for most men, "talk is primarily a means to preserve independence and negotiate and maintain status in a hierarchical social order" (p. 77). Both men and women are concerned about the dual dimensions of status and connection during conversation, but status is usually given far more relative weight by men and connection is usually given far more relative weight by women (Tannen, 2010; see also Coates, 1993). The status dimension is very different from the connection dimension, as indicated below. Therefore, each produces very different communication expectations and patterns.

Status	Connection
Independence	Interdependence
(separateness)	*(intimacy)*
Competition	Cooperation
(contest)	*(consensus)*
Power	Empowerment
(control)	*(choices)*

In mixed-sex groups, men's speech consists mostly of task-oriented, instrumental communication that is exhibited by giving information, opinions, and suggestions (James & Drakich, 1993). Men usually see talk as a contest, an opportunity to establish or increase status in the eyes of group members. Thus, men report their knowledge to the group. They talk more than women, tell more jokes, impart more information and advice, and offer more solutions to problems. Why? Because this spotlights them as experts and raises their status in a group (Tannen, 2010).

Conversely, women's speech in mixed-sex groups consists more of supportive and facilitative communication such as agreeing, indicating interest in what others are saying, and encouraging others to participate in group discussions (James & Drakich, 1993). Women try to connect with other speakers, share feelings, and listen intently to establish rapport. Displaying interest in other group members and offering encouragement to them establishes a connection.

Gender differences in uses of social networking technologies also illustrate these differences in communication styles. Women are the majority of users on Facebook, Twitter, and Flickr. Women use social media primarily to socialize. Facebook COO Sheryl Sandberg notes that women engage in 62% of the sharing, of connecting with friends and family, on the Facebook networking site (Goudreau, 2010). Conversely, Villanova University communication professor Sherry Perlmutter Bowen concludes that men use social media primarily to garner information and increase their influence. "I see males espousing their wisdom on social media sites and using social media to sell, compete, to 'climb the ladder'" (quoted in Goudreau, 2010).

So are men jerks for seeing conversation as an opportunity to enhance status? Are women meek and emotional for seeing conversation as an opportunity to bond with others? Such interpretations are extremely limiting and simplistic. Consider the tendency of women to encourage member participation in group discussions, whereas men rarely show such a tendency (Taylor, 2002). How should this be interpreted? From the connection perspective, women appear to be highly sensitive, caring group members and men seem to be insensitive clods. From the status perspective, however, women may appear to be the insensitive ones. Inviting a man into a group discussion may diminish his status. It calls attention to his nonparticipation, making him appear unassertive. He may have little or no knowledge on the subject of conversation. Spotlighting his lack of knowledge in front of the group could be embarrassing. When men and women approach simple conversation from conflicting perspectives, it is not surprising that misunderstanding and ridicule result.

Not all men and women will follow the male and female communication styles, bringing into question whether such gender styles actually exist. The gender communication styles perspective has received two main criticisms. First, it seriously underemphasizes the role of unequal power. That is, women's style of communication is typical of relatively powerless people (Freed, 1992; Tavris, 1992)—for example, higher status, more powerful individuals typically interrupt more than lower status, less powerful individuals (Hall, 2006). This *dominance perspective* is partly true, but not the entire explanation for gender differences in communication (Mulac & Bradac, 1995; Noller, 1993). As Tannen (1990) explains: "Male dominance is not the whole story. It is not sufficient to account for everything that happens to women and men in conversation, especially in conversations in which both are genuinely trying to relate to each other with attention and respect" (p. 18). Research on leadership in groups also weakens this perspective. "Rather than being less powerful, women may in fact be equally or more powerful than their male counterparts" because the typical leadership style of women that is friendly and supportive (connecting) is better suited to today's business and institutional climate than the more competitive male style (status enhancing) (Kalbfleisch & Herold, 2006). This research suggests that women may still focus on connection when they attain leadership (and gain greater power) because that is what works for them. If true, then as equality between men and women improves, the gender differences in communication may still remain apparent.

Second, some communication experts argue that contrary to the different communication styles perspective or the dominance of men perspective, gender differences in communication occur primarily because of *skills deficiencies.* "Members of each sex tend to specialize in some skills while having comparative deficits in other skills" (Kunkel & Burleson, 2006, p. 151). Men may exhibit poor listening skills. Women may exhibit lack of assertiveness skills. Again, this does not explain all of the communication differences between men and women. When a person displays knowledge during a group discussion (enhancing status) or listens intently (inducing connection), these behaviors are not usually perceived as skill deficiencies. They may be effective and appropriate communication depending on the context, but men tend to do the former and women tend to do the latter more often. Men and women may have the skill to do either, but both may merely choose what they are most accustomed to doing (communication styles).

Given their differences, how do men and women communicate competently with each other? They have to allow for differences, combat dominance, and correct deficiencies. This can be accomplished in a number of ways. First, knowledge of the different conversational assumptions made by men and women has to be broadened. Applying the standards of one group to the behavior of the other can create misunderstanding (Wood, 2015). Women will continue to misjudge men if they apply the single standard of connection to all group discussions, and men will continue to misjudge women if they continue to apply the single standard of status to all group discussions. Both status and connection are legitimate standards for assessing conversations, but we all can look silly to the other sex when only one standard is applied.

Second, adaptation to each other's style of conversation would display skills proficiency, and thus be beneficial. Men could make fewer interruptions that seize conversational control, be more attentive listeners during group discussions, ask more questions to clarify points or

(Continued)

seek information, and encourage women to join the group discussion when appropriate. These adaptations show flexibility and a concern for connection without the appearance of subservience. Women who learn assertiveness skills expand their opportunities to be heard during group discussion and to be taken seriously

(enhancing status) without losing their sensitivity to the importance of connection.

Third, equalizing power imbalances that often put women at a disadvantage will diminish some of the gender differences in communication. How this can be done is discussed at length in Chapter 10.

QUESTIONS FOR THOUGHT

1. Can you think of additional ways men and women can adjust their conversational styles to reduce misunderstandings and increase effectiveness in groups?
2. Do the typical male–female patterns of conversation identified by the different styles perspective correspond with your experience of communicating in mixed-sex groups?
3. Do you think the criticism of the different styles perspective is justified? Apply your own experiences.

Group communication is so complex, however, that any list of standards used to judge members' communication ethics, applied absolutely, would immediately create problems. Ethical communication is a matter of context. A lie that accuses a member of your study group of cheating on a test is different from a lie that covers up an embarrassing event that is private and none of the group's business. Exceptions also will inevitably surface. Students don't have complete freedom of choice to learn what they want to learn, nor should they. Few would freely take a public speaking course unless mandated by general education requirements, because most people fear giving speeches. Honesty, respect, fairness, choice, and responsibility, however, are strong values in most cultures, and they should act as basic standards for evaluating our communication behavior.

Definition of a Group

Both communication and communication competence have been defined. In this section, for clarification, the definition of a group is offered and distinguished from interpersonal communication and public speaking.

▶ Groups: More than People Standing at a Bus Stop

A **group** is a human communication system composed of three or more individuals, interacting for the achievement of some common goal(s), who influence and are influenced by each other. A group is different from a mere collection of individuals, called an

aggregation (Goldhaber, 1990). Twenty-five people standing in line to buy tickets for a movie are not a group, but simply an aggregation. Because they do not interact with and influence each other to achieve a common goal (strangers standing in line are not there expressly to help each other secure tickets), they do not qualify as a group. The same holds for a crowd shopping in a mall or waiting for a plane departure delayed by fog, or people sitting on benches in a public park. In such cases, the presence of other people is irrelevant to the achievement of the specific goal (buying clothes, traveling from point A to point B, or enjoying the outdoors). To be called a group, a collection of individuals must succeed or fail as a unit in a quest to achieve a common goal(s). Crowds, of course, can become groups if they satisfy the definition provided (e.g., flash mob).

The transactional view of communication posits that each participant influences the other, so it should not be surprising that this definition of a group includes the influence group members have on each other. This aspect of the definition of a group

Andersen Ross/Iconica/Getty Images

This photo illustrates which elements of how a group is defined?

1. Three or more individuals
2. Interacting for the achievement of some common goal
3. The bartender is influenced by the two women
4. The two women are influenced by the bartender

Answers are given at the end of the chapter.

is explored extensively in later chapters when norms, roles, leadership, and power are discussed. Explaining how a group is a human communication system, another aspect of the definition of groups, is the subject of Chapter 2.

This text will focus on *small* groups, with special emphasis in Chapters 8 and 9 given to decision-making and problem-solving groups. **Trying to draw a clear line between small and large groups, however, can prove to be difficult.** When does the addition of one more member transform a small group into a large one? When you attend a group meeting and you can't remember afterward whether some members were even present, you've probably reached large-group status. When groups grow to the point where problems of coordination emerge and formal rules for discussion and debate (parliamentary procedure) during meetings become necessary, the group can reasonably be designated as large. To borrow the words of Sir Francis Bacon, when members' "faces are but a gallery of pictures, and talk but a tinkling cymbal," small doesn't seem like an appropriate designation for a group.

▶ Interpersonal Communication and Public Speaking: Ungroups

You may have noticed that the definition of a group sets the minimum number of participants at three. That is because communication between only two individuals is usually referred to as **interpersonal communication** (Adler & Proctor, 2013). Conventional academic terminology also refers to a two-person transaction as **dyadic**. Distinguishing interpersonal communication and group communication, however, is more than quantitative (two individuals versus three or more). **There is an important qualitative dimension as well** (Moreland, 2010). As most couples experience, interpersonal communication between spouses is massively changed with the addition of a child. In such cases, three individuals seem like many more than two. Communication between two individuals is far less complex

---

SECOND LOOK

Groups versus Aggregations

Groups	Aggregations
Crowd doing "the wave"	Crowd in a shopping mall
Cheerleading squad	Individuals waiting for cheerleading tryouts
Crossing guard leading children	Children waiting at stop signal to cross street
Jury	Individuals waiting for jury duty assignment

than the complicated network of transactions found in groups of three or more. As the old saying goes, "Two's company, three's a crowd." Thus, the unit of analysis is structurally different when focusing on three or more individuals, not just two (see Chapter 2 for more detailed discussion). Coalition formation and majority–minority influence occur in groups, not dyads. A group dynamic seems to begin with no fewer than three individuals. For example, one study showed that two individuals working together to solve a complex problem performed no better than two individuals working apart. Three individuals working together, however, proved to be the point at which superior problem solving begins (Laughlin et al., 2006). I doubt that you would deem it unusual to refer to a family as a group, but you might think it odd to label a married or dating couple as a group. We typically say, "Aren't they a cute couple" but not "Aren't they a cute group." The dynamics between two people are qualitatively different from the dynamics experienced among three or more people.

Group communication is also distinct from **public speaking**. With public speaking, the speaker and the audience are clearly indicated, and the speaking situation is far more formal than what is usually found in group discussions. Verbal feedback is often delayed in public speaking events, but during group discussions verbal feedback often is almost immediate. Public speakers usually prepare remarks in advance and speak from notes or even a manuscript. Group members usually don't make formal preparations to speak during group discussions, but may do so when participating on group panels, symposiums, or public forums (see Appendix A for details).

In summary, human communication is a transactional process of sharing meaning with others. Communication competence, a recurring theme throughout this book, is communicating effectively and appropriately in a given context. It is achieved generally through knowledge, skills, sensitivity, commitment, and ethics. Learning to communicate competently in groups is of vital importance to all of us. With this as a backdrop, let's explore in the next chapter how groups function as systems.

In Mixed Company

MindTap™
Reflect on what you've learned online.

▶ Online

Now that you've read Chapter 1, access the online resources that accompany *In Mixed Company* at **www.cengagebrain.com**. Your online resources include:

1. Multiple-choice and true-false **chapter practice quizzes** with automatic correction
2. Digital **glossary**
3. **Interactive Flashcards**

QUESTIONS FOR CRITICAL THINKERS

1. Are there any circumstances in which a Me-orientation becomes necessary when participating in a small group?
2. Does competent communication ever necessitate dishonesty? Explain.
3. When you are a member of a group, should you always exhibit commitment to the group or are there exceptions? Explain.

VIDEO *Case Studies*

This activity presents video case studies from a variety of films for you to analyze. A movie rating (PG-13, R, etc.) and category (drama, romantic comedy, etc.) are included to help you decide which movies are suitable for your viewing. You are asked to analyze each video case study, applying key material presented in each chapter.

Definitely Maybe (2008). Romantic Comedy; PG-13

Sweet story of a divorcing father whose little girl wants him to tell the story of his romantic life before meeting her mother, and how he met and married her mother. Analyze the appropriateness of the father's story as he tells it to his daughter. What rules are operating here? Does he violate any rules of appropriateness?

Home for the Holidays (1995). Comedy/Drama; PG-13

Uneven, but ultimately entertaining movie about a family that experiences a stressful Thanksgiving weekend. Analyze family members' communication competence, especially during the disastrous dinner segment. What rules operate during the dinner? Which ones are violated? Does any family member exhibit effective and appropriate communication? Explain.

I Love You, Man (2009). Comedy/Romance; R

Hilarious, but sometimes crude, tale of a guy (Paul Rudd) who gets engaged to his dream woman but doesn't have a male friend to serve as his best man. His quest to rectify this situation leads to the development of an odd friendship with a character played by Jason Segal. Are gender differences depicted in the movie mere stereotypes or are they accurate based on the research and discussion presented in this chapter?

The Hunger Games: Catching Fire (2013). Action-Adventure; PG-13.

Katnis (Jennifer Lawrence) and Peeta (Josh Hutcherson) become enemies of the Capitol and must participate in a second Hunger Games pitting previous winners against each other. Examine the ethics of the Hunger Games participants, applying the five standards of ethical group communication. Identify instances in which communication is interpersonal and when it is small group. Are participants ever just an aggregation?

Return to Paradise (1998). Drama; R

Underrated film about a harrowing ethical dilemma involving three friends who vacationed in Malaysia. You'll be contemplating what action you would take in the same circumstances. Analyze this film from a communication ethics perspective. Is Anne Heche's character justified in lying to the Vince Vaughn character? Does Vince Vaughn's character have a choice, or is he being coerced unethically? Does he have a responsibility to return to save his friend?

Hindsight Bias Test Answers

All false except #14.

To determine your grade, deduct 2 points for each incorrect answer. Total possible points = 30. Your grade is calculated by subtracting the sum of all points deducted for wrong answers from 30 possible points, then dividing that number by 30. For example, five incorrect answers result in a 10-point deduction. Subtracting that 10-point deduction from 30 equals 20 points. Your 20 points divided by 30 equals 67%.

Answers to Multiple-Choice Questions in Captions

Cartoon (p. 15): 2, 4; Photo (p. 33): 1, 3, 4.

2

Groups as Systems

MindTap™
Start with a
quick warm-up
activity.

I n one of my small group communication courses, six women formed a project group. During their first meeting in class, communication was warm, friendly, and task oriented. They accomplished a great deal in a short period of time: deciding which of the five project options they would pursue, dividing labor to develop the project, and setting deadlines for accomplishment of specified tasks. They told me that they all were very pleased with their new group.

During the next week, the six women met one more time for a lengthy session, and again they were pleased by their progress on the project and increasingly comfortable with their harmonious interactions. Then a male student who had missed a week of class and had no project group approached me and asked which of the four class groups he should join. I told him to join the all-women group for two reasons: I typically encourage mixed-sex, not same-sex, groups (there were far more women than men in the class), and the other groups had seven members already. From the moment he joined the six women he transformed this harmonious, task-effective group into a frustrating experience for every group member. His opening introductory remark upon joining the group of women was, "I hope PMS won't be a problem for us." He guffawed at his supposed humor, but all six women seemed stunned. During the group meeting he made sexist remarks, offered derogatory comments about the choice of project already decided by the women, and made a complete nuisance of himself. As he left class, he loudly proclaimed to everyone that he was "leader of a chicks group."

All six women bolted to the front of the class and begged me to assign this disruptive individual to another group. I explained that moving him to another group would make the other groups too large and would merely pass the problem to another group, not solve it.

The problem became more complex because at midterm I have students form new project groups. Nobody wanted this disruptive individual as a group member. When he joined a new group, a woman in that group immediately shot out of her chair and confronted me with the ultimatum: "Either you move that guy to another group or I'm dropping this class." With no small effort I managed to convince her to remain in the class.

This example illustrates that every group is a system. A **system** is a set of interconnected parts working together to form a whole in the context of a changing environment (Littlejohn & Foss, 2011). A group is composed of individual members interrelating with each other as a whole entity, not as individual parts operating in isolation from each other. The behavior of one member affects the entire group because of the interconnectedness of system parts (all group members), especially if the behavior is disruptive. In this opening case, the six women could not ignore their obnoxious individual. They had to adapt to the jarring change that occurred once he joined their group. Their disruptive member changed the group environment, and the communication dynamics also changed from warm and friendly to defensive and strained.

In general, a system is composed of input, throughput (processes), and output (Katz & Kahn, 1978). **Input** consists of resources that come from outside the system, such as energy (sunlight, electricity), information (Internet, books), people (a new group member), and environmental influences (organizations, society, culture). **If input ceases, a system deceases.** A system inevitably wears down without continuous input. This wearing-down process is called **entropy**—a measure of a system's movement toward disorganization and eventual termination. **All living systems combat entropy with input.** No group, for example, can survive without new members. The group will dismantle because current members will lose interest and leave, join different groups, or the members themselves will eventually die. Consider the religious sect called the Shakers (members shook to rid themselves of evil). Now near extinction, their inevitable demise is foreordained by three Shaker decisions: a belief in celibacy, a complete withdrawal from mainstream society, and a group decision in 1965 to admit no new members (Melton, 1992). From a peak membership of 6,000 in the 1830s, there were only three remaining members at the Sabbath Day Lake, New Gloucester, Maine, community in 2013 (Grondahl, 2013). Contrary to the Shakers' aversion to new members, interjecting "new blood" into a group can bring new information, new ideas, new experiences, new energy, and even different values and perspectives. New members can thwart entropy, energize, and revitalize a group. New members, however, can also shake up the system by disrupting traditions and stable patterns of behavior.

Throughput is the *process* of transforming input into output to keep the system functioning. Input is transformed in a group by its members engaging in communication activities, such as presenting information during group discussion and then taking that information and engaging in creative problem solving. According to **structuration theory**, a system, such as a small group, establishes structures for such discussion and problem solving in the form of rules, roles, norms, and power distribution (all subjects for later development) (Poole et al., 1996). These structures are used to permit the system (the small group) to function effectively and to sustain itself. These structures, however, also constrain the process (West & Turner, 2014). For example, establishing rules for group discussion (e.g., "meetings will follow a prepared agenda"; "the chairperson will lead the group discussion"; "interruptions will be kept to a minimum") permits an orderly dialogue to occur among group members—it gives it a clear form. At the same time, however, it constrains unfettered discussion from occurring. Rules permit certain communication behaviors (polite discussion) while restricting others (raucous debate). Through the discussion process, the rules, roles, norms, and distribution of power may be reinforced even institutionalized within an organization, or they may change over time. This means that a group is in a perpetual state of becoming (change is inevitable).

Output comprises the continual results of the group's throughput (transformation of input). Group outputs include decisions made, solutions to problems created and implemented, projects completed, group procedures modified, team member cohesiveness enhanced, member relationships improved, and so forth. Again, these outputs are discussed in detail in later chapters.

As my colleague Mark Murphy has noted, if groups mess up their input, throughput, and output, they're going to be kaput. **My principal purpose in this chapter is to avoid such an outcome by explaining and discussing systems theory and how it can be applied to groups.** This is not merely an abstract exercise for the intellectually curious. Understanding at least the basics of systems theory provides useful insights into why some small groups succeed and others fail.

There are three chapter objectives:

1. To explain interconnectedness of parts in a system,

2. To discuss how groups must adapt to a changing environment,

3. To explore the influence of size on a group's ability to function effectively.

Interconnectedness of Parts

Interconnectedness of parts is a major element of systems theory. The effects of interconnectedness can be seen in two ways: the ripple effect and synergy.

MindTap™
Read, highlight, and take notes online.

Focus Questions

1. What is the ripple effect and how does it affect groups?

2. What is synergy? What is negative synergy? How is each produced?

▶ Ripple Effect: A Chain Reaction

In a system, one part can have a significant impact on the whole. This **ripple effect** or chain reaction spreads across the entire system, much the way a pebble tossed into a pond disturbs the water and forces adjustments. This ripple effect can be plainly seen from a historical example. The influenza pandemic of 1918–1919 killed 50 million people globally. This was more than the total deaths from both world wars of the twentieth century (Vergano, 2014). This flu pandemic rippled through every part of society. In the United States, enormous stress was placed on healthcare systems that nursed the sick and on economic systems that struggled with a major portion of the workforce incapacitated. Even social relations were affected. People avoided contact with each other or, when forced to interact, commonly wore cloth masks across their faces, which they hoped would protect them from the virus (Kolata, 1999). Subsequent flu pandemics in 1957, 1968, and 2009, although far less lethal and catastrophic, have also produced significant ripple effects.

The ripple effect from cyberattacks on U.S. businesses and vital industries recently became a subject of intense concern. President Obama called such attacks "one of the gravest national security dangers that the United States faces." Homeland Security Secretary Jeh Johnson explained, "We are all connected online and a vulnerability in one place can cause a problem in many other places" (quoted by Pickler, 2014, p. B8).

A small part of a huge system can generate an enormous ripple effect. The Writers Guild of America went on strike in late 2007, and didn't settle its strike until mid-February 2008. If you look at the screen credits for movies and television programs, screenwriters are but a blip among the vast network of individuals and groups that compose the system required to complete a single film or an episode of a TV series. Yet this strike shut down film and television production, cost an estimated $3.5 billion in lost revenue, forced a starkly abbreviated Golden Globes award ceremony, threatened the cancellation of the Academy Awards ceremony, and required viewers to watch endless reruns and banal "reality shows." Entire production crews, caterers, gardeners, agents, and actors were out of work during the strike ("Striking Numbers," 2008).

The ripple effect, of course, does not have to be a negative experience. When a parent gets a job promotion or a significant raise in pay, all members of the family stand to gain from the good fortune. If a child wins a scholarship to a major university, the entire family potentially benefits from the news. Accomplishments of individual family members may motivate others in the group to seek similar goals. When a group leader who provokes dislike comparable to a skunk in your clothes closet is replaced with a competent, well-liked leader, optimism and enthusiasm can spread throughout a group.

The H₁N₁ epidemic prompted people in Mexico to wear gauze masks to prevent the ripple effect.

Recognizing the significance of the ripple effect means paying close attention to your own impact on groups (see Box 2.1). Your level of communication proficiency or deficiency can mean success or failure of the entire group. "The power of one" should not be underestimated.

▶ Synergy: One Plus One Equals a Ton

James Surowiecki (2005), author of *The Wisdom of Crowds*, asserts that groups can often perform better than individuals working alone (see also Laughlin et al., 2006). He offers the television game show *Who Wants to Be a Millionaire?* as an example, among others, of the superiority of groups. When contestants are unable to answer a question, they may contact a trusted friend or family member (allies) or the studio audience. The trusted allies are correct 65% of the time, but the studio audience is correct 91% of the time. Psychologist Keith Sawyer (2007) calls this collective wisdom "group genius."

Groups often outperform individuals working alone, and sometimes they produce spectacularly superior results. This group genius is called synergy. **Synergy** occurs when group performance from joint action of members exceeds expectations based on perceived abilities and skills of individual members (Salazar, 1995). Thus, the whole is not necessarily equal to the sum of its parts. It may be greater than the sum of its individual parts.

The synergistic quality of group decision making is analogous to mixing drugs or chemicals. Some combinations of drugs, such as those used in chemotherapy, can

BOX 2.1

Are You a Difficult Group Member?

Instructions: Rate honestly your likely behavior in each of the scenarios below. This should reveal whether you are a difficult group member. Optional Alternative: After answering this questionnaire, ask fellow class or team members to complete this same assessment about you, but only if you feel comfortable making such a request. If team members are hesitant, encourage them to complete the assessment without identifying themselves in the questionnaire (ideally, all team members should complete the assessment to preserve anonymity). Compare the results by following the scoring system at the end of this assessment.

1. When a topic of great interest to me is discussed in my group, I tend to talk much longer and more forcefully than I know I should.

FREQUENTLY			RARELY	
5	4	3	2	1

2. During group discussions, I typically remain silent, exhibiting lack of interest in the proceedings.

FREQUENTLY			RARELY	
5	4	3	2	1

3. When my group attempts to work on a task, especially one in which I have little interest, I prefer to joke around and be comical instead of focusing on the task.

FREQUENTLY			RARELY	
5	4	3	2	1

4. When I oppose what my group decides, I am inclined to reintroduce the issue already decided even though I know there is little chance the group will change its decision.

FREQUENTLY			RARELY	
5	4	3	2	1

5. I often quarrel openly with group members by raising my voice, interrupting other members to forcefully interject my own opinion, and criticizing those who disagree with me.

FREQUENTLY			RARELY	
5	4	3	2	1

6. I have strong opinions that often color my participation during group discussions, and I attempt to convert group members to my way of thinking even if they are unresponsive.

FREQUENTLY			RARELY	
5	4	3	2	1

7. I'm inclined to predict failure of the group, especially if a risk is involved, and I tend to focus on what will go wrong, not on what will go right with my group's decisions.

FREQUENTLY			RARELY	
5	4	3	2	1

Total your responses for all seven of your answers (maximum score = 35; minimum score = 7). Determine your average score (total score divided by 7). If your average score is 3.0 or higher, you tend toward being a difficult group member. Any single answer that is 3, 4, or 5 indicates trouble for your group on that particular behavior. These seven scenarios correspond to the seven disruptive informal roles discussed in Chapter 5.

The 1980 U.S. Olympic hockey team was a classic example of group synergy. Not expected to progress beyond the preliminary rounds, the team knocked off the powerful Soviet team 4-3 in the semifinals and went on to win the gold medal, completing the "miracle on ice."

produce more effective results than two or more drugs taken separately. Combining some pesticides can dramatically increase potency. One study at Tulane University found that mixing two common pesticide chemicals, endosulfan and dieldrin, didn't just double the potency of each—it increased their potency by as much as 1,600 times. As endocrinologist John A. McLachlan, who led the Tulane University team that did the study, explains, "Instead of one plus one equaling two, we found that one plus one equals a thousandfold" (cited in "Playing Havoc," 1996, p. 14A).

Habitat for Humanity is a case study in synergy. Habitat was begun in 1976. It has constructed more than 800,000 modest homes for almost 3 million poor people in nearly 90 countries around the world, and it expects to hit the one million new homes milestone by 2015. It has become one of the largest homebuilders in the United States ("Habitat for Humanity," 2013). Habitat work crews composed of volunteers divide the labor, with each small subgroup erecting portions of the total structure a section at a time. Most volunteers who build Habitat homes have no expertise in such tasks. The aggregate of individual skill levels of typical Habitat team members doesn't exactly suggest success, but admirable success does occur.

Synergy is produced in primarily three ways. First, when group members are highly motivated to achieve a common goal, such as when grades, jobs, or lives are at stake, synergy may occur (Forsyth, 2014). Habitat achieves admirable results because group members are highly motivated to build decent housing for poor people.

Kim Macdonald/Habitat for Humanity

An all-women construction team works cooperatively to build a Habitat home.

Second, synergy is produced from group effort, not individual, independent effort (Carey & Laughlin, 2012). Habitat members work together in subgroups, not by themselves. If group members work independently by completing individual assignments on their own, and the group merely compiles the results without the benefit of group discussion, no synergy will occur (Fandt, 1991). For instance, if your group took an essay test and each member was assigned one question to answer, no synergistic benefit would occur if group members did not discuss rough draft answers with the whole group and make improvements prior to a final draft.

Third, groups whose members have deep diversity have greater potential to produce synergy than groups with little such diversity. **Deep diversity** is substantial variation among members in task-relevant skills, knowledge, abilities, beliefs, values, perspectives, and problem-solving strategies (Harrison et al., 2002). For synergy to occur, you need to have a wide variety of skills and abilities among your group membership. In a simulation study comparing groups with deep diversity and those without, the groups with deep diversity were synergistic and outperformed even their best individual member. Groups without deep diversity performed much more poorly (Larson, 2007). If Habitat crews were composed entirely of construction workers with a wide variety of home-building skills (e.g., electricians, plumbers, etc.) instead of mostly eager but unskilled volunteers, the synergistic effect would likely mushroom beyond the already impressive results. The voluntary nature of Habitat's undertaking, however, makes widespread deep diversity generally impractical even for relatively small work crews.

▶ Negative Synergy: Results Beyond Bad

Systems don't always produce synergy. **If you're sharing ignorance (misinformation based on lack of knowledge), no group genius is likely to emerge** (Krause et al., 2011). The National Geographic-Roper Public Affairs Geographic Literacy Study (2006) revealed some major gaps in geographic knowledge of young Americans ages 18 to 24. The 510 randomly selected respondents answered only slightly more than half of the geography questions correctly. Half of the respondents could not find Japan on a map, and 65% did not know where our "Mother Country" Great Britain is located. More locally, half did not know where New York is and *6% were unable to locate the United States.* (When asked the trivia question on a roll sheet I circulate in each of my classes, "What is the tallest mountain in the world?" one student wrote Mountain Dew. I laughed, then remembered the results of this geography study. I wasn't completely sure this answer was meant as a joke.) Authors of this report note: "Americans are far from alone in the world, but from the perspective of many young Americans, we might as well be" (p. 6). Fortunately, those with at least some college education performed better on the test. Nevertheless, groups with limited knowledge on a subject of interest aren't likely to perform magic. That is why it would be folly to have a group of geography challenged individuals making decisions, for example, about U.S.–Middle Eastern policy. If you can't locate a country on a map, you probably know next to nothing about that country's culture, government, values, and the like. No good would likely come from shared ignorance.

Shared ignorance among group members can produce negative synergy. **Negative synergy** occurs when group members working together produce a worse result than expected based on perceived individual skills and abilities of members (Salazar, 1995). The whole is worse than the sum of its parts. Negative synergy is like mixing alcohol and tranquilizers, causing suicidal effects. When group members know little about a subject, compete against each other (Me-orientation), resist change, or share a collective bias or mindset, the result of mixing their individual contributions can produce decisions beyond bad. As David Lykken (1997) observes, "A gang is more dangerous than the sum of its individual parts." Even groups uniquely talented and trained for a specific task may fail disastrously at a distinctly different task that requires other specialized knowledge and skills. For example, military groups may be quite effective in warfare but inept as a peacekeeping police force that requires cooperation, diplomacy, and creative problem solving (Weiss, 2011).

In February 2003, the Department of Homeland Security encouraged Americans to choose a "safe room" (an inner closet or the like) in their homes to seek protective shelter in case of a bioterrorist attack. The safe room was to be sealed with plastic sheeting and duct tape. This protection against a bioterrorist attack seemed to ignore the obvious downside of this recommendation: oxygen deprivation leading to death.

The rollout of the website for the implementation of the Affordable Care Act (Obamacare) on October 1, 2013, was a disaster. Almost no one was able to enroll in a health insurance option, the system crashed, and most people got to stare at a frozen screen even after repeated, frustrating attempts. The massive problems continued for weeks. Clay Johnson, a former member of President Obama's technology team and a Presidential Innovation Fellow, blamed a "sloppy" team of contractors who may simply have been unqualified for the job (Liptak & Acosta, 2013). There weren't just a few "glitches"; the system suffered a meltdown and took months to repair.

On a more narrow scale, negative synergy can be seen in a recorded dialogue of a group deliberating a winter survival task in which items must be ranked according to their utility in improving the group's survival in a wilderness area. Here, the actual process of negative synergy becomes apparent.

B: This may sound crazy, but I say we go for the radio.

A: Why the radio? It's broken.

B: I know, I know . . . but that doesn't mean we can't use it.

C: I don't understand.

A: I think I do . . . but go ahead.

B: OK, like here's what I'm thinking . . . we could use the parts to build our own transmitter.

A: Right . . . like we could take the antenna and place it on a high tree . . . run wires down, and start building a transmitter, maybe then send Morse codes. We wouldn't have to talk.

B: What about power, though?

A: We could use the battery from the plane.

B: But that's not on the list here, and we were told not to assume other things aside from the list.

C: We could use solar power.

B: Yeah, the sun . . . or electrical power . . . build our own generator . . .

A: Do we know codes?

C: I know SOS . . . three dots, three dashes, three dots . . .

B: Anyway, no matter. Just keep sending signals—any signals. . . .

C: So we go with the radio?

B: Yeah, I bet no one else thought of it. (Hirokawa, 1987, p. 22)

In this illustration, there is no indication that any of the group members knows anything about building a transmitter or generator. Bad ideas in this group are simply compounded one upon the other—negative synergy at work.

This cartoon illustrates:
1. Synergy
2. The ripple effect
3. Negative synergy
4. Entropy

Answers are given at the end of the chapter.

Adaptability to a Changing Environment

Systems are never in a static state. They are in a constant state of becoming until they terminate. They have to adapt to their changing environment. The **environment** is the context within which a system operates, such as a team within an organization or a student project group within a college class. You do not have a choice between change and no change. The relevant choice is, can a system (group) adapt to the inevitable changes that are certain to occur?

Every system reacts to change in its own way. For instance, two groups that begin at the same point and experience similar environmental conditions may turn out very differently. Conversely, two groups that begin at very different points and experience dissimilar environmental conditions may turn out very similarly. In other words, groups with a similar or identical final goal (e.g., financial security) may reach that end in highly diverse ways (one family may invest in the stock market; another family may rely on retirement plans or real estate investments). This process is called **equifinality**, in the somewhat ponderous systems lingo. In this section, the process of adapting to change in a system is discussed.

Focus Questions

1. What relationship do stability and change have in groups?
2. Why do groups establish boundaries? How do they control boundaries?
3. In what circumstances can groups become too open? Too closed?
4. Is it better for a group to be more open than closed? Explain.

▶ Dynamic Equilibrium: Managing Stability and Change

There is always a dynamic tension between stability and change in any system (Dovidio et al., 2009). All systems attempt to maintain stability and to achieve a state of equilibrium (*homeostasis*) by resisting change, but no system can avoid inevitable change (Wood, 2004). Too much stability can produce stagnation and tedium. Too much change can produce chaos and group disintegration. **There is no perfect balance point between stability and change in any system, but there is a range in which systems can manage change effectively to promote growth and success without destroying the system with too much instability.** This range is called **dynamic equilibrium** (Forsyth, 2014). A system sustains dynamic equilibrium when it regulates the *degree, rate,* and *desirability of change,* allowing stability and change to coexist (see Closer Look: "Dealing with Difficult Group Members").

Consider what happens when the three variables of change are not sufficiently regulated. As the owner of a small business, a friend of mine decided to go high tech and computerize his office with the very latest, most sophisticated equipment. At the same time, he embarked on an office renovation project. To add to the disruption, he moved in a new partner. His office staff went berserk. Staff members hadn't been trained to run the sophisticated computer programs and equipment. They resented the renovation, which displaced them from their normal work areas and created a huge mess that interfered with their efficiency. The new partner turned out to be a very demanding individual who expected instant results from the beleaguered staff. His favorite saying, posted on the wall of his office, was "Impossible is a word found only in a fool's dictionary." The final change, however, that toppled this house of horrors was my friend's insistence that his staff work half-days on weekends until the office was returned to a more normal state. Three of the four members of his staff quit, and they were spitting fire as they stomped out of the office, never to return. They left a gift for my friend's partner—a thesaurus renamed with black marker pen *Fool's Dictionary* with words such as *idiot, pompous, twit, jerk,* and *moron* highlighted. The business had to be shut down for two weeks, resulting in a substantial loss of revenue.

CLOSER LOOK

Dealing with Difficult Group Members: A System Perspective on "Bad Apples"

This chapter opened with a narrative about a difficult group member. One troublesome member's inappropriate behavior can ripple throughout the group, causing disharmony and dissension, disrupting the equilibrium of the group, and preventing a group from operating as a cohesive, fully functioning team. Research by Will Felps and his colleagues (2006) on "bad apples"—disruptive members who poison the group ("One bad apple spoils the barrel")—demonstrates just how disturbing such a group member can be. Their study was featured on the public radio show *This American Life* ("Ruining It for the Rest of Us," 2008) where Felps provided additional details about the study. A skilled student actor portrayed three versions of disruptive, or "bad apple" behavior in several groups. He played a *jerk* who made insulting remarks to other group members, such as "Do you know anything?" and "That's a stupid idea." He played a *slacker* who wouldn't contribute during a 45-minute challenging group task, text messaged a friend, and responded with "whatever" or "I really don't care" to other group members' ideas. Finally, he played a *depressive pessimist* who put his head on the table, complained about the task being boring, and predicted group failure. (For additional versions of bad apple behavior see "disruptive roles" discussed in Chapter 5.)

The results were startling. No matter how talented team members were, those groups that had to deal with the one bad apple scored 30% to 40% lower on a challenging task than teams with no bad apple. Disruptive behavior was also contagious. When playing the jerk, group members would respond to insults from the bad apple with insults of their own; when playing the slacker, group members would assume slacker behavior and say, "Let's just get this over with. Put down anything"; and when playing the depressive pessimist, other group members became cynical and disengaged. One group began its task alert and enthusiastic with members leaning forward in their chairs, completely engaged on the task. When confronted with the depressive pessimist, however, within 45 minutes all group members were sprawled out on the table looking depressed and disengaged.

Another study showed that one disruptive team worker who exhibited incivility, or rude behavior, toward fellow team members had prompted half of those who were interviewed to contemplate leaving their jobs and 12% actually had quit (Pearson et al., 2000). To work with a jerk can drive you berserk. Who needs that? Since the best employees are likely to have greater job opportunities because they are desirable applicants, they are frequently the most likely to leave to escape the disrupter's cancerous effect on the team (Mitchell & Lee, 2001). This leads to a further deterioration in group performance (Felps et al., 2006).

Jerry Talley of Edgewise Consulting in Mountain View, California, estimates that dealing with bad apples consumes a minimum of 10% of a company's time, and that can easily grow to 30% to 40% if the company is truly dysfunctional (Townsend, 1999a). Most group members in decision-making and problem-solving groups feel ill-equipped to handle disruptive behavior (Felps et al., 2006). When the entire group is affected, it becomes a systemic problem.

Dynamic equilibrium in a group is sustained by regulating the degree, rate, and desirability of change within the system. In the chapter-opening bad apple case study, the degree of disruption was significant, even tumultuous, for the six women faced with the male who behaved like a jerk; thus, the change produced in the group's dynamic was substantial. The rate of change brought about by the disruptive new member was abrupt and wholly unanticipated. The disruption shattered the group equilibrium, forcing a response to this sudden change. The change produced by the disruption was also extremely undesirable. To restore the dynamic equilibrium in the group, the six women working together needed to reduce the degree of disruption and encourage more desirable behavior.

There are several fundamental steps that should be taken by a group when dealing with a difficult member who threatens the group's dynamic equilibrium, even its ability to function.

First, make certain the group climate is cooperative. Chapter 4 discusses group climate in depth. Most difficult people are created by a competitive system (Aguayo, 1990). If your group creates a ruthlessly competitive, politicized climate where decision making is influenced by rumor mongering, backstabbing, deal making, and sabotaging the efforts of other members, then difficult group members will appear like flies at a summer picnic (Lafasto & Larson, 2001). The group of six women had established a very cooperative group climate, so this was not what precipitated their troublemaker's offensive behavior. Nevertheless, they did make some mistakes, as we'll see—some that they corrected, and others that they did not.

Second, the group should establish a clear code of conduct for all group members. This code should spell out specific unacceptable behaviors (insults, rudeness, threats, bigoted statements, and any other disrespectful communication).

The Joint Commission on Accreditation of Healthcare Organizations required just such a code of conduct for its 15,000 healthcare organizations because of disruptive behavior between doctors and nurses. The code is viewed as "an essential element" in addressing such disruptive behavior (Grenny, 2009). A code of conduct takes a systems approach to the problem by viewing disruption as every member's concern.

Third, change your communication in relation to a difficult person's behavior, such as:

a. *Don't placate the troublemaker.* Laughing nervously when the disrupter cracks sexist or racist jokes or makes offensive remarks about group members merely encourages further moronic behavior. Permitting frequent interruptions from the offending party—enduring this ploy for conversational control—is a strategy of appeasement with little potential for success. Allowing the disrupter to manipulate the group so an illusion of harmony can be maintained rewards the troublemaker for objectionable behavior. Initially, all six women were stunned by their disruptive new member, then they laughed nervously at their troublemaker's sexist "jokes" and comments, and they let him dominate conversations. Soon, they stopped laughing and collectively they wouldn't let him interrupt, as he was prone to do. They began saying to him, "Please wait; I'm not finished speaking."

b. *Refuse to be goaded into a reciprocal pattern.* Be unconditionally constructive (Ury, 1993). Don't counter abusive remarks with abusive remarks of your own. Disrupters thrive on provoking retaliation. Becoming aggressive with aggressors escalates into intractable power struggles. So don't take the bait. Keep telling yourself that if you do, you're engaging them on their terms and on their familiar ground, to your disadvantage. Fighting fire with fire produces a firestorm. Resist the temptation. This requires self-control (and in some cases deserves a medal of commendation). In some extreme cases it won't be possible. To their great credit, none of the six women reciprocated the inappropriate behavior of their tormenter. It required a group effort (a systems approach) because had even one member taken the bait and reciprocated the inappropriate behavior, the disrupter would have been encouraged, not discouraged, to continue exhibiting his sophomoric behavior.

c. *Have an out-of-body experience* (Lulofs, 1994). Remove yourself mentally from the conflict. Listen to the disrupter as if you were an uninvolved third party with no energy in the outcome. Picture yourself as a mediator whose job it is to resolve the problem. Only one group in Felp's "bad apple" study was able to resist the disrupter's negative influence. This group had a strong member who didn't return insults with insults, didn't get angry, but instead listened carefully to everyone and asked lots of probing questions. He was the antidote to the contagious "disease of me" of the poisonous apple. He set a constructive tone and would not be sidetracked. His father was a diplomat, so perhaps he learned from him how to handle a bad apple.

d. *Don't provide a soapbox for the troublemaker.* On two occasions in my teaching career, I have had a disruptive student interrupt me in the middle of a lecture/discussion to complain about the class. On the first occasion, I handled the situation poorly. My difficult student blurted out in a loud voice, "Can we do something relevant for a change? I'm tired of discussing other people's problems." I mistakenly took the bait and tried justifying what I had been doing in the class. Not surprisingly, he was unmoved by my response and undeterred in his obnoxious behavior.

On the second occasion, my disrupter demanded to know why I was "wasting so much time on the relationship between gender and communication patterns." In this instance, I immediately deferred to the entire class, "Do the rest of you agree that this is a waste of time?" When they indicated that they did not, I then asked the class, "Do you want to take class time to discuss his complaint?" They again indicated that they did not. With the support of the group (a system approach), I then deferred a confrontation with this student until the class was over. He was ill prepared to challenge the entire group. Notice, however, that I said I deferred the confrontation. You can't ignore disruptive behavior, especially when it becomes chronic.

Fourth, attempt to convert disruption into a constructive contribution (Gouran, 1988). Suppose in the middle of a group discussion your disrupter blurts out, "That's a completely stupid suggestion." You could reply in kind, thereby setting in motion a reciprocal pattern of derision. Instead, you could attempt to divert the disrupter away from abusive remarks and toward constructive contributions to the group by responding, "Perhaps you could provide a better suggestion." This response does not invite your obnoxious member to mount a soapbox and launch into an irrelevant monologue. You are requesting a pertinent contribution. Research indicates that substantive comments in a group discussion encourage a focus on content, not on relationship conflicts (Bell, 1974). Disrupters are less likely to continue their abuse when they are focused on the substance of the discussion. If the disrupter does not respond appropriately to your invitation to be constructive, then you can proceed to the next step.

Fifth, confront the difficult person directly. If the entire group is upset by the behavior of the difficult person (the system is disrupted, not just an individual), then the group should confront the disrupter. The group's code of conduct should be enforced systemwide. Even truly abrasive individuals whose behavior seems to indicate a complete lack of regard for the group will find it tough to ignore pressure from group members. Be descriptive. State what behavior is offensive and encourage more constructive behavior. For example: "Your comments about women offend me. Please stop." Do not get abusive or nasty with the troublemaker. I strongly encouraged the six women to confront their troublemaker as a group. I presented this as an opportunity to experiment with communication strategies for dealing with difficult members. Unfortunately, they never directly confronted him.

Sixth, **separate yourself from the difficult person if all else fails.** Communication is not a panacea for every problem that comes up in groups. Some individuals leave no other option except removal from the group, and this may be very positive for the group. One clothing retailer, for example, fired his top-selling employee who was a bad apple. The sales at the store skyrocketed nearly 30% once the bad apple was jettisoned from the group (Sutton, 2011).

If the difficult person is powerful, expulsion may not be an option. In this case, try putting physical distance between you and the problem person. Stay out of each other's way whenever possible. Keep interactions to a minimum. In a few instances, you may have to leave the group to restore your sanity. Some jobs, for instance, are just not worth keeping when abuse is heaped on you daily by an individual with more power than you have.

I have presented you with a rational model for handling troublemakers. Try these methods. They will work well for you in most situations. Nevertheless, we are not strictly rational beings. Difficult people can provoke intense anger and deep frustration from group members. In my own experience, I have found that even if I lost my temper and let my emotions get the better of me, this response is not as problematic as simply ignoring or enduring the disruptive behavior. Even if your anger translates into personal attacks (not a good choice), at the very least you have served notice on the troublesome group member that his or her pattern of behavior is unacceptable and will not be suffered in silence.

QUESTIONS FOR THOUGHT

1. What are some possible disadvantages of expelling a difficult group member? Why should this be a last resort, not a first choice?
2. Have you ever had to deal with a difficult group member? What seemed to work best to manage this challenge?

Too much change (degree) was required in too concentrated a period of time (rate) without a concerted effort to persuade the staff of the value (desirability) of the changes demanded. Groups can often adapt even to large changes if given sufficient time to absorb them and if members are convinced the changes have merit. In some instances, of course, the dismantling of an ineffective system may be necessary to replace it with a better system—one that institutes wholesale change and radical departure from the way things were. Sports teams, for example, may fire entire coaching staffs, dump numerous weak-performing players, and begin from the ground up rebuilding a losing team.

▶ Boundary Control: Regulating Input

Openness and change go hand in hand in a system. **Openness** refers to the degree of continuous interchange with the outside environment. As systems open to the outside, new input enters the system, inevitably disturbing it. Admit women into a previously all-male club, boardroom, or law firm and change is inevitable. Add a single member to your small group and, as powerfully illustrated in the chapter opening case study, massive disturbance can occur. A group must adapt to change or suffer strife, even possible demise. **Adaptability to change** is the adjustment of group boundaries in response to changing environmental conditions.

Boundaries regulate input and consequent exposure to change in a system. When groups establish boundaries, they regulate the degree, rate, even the desirability of change. This **boundary control** determines the amount of access a group has to input, and thus influence, from outsiders.

Every group maintains boundary control to some extent. It is a critical group function. The cast of the television sitcom *Friends* showed keen awareness of the necessity of maintaining boundaries (Chin, 2000). Matthew Perry, the self-deprecating Chandler Bing character in the series, became addicted to painkillers following a Jet Ski accident, and he subsequently lost a shocking amount of weight. Fellow cast members became intensely protective and supportive of Perry during his recovery. They erected strict boundary control to maintain group solidarity and personal friendships among cast members by communicating little information to the press and public about his ordeal.

Boundaries, however, are permeable. They leak. No group can close off so completely to its environment that no change is possible. There is always some interchange with the environment that leaks through the boundaries. Sometimes this is cause for real concern. Twitter tweets, Internet searches, and text messaging all have become sources of concern in court cases (MacLean, 2011). Breakdowns in jury boundary control have occurred repeatedly in the United States (Bowcott, 2013). In Florida, nine jurors in a big federal drug trial admitted that they had conducted "research" on the case by searching the Internet for information, directly violating the judge's instructions not to do so. A mistrial had to be declared. Two appeals courts, in Maryland and New Jersey, reversed criminal convictions because jurors accessed information by using social networking technology (Elias, 2010). As Douglas Keene, president of the American Society of Trial Consultants, notes, "It's important that they (the jurors) don't know what's excluded, and it's important that they don't know why it's excluded" (quoted in Schwartz, 2009). A fair, unbiased trial is at stake (St. Eve & Zuckerman, 2012).

▶ Communication Methods of Boundary Control: Erecting Barriers

Groups establish boundaries by using a variety of communication methods. They can erect physical, psychological, and linguistic barriers, and they can establish rules, roles, and information networks.

Physical Barriers: Protecting Group Space There are many possible physical barriers that can communicate "stay out" to those outside a group. These physical barriers include locking group meeting rooms or choosing an inconvenient location in a building to discourage people from just dropping by and disturbing a group meeting. A board of supervisors' public meeting might place the board on a raised stage or rope off audience members from direct access to board members. Physical boundaries are not always quite so obvious. Gangs may designate a few city blocks as their turf (Conquergood, 1994). Graffiti painted on signs or buildings serves to mark the gang's turf. Removing or painting over a rival gang's graffiti scrawlings can get a gang member killed (Murphy, 2013).

Psychological Barriers: Member in Name Only Groups can communicate to an individual that they do not belong in the group (Nezlek et al., 2012). When this occurs, the group is erecting a psychological barrier. Such barriers occur when a member's contribution during group discussion is ignored or the member is treated as an outcast. The group may even tell the member directly to leave the group. Women and ethnic minorities historically have been made to feel like outsiders and tokens when first joining mostly white, male groups.

Linguistic Barriers: Having to Speak the Language Groups erect linguistic barriers when members use a private vocabulary or slang meant to camouflage meaning outside of the group. Cyberbanging, the high-tech tagging on thousands of gang-related websites, creates virtual turf warfare (Carreon, 2005). Rival gang members exchange threats and "throw up" gang numbers and names on sites operated by the Crips, Bloods, Norteños, Sureños, and various Asian and lesser known gangs. Police seeking to address gang warfare effectively must attempt to decipher street lingo found on various social media used by gangs. This street talk can vary widely among gangs and their geographic locations. In Chicago, for example, a gun may be referred to as a cannon or thumper. In Houston, it may be referred to as a burner, chopper, pump, or gat. In New York, it might be a drum set, biscuit, shotty, rachet, ratty, or flamingo ("Tweets and Threats," 2014). Those who understand the lingo are presumed to be group members. Those who don't are clearly outsiders.

Sandy Huffaker/Getty Images News/Getty Images

This photo of a barrier between the United States and Mexico illustrates

1. Permeable boundaries
2. Attempted regulation of change in a system
3. Boundary control
4. Equifinality

Answers are given at the end of the chapter.

Rules: Permission Not Granted Membership rules establish who can join a group and who is barred. They also define appropriate behaviors in specified social situations. Rules can establish what constitutes disruptive and inappropriate behavior, thus drawing boundaries regarding what will and will not be tolerated by the group. Rules may also specify who can talk to whom, thus controlling input from outside. The Federal Judicial Center's publication, *Benchbook for U.S. District Court Judges*, offers this suggested jury instruction: "You may not communicate with anyone about the case on your cell phone, through email, Blackberry, iPhone, text messaging, or on Twitter, through any blog or website, including Facebook, Google+, MySpace, LinkedIn, or YouTube" (Yurkiw, 2013). In other words, unplug yourself from the world of electronic communication. These judicial rules are meant to prevent juror misconduct and consequent mistrials and reversals.

Roles: Staying in Bounds A **role** is a pattern of expected behavior associated with parts we play in groups. The expectations attached to group roles specify appropriate behavior, thereby fostering predictability and controlling variability. Once the pattern of behavior is associated with a group member, a boundary is set.

In the United States, managers are expected to respect the boundary between an employee's work life and private life. Commenting on a female employee's lack of a husband and informing her that she will be attending a luncheon to meet an eligible male would be viewed as clearly overstepping the boundaries separating supervisor and employee. The same reaction may not occur, however, in India, where a leadership style called *paternal authoritativeness* is often preferred. Indians expect that someone in a supervisory leadership role, typically a male, will act like a father who cares about a family member. Going to the trouble of arranging a luncheon for a female employee to meet an eligible male would likely be perceived as showing personal interest and concern for the employee's welfare (Brislin, 1993). The employee would likely appreciate the gesture (and attend the luncheon), whereas in the United States charges of sexual harassment might be filed. **Role boundaries and culture are inseparably interconnected.**

Networks: Controlling Information Flow Groups set boundaries by establishing networks. A **network** is a structured pattern of information flow and personal contact. Networks control the access and flow of information within the group, and they may also isolate the group from outside influences. Facebook, for example, was originally limited to Harvard students only. Outsiders could not get access. It was a relatively closed network. Quickly, Facebook broadened to include more than a billion users and counting, but each participant can control who has access to his or her home page by either accepting or rejecting a request for access to become a Facebook "friend" (Martin, 2014). The more open the network, the more accessible information is to a broad range of individuals. **Open networks encourage change and potential disruption; closed networks emphasize stability, privacy, and permanence.**

▶ Boundary Control and Group Effectiveness: Open and Closed Systems

Although all groups set boundaries, there is a strong bias in American culture that encourages openness, or loose boundaries, and discourages closedness, or rigid boundaries. We preach the value of fostering an open society and maintaining an open mind. Having a closed mind is linked to an authoritarian personality and dogmatism. A closed society is likened to North Korea. The belief that openness is always good and closedness is always bad is a faulty one (Klapp, 1978). No group can long endure unless it closes off to *some* outside influences and restricts access to *some* information (Galanter, 1999). This is why boundary control is an essential group function.

A group must close off when both the quantity and type of input place undue stress on the group and/or prevent it from accomplishing its task. There are times, for instance, when a family seeks advice and counsel from friends and relatives (input), but there are also times when a family should close itself off to intrusion from outsiders. In-laws who are overly free with advice and criticism impose stress on the family. Permitting even well-intentioned relatives and friends to hammer immediate family members with unsolicited counsel can easily lead to bickering, increased tension, conflict, and even family disintegration.

Despite the popularity of shows such as *Survivor, Big Brother, The Apprentice,* and the *Real Housewives of New Jersey, Atlanta, D.C.,* or name the city, and their billing as "reality television," participants do not act naturally when cameras and microphones record their every move and conversation. It's too intrusive. Competing for huge prize money also makes for "unreality television." We need our boundaries to live our lives without the increased stress from probing eyes of strangers.

Group members should watch for signs of excessive openness or closedness, such as when groups experience debilitating stress and tension, divisive conflicts, boredom and malaise, and poor productivity. Loosening or tightening boundaries may be in order. Whether to relax or tighten boundaries depends on whether the group is already very closed or very open.

Unreality TV programs, such as *Survivor,* loosen boundaries and create extreme openness to the probing eyes of viewers.

SECOND LOOK

Openness and Group Boundary Control

Types of Group Boundaries Regulating Change

Physical Barriers	Psychological Barriers
Linguistic Barriers	Rules
Roles	Networks

Boundary Control and Group Effectiveness

- Signs of Excessive Openness or Closedness:

Debilitating Stress	Divisive Conflicts
Boredom	Malaise
Poor Productivity	

- Adjust boundaries when signs of excessive openness/closedness occur.

Influence of Size

Size is a central element in any human system. Fluctuations in size have enormous influence on the structure and function of a group (Laughlin et al., 2006; Lowry et al., 2006).

Focus Questions

1. **What is the most appropriate size for a decision-making group?**
2. **What distinguishes a small group from a large one?**
3. **How are groups and organizations different?**

▶ Group Size and Complexity

As groups increase in numerical size, complexity increases. Try scheduling a meeting for a group of 15 or 20 members. Consider how difficult it would be to find a time that doesn't conflict with at least one or more members' personal schedules and preferences. There are numerous complications that increased complexity produces. This section discusses these complications.

Quantitative Complexity: Exponentially Complicated As the size of a group increases, the possible number of interactions between group members increases exponentially (Bostrom, 1970). The calculations are as follows:

Number in Group	Interactions Possible
2	2
3	9
4	28
5	75
6	186
7	441
8	1,056

In a dyad, only two relationships are possible, namely, person A to person B, and vice versa. A and B may not have the same perception of their relationship. Person A may perceive the relationship with B as a close friendship, whereas B sees the relationship with A as merely acquaintanceship. In a triad, or three-member group, there are nine possibilities:

1. A to B	4. C to A	7. A to B and C
2. B to A	5. B to C	8. B to A and C
3. A to C	6. C to B	9. C to A and B

Adding even a single member to a group enormously complicates the group dynamics. In a study investigating why groups fail, one notable factor was the difficulty of scheduling meetings when groups grew to eight members (Fiechtner & Davis, 1992).

Imagine the difficulty Diane and Stanley Cook experienced raising their ever-expanding family (McLaughlin, 2004). As college sweethearts they began dreaming of raising a large family. Their wish was granted—in a big way. They raised five biological children and *106 foster children!* Many of the foster children were developmentally disabled, physically or mentally. This amazing couple adopted 13 of these foster children. Living in a 2,000-square-foot home, "only" 13 children lived under the same roof at the same time. Nevertheless, preventing sheer chaos would be a substantial challenge. "It was organized," Diane Cook explains. "Everybody chipped in" (p. 19A).

Complexity and Group Transactions: Size Matters Variations in size affect group transactions in several specific ways. First, **larger groups typically have more nonparticipants than smaller groups** ("Is Your Team too Big?" 2006). This occurs partly because in larger groups there is more intense competition to seize the floor (Carletta et al., 1998). More reticent members are apt to sit quietly rather than fight to be heard. This also means that the more talkative members are likely to emerge as leaders of larger groups because influence on the group comes partly from speaking (Kolb, 1997).

Second, **smaller groups inhibit overt disagreement and signs of dissatisfaction more than larger groups.** Smaller groups can apply more intense pressure to conform to majority opinion than can be applied in larger groups (Bettinghaus & Cody, 1987). Splinter groups and factions are more likely to emerge in larger groups. In a 6-person group, there may be only a single deviant who must stand alone against the group. In a 12-person group, however, two or more deviants may more easily emerge, forming a supportive faction ("Are Six Heads as Good as Twelve?" 2004).

In the movie *12 Angry Men,* only one juror votes "not guilty" on the first vote. Hailed by many as a dramatization of the importance of one person standing against the many in a fight for truth and justice, one scene is often overlooked. The lone holdout debates with fellow jurors for a while, but eventually indicates that he is unwilling to continue if no other juror will support his position. He makes a deal with the jury. If no other juror votes not guilty on the next ballot, then he will join the majority and also vote for conviction, thereby sending the defendant to death row. When he gains an ally, the fight is continued to its dramatic conclusion. Nonconformity is easier when you don't have to stand alone against the group.

Third, **group size affects levels of cooperation** (Benenson et al., 2000; Stahelski & Tsukuda, 1990). When groups of 12 to 30 members were compared, the smallest groups were found to be the most cooperative, meaning they worked together on tasks more interdependently, engaged in collaborative effort, and exhibited consensus leadership. As groups increased in size, cooperation decreased. This resulted in diminished task effectiveness, unmet goals, and increased conflicts. Other studies have found that larger groups encourage formation of **cliques** or small, narrowly focused subgroups (factions) that create a competitive atmosphere (Carron & Spink, 1995).

Fourth, **group members tend to be less satisfied with groups of 10 or more** (Carter & West, 1998). The overall group climate often deteriorates when groups become large (Aube et al., 2011; De Cremer & Leonardelli, 2003). Tasks become more complex to perform, tension mounts, and dominant group members can trigger interpersonal disharmony by becoming too aggressive and forceful with other members while trying to impose order (Pavitt & Curtis, 1994).

Thus, **decreased participation, inhibition of overt disagreement, diminished levels of cooperation, and reduced levels of satisfaction characteristic of larger groups all lead to significantly diminished group productivity** (Aube et al., 2011; Stahl et al., 2010). Research by Marcia Blenko and her colleagues (2010) shows that each member added to a decision-making group that starts with seven members reduces decision effectiveness by about 10%. If this **rule of seven** is taken to its logical conclusion, they explain, a group of 17 members or more "rarely makes any decisions" (p. 88). Too many group members can create decision paralysis, not cooperative decision making. Another study of 2,623 members in 329 work groups shows that groups composed of 3 to 8 members are significantly more productive than groups composed of 9 or more members. Groups of 3 to 6 members are the most productive, according to one other study (Wheelan, 2009).

So what is the ideal size for a group? Is it 3 to 6, or maybe 7 or 8? There is no perfect number. Amazon.com CEO Jeff Bezos follows the "two pizza rule." A group is too large if two pizzas are insufficient to feed all members (Yang, 2006). Obviously, this rule is an imprecise standard for determining ideal group size (small, medium, or large pizzas? Thin crust or deep-dish?). **The best size for a group is the smallest size capable of performing the task effectively** (Sawyer, 2007; Sundstrom et al., 1990). This admittedly is also somewhat imprecise advice, but there is a trade-off between *quality* and *speed* when trying to determine ideal group size (Pavitt & Curtis, 1994). If the primary group goal is the quality of the decision, then a group of 7 to 8 members is advisable. These smaller groups are especially effective if there is little overlap of knowledge and skills among group members and the group task requires substantial deep diversity in knowledge and skills (Larson, 2007; Valacich et al., 1994). If the primary goal of the group is speed, however, then very small groups of 3 or 4 members are advisable. Larger groups, especially those with a dozen or more members, potentially provide a diversity of resources but typically slow decision making and problem solving, sometimes maddeningly so.

In a comparison of 6-member and 12-member mock juries, the larger juries took much longer to deliberate and they took more votes (Davis et al., 1997). Because juries are faced with momentous choices that significantly affect people's lives, however, the 12-member jury has been the norm. If your freedom depended on a jury verdict, you would certainly want the primary group goal to be the quality and not the speed of the decision. Consensus (unanimous agreement) becomes difficult when groups are large. Juries are structured so quick decisions are unlikely and consensus is difficult to achieve. Requiring a unanimous vote from 12 jurors requires careful deliberation on key issues and evidence to achieve consensus.

Contextual factors (politics, legal requirements, institutional norms, availability of members, task complexity, etc.) may necessitate groups larger in size than what works for greatest efficiency. I once worked on a campus task force on hiring practices. Initially, the task force began with seven members. Howls of displeasure erupted across campus. Many segments of the campus strenuously objected to a lack of representation on the task force. Ultimately, what began as a small group became a rather cumbersome 20-member large group because of important political considerations. Not once in months of meetings did all 20 members attend the same meeting, and discussions were often exercises in cross-talk and interruptions. Competent communicators can work effectively in larger groups, although increased size magnifies the challenges.

▶ An Organization: A Group of Groups

When groups grow, they reach a point where they may become organizations with bureaucracies. For instance, suppose you and two friends decide to open a small business together. Let's say you call it Computer Repair Use and Distribution (CRUD for short). In its initial stages, the structure of your group is informal and the division of labor is most likely equal. Since the three of you work together as friends (Crud Buds), communication is not hampered by cumbersome chains of command, middle managers, and the bureaucratic complexities of a large, formal organization. Standards of operation and procedures for decision making are informally negotiated among the three of you as situations occur.

If your little enterprise booms, employees will have to be hired, thus expanding the business and increasing the complexity of the entire operation. Work schedules will have to be coordinated. Perhaps a fleet of vans (Crudmobiles) will have to be purchased to form a computer repair "strike team." Standardized codes of dress (Crud Duds) and conduct on the job (Crudiquette) may be required. Constant training (Cruducation) in ever-changing computer technology will be necessary. Formal grievance procedures may also be required to settle disputes among employees and management. You may decide to open additional CRUD outlets (Crudlets), and even become a chain, selling franchises around the country. Now you must hire managers, accountants, and lawyers; establish a board of directors; sell stock in the company; and become business executives. What began as a small enterprise can grow into a large organization.

Consider Facebook, which became the world's largest social networking site. Facebook began as a small enterprise in 2004 at Harvard University. Creator Mark Zuckerberg, along with fellow roommates and classmates Eduardo Saverin, Dustin Moskowitz, and Chris Hughes, developed Facebook as an online Harvard student directory that quickly mushroomed into a dominant global social networking site. Despite disputes regarding whether Zuckerberg stole the original idea for Facebook, no one can dispute the meteoric rise of Facebook from a small group effort of four roommates into a large organization of more than 6,300 employees worldwide in just its first decade of operation (Martin, 2014).

When small groups grow into larger groups, finally graduating into complex organizations, the structure and function of these human systems change. Small groups are more personal than large organizations. Small groups usually can function well as a committee of the whole, with relatively equal distribution of power. **With increasing group size comes greater formality.** Traditional large organizations become hierarchical (members of the organization are rank ordered from top to bottom), with clearly demarcated power structures, lines of authority, and top-down communication networks (Tapscott & Williams, 2006), although recently there has been a trend toward *flattening the hierarchy* by moving away from tightly defined roles of superiors and subordinates and placing greater emphasis on teamwork. Using social networking sites for intraorganizational communication has also encouraged a flattened hierarchy (Shih, 2010). In traditional organizations, the company is more important than any single individual. Employees can be replaced with relative ease, whereas in a small intimate group, loss of a single member may bring about the demise of the group.

The flow of information is one of the most important differences between small groups and complex organizations. Normally, little negative information from below reaches the top of the corporate hierarchy, or, if it does, it is delayed (Adler & Elmhorst, 2008). Who wants to be the bearer of bad tidings? They often shoot (figuratively speaking) the messenger who brings bad news.

Bad decision making cannot be hidden easily when the group is small. Almost any blunder will become incandescent when the black hole of bureaucracy is not present to shroud it. If you have three people running a small business and one of the three does something boneheaded that affects the enterprise, your choices immediately narrow to two possibilities (unless, of course, you are guilty but playing dumb). One of your two partners has to be the culprit.

Information distortion usually is a bigger problem in organizations than in smaller groups. Managers act as gatekeepers, screening messages, selecting which ones will be brought to the attention of higher-ups. By the time a message from below reaches top executives in an organization, it can easily become unrecognizable nonsense. Similarly, information from the top can be distorted by the time it filters down to the bottom of the organization (Adler et al., 2013).

In smaller groups, the communication is usually more direct, with fewer opportunities for distortion from messages being transmitted serially through several people. If the message is communicated to the entire group at the same time—a comparatively easy task if the gathering is small—then the problems of message distortion are reduced.

Although organizations are not emphasized in this text, I include examples from organizational settings because many of you can relate meaningfully to such an environment. Virtually all of what is discussed is immediately relevant to enhancing communication competence in organizations. After all, "an organization itself may be viewed as a group of groups" (Haslett et al., 1992, p. 103). Work is often performed in teams (subsystems) within the larger organizational system (an environmental influence), a subject for later discussion in Chapter 7.

In summary, groups are systems. The three main elements of a system are interconnectedness of parts, adaptability to change, and the influence of size. There is no precise dividing line between small and large groups, and the ideal size for most decision-making and problem-solving groups is the smallest group capable of performing the task effectively. Having now laid the theoretical foundation for analyzing small groups, I discuss the process of group development in the next chapter.

SECOND LOOK

Effects of Increasing Group Size

Increases

Complexity

Factionalism/cliques

Formality—more hierarchical

Information distortion

Quality decision making (unless group becomes too large and unwieldy)

Difficulty achieving consensus/majority vote often substituted

Likelihood that talkative members become leaders

Decreases

Participation in group discussion

Cooperation (in very large groups)

Pressure to conform—coalitions likely to form in opposition to group norms

Member satisfaction with group experience (10 or more)

Access to information

Flow of negative information to top of hierarchy

Speed of decision making

MindTap

Reflect on
what you've
learned.

In Mixed Company

▶ Online

Now that you've read Chapter 2, access the online resources that accompany *In Mixed Company* at **www.cengagebrain.com**. Your online resources include:

1. Multiple-choice and true-false **chapter practice quizzes** with automatic correction

2. Digital **glossary**

3. **Interactive Flashcards**

QUESTIONS FOR CRITICAL THINKERS

1. How does the effect of a disruptive group member demonstrate the interconnectedness element of a system?
2. In groups you belong to, what boundaries are erected?
3. Have you experienced group boundaries that are too rigid in any groups to which you belong? How can you tell that the boundaries are too rigid?
4. What's the largest group you've ever belonged to that didn't experience serious problems because of its size? Why did it work?

VIDEO *Case Studies*

City Island (2010). Comedy-Drama; PG-13

Vince Rizzo, played by Andy Garcia, is a corrections officer who secretly wants to be an actor. He hides this fact and his secret acting lessons from his wife Joyce, played by Julianna Margulies, so she thinks he is having an affair. Secrets abound between Vince and Joyce, and the spillover ensnares other family members with their own secrets. Analyze boundary control issues and openness versus closedness concerns from a systems perspective.

Contagion (2011). Drama; R

Horrific presentation of a pandemic virus and its consequences. You have to have a strong stomach to watch this movie. Analyze this film for the ripple effect and systems theory dynamics.

Freedom Writers (2007). Drama; PG-13

This is the story of a young, idealistic teacher (Hilary Swank) who lands her first job at a Long Beach high school dominated by racial tension and gang violence. Based on the true story of Erin Gruwell, this depiction avoids condescension and phony emotional displays. Analyze Gruwell's class as a system. Apply the three main components of systems.

In Good Company (2004). Comedy/Drama

Dennis Quaid plays an advertising sales executive whose life at work and home is upended when his new boss, played by Topher Grace, turns out to be a 20-something, inexperienced doofus, who even begins seeing Quaid's daughter (Scarlett Johannson). Examine the adaptability to change in both the family system and the organizational system. Consider issues of boundary control. Finally, analyze appropriateness of the Topher Grace character's behavior in the small group (Quaid's family) versus the organization (ad agency).

The Host. (2013). Adventure/Sci-Fi/Romance. PG-13

Average but intriguing story about the human race being infected with small parasitic aliens called "souls." Analyze from a systems perspective the isolated cave-dwelling humans who have created a protective enclave from the aliens. What are the interconnected parts, adaptability to change, boundary control, and influence of size elements? How does environment influence the group?

Answers to Multiple-Choice Questions in Captions

Cartoon, p. 49, 3; Photo, p. 57, 1, 2, 3.

3
Group Development

O n April 24, 1997, the board of directors for Delta Air Lines announced the unanimous decision not to renew the contract of Delta's chairman, Ronald Allen. Allen was forced out because, as one board member put it, there was "an accumulation of abrasions over time" (Brannigan, 1997, p. A8). So what were these "abrasions" that led the board to replace Allen? In a memo released to Delta employees, the board, without making direct reference to Allen, stated that it placed "a high value on Delta's culture of respect, unity, and deep regard for our heritage." The board went on to say that it intended "to select a person as our next leader who will work well within this culture we all value so highly" (cited in Brannigan, 1997, p. A8).

Ronald Allen clearly did not engender respect, unity, and a deep regard for the worker-friendly, family atmosphere valued by the board. Allen had a caustic management style that concentrated on the financial "bottom line" at the expense of relationships with workers. He developed a reputation for berating employees in front of other workers. He was known as autocratic, intolerant, and harsh (Brannigan, 1997). When Hollis Harris revealed to Allen that he was resigning as Delta's president to head Continental Airlines, Allen demanded that Harris relinquish the keys to his company car on the spot, leaving him stranded without transportation home. Allen cut thousands of jobs. Employees were extremely upset with this cost-cutting measure and the heavy-handed way in which it was done. Allen acknowledged that workers were upset with his slash-and-burn tactics, but his glib response was "so be it." Soon, buttons reading "So Be It" began appearing on the chests of pilots, flight attendants, and mechanics.

MindTap
Start with a
quick warm-up
vactivity.

Worker morale plunged. An exodus of senior managers began. Many experienced workers were laid off or quit. Delta service, once the envy of the airline industry, rapidly deteriorated. Dirty planes and frustrated flight attendants became the norm. On-time performance of flights sank from the top to the bottom of the industry. Passengers began joking that Delta stood for "Doesn't Ever Leave The Airport." Tough measures were necessary to save Delta financially when Allen took over, but, as Wayne Horvitz, a Washington, D.C., labor relations consultant notes, "You don't have to be an SOB to be tough" (Brannigan, 1997, p. A1). Allen had "broken the spirit" of this once proud company. Under his direction, "What the airline embarked on was nothing less than a suicidal mission" ("Plane Business Ron Allen," 2008). His narrow focus on the task of returning Delta to profitability ignored the vital role interpersonal relations play in group success.

Delta filed for bankruptcy protection and reorganization in 2005. "After the bankruptcy, Delta spent millions to rebuild morale, flying in many of its 47,000 employees for a series of events that were equal parts team-building and tent revival. Delta also convinced creditors to cede 15% ownership to employees" (Foust, 2009). Richard Anderson became CEO of Delta in 2007. He established the practice of flying in a Delta cockpit jump seat once a month to solicit suggestions for improving the company from pilots in flight, and he spent a two-day stretch soliciting suggestions from 2,000 employees. Delta posted its first profit since bankruptcy, $500 million, in 2007. Delta made an aggregate profit of $3.2 billion between 2010 and 2013 with Anderson at the helm, surviving the "Great Recession" that hit hard in 2008 (Caulderwood, 2013).

This example highlights the strong connection between the task and social dimensions of groups. Put simply, how group members are treated and the quality of their relationships within a group can markedly affect task accomplishment. Try getting your housemates to keep your joint apartment clean and tidy (task) when relationships among housemates are strained. One study showed that high-quality relationships with coworkers encourage high job motivation; low-quality relationships predict job burnout and a desire to quit (Fernet et al., 2010). As groups move through phases of development, the relationship between task and social dimensions of every group can become a critical factor in achieving success or experiencing failure. **The primary purpose of this chapter is to explore this interconnectedness of task and social dimensions through phases of group development.** There are two related chapter objectives:

1. To explain the connection between task and social dimensions of a group,

2. To discuss task and social dimensions within the periodic phases of group development.

Primary Dimensions of Groups

The Ronald Allen case study illustrates the importance of social relations to group performance and effectiveness. This is not a unidirectional process, however. Social relations in groups affect the task, but the reverse is also true. In this section, the systemic interconnection between the two primary dimensions of groups, task and social, are explored.

> ## Focus Questions
>
> 1. **How do the task and social dimensions of groups interconnect?**
> 2. **How are the task and social dimensions integral to both the formation and development of decision-making groups?**
> 3. **How does a group build cohesiveness?**

▶ Task and Social Dimensions: Working and Socializing

All decision-making groups have both task and social dimensions. The **task dimension** is the work performed by the group. The **social dimension** is the relationships that form between members in the group and their impact on the group as a whole. **Because groups are systems, the task and social dimensions are interconnected.** Thus, degree of concern for a task affects the social or relationship aspects. Conversely, degree of concern for relationships in the group affects the accomplishment of the task.

The output from a group's task dimension is productivity. **Productivity** is the result of the efficient and effective accomplishment of a group task. The output from the social dimension is cohesiveness. **Cohesiveness** is the degree to which members feel a part of the group, wish to stay in the group, and are committed to each other and to the group's work (Lanfred, 1998; Wech et al., 1998). Cohesiveness is produced primarily by attention to social relationships.

Neither the task nor the social dimension can be ignored for a decision-making group to be successful. **Finding the optimum balance between productivity and cohesiveness is an important goal for all groups** (Hardy et al., 2005). Too much attention to productivity can diminish cohesiveness by producing stress and conflict. Ronald Allen's single-minded focus on the task of returning Delta Air Lines to profitability disrupted the interpersonal harmony within the company. This disruption ultimately led to poor service, diminished worker morale, loss of valuable employees, and a negative image within the industry and among passengers. Conversely, too much emphasis on cohesiveness can produce a group of socializers ("It's party time!") who like each other a great deal but accomplish nothing in particular (Hardy et al., 2005). This is a problem unless, of course, the purpose of the group is merely to have a good time and no task needs to be accomplished, in which case knock yourself out.

In general, cohesiveness enhances group productivity unless overemphasized (Beal et al., 2003; Evans & Dion, 2012). This relationship is stronger in smaller groups than in larger ones, for ongoing natural groups than for artificially created groups, and for cooperative groups than for competitive groups (Klein, 1996). The nature of the task and type of group also affect the relationship between cohesiveness and productivity (Chiocchio & Essiembre, 2009). The more interconnected group members must be to accomplish a task (e.g., flying a passenger jet, performing surgery, playing team basketball) the stronger is the cohesiveness–productivity relationship (Gully et al., 2012).

▶ Building Cohesiveness: Bringing Us Together

So how do groups build cohesiveness? The main strategies are:

1. **Encourage compatible membership**. When group members enjoy each other's company and share an attraction for one another, cohesiveness can be easily built. When difficult, disruptive individuals join the group, cohesiveness can suffer. Of course, a group doesn't always have the luxury of choosing who can join. Sometimes membership is mandated by the environment within which the small group operates (e.g., an institution or corporation).

2. **Develop shared goals**. One aspect of cohesiveness is sharing a common vision. When all group members are pulling together to achieve a goal valued by all, cohesiveness is likely to increase (Hardy et al., 2005).

3. **Accomplish tasks**. Productive groups usually become more cohesive as a result of task accomplishment. If group members feel good about work accomplished, this often pulls the group together and promotes team spirit. This is true unless some members suspect that they are doing the lion's share of the work and others are slackers. This can promote disgruntled feelings and may diminish the effort of the hard-working members, which in turn may lead to poor group performance and subsequent diminished cohesion (Hoigaard et al., 2006). As a rule, successful teams exhibit harmony. Unsuccessful teams, however, frequently manifest frustration and disappointment by sniping, sniveling, and finger-pointing (Van Oostrum & Rabbie, 1995). Poor productivity can lead to group disintegration.

4. **Develop a positive history of cooperation**. If group members work together cooperatively rather than competitively, cohesiveness can flourish (Klein, 1996). Constructing cooperation in small groups is discussed in Chapter 4.

5. **Promote acceptance of group members**. Make each other feel valued and welcomed in the group. Make an effort to engage in friendly conversation. Cohesion is disrupted if some members feel that cliques have developed and that they are outsiders, not members embraced by others (Hardy et al., 2005).

The task and social dimensions are integral to both the formation and development of decision-making groups. Just where these two dimensions fit into the life of a group can be ascertained by exploring the periodic phases of group development.

Periodic Phases of Group Development

Tuckman (1965) describes the four phases of group development as forming, storming, norming, and performing (see also Wheelan et al., 2003). These phases should not be viewed as sequential. Groups do not necessarily pass through these phases of development in linear fashion like a person does when growing older (i.e., youth, middle age, old age). Groups tend to be far messier than this, sometimes cycling back around to a previous phase that was seemingly completed (Hare, 1994). (Unhappily, such cycling back is not possible with aging.)

Admittedly, group development can be classified in terms of an initial phase where individuals join together for some reason (forming), a tension phase (storming), a standards and rules of conduct for members phase (norming), and a phase where effort is targeted toward goal achievement (performing). These phases can be periodic, meaning that they are apt to appear, disappear, reappear, and even overlap (Chang et al., 2006). Forming, storming, norming, and performing are also global phases of group development relevant to groups in general, large or small. Specific phases relevant to the process of decision emergence in small groups are discussed in Chapter 9.

Focus Questions

1. Does why we join a group make any difference to the group? Explain.
2. How does group composition affect group efficacy?
3. Is tension in a group always undesirable? Explain.
4. Where do group norms come from? Why do we conform to group norms?
5. Under what conditions do groups outperform individuals?

▶ Forming: Gathering Members

A group begins with its own formation. In this section, two issues are addressed: (1) why we join groups, and (2) how diverse membership affects groups.

Reasons We Join Groups: Motivation The reasons we join groups act as catalysts for group formation. We join groups to satisfy some need (Shaw, 1981). There are six main reasons we join groups. They are:

1. **Need to Belong: No One's an Island** Humans are communal beings. We have a powerful need to belong, one that is as much an imperative as the need for food. This innate need is universal, not specific to any culture (Baumeister & Leary, 1995). It has survival value for humans. Forming social bonds with group members can provide protection from outside threats to one's person and possessions. Group membership can stave off the "lethal poison" of chronic loneliness (Lynch, 2000). We find mates by joining groups (e.g., Parents Without Partners), and we satisfy our desire for affection from family and groups of friends. American culture lauds individualism, but, as evolutionary biologist George Gaylord Simpson (1994) observes, "The quest to be alone is indeed a futile one, never successfully followed in the history of life." Joining a group provides an opportunity to satisfy our deep need to belong (Hill, 2009). Feeling as though we belong also maintains a desire of group members to remain in a group, more so than financial rewards (Stewart et al., 2012).

2. **Interpersonal Attraction: The Drawing Power of Others** We join a group because we are drawn to its members. We seem drawn to others who are similar in personality, attitudes and beliefs, ethnic origin, sexual orientation, and economic status (Berscheid & Reis, 1998; McCrae et al., 2008). Many campus clubs and support groups are attractive because of member similarity. Physical attractiveness may also draw us to join a group. We may have no other reason to join a group than that we'd like to get to know a particular attractive group member. Although there is a popular belief that physical attractiveness is more important to men than it is to women as a factor influencing interpersonal attraction, reviews of hundreds of studies show otherwise (Langlois et al., 2000).

3. **Attraction to Group Activities: Joining for Fun and Frolic** Sometimes we join groups to participate in the group's activities. This is a primary motivation for joining most college athletic teams, fraternities, and sororities. Joining a group because you are attracted to the group's activities doesn't preclude the additional draw from social connection among members. When I coached intercollegiate debate, students joined primarily for the academic competition. Secondary motivations, however, developed along the way, such as traveling around the country, cultivating friendships, falling in love, and engaging in the inevitable social activities that are attached to debating. Softball leagues are frequently rated A, B, and C so the hardcore athletes can be separated from the Budweiser crowd. Some players are drawn to the physical activity, and others are drawn more to the social activities.

4. **Attraction to Group Goals: A Purpose-Driven Membership** Another reason we join groups and wish to remain as members is an attraction to the group's goals. Political groups gain members because individuals are drawn to the cause or the candidate. We join most volunteer groups because we are attracted to the groups' goals.

   When you join a group for a worthy cause, you don't have the luxury of interacting only with members that you'd enjoy inviting to dinner. You're stuck adapting to the various personalities and quirks of fellow members. Your commitment to the goal of the group, however, may be enough to keep you coming back despite the obnoxious character who insists on showing his proficiency at nose humming.

5. **Establishment of Meaning and Identity: Groups-R-Us** When situations are ambiguous, and we're looking for answers, we often join groups as a means of better understanding ourselves, our world, and others who cross our paths (Goethals & Darley, 1987). A study of youth violence by former Massachusetts Commissioner of Public Health Deborah Prothrow-Stith (1991) draws this similarity between antisocial groups such as gangs and prosocial groups such as fraternities: "They provide young people with goals and objectives, a world view, and a place where they are valued (p. 97)." You may join a choir, a marching band, or an athletic team for similar reasons.

6. **Fulfillment of Unrelated Needs: Our Miscellaneous Reasons** Finally, we join groups to satisfy needs that are unrelated to the group's task, goals, members, or even our desire to belong. We may become group members to enhance our résumé or establish business contacts. Sometimes we join a group because other members familiar to us have joined, removing some of the uncertainty associated with group formation (Arrow & Crosson, 2003). In some cases, we are told by persons in authority to join a group. You may be summoned for jury duty. It is wise to comply. The instructor of your class may put you into a group of people who interest you very little. If you are pragmatic, you will make the best of a less than satisfactory situation because your grade may depend on it.

The reasons individuals join groups have noticeable effects on the productivity and cohesiveness of those groups. If they join because they are attracted to the other members, the likelihood of cohesiveness in the group is certainly more probable than if they join to meet self-oriented needs. If they join because they are attracted to the group's goals, productivity is likely to be enhanced. If they join groups for personal gain only, they'll likely end up as deadweight and drag down the entire group.

Member Diversity: The Benefits and Challenges of Difference According to the U.S. Census Bureau, more than a third of this country's population is non-white. By 2043, minorities composed largely of Mexican Americans and other

©Jamie Roach/Shutterstock.com

We join groups for all sorts of reasons. Which reasons might be true for members of this team: Need to belong? Interpersonal attraction? Attraction to group activities? Attraction to group goals? Establishment of meaning and identity? Fulfillment of unrelated needs?

Latinos, African Americans, and Asian Americans will constitute the majority of the population (Kayne, 2013). In addition, with the advent of virtual groups whose members may vary widely in age, ethnicity, and culture, the likelihood that you will participate in groups whose membership mirrors yourself is becoming ever more remote. This offers opportunities and challenges.

Groups usually benefit significantly from diverse membership (Gastil et al., 2007). **Diverse membership** is defined as proportional representation by culture, ethnicity, gender, and age (Karakowsky & Siegel, 1999; McLeod et al., 1996). Heterogeneous (diverse membership) groups are more likely to have members with *deep diversity*— varied skills, perspectives, backgrounds, information, and experiences (discussed in Chapter 2).

This deep diversity can provide a wider array of problem-solving and decision-making resources than are likely to be found in homogeneous (nondiverse membership) groups (Haslett & Ruebush, 1999; Homan et al., 2007). For example, research shows that gender diversity in small groups enhances team performance (Curseu & Schruijer, 2010). Groups whose membership includes a rich mixture of Asian, African, Latino, and Anglo Americans have superior performance to groups that include only Anglos (McLeod et al., 1996). Professor Samuel R. Sommers (2006) of Tufts University summarizes his findings in one study of 200 participants on 29 racially diverse mock juries: "Such diverse juries deliberated longer, raised more facts about the case, and conducted broader and more wide-ranging deliberations." More important, "They also made fewer factual errors in discussing evidence and when errors did occur, those errors were more likely to be corrected during the discussion" (quoted in "Racial Diversity," 2006). Finally, groups with a mix of males, females, and various ethnicities also counteract biases more effectively than more homogeneous groups (Marcus-Newhall et al., 1993).

Diversity in group membership, however, poses significant challenges (Chao & Moon, 2005; Mannix & Neale, 2005). Diversity may result in increased difficulty achieving agreement, especially considering individualism–collectivism cultural value differences discussed in Chapter 1, and power–distance value differences discussed in Chapter 9 (Hofstede & Hofstede, 2010). Cohesiveness and group satisfaction may also be more challenging to develop and maintain (Barker et al., 2000). A competition for power and resources between majority and minority members may emerge and result in hostile communication and discrimination (Mannix & Neale, 2005). With group diversity comes the potential for conflict and misunderstanding. Hackman (2003), for example, studied gender diversity in concert orchestras and found strong resistance from entrenched male members to the entrance of large numbers of women into the orchestras. He concluded:

> Life in a homogeneously male orchestra surely is not much affected by the presence of one or two women, especially if they play a gendered instrument such as the harp. Larger numbers of women, however, can become a worrisome presence on high-status turf that previously had been an exclusively male province, engendering intergroup conflicts that stress all players and disrupt the social dynamics of the orchestra (p. 908).

Consider one other challenge posed by diversity in age (Timmerman, 2000). A Pew Research Center study (2009) reported the largest generational differences in the United States in 40 years. Those 65 years and older differ significantly from those 18 to 29 on issues of politics, religion, social relationships, use of technology, and other topics (see also Leonhardt, 2012). Generalizations based on generation gaps should be embraced cautiously, but generational differences do pose significant challenges for groups. Older members in college groups composed mostly of teens and 20-somethings may have a tough time identifying with younger members, and vice versa. Older members may feel isolated and become nonparticipants, or they may "take charge" as in a parental role without the willing acceptance of younger members. Individuals fresh out of college who join the business and professional world may find it intimidating working with more mature, experienced group members. Issues associated with following rules, respect for authority, and attention to task and details may trigger clashes. **Despite these challenges, diverse membership in groups is generally a positive influence.**

There is no magic, however, from merely adding traditionally excluded members to decision-making and problem-solving groups. Sexism, sexual harassment, and stereotyping continue to plague mixed-sex groups (Raghubir & Valenzuela, 2010). Adding a single ethnic minority, woman, or person of a markedly different age to a group can easily appear to be tokenism. Tokens are often the targets of prejudice and discrimination (Fiske, 1993). They can be easily ignored, harassed, or silenced.

In situations where group composition can be considered during the forming phase (e.g., task force or ad hoc groups), a maximum effort should be made to have a diverse membership (Karakowsky & Siegel, 1999). The **20 percent rule** is an important minimum standard to achieve in this regard. Researchers have observed that discrimination against minorities and women drops substantially when no less than 20% of a group, and no fewer than two members, are ethnic minorities and/or women (Pettigrew & Martin, 1987).

In addition, negative side effects of group diversity can be addressed by recognizing that initially team members will need some time to address any friction that emerges because of broad category differences (race, age, and so forth). Also, these category differences, instead of being highlighted (e.g., "People of my generation believe…"), can be minimized during group discussion and problem solving, making conflict less likely (Homan et al., 2010).

In conclusion, the competent communicator can show sensitivity to the needs of the group during the forming phase in the following ways (Andersen, 1988; Mannix & Neale, 2005):

1. **Express positive attitudes and feelings**. This phase is the getting-acquainted stage of group development. This is not an appropriate time to be deviant (e.g., displaying embarrassing lapses in social etiquette, making abrasive remarks or provocative statements, or wearing outrageous dress). Don't put your foot in your mouth. Put your best foot forward.

2. **Appear friendly, open, and interested**. Be approachable by establishing eye contact with group members, initiating conversation, and responding warmly to interactions from others.

3. **Encourage a "getting-to-know-you" conversation**. This places the initial emphasis on the social dimension of the group before delving into the task immediately. As noted in Chapter 1, this may be more of a stretch for men than women, generally, because men often place greater emphasis on status than connection during conversation. A getting-acquainted conversation allows you to explore interesting differences that accompany diverse membership. View diversity as an opportunity instead of an irritation. Different perspectives can improve group decision making and problem solving.

4. **Find areas of commonality and cooperation**. Problems mostly arise when group members concentrate on differences, not similarities, among members. **Ethnocentrism**—the belief that one's own culture is superior to others, especially when two cultures have large differences—should be avoided. Cultural difference is not deficiency. Try finding commonalities in values and perspectives and explore ways to cooperate. Chapters 4, 10, and 11 explore commonality and cooperation in detail.

5. **Establish clear group goals** (Crown, 2007). Both heterogeneous (diverse membership) and homogeneous (nondiverse membership) groups function better when clear group goals are established early in the formation phase. Developing clear goals is discussed in Chapter 7.

▶ Storming: Feeling the Tension

All groups experience some social tension because change in any system can be an ordeal. Tension can be a positive force. We are usually at our best when we experience some tension. Athletes perform best when they find the proper balance between complete relaxation and crippling anxiety. Excessive tension, however, can produce damaging conflict that may split the group apart. The relative absence of tension in a group can result in lethargy, haphazard attention to the task, and weak productivity. **Finding both the level of tension that galvanizes the group and effectively managing group tension are important factors in successful group development.**

There are two types of social tension: primary and secondary (Bormann, 1990). All long-term groups experience both types.

Primary Tension: Initial Uneasiness When you first gather in a group, you normally feel some jitters and uneasiness, called **primary tension**. Instructors meeting classes for the first time usually experience some primary tension. When you initially meet roommates, classmates, or teammates, primary tension occurs. Even groups that have a lengthy history can experience primary tension at the outset of every meeting. This is especially true if groups such as the PTA, homeowners associations, or student senate meet infrequently. Also, when virtual group members connect, if contact with an online group is infrequent, primary tension can emerge.

There are many signs of primary tension. Group members may become cautious and hesitant in their communication. Long periods of uncomfortable silence and tentative statements are all indicators of primary tension. Group members are often overly polite and careful to avoid controversy. Interruptions normally invoke immediate apologies.

Primary tension is a natural dynamic of group life. In most instances it tends to be short-lived and cause for little concern. With time, you become comfortable with the group and your primary tension diminishes. **Joking, laughing, and chatting about your interests, experiences, and beliefs on noncontroversial subjects all serve to reduce primary tension.** You're not trying to "support gay marriage," "promote intelligent design," or "raise an alarm about climate change." "Hi! My name is Malcolm; what's your position on abortion?" is not a good way to begin in a group. Controversial subjects can increase tension among members. Your purpose is to become acquainted with other group members. As you get to know each other better, there is less perceived threat and, consequently, less primary tension.

If a group is too anxious to get down to business and foregoes the small talk, primary tension is likely to create an atmosphere of formality, stiffness, and insecurity. Communication will be stilted and hesitant. The ability of the group to work on a task will be hindered by excessive and persistent primary tension.

Engaging in small talk to relieve primary tension has cultural variations. In the United States, we tend to view small talk as wasting time, especially if our primary focus is on a task (e.g., finalizing a business agreement), not social interaction. Many Asian (e.g., Japanese, Chinese, and Korean), Middle Eastern (e.g., Saudi Arabian), and Latin American (e.g., Mexican, Brazilian, and Chilean) cultures view small talk as a necessary ritual engaged in over many cups of coffee or tea for several hours or several meetings, during which the group's task may not even be mentioned. Ethiopians attach prestige to tasks that require a great deal of time to complete. Lengthy small talk, viewed by most Americans anxious to do business as "doing nothing," is considered highly significant and purposeful (Samovar & Porter, 2010).

Secondary Tension: Later Stress and Strain The stress and strain that occur within the group later in its development is called **secondary tension**. Having to make decisions produces secondary tension. Disagreements and conflicts—*storming*—inevitably emerge when group members struggle to define their status and roles in the group. Tight deadlines for task completion can induce tension. Intense time pressure also can produce poor small group performance on tasks (Bowman & Wittenbaum, 2012). Whatever the causes, you should expect some secondary tension in a long-term group. Low levels of secondary tension may mean that the group is highly harmonious. It may also mean that group members are unmotivated, apathetic, and bored.

Signs of secondary tension include a sharp outburst, a sarcastic barb, hostile and antagonistic exchanges between members, or shouting matches. Extreme secondary tension is unpleasant for the group. If it is left uncontrolled, the group's existence may be threatened.

Secondary tension has become an issue in jury deliberations (Weingart & Todorova, 2010). This is particularly true in cases involving controversial statutes such as "three strikes" and death penalty laws. Even in relatively minor cases, however, secondary tension can produce juror warfare. For example, during a Manhattan, New York, jury deliberation involving a man charged with selling a $10 bag of heroin, jurors yelled at each other, and after four days of antagonistic debate a note was sent to the judge complaining about the lone holdout juror. It read: "Tension is high, nerves are frayed, and all minds are not sound" (Finkelstein, 2001). In other instances, court officers have broken up fistfights, jurors have flung chairs through windows, and some jurors have screamed so loudly that they could be heard on other floors of the courthouse. In the 2008 corruption trial of former Alaska Senator Ted Stevens, 11 members of the jury sent a note to the judge about their 12th member that read, "She has had violent outbursts with other jurors, and that's not helping anyone" ("Stevens Trial Jurors Warned," 2008, p. 3A). Jurors have been caught wandering away from the jury room, and in one case a juror tried to escape the deliberations permanently by leaping off the jury bus. Courts all around the United States have begun providing booklets to jurors detailing how to deliberate while remaining courteous and even-tempered.

The goal is not to eliminate secondary tension in groups. Most decision-making groups experience secondary tension. Within tolerable limits, such tension can be a positive force. Tension can energize a group, challenge the members to think creatively, and bring the group together. Trying to avoid or to camouflage secondary tension merely tricks us into believing that the group is functioning well. Beneath the surface, the group may be disintegrating or the decisions coming from the group may be ill conceived, even disastrous.

The real challenge facing competent communicators is to manage secondary tension within tolerable limits. But how do we know when tension exceeds the limits? There is no mathematical formula for such a determination. Some groups can tolerate a great deal of disagreement and conflict. Other groups are more vulnerable to disintegration because members are more thin-skinned or insecure and view disagreements as personal repudiations and attacks.

A group's inability to accomplish tasks and to maintain a satisfying social climate is a general rule of thumb for determining excessive tension in a group (Wilson & Hanna, 1990). In a Los Angeles trial of defendants charged with seriously beating a trucker named Reginald Denny, jurors clearly experienced excessive tension. One juror was dismissed by the judge at the request of the other 11 exasperated jurors for "failure to deliberate." One female member of the sequestered jury became so upset about not being able to see her boyfriend that she ran down a hallway of the courthouse yelling, "I can't take it anymore" (Kramer, 1993, p. 1A). The judge gave jurors the weekend off from their deliberations to recharge their batteries and to reduce the tension so they could finish their task.

A competent communicator can handle secondary tension as follows (Andersen, 1988):

1. **Tolerate, even encourage, disagreement**. Suppressing differences of opinion will likely increase tension and exacerbate conflict. The trick is to keep the disagreement within tolerable limits. One way to do this is to focus the disagreements on the task (unless, of course, the conflict is social in nature). Resist the temptation to drift into irrelevant side issues, especially contentious ones.

2. **Keep a civil tongue**. Disagree without being disagreeable. You want to foster a cooperative, not a competitive, atmosphere for discussion. You can express opinions with conviction and exuberance without raging against those who do not agree with you.

3. **Be an active listener**. Encourage all group members to express their opinions and feelings. Clarify significant points that are confusing. Resist the temptation to interrupt, especially if this produces defensive behavior from group members. Make an honest effort to understand the point of view that is in opposition to your own.

4. **Use humor** (Romero & Pescosolido, 2008). In a study of the 414-page transcript of a real death penalty trial, 51 instances of laughter, not all involving humor (some revealed embarrassment), were identified. Tension release was the most common reason for the laughter (Keyton & Beck, 2010). Humor, of course, can increase tension if it is used as a weapon to put down other group members. Self-deprecating humor works well to avoid the negative uses of humor. In the death penalty trial, one juror misstated another juror's position on sentencing, stating "30 days" as the preferred penalty instead of "30 years." Laughter ensued, but you could imagine self-deprecating humor here lightening the tension of a serious discussion on life or death: "Sorry, 30 years. I stand corrected. Wow, 30 days for a homicide. That's almost as serious as a stack of unpaid parking tickets. How could anyone think I'm soft on crime!"

There are numerous sources of conflict within a group that raise the level of tension. Reasons for stormy transactions in groups and strategies for effectively managing them are discussed in greater detail in Chapters 10 and 11. For now, recognize that conflict and tension are a normal part of the group experience. Dealing with tension may be smooth sailing for some groups and white-water rafting for others.

▶ Norming: Regulating the Group

In groups, rules that establish standards of appropriate behavior are called norms. In this section, types of norms, their purpose and development, and conformity and nonconformity to norms are discussed.

Types of Norms: Explicit and Implicit There are two types of norms: explicit and implicit. **Explicit norms** are rules that expressly identify acceptable behavior. Such rules are codified in constitutions and bylaws of fraternal organizations, religious orders, and the like. All laws in our society act as explicit norms. Most norms in small groups, however, are not so obvious. **Implicit norms** are rules that are indirectly indicated by uniformities in the behavior and attitudes of members.

A college seminar illustrates the difference between explicit and implicit norms. If participating in a seminar qualifies as a new experience for you, group norms could be determined in several ways. Usually, the professor teaching the seminar will provide a syllabus explicitly specifying what students are expected to do during the term. Such norms as "Refrain from tardiness and absenteeism," "All assignments must be turned in on time," "All papers must be typed—no exceptions," and "Active participation in class discussions is expected" are some of the possible explicit rules.

The implicit rules for the seminar class might be such things as "Don't interrupt the professor when he or she is speaking," "Sit in chairs stationed around the table," "Be polite when disagreeing with classmates," and "Don't hide the professor's notes, even in jest" (it happens). These norms are ascertained by observing the behavior of your classmates and the professor.

Purpose and Sources of Norms: Achieving Group Goals The general purpose of norms is to achieve group goals. Consider the group Overeaters Anonymous (Shimanoff, 1992). Change (i.e., losing weight) is regulated by rules, one of which is that members are permitted to talk about food only in generic terms (carbohydrates, protein, etc.) but not in terms of specific foods (Twinkies, burgers, cookies). The rule is based on the assumption that references to particular foods will stimulate a craving for those foods and make goal achievement more difficult, while references to foods in generic terms will produce no such cravings. Apparently, you won't hear the refrigerator calling your name when merely talking about carbohydrates, but mention Häagen-Dazs and there better be a clear path to the Frigidaire or someone is going to get trampled.

The norming process takes place almost immediately in groups. When a group is formed, members cast about trying to determine what behavior will be acceptable and what will be unacceptable. Part of the primary tension in a group may stem from this concern for proper group etiquette.

There are three principal sources of norms in small groups. **The first source of norms is from systems outside the small group.** Standards of excellence and specific norms of performance for work teams within organizations often are externally influenced by management outside of the team (Sundstrom et al., 1990). Charters and bylaws of local chapters of fraternal organizations, therapeutic groups, and others are usually set by parent organizations or agencies.

A second source of small group norms is the influence of a single member. Research shows that a single person can influence the group to accept higher standards of behavior and performance than would exist without the influence of this member. Even when that influential member leaves the group, the norm typically remains (MacNeil & Sherif, 1976). Sometimes these influential individuals are designated group leaders and sometimes they are newcomers joining an established group.

A third source of small group norms is the group itself (Jetten et al., 1996). Small group norms most often develop from transactions within the group. Sometimes this is explicitly negotiated (e.g., juries deciding what procedures will be used to arrive at a verdict), but most often it emerges implicitly from trial and error. ("Oops, the group is looking at me like I just suggested euthanizing all family pets; guess I shouldn't share every thought that comes into my head.")

Degree of Conformity: Strength of Group Pressure Solomon Asch (1955) found that when a group composed of confederates of the experimenter unanimously judged the length of a line incorrectly, naive participants unaware of the setup chose the obviously erroneous group judgment 35% of the time. Most of these same participants (75%) conformed to the group error at least once during the study. Social psychologist Anthony Pratkanis of the University of California, Santa Cruz, replicated this study for *Dateline NBC* in August 1997. In his study, 9 of 16 college students studied fell in line with the unanimous choice made by 6 other group members, even though the choice was clearly incorrect. Ironically, one participant interviewed beforehand characterized himself as a nonconformist. During the study, he conformed earlier and more often than any other student. **Conformity** is the adherence to group norms by group members, in this case "following the crowd" by choosing the wrong answer.

Although the degree of conformity in the United States is fairly high (Baron et al., 1996), **it is significantly higher in other cultures.** A review of 133 conformity studies found significantly higher rates of conformity in collectivist cultures compared to individualist cultures (Bond & Smith, 1996). This, of course, makes sense. Collectivist cultures place greater emphasis on group harmony and on individuals blending into groups than do individualist cultures.

The serious negative consequences of conformity can be seen from a major study of binge drinking by college students. Defined as "five or more drinks in a row at least once in the two weeks prior to completing the survey," the study found that 37% of college students in the United States binge drink. The same study reported that 14% of college students consumed 10 or more drinks in a row at least once in the two weeks prior to the survey and 5% reported consuming 15 or more drinks in a row ("Binge Drinking

Statistics," 2013). More than 80% of students living in fraternities and sororities report binge drinking (Wechsler & Wuethrich, 2003). An estimated 1,825 college students die each year from heavy drinking, about 600,000 are injured because of it, about 700,000 college students are physically assaulted by an intoxicated student, and almost 100,000 college students are sexually assaulted or raped because of binge drinking (Hingson et al., 2009). Aside from personal injury and death, binge drinking diminishes sound judgment. In a Harvard University study (Wechsler & Wuethrich, 2003), 37% of binge drinkers reported that they had done something they regretted afterward (e.g., argued with friends, engaged in unprotected sex). Drinking to excess is encouraged by group norms (Kinard & Webster, 2010; Wechsler & Nelson, 2008). A Zogby International poll reported that 56% of 1,005 college students surveyed felt group pressure to drink ("Poll," 2000).

Conformity isn't always a negative experience. Group pressure can be applied for prosocial reasons. At Shaker Heights High School in Ohio, the Minority Achievement Committee (MAC), a small group of high-achieving African-American male students, is working to establish the norm that being smart and doing well in school is cool, not "acting white." Students must earn at least a 2.8 GPA to gain membership into the MAC. Weekly MAC meetings begin with a firm handshake and the MAC credo, "I am an African American and I pledge to uphold the name and image of the African-American man. I will do so by striving for academic excellence, conducting myself with dignity, and respecting others as if they were my brothers and sisters" ("The MAC Scholars Program," 2014). MAC is fighting a trend that moves in the opposite direction. One national report on minority academic achievement gaps in high schools notes that

Andrew Lichtenstein/Sygma/Corbis

Peer pressure in groups is a key cause of binge drinking.

Tokyo Space Club/zefa/Corbis

In what ways are individuals in this photo illustrating conformity to group norms?

"hunger for peer approval" can be a disincentive to learn when the peer group does not value academic excellence (Poliakoff, 2006).

Why We Conform: Fitting In So why do we conform to norms, especially in a society as individualistic as the United States? We conform for two principal reasons. First, **we conform to norms to be *liked*** (Aronson et al., 2013). We want social acceptance, support, companionship, and recognition (Baumeister & Leary, 1995). We must "go along to get along." (See Closer Look: "High School Cliques.") Loyalty to the group is manifested in conformity to group norms and is rewarded with approval from the members. Norms create solidarity with group members. Our natural desire to belong and to be liked makes such solidarity attractive. Individual goals, such as making friends or increasing social activities, can be satisfied by conforming to group norms. As Walter Kirn (1997) notes, college students don't usually binge drink just to get drunk and feel the buzz: "They think they are doing something more meaningful: vowing their loyalty to new friends, winning the respect of others, building a zany memory they'll cherish. Fraternities and selective social clubs exploit students' desperate hunger to fit in" (p. A11).

Second, **we conform to norms because we want to be *right*** (Aronson et al., 2013). Acting incorrectly can be embarrassing and humiliating. Group norms identify correct behavior. In this case, we may not want to be liked by group members as much as we want to avoid social disapproval by being ridiculed or harassed. Few people enjoy appearing to be a fool.

CLOSER LOOK

High School Cliques: A Lesson in Conformity

When the school lunch bell rings at high schools across the country, kids pour out of their classrooms and almost instantly sort themselves into small groups or cliques. In a field investigation of cliques at three Santa Cruz County, California, high schools, students split into a myriad of small groups—jocks, preps, dirts, surfers, skaters, Goths, nerds, and a variety of ethnic groupings (Townsend, 1999b). We all remember cliques in high school. For some of you it may still be a fresh memory.

Cliques are subgroups of interconnected members within the larger group system (Forsyth, 2014). Students join cliques because the pressure to belong, to be accepted by peers, is intense (Mandel, 2010). In some cases, the outcasts rejected by more established cliques form their own group. As one girl at Soquel High School revealed, "We're outcasts, but at least we're outcasts together" (Townsend, 1999b, p. A8). As Margarita Azmitia, professor of developmental psychology at University of California, Santa Cruz, notes, "Some kids don't want to be in deviant cliques, but that's their only option" (Townsend, 1999b, p. A8). The clique gives them an identity, and some protection from harassment by more favored cliques on campus.

High school cliques typically divide into a competitive hierarchy, with jocks on top and nerds on the bottom. This competitive hierarchy often leads to in-group versus out-group hostility. Name-calling, threats, water balloons, and food rain down on those who belong to the less popular cliques. "They throw stuff at us all the time" says one 18-year-old male student, indicating a collection of surfers, jocks, and popular kids.

"I've had yogurt thrown at me, apples, oranges," says another student dressed entirely in black. "They call me dirt, faggot, queer" (Townsend, 1999b, p. A1). A student athlete, one of the popular kids at Aptos High School, looks across the open quad where cliques have fanned out like ripples on a pond and says, "I hate 'em, I don't care." Another jock adds, "They smell... and they don't wear shoes." A 15-year-old female student expresses her anguish regarding the abuse heaped on her by competing cliques, "A lot of people yell at us. They say, 'You freak of nature. You Satanist.' We've had people harass us to tears. I've come back crying. They yell, 'Go back to hell, no one wants you.' It hurts." "It's almost as bad as racism," says an 18-year-old male student who is one of the objects of jock derision. "We are who we are, and we can't be someone else" (Townsend, 1999b, p. A8). Misery loves miserable company (Forsyth, 2014), so the outcasts and the derided join cliques for identity and for self-protection.

Conformity to the norms of the clique is strong. At least there is some protection from harassment when you aren't facing it alone. Some students are so desperate to fit in that they will do almost anything to gain membership and to remain in a clique. Professor Azmitia explains that cliques are typically only 10 to 12 members in size. This sets up an intense competition to get into the cliques, especially the most favored ones, and to remain members once admitted. Even minor deviance from clique norms, such as wearing the wrong clothes, hanging with someone from an outcast clique, or missing a clique party can get a member ousted. As a ninth grader at Aptos High confessed, "I wasn't comfortable with myself, so I tried to conform. I felt pressure to look a certain way. To party, to use drugs and alcohol." She would get "weird looks" when she wore a colorful scarf wrapped around her short blond hair. "They were too uptight about everything" (Townsend, 1999b, p. A8). Eventually she left her popular clique, but she quickly joined an outcast group.

Although cliques are common in high school, a survey by CareerBuilders of almost 3,000 U.S. workers found that 43% responded that their workplace is populated with cliques. One in ten workers felt intimidated by cliques, 20% said they did something they really didn't want to do to

fit in with a clique, and 19% "made fun of someone else or pretended not to like them" to accommodate a clique (Hunt, 2013).

Cliques can boost self-esteem by providing social acceptance, a sense of identity and belonging, support, companionship, and recognition for members (Mandel, 2010). Friendships can blossom from participation in cliques. Nevertheless, cliques can isolate those who are socially ostracized from clique membership (Hardy et al., 2005; Mandel, 2010), and they can encourage blind, desperate conformity, especially when intergroup competition erupts into hostility toward and abuse of those who don't "fit in."

QUESTIONS FOR THOUGHT

1. Do you remember your experiences with cliques? Were your experiences mostly positive or negative?
2. Did you experience an intense pressure to conform as a clique member? Did intergroup rivalry exist that produced harassment of members from other cliques? How did you respond?
3. Are there ethical issues involved in joining cliques and rejecting others from joining? Apply the five criteria for ethical communication discussed in Chapter 1.

Conditions for Conformity: When We Bow to Group Pressure There is greater conformity to group norms when certain conditions exist. First and foremost, **the stronger the cohesiveness in the group, the greater is the conformity to group norms** (Prapavessis & Carron, 1997). The relationship between cohesiveness and conformity is hardly surprising. Cohesiveness, by definition, is the degree of attraction we have to a group and our desire to be a member. If there is minimal attraction to the group and nebulous desire to be a member, then there is scant reason to adhere to the rules of behavior. A group has little leverage against apathetic or scornful members. Conversely, individuals who are strongly attracted to the group and wish to remain members in good standing are much more likely to conform and to bow to peer pressure for uniformity of opinion and behavior.

Second, **conformity increases as the task importance increases** (Baron et al., 1996). When accurately performing the group task assumes great importance, we tend to conform even when other group members confess to a general lack of confidence in the accuracy of their own judgments (Baron et al., 1996).

Third, **conformity is greater when individuals expect to be group members for a long time** (Smith, 1982). After all, you must live with this group. Why make your life unpleasant by not conforming, particularly in job situations in which economic considerations may make job switching impractical?

Fourth, **conformity is greater when individuals perceive that they have somewhat lower status in the group than other members or that they are not completely accepted by the group** (Smith, 1982). Higher-status members have earned the right to dissent, but lower-status members must still earn that right to occasional nonconformity. Lower-status members also feel a greater need to prove themselves to the group, to show fealty.

Addressing Nonconformity: When Groups Get Tough Because behavior in groups is governed by rules, a violation of a norm can be quite unsettling for group members. Nonconformity disturbs the system. Groups usually do not appreciate such violations, called **nonconformity**, except within fairly limited boundaries. There are four communication strategies groups typically use to command conformity from nonconforming members (Leavitt, 1964; Lipman-Blumen & Leavitt, 1999). These strategies tend to follow a sequential order, although there may be variation in some circumstances.

First, **group members attempt to *reason* with the deviant.** The quantity of talk aimed at the nonconformist initially increases substantially (Schachter, 1951). Groups show an intense interest in convincing nonconforming members of their folly. Clearly, groups expect their troublesome members to change their point of view and behavior.

Second, if reason fails to sway a nonconforming member, **a group will often try *seduction*.** This is usually a ploy to make the deviant feel guilty or uncomfortable because the group is made to look bad in the eyes of outsiders. Telling the nonconformist that his or her efforts are wasted and will accomplish nothing is another form of the seduction strategy. "You won't get anywhere anyway, so why cause such turmoil?" is the seduction strategy at work. Offers of promotions, perquisites, monetary incentives, and the like in exchange for conformity are other examples of seduction.

The third line of defense against nonconformists is *coercion*. This is where groups begin to get rough. Communication turns abusive and threatening. Groups attempt to force conformity by using nasty and unpleasant tactics. For example, whistleblowers are individuals who expose to the light of public scrutiny such abuses as waste, fraud, corruption, and dangerous practices in corporations and organizations. Coercive tactics used against whistleblowers often include threats of firing and sometimes actual terminations. In addition, some are transferred to undesirable jobs and locations, demoted, harassed, and intimidated by supervisors and peers (Levin, 2010).

The final stage of group pressure to induce conformity is *isolation*. Often referred to as *ostracism*, this strategy ignores or excludes a member by giving the silent treatment or isolating the member from social interaction with the group. It is a kind of social death that produces significant psychological pain (Williams, 2007; Williams, 2011). Even being ostracized by a despised group such as the Ku Klux Klan hurts the rejected individual (Gonsalkorale & Williams, 2007; Williams, 2011). Ostracism is "an exceptionally potent form of social influence" (Williams et al., 2000, p. 760). A member's sense of belonging to the group is severed. When coercion doesn't gain conformity from whistleblowers, for example, ostracism is often the next strategy used (Miceli & Near, 1992). When an opportunity arises to get back into the good graces of the group, members will often seize that opportunity by conforming to group norms (Williams, 2007).

Studies show that even **cyberostracism**, a remote form of ostracism that occurs on the Internet, can be quite potent (Smith & Williams, 2004; Abrams et al., 2010). Acts of cyberostracism occur when a group of online team members or chat room users deliberately ignore a member who violates the group's norms (e.g., by incorrect use of technology, straying from the topic, using profanity, flaming). Even when the ostracism isn't clearly deliberate (using English when a member speaks primarily Spanish or vice versa), the negative effects occur (Dotan-Eliaz et al., 2009; Hitlan et al., 2006).

The norming periodic phase of group development provides a structure for appropriate and effective communication. A competent communicator should do the following during the norming phase of group development to be appropriate and effective:

1. **Adapt communication to the norms of the group.** As previously noted, communication becomes inappropriate when, without sacrificing goals, violation of norms could be averted by more prudent action.

2. **Encourage change when norms are excessively rigid.** Norms are not sacrosanct. Some norms can be suffocatingly rigid—too closed to permit adaptation to change in the system. Norm rigidity fosters nonconformity and disruption. Violating the norm is one avenue of change if rational argument proves unsuccessful, but expect backlash from the group. Leaving the group is certainly an option. Failure to loosen norms from within may require intervention from without, such as court suits and protests.

3. **Encourage change when norms are too elastic.** Excessive openness in a system can be counterproductive. Apply the same guidelines for changing overly rigid norms.

▶ Performing: Group Output

If I had a dollar for every time I have been told that a camel is a horse designed by a committee, I'd be downing dark beers on a white sand beach in the tropics, enjoying a blissful life of leisure. Then there is the equally moth-eaten description of a

SECOND LOOK

The Norming Process

Types of Norms

Explicit—Preferences and prohibitions specifically stated in some form

Implicit—Preferences and prohibitions determined from observation

Sources of Norms

Other larger systems outside the small group

Influence of a single member

Transactions within the group

Why Group Members Conform to Norms

Desire to be liked

Desire to be right

Conditions for Conformity to Norms

The stronger the cohesiveness, the greater the conformity

Greater conformity when individuals expect to be group members for a long time

Greater conformity when individuals perceive they have lower status in groups

Addressing Nonconformity

Reason

Seduction

Coercion

Isolation/Ostracism

committee as "a group of people who can do nothing individually but, as a group, can gather and decide that nothing can be done." Along the same line is this anonymous offering: "Trying to solve a problem through group discussion is like trying to clear up a traffic jam by honking your horn." Winston Churchill, always armed with his sardonic wit, fired this salvo: "A committee is the organized result of a group of the incompetent who have been appointed by the uninformed to accomplish the unnecessary." On my own campus, committees metastasize like cancer, eating up professors' and administrators' time and sucking the lifeblood from the institution. At last count there were 63 committees. There was even a recent proposal to establish a committee on committees, ostensibly to bring this energy-sucking monster under control, but nothing ever came of the proposal.

In terms of performance, groups as decision-making units are in need of better public relations. Too many people are inclined to believe that groups are assembled to stymie progress and to serve as roadblocks to decision making, not to produce better alternatives. Grouphate is real.

So, are groups inevitably the great roadblock to effective decision making and problem solving, leaving us to conclude that individual performance is superior to group performance? One of the most researched areas of group communication is the comparison of individual to group performance. **The key issue from**

Bill Varie/Cusp/Corbis

Social loafing

This photo shows a form of social loafing. Social loafing:

1. Decreases as the size of the group increases
2. Is the same as shyness
3. Occurs because specific group members often do not see the connection between personal effort and group outcomes
4. Is fundamentally a lack of motivation by the loafer

Answers are given the at end of the chapter.

this research is not whether individuals or groups are superior performers, but rather, under what conditions groups outperform individuals and vice versa. Since grouphate is often a result of poor group productivity, group versus individual performance is a significant issue to explore.

Motivation to Perform: Social Loafing and Social Compensation Lackluster effort from some group members is but one reason for the negative views of group decision making and problem solving. Undoubtedly, you have participated in groups in which your enthusiasm for a group task has been blunted by the lifeless response from other group members. Grouphate is fueled by this all too common experience. Why are some group members strongly motivated to work hard on a task, but other members are not? The **collective effort model (CEM)** suggests that group members are strongly motivated to perform well in a group if they are convinced that their individual effort will likely help in attaining valued results (Hart et al., 2001). **If members view the task as unimportant or meaningless (mere busywork) or a member's effort is expected to have little effect on the group outcome even when the outcome is highly valued (a person of low ability working with high-ability members), then social loafing will likely occur.**

Social loafing is the tendency of a group member to exert less effort on a task when working in a group than when working individually (Karau & Hart, 1998). It is particularly problematic in virtual groups (online groups). In a survey of 600 employees of multinational corporations who participate actively in virtual groups, 75% indicated that social loafing is a serious challenge (Solomon, 2010). The reasons are discussed in Chapter 12. Groups in general display social loafing by missing group meetings, showing up late to meetings, performing and participating in a lackluster manner, or failing to start or complete individual tasks requested by the group. Please note here that reticence to participate during group discussions because of shyness does not constitute social loafing. Loafers put out little effort because of poor motivation, disinterest, or a bad attitude.

Social loafing is more common in individualist cultures than in collectivist cultures (Early, 1989; Gabreyna et al., 1985). Personal efforts and achievements are less visible in a group and more likely to go unrecognized, so social loafing is more likely in an individualist culture. In a collectivist culture, social striving or the desire to produce for the group because group membership is highly valued is strong.

So what can you do about social loafers? Here are several steps that can be taken to address the problem (Forsyth, 2014; see also Lumsden & Lumsden, 1993):

1. **Choose meaningful tasks** (Karau & Williams, 2001). Groups can't always choose their tasks, and sometimes they are given unchallenging tasks to perform by those with higher authority. If required to choose a project from a list of several options, choose the option most interesting to the group as a whole, not the option interesting to only one or two relatively dominant members.

This is a China-Guizhou-Miao ethnic group tug of war. Social loafing is a common problem in groups. Social loafing is

1. More common in collectivist cultures
2. More common in individualist cultures
3. No more common in collectivist cultures than in individualist cultures
4. Never a problem in highly competitive situations

Answers are given at the end of the chapter.

2. **Establish a group responsibility norm** (Hoigaard et al., 2006). Emphasize individual responsibility to the team and the importance of every member contributing a fair share to the successful completion of a task. Fairness and responsibility are important ethical concerns.

3. **Note the critical importance of each member's effort.** Impress upon all members that their individual effort is special and essential to the group's success. When group members believe that their contribution is indispensable to group success, they typically exert greater effort (Henningsen et al., 2000; Johnson, 2003). This is especially true if the task is difficult (Matsui et al., 1987) and the member feels uniquely capable (Huguet et al., 1999).

4. **Hold members accountable.** Provide each member with specific and easily identifiable tasks, and set aside time for the group to assess each member's contribution to the overall project (Gammage et al., 2001). Face-to-face peer appraisal that focuses on development of each group member's abilities, not on criticizing weak effort, diminishes social loafing (Druskat & Wolff, 1999).

5. **Enhance group cohesiveness**. Members of weakly cohesive groups are more prone to social loafing than members of highly cohesive groups (Karau & Hart, 1998). Highly cohesive groups, however, with a mediocrity norm that sets low expectations on members for performance could produce an entire group of social loafers (Hoigaard et al., 2006). See the steps for enhancing cohesiveness discussed earlier in this chapter.

6. **Confront the loafer**. If the steps above are insufficient, either the leader of the group, a designated member, or the group as a whole should approach the loafer and ask why the lethargic attitude exists. Encourage stronger participation, reaffirm the importance of the loafer's contribution to the team effort, and solicit suggestions regarding how the group might help the person become a contributor. Do not name-call or personally attack the loafer.

7. **Consult a higher power** (not to be confused with divine intervention, although that would be impressive). When all of the above steps fail, consult a supervisor, teacher, or someone with greater authority than the group members and ask for advice. The authority figure may need to discuss the problem with the loafer.

8. **Boot out the loafer**. This is a last resort. Do not begin with this step, as many groups would prefer to do. You may not have this option available, however.

9. **Sidestep the loafer**. Reconfigure individual responsibilities and tasks so even if the loafer contributes nothing to the group effort, the group can still maneuver around the loafer and produce a high-quality result.

Social loafing from some group members can produce an opposite reaction from other group members called **social compensation**—an increased motivation to work harder on a group task to counterbalance the lackluster performance of others. Several studies show that when group members expect listless effort from others in the group, they display greater motivation to work harder and exhibit higher than expected productivity compared to when they work alone (Williams & Karau, 1991; Williams & Sommer, 1997). **Social compensation is especially likely when a high-ability group member senses that his or her maximum effort is required for the group to be successful on a meaningful task because other group members have less ability to perform effectively** (Hart et al., 2001). If poor performance from low-ability group members is perceived to be caused by external forces (bad luck, life stresses), then compensation is likely. If, however, the poor performance is attributed to internal causes (laziness), then compensation is unlikely. **Compensation is especially unlikely when high-ability group members are suspected of loafing.** Few wish to play the sucker and cover for the able but unwilling sluggards in the group (Hart et al., 2001; Hoigaard & Ommundsen, 2007).

When Groups Outperform Individuals: Three Heads Are Better than One

Groups often outperform individuals. Even groups whose members have imbibed enough alcohol to reach the legal limit of .08 blood alcohol level ("groupdrink") perform as well as groups whose members are not alcohol impaired, and they outperform intoxicated individuals working alone. The cognitively impairing effects of alcohol are neutralized by group processes (Frings et al., 2008). This is not a justification for members of small groups getting smashed on liquor, of course, but it does reveal the potency of groups compared to individuals even under challenging circumstances.

Groups usually outperform individuals when certain conditions exist (Laughlin et al., 2006; Pavitt & Curtis, 1994; Sawyer, 2007). First, **when the task requires a wide range and variety of information and skills, groups tend to be superior to any individual.** One study found that the group scored significantly higher than its highest-scoring member (Laughlin et al., 2006). It did this by *pooling knowledge.*

Social Loafing: A Self-Assessment

Make honest assessments of your participation in small group decision making and problem solving.

1. I am on time for small group meetings.

   RARELY   ALMOST ALWAYS

   1   2   3   4   5

2. I leave small group meetings early.

   RARELY   ALMOST ALWAYS

   1   2   3   4   5

3. I am quiet during small group discussions.

   RARELY   ALMOST ALWAYS

   1   2   3   4   5

4. My attention during small group discussions is focused on the task.

   RARELY   ALMOST ALWAYS

   1   2   3   4   5

5. I am strongly motivated to perform well in small groups.

   RARELY   ALMOST ALWAYS

   1   2   3   4   5

6. When other group members show little interest in accomplishing a task successfully, I lose interest in achieving success.

   RARELY   ALMOST ALWAYS

   1   2   3   4   5

7. When other group members seem uninvolved in participating on the group task, I also reduce my participation.

   RARELY   ALMOST ALWAYS

   1   2   3   4   5

Your scores on statements 1, 4, and 5 should be high (4–5), and your scores on statements 2, 3, 6, and 7 ideally should be quite low (1–2)—little social loafing.

When the highest-scoring member didn't know the answer to a question, another member typically did. Thus, the group as a whole benefited because members had non-overlapping knowledge. As humorist Will Rogers once said, "Everybody is ignorant, just on different subjects." A key to successful group performance is putting together a team composed of members who do not share ignorance, but instead exhibit deep diversity by pooling nonoverlapping areas of knowledge (Stasson & Bradshaw, 1995).

Second, **groups generally outperform individuals when both the group and any individual compared are without expertise on the task** (Laughlin et al., 2006). Here *synergy* is at work. As Johnson and Johnson (1987) remark in somewhat overstated fashion, "None of us is as smart as all of us" (p. 131). In one study, even though no individual group member knew the correct answer on a test question, the group as a whole selected the correct answer in 28% of the cases. Individual members working alone selected the correct answer only 4% of the time (Stasson & Bradshaw, 1995). The longer group members work together, the greater is this result (Watson et al., 1991). Long-term groups typically score significantly higher than even their best member.

Third, **groups will usually outperform an individual when both the group and the individual have expertise and the task is an especially large and complex one.** The ability of a group to divide labor, to *share the load*, will normally result in a better decision than any overburdened individual could manage. Shaffner (1999) provides the arithmetic logic for sharing the load. If one person had all the knowledge and skills to single-handedly build a Boeing 777, it would take about *250 years* to deliver one plane. The logic of working in groups is indisputable when the task is large and complex.

A group of experts is especially effective when members are highly motivated and they are trained to work as a team. One study found that expert groups outperform their best member 97% of the time (Michaelson et al., 1989). *Teamwork* allows a group to coordinate efforts and to work at optimum effectiveness.

Fourth, **even when comparing a group of reasonably bright and informed nonexperts to an individual with special expertise, group decisions are sometimes superior.** One of the reasons for this superiority is that when groups are functioning effectively, members perform an *error correction* function for the group (Hastie et al., 1983). Assumptions are challenged and alternatives are offered that an individual might overlook. This was the primary reason that accounted for the "groupdrink" result discussed earlier (Frings et al., 2008). In addition, the collective energy and chemistry of the group may produce a *synergistic result.*

When Individuals Outperform Groups: No Magic in Groups Although groups frequently outperform individuals, this is not always the case. There are five conditions supported by research in which individuals outperform groups.

First, **groups composed of uninformed laypersons will not usually outperform someone with special expertise, such as a doctor or lawyer, on issues of medicine and law.** There is certainly no advantage to be gained from *pooling ignorance*. As already noted, however, even in uninformed groups, synergy sometimes compensates for lack of knowledge. *Negative synergy,* nevertheless, is more likely when group members are uninformed.

Second, **individuals outperform groups when groups establish norms of mediocrity.** Some groups are composed of members who are satisfied with relatively low productivity. If norms of mediocrity prevail in a group, performance will be sluggish or worse (Stogdill, 1972). Even individual members who may wish to perform at a higher level will become discouraged because of *insufficient motivation* to excel. Since the group rewards middling performance, why bother trying harder than the rest?

Third, **when groups become too large, individuals outperform groups.** Again, the rule of thumb is to select the smallest group capable of performing the task effectively. Quality performance is usually enhanced in moderately sized groups (i.e., 7 to 8 members). Much larger than this and *problems of coordination and efficiency* increase. *Social loafing* also becomes a bigger problem in large groups (Chidambaram & Tung, 2005). Loafers can hide their anemic effort more easily in large groups.

Fourth, **when the task is a simple one, groups are not superior to individuals.** There is no special advantage in having a group work on a remedial task. *Minimal resources* are required. If any individual can likely do the task, why involve a group?

Finally, **when time is a critical factor, groups usually perform less effectively than individuals.** In emergency situations or in circumstances where speed and efficiency are paramount, individuals can often perform better than groups, especially large groups. The reason is simple. *Groups tend to be abominably slow,* and larger groups usually take longer to make decisions than smaller groups (Davis et al., 1997). There are exceptions, such as disaster teams and emergency surgical teams trained to perform under pressure and time constraints. Most groups, though, are not trained to operate swiftly and efficiently under pressure. As previously noted, small groups are usually faster than larger groups, but even small groups can lag behind a single individual in the performance of a task.

The performance phase of group development is a complex process. I have merely laid the groundwork for more detailed discussion of group performance in later chapters. Nevertheless, some general advice regarding communication competence can be offered. A competent communicator does the following to enhance group performance:

1. **Focus on the task**. Because task and social dimensions of groups are interconnected, focusing on the task to the detriment of social relationships among members obviously makes little sense. Nevertheless, when there is work to be

done, the primary focus is on the accomplishment of the task. Cohesiveness can be built when the pressure to perform has lessened. Task accomplishment also increases cohesiveness.

2. **Encourage participation from group members**. The group needs to utilize its resources fully, which means that even social loafers may have much to contribute. A note of caution here: Encouraging member participation should not be a blanket rule. Some group members should not be encouraged to participate because they disrupt the group's decision-making process (more on this in Chapter 8).

In summary, all groups have a task dimension and a social dimension. The output of the task dimension is productivity. The output of the social dimension is cohesiveness. Productivity can affect cohesiveness and vice versa. Group development encompasses four periodic phases: forming, storming, norming, and performing. These periodic phases do not occur in rigid sequence. They frequently overlap, and groups may jump around between phases depending on the circumstances and situations groups face. Some groups never progress beyond the forming and initial storming phases. These are groups that dissolve because they do not work.

SECOND LOOK

Group Versus Individual Performance

Group Superior to Individual Conditions	Reason(s)
Broad-range task	Pooling knowledge, group remembering
Neither have expertise	Synergy
Experts, complex task	Sharing the load, teamwork
Individual expert, informed group	Error correction, synergy

Individual Superior to Group Conditions	Reason(s)
Individual expert, uninformed group	Pooling ignorance, negative synergy
Groups establish mediocrity norms	Insufficient motivation to excel
Group becomes too large	Difficulty coordinating, social loafing
Simple task	Minimal resources required
Time is a critical factor.	Groups are too slow.

SECOND LOOK

Competent Communication and Group Development

Forming Periodic Phase

Express positive attitudes and feelings

Appear friendly, open, and interested

Encourage a "getting-to-know-you" conversation

Find areas of commonality and cooperation

Establish clear group goals

Storming Periodic Phase

Tolerate, even encourage, disagreement and deviance

Keep a civil tongue

Be an active listener

Use humor, especially self-deprecation

Norming Periodic Phase

Adapt communication to the norms of the group

Encourage change when norms are excessively rigid

Encourage change when norms are too elastic

Performing Periodic Phase

Focus on the task

Encourage participation from group members (in most instances)

MindTap
Reflect on what you've learned.

In Mixed Company

▶ Online

Now that you've read Chapter 3, access the online resources that accompany *In Mixed Company* at **www.cengagebrain.com**. Your online resources include:

1. Multiple-choice and true-false **chapter practice quizzes** with automatic correction

2. Digital **glossary**

3. **Flashcards**

QUESTIONS FOR CRITICAL THINKERS

1. When is it appropriate to be a nonconformist in a small group?
2. Are there ever times when the task is so important that concern for the social dimension of the group must be ignored?

VIDEO *Case Studies*

My Cousin Vinny (1992). Comedy; R

If you don't laugh repeatedly while watching this movie, then you should have your funny bone checked by a specialist. Vinny is an inexperienced Brooklyn lawyer asked to defend his cousin on charges of murder in a backwater town in Alabama. Analyze this movie in terms of norms and conformity. Which norms are explicit and which are implicit? Is the stuttering defense lawyer a nonconformist?

Bulworth (1998). Comedy; R

Warren Beatty is hilarious as a lackluster U.S. senator who revives his failing reelection campaign by speaking his mind—without editing anything. Which norms does Bulworth violate and with what effects?

Easy A (2010). Comedy; PG-13

Hilarious take on high school in the land of Twitter, texting, and YouTube. Emma Stone, in a stunningly sharp depiction, plays a high schooler who begins to "act out" the *Scarlet Letter,* the famous novel that is assigned in her favorite class. Her lies about having sex get her noticed, then eventually ostracized. Analyze the stages of reactions to her nonconformity and how she addresses the group's reactions.

Hairspray (2007). Musical; PG

You really have to like musicals as a film genre to enjoy this story of Baltimore teen life in 1962. Nevertheless, there is much to analyze from the standpoint of norms and conformity. Examine explicit and implicit norms. What are some reactions to norm violations and how do these reactions parallel research on the four typical group reactions to nonconformity?

Lord of the Flies (1963). Drama; NR

There is a 1990 remake of William Golding's grim allegory of schoolboys stranded on a deserted island, but it is a pale, lifeless effort compared to the splendid original film. Analyze in detail all four phases of group development.

Lord of the Rings: The Fellowship of the Ring (2001). Drama; PG-13

Movies don't get much better than this fantasy epic. Analyze this first-rate thriller in terms of the four global phases of group development (forming, storming, norming, and performing). This film is rich with applications to group development.

Mean Girls (2004). Comedy/Drama; PG-13
Lindsay Lohan plays a teen who has been home-schooled in Africa, then enters an Illinois public school. Analyze this film for the power and influence of cliques and the difficulties outsiders face dealing with cliques.

The Croods (2013). Animated comedy; PG
Animated story of early cave-dwelling family abruptly forced to journey through an unfamiliar fantasy world with the help of an inventive boy. Hilarious group dynamic that offers plentiful examples of conformity and nonconformity to norms. Also, examine cohesiveness of the group, group diversity, and task and social dimensions of the family.

Answers to Multiple-Choice Questions in Captions
Photo (man drawing cartoon page 92), 3 and 4; photo (p. 94 tug of war photo), 2.

4

Developing the Group Climate

Nathan King/Alamy

I DEO is "the largest and most influential product design firm in the world" (Myerson, 2001, p. 11). The company's 500 designers in 10 cities (Palo Alto, San Francisco, Chicago, Boston, New York City, London, Munich, Singapore, Tokyo, and Shanghai) work on hundreds of projects each year (Flinn, 2010). IDEO has won more design awards than any competing design firm (**www.ideo.com**).

● MindTap™
Start with a quick warm-up activity.

What IDEO has accomplished, however, is not nearly as impressive as how the firm has accomplished it. David Kelley, the founder and driving force behind IDEO, is the most unique corporate executive you're likely to find. Kelley has established a corporate climate that is the antithesis of most companies and small businesses. Kelley wanted three things when he established IDEO: to work with friends, to have no bosses in charge of employees' lives, and to eliminate jerks from the workplace (O'Brien, 1995).

Kelley organizes weekly company bike rides, hosts birthday celebrations for workers according to their zodiac signs, and often conducts Monday morning meetings seated on the floor of a room devoid of furniture. IDEO teams go to baseball games, movies, and take field trips to recharge team members' creative energy. Teams engage in poetry slams and "IDEO-centric parties." The IDEO atmosphere is laid back and fun loving. One IDEO designer notes, "It was only slightly surprising to get mimosas during one of our monthly meetings." At IDEO, developing and maintaining a positive group climate of fun, excitement, and support that is free of negative infighting is essential (Chion, 2013).

A **group climate** is the emotional atmosphere, the enveloping tone that is created by the way we communicate in groups. A communication climate permeates all groups and affects every aspect of a group's social and task dimensions. A **positive climate** exists when individuals perceive that they are valued, supported, and treated well by the group. A **negative climate** exists when group members do not feel valued, supported, and respected, when trust is minimal, and when members perceive that they are not treated well.

The purpose of this chapter is to identify and explain why a positive group climate is far more likely to develop when cooperative communication patterns are emphasized and competitive communication patterns are deemphasized. There are two objectives related to this purpose:

1. To discuss the effects of competitive and cooperative communication patterns on group climate and group effectiveness, and,

2. To explore ways to construct cooperation in small groups.

Read, highlight, and take notes online.

Competition and Cooperation

This section compares competition and cooperation in small groups. The effects of competition and cooperation on small group climate and goal attainment are presented.

Focus Questions

1. In what circumstances might competition be constructive in small groups?

2. What is the relationship between communication competence and competition/cooperation?

3. What is the relationship between competition and motivation to succeed?

4. What is the relationship between competition and achievement and performance?

▶ Definitions: Conceptual Clarity

Although seemingly straightforward, the terms *competition, cooperation,* and *individual achievement* aren't always used in a conceptually clear manner. To avoid any confusion, these three terms are defined, and the term *hypercompetitiveness* is introduced. The relationship of these concepts to small group communication is explored as this chapter unfolds.

Competition: Winners Take All Alfie Kohn (1992) defines **competition** as a mutually exclusive goal attainment (MEGA) process. When transactions in groups are competitive, individual success is achieved at the expense of other group members. **Competition, by definition, necessitates the failure of the many for the success of the few.** When the city of San Francisco solicited applications for 50 new firefighters, more than 10,000 individuals applied. That's 50 winners and more than 9,950 losers. Pick any contest and the disproportionate number of losers compared to winners is usually enormous.

Cooperation: Winners All Distinctly unlike competition, **cooperation** is a mutually inclusive goal attainment (MIGA) process. Individual success is tied directly to the success of other group members. **Group members work together, not against each other, when attempting to achieve a common goal.** The phenomenally successful Mars rover called *Sojourner,* which explored the surface of Mars in 1997, served as the model for future equally successful rovers in NASA's Mars Exploration Rover Mission that continues today. The *Sojourner* project was a cooperative team effort under the direction of Donna Shirley (1997). *Sojourner*'s challenge was to take pictures, measure the chemistry of Martian rocks, and test the difficulty of maneuvering the rover on Martian soil. *Sojourner,* which looked like a stripped-down microwave oven on four wheels, was built at a cost of $25 million, a mere pittance for an interplanetary project. *Sojourner* had to weigh less than 22 pounds, survive 150-degrees-below-zero temperatures, and operate at a peak power of 16 watts. Expected to operate for only 1 week and travel no more than 10 meters from its mother spacecraft, *Sojourner* lasted 3 months and explored 100 meters across the surface of Mars. Every team member had the exact same goal—to successfully explore Mars with the rover they built from scratch (sometimes using parts from local hardware stores to keep within their meager budget). The team members succeeded as a unit in attaining their goal. Team members helped each other on every part of the project; to do otherwise might have sabotaged the success of the entire mission.

The *Sojourner* project was successful because team members worked cooperatively. Goals, however, are not always reached even when group members' cooperative effort is stellar. That is because **cooperation is a process, not an outcome** (King et al., 2009). Cooperation is a means to an end but not an end in itself. It is a powerful means to achieving important group goals, but two groups can negotiate cooperatively and still end up agreeing to disagree.

Individual Achievement: Going It Alone Independently accomplishing a goal previously unrealized, such as performing your best dance routines or earning a

This is the Mars rover Sojourner, a model of success achieved by group cooperation.

higher grade on a calculus exam than at any other time in your academic life, is neither competition nor cooperation. It is **individual achievement**—the attainment of a personal goal without having to defeat another person. It is, however, often mistakenly referred to as "competing with oneself." When Mariah Nelson (1998) asked 1,030 girls and women from ages 11 to 49 to indicate with whom they compete generally, 75% responded "with myself; my own standards and goals." **For conceptual clarity it is important that we understand the difference between competition and individual achievement.** If you "compete with yourself," you will be both the victor and the vanquished—a conceptual contradiction. As Kohn (1992) notes, competition is not a solitary undertaking. Claiming that we compete with ourselves is like saying we arm wrestle with ourselves. Arm wrestling, and all competition, is an interactive phenomenon necessitating at least one other adversarial party.

Hypercompetitiveness: Winning Is Everything In a study of 198 of the world's top athletes, more than half of the participants said that they would take a drug that would improve their chances of winning every competition for a five-year period. Here's the stunner: these same top athletes would take the performance-enhancing drug even if they knew that it would kill them at the end of the five years ("Superhuman Heroes," 1998). The excessive emphasis on defeating others to achieve one's goals is called **hypercompetitiveness**. Psychologist Elliot Aronson (2012) claims, "We manifest a staggering cultural obsession with victory" (p. 258).

Competition in the United States is everywhere. A high school athlete has only a 1 in 300 chance of receiving a "full-ride" athletic scholarship to college. Nevertheless, parents increasingly sign up their kids when they are preadolescents for expensive private lessons. They also enroll their children in club programs and "traveling teams" that supplement traditional athletic experiences such as Little League, all to enhance the mistaken belief that this will improve their children's chances of becoming star athletes (Emmons, 2005; Hyman, 2009). There is a "youth sports juggernaut that puts a premium on hypercompetitive training and playing at the earliest ages" (Goldman, 2014). Every year about 3.5 million young athletes under the age of 15 suffer sports injuries, and half of these injuries result from intense overuse of their still-developing bodies (Hyman, 2009; Jayanthi et al., 2012). In the elusive drive to win a future scholarship to college, children are being put at risk for overuse injuries and emotional and psychological abuse from hypercompetitive coaches. As Nancy Lazenby Blaser, commissioner of the Central Coast Section of California High School Athletics, notes, "It's almost like prostituting your children for the family benefit of getting a scholarship. How could volleyball or soccer be so important that you put your kid in a situation like that?" (quoted in Emmons, 2005, p. 13A).

Our educational, economic, judicial, and political systems are also based on intense competition. U.S. universities are "intensely individualistic and highly competitive. Student is pitted against student through the grading system, and faculty member against faculty member for promotion and other academic favors" (Smith, 1990, p. 13). The competition for coveted academic scholarships at the nation's highly ranked universities can be ruthless (Poto, 2010).

▶ Constructive Competition: Tempering the Need to Win

It is hypercompetitiveness, not competitiveness itself, that poses the greatest challenge to establishing a positive group climate of trust, openness, directness, supportiveness, and accomplishment. Arguing that all competition is bad and that our goal should be to replace every instance of competition with cooperation is unrealistic and pointless. There will be numerous times in groups where, despite Herculean efforts to cooperate, competition prevails. In some cases, a cooperative alternative may not exist. How does a hiring committee, for example, transform the competition among hundreds of candidates into a cooperative endeavor when there is only a single position? In such cases, the competent communicator has to have the flexibility of skills to adapt to an adversarial, competitive situation. As will be discussed in Chapter 11, sometimes a competitive communication style is required to manage a conflict effectively.

When competitiveness increases, constructive competition tends to decrease.

Aside from the inevitability of competition in some circumstances, competition can be constructive. **Constructive competition** occurs when competition produces a positive, enjoyable experience and generates increased efforts to achieve without jeopardizing positive interpersonal relationships and personal well-being (Tjosvold et al., 2003, 2006).

Necessary Conditions: A Trinity Under certain conditions, competition can be constructive and won't create a negative group climate (Johnson, 2003). These conditions are as follows:

1. *When winning is deemphasized.* The less group members emphasize winning as the primary goal of competition and instead focus more on having fun and developing skills while competing, the more positive will be the group climate. A study of kids involved in Little League revealed that the more winning is emphasized, the higher is the dropout rate. Hypercompetitive managers who made winning the central goal had a team dropout rate *five times greater* than teams whose manager emphasized having fun and developing skills, not winning ("Put Enjoyment Ahead," 1994). There was no difference in the win–loss records of the two comparison groups. More than 41 million youths ages 18 and younger participate in organized sports programs in the United States, but 70% of these kids quit by age 13. Many quit because their interests change to other pursuits over time (Fullinwider, 2006), but many others quit because the pressure to win is too great, and consequently they aren't having fun (Emmons, 2005; see also Goodwin, 2010).

Legendary college basketball coach John Wooden validates the importance of deemphasizing winning: "Many people are surprised to learn that in 27 years at UCLA, I never once talked about winning" (quoted in Aguayo, 1990, p. 99). Wooden instead emphasized that every team member learn offensive and defensive skills and give his best effort. The results of Wooden's coaching philosophy are, to this day, jaw-dropping: 10 national championships in his last 12 years at UCLA, including an 88-game winning streak—still the record for men's major college basketball.

2. *When opponents are equally matched, allowing all participants a reasonable chance to win.* Professional athletes will sing the praises of competition. Why wouldn't they? Their phenomenal ability to win against the very best athletes in the world has propelled them to superstardom and staggering wealth. Clearly, competition is often rewarding for those who have a reasonable shot at winning. Even those individuals who are not the best but are a tier below the superstars, with great effort and perhaps some luck, can become winners at least occasionally (see Figure 4.1). They will likely find competition fun and enjoyable, challenging, motivating, and personally gratifying. But what about the vast majority of people who have no special talents; who are average or worse? If the driving force of competition is winning and attaining the rewards that go with victory, why would those who know that they will never reap such rewards be motivated by competition to excel? In fact, why wouldn't the prospect of being a persistent "loser" demoralize and deject competitors? In the workplace, employees who feel unable to compete effectively want to quit their jobs (Tjosvold et al., 2003).

3. *When there are clear, specific rules that ensure fairness.* When there are clear rules enforced without bias, competition can be a constructive enterprise. When there are no rules, or rules are enforced selectively or haphazardly, competition induces strong dissatisfaction with remaining a member of a group (Tjosvold et al., 2003), and it promotes cheating. David Callahan (2004), in his book *The Cheating Culture,* concludes, "Cheating thrives where unfairness reigns" (p. 263). Callahan documents widespread cheating in America. One study of college alumni reports that a whopping 82% of those surveyed cheated in college, the vast majority more than once (Yardley et al., 2009).

Cheating proliferates when, in a pervasive atmosphere of hypercompetitiveness, rules of fair play are either nonexistent or unenforced (Callahan, 2004). The steroid scandal in professional baseball is a prime example. Until congressional hearings in 2005, little effort was made to stem the tide of rampant steroid use in the major leagues. As a result, those players who may have wanted to "stay clean" were tempted to use

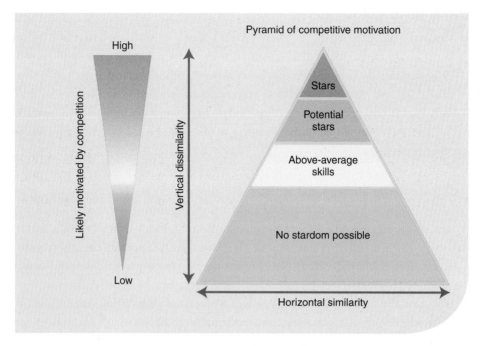

FIGURE 4.1
Pyramid of competition. Competition will likely motivate performance and achievement for those at the top of the pyramid, but increasingly less so as vertical dissimilarity (differences between competitors in skill levels) increases. Stars usually find competition against those of significantly lesser skills unchallenging; those of lesser skills are usually intimidated by stars. Horizontal similarity (individuals with equivalent skills) may motivate achievement and performance to some degree.

steroids to prevent losing the competitive edge against those who were cheating with performance-enhancing drugs (Callahan, 2004).

All three of the above conditions must be satisfied for constructive competition to occur. Remove one condition and constructive competition erodes. Apply rules unfairly, for example, and watch mildly competitive teams transform into hypercompetitive monsters, as we have all observed so often in professional sporting events. Also, the less these three conditions for constructive competition are met, the more likely that competition will turn negative. Being "a little bit fair" or a little less intensely competitive might reduce the negative effects, but it won't likely eliminate them and replace them with constructive outcomes.

Competition and Communication Competence: Can Me Be We? If cooperation is We-oriented (working together) and competition is Me-oriented (working against others for one's own sake), how can competitive patterns of interaction be anything but incompetent communication? First, **communication competence is a matter of degree.** Drinking a small amount of alcohol does not make you an alcoholic, and it may be beneficial in some instances, if kept to a minimum. Likewise, a small amount of competitiveness in groups usually does no harm and may be beneficial to the group (Tauer, 2004). Second, **although competent communication requires a We-orientation (rather than a Me-orientation), this does not exclude any consideration of individual needs.** Orientation implies primary, not exclusive, focus. The emphasis matters, not the mere presence of occasional competitive, individualistic communication patterns. Third, **many activities combine both competition and cooperation.** *Intergroup* (between groups) competition usually requires a great deal of *intragroup* (within a group) cooperation.

▶ Intragroup Competition and Cooperation: Challenging Orthodoxy

The pervasiveness of competition in American society and the vehemence with which it is defended make competition difficult to challenge. Nevertheless, a sober, analytical review of the research comparing the effects of competition and cooperation is warranted, if for no other reason than to base common beliefs on credible evidence, not mere anecdotal experiences. More than 1,200 research studies have been conducted on the relative merits and demerits of competition and cooperation (Johnson, 2009). This section discusses intragroup (within a group) effects derived from this voluminous research. The subsequent section addresses intergroup effects.

Group Productivity: Achievement and Performance on Tasks Reviews of hundreds of studies clearly show that cooperation, not competition, produces higher levels of group achievement and performance on a wide variety of tasks (Johnson, 2003). For example, cooperative, not competitive, learning clearly leads to higher academic achievement (Johnson & Johnson, 2009). One study determined that when competitive groups were compared to cooperative groups within an organization, overall the cooperative groups vastly outperformed the competitive groups. Even the *worst* cooperative groups that were relatively weak on task accomplishment, on average, outperformed the *best* competitive groups (Van Oostrum & Rabbie, 1995). **The cooperative advantage is especially significant when compared to the disadvantages of competition that is hypercompetitive, between unequal opponents, and conducted unfairly** (Stanne et al., 1999).

There are two primary reasons cooperation promotes and competition dampens achievement and performance for most groups and individuals (Kohn, 1992). First, **attempting to achieve excellence and trying to beat others are different goals.** A series of studies conducted at a business school at Cambridge University makes the point. Teams composed of members with high IQ scores performed worse than teams whose members had more ordinary IQ scores. (The groups did not compete against each other, but were merely compared on the basis of results.) Why did the high-IQ groups perform relatively poorly? High-IQ members spent a great deal of time in hypercompetitive debate, attempting to outshine each other. Moderate-IQ members worked as a team, uninterested in competing with each other for intellectual star status (Belbin, 1996). Trying to beat other group members diverts attention from achieving group excellence.

Second, **resources are used more efficiently in a cooperative climate.** A cooperative climate promotes the full utilization of information by a group, whereas a competitive climate typically promotes information hoarding (Johnson & Johnson, 2005; Stanne et al., 1999). When group members work together toward a common goal, not competitively to advance individual goals, there is likely to be less duplication of effort, better utilization of members' skills, and greater pooling of information and knowledge. Synergy is more likely to occur in a cooperative climate.

Group Cohesiveness: Social Relationships among Group Members Closely associated with group achievement and performance is group cohesiveness. When group members feel liked, valued, supported, and accepted, cohesiveness is strong. When group members feel disliked, unvalued, unsupported, and rejected, cohesiveness suffers. Does competition enhance intragroup cohesiveness? A review of more than 180 studies concluded that cooperative communication promoted significantly greater liking, support, and acceptance of group members than did competitive communication (Johnson, 2003).

Jules Henry (1963) noted that "a competitive culture endures by tearing people down." Although many adolescents quit sports because they fear failure and they can't handle the pressure of intense competition, many others never try out because they wish to avoid embarrassment and the ridicule of team members. Remember those agonizing moments in childhood when you engaged in the ritual of choosing up sides for basketball, soccer, or some other competitive game? If your schoolmates considered you a star, your inclusion on the team was assured. Your main concern was the prestige and enhanced self-esteem that accompanies being chosen first, second, or third. If your schoolmates viewed you as inept at sports, however, then your main concern was whether you would suffer the humiliation of being taken last in the playground draft.

In a competitive environment, the most skillful are valued. The less skillful just make defeat more probable and thereby become a burden on the team. Most people quit rather than absorb the torment of being called a loser. "We reward winners and are disdainful of losers" (Aronson, 2012, p. 258).

▶ Intergroup Competition and Cooperation: Them versus Us

In one of my group communication classes, students were assigned a symposium project. When we discovered that two of the four groups had chosen the same topic, hypercompetitiveness erupted. One of the two groups immediately negotiated with me to present its symposium first, thereby hoping to steal the thunder of the other group. When members of the competitor group overheard the negotiations, they screamed foul. Bitter recriminations flew between the antagonists. I stepped in to calm tempers. I instituted a random drawing to designate the order of presentations. Despite my assurance that both groups could work on the same topic and that grades would not be determined on any comparison between groups, the competitors seemed unsatisfied.

Outside of class the antagonism continued. Members of the two competing groups verbally accosted each other during lunch in the cafeteria. When class resumed, both groups could be heard muttering unflattering comments about their adversaries. Information from researching was jealously guarded by each group. On her own initiative, one member asked to speak to the rival group, but her rivals rudely rebuffed her.

Neither group needed to compete, yet compete they did. By pooling resources and emphasizing different aspects of the topic, they could have improved both of their final presentations. Instead, the two groups became instantly rigid and systemically hostile, each demanding that the other group choose a different topic. The result? Both groups gave mediocre symposium presentations.

A huge body of research shows conclusively that **intergroup interactions are generally far more competitive than interactions between individuals** (Wildschut et al., 2003). Plato in his *Republic* has Polemarchus stating that "justice consists of helping one's friends and harming one's enemies." This is an ancient statement of what is now referred to as the **norm of group interest**—a collective prescription that group members should pursue maximum group outcomes (winning at all costs), even if this means acting hypercompetitively against other groups when members may privately not wish to do so (Wildschut et al., 2002). We want to help our group succeed, even if we may disagree with the ultimate goal of defeating another group and preventing its success. Just in the last decade of the twentieth century, this intergroup hypercompetitive hostility claimed the lives of 30 million people worldwide (McGuire, 1998).

Despite the intergroup hostility, doesn't wanting to defeat another group increase cohesiveness within your own group? This is true to an extent. There are "weak indications" that intergroup competition generates internal group cohesion. This is primarily true when your group has to pull together to face a common foe. In the long run, however, **cohesiveness is enhanced primarily for winning teams.** Losing teams typically fall apart and members look for someone to blame (Van Oostrum & Rabbie, 1995). Competition is simply more enjoyable for winners than it is for losers.

Even if intergroup competition stimulates internal group cohesion, this method is a questionable way to achieve such a result. The group will have to manufacture enemies to defeat in order to maintain cohesion within the group. Cohesion, then, is artificially induced. It doesn't flow naturally from group interaction. Once the foe has been bested, the reason for cohesion is removed. A cooperative group climate, on the other hand, enhances the social relationships within the group, thereby increasing cohesiveness and group productivity as a by-product (Rabbie, 1993).

Wong Adam/Redlink/Redlink/Corbis

Intergroup competition can be fierce. Winning teams are usually cohesive, but losing teams often lose cohesiveness and group members look to blame each other for losing.

Focus on Culture

Competition and Culture

The pervasiveness of competition in the United States can easily trick us into believing that humans are competitive by nature. But where is the evidence that humans must compete because nature makes it inescapable? Brain research suggests that humans are neurologically wired for cooperation, not competition (Tomasello, 2009). Even the depiction of life in the animal world as "survival of the fittest" and "red in tooth and claw," to use Tennyson's metaphorical description, vastly overstates the competitive aspects of life on earth. Zoologist Frans de Waal notes, "Aiding others at a cost or risk to oneself is widespread in the animal world" (quoted by Boyd, 1996). Cooperation, according to this new school of thought, has survival value (de Waal, 2010). Animals that help each other find food and ward off predators do better than those that go it alone (Boyd, 1996). This "cooperation has survival value" perspective also holds true for human societies (Tomasello et al., 2012).

Comparing cultures reveals that "it is the norms of the culture that determine its competitiveness" (Kohn, 1992, p. 39), not human nature. Anthropologist Margaret Mead (1961) claimed that "it is the way the structure of the society is built up that determines whether individual members shall cooperate or shall compete with one another" (p. 481).

Consider the typical case of an elementary student who experiences difficulty discerning the correct answer to a math problem. The teacher urges the student to "think harder," applying further pressure to the intimidated youngster, who desperately hopes for a flash of brilliance. Meanwhile, fellow classmates are frantically waving their hands, certain in their own minds that they have deduced the right answer. Finally, giving up on the perplexed child, the teacher recognizes another student who excitedly shouts the correct answer. One child's misery is another child's triumph. Henry (1963) summarizes this commonplace competitive situation in U.S. classrooms this way: "So often somebody's success has been bought at the cost of our failure. To a Zuni, Hopi, or Dakota Indian, [besting another student] would seem cruel beyond belief, for competition, the wringing of success from somebody else's failure, is a form of torture" (p. 35).

There is abundant evidence demonstrating that American hypercompetitiveness flows primarily from an individualist cultural value system, not a biological imperative (Chatman & Barsade, 1995). Collectivist cultures tend to be far less competitive than the United States (Cox et al., 1991). Two separate studies comparing American groups (highly individualist) with Vietnamese groups (highly collectivist) found that Americans were competitive but the Vietnamese exhibited an "extraordinarily high rate" of cooperation, even when faced with competitive strategies from others. The authors of these studies concluded: "The difference between the extremely individualist and extremely collectivist cultures was very large and consistent with cultural norms" (Parks & Vu, 1994, p. 712). Cultural norms heavily influence the degree of competitiveness in a society.

QUESTIONS FOR THOUGHT

1. Can you imagine any culture entirely free from competition? In what ways would that be desirable and in what ways might that be undesirable?
2. Have you had experience with other cultures in which cooperation is emphasized? If so, how did you react to it?

Communication and Group Climate

Urgent pleas and pious pronouncements ("Let's all just get along") rarely produce cooperation in groups, even if our intentions are noble. Learning cooperative communication skills, however, is critical to the establishment of a positive group climate (Johnson, 2003).

> ## Focus Questions
>
> 1. In what ways might positive evaluation of others produce defensiveness?
> 2. When is controlling communication appropriate and when is it inappropriate?
> 3. What's the difference between a shift response and a support response?

▶ Defensive and Supportive Communication: Shaping Group Climate

Jack Gibb (1961), in an eight-year study of groups, identified specific communication patterns that both increase and lessen **defensiveness**—a reaction to a perceived attack on our self-concept and self-esteem. We feel personally diminished by communication patterns that ignite defensiveness. Typical responses to such diminishment include *denying* the truth of the attack, *counterattacking* or striking back at those who diminish us, and *withdrawing* from defensive situations (Ellison, 2009). One study reported that defensive communication patterns lead to worker burnout and a desire to leave the job (Becker et al., 2005).

Defensive provoking communication patterns invite a hypercompetitive response to protect our self-image. Supportive communication patterns invite cooperation. As each of these communication patterns is discussed, see if you recognize any of them in your own experience with groups (take the self-assessment test in Box 4.1).

Evaluation versus Description A friend of mine was in his townhouse when the 6.9-magnitude Loma Prieta earthquake hit Santa Cruz, California, in October 1989. Objects flew across the rooms, kitchen cabinets emptied onto the counters and floor, and glass shattered throughout his home. When the 15 seconds of rocking and rolling to Mother Nature's syncopation subsided, a momentary quiet ensued. Then from the back room came the timid, frightened little voice of his

BOX 4.1

Reactions to Defensive and Supportive Communication

Project yourself into each situation below and imagine how you would react. Choose a number for each situation that reflects how much you would like or dislike the statements presented.

1. You live with two roommates in an apartment. You forgot to clean your dishes twice this week. One of your roommates says to you, "Do your dishes. I'm tired of cleaning up your mess."

   STRONGLY DISLIKE   STRONGLY LIKE

   5   4   3   2   1

2. You're working with your team on a group project. One member says to the group, "I'm feeling very concerned that we will not finish our project in time. We're about halfway and we only have two days before our presentation. What do the rest of you think?"

   STRONGLY DISLIKE   STRONGLY LIKE

   5   4   3   2   1

3. You are a member of a softball team. Your coach says to you in front of the team, "You blew the game last week. Are you prepared to do better this game?"

   STRONGLY DISLIKE   STRONGLY LIKE

   5   4   3   2   1

4. At work, you tripped and badly bruised your shoulder. Your boss says to you, "I heard that you injured yourself yesterday. Do you need time off? That must really hurt. Can I

do anything to make you more comfortable while you work in your office?"

   STRONGLY DISLIKE   STRONGLY LIKE

   5   4   3   2   1

5. Your support group meets once a week to share experiences and solve personal problems. The group facilitator announces to the group, "We haven't got time to hear from (*your name*). We have more important things to consider."

   STRONGLY DISLIKE   STRONGLY LIKE

   5   4   3   2   1

6. During a group problem-solving session, one member says to the group, "I have a suggestion that might solve our problem. Perhaps this will move us forward."

   STRONGLY DISLIKE   STRONGLY LIKE

   5   4   3   2   1

7. You are a member of the student senate. During discussion on a controversial campus problem, the senate president says to the group, "We're obviously divided on this issue. Because I'm the president of this body, I'll have to make the final decision."

   STRONGLY DISLIKE   STRONGLY LIKE

   5   4   3   2   1

8. During a dorm council meeting, one member says to the council, "I know we all have strong feelings on this issue, but let's put our heads together and see if we can find

a solution everyone can support. Does anyone have ideas they wish to share with the group?"

STRONGLY DISLIKE   STRONGLY LIKE

5   4   3   2   1

9. During a heated group discussion with fellow classmates, one group member says, "I know I'm right and there's no way any of you will convince me that I'm wrong."

STRONGLY DISLIKE   STRONGLY LIKE

5   4   3   2   1

10. Your class project group approaches your teacher and proposes an idea that your teacher initially dislikes. She says to your group, "I can see that you really like this idea, but it doesn't satisfy the requirements of the project. I suggest that you keep brainstorming."

STRONGLY DISLIKE   STRONGLY LIKE

5   4   3   2   1

11. You're a member of a hiring panel. During a break from an interviewing session, one member of the panel takes you aside and says, "Look, I want you to support my candidate. We've been friends a long time.

This is important to me. Whaddaya say? Can I count on you to back me up?"

STRONGLY DISLIKE   STRONGLY LIKE

5   4   3   2   1

12. You've been asked to work on a committee to solve the parking problem on campus. The chair addresses the committee: "It is my hope that this committee can come to a consensus on solutions to this parking problem. I'll conduct our meetings, but I only have one vote, the same as everyone else."

STRONGLY DISLIKE   STRONGLY LIKE

5   4   3   2   1

Answers 1, 3, 5, 7, 9, and 11 5 **defensive communication** (control, evaluation, indifference, superiority, certainty, and manipulation—in that order); 2, 4, 6, 8, 10, and 12 5 **supportive communication** (description, empathy, provisionalism, problem orientation, assertiveness, and equality—in that order). Find your average score for each set (divide by six both the sum of the odd-numbered items and the sum of the even-numbered items). Which do you like best (lower average score)—defensive or supportive communication?

five-year-old daughter: "Daddy, it wasn't my fault." We are quick to evaluate each other in American society, especially negatively, and we are ready to defend ourselves with **self-justification**—providing excuses that absolve us of blame—even when no evaluation is offered (Tavris & Aronson, 2007). **Negative evaluations include criticism, contempt, and blame. Positive evaluations include praise, recognition, and flattery.** Negative evaluations produce defensiveness (Gottman & Gottman, 2006; Robbins et al., 2000). Criticism produces more conflict in the workplace than mistrust, personality clashes, pay, or power struggles (Baron, 1990), and harsh criticism demoralizes participants, reduces their work effort, and leads to refusals to work with criticizers on future tasks (Baron, 1988). Criticism from out-group members (those from another group) provokes considerably greater defensiveness than from in-group members (those from your own group) (Sutton et al., 2006). Criticism from an in-group member may also provoke considerable defensiveness if the in-group member is either a newcomer to the group (Hornsey et al., 2007) or seems uncommitted to the group (Hornsey et al., 2004). In either case, the criticizer's identification with the group is suspect.

Praise, on the other hand, is usually highly desired but often absent ("Survey Shows," 2012; Weisser, 2013). Surveys consistently reveal that scant praise and limited recognition for quality performance produce job dissatisfaction and a desire to leave (Lipman, 2013; Kjerulf, 2012). A Gallup study of more than 80,000 managers concluded: "Praise and recognition are essential building blocks of a great workplace" (Buckingham & Coffman, 2002b).

Nevertheless, even praise can induce defensiveness, especially when one group member receives praise and others don't ("Hey, how come I didn't get complimented?") or when we suspect an ulterior motive prompts the positive evaluation (Kjerulf, 2012). Note also that praise should accompany real accomplishments (Bronson & Merryman, 2011). Praising that which is not praiseworthy merely encourages false hope and future disappointment, as anyone can witness from watching numerous talentless individuals compete on *American Idol*. Effusively praised by family and friends in an understandable but misguided effort to be supportive, the painful attempts by some contestants who screech and croak a tune inevitably lead to crushing, demoralizing disappointment when the panel of judges mercifully (for the viewing audience) bounces them from the competition. Suffering such disappointment may not produce a soul-searching personal reappraisal of their talent, but it often seems to trigger a defensive counterattack from distraught contestants against the judges.

Description can minimize defensiveness. **Description** is a first-person report of how an individual feels, what he or she perceives to be true, and what behavior is desired from others. When *American Idol* judges focus on actual singing of contestants ("Forgetting the lyrics isn't helpful at this stage of the competition"), the comments are more constructive and less defensive producing than personal assaults ("You sound like a dog in heat") and sarcasm ("Pretty good for a person with absolutely zero talent").

Consider these four steps for achieving descriptive effectiveness:

1. *Praise first, then describe.* Try beginning with praiseworthy behavior before describing behavior that is problematic ("This is a well-written task force report. I do have a few suggestions, however, for improvement"). When praise is used before negative feedback, there is greater likelihood that the recipient will agree with the negative feedback. Motives of those group members providing the negative feedback are also more likely to be assumed to be constructive than destructive when praise precedes negative feedback (Hornsey et al., 2008). There is the risk, of course, that this "praise first" strategy might be seen as patronizing and

manipulative. Praise that is genuine, however, does minimize defensiveness (Hornsey et al., 2008).

2. *Use I-statements, not You-statements* (Narcisco & Burkett, 1975; Notarius & Markman, 1993). I-statements may begin with an identification of the speaker's feeling, followed by a description of behavior linked to the feeling. "I feel excluded and isolated when my contributions receive no response from the group" is an example. Such an I-statement focuses the attention on the person speaking. If there are no important feelings involved, simply offer recommendations for improvement ("I have a few changes I'd like you to consider"). Suggestions for change imply that a group member has "not measured up" in some ways (negative evaluation), but framing your message as an I-statement can seem less like an accusation ("You need to make these changes"). If you are speaking on behalf of your group, I-statements shift into We-statements ("We are very concerned that our presentation will not be finished on time"). We-statements are simply the plural form of descriptive I-statements.

A You-statement of negative evaluation, on the other hand, places the focus on someone who is an object of attack. "You have excluded me from the group and you make me feel isolated" is a statement that blames. Expect denial from group members so accused ("We've never excluded you") or a counterattack ("If you've been excluded, it is because your comments sound like those of a simpleton in a *Jackass* movie"). Any statement that begins with "You didn't …" or "You shouldn't …" or "You haven't …" can instantly put the receiver on guard because it can seem like an accusation will follow. Avoiding You-statements is not always warranted to minimize defensiveness ("You might consider these changes," for example), but try developing the habit of using I-statements instead.

3. *Make your descriptions specific, not vague.* Strive for clarity (Baron, 1988). "I feel weird when you act inappropriately around my boss," is an inexact description. "Weird" and "inappropriately" require specific elaboration. Get to the point. "I feel awkward and embarrassed when you tell my boss jokes that ridicule gays and women" is more specific.

4. *Eliminate editorial comments from descriptive statements.* Some I-statements are undisguised personal assaults. "I feel ashamed when you act like an idiot in front of my colleagues" uses the I-statement form without the supportive intent or phrasing. Even an I-statement that may appear to be a specific description devoid of judgment sometimes inadvertently travels into evaluative territory. "I get irritated when you waste the time of this committee by commenting on trivial side issues" loads the statement with provocative phrasing. "Waste time" and "trivial" retain the evaluative and attack elements likely to induce defensive responses. Simply jettison the loaded language.

Textbook-perfect, praise-first, first-person-singular, specific, editorial-free statements, of course, induce no supportive climate if the tone of voice used is sarcastic or condescending, eye contact is threatening, facial expressions and body language are intimidating, and gestures are abusive. Focus on your own feelings and spotlight the specific behaviors you think need improvement without sending mixed messages composed of verbal descriptions and nonverbal, negative evaluations.

Control versus Problem Orientation English poet Samuel Butler once said, "He who agrees against his will, is of the same opinion still." **Issuing orders and demanding obedience, especially when no input was sought from group members who were told what to do, is controlling communication.** Dictatorial, demanding behaviors from teachers are poorly received by students (Schrodt et al., 2008). Jack Brehm (1972) developed a theory of psychological reactance to explain our resistance to efforts aimed at controlling our behavior. Simply put, **psychological reactance** means the more someone tries to control us by telling us what to do, the more we are inclined to resist such efforts or even to do the opposite (Rains & Turner, 2007). The following bit of wisdom captures this well: "There are three ways to make sure something gets done—do it yourself; hire someone to do it; *forbid* your kids to do it" (Landers, 1995). The more intensely parents admonish their kids not to smoke, ingest drugs, or get various parts of their anatomies pierced, the more likely their children are to do these behaviors so they can assert their sense of personal freedom (Dowd et al., 1988).

Tell someone they can't do something and, typically, it is what they want to do most. A 15-year study of "radical groups," involving more than a thousand subjects, concluded that the coercive practice of "deprogramming" individuals to give up their cult membership "can drive young people back into their group, or into a pattern of cult-hopping, for years" (Levine, 1984, p. 27).

We help prevent a defensive climate from emerging when we collaborate on a problem and seek solutions cooperatively. The orientation is on the problem and how best to solve it, not on how best to control those who have less power. All controlling communication can't be eliminated (parents want to protect their children from foolish or dangerous behavior), but it can be kept to a minimum (LaFasto & Larson, 2001). Group members who are not acting responsibly (for example, being late with reports due to laziness) may have to be told to change their behavior by the group leader or the group as a whole: "We need your report so our group can finish this project. Is there a problem, and can we help?" Generally, however, by focusing on problem solving, personality conflicts and power struggles should fade into the background.

A study of decision making at 356 U.S. companies discovered that 58% of strategic plans were rejected when executives overseeing the plans attempted to impose

This cartoon illustrates:

1. Defensiveness
2. First-person-singular language
3. Criticism
4. Psychological reactance

Answers are given at the end of the chapter.

their ideas on colleagues. When executives asked instead for problem-solving ideas from colleagues, 96% of the plans were approved (McNutt, 1997). Ownership of a solution to a problem comes not from mandating it ("This is what I've decided and you must do it"), but from collaborating as a group and brainstorming possible solutions.

Wanting to be less controlling and more oriented toward problem solving is not the complete answer. The competent communicator must know how to problem-solve, have the requisite skills, and be committed to finding solutions. More will be said about these in later chapters.

Manipulation versus Assertiveness Most people resent and resist being manipulated. If you are like most people, simply knowing that someone is attempting to influence you for his or her own benefit is repellent. I experienced my own private purgatory when I sold encyclopedias door to door for a brief time one summer following graduation from college (when door-to-door sales were common). After I suffered many rude comments and slammed doors, the first person to invite me in was a young, friendly woman who had no idea I hoped to sell her encyclopedias. I was trained to camouflage my real purpose to avoid immediate rejection (rarely successful). Upon entering her home, I noticed the woman's inebriated husband and his snarling German shepherd. "If you're selling something," the unpleasant husband snapped at me, "you'll be dealing with my dog." I concocted a quick excuse and exited. I immediately sought sanctuary but found no churches in the vicinity. I luckily found refuge in the house of an older Czechoslovakian couple. I was served tea and cookies while I engaged in friendly conversation about "the old country" for almost three hours. I gave up trying to sell encyclopedias for the evening, having recognized how intensely people in my sales territory resented being disturbed by a stranger attempting to sell them something. To this day, I wonder if that sweet couple ever thought of the young man who came to visit them for no apparent reason. I quickly retired from the encyclopedia business.

A study of 6,000 team members in 600 organizations found that playing politics, an especially cutthroat version of manipulative communication, destroys social relationships and team effectiveness (LaFasto & Larson, 2001). **Hidden agendas**— personal goals of group members that are not revealed openly and that can interfere with group accomplishment—can create a defensive atmosphere. When you suspect that a team member is complimenting your performance merely to gain an ally against other members in a dispute, this hidden agenda will likely ignite defensiveness.

Assertiveness is the alternative to manipulation. Assertiveness is honest, open, and direct, but not aggressive, communication. It is the opposite of game playing and strategic manipulation. An assertive message says, "This is how I feel and this is what I need." A much more extensive discussion of assertiveness appears in Chapter 10.

Indifference versus Empathy We like being acknowledged when we are present in a group. We dislike being treated like a piece of furniture, sitting alone in a corner. Indifference from group members, or what Gibb (1961) calls neutrality, makes us defensive. Making little or no effort to listen to what a member of your group has to say exhibits indifference and treats the communicator as a nonperson. Failure to acknowledge another person's communication effort either verbally or nonverbally is called an **impervious response** (Sieberg & Larson, 1971). Such indifference is disconfirming. This is a common complaint from students working in virtual groups. When your online class team members don't respond to your phone calls, emails, text messages, or postings on social media, this apparent indifference can be a frustrating experience and a huge impediment to group success.

You counter indifference with empathy. Howell (1982) defines **empathy** as "thinking and feeling what you perceive another to be thinking and feeling" (p. 108). Empathy is built on concern for others (Rifkin, 2009). **It requires that we try to see from the perspective of the other person,** perceiving the needs, desires, and feelings of a group member because that is what we would want others to do for us (Fisher & Shapiro, 2005). "How would you like it if I treated you the way you treat me?" is a plea for empathy from others.

Superiority versus Equality Communicating superiority sends the message that one is Me-deep in self-importance. It can be a tremendous turnoff for most people. Group leaders who exhibit superiority to group members undermine their credibility and influence (Reicher et al., 2007). Rosenfeld (1983) found that the

Texting in class sends the message: "I don't care enough to pay attention to the instructor. Texting is more important." This communicates indifference and is disrespectful.

Ariel Skelley/Blend Images/Getty Images

behavior of instructors in classes that are disliked by students is characterized as predominantly superior. One of the key factors characterizing classes that were liked was "My teacher treats us as equals with him/her." Whatever the differences in our abilities, talents, intellect, and the like, treating people with respect and politeness—as equals on a personal level—encourages harmony and productivity. Treating people like they are IRS agents at the award ceremony for the state lottery winner will invite enmity and retaliation. One study showed that embarrassing and belittling students for "inferior" performance in the class produced negative student evaluations of teachers (Schrodt et al., 2008).

Equality does not mean we all have the same abilities. I will never swim with the grace and speed of Olympic gold-medalist Michael Phelps. Despite three sets of swimming lessons when I was a child, I sank to the bottom of the pool every time the instructor tried to teach me to float on my back. I had the buoyancy of a granite slab. Equality from the standpoint of group climate means that we give everyone an *equal opportunity to succeed and exhibit whatever potential they possess.* We recognize that everyone has faults and limitations. In fact, one way of demonstrating equality as a means of minimizing defensiveness is to share your own shortcomings with group members (Hornsey et al., 2008). Self-deprecating humor that makes fun of your own failings is also an effective means of communicating equality, not superiority (Greengross & Miller, 2008). Comedian Wendy Liebman demonstrates self-deprecating humor: "I've been getting back to nature ... well I was evicted ... from my parent's house ... but we're still very close ... genetically ... I'm engaged now ... it was so romantic ... he turned off the TV ... well he muted it ... during the commercials." Poking fun at yourself just makes you seem more human and likable if it's done occasionally. It is the antithesis of ego. If it is done frequently, however, you may come off as a loser.

Certainty versus Provisionalism There are very few things in this world that are certain—death, taxes, your clothes dryer will eat your socks, your toast will fall buttered-side down, and your technological devices will fail at the most inopportune times are a few that come to my mind. Communicating certainty to group members is asking for trouble. I listened to students in my class argue with one of their group members who insisted that crystals really do have healing powers and that only pigheadedness kept the group from accepting the truth of what he was adamantly asserting. This individual would entertain no contrary point of view, so certain was he of the unalterable correctness of his belief, nor would he accede to requests from members for hard evidence of crystals' healing power. He was certain he was right and anyone who couldn't accept this truth must be stupid.

SECOND LOOK

Defensive versus Supportive Communication Patterns

Defensive	Supportive
Evaluation	Description
Control	Problem orientation
Manipulation	Assertiveness
Indifference	Empathy
Superiority	Equality
Certainty	Provisionalism

Certainty is reflected in terms such as *never, always, impossible, can't,* and *won't.* "We'll never finish this project on time" and "We can't get an A" are two examples of using terms of certainty. These terms of certainty may shut down group discussion and kill motivation to succeed.

Provisionalism counters certainty. **Provisionalism** means you qualify statements, avoiding absolutes. Provisionalism is reflected in the use of qualifying terms such as *possibly, probably, perhaps, occasionally, maybe, might,* and *sometimes.* "We may have difficulty finishing this project on time unless we organize our effort" and "We might get an A if we keep working" are provisional statements. This is the language of precision, not fence-straddling. Problems are approached as interesting issues to be investigated and discussed, not defensive power struggles regarding who is right or wrong.

Once a group climate develops from the six defensive inducing or supportive patterns of communication just discussed, it can set in motion a **reciprocal pattern**—tit for tat. One famous tit-for-tat exchange occurred between Lady Astor, the first female member of the British Parliament, and Winston Churchill. Exasperated by Churchill's opposition to several of the causes she espoused, Lady Astor acerbically remarked, "Winston, if I were married to you, I'd put poison in your coffee." Churchill replied, "And if you were my wife, I'd drink it" (Fadiman, 1985, p. 122). Verbal attack begets verbal attack.

One study found that supportive/confirming communication patterns by one party during a conflict elicited similar responses from the other party (Burggraf & Sillars, 1987). The same held true for defensive/disconfirming communication patterns (Sundell, 1972). Remember the "bad apple" research of Felps and his colleagues

(2006) discussed in Chapter 2? Insults (evaluation) from the bad apple begat insults from other group members, slacker behavior (indifference) begat slacker behavior, and cynical behavior (indifference and certainty) begat reciprocal cynical behavior from others in the group.

The challenge in any group is to maintain the positive reciprocal pattern of support and to break the cycle of the negative reciprocal pattern of defensiveness. A positive reciprocal pattern of support and cooperation should emerge from the communication transactions among group members. Group leaders may play an important role in this process by setting a cooperative tone for the group. The responsibility for establishing a positive group climate, however, rests on all group members.

▶ Competitive and Noncompetitive Listening: Shifting and Supporting

Listening effectively is one of the most critical on-the-job communication skills you can exhibit (Darling & Dannels, 2003; Landrum & Harrold, 2003). "Good listening skills can help you to feel easy in all sorts of social situations, and to build the kind of rapport that leads to solid emotional bonds" (Gottman & DeClaire, 2001, p. 198). Despite the obvious importance of listening well in groups, evidence shows that for the most part we don't listen effectively. A study of 269 college students revealed that 90% of those surveyed admitted to text messaging during class lectures. It is now the top classroom distraction. Despite the common belief that you can multitask effectively (texting and listening to group members simultaneously), research debunks this belief. As Stanford psychologist Clifford Nass notes based on his research, "It turns out multitaskers are terrible at every aspect of multitasking. They're terrible at ignoring irrelevant information; they're terrible at keeping information in their head nicely and neatly organized; and they're terrible at switching from one task to another" ("Interview: Clifford Nass," 2010).

Active listening is focused listening. We make a conscious effort to focus our attention on the speaker and his or her message. Too often when sitting in groups we do not make the effort to listen actively. We allow our minds to wander and our attention to be distracted.

Competent listening, however, goes far beyond actively listening to other group members. **How we listen is also extremely important.** In this section I will briefly discuss competitive and noncompetitive listening.

Shift Response versus Support Response: Focusing on Me or Thee

Listening can become a competitive event. When we vie for attention during a group discussion, our listening becomes competitive. Conversation becomes a contest. An attention-*getting* initiative by a listener, called the **shift response,** is a key competitive listening strategy. Here the listener attempts to shift the focus of attention from others to oneself by changing the topic of discussion. The shift response is Me-oriented. The **support response,** in contrast, is an attention-*giving,* cooperative effort by the listener to focus attention on the other person, not on oneself (Derber 1979; Vangelisti et al., 1990). Consider the following example:

Maria: I'm feeling very frustrated by our group's lack of progress on our project.

Michael: I was more frustrated by Jerry's snotty attitude during yesterday's meeting. (*Shift response*)

Notice how Michael does not respond to Maria's frustration. Instead, he shifts the focus to his own frustration about another issue in the group. Now compare this shift response with a support response, as follows:

Maria: I'm feeling very frustrated by our group's lack of progress on our project.

Michael: I hear you. What do you think we should do about it? (*Support response*)

Here, the response from the listener keeps the focus on the speaker and encourages Maria to explore the topic she initiated.

A shift response can easily provoke shift responses from other group members in a hypercompetitive battle for attention, such as in the following example:

Beth: I don't think our project fulfills the requirements of the class assignment. I'm worried that we will get a bad grade.

Greg: The assignment is too difficult. I don't understand what we are supposed to do. (Shift response)

Carla: The project isn't too difficult. It is really interesting and fun. I'm looking forward to the next project, aren't you? (Shift response)

Beth: But what about our report on this current project? I still don't think we've fulfilled the assignment. (Shift response to refocus attention on initial topic)

Greg: You worry too much. I need help on my speech. What's the main point I need to make first? (Shift response)

Although the shift response may be appropriate in some instances where individuals drift from the main topic of conversation and need to be refocused, **competent communicators emphasize support responses and use shift responses infrequently.** *Background acknowledgment* ("really," "uh-huh," "yup"), a *supportive assertion* ("That's super," "Nicely done"), and a *supportive question* ("How do you think we should proceed?") are the types of supportive responses that encourage cooperative discussion, not competitive struggles for attention.

Competitive Interrupting: Seizing the Floor Nathan Miller bitingly asserts that "conversation in the United States is a competitive exercise in which the first person to draw a breath is declared the listener" (cited in Bolton, 1979, p. 4). Competitive interrupting is closely related to the shift response. It differs, however, in one key way. **Listeners who use the shift response usually observe the "one speaker at a time" rule of conversation. Competitive interrupters do not.**

Interrupting becomes competitive when the listener attempts to seize the floor from the speaker and dominate the conversation. Not all interrupting, of course, is competitive. Sometimes group members interrupt to express support ("I agree with Joe") or enthusiasm ("Great idea"), seek clarification ("I'm confused. Could you explain that again before we move on?"), warn of danger ("Look out. You're falling over backward"), or cut short a "talkaholic's" nonstop monologue that prevents other group members from participating (James & Clarke, 1993).

Competitive interrupting is Me-oriented. The focus is on individual needs, not group needs. Competitive interrupting creates antagonism, rivalry, hostility, and in some cases withdrawal from group discussion by frustrated members. Group members often mirror the interrupting patterns of others. If one member interrupts to seize the floor, another member will likely interrupt to seize it back. If members rarely interrupt, and when they do, primarily offer support, others will likely follow suit and keep the conversation supportive and cooperative.

Ambushing: Preparing Rebuttals When a group member is ready to pounce on a point made by a speaker, that member is listening with a bias. The bias is to attack the speaker verbally, not try to understand the speaker's point of view. This is called **ambushing**. Ambushing is clearly competitive listening. Ambushers aim to defeat a speaker in a verbal jousting match. Preparing a rebuttal while a speaker is still explaining his or her point shows little interest in comprehending a message. In competitive debates, message distortion is a common problem. The focus is on winning the argument, not discerning a message accurately.

Debating ideas is a useful and important process in a democratic society. Ambushing, however, puts the caboose in front of the train engine. Defeating an opponent becomes the driving force for ambushers, not clarity of messages. During group discussion, try to understand messages clearly and accurately *before* evaluating them. Otherwise, you may be evaluating and refuting ideas that were never advanced by any group member.

Probing and paraphrasing can short-circuit ambushing. **Probing** means seeking additional information from a speaker by asking questions. Probing includes clarifying questions ("Can you give me an example of an important goal for the group?"), exploratory questions ("Can you think of any other approach to this problem?"), and encouraging questions ("Who can blame us for making a good effort to try a new approach?").

Paraphrasing "is a concise response to the speaker which states the essence of the other's content in the listener's words" (Bolton, 1979, p. 51). Paraphrasing should be concise and precise. For example:

Gabriela: I'm so sick and tired of working and working on this report and we have so little to show for it. If we'd started earlier, we would be done by now.

Frank: You seem frustrated and unhappy with the group's effort.

Gabriela: I am frustrated, but I'm not unhappy with our group. We've all worked hard. None of us could arrange our schedules to begin any sooner on this.

Paraphrasing can reveal misunderstanding. Ambushing merely assumes a message is understood without checking. Noncompetitive listening is a useful communication skill.

In summary, there is perhaps no greater challenge or more important task in a group than establishing a positive, cooperative climate. A negative, competitive climate will bode ill for your group. Defensive climates promote conflict and disharmony in groups. Supportive climates do not free groups entirely from conflict, but such an atmosphere enhances the likelihood of constructive solutions to conflict in groups.

Reflect on what you've learned

In Mixed Company

▶ Online

Now that you've read Chapter 4, access the online resources that accompany *In Mixed Company* at **www.cengagebrain.com**. Your online resources include:

1. Multiple-choice and true-false **chapter practice quizzes** with automatic correction
2. Digital **glossary**
3. **Flashcards**

QUESTIONS FOR CRITICAL THINKERS

1. Why do you think supervisors faced with poor employee performance use predominantly controlling, not problem-solving, strategies?
2. Are there instances when you should act as a model of cooperative behavior even though other group members will take advantage of you?
3. Is hypercompetitive communication ever ethical? Explain.

VIDEO *Case Studies*

August: Osage County (2013). Drama; R
A Meryl Streep and Julia Roberts vehicle depicting family dysfunction. Focus on the abundance of defensive versus supportive communication patterns and competitive and noncompetitive listening examples.

Authors Anonymous (2014). Comedy; PG-13

A dysfunctional group of hopeful, unpublished writers attempts to remain unconditionally positive and supportive in their communication in the face of constant rejection. Not for everyone, but this movie has many amusing moments. Analyze the effects of unconditionally supportive communication and what occurs when praise turns to criticism and envy.

Leatherheads (2008). Comedy; PG-13
Goofy comedy about the early days (1920s) of professional football, starring George Clooney. Is the competition in all of its aspects depicted as constructive or destructive? Apply the three criteria for constructive competition.

Who's Afraid of Virginia Woolf? (1966). Drama; R
Engrossing but lengthy film depicting George and Martha, a troubled couple, "entertaining" another couple in the wee hours of the morning. This film is loaded with examples of defensive communication. Identify as many examples as you can find.

Playing by Heart (1998). Romantic Comedy; R
This is a wonderful romantic comedy about people's lives intersecting, sometimes poignantly. Look for defensive and supportive communication patterns.

Remember the Titans (2000). Drama; PG
Feel-good true story of a black football coach who has to deal with racism in a newly integrated high school in Virginia. Examine this film for both intragroup and intergroup competition. Do the results of competition depicted in the movie parallel the research in this chapter? Is the competition constructive? Explain.

Answers to Multiple-Choice Question in Cartoon Caption:
Cartoon, p. 124, 1, 4

5

Roles in Groups

I n a study of a surgical team at St. Joseph's Hospital in Ann Arbor, Michigan, the distinction between the roles of doctor and nurse was evident. During a coronary bypass operation, the two surgeons began swapping stories about the Detroit Tigers while loud rock music played in the background. Two nurses assisting with the operation began a quiet discussion of their own, only to be reprimanded by the head surgeon, who bellowed, "Come on, people; let's keep it down in here!" (Denison & Sutton, 1990, p. 301). Nurses did not have the same leeway to talk, laugh, and joke with each other as surgeons did. Surgeons, by necessity, were in charge of the operation. Surgeons were in the leader role and nurses were in the follower role, expected to do the bidding of the surgeons without question.

In the drama of life, we play many roles often with telling consequences. A group **role** is the pattern of expected behavior associated with parts that we play in groups. There are expectations for playing the role of a doctor (in charge) and for that of a nurse (follow doctors' orders). These expectations may not always be constructive. Individuals act out their roles in transactions with group members. What might have begun as a casual or unnoticed pattern of behavior may quickly develop into an expectation. For example, when you tell a few jokes during the initial meeting of your group, you may be assuming the role of tension reliever without even noticing. Other group members may come to expect you to interject humor into tense situations.

Roles are not static entities. When the composition of your group changes, when phases of development change, when the group climate shifts either toward or away from a cooperative/supportive one, or when you move from one group to another, you

MindTap

Start with a
quick warm-up
activity.

have to adapt to these changes in the system. The required behaviors for your role may change as a consequence, or the roles members play may change.

The principal purpose of this chapter is to discuss group roles. There are five objectives relevant to this purpose:

1. To explain the significance of roles in groups,
2. To identify the different types of group roles and their corresponding communication patterns,
3. To discuss role adaptability in the group system,
4. To explore the role emergence process,
5. To explain the newcomer role and the socialization process in groups.

Norms and roles form the basic structure of a group. **Structure** is the systematic interrelation of all parts to the whole. Structure provides form and shape for a group. **Norms are *broad* rules that designate appropriate behavior for *all* group members, while roles stipulate *specific* behaviors that are expected for *individual* group members.** A norm for a group might be that every member works hard on all tasks. Roles, however, specify different task behaviors for a vice president, a middle manager, and an office worker. In this section, the influence of roles on behavior is explored.

Influence of Roles: Not Just Playing Games

The expectations attached to roles can have a marked influence on group members' perceptions (see Closer Look: "The Stanford Prison Study"). This influence was demonstrated in a study in which pairs of students performed the roles of questioner and contestant in a college bowl type of quiz game (Ross et al., 1977). Questioners were instructed to think of 10 difficult questions for which they knew the answers. They then were to ask contestants these questions. Both students and the audience knew that the roles of questioner and contestant were randomly assigned. Yet, both the audience and the contestants thought that those students playing the questioner role were smarter than those students playing the contestant role. Questioners, of course, looked more impressive asking difficult questions for which they already knew the answers, while contestants looked less impressive trying to answer the questions and sometimes making mistakes. Despite the obvious advantage given to the questioners and despite the fact that students playing both roles were equally intelligent, the predominant perception was markedly influenced by the role each student played.

Focus Questions

1. Are some roles more prestigious than others?

2. When two roles conflict, which role is likely to prevail?

▶ Role Status: Playing by Hierarchical Rules

Not all roles are valued equally. Presidents and CEOs of companies are accorded greater status than middle managers or the average worker. This status difference is amply illustrated by the pay disparity. In 2014, the average CEO salary was *331 times* that of the average worker's wage—$11.7 million versus $35,293 annual pay— and 774 times that of a minimum wage worker (Hall, 2014). Middle managers have higher status than staff members. College professors usually are accorded greater status than elementary school teachers. Teachers typically have greater status than students, although one disturbing study showed that status differences are not always respected. A survey of 4,735 K–12 teachers found that 27% had been verbally threatened by students and 37% had been the target of obscene remarks or gestures (Chamberlin, 2010). Higher societal status doesn't always translate into respect from all those in lower-status roles who are expected to comply with the wishes and directions of higher-status individuals.

One study showed the power of **role status**—the relative importance, prestige, or power accorded a particular role (Geis et al., 1984). When viewers saw television commercials depicting a man in a high-status, important person role (his wishes, needs, and preferences were the central concern of the commercial) and a woman in the relatively low-status, helpmate role (her wishes, needs, and preferences were never addressed or acknowledged), they described the man as a "rational, independent, dominant, ambitious leader." The woman, by contrast, was described as an "emotional, dependent, submissive, contented follower." A markedly different result from these stereotypic depictions of male–female interactions occurred when the roles were exactly reversed. When the woman in the commercial performed the high-status role and the man acted out the low-status role, viewers described the woman as a "rational, independent, dominant, ambitious leader" and the man as an "emotional, dependent, submissive, contented follower."

Role status can be a source of great discontent in groups. For example, surgical teams, by necessity, have clearly defined roles. Nurses, nevertheless, complain bitterly that doctors are unnecessarily oppressive in exercising their superior power (that is, they used defensive communication patterns of control and superiority). As illustrated in the opening chapter case study, nurses describe being treated like slaves, and often are expected

Roles in groups can vary widely in status. A college professor has far more status than students in a class.

to perform demeaning tasks when ordered by surgeons to do so. The power disparity between the higher-status physician role and the lower-status nurse role "can cause a great deal of resentment and impede successful collaboration" (Ellington, 2008, p. 185).

The power disparity can also lead to abusive behavior by the more powerful doctors. Social psychologist Dacher Keltner (2007) observes "that most rude behaviors—shouting, profanities, bald critiques—emanate from the offices and cubicles of individuals in positions of power." Results from a survey of more than 2,100 physicians and nurses conducted by the American College of Physician Executives, show that the clash of roles between doctors and nurses and the abusive behavior it produces is stunningly frequent. Almost 98% of those surveyed reported witnessing bad behavior between physicians and nurses. A surprising 40% said that these clashes occurred at least weekly or daily. Typical bad behavior included cursing, yelling, and demeaning behavior, and doctors initiated most of it. In one case, a doctor told a nurse, "You don't look dumber than my dog. Why can't you at least fetch what I need?" In another instance, a surgeon shouted for all to hear that "monkeys could be trained to do what scrub nurses do" (Johnson, 2009; see also Brewer et al., 2013). "While there were complaints about nurse behaviors, both doctors and nurses who filled out the survey said physicians were to blame for a large part of disruptive behaviors" (Johnson, 2009). Many survey respondents claimed that doctors acted as though they should be granted special treatment befitting their superior role and status.

Abuse by doctors has consequences. The more that abuse is heaped on nurses, the more likely they are to quit their jobs (Grenny, 2009). Aside from the deleterious effects on nurses, patient care is also at risk from the bad behavior of "superior" doctors. A study called "Silence Kills," conducted by VitalSmarts and the American Association of Critical-Care Nurses, reports that more than 20% of healthcare professionals have witnessed harm to patients because of disrespectful and abusive treatment mostly by doctors toward nurses (Maxfield et al., 2005). Nevertheless, studies of doctor–nurse communication clearly show that lower-status nurses continue to defer to high-status physicians "despite believing their expertise to be more appropriate in a particular situation" (Sirota, 2007, p. 54).

CLOSER LOOK

The Stanford Prison Study

It happened one Sunday morning. Police officers, with vehicle sirens screeching, swept through the college town and arrested 10 male college students. Charged with a felony, the students were searched, handcuffed, and taken to police headquarters for booking. They were blindfolded and transported to the "Stanford County Prison," located in the basement of the Stanford University psychology department building. Upon arrival they were stripped naked, issued a smock-type uniform with an ID number across the front and back, and forced to wear a cap made out of nylon to simulate a shaved head. Each prisoner received towels, soap, a toothbrush, and bed linen. Jail cells were sparsely furnished—cots and bucket toilets. Personal belongings were prohibited.

The 10 inmates were guarded by 11 other college students. These guards carried nightsticks, handcuffs, and whistles. They dressed in khaki uniforms and wore reflecting sunglasses to make eye contact difficult. They remained nameless.

Guards established a set of rules that the prisoners were to follow without hesitation or resistance. The rules were rigid: no talking during meals, rest periods, or after lights were out. Head counts were taken at 2:30 A.M. Troublemakers

faced loss of "privileges." At first, these privileges included opportunities to read, write, or talk to other inmates. Later, privileges were defined as eating, sleeping, and washing.

The inmates revolted against the repressive conditions. Some barricaded the doors of their cells with cots. Some engaged in hunger strikes. Several tore off their ID numbers. The guards became increasingly abusive and authoritarian in response to the revolt. They used a fire extinguisher to quash the rebellion. Punishment for disobedience included cleaning toilets with bare hands, doing push-ups, and spending time in solitary confinement (a closet). Head counts were used as a means of harassment. Head counts took 10 minutes or less on the first day. By the fifth day, the head counts lasted several hours as the guards vilified prisoners, who were standing at attention the entire time, for minor infractions of the rules.

Within a short time, some of the prisoners began to act depressed, dependent, and disturbed by their incarceration. Several prisoners experienced severe stomach cramps. One prisoner wept uncontrollably. He flew into fits of rage and experienced disorganized thinking and bouts of severe depression. Three other inmates developed similar symptoms. Another inmate developed a psychosomatic rash over his entire body when his "parole" was denied.

The chief form of communication initiated by the guards to the prisoners consisted mostly of commands, insults, verbal and physical abuse, degrading references, and threats. The principal form of communication used by the prisoners when interacting with the guards consisted mostly of resistance and ridicule in the beginning, but became more compliant later (e.g., answering questions and giving information). Prisoners even turned on each other, engaging in far more uncomplimentary and negative evaluations than supportive and complimentary communication.

Stanford psychologist Philip Zimbardo (2007), who conducted this mock prison study, terminated the experiment after only six days. The study was originally planned for a two-week period, but he decided that the roles had become real. "In guard roles, college students who had been pacifists and 'nice guys' behaved aggressively—sometimes even sadistically.... As prisoners, psychologically stable students soon behaved pathologically, passively resigning themselves to their unexpected fate" (Gerrig, 2013). Zimbardo had taken 21 healthy, well-adjusted male students who exhibited no signs of emotional instability or aberrant behavior when given extensive personality tests and clinical interviews prior to the experiment, and he had transformed them into pathological guards and compliant prisoners. The guard and prisoner roles were randomly assigned by the flip of a coin, so pathological behavior cannot be explained by looking for character flaws in the men acting as guards. Clearly, the young men in this controversial field study became the product of their designated roles. As one guard in the prison study explained afterward, "Once you put a uniform on, and are given a role ... then you're certainly not the same person if you're in street clothes and in a different role. You really become that person once you put

on the khaki uniform, you put on the glasses, you take the nightstick, and you act the part" (quoted in Zimbardo, 2007, p. 213).

The parallels of the Stanford study to the shocking abuse by American soldiers of Iraqi inmates at Abu Ghraib prison near Baghdad in 2004 are stunning (Zimbardo, 2007). In both the real and the experimental prison, guards stripped prisoners naked, forced them to wear bags over their heads, chained prisoners together, and finally forced prisoners to endure sadistic sexual degradation and humiliation. Guards said to a group of prisoners, "Now you two, you're male camels. Stand behind the female camels and *hump* them."

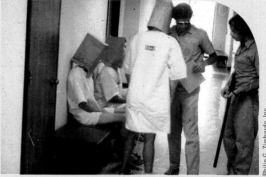

The Stanford prison study and Abu Ghraib prison in Iraq showed chillingly similar results.

This was just one of the many examples of abuse heaped upon prisoners, not by guards at Abu Ghraib, but by college students playing the role of guards in the Stanford prison study. In both the Stanford "prison" and Abu Ghraib, the guards were ordinary individuals placed in extraordinarily bad situations, and they acted brutally.

As Zimbardo (2007) notes, although students are unlikely ever to play the roles of prisoner or guard in real life, this study is analogous to more commonplace role status differences. Whenever the power accorded certain roles establishes unequal power distribution, the potential for abuse is real. Teacher–student, doctor–patient, supervisor–employee, and parent–child relationships are just a few examples of role status differences that can potentially lead to verbal, even physical, mistreatment.

QUESTIONS FOR THOUGHT

1. Considering the effects this experiment had upon its subjects, do you have any ethical concerns about conducting similar studies?
2. Would you have preferred to be a prisoner or a guard? Why?
3. How do you think you would have acted in the guard role and in the prisoner role? How confident are you that you would not act as most prisoners and guards did in the experiment? On what is this based?

▶ Role Conflict: Torn between Two Roles

The influence of roles can be seen in another way. When we find ourselves playing roles in different groups that contradict each other, we experience **role conflict**. Usually, we are forced to make a choice between the two roles. Students who have children are often faced with conflict between their student role and their parent role. Do you take the final exam or do you stay home with your sick child? Women with careers and families are increasingly concerned with this perceived role conflict. When a woman is in an important business meeting in which colleagues depend on her input and she receives a phone call from her child's school, what does she do? Let me note that the same role conflict could also exist for a man, but women are still typically cast as the primary caregiver except in single-parent situations. The perception that family demands will intrude upon a woman's work world more than on a man's can impede women's advancement in organizations (Eagly & Carli, 2007).

Students increasingly find work–family and student–work role conflicts emerging (Lenaghan & Sengupta, 2007). As the cost of a college education skyrockets, students must work full- or part-time to cover the costs of higher education and living expenses. Work obligations can interfere with students' need to meet with their group to work on projects for class. This is a common source of tension within small student groups, whose members' grades may depend on responsible and enthusiastic participation from everyone involved.

An extensive review of 42 studies on role conflict showed significant effects (Fisher & Gitelson, 1983). When individuals felt role conflict within organizations (family role versus professional role), they exhibited an increased tendency to leave an organization. They also showed decreases in commitment to the organization, involvement in the job, satisfaction with the job, and participation in decision making (see also Naus et al., 2007). Role conflict in organizations, with all its negative consequences, is usually chronic not temporary (Perrewe et al., 2004).

Some roles have a greater impact on us than others. **The role that has the greatest importance and most potent effect on us is usually the one we choose when we have to decide between conflicting roles.** The expectations associated with group roles and the perception of the value, prestige, influence, status, or stigma attached to each role by both the group and the individual can strongly affect us. Finding a balance between conflicting roles and adjusting to inevitable changes in the small group system are keys to addressing role conflict (Lenaghan & Sengupta, 2007).

▶ Role Reversal: When Students Become Teachers

The effects of roles on perceptions can be seen in a dramatic way by doing a role reversal, which is stepping into a role distinctly different from or opposite of a role

First responders to an emergency may experience role conflict—a desire to play the role of parent or spouse by responding to family safety before playing the role of first responder when the two roles clash.

we're accustomed to playing (from child to parent, student to teacher, and employee to employer or vice versa). The CBS show *Undercover Boss* uses role reversal to dramatize how different it is for CEOs of companies to experience the day-to-day trials of ordinary workers. The boss, unbeknownst to employees, becomes an ordinary worker at his or her own company. The insight gained from reversing roles from CEO to worker is often profound.

As a student, I complained on more than one occasion about the quality of instruction I was receiving from my college professors. When I became a college professor myself, however, similar complaints from students seemed unjustified, and I initially made excuses for some ineffectual teaching practices. As a teacher, I began to appreciate on a more personal basis the many challenges instructors face when attempting to motivate student interest in class. Reversing roles can promote a real appreciation for the *constraints of roles* on your behavior (e.g., you're required to grade students even if you dislike the practice because of its potential for triggering defensiveness). Role reversal can also promote changes in behavior, as it thankfully did early on in my teaching career.

Types of Roles: There Is a Part for Everyone

It is not possible to enumerate here all the roles a person can play in groups. In the broadest sense, there are two types of roles: formal and informal. A **formal role** is a *position* assigned by an organization or specifically designated by the group leader. Titles such as president, chair, and secretary usually accompany formal roles. Especially within larger organizations, a set of expected behaviors to fulfill the role is explicitly spelled out. A job description used to hire an individual to fill a specific position is an example. Formal roles exist within the structure of the group, team, or organization. They are designated; they do not emerge naturally from communication transactions. Formal roles are often independent from any person filling the role.

In most small groups, the roles are usually informal. An **informal role** emerges from the group transactions, and it emphasizes *functions*, not positions. A group member may fulfill leadership functions, that is, perform as a leader, without any formal designation. Actual duties and specific behaviors expected from a group member playing an informal role are implicitly defined by communication transactions among members. The group does not tell an individual explicitly how to play a specific role, but members do indicate degrees of approval or disapproval when an individual assumes the role. Informal role-playing is improvisational, not scripted.

Informal roles, the principal focus of this discussion, are typically classified into three types: task, maintenance, and self-centered (Benne & Sheats, 1948; Mudrack & Farrell, 1995).

Focus Questions

1. Are there some group roles that the competent communicator should avoid?

2. How do communication patterns differ among task, maintenance, and disruptive roles?

▶ Task Roles: Focusing on Maximum Productivity

Task roles move the group toward the attainment of its goals. **The central commu-nicative function of task roles is to extract the maximum productivity from the group.** Consider a sample of the most common task roles:

1. *Initiator-Contributor.* This person starts the ball rolling by offering lots of ideas and suggestions. Trying to come up with an idea for a group project in class requires an initiator. Imagine the uncomfortable silence that occurs without an initiator in the group. The group becomes mired in a state of dysfunctional inertia. When your instructor poses a question for class discussion, if no one responds, this lack of an initiator-contributor kills the learning process. When a group has one or more initiators, fruitful discussion can ensue. Groups typically function more effectively when the initiator-contributor role is shared and rotates depending on the context. At some point, however, contributions need to stop and decisions need to be made. Proposing numerous solutions and new direc-tions indefinitely can scatter the focus and splinter a group down myriad paths with no resolution in sight.

2. *Information Seeker.* When a group begins a task, the information seeker takes an inventory of the knowledge base of group members, such as: "So, does any-one know why textbooks are so expensive?" The information seeker solicits research, experiences of group members, and any supporting materials to bol-ster ideas once they have been initiated. Informational deficits quickly become apparent once information seekers probe the level of knowledge of group members.

3. *Information Giver.* The information seeker and the information giver roles have a symbiotic relationship. They feed off of each other in an interdependent relation-ship. When a group member seeks information and receives that information from another member, the group advances in its knowledge on a subject under discussion, as long as the information is relevant and credible. If no member is qualified to provide such information, the role of information giver becomes one of researching the topic to provide credible information for the group. In a group

devoid of expertise, lack of at least one information giver results in sharing igno-rance or group impotence.

4. *Opinion Seeker.* Without an opinion seeker, a group can assume agreement where none exists. Dominant members may squelch or discourage the viewpoints from others. The opinion seeker helps the group determine where agreement and per-haps disagreement exist. For example, "Does everyone agree or does anyone have a differing opinion on the subject?" The false assumption that agreement is uni-versal within the group can lead to disastrous groupthink, a topic discussed at length in Chapter 8.

5. *Clarifier-Elaborator.* A group member playing this role explains, expands, and extends the ideas of others and provides examples and alternatives that piggy-back on the ideas of others. During heated disagreements, group discussion can deteriorate into murky confusion. The clarifier can step in and provide refresh-ing clarity, such as: "I actually don't believe we are as far apart as everyone seems to believe. Consider how similar we are on the following issues...."

6. *Coordinator.* This role requires organizational skills. Scheduling issues need to be resolved and the coordinator organizes where, when, and how a meeting will take place. The coordinator encourages teamwork and cooperation among group members.

7. *Secretary-Recorder.* This role serves a group memory function. The secretary-recorder takes minutes of meetings, prepares reports for further discussion and decision making, and reminds members of past actions that may have been for-gotten as time passes. For example, "That was an information item only in our last meeting. No action was taken."

8. *Facilitator.* A group member playing this role keeps participants on track, guides discussion, reminds the group of the primary goal that informs the discussion, and regulates group activities. For example, "I think we've drifted from our main focus. Let's bring back the discussion to what we can actually accomplish in the next two weeks."

9. *Devil's Advocate.* This is a critical role for any group, and one that is often absent from group decision making. A devil's advocate gently challenges a prevailing point of view for the sake of argument to test and critically evaluate the strength of ideas, solutions, or decisions. You raise questions and potential objections, not because you necessarily disagree with the other group members, but because you don't want the group to rush headlong into making a rash decision that has not been carefully considered. "So, what happens if our plan doesn't work the way we think it will? Do we have a backup strategy?" are the kind of questions a devil's advocate asks. Chapter 8 discusses this role in more detail.

▶ Maintenance Roles: Focusing on Cohesiveness

Maintenance roles focus on the social dimension of the group. **The central communicative function of maintenance roles is to gain and maintain the cohesiveness of the group.** Consider a sample of common maintenance roles:

1. *Supporter-Encourager.* A group member playing this role bolsters the spirits and goodwill of the group, provides warmth, praise, and acceptance of others, and invites reticent members into the discussion. For example, "Good job everyone. Great group!"

2. *Harmonizer–Tension Reliever.* When you assume this role you attempt to maintain the peace and reduce secondary tension by using humor and by reconciling differences between members. This isn't just a "can't we all just get along" approach. This role also doesn't require squelching all conflict and disagreement among group members. Sometimes conflict can be constructive (see Chapter 11). When tempers flare and communication turns defensive, however, a harmonizer-tension-reliever can call for a brief break to calm anger ("Let's try not to make this personal, and perhaps we need to take a break. I think we are getting weary").

3. *Gatekeeper-Expediter.* Someone playing this role controls channels of communication and flow of information, regulating the degree of openness within the group system. When member participation seems uneven, the gatekeeper encourages contributions from quieter members. Rules may be suggested to expedite efficient meetings, such as: "Perhaps we should set a time limit for discussing this item."

▶ Disruptive Roles: Focusing on Self

Self-centered or disruptive roles serve individual needs or goals (Me-oriented) while impeding attainment of group goals. Individuals who play these roles often warrant the tag "difficult group member" or "bad apple." **The central communicative function of self-centered, disruptive roles is to focus attention on the individual.** This focus on the individual can diminish group productivity and cohesiveness. Competent communicators avoid these roles (see Chapter 2 for ways to deal effectively with disruptive, bad apple group members).

1. *Stagehog.* An individual playing this role seeks recognition and attention by monopolizing the conversation and preventing others from expressing their opinions fully. The stagehog seeks the spotlight like a moth to a flame.

2. *Isolate.* An isolate deserts the group and withdraws from participation. He or she acts indifferent, aloof, uninvolved, and resists efforts to be included in group decision making. A person playing this role is a group member in name only. Isolates can be dead weight on a group.

3. *Clown.* This role is not merely one of offering humor to lighten the tension in the group. The clown engages in horseplay, thrives on practical jokes and comic routines, diverts members' attention away from serious discussion of ideas and issues, and steps beyond the boundaries of mere tension reliever. Humor taken to extremes says, "Look at me. I'm so funny." This is self-centered not group centered.

4. *Blocker.* This role is obstructionist in nature. The purpose is to prevent the group from taking action, especially action the blocker finds objectionable. In Congress it is called a filibuster. A person who plays the blocker thwarts progress of the group by refusing to cooperate, opposes much of what the group attempts to accomplish, and incessantly reintroduces dead issues of interest to the blocker.

5. *Fighter-Controller.* Some group members love to fight and control group discussions. A fighter-controller tries to dominate group discussion, competes with members, picks quarrels, interrupts to interject his or her own opinions into discussion, and makes negative remarks to members ("You're really kind of slow on the uptake aren't you? Try keeping up."). The fighter-controller is a bully.

6. *Zealot.* When a group member plays this role he or she tries to convert members to a pet cause or idea, delivers sermons to the group on the state of the world, and often becomes obsessively political in remarks ("Once again, politics reigns supreme. I've been telling you this all along, haven't I?"). It is one thing to be enthusiastic when expressing a point of view, but it is quite another when one's zeal becomes that of a true believer. As Winston Churchill once remarked, a true believer is "one who can't change his mind and won't change the subject."

7. *Cynic.* This role is a climate killer. A cynic displays a sour outlook, engages in faultfinding, focuses on negatives, and predicts group failure ("We're never going to agree on a decent topic"). H. L. Mencken described a cynic as someone who "smells flowers [and] looks around for a coffin." When the group may need a cheerleader, the cynic provides a disheartening message ("I told you we wouldn't succeed. This was a stupid idea in the first place").

This is a static list and description of task, maintenance, and disruptive roles. These roles, however, become actualized within the group system during a series of

SECOND LOOK

Sample of Informal Roles in Groups

Task Roles

1. *Initiator-Contributor:* Offers lots of ideas and suggestions; proposes solutions and new directions.
2. *Information Seeker:* Requests clarification; solicits evidence; asks for suggestion.
3. *Information Giver:* Provides information based on research, expertise, or personal experience.
4. *Opinion Seeker:* Requests viewpoints from others; looks for agreement and disagreement.
5. *Clarifier-Elaborator:* Explains, expands, and extends the ideas of others.
6. *Coordinator:* Draws together ideas of others; organizes and schedules meetings; promotes teamwork and cooperation.
7. *Secretary-Recorder:* Takes minutes of meetings; keeps group's records and history.
8. *Facilitator:* Keeps group on track; guides discussion; reminds group of goal; regulates group activities.
9. *Devil's Advocate:* Gently challenges prevailing point of view for the sake of argument to test and critically evaluate the strength of ideas, solutions, or decisions.

Maintenance Roles

1. *Supporter-Encourager:* Bolsters the spirits and goodwill of the group; provides warmth, praise, and acceptance of others; includes reticent members in discussion.
2. *Harmonizer-Tension Reliever:* Reduces tension through humor and by reconciling differences.
3. *Gatekeeper-Expediter:* Controls channels of communication and flow of information; encourages evenness of participation; promotes open discussion.

Self-Centered/Disruptive Roles

1. *Stagehog:* Monopolizes conversation; prevents others from expressing their opinions.
2. *Isolate:* Withdraws from participation; acts indifferent, aloof, uninvolved.

3. *Clown:* Engages in horseplay; diverts members' attention from serious discussion of ideas and issues.

4. *Blocker:* Opposes much of what group attempts to accomplish; incessantly reintroduces dead issues; makes negative remarks to members.

5. *Fighter-Controller:* Tries to dominate group; competes with members; abuses those who disagree.

6. *Zealot:* Tries to convert members to a pet cause or idea; exhibits fanaticism.

7. *Cynic:* Displays sour outlook; engages in faultfinding; focuses on negatives; predicts failure.

transactions among members. Roles unfold in the context of discussion, debate, and disagreement. Consider the following brief group transaction as a sample illustrating this process of role-playing:

Jeremy: I think we should do our project on campus safety. (Initiator)

Maria: Do any of you know anything about campus safety? (Information seeker)

Charlise: I did a survey last semester in another class and discovered some interesting results. (Information giver)

Peter: That just sounds boring, just like this project. (Cynic)

Darnell: I don't see you offering anything constructive to this conversation. So why don't you give it a rest? (Fighter-controller)

Peter: And I suppose you love this project? (Fighter-controller)

Maria: Come on you guys, this isn't getting us anywhere. Let's calm down, Okay? This isn't bare-knuckle cage fighting. (Harmonizer-tension reliever) We can do better than this. (Supporter-encourager) So, can we get back to discussing Jeremy's idea for a topic? (Facilitator) I think it has promise and could be interesting. What do the rest of you think? (Opinion seeker; Facilitator)

In this brief sample discussion, you see some group members assuming roles in response to other members. There are task, maintenance, and disruptive roles represented, and some members play more than one role in rapid-fire succession while other members play a single role. Role-playing in small groups is a dynamic, transactional process.

Playing by the Roles: A Self-Assessment

Fill out the self-assessment on roles for any important group that you choose: family, study group, project group, and so on. This should reveal which roles you play most often in your group. **Optional Alternative:** After answering this questionnaire, ask fellow class or team members to complete this same assessment about you, but only if you feel comfortable making such a request. If team members are hesitant, encourage them to complete the assessment without identifying themselves in the questionnaire (ideally, all team members should complete the assessment to preserve anonymity). Compare the results.

1. My degree of participation in group activities was

LOW				HIGH
1	2	3	4	5

2. How task-oriented (showed interest in meeting group goals) were you?

LOW				HIGH
1	2	3	4	5

3. How socially oriented (concerned about the relationships among group members) were you?

LOW				HIGH
1	2	3	4	5

4. How much influence did you have on the group's decisions?

LOW				HIGH
1	2	3	4	5

Using the same 1–5 scale, indicate the degree to which you played the following roles (see Second Look 5.1) by writing the appropriate number:

TASK

____ Information giver
____ Initiator-contributor
____ Clarifier-elaborator
____ Devil's advocate
____ Secretary-recorder

____ Information seeker
____ Coordinator
____ Facilitator
____ Opinion seeker

MAINTENANCE

____ Supporter-encourager
____ Gatekeeper
____ Harmonizer–tension reliever

DISRUPTIVE

____ Stagehog
____ Fighter-controller
____ Zealot
____ Cynic

____ Isolate
____ Blocker
____ Clown

Role Adaptability: Staying Loose

Playing roles is a fluid, dynamic process. Individuals in a system are so interconnected that what one group member does can influence significantly the roles other group members play. Clashes regarding who gets to play a particular task role, for example, may ignite disruptive role behavior from the "losing" group member.

Focus Questions

1. Why should group members exhibit role flexibility?

2. What are the disadvantages of role fixation?

▶ Role Flexibility: Adapting to Context

The most competent small group members are the ones who exhibit **role flexibility**—"the capacity to recognize the current requirements of the group and then enact the role-specific behaviors most appropriate in the given context (Forsyth, 2014, p. 177). For example, if group discussion becomes confusing, an alert member recognizes the need to play the clarifier role. If members' discussion veers off topic, a competent member recognizes the need to play the facilitator role and refocus the discussion. Playing devil's advocate by challenging a group idea in its formative stage may squash creativity and the generation of further innovative ideas. Having your ideas challenged immediately by a devil's advocate will likely discourage further contributions to idea generation during brainstorming sessions for fear of evaluation. There is a time and place for playing specific informal roles.

▶ Role Fixation: Stuck Playing One Part

Sometimes, the necessary flexibility of small group roles escapes individual members and they become so enamored with a single role that they exhibit **role fixation**—the acting out of a specific role and that role alone no matter what the situation might require (Postman, 1976). Professional comedians sometimes don't know when to be serious in social gatherings. They are always "on." Lawyers who cross-examine their spouses and children as they do hostile witnesses on the stand at a criminal trial may find their role fixation is a ticket to a court of a decidedly civil sort. Competent communication requires the ability and the willingness to adapt communication behavior to changing situations. Some individuals, however, get locked into the mindset that they must play a certain role and there are no good substitutes. Leader, information giver, feeling expresser, and tension reliever are among the most likely candidates for role fixation.

Role fixation in decision-making groups can occur when an individual moves from one group to another, or it can happen within a single group. If you were a gatekeeper in your last group, you may insist on performing the same role in your new group. There may be another member, however, who can play the role better. If you insist on competing for the role instead of adapting to the new group by assuming another role, you will be a source of conflict and disruption. If the other member is truly better in the role than you are, then the resources of the group will not be utilized to their fullest if you continue to fight for the role.

Sometimes the group insists on role fixation to its own detriment. The reluctance of men to accept women in high-status roles, for instance, can lead to role fixation against a woman's wishes. Women should have the opportunity to play roles that require more than nurturing (e.g., supporter-encourager) or low involvement (e.g., secretary-recorder).

In a larger sense, as explained in Chapter 3, you don't want to become fixated on even a category of roles. Those members who become fixated on task roles to the virtual exclusion of maintenance roles, or vice versa, exhibit a counterproductive imbalance between productivity and cohesiveness.

Role Emergence: Learning Our Parts

In large groups and organizations, roles are largely determined by their formal structure. Even within this formal structure, however, role emergence occurs. Functional roles operate in smaller group meetings within the organization or in factional subunits of large groups.

Role emergence, however, is a relevant concern primarily to small, informal, leaderless groups without a history. These groups could be ad hoc project groups set up within formal organizations (e.g., self-managed work teams), classroom discussion groups formed for the purpose of completing a class project, or a jury in a criminal trial. The roles each member will play have not been designated in advance but emerge from the transactions conducted among group members. How roles emerge in zero-history groups has been studied extensively at the University of Minnesota (Bormann, 1990).

Focus Questions

1. **How do roles emerge in small groups?**
2. **What is role specialization and why is it important?**

▶ Group Endorsement: Accepting a Bid

Individuals initially make a bid to play a role. They may bid for a role because they have special skills that suit the role, or they may succumb to gender role stereotyping. Group endorsement of the bid to play a specific role must occur before a person gets to play that role. In a competitive culture, high-status roles are generally perceived to be those that are task oriented. Accomplishing tasks brings victories, tangible accomplishments, and recognition. The roles of facilitator, initiator-contributor, information giver, and devil's advocate are high-status roles because individuals are perceived as doers—they accomplish important tasks for the group's success.

Despite their critical importance to group success, maintenance roles are often viewed as lower status in a competitive culture such as the United States. Those who play maintenance roles are viewed as the helpers, not the doers. Helpers typically receive less status than doers in our society (e.g., surgeons are viewed as the doers and nurses are seen as the surgeon's helpers). Women have been socialized to play primarily the lower-status maintenance roles. As Wood (2015) notes, "Women remain disproportionately represented in service and clerical jobs, whereas men are moved into executive positions in for-profit sectors of the economy. Women are still asked to take care of social activities on the job, but men in equivalent positions are seldom expected to do this" (p. 50). Thus, group roles such as supporter-encourager, harmonizer–tension reliever, and secretary-recorder (a task role that is lower status and helping in nature) are roles traditionally played more by women than men. When women are underrepresented in groups, it is particularly difficult to break through the stereotyping and receive the endorsement of the group to play nonstereotypic, higher-status roles or to enhance the perceived status of maintenance roles.

The endorsement process proceeds by trial and error. A group member tries out a role, perhaps initiator-contributor, for example. If the group does not reinforce the effort (members ignore the contributions), then the member will try another role, hoping to get an endorsement. An individual who persists in an effort to play a specific role in the face of group resistance may be characterized as inflexible and uncooperative.

▶ Role Specialization: Settling into One's Role

Once a role for a member has been endorsed by the group, **role specialization**—when an individual member settles into his or her primary role—occurs. If the group wants you to be an information giver, then that will be your principal function. This specialization doesn't preclude you from assuming other roles, however. Role specialization does not grant a monopoly to a single member. There may be more than one harmonizer in the group, although there is likely to be only one member with the primary responsibility. Too much effort to operate in what is perceived to be another member's primary role territory can invite negative feedback from the group.

Newcomers: Disturbing the System

Group members learn their roles over time as they emerge from group transactions. Once established, members' roles can become solidified and resistant to change. Consequently, the interconnectedness of all components of a system makes the entry of even a single new member into an established group a highly significant event (Delton & Cimino, 2010). As groups develop, relationships among members stabilize and the roles and norms in the group become more complex. "The entry of a newcomer into the group can threaten this development by forcing members to alter their relationships with one another" (Moreland & Levine, 1987, p. 156). The newcomer role is particularly challenging for anyone entering an established group, and it forces change on the group as a whole.

Focus Questions

1. **What aspects of a group contribute to or thwart acceptance of a newcomer into the group?**
2. **What responsibilities should newcomers and longstanding group members have to make the socialization process work?**

▶ Nature of the Group: The Challenge of Acceptance

Several characteristics of a group directly affect the acceptance of a newcomer (Moreland & Levine, 1987). First, **the level of group development has a direct bearing on newcomer acceptance.** Several research and development groups in a large corporation were studied for four months (Katz, 1982). Members of the groups that had been in existence for a relatively short time communicated more with newcomers and were more open to their ideas than were members of older groups. A newcomer in a younger group is less disruptive because he or she enters early on in the group development process. Entering a longstanding group, where development has progressed far beyond the initial stages, can be a much greater shock to the system and requires greater adaptation by the members. The newcomer seems more like an outsider in older groups than in younger ones.

Second, **the level of group performance affects the acceptance of newcomers.** When the system is functioning well, group members may not want to take a chance on altering a successful formula. Accepting a newcomer may pose a big risk. When a group is performing poorly, however, there is a strong impetus for change. The arrival of a newcomer may be perceived as a welcome addition. The newcomer might turn the group around (Phillips et al., 2009).

Third, **the number of members affects acceptance of a newcomer into a group.** Groups that have too few members to perform necessary tasks well are usually eager to accept newcomers. Newcomers mean less work for each member and potentially greater success for the group. Groups that have too many members to function efficiently, however, will probably view a newcomer as an additional burden.

Fourth, **the degree of turnover in a group also affects acceptance of newcomers.** Groups accustomed to frequent entry and exit of members will accept newcomers more readily than groups unaccustomed to turnover.

Finally, **groups are more accepting of a newcomer when members believe the newcomer accepts and will conform to the norms, values, and practices of the group.** One method for determining such acceptance and willingness to conform in advance of actual membership is using hazing or initiation rituals (see Closer Look: Hazing").

CLOSER LOOK

Hazing Newcomers: From Water Torture to Liver Swallowing

Chen "Michael" Deng, a first-year student at Baruch College in Manhattan, New York, was a fraternity pledge subjected to a hazing ritual that cost him his life in December 2013. Deng traveled to an isolated part of the Pocono Mountains in Pennsylvania. Pocono Mountain Regional Police Chief Harry Lewis described what Deng was subjected to by almost 30 fraternity brothers: "He was blindfolded, in the dark, carrying some weight and asked to get from point to point while several of his brothers were striking, tackling, punching, and pushing him." Deng fell, hit his head on a rock, and died (Muskal, 2013). There have been 59 deaths from hazing since 2005 (Glovin, 2013), the year Matthew Carrington, a student at Chico State University in Northern California died from hyponatremia, a deadly drop in sodium levels in the bloodstream caused by drinking massive quantities of water in a short period of time—in this case five gallons in a few hours (May, 2005).

Hazing newcomers who are trying to gain final membership to groups may not turn lethal, but serious injuries can result from such practices. A Florida court convicted two former fraternity brothers at Florida A & M University for causing "serious bodily harm" to a student named Marcus Jones. Jones was beaten severely during fraternity hazing. He suffered a ruptured eardrum and a blood clot that required surgery ("Florida Jury Convicts," 2006). A Drake University student, Nate Erickson, was hospitalized for alcohol poisoning as the result of hazing by two members of the Phi Delta Theta fraternity. Sgt. Lori Lavorato, public information officer for the Des Moines Police Department, explained, "He was not physically forced to consume alcohol. It was more a case of peer pressure, where he thought that, in order to become a member, he felt it was a necessity to do so" (quoted in Vasilogambros, 2009). Students at Birmingham University have suffered frostbite from walking barefoot through snow, have been waterboarded, and have required emergency treatment from running across a bed of sharp rocks barefoot (Gonchar, 2012).

Hazing, or an initiation rite, is defined as "any activity expected of someone joining or participating in a group that humiliates, degrades, abuses, or endangers them regardless of a person's willingness to participate" (Allan et al., 2008). According to the National Study of Student Hazing in its investigation of 11,482 undergraduate students enrolled at 53 colleges and universities, 55% of college students who are involved in clubs, teams, and campus organizations experience hazing. In more than half of these hazings, someone from the "offending group" posted pictures on YouTube or a social networking site of the victims engaged in humiliating and dangerous activities. The most common groups guilty of hazing are, in order of frequency, varsity sports teams and social organizations such as fraternities and sororities, club sports teams, performing arts groups, intramural teams, academic clubs, and honor societies (Allan & Madden, 2008). Hazing purposely subjects prospective group members to a series of activities designed to test the limits of physical exertion, psychological strain, and social embarrassment.

The list of silly, stupid, dangerous, illegal, and even lethal activities actually required by some groups as a rite of passage into groups is long. Examples include forcing students to swallow quarter-pound hunks of raw liver slathered with oil; abandoning students on mountaintops or in remote areas in bitter cold conditions without suitable clothing; repeatedly punching the stomach and kidneys of students who forget parts of ritual incantations; incarcerating initiates in a locked storage closet for two days with only salty foods, no liquids, and only a small plastic cup to catch urine; requiring initiates to consume a mixture of urine, spoiled milk, and eggs; forcing initiates to steal; forcing initiates to abuse alcohol or illegal drugs; and requiring initiates to engage in unprotected sex or sex with multiple partners (Allan & Madden, 2008; Forsyth, 2013).

Hazing raises serious ethical questions. Is it respectful to treat newcomers to groups by torturing, humiliating, and shaming them? Is endangering newcomers' lives responsible behavior even if the intentions are worthwhile? If membership in a highly desirable group is dependent on debasing oneself or engaging in high-risk or illegal activities, does this not remove choice from the equation? *Is it ethical*?

Forty-four states have outlawed hazing ("State Anti-hazing Laws," 2010). Numerous colleges and universities have followed suit. Stopping hazing, however, is not easy. When Richard Swanson, a University of Southern California student, gagged on an oil-soaked hunk of liver, then choked to death before anyone could help him, the university applied stringent rules to initiation practices. Students rioted in protest. Outlawing hazing is more likely to drive it underground than to eliminate the practice.

This is a *Wizard of Oz* hazing of New York Yankee rookie baseball players.

Why do groups insist on such harsh and risky membership rituals? There are several reasons (Keating et al., 2005; Moreland & Levine, 1987). First, the harder it is to get into a group, the greater will be the loyalty and commitment to the group once membership has been attained. We tend to place greater value on that which is difficult to achieve than that which requires minimal effort (Prapavessis & Carron, 1997). The more severe the hazing ritual, the more desirable a group appears to be. In one classic experiment, the more electric shock a woman received as part of the hazing ritual, the more she convinced herself that the group and its activities were valuable, interesting, and desirable despite the clear effort of the experimenters to make the group appear uninteresting and worthless (Gerard & Mathewson, 1966).

Second, **hazing creates group cohesiveness and conformity** (Lodewijkx et al., 2005). If you had to swallow a slimy, oil-soaked slab of raw liver, freeze off the south side of your anatomy, or risk your life to gain membership, chances are quite good that you would slavishly conform to the norms of the group once you were admitted as a full-fledged member. Deviance is not likely to emerge from a tight-knit group bonded by ordeals.

Third, a harsh initiation provides the group with valuable information about the newcomers. If newcomers refuse to be initiated, fail the initiation tasks, or participate in the rites of passage grudgingly, this informs the group that such newcomers are not likely to fit in with the group. They probably will not conform to group norms.

Fourth, a harsh initiation may convince newcomers how dependent they are on longtime members (old-timers). The old-timers make the decisions regarding who is granted membership and who is not. The old-timers must be convinced that the newcomers are worthy of that membership.

QUESTIONS FOR THOUGHT

1. Have you ever participated in hazing, either as the perpetrator or the recipient? What were the reasons?
2. Should hazing rituals, especially the high-risk ones, be outlawed? Would outlawing such practices ever stop them?
3. Can you think of any hazing rituals that are not unethical? Explain. Is it possible to have hazing rituals that are not dangerous, illegal, or abusive and still serve the purpose of creating cohesiveness and subsequent conformity in the group?

▶ Group Socialization: Mutual Adaptation to Change

In any system, interconnected parts must adapt to changing conditions. Newcomers require adaptation in a group because they inherently produce change by their mere presence. The communication process in which new and established group members adjust to one another is called **group socialization** (Anderson et al., 1999).

This process is one of mutual adaptation. Newcomers must "learn their place" in the group. They must play the role of newcomer, not act initially like an established group member. Established members must also adjust to the newcomers. This may include changing roles that may require learning new skills when replaced by a newcomer (Forsyth, 2014).

For their part, **newcomers can employ several strategies to improve their chances of gaining acceptance from a group** (Dean, 2009; Moreland & Levine, 1987).

1. ***Conduct a thorough reconnaissance of the group.*** Most newcomers do a poor job of scouting out a group to determine whether they and the group are a good match (Wanous, 1980). Newcomers should exploit all available sources of information about the group to form a reasonably accurate assessment of the group they contemplate joining.

2. ***Play the role of newcomer.*** "The temptation when joining a new group is to try and make a splash, to impress others.... Groups are hostile to criticism from newcomers and are likely to resist, dismiss, or ignore it" (Dean, 2009). Seek the advice of longtime members, avoid disagreements with old-timers, and talk less than they do. Listen, to show respect and to learn valuable information. Emphasize similarities to other members in the group, and seek information from old-timers (Burke et al., 2010). As you become more accepted by the group, your communication can move away from the newcomer role pattern.

3. ***Embrace your new group; distance yourself from previous groups.*** "This is the way we successfully met this challenge where I used to work" is unlikely to be a welcomed comment from a newcomer. It suggests superiority of your previous group that likely evokes defensiveness from your new group members. Embracing your new group and distancing yourself from a previous group ("This group is much better prepared to handle this challenge than my previous group") inclines group members to listen, even accept suggestions or criticism more readily (Horney et al., 2007).

4. ***Seek mentors within the group.*** Mentors are old-timers who develop a close personal relationship with the newcomer and assist the newcomer's entry into the group (Oglensky, 2008). The mentoring process can increase the newcomer's understanding of the group and enhance his or her level of group satisfaction (Allen et al., 1999; Oglensky, 2008).

5. ***Collaborate with other newcomers.*** When more than one newcomer enters a group, they stand to gain from banding together. Newcomers can lend emotional support and encouragement to each other. They can provide useful information about the group. They can act as a friendly face, making the group climate more inviting.

Established group members also have a responsibility to engage in the socialization process. Old-timers may have expectations regarding how newcomers should act that may not be shared by new members. A period of adjustment occurs as new and older members adapt to one another. **There are several strategies that established members of groups can employ to make the role of newcomer less challenging and intimidating** (Anderson et al., 1999).

1. *Welcome new members into the group.* An initial meet-and-greet gathering of group members in which newcomers introduce themselves and old-timers provide brief narratives about themselves works well. Providing opportunities for socializing outside of group task responsibilities also helps. Informal social activities can send a welcoming message to newcomers.

2. *Orient new members.* Provide a tour of the facilities, offer a brief history of the group, and discuss expectations the group has for newcomers. Inform newcomers of any politics or other environmental influences from outsiders that may provide challenges and potential pitfalls.

3. *Mentor newcomers.* Have a structured mentoring process for newcomers if this is a longstanding group; brief ad hoc groups typically do not require mentoring programs.

Competent communicators learn about the nature of the group to which they seek membership, and they learn the strategies that will assist their acceptance into the group. Women and ethnic minorities, who are often in the newcomer role, add diversity to a group, which presents challenges but usually benefits group decisions (Phillips et al., 2009). It should be the goal, however, of both newcomers and long-standing members of a group to work together to make the socialization process successful for all.

In summary, there are many roles to play in small groups. Competent communicators learn to play a variety of roles. I've explained the roles we play during the life of a group and how to function effectively in those roles. In the next chapter, the leader role, often the most coveted of all the roles in groups, is discussed.

In Mixed Company

▶ Online

▶ MindTap™

Reflect on what you've learned.

Now that you've read Chapter 5, access the online resources that accompany *In Mixed Company* at **www.cengagebrain.com**. Your online resources include:

1. Multiple-choice and true-false **chapter practice quizzes** with automatic correction

2. Digital **glossary**

3. **Flashcards**

VIDEO *Case Studies*

The Hunger Games: Catching Fire (2013); Action/Adventure/Sci-Fi; PG-13

This is the second in the *Hunger Games* series. Katniss and Peeta become targets of the Capitol following their victory in the 74th Hunger Games, which ignites rebellion. Identify and analyze informal role emergence and roles that each character plays as a new *Hunger Games* composed only of past winners is instituted. Is there role status? Role conflict? Role reversal? Role fixation?

The Jane Austen Book Club (2008). Romance; PG-13

A group of women and one guy form a book club to read and discuss all six books by Jane Austen. Examine the roles that develop in the group. Identify who plays task, maintenance, and disruptive roles.

The Saffires (2013). Biography-Drama; PG-13

Based on a true story, in 1968, four young, talented Australian Aboriginal girls become a singing group called The Saffires, who entertain U.S. troops during the Vietnam War. Analyze role emergence and informal roles played by each of the women. Does role status emerge as an issue? How does the group respond to the newcomer played by Chris O'Dowd as the group manager?

12 Angry Men (1957; 1997). Drama; PG-13

Either version of this taut drama that depicts a jury locked in animated argument because one juror votes "not guilty" in a capital murder case is wonderful entertainment. Which informal roles—task, maintenance, and disruptive—do each of the characters play? Are there any formal roles depicted? Explain the role emergence process.

6 Group Leadership

MindTap

Start with a quick warm-up activity.

S cholars, philosophers, social scientists, even novelists have exhibited an intense interest in leadership. In politics, leadership is a buzzword and a subject of intense, although not always informed or fruitful debate. In 2014, after Russian President Vladimir Putin invaded Crimea in the Ukraine, the question, "Is Putin a stronger leader than Obama" became a subject of political posturing. Not surprisingly, the answers tended to fall along partisan lines ("Obama Approval Inches Up, Tied with Putin as Leader," 2014).

"Authors have offered up over nine thousand different systems, languages, principles, and paradigms to help explain the mysteries of management and leadership" (Buckingham & Coffman, 1999, p. 53). Conduct a Google search of articles, books, and viewpoints on leadership and you'll get millions of hits. Business executives and management consultants regularly author books on leadership, mostly consisting of anecdotes that purport to prove allegedly sage advice garnered from years of corporate experience or management training. Matthew Stewart (2009), a former management consultant turned disapproving critic, comments: "Upon putting the gurus' books down, however, I find that I get the same feeling I get after reaching the bottom of a supersized bag of tortilla chips. They taste great while they last, but in the end, what am I left with?" (p. 8). He later answers: "platitudes," "bundles of nonfalsifiable truisms," and "transparently unsubstantiated pseudotheories."

Echoing Stewart's criticism, what I see most of these business executives and management consultants too frequently offering is ego gratification for the authors who endlessly tout their self-proclaimed mastery of leadership based on experience only as

CEOs, and sometimes not even that. Untroubled by the lack of social scientific research to support this supposed mastery of leadership, they provide advice that may have worked for them but doesn't readily translate to others who must adapt to markedly different situations and circumstances than a corporate CEO might face (Vroom & Jago, 2007). Stewart argues that they "write with complete indifference to or even against the academics" (p. 249). I present this assessment because careful, insightful academic research on leadership effectiveness too often is ignored while these flashy, quick-fix books are lionized by the press and the popular culture. With few exceptions (some referenced later in this chapter), they have minimal merit.

Fortunately, you don't have to depend on the self-promotional and self-congratulatory peppy platitudes of these personal testimonials on leadership. One communication scholar estimated more than a decade ago that nearly 8,000 research studies had been published on group leadership (Pavitt, 1999), and hundreds more have been produced since this estimate was offered (Vroom & Jago, 2007). One highly acclaimed reference book on leadership takes more than 1,500 pages to review the vast research and theory on leadership (Bass & Bass, 2008).

This reservoir of research serves as the foundation for my discussion of this chapter's principal purpose, namely, to explore leadership effectiveness in groups. In far fewer than 1,500 pages, much to your relief I'm sure, three objectives are addressed:

1. To define leadership,
2. To discuss how to gain and retain leadership,
3. To explore several perspectives on what constitutes effective group leadership that have evolved one from the other.

Definition of Leadership: An Evolving Consensus

MindTap™

Read, highlight, and take notes online.

As far back as 1949, there were at least 130 different definitions of leader and leadership (Bass, 1960). The number has continued to grow since (Northouse, 2013). Despite the numerous definitions, there is an evolving consensus on what leadership is and is not.

Focus Questions

1. What is meant by "leadership is a process not a person"?
2. What are the key differences between managing and leading a small group?
3. What role does communication play in leadership of small groups?

▶ Leadership and Influence: A Two-Way Process

There seems to be agreement that leadership is a social influence process (Northouse, 2013; Vroom & Jago, 2007). Leadership experts Hackman and Johnson (2013) proclaim, "Exercising influence is the essence of leadership" (p. 166). This influence can come from status, authority, personality, interpersonal and group communication skills, and a host of other factors.

"Credibility is the foundation for successful influence ..." (Hackman & Johnson, 2013, p. 166). The ancient Greeks called it *ethos*, defined by Aristotle as good will, good character, and good intellect. More recently, communication scholars have defined **credibility** as a composite of competence (knowledge, skills), trustworthiness (honesty, consistency, character), and dynamism (confidence, assertiveness). "We want to believe in our leaders. We want to have faith and confidence in them as people. We want to believe that their word can be trusted, that they have the knowledge and skill to lead" (Kouzes & Posner, 2003, p. 22).

The social influence, however, occurs with the consent of the governed (Bennis, 2007). Leaders influence followers, but followers also influence leaders by making demands on them, requiring them to meet members' expectations, and evaluating their performance in light of these expectations (Avolio, 2007; Nye, 2002).

▶ Leadership and Followership: It Takes Two to Tango

The leader and follower roles either exist together or they exist not at all. A leader must have someone to lead and followers must have someone to follow. As House Speaker John Boehner remarked on the "Tonight Show," referring to his many challenges with his Republican caucus, "You learn that a leader without followers is simply a man taking a walk" (quoted by Mimoli, 2014). "The only person who practices leadership alone in a room is the psychotic" (Bennis, 2007, p. 3).

Negative connotations have been associated with the term *follower,* such as passive, pliable, sheep-like, even unintelligent. Henry Ford, who pioneered the mass-production assembly line, articulated an apparent contempt for his workers who he expected to follow directions from their supervisors without thinking: "The average worker," Ford asserted, "wants a job ... in which he does not have to think." Ford further claimed that, of the 7,882 operations necessary to construct a Model T automobile, 2,637 could be completed by "one-legged men," 670 by "legless men," 715 by "one-armed men," 2 by "armless men," and 10 by "blind men." Continuing in this vein of supposedly amusing contempt for the worker/follower, he asked, "Why is it that when I ask for a pair of hands, a brain comes attached?" (Ford, 2003). This vision of followers parking their brains at the door and mindlessly moving in whatever direction leaders coercively tell them to go has been relegated to the trash can of archaic thinking.

Modern researchers and scholars see leadership as a partnership. Leaders and followers are like ballroom dancers. One leads and the other follows, but they influence each other, and they must work in tandem to be effective. "Leader-centricity tends to obscure, if not completely overlook, the role that followers play in this process.... we see that followers must be central to any act of leadership. This is for the simple reason that it is their labor that provides the proof of leadership. Without this labor there could simply be no leadership (Haslam et al., 2011, p. 17).

Thus, **"Leadership is a process and not a person"** (Hollander, 1985, p. 487; see also Vroom & Jago, 2007). When you look at leadership from this angle, there can be no doubt that focusing only on leaders without analyzing the complex social transactions that take place between leaders and followers misses the mark. For example, one study investigated whether angry leaders (Chef Gordon Ramsay on *Hell's Kitchen*, for example) motivate followers better than leaders who are generally positive (such as Barack Obama). The answer depends on levels of agreeableness among followers. *Agreeableness* is a tendency to be pleasant and accommodating with others. Groups composed of members with higher average levels of agree-ableness performed more effectively when their leader expressed support and was positive, whereas groups composed of members low on agreeableness performed more effectively when their leader expressed anger, even though they may have disliked the emotional outbursts (Van Kleef et al., 2010). **There is no one-size-fits-all leader–follower relationship.** Some followers can easily handle a leader's anger and be motivated to improve personal performance, although disrespectful expressions of anger (such as screaming "You moron") are generally a questionable practice. Other followers may fall apart and become demoralized by leader anger.

Although some authors and scholars offer special advice on how to be a good follower, that seems unnecessary and redundant. **There are no special guidelines for being an effective follower that diverge from what makes an effective team member** (see Chapter 7) and a competent communicator in small groups. Leaders and follow-ers are interconnected parts of a system, not separate entities (Balkundi et al., 2009).

▶ Leader versus Manager: Interpersonal versus Positional Influence

There are two primary differences between a leader and a manager (Hackman & Johnson, 2013; Rost, 1991). First, **a leader does not ordinarily operate from posi-tional authority; a manager does.** Anyone in a group can exhibit leadership even without being designated the leader. Only a manager is permitted to manage. Thus, managers are formally assigned the position of authority. A leader exercises inter-personal influence (leader–follower relationship), but a manager exercises positional influence (supervisor–subordinate relationship). "Persons who can require others to do their bidding because of power are not leaders" (Hogan et al., 1994). This means that as a student you won't exercise managerial authority, but you can become a leader on your project team, during discussion sessions, or in study groups through your communication with group members.

Second, **leaders work to change the status quo; managers typically maintain it.** Managers implement "the vision and strategy provided by leaders" (House & Aditya, 1997, p. 445). They do this by working with budgets, by organizing tasks, and by carrying out policies and plans devised by leaders. Managers enforce rules when they are broken, but they don't create the rules (Bryant & Higgins, 2010; Powell & Graves, 2006). Their primary goal is efficiency, not transformation. "There are many institutions that are very well managed and very poorly led. They may excel in the ability to handle all the routine inputs every day, yet they may never ask whether the routine should be preserved at all" (Bennis, 1976, p. 154).

Leadership implies change because influence inherently means change—a change in attitude, belief, or behavior (Haslam et al., 2011). "People expect leaders to bring change about, to get things done, to make things happen, to inspire, to motivate" (Husband, 1992, p. 494). Some have called this **transformational leadership**, and they have distinguished it from transactional leadership (Bass, 1990; Burns, 1978). **Transactional leadership** is described in terms that are similar to what I've described as management, not leadership. I agree with Rost (1991) and his postindustrial model of leadership, when he claims, *"Leadership, properly defined, is about transformation, all kinds of transformations"* (p. 126). Change, small and large, brought about through the leadership process is inherently transforming. Influencing group members through persuasion (not coercion) transforms them from what they were to what they become. **All leadership, therefore, is transformational to a greater or lesser degree.**

This doesn't mean that every leader must have charisma. Leaders perceived to be *highly* transformational, however, are sometimes referred to as charismatic leaders (Judge & Piccolo, 2004). Hackman and Johnson (2013) label them the "superstars of leadership" (Gandhi, Martin Luther King, Mother Teresa, Nelson Mandela, or Pope Francis, for example). **Charismatic leaders** are visionary, decisive, inspirational, and self-sacrificing (House & Javidan, 2004). They exhibit strong listening skills, empathy, self-confidence, and skillful speaking (Levine et al., 2010).

Charismatic leaders have a significant impact on group members' lives and they provoke fierce loyalty, commitment, and devotion from followers. A strong identification with the leader develops, and the followers' goals, self-esteem, and values become entangled with the charismatic leader–follower relationship (Fiedler & House, 1988). Charismatic leadership includes two essential elements: group identity and successful advancement of top group goals (Steffins et al., 2013). **The group confers charisma upon the leader.** If group members identify with the leader or the leader is successful in advancing key group goals, members will likely perceive the leader as charismatic. Recent research confirms this: "The more successful the group, the more charismatic the leader was seen to be" (Haslam & Reicher, 2012, p. 45).

These distinctions do not exclude managers from being leaders, any more than being a leader excludes you from being a manager (Dubrin, 2010). One person can be both (House & Aditya, 1997). Some even argue that being both a strong leader and a manager is the ideal (Kotter, 1990). The point is not to denigrate managers in order to exalt leaders. The two can overlap, and often do. Leaders who inspire and motivate followers to strive for wholly unreachable goals, who can't organize a plan of action, or who quickly lose focus on one challenge when a new challenge emerges will have very limited effectiveness because they lack management skills. Conversely, a manager may be interested in more than merely maintaining the status quo. When a manager seeks positive change, motivates and inspires followers, and creates direction for the group, however, he or she is acting as a leader, not a manager.

▶ Leadership and Communication: Duct-Taped Together

Leadership is fundamentally a communication process exercised within the group (Barge & Hirokawa, 1989). *"Extraordinary leadership is the product of extraordinary communication"* (Hackman & Johnson, 2013, p. 252). **Competent communication is a necessary precondition for a high-quality leader–follower relationship to develop** (Flauto, 1999). Those leaders rated as the most skillful communicators are deemed the most effective leaders (Riggio et al., 2003). A survey of 1,400 leaders, managers, and executives found that the "most critical leadership skill" by far was the ability to communicate effectively and "the biggest mistake leaders make" is "inappropriate use of communication" ("Critical Leadership Skills," 2014).

The leader sets the emotional tone for the group. When discussing *emotional intelligence,* Daniel Goleman (1998) notes: "Interpersonal ineptitude in leaders lowers everyone's performance: It wastes time, creates acrimony, corrodes motivation and commitment, builds hostility and apathy" (p. 32). Leaders who fail typically do so because they exhibit insensitivity toward group members, are brutally critical, and are too demanding (Goleman, 1998). As Goleman (2013) further notes, "The common cold of leadership is poor listening" (p. 226). In other words, inept leaders do not respect their followers. They don't care what they think or how they feel.

Showing respect for followers is a critical communication imperative for leaders (van Quaquebeke & Eckloff, 2010) and a key element of ethical communication (see Chapter 1). Leaders exhibit respect by recognizing and appreciating the importance and worth of others. You compliment good work, and when mistakes occur you engage in constructive dialogue to correct the error instead of criticizing and deflating the individual. You act politely toward group members. You show a genuine interest in others' opinions, and you don't blame others for your own mistakes. In short, you exercise supportive communication not defensive communication patterns (see Chapter 4). Because of the interconnectedness of leaders and followers, the more followers "feel respected by their leaders, the more they will 'return the favor' by being open to their leader's influence" (van Quaquebeke & Eckloff, 2010, p. 352). **Unfortunately, respect from leaders is highly desired by followers but too rarely experienced** (van Quaquebeke & Eckloff, 2010).

Consider the president of a large organization whose open contempt and disrespect for his employees was reflected in his oft-stated motto: "Bring 'em in and burn 'em out." He seemed to enjoy bullying and abusing his workers. A junior staff member, for instance, announced that it was her birthday and offered pieces of cake to fellow workers, including the president. The president's response was to complain loudly to a nearby manager, "Can't you get your staff to work?" Then, to the junior staffer, he looked at her derisively and said, "And you sure don't need the calories in that cake" (quoted by Goleman et al., 2002, p. 194).

Emotional outbursts, or what Birgitta Wistrand, CEO of a Swedish company, calls "emotional incontinence," also create a ripple effect that spreads fear, mistrust, and anger in all directions. This is not a climate conducive to effective leadership and group performance. As the old maxim goes, "A fish rots from the head down." **Ineffective leaders are ineffective communicators.** Effective leaders create a supportive, cooperative group environment through their communication with others (Goleman, 2013).

Leadership, then, is a leader–follower influence process, directed toward positive change that reflects mutual purposes of group members and is largely accomplished through competent communication (Hackman & Johnson, 2013; Rost, 1991). Conceptualizing what constitutes leadership, however, is a far cry from knowing how to exercise leadership in a group. How leaders emerge and the ways to retain leadership in groups are discussed next.

Gaining and Retaining Leadership: Getting There Is Just the Start

Gaining and retaining leadership in a small group are different communication processes. In this section, those differences are explored.

Focus Questions

1. **What should you avoid if you want to emerge as a leader of a group?**
2. **How is the process for retaining the leader role different from the process for emerging as group leader?**

▶ How Not to Become a Leader: Thou Shalt Not

Why do people want to be leaders? There are numerous reasons, but the most obvious ones are *status* that comes from running the show, *respect* from group members for doing a good job of guiding the group, and *power* accorded leaders that allows them to influence others and produce change.

It is often easier to determine what you shouldn't do more than what you should do if you wish to become a leader. We know that corruption or sex scandals, for instance, can send the media into a feeding frenzy and can torpedo a promising political career, but the absence of such scandals won't capture any headlines ("Candidate X still hasn't been caught doing anything corrupt"). Having a spotless character may just brand you as dull in some people's minds. Lack of negatives does not necessarily equal leadership potential.

There are important negatives to avoid, however, if you hope to have a chance to become group leader. The competent communicator who wishes to emerge as group leader should heed the following dictums (Bormann, 1990; Fisher & Ellis, 1990; Geier, 1967):

1. *Thou shalt not show up late for or miss important meetings.* Groups choose individuals who are committed, not members who exhibit insensitivity to the group. As an anonymous wit once observed, "Absence makes the heart grow fonder—of someone else."

2. *Thou shalt not be uninformed about a problem commanding the group's attention.* Knowledgeable members have a greater chance of emerging as leaders. The clueless need not apply.

3. *Thou shalt not manifest apathy and lack of interest by sluggish participation in group discussions.* Group members are not impressed by "vigor mortis." Indifference provokes defensiveness. Participation is a sign of commitment to the group, and commitment to the group and its goals is part of the leadership process (De Souza & Kline, 1995).

4. *Thou shalt not attempt to dominate conversation during discussion.* Leadership is not "loudership" (Kluger, 2009). Loudmouths who won't dial down the volume and the intensity of their speech can be annoying. Raising your armor-piercing voice to demand unyielding attention alienates group members. Learning when to shut up is a useful skill.

5. *Thou shalt not listen poorly* (Bechler & Johnson, 1995). Leadership is not a monologue; it's a dialogue. As someone once said, a monologue is "the egotist's version of a scintillating conversation." Dialogue means leaders and followers listen carefully to each other.

6. *Thou shalt not be rigid and inflexible when expressing viewpoints.* A hardened position is plaque on the cortex. It decays the mind and contracts the brain. Group members prefer open not closed minds. For example, a national report using surveys and focus groups of college Republicans following the 2012 presidential defeat of Mitt Romney by Barack Obama found that respondents viewed the Republican Party as "closed-minded" and "rigid." "Open-minded," "caring," and "cooperative" were attributes that least described the party. The report was viewed by the Republican National Committee as a call to "repair the brand" of the Republican Party for fear of future election debacles and loss of national leadership (Dann, 2013).

7. *Thou shalt not bully group members.* Browbeating members to do your bidding will gain few admirers. There may be no way to avoid issuing orders in some situations (e.g., in the military), but watch out for psychological reactance (see Chapter 4). Bullies get banished to the playground.

8. *Thou shalt not use offensive and abusive language.* Blue language produces red faces. This will surely alienate many, if not most, group members, except in rare instances such as locker room talk within some sports teams. Embrace civility.

Some of these counterproductive communication patterns are more likely than others to prevent an individual from becoming a group leader (Geier, 1967). The three most relevant, in order of importance, are: being uninformed, not participating, and being rigid and inflexible.

▶ General Pattern of Leader Emergence: Process of Elimination

The extensive research conducted at the University of Minnesota under the direction of Ernest Bormann (1990) discovered a pattern of leader emergence in small zero-history groups. **In general, a group selects a leader by a process of elimination.** Potential candidates are systematically removed from consideration until only one person remains to be leader. We may be quite clear on what we don't want in a leader but not as sure about what we do want. This narrowing of the candidate field makes good sense. As we eliminate candidates, complexity is reduced. The breadth of possibilities is narrowed, while the depth of understanding of each candidate's qualifications for the role is increased.

There are two phases to the process-of-elimination explanation of leader emergence. During the first phase, roughly half of the members are eliminated from consideration. The criteria for elimination are crude and impressionistic. Negative communication patterns—the "thou shalt nots"—weigh heavily. **Quiet members are among the first eliminated.** Nonparticipation will leave the impression of indifference and noncommitment. It also gives the impression that such individuals hiding in the shadows do not perceive themselves as leaders. Research shows that perceiving yourself as a leader improves your chances of emerging as a group leader (Emery et al., 2011). There was not a single instance in the Minnesota studies of a quiet member who became a leader.

Conversely, talkativeness also influences the leadership emergence process. **Those who talk the most are perceived initially as potential leader material** (Jones & Kelly, 2007; Riggio et al., 2003). The group will quickly eliminate a group member from consideration, however, if he or she blathers or makes pronouncements on subjects without making a great deal of sense. Such individuals are reminiscent of William Gibbs McAddo's characterization of President Warren G. Harding as "an army of pompous phrases moving over the landscape in search of an idea." Windbags gain no favor. Quality of contributions plays an important part in determining who emerges as group leader (Jones & Kelly, 2007).

The members who express strong, unqualified assertions are also eliminated These individuals are perceived to be too extreme and too inflexible in their points of view to make effective leaders. The attitude of certitude will provoke defensiveness from group members. **The uninformed, unintelligent, or unskilled are next in line for elimination** (Riggio et al., 2003). Groups look for task-competent individuals who are committed to the group goals to emerge as leaders (De Souza & Klein, 1995). Inept members distract the group from goal attainment.

In the second phase, about half the group still actively contend for the leader role. This part of the process can become quite competitive. Frustrations and irritations can mount. Of these remaining contenders, **those who are bossy or dictatorial and those whose communication style is irritating or disturbing to group members are eliminated.**

So who emerges as leader if more than one member survives the elimination rounds? There are several possibilities. First, if the group feels threatened by some external or internal crisis (e.g., the inability to choose a topic for a symposium presentation, or if members with expertise fall sick or leave the group), **the group often turns to the member who provides a solution to the crisis,** and he or she becomes the leader. Second, **those members perceived to be effective listeners can make a strong bid to be chosen leader** (Johnson & Bechler, 1998). Effective listening establishes connections with followers. Listening skills display empathy, and those who exhibit greater empathy are more likely to emerge as leaders (Kellett et al., 2006). Third, **those individuals who exhibit high levels of *emotional intelligence*—**"the ability to perceive, glean information from, and manage one's own and others' emotions"—emerge as group leaders more readily than those who don't (Lopez-Zafra et al., 2008; see also Goleman, 1995). This affirms the importance of competent communication. Fourth, **members who remain active contenders for**

the leader role often acquire lieutenants. A *lieutenant* is an advocate for one of the contenders. He or she boosts the chances of the contender becoming the group leader. If only one of the members gains the support of a lieutenant, then this person will likely become the leader. If two members each gain a lieutenant, then the process of leader emergence can be drawn out or can even end in stalemate.

Research on leader emergence in virtual groups parallels these findings of leader emergence in standard, face-to-face groups. Degree of participation was considered to be an important consideration, as it is in standard groups. The type and quality of the participation, however, mattered. Virtual group participants had a negative view of those positioning themselves to emerge as leaders when they were perceived to be "dominant, opinionated, outspoken, uncompromising, and pursuant of their own agenda." Virtual group participants had a positive view of those who were "inclusive, collaborative, concerned about others, good listeners, and in search of consensus" (Shollen, 2010).

The general tendency in both standard and virtual groups is for members to accept as leader the person who provides the optimum blend of task efficiency and sensitivity to social considerations. This tendency, of course, does not translate into a tidy formula or precise recipe. Some groups prefer a leader who concentrates more on task accomplishment and less on the social dimension of the group. Other groups prefer the opposite.

Ultimately, if you want to become the leader of a group, you should take the following steps (Bormann, 1990):

1. Manifest conformity to the group's norms, values, and goals.

2. Display proper motivation to lead.

3. Avoid the "thou shalt nots" previously identified.

Deviants, dissenters, and disrupters will be eliminated early as potential leaders. Women and ethnic minorities may also have greater difficulty emerging as leaders (see Focus on Gender/Ethnicity: "Gender and Ethnic Bias in Leader Emergence"). Groups prefer leaders who will assist them in the attainment of their goals, who will defend the group vigorously against threats, and who will remain loyal to the group. Since most group members think of a leader as the single individual who does most of the work, anyone hoping to be leader must also demonstrate a willingness to work hard for the group (Hollander, 1978).

▶ Retaining the Leader Role: Hanging onto Power

The process for retaining the leader role is not the same as the process for emerging as the group leader. An individual could conform to group norms, display a strong motivation to lead the group, and avoid the "thou shalt nots"

SECOND LOOK

Pattern of Leader Emergence

General Pattern

(Process of Elimination)

Phase One

   Quiet members eliminated

   Members who express strong, unqualified assertions eliminated

   Uninformed, unintelligent, and/or unskilled eliminated

Phase Two, part one

   Bossy, dictatorial members eliminated

   Members with irritating or disturbing communication style eliminated

Phase Two, part two

   Member who provides solution in time of crisis considered

   Member who exhibits effective listening skills considered

   Member who exhibits emotional intelligence considered

   Member who acquires a lieutenant considered

   If more than one member acquires lieutenant—possible stalemate

How to Become a Leader

   Manifest conformity to group norms, values, and goals.

   Display proper motivation to lead.

   Avoid the "thou shalt nots."

Modifying Factors of Leader Emergence

   Gender bias

   Ethnic bias

and still not retain the role of leader, as many political leaders have learned. A leader is sometimes deposed if his or her performance is felt by members to be unsatisfactory. **There are three primary qualifications for retaining leadership** (Wood et al., 2006):

1. You must demonstrate your competence as leader.

2. You must accept accountability for your actions.

3. You must satisfy group members' expectations.

Focus On Culture

Gender and Ethnic Bias in Leader Emergence

Cornelia Dean (2005) was the *New York Times* science editor from 1997 to 2003. At a dinner for the superstars of the scientific community, a colleague introduced Dean to one of America's foremost neuroscientists without indicating her title. "Oh yes," the self-important scientist muttered as he surveyed the room for someone more noteworthy to converse with than this apparent nobody. He then asked, "Who is the new science editor of the *New York Times,* that twerpy little girl in the short skirt?" Flabbergasted by this clueless inquiry, Dean responded, "That would be me" (p. F3).

Bias against women and ethnic minorities is a significant issue in the leadership emergence literature. The research on gender bias is far more voluminous than it is on ethnic bias (Northouse, 2013). Studies of gender bias in the workplace, where emerging leaders live their daily lives and engage in small group communication, provide mixed results. The issue of a glass ceiling, an invisible barrier of subtle discrimination that excludes women from top jobs in corporate and professional America, remains relevant. Only 23 women were CEOs of the 500 largest companies in the United States in 2014, and only five women headed one of the 50 largest companies. An additional 23 women were CEOs of the next 500 largest U.S. companies. *That's a total of 46 women (4.6%) and 954 men (95.4%) running our largest 1,000 corporations* ("Women CEOs," 2014). A mere 16.9% of Fortune 500 corporate board seats were occupied by women in 2013, and only 14.6% of executive officers at these same companies were women ("Women in U.S. Management," 2013). In politics, women in 2014 held only 20 (20%) of the 100 U.S. Senate seats, 78 of the 435 House seats (17.9%), 1,784 (24.2%) of state legislative seats, and 74 (22.5%) of statewide elective executive offices ("Women in Statewide Elective Executive Office 2014"; Women in State Legislatures," 2014; "Women Serving in the 113th Congress 2013–2015"). These figures represent very slow progress for women.

That's the bad news. The encouraging news is that women are poised to make huge strides. Women are well positioned to advance in the information-based economy driven by the microchip. The new economy is based primarily on the knowledge and skills of the workers instead of seniority, and women are poised to take advantage of this trend (Eagly & Carli, 2007; Rosin, 2010).

Consider the evidence of such a trend. Women in 2012 held more than half (51.5%) of all managerial and professional positions in the United States ("Women in U.S. Management," 2013). This trend is very likely to continue, even to grow more robust in the immediate future because women are receiving more education than men in preparation for the developing job market. Women earn almost 62% of associate degrees, 60% of all bachelor's degrees, 60% of master's degrees, and 52% of all doctoral degrees. Since 1982, women have earned 9 million more college degrees than men (Perry, 2013).

Nevertheless, women still have difficulty becoming leaders. When individuals think of "leader" they typically think "male" (Koenig et al., 2011). Nevertheless, abundant research shows that women in many respects make better leaders than men (Eagly et al., 2003; Eagly, 2007). One study of 58,000 individuals revealed that women outranked men on 20 of 23 leadership skills. Another study of 2,482 executives revealed that women again outranked men on 17 of 20

(Continued)

leadership skills (Sharpe, 2000). Finally, a study of 7,289 leaders shows that women outranked male leaders on 15 of 16 core leadership competencies (Zenger & Folkman, 2012). Despite research findings on the leadership effectiveness of women, in a variety of group settings, men are typically favored over women when leaders are selected and evaluated, even when no differences in actual leadership behavior occur (Eagly & Karau, 2002; Forsyth et al., 1997). Gender bias, although diminished in recent years, remains a barrier to the upward advancement of women into positions as upper-level leaders (McEldowney et al., 2009). Even when women do emerge as leaders, they suffer penalties. When women exercise leadership by being assertive, reactions are often negative, but if they behave in stereotypic ways by exhibiting a kind, gentle, empathic approach, they are often seen as ineffectual and a poor leader (Eagly & Carli, 2007; Hoyt, 2010).

The "Ban Bossy" campaign started in 2014 by Facebook COO Sheryl Sandberg aimed to combat this double standard by highlighting and trying to combat the strong tendency, even as early as elementary school, to label young girls "bossy" when they attempt to be leaders. As Sandberg explains, "We know that by middle school, more boys than girls want to lead, and if you ask girls why they don't want to lead, whether it's the school project all the way to running for office, they don't want to be called bossy, and they don't want to be disliked" (quoted by McFadden & Whitman, 2014).

Female leaders are scrutinized more, especially when they take leadership positions that are usually held by men (Brescoll et al., 2011). Women are less liked and more personally disparaged than equivalently successful men. These penalties can negatively affect the careers of female leaders both in advancement and in

Paul Morigi/Getty Images Entertainment/Getty Images

Fortune magazine's "Most Powerful Women Summit" featured Facebook Chief Operating Officer Sheryl Sandberg, whose best-selling book, *Lean In,* details the challenges women face rising to the highest levels of leadership in business and industry and approaches to improving gender inequality.

recommendations for pay increases (Heilman et al., 2004).

This is a good news/bad news record, but, overall, the outlook for women in leadership positions, at least white women, is optimistic. The outlook for ethnic minorities in leadership positions is less optimistic. In 2012, there were only 24 people of color (4.8%) who were CEOs of Fortune 500 companies and only four of these were woman of color (Crosby et al, 2012). In 2013, women of color held a mere 3.2% of all boards of directors seats in business. More than two-thirds of top companies had no women of color as directors (Clawson, 2013). People of color make up 25% of law school student enrollments, 20% of all associates in law firms, but only a measly 7% of all partners. Of all law firms employing associates, 16% have no associates who are people of color ("Legal Professions: Status of Women and Men," 2014). The percentage of African Americans on Fortune 500 boards of directors is less than 8% ("Black Enterprise Publishes Exclusive Registry," 2013). The situation for Hispanic Americans and Asian Americans is even worse ("Missing Pieces," 2014).

How do we combat gender and ethnicity bias in emergent leadership in groups? First, the **20 percent rule** again comes into play. When women and minorities find themselves flying solo in groups, the chance that they'll land in a leadership position is remote. As the number of women and ethnic minorities increases in a group to as much as 20% of the membership, however, the likelihood that a woman or a minority will emerge as leader also increases because bias decreases (Shimanoff & Jenkins, 2003). When women and ethnic minorities are no longer perceived as tokens, but instead form a substantial portion of group membership and increasingly occupy top leadership positions, then competence will be judged less on gender

and ethnic bias and more on actual performance (Karakowsky & Siegel, 1999).

Second, if group members are allowed to mingle, interact, and work on a project before determining a leader, the decision is more likely to be made on the basis of individual performance rather than gender (or ethnicity, if we extrapolate the research findings). Small groups that met for 6 to 15 weeks on a project were as likely to name a woman as their leader as they were a man (Goktepe & Schneier, 1989). Allowing women and minorities to display their strengths increases their chances of emerging as group leaders.

Third, engaging in task-relevant communication behavior is a key to emerging as leader of a small, task-oriented group (Hawkins, 1995). Task-relevant communication includes initiation and discussion of analysis of the group problem, establishment of decision criteria, generation of possible solutions to problems, evaluation of possible solutions, and establishment of group operating procedures. Task-oriented female group members are as likely to emerge as leaders of small task groups as are task-oriented male group members (Hawkins, 1995). This finding is bolstered by 2013 Gallup poll results that show 41% of respondents have no preference for either a male or female boss and 23% prefer a female boss, the highest percentage ever recorded in this annual survey that dates back to 1953. Men were actually more accepting of female bosses than women (Newport & Wilke, 2013). Fourth, if women and minorities are among the first to speak in the group and they speak fairly frequently, their chances of emerging as leaders increase (Shimanoff & Jenkins, 2003). Speaking early and often without dominating discussion is perceived as assertive. Speaking early is more important for women and minorities than it is for men.

(Continued)

Finally, women and ethnic minorities can advance their chances of becoming leaders in small groups by honing their communication skills and abilities. Developing competence in communication by using skills appropriately and effectively can go a long way toward combating gender and ethnic leadership bias (Hackman & Johnson, 2013).

QUESTIONS FOR THOUGHT

1. Should group members encourage women and minorities to speak early and often by inviting their participation?
2. Do you feel that the glass ceiling will shatter soon, as the number of women and minorities in the middle ranks of leadership swells? What might prevent this from happening?
3. What responsibilities do white males have regarding the issue of leadership bias?

Retaining the role of leader can be a tricky business. Groups can be fickle. Carly Fiorina was named CEO of Hewlett-Packard (HP) in 1999, one of only a handful of women leading a Fortune 500 company. Expectations were high that Fiorina, a charismatic and articulate leader in her previous positions, would reverse the gradual downward slide the company had been experiencing. Her signature decision was the controversial purchase of Compaq Computer in 2002. "Fiorina was a controversial figure at HP, partly because of the abrasive manner in which the takeover of Compaq was fought in 2001 and 2002" (Oates & Cullen, 2005). In February 2005, Fiorina was forced to resign her position. She failed to meet expectations and to demonstrate her leadership competence in a cutthroat business. Her vision clashed with that of stockholders and employees, thousands of whom were forced out of HP in painful cost-cutting measures. As a *San Jose Mercury News* editorial summed it up, "In the corporate world, change must be a catalyst for results, and at HP, it wasn't. And so Fiorina was asked to leave" ("Out of 'Internet Time,'" 2005, p. 6B). In 2010, Fiorina tried to parlay her business experience into a political leadership position. She ran for United States senator in California, only to be overwhelmed by the incumbent Barbara Boxer. Her competence as a business leader was a central issue and haunted her campaign.

Group expectations of a leader may shift as circumstances alter. Members' confidence in and loyalty to their leader may be shaky. A leader must demonstrate competence and satisfy group expectations on a continuing basis or member loyalty may disappear quickly. Last year's success may not compensate adequately for this year's failure, as Fiorina and many athletic coaches and political leaders have learned.

Perspectives on Effective Leadership: An Evolving View

Scholarly perspectives on leadership effectiveness have changed greatly over the three-quarters of a century since the first serious research was conducted. In this section, the primary perspectives that have generated considerable interest are discussed. I begin with the most basic perspective and show how each perspective evolves from previous efforts to explain what constitutes effective leadership in groups.

▶ Traits Perspective: The Born Leader View

This is the "leaders are born not made" perspective; sometimes referred to as the "heroic model" of leadership (Vroom & Jago, 2007). **This perspective views leadership as a person, not a process.** Thus, we hunt for the "heroic" and exceptionally talented individuals to idolize as model specimens of leadership. This journey has taken us to strange places. You can buy books on the leadership secrets of Jesus, Colin Powell, Meg Whitman, Donald Trump, Attila the Hun, and Osama bin Laden. A Quinnipiac University poll found that 80% of American respondents viewed Russian President Vladimir Putin as dishonest and untrustworthy and 33% weren't sure about his mental stability, yet 57% saw him as possessing "strong leadership qualities" ("Obama Approval Inches Up, Tied with Putin as Leader," 2014). *Fortune* magazine identified New York Yankees shortstop, Derek Jeter, as 11th on a list of the world's 50 greatest leaders for being inspiring and not using steroids ("The World's 50 Greatest Leaders," 2014). One survey of CEOs in 60 countries asked which leaders respondents most admired. The top 10 list included Winston Churchill, Mahatma Gandhi, and Napoleon Bonaparte. Among the same respondents, 96% of the male CEOs failed to mention a single female leader and 83% of the female CEOs did likewise ("Leaders CEOs Most Admire," 2014). Clearly, such vastly disparate, male-dominated lists of model leaders suggest a perspective with substantial limitations.

Nevertheless, the earliest academic studies on leadership set out to discover a universal set of traits applicable to all those who become leaders. **Traits** are relatively enduring characteristics of an individual that highlight differences between people and that are displayed in most situations. There are physical traits such as height, weight, physique, beauty, and attractiveness. There are personality traits such as being outgoing, sociable, or introverted and shy. There are traits associated with inherent capacities of an individual such as intelligence and quick-wittedness. There are also traits associated with consistent behaviors such as confidence, trustworthiness, and integrity. A huge number of traits were studied. We know, for instance, that height, weight, and physical attractiveness have a bearing on social influence (White et al., 2013). Tall individuals usually have greater influence with others than do shorter individuals. Very heavy or skinny people have less influence than more "ideal weight" types (Hickson & Stacks, 1989). Good-looking individuals can influence a group. So why don't all tall, fit, and physically attractive individuals become leaders instead of short, dumpy, plain-looking individuals?

Will any single trait likely make a person an effective leader? Clearly not (Hackman & Johnson, 2013; Northouse, 2013). One study by John C. Turner and Alexander Haslam showed that when students were faced with a rival group that had an intelligent leader who also exhibited inconsiderateness, they wanted their own leader to be *un*intelligent. Conversely, when the rival leader was perceived to be unintelligent, they preferred an intelligent leader for their own group (cited in Reicher et al., 2007). What is usually considered a desirable leader trait can become undesirable when other traits intrude. A trait such as intelligence could be neutralized by unfriendliness, ethical indifference, laziness, arrogance, or insensitivity.

One disturbing study of 200 business executives showed this clash of opposing traits (Babiak & Hare, 2006). Nearly 4% of these business executives qualified as **psychopaths**—"someone who has no conscience and feels no remorse or empathy" (Perman, 2011). These are "horrible bosses" not cold-blooded killers. "The only thing that counts for these people is to win" (Kets de Vries, 2014). Yet, they are typically charming, but ruthless and manipulative. They make terrible leaders, especially because they cannot abide working in teams. Qualities often associated with leadership by many (charm, confidence, aggressiveness, and decisiveness) are counterbalanced by repellant qualities (being antisocial, bullying, manipulative, and unethical),

Is there a combination of traits that might make a leader effective? Fiedler and House (1988) claim that "effective leaders tend to have a high need to influence others, to achieve, and they tend to be bright, competent, and socially adept, rather than stupid, incompetent, and social disasters" (p. 87). Stogdill (1948, 1974), however, twice reviewed hundreds of studies on the relationship between traits and leadership and concluded that no universal set of traits assures leader emergence or leader effectiveness.

How could it be otherwise? One study of 3,700 business executives, for example, used 60 traits to assess leadership (Stamoulis & Mannion, 2014). Who could possibly possess all 60 traits or even a vast majority of such a huge list? "To expect that a person would be born with all of the tools needed to lead just doesn't make sense based on what we know about the complexity of social groups and processes" (Riggio, 2009). A 25-year study by the Gallup Organization of 80,000 leaders found that the greatest leaders in the world don't share a common set of characteristics (Buckingham & Coffman, 1999).

Certain basic traits (intelligence, social and verbal skills, extroversion) may be the irreducible minimum qualifications to become a leader, but to retain the role of leader and ultimately to perform effectively requires much more.

The traits perspective explains relatively little about effective leadership in groups. Which traits, for instance, do Facebook founder and CEO Mark Zuckerberg, Pope Francis, Hillary Clinton, Barack Obama, Sarah Palin, and Supreme Court Justice Sonia Sotomayor share that explain their leadership position: Good looks? Intelligence? Physical size? Charisma? Personality? Age? Ethnicity? Gender? Verbal skills? Can they possess any or all of these traits and still be ineffective leaders?

The principal problem with the trait approach to effective leadership is the assumption that leadership resides in the person, not in transactions between leaders and followers conducted within the group system (Northouse, 2013). No one set of leadership traits will fit every situation and group. Although the trait perspective is not entirely without merit, there's much more to leadership effectiveness. **Leaders are not born; they are developed** (Ruvolo et al., 2004).

▶ Styles Perspective: One Style Doesn't Fit All

Unsatisfied with the trait approach to leadership, Kurt Lewin and his associates developed a new approach based on three leadership styles: autocratic, democratic, and laissez-faire (Lewin et al., 1939). **Autocratic style** exerts control over group members. The autocratic leader is highly directive. This leadership style does not encourage member participation. Autocratic leaders are not concerned about making friends or getting invited to parties. The autocratic style (usually referred to more neutrally as the *directive style*) puts most of the emphasis on the task, with little concern for the social dimension of the group (high task, low social).

The **democratic style** encourages participation and responsibility from group members. Democratic leaders work to improve the skills and abilities of group members (Gastil, 1994). Followers have a say in what the group decides. The democratic style (usually referred to more neutrally as the *participative style*) puts a balanced emphasis on both the task and social dimensions of the group (high task, high social).

The **laissez-faire style** is a do-nothing approach to leadership. It is "the avoidance or absence of leadership" in which individuals "avoid making decisions, hesitate in taking action, and are absent when needed" (Judge & Piccolo, 2004, p. 756). Laissez-faire amounts to a sit-on-your-derriere style. This style doesn't try to influence anyone, *so it is by definition non-leadership.* "Without influence, leadership does not exist" (Northouse, 2013, p. 5). Thus, it has been dropped from serious consideration in most of the research.

The extensive research comparing autocratic-directive and democratic-participative leadership styles shows mixed results (Northouse, 2013). Both directive and participative styles can be productive, and although the participative style fosters more member satisfaction than does the directive style (Van Oostrum & Rabbie, 1995), the difference is neither large nor uniform (Gastil, 1994). Participative leadership seems to work best when it springs naturally from the group itself. Not all small groups, however, want or expect their leaders to adopt the participative leadership style (see Box 6.1). Some cultures prefer the "paternal authoritative" (benevolently directive) style to the participative style (Brislin, 1993). In such cultures, the participative style may not work as well as the directive style.

BOX 6.1

What Is Your Leadership Style Preference?

Fill out the self-assessment on leadership styles. Note: The rating scale changes.

1. I like it when my supervisor at work admits openly that he/she made a mistake.

STRONGLY DISAGREE			STRONGLY AGREE	
1	2	3	4	5

2. I want to be told what to do on the job, not have to figure it out for myself

STRONGLY DISAGREE			STRONGLY AGREE	
5	4	3	2	1

3. If my team were hiring a new applicant, I prefer that the entire team interview the candidate and make the final decision, not the team leader only.

STRONGLY DISAGREE			STRONGLY AGREE	
1	2	3	4	5

4. I don't want my boss to be my friend; I prefer that my boss remain aloof from the group so he/she can be objective when decisions need to be made.

STRONGLY DISAGREE			STRONGLY AGREE	
5	4	3	2	1

5. I do not think that my boss should reverse the decision of his/her team except in extraordinary circumstances (dangerous mistake).

STRONGLY DISAGREE			STRONGLY AGREE	
1	2	3	4	5

6. I prefer to be told what decisions have been made then informed what I should do to implement these decisions, not engage in time-consuming debate.

STRONGLY DISAGREE			STRONGLY AGREE	
5	4	3	2	1

7. I prefer having many opportunities to provide input before my team leader makes a final decision.

STRONGLY DISAGREE			STRONGLY AGREE	
1	2	3	4	5

8. I want my boss to make the important decisions, not get me and others on our team involved; that's why he/she gets paid the big bucks.

STRONGLY DISAGREE			STRONGLY AGREE	
5	4	3	2	1

9. I want my boss to encourage robust debate and differences of opinion before any decisions are made.

STRONGLY DISAGREE			STRONGLY AGREE	
1	2	3	4	5

10. I want my boss to be decisive, to make decisions confidently, and model a person who is totally in charge.

STRONGLY DISAGREE			STRONGLY AGREE	
5	4	3	2	1

Tally your total score and divide by 10. The higher your average score, the more you prefer participative leadership from supervisors/bosses/team leaders. The lower the average score, the more you prefer the directive leadership style.

Gender also plays a role in the leadership style–effectiveness equation. Male and female leaders are evaluated by group members as equally competent when the democratic-participative style is used. When the autocratic-directive style is used, however, group members evaluate women as substantially less competent leaders than men (Eagly & Carli, 2007; Van Engen & Willemsen, 2004). Apparently, group expectations influence judgments of leader competence. Female leaders are expected to adopt the participative leadership style, which complements the desire for connection, but groups are less accustomed to seeing women use the directive style, which places more emphasis on independence and power than on connection (Tannen, 2010). Men clearly have more flexibility in choice of leadership style. With time, this stereotype that locks women into a single style of leadership should virtually vanish as women challenge the expectation.

One weakness of the participative/directive leadership style duality is that these styles are viewed as extreme opposites. Individuals operate as either participative or directive leaders, but not both. **Realistically, though, a combination of participative and directive leadership styles is required in small groups.** In organized sports, the autocratic leadership style is preferred by some athletes but not by others, and among high school wrestlers, autocratic is preferred toward the end of the season but not at the beginning (Turman, 2003). Also, consider a "temp worker" who is new on a job. Should this person be consulted on how the job should be accomplished when he or she doesn't even have a good idea what the job entails? Should teachers consult their students before determining course content when the students know little or nothing about the subject? Should military commanders seek the advice of their troops before launching an offensive? "All those in favor of attacking the heavily armed enemy signal by saying aye; those opposed, nay. Okay, the nays have it. We'll stay put and live another day." Group members can't always meaningfully participate in decision making.

No one style of leadership will be suitable for all situations any more than one set of leadership traits will mesh with every situation. This realization has led researchers to explore yet another approach to leadership—the situational or contingency perspective (Vroom & Jago, 2007).

▶ Situational (Contingency) Perspective: Matching Styles with Circumstances

This is the "it depends" approach to leadership. Since no one style of leadership is appropriate for all situations, effective leadership is contingent upon matching styles with situations. Those leaders whose style fits well with their situation exhibit strong confidence and perform at a high level (Chemers, 2000). One caveat, however, should be noted at the outset of this discussion of situational leadership:

What style of leadership is depicted in this photo?

1. Democratic/participative
2. Laissez-faire/sit-on-your-derriere
3. Functional
4. Autocratic/directive

Answers are given at the end of the chapter.

In open systems, leadership effectiveness may be influenced by situational forces beyond the control of any leader (Vroom & Jago, 2007). Military officers, coaches of sports teams, orchestra conductors, and others receive adulation for successes and blame for failures, but group success or failure is largely systemic. Even the most gifted and capable leaders can be victimized by the harsh situational realities of inadequate resources, adversarial hostilities, weak systemic support, and the like. Nevertheless, leaders who can adapt flexibly to systemic situations have the best chance of success.

There are two principal situational models of leadership effectiveness. The first is Fred Fiedler's (1967) contingency model. Fiedler's model, however, does not offer guidance on how to become a more effective leader once you're in a group. In this sense it has rather limited application for our purposes, so I will spare you an explanation of his complicated, difficult-to-apply model (Northouse, 2013).

A more flexible and useful situational model of leadership effectiveness has been offered by Hersey and Blanchard (see Hersey et al., 2001). Although their model is targeted at organizations, it applies well to groups large and small, especially ones with long life cycles. **Hersey and Blanchard have combined three variables in their situational model:**

1. The amount of guidance and direction (*task emphasis*) a leader provides
2. The amount of relationship support (*socio-emotional emphasis*) a leader provides
3. The *readiness level* in performing a specific task, function, or objective that followers demonstrate

There are four leadership styles in the Hersey and Blanchard model that flow from the first two variables. The **telling style** (high task, low relationship emphasis) is directive. A leader using this style provides specific instructions regarding a task and closely supervises the performance of followers but places minimal focus on developing social relationships with followers. The **selling style** (high task, high relationship) is also directive. A leader using this style explains and clarifies decisions but also tries to convince followers to accept directives. The **participating style** (low task, high relationship) is nondirective. A leader using this style encourages shared decision making with special emphasis on developing relationships in the group. The **delegating style** (low task, low relationship) is nondirective. A leader using this style allows the group to be self-directed. Responsibility for decision making and implementation of decisions rests with the group. **The key to leadership effectiveness is matching the appropriate style to the group environment.** One survey of business leaders reported that 76% of 1,400 respondents viewed use of an inappropriate leadership style to be among the biggest failures of leaders ("Critical Leadership Skills," 2014).

Fisher (1986) criticized the situational approach to leadership by contending that no leader could consider all possible situational variables to know which style to use. Hersey and Blanchard agree with the thrust of Fisher's criticism. They contend, however, that there is no need to consider all or even most variables. The relationship between the leader and followers is the prime consideration because if group members decide not to follow the leader, then all other situational variables (nature of the task, time involved, expectations, etc.) are irrelevant.

The primary situational variable that the leader must consider when adapting leadership styles to the specific group is the readiness level of followers. Readiness is "the extent to which a follower demonstrates the ability and willingness to accomplish a specific task" (Hersey et al., 2001, p. 175). *Ability* "is the knowledge, experience, and skill that an individual or group brings to a particular task or activity" (p. 176). *Willingness* "is the extent to which an individual or group has the confidence, commitment, and motivation to accomplish a specific task" (p. 176). *This all sounds remarkably like communication competence.*

Decisions are leader directed at lower levels of readiness; decisions are follower directed at higher levels of readiness. As readiness levels increase, effective leadership

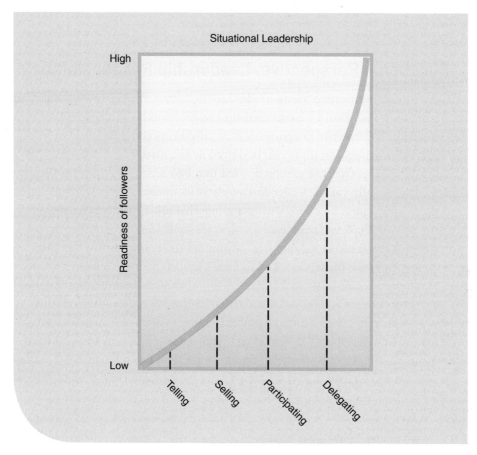

FIGURE 6.1
Note the telling (S1), selling (S2), participating (S3), and delegating (S4) leadership styles
related to follower readiness based on Hersey and Blanchard's situational model.

requires reduced guidance and direction from the leader and less socio-emotional support for followers. These relationships are depicted in Figure 6.1.

Followers, for whatever reasons (e.g., divorce, midlife crisis, lack of challenges), may
regress in their readiness levels, losing motivation or slipping in their skill performance.
In such cases, the leader moves backward through the styles curve (i.e., from delegating
to participating or even to telling), adapting to the change in circumstances.

The situational leadership model makes sense, but is it supported by research? The
research on situational leadership is skimpy and contradictory (Northouse, 2013;
Vecchio et al., 2006; Yukl, 2006). Nevertheless, clearly one leadership style does not fit
all situations. Newly formed groups typically require greater supervision and direction
than experienced groups. Experienced, capable groups work best when a leader is more

a "guide on the side" than a "sage on the stage." The situational leadership model rightly emphasizes the significance of context to leadership effectiveness.

▶ Functional Perspective: Leadership Responsibilities

The functional perspective views leadership in terms of certain functions, or responsibilities, that must be performed for the group to be successful. Typically, these functions fall into two categories: task requirements and social needs. **Finding the right balance between these two is viewed as essential.**

The functional perspective can be divided into two schools of thought. William Schutz dubbed the first as the **leader-as-completer** viewpoint. Leaders are thought to perform those essential functions within a group that other members have failed to perform. The list of task and maintenance roles previously identified in Chapter 5 indicates functions essential to a group (e.g., giving information, coordinating, facilitating, gatekeeping, relieving tension, and so forth). Leader, then, is seen as an adaptive role. **Leadership is demonstrated when** *any member* **steps in and assumes whatever role in the group is required at a particular time that has not been filled by any other member.** When a group member dominates discussion, any other member can act as a gatekeeper ("I'd like to hear from some other members, and can we agree to keep our comments short, perhaps no longer than two minutes?"). When the group seems inclined to make a specific decision but no mention has been forthcoming about possible disadvantages or potential pitfalls of such a decision, anyone can play devil's advocate ("I know this looks like a good decision, but have we considered what might go wrong if we implement it, and do we have a backup plan if things don't work out as planned?"). A second school of thought, the **vital functions** viewpoint, sees leaders performing key responsibilities different in kind and/or degree from other members. A large-scale investigation, however, of the question "Which communicative functions do leaders perform more frequently or more characteristically than non-leaders?" revealed no significant, unique functions associated with the leader role (Drecksel, 1984).

Of the two functional viewpoints, the leader-as-completer seems to have the greater merit. During the 9/11 terrorist attacks in 2001, many ordinary people exhibited extraordinary leadership. Office workers carried injured coworkers down daunting flights of stairs. Heroes emerged to rescue strangers because everyone, not just designated leaders (managers, fire battalion chiefs), felt responsible for the lives of fellow citizens and coworkers. They completed what was needed.

From the leader-as-completer functional perspective, leadership is a shared responsibility, not a specific individual's responsibility. **This perspective truly embraces the view that leadership is a process, not a person.** No one person can provide a group with everything that it needs to be successful. A designated leader has a few procedural duties such as setting an agenda, conducting an efficient meeting, guiding group

The Dalai Lama typifies servant leadership. He seeks to serve others, not himself. This is ethical leadership of the highest order.

discussion, and seeing that minutes of formal meetings are prepared and distributed. All the members, however, especially in informal small groups, have the responsibility for leadership. This is especially true of teams (Pearce & Sims, 2002; see also Chapter 7).

▶ Servant Leadership Perspective: Ethics in Leadership

He was called "the most cold-blooded businessman around … brutal, heartless, and arrogant" (Plotz, 1997, pp. 1, 3). He received the nicknames "Rambo in Pinstripes," "the Shredder," and "Chainsaw Al" for his "downsizing" tactics when he was called in to "save" a company. He wrote a self-promoting book entitled *Mean Business*. *Time* magazine in 2010 offered its "Top 10 Worst Bosses" list as a reminder of how not to be a great leader. Al Dunlap was first of the worst (Fastenberg, 2010).

Albert Dunlap was a notorious corporate turnaround specialist, a hired gun who was given the position of CEO in a company. He used this position to "turn around" a company by eliminating thousands of employees' jobs, increasing stock values, and selling off the remaining business. Dunlap slashed 35% of the workforce when he was CEO of Scott Paper Company (Fastenberg, 2010). He cut more than 6,000 jobs when he took over the helm at Sunbeam. In the bargain, he received a $70 million contract with Sunbeam. He bragged, "You can't overpay a great executive … Don't you think I'm a bargain?" (quoted in Byrne, 1999, p. 185).

"Nothing that is valued by less steely businessmen—loyalty to workers, responsibility to the community, relationships with suppliers, generosity in corporate philanthropy—matters to Dunlap" (Plotz, 1997, p. 2). In his book, Dunlap offered this glib advice to those who lost their jobs and livelihood to his slash-and-burn tactics: "A company is not your high school or college alma mater. Don't get emotional about it" (Dunlap, 1997, p. 272). "Don't get emotional," he tells workers who must find a way to pay their mortgages and support their families after abruptly losing their jobs in a tight job market—this flippant advice coming from a multimillionaire. As former Labor Secretary Robert Reich remarked when he heard that Dunlap planned to cut thousands of employees at Sunbeam, "There is no excuse for treating employees as if they are disposable pieces of equipment" (quoted in Byrne, 1999, p. 68).

Those who studied Dunlap's autocratic leadership style claim that it consisted of intimidation and fear (Byrne, 1999). As Richard Boynton, president of the household products division of Sunbeam Corporation, put it, "It was like a dog barking at you for hours. He just yelled, ranted, and raved. He was condescending, belligerent, and disrespectful" (Byrne, 1999, p. 5).

Ironically, Dunlap himself was fired as CEO of Sunbeam in June 1998 and he subsequently retired. His trademark downsizing strategy faltered. The company's board of directors apparently lost faith in Dunlap's leadership. Those employees who remained at Sunbeam after the downsizing reportedly cheered when they heard that he had been fired.

Al Dunlap's leadership approach raises ethical concerns. Dunlap's communication exhibited little apparent respect for workers. He told them that if they wanted a friend "get a dog." He created a defensive work climate that squelched personal choice. Dunlap came into an organization ready to wield the downsizing axe, and those most affected by his "burn the walls to heat the house" (Fenton, 2005) tactics were given little say in the matter. He showed "the worst kind of corporate irresponsibility" (Fenton, 2005). Even his honesty became an issue. In 2002, Dunlap paid $500,000 to settle charges by the Securities and Exchange Commission of defrauding investors by inflating sales at Sunbeam. He also paid $15 million to settle a class-action shareholder lawsuit that was based on similar charges (Roland & Mathewson, 2002). As a condition of the settlement, Dunlap was barred from working as an executive at a public company.

A key principle of ethical leadership recently gaining popularity is the dictum to "serve others." Ethical leaders are **servant leaders** who "place the good of followers over their own self-interests and emphasize follower development ... They demonstrate strong moral behavior toward followers" (Northouse, 2013, p. 220). Initially offered by Robert Greenleaf (1977), the concept of servant leadership has been studied and developed more recently (Spears, 2010; Walumbwa et al., 2010). Heavy emphasis is placed on caring for others, not advancing one's own self-interest. Servant leadership embraces the five elements of communication ethics (see Chapter 1; see also Northouse, 2013). A servant leader is scrupulously honest, respectful, and fair toward followers, provides choices for followers when possible, and is responsible for helping the group achieve goals in ethically acceptable ways. These are all important elements to consider when acting as a leader in a small group. "A servant leader is therefore a moral leader" (Dubrin, 2010, p. 108). As Facebook Chief Operating Officer Sheryl Sandberg explains, "Leadership is not bullying and leadership is not aggression. Leadership is the expectation that you can use your voice for good. That you can make the world a better place" (quoted by McFadden & Whitman, 2014).

If reports are accurate, Albert Dunlap, from the point of view of servant leadership, failed. He exhibited little apparent interest in serving others (except perhaps for shareholders), made no obvious attempt to accept social responsibility for those most damaged by his decisions, provided little or no opportunity for anyone to influence or even discuss his choices, and seemed to care little that inequalities and social injustices might occur because of his actions. He was a bully. He earned his "worst boss" designation.

▶ Culture and Leadership: Are Leadership Effectiveness Theories Universal?

"Almost all of the prevailing theories of leadership, and about 98% of the empirical evidence at hand, are rather distinctly American in character" (House & Aditya, 1997, p. 409). This hasn't changed appreciably in recent years. Can we apply the leadership effectiveness theories discussed in this chapter universally across cultures? At this point we simply don't know.

Nevertheless, research does suggest that some differences across cultures regarding leadership do exist. Even though in the United States the importance of leadership is widely taken for granted, other cultures do not necessarily share this view. A huge research project called GLOBE, conducted by a collaborative group of 170 scholars worldwide, studied 62 cultures and 17,300 individuals in 951 organizations. It revealed that status and influence accorded leaders vary widely among cultures (House, 2004). Americans, Arabs, Asians, the British, Eastern Europeans, the French, Germans, Latin Americans, and Russians tend to idealize strong leaders, erecting statues and naming streets and buildings after those thought to be extraordinary. German-speaking parts of Switzerland, the Netherlands, and Scandinavia, however, are generally skeptical of strong leaders and fear their abuse of power. In these countries, public commemoration of leaders is sparse. Leadership characterized as elitist, self-centered, and egotistical is perceived to be slightly effective in Albania, Taiwan, Egypt, Iran, and Kuwait. All other countries in the GLOBE study, however, especially Northern European countries, had a very negative opinion of such leadership.

The participative leadership style, typically accepted or even preferred in Western cultures, is questionably effective in Eastern cultures (Dorfman, 2004). Directive leadership is strongly favored more in Middle Eastern cultures (Scandura et al., 1999).

Listening carefully is also more preferred in the United States than it is in Asian cultures such as China (Jones et al., 1990). This could have implications for leader emergence because being a good listener correlates with assuming a leader role in groups, at least in the United States, as previously noted.

There do seem to be some universals in the cross-cultural research on leadership. The GLOBE study revealed strong endorsement by all cultures examined of such leadership attributes as having foresight and planning ahead; being positive, encouraging, dynamic, motivating, communicative, and informed; and being a team builder. Conversely, "the portrait of an ineffective leader is someone who is asocial, malevolent, and self-focused. Clearly, people from all cultures find these characteristics to hinder effective leadership" (Northouse, 2013, p. 403). Less clearly, being individualistic, status conscious, and a risk taker was viewed as enhancing outstanding leadership in some cultures but impeding outstanding leadership in other cultures (Dorfman et al., 2004). Also, an in-depth study of 1,500 corporate executives and public sector leaders in 60 countries and 33 industries found that among the North American CEOs, 65% viewed integrity as a top trait for tomorrow's leaders, but only 29% to 48% of CEOs from other countries shared this view (Carr, 2010).

Again, even if agreement on a certain set of leadership traits existed across cultures, this would be a far cry from actually demonstrating effective leadership in actual practice. In any case, we still have much to learn about effective leadership and cultures.

With so many perspectives and viewpoints, what do we really know about leadership in groups? **The central, overriding point to make about leadership is that effective leaders adapt to changing situations.** Leaders have to function within a system (leadership is a process not just a person), and change is unavoidable in any system. The "one leadership style fits all" approach is doomed to fail much of the time. Leadership and communication competence are inextricably bound. No specific set of traits, particular style, situational readiness, or set of functions or services will produce effective leadership without the knowledge, skills, sensitivity, commitment, and ethics of all group members participating in the leadership process together.

In summary, leaders emerge in a process of elimination. There are different requirements, however, for gaining the leader role and retaining it once the role has been secured. The key to effective leadership is the ability to adapt to changing situations and to exhibit communication competence in the process.

In Mixed Company

Reflect
on what you've
learned.

▶ Online

Now that you've read Chapter 6, access the online resources that accompany *In Mixed Company* at **www.cengagebrain.com**. Your online resources include:

1. Multiple-choice and true-false **chapter practice quizzes** with automatic correction
2. Digital **glossary**
3. **Flashcards**

QUESTIONS FOR CRITICAL THINKERS

1. Do Adolf Hitler, Joseph Stalin, and Charles Manson qualify as leaders? Explain your answer.
2. If you worked in a culture that has difficulty accepting women as leaders, how should you address this issue?
3. Are there any instances in which being a servant leader might prove to be ineffective, even counterproductive for the group? Explain.

VIDEO *Case Studies*

The American President (1995). Comedy-Drama; PG

Michael Douglas plays the president of the United States as a noble character. Analyze his leadership as an influence process. What style of leadership does he exhibit? Does his leadership seem more managerial/transactional or charismatic?

Horrible Bosses (2011). Dark comedy; R

Three friends decide to murder their horrible bosses. This is a very funny movie in a very dark way. Beware the vulgarity. Examine the depiction of horrible bosses from the perspective of psychopathic leaders.

Jobs (2013). PG-13; Biography/Drama

A fairly bland, but still interesting, retelling of Steve Jobs' ascension from being a college dropout to one of the most influential and recognizable entrepreneurs of the twentieth century. Analyze Jobs' leadership style. Consider all perspectives (traits, style, etc.). Examine how he gains and especially tries to retain leadership.

Star Trek: Into the Darkness (2013). PG-13; Action/Adventure/Sci-Fi

This is a terrific sequel to the initial reboot of the *Star Trek* motion picture series. Analyze Captain Kirk's (Chris Pine) leadership style. Does he adapt to the situation by changing his style to meet changing circumstances? Contrast Kirk's leadership style with Spock's style. Apply the functional perspective and the servant leadership perspective to both individuals.

The Wolf of Wall Street (2013). Biography/Comedy; R

This is a depiction of a true story—the rise and fall of stockbroker Jordan Belfort (Leonardo DiCaprio). This movie is not for the faint at heart. There is very graphic sexual content and vulgarity. Is Belfort a psychopathic leader? Compare his positive traits with his negative qualities and analyze his leadership effectiveness.

Answer to Multiple-Choice Question in Caption on page 185: 4

7 Developing Effective Teams

It began as a ragtag group of street performers led by Guy Laliberte. It grew into something wild and wonderful. In 1984, Laliberte contacted the government in Quebec, Canada, to sponsor a show he called Cirque du Soleil (Circus of the Sun). With a small grant from the government to perform as part of Quebec's 450th anniversary celebration of Jacques Cartier's discovery of Canada, Laliberte's vision came to fruition. His vision was to create a circus of a much different sort, one that would mix street entertainment with traditional circus acts. The success of Cirque du Soleil is unparalleled. It is the largest theatrical production in the world (Jean-Arsenault & Conseil, 2007). It is also a grand exercise in teamwork. Lyn Heward, the creative director at Cirque du Soleil, explains that teamwork is critical. She notes that "no matter what your product is, whether it's computers, cars, or anything else, your results lie in having a passionate strong team of people" (quoted by "Cirque du Soleil," 2011).

Conversely, a disturbing study revealed the alarming statistic that more than 400,000 patients die each year from medical errors in hospitals (James, 2013). Although the causes of this stunning situation are complex, poor teamwork is emerging as a major cause (Catchpole et al., 2008; Nurok et al., 2011). "Teamwork is an important component of patient safety. In fact, communication errors are the most common cause of sentinel events and wrong-site operations in the United States" (Makary et al., 2006). So connected are teamwork and patient safety that the American Heart Association issued a "scientific statement" on teamwork and patient safety in the cardiac operating room. In part it reads: "Nontechnical skills such as communication, cooperation, coordination, and leadership are critical components of teamwork, but limited

MindTap™
Start with a quick warm-up activity.

interpersonal skills underlie adverse events and errors" (Wahr et al., 2013). Others have stated, "Healthcare must have as much improvement in teamwork skills as there has been in technical skills" (Pronovost & Fleischlag, 2010).

What distinguishes successful from unsuccessful teams? Although there are certainly differences between circus teams and surgical teams, **one key to successful teams resides in the communication competence of members** (LaFasto & Larson, 2001). There is a wide variety of teams: sports, legal, classroom project, and creative design, to mountain climbing, surgical, computer programming, and script-writing teams. This wide variety makes team effectiveness a challenge. **The primary purpose of this chapter is to explore how to build and sustain a wide variety of effective teams.** Toward this end, there are four chapter objectives:

1. To describe what is likely to make effective team members,

2. To discuss ways to develop competent team relationships,

3. To explain what structures and functions should be established to build and sustain effective teams,

4. To identify what constitutes effective team leadership.

The need for effective teams increases as our society and world become ever more complex. This is what Maxwell (2001) calls the law of Mount Everest: "As the challenge escalates, the need for teamwork elevates" (p. 52). This is especially true in "high-pressure workplaces, such as nuclear plants, aircraft cockpits, or the military [in which] teamwork is essential to survival" (Appleby & Davis, 2001, p. B2).

The wisdom of teams, however, is sometimes a tough sell in an individualistic culture such as the United States, where individual performance is extolled and personal ego is celebrated (Acuff, 1997). The wisdom of teams, nevertheless, is an underlying theme of this chapter and it will be explored further in subsequent chapters on decision making and problem solving.

How Teams Differ from Groups

All teams are groups, but not all groups are teams. Teams are specialized groups. In this section, we discuss four principal characteristics that identify differences between standard groups and teams.

► Level of Cooperation: The Working Together Imperative

Teams typically manifest a higher level of cooperation than standard groups. Members of standard groups may actually oppose each other, not work together on a common goal. Senate and House committees regularly battle over confirmation of presidential appointees, issues of taxes and spending, the size of government, and the like. Committee members act as adversaries, not team members.

The essence of all teams is collaborative interdependence (Guzzo & Dickson, 1996; Kelley & Littman, 2005). Team members generally must work together or they will be unsuccessful in achieving their goals. When members work mostly for themselves, attempting to advance individual agendas (scoring more points than other teammates), the essence of a team, collaborative interdependence, is missing. The 2004 U.S. men's Olympic basketball team was a huge disappointment (some would say an embarrassment compared to "Dream Teams" of past Olympics). Composed of NBA players such as Tim Duncan and Allen Iverson, American players displayed individual prowess at times, but little actual teamwork (Killion, 2004). Dismantled 92–73 in a preliminary round game by Puerto Rico, a team with just one NBA player, the United States went on to lose three games (equal to the total number of losses in all previous Olympics). Coach Larry Brown remarked after the loss to Puerto

U.S. Navy/Getty Images News/Getty Images

Collaborative interdependence is the essence of teamwork. Each member of the Blue Angels must operate with exact precision in concert with other team members or disaster would strike.

Rico, "We have to become a team in a short period of time. Throw your egos out the window" (quoted by Killion, 2004, p. 3D). Beginning to play more like a team in the medal bracket, the United States won the bronze medal, much better than another group of NBA players who couldn't do better than sixth place for the United States in the 2002 World Games. When you don't work together, regardless of individual skill levels, you're a team in name only.

In contrast, the 2008 U.S. Olympic basketball team concentrated on developing teamwork and foregoing individual stardom. In its eight games, all victories, the U.S. team had more assists than its opponents in every game, emphasizing the players' willingness to pass and engage in team play. In the final against Spain, all five start-ers scored in double figures, exhibiting a willingness to spread the scoring around, not seek personal glory ("Olympic Basketball/2008 Olympics," 2008). This "redeem team" won the gold medal with teamwork. Using a similar teamwork formula, the U.S. repeated its gold medal performance in 2012, defeating eight opponents by an average of 32 points per game.

▶ Diversity of Skills: Looking for Complementarity

Teams usually consist of members with more diverse skills than those found in standard groups. In standard small groups, membership is usually a potluck. You may have lots of desserts but few main dishes. Project groups in my classes have often been stymied because no member has sufficient technical skills to permit the group to choose some of the project options. New members of the student senate are not typically chosen for how well they might blend with and complement other sen-ate members. Often they are chosen because no one else wants the job.

A team requires complementary, not identical, skills. At the IDEO design firm, diverse teams are essential to success (Chion, 2013). When ABC's *Nightline* with Ted Koppel challenged IDEO to redesign the common grocery store shop-ping cart to "see innovation happen," a diverse team of individuals was assembled for the five-day challenge captured on camera. Engineers and industrial designers collaborated and brainstormed with team members whose backgrounds included psychology, architecture, business administration, linguistics, and biology. Peter Skillman led the team because he "had proved an able facilitator under fire, great at leading brainstorms and bringing disparate teams together" (Kelley & Littman, 2001, p. 9).

Scouts looking for talented individuals to join the Cirque du Soleil teams don't seek just dancers, gymnasts, or athletes. The list of team members include contortionists, pickpockets, skateboarders, clowns, "giants," whistlers, fire jugglers, martial artists, even a septuagenarian husband-and-wife acrobatic team and a 3-feet-10-inches tall Brazilian acrobat (Baghai & Quigley (2011).

▶ Group Identity: Operating as a Unit

Teams typically have a stronger group identity than standard groups. In a standard small group, there are only superficial indicators of identity. I serve on the bookstore committee on my campus, whose purpose has been to explore ways to reduce the costs of textbooks for students. No one would recognize from mere appearances what group is meeting. Members certainly don't wear uniforms, brandish a team tattoo, sing a fight song, participate in team cheers ("Go e-books?"), or exhibit anything that might identify the group to the casual observer. Members would have to tell outsiders what group this is and what is our primary purpose. A small group may not even have a specific name. Teams, however, are almost always easily identified. Team names are important and often the subject of intense debate. Consider the national kerfuffle in 2014 regarding whether the name of the Washington *Redskins* NFL football team is racist. Team members have a sense of cohesiveness and oneness that exceeds the typical, standard, small group.

▶ Time and Resources: Commitment to the Team

Most small groups that we join require a limited time commitment and few resources to function. A hiring committee normally requires a few meetings. Once the decision has been made, the committee disbands. Little or no money is necessary to sustain the panel. Teams, however, often require substantial resources and long-term time commitments. Sports teams play for a season and return the next year. Some members may change, but the team remains intact. Team members may devote huge time allotments to perfecting skills to help the team succeed. Teams in organizations may require substantial financial resources, even if the team was formed to work on a specific project, such as the Mars rover team at NASA.

With the four characteristics that distinguish teams from standard groups in mind, I define a **team** as a small number of people with complementary skills who act as an interdependent unit, are equally committed to a common mission, subscribe to a cooperative approach to accomplish that mission, and hold themselves accountable for team performance (Katzenbach & Smith, 1993).

Given this definition, obviously not all small groups can become teams. Boards of directors, student and faculty senates, class discussion groups, task forces, and standing committees are not usually teams because members may simply represent diverse factions at odds with each other. Such groups often lack cohesiveness and cooperation, and group members are usually chosen for reasons other than complementary skills that they bring to the group. Members are expected to attend periodic meetings in which discussion occurs and an occasional vote is taken, but members do not have to work together to accomplish the group's primary goals.

Similarly, not every group dubbed a team truly qualifies. Those small groups that only half-heartedly exhibit the several criteria included in the preceding definition are more pseudo-teams than actual teams. **Pseudo-teams** give the appearance of being teams and of engaging in teamwork without exhibiting the substance of teams. This doesn't mean that every team that fails to meet its goals is a pseudo-team. When small groups truly incorporate all the elements of the definition of teams, yet fail, they are still teams, just relatively ineffective ones for whatever reasons. Sometimes the challenge is simply too great for any team to be successful.

Teams embody a central theme of this text—that cooperation in groups has distinct advantages that should be pursued. Although most material presented in other chapters applies to teams, the analysis and advice is sometimes too general to be practical enough to make teams successful. This chapter offers more specific detail to respond to the unique differences between teams and small groups.

Finally, all groups cannot be teams, but small groups usually benefit from acting more teamlike. Ways that you build teams and induce teamwork are now addressed.

Team Members

Group members are the raw materials of any successful team. Assembling the optimum combination of individuals is the starting point for team building. "Among the top predictors of a team's effectiveness are the qualities of the individuals who make up the team: the skills and competencies they possess, the attitudes they display, the behaviors they engage in" (LaFasto & Larson, 2001, pp. 2–3). Notice that personality traits were not specifically included on this list. There is no solid evidence that any specific personality trait such as conscientiousness, extroversion, agreeableness, and so forth likely contributes significantly to team success (Kichuk & Wiesner, 1998).

Focus Questions

1. **What is the ideal team member?**
2. **Why is the attitude of team members at least as important as their aptitude for decision making and problem solving?**
3. **Should ineffective team members ever be removed from the group?**

▶ Team Slayers: Members' Bad Attitudes and Bad Behavior

For teams to be effective, **attitude is at least as important as aptitude.** A member's natural ability and potential can't compensate for a bad attitude. "Good attitudes ... do not guarantee a team's success, but bad attitudes guarantee its failure" (Maxwell,

2001, p. 106). Corresponding bad behavior that easily flows from bad attitudes diminishes the team process even further.

Egocentrism: Me-Deep in Omnipotence Those who communicate egocentrically reveal the "Me-first" attitude that promotes team friction and weakens team cohesiveness. Egocentrics may even ridicule the fundamental underpinnings of teamwork, namely cooperation. As one T-shirt trumpeted, "My idea of a team is a whole lot of people doing what I tell them to do."

Egocentrism can be a significant problem. Physicians are "steeped in a culture of quiet heroism and taught to exude a confident omnipotence" ("Medical Mistakes," 2003, 4C). This erodes necessary teamwork and contributes to the shocking number of patient deaths from surgical errors. Dr. Dennis O'Leary, president of the Joint Commission on Accreditation of Healthcare Organizations, comments: "Right now, we're dealing with the problem of retraining surgeons who were taught to believe they were the center of the universe, and they're not" (Altman, 2001). O'Leary notes that about 40% of orthopedic surgeons refuse to mark the site of an operation because they are convinced that they could never make a serious site error. Instead of doctors acting godlike, they need to set aside their egos and become team members. As Dr. Martin Makary, a surgeon at John Hopkins and author of one study on poor teamwork and surgical errors notes, "There's a lot of pride in the surgical community. We need to balance out the captain-of-the-ship doctrine" (quoted by Nagourney, 2006). Bloated egos can destroy teams. They can foster defensiveness and perpetuate errors from egocentric control freaks who desire to protect their image more than correct their mistakes.

Team members with a We-orientation have a very different effect on a team than egocentric team members. We-oriented team members typically are more inclined than egocentric members to improve their own performance and to enhance other members' performance (Driskell & Salas, 1992).

Cynicism: Communicating a Can't-Do Attitude Teams are systems, so even a single member can demoralize an entire team. **The attitude that most destroys teamwork and team effectiveness is cynicism.** Cynics communicate negativity by predicting failure and looking for someone or something to criticize, sapping the energy from the team with their negativity. "Cynicism, like a disease, constantly spreads, seeking new receptive hosts. The attitude and the behavior associated with it are contagious" (LaFasto & Larson, 2001, p. 23).

Experience and talent are not contagious, but attitude is. **What you want in a team member is the communication of an optimistic, can-do attitude, not a cynical can't-do attitude.** An optimistic attitude nourishes a team's spirit, braces it for coming challenges, and encourages aspirations to rise and motivation to increase. For example, on April 29, 2007, an overturned gas tanker-truck burst into a fireball and literally melted 165 feet of elevated freeway on the Interstate 80/I-580 connector ramp in the San Francisco Bay area. Initially predicted to take many months and create a gridlock traffic nightmare, the repair of this collapsed section of roadway was completed in an astounding 18 days. Clinton C. Meyers, the contractor on the job, explained how his crew managed to complete the monumental repair in so short a time: "I've got a tremendous organization behind me of dedicated can-do people.... This shows what you can accomplish when everyone works together as a team" (quoted in May, 2007, p. 6B).

Verbal/Nonverbal Abuse: Bad Behavior Kills Teams The 2009 survey by American College of Physician Executives of 2,100 doctors and nurses discussed in Chapter 5 found that 85% of respondents experienced degrading comments and insults, 73% yelling, and 50% cursing (Johnson, 2009). Some nurses were groped by doctors, and one physician reportedly became so enraged over some nurse's perceived inadequacy that he stuffed her head-first into a trashcan ("New Survey," 2009). These and other bad behaviors such as spreading malicious rumors, refusing to work together, inappropriate joking, and throwing objects create a group climate that is the antithesis of teamwork. Hospitals across the country, as a result of these survey findings, are instituting zero-tolerance policies to stamp out such team-killing behavior. Doctors, and some nurses, have been terminated for abusive behavior. No team should permit such bad behavior. It creates defensiveness, when instead you want a supportive, cooperative communication climate for your team to be successful.

Team Member Removal: Expelling the Bad Apple Because even a single member can destroy a system, the "weakest link" in the chain may have to be removed if it prevents the team from being effective (Coutu, 2009). This action, however, should never be taken casually. Removal should be a last resort after efforts to correct problem behavior have been undertaken (see Chapter 2).

The principal candidates for expulsion from a team should be those who persistently display incompetent communication, especially if they show no interest in improving, and those with egocentric and cynical attitudes that disrupt team relationships. Even knowledgeable and highly skilled team members who communicate cynicism may need to be removed. Team members with only average skills and knowledge but who have optimistic, contagious attitudes are far more valuable. Bad attitudes are poison for a team. Those with skills and knowledge deficits can be trained to become more effective team members. Those with poisonous attitudes must either make an attitude adjustment or be expelled before they irreparably ruin the team. Necessary steps to expel these disruptive team members were discussed in detail in Chapter 2.

▶ Team Builders: Choosing and Developing Team Members

Unlike standard groups, teams aren't usually stuck with potluck when member composition is the focus. There are usually choices to be made. Who should become a team member depends on what each potential member has to offer the team.

Experience and Problem-Solving Abilities: Core Competencies "Experience and problem-solving ability are the core competencies that move a team toward its objective" (LaFasto & Larson, 2001, p. 7; see also Ellis et al., 2005). We look for experienced members when forming teams. No one wants a cardiac surgeon who is performing his or her first operation. Who wants to fly with an inexperienced pilot, copilot, or navigator handling the plane? You don't want to mountain climb with a bunch of inexperienced team members. In each case you may forfeit your life. Experience counts because with experience comes knowledge and from knowledge comes problem-solving ability. Experienced group members "have been here before." Those who have limited experience may compensate by demonstrating a strong problem-solving aptitude.

Although the problem-solving potential of technical experience is necessary for team effectiveness, other elements are also required (Marks et al., 2002). In a study of high-performing and low-performing surgical teams, it was found that high-performing teams had handpicked their team members. Members were chosen not on the basis of surgical experience, because all members had such experience, but on the basis of prior experience working together as a team and the demonstrated ability of each member to work well in a group. Low-performing teams picked members mostly on the basis of availability. As one nurse commented about her hospital's method of choosing surgical group members, "We don't have any real teams here. It's just who gets assigned on any given day" ("Teamwork," 2002, p. 5). Without appropriate teamwork knowledge and skill development, members of action teams (surgical teams, military units, expedition teams, rescue teams, and the like) "can be unprepared to work as an interdependent unit" (Ellis et al., 2005, p. 642; see also Hollenbeck et al., 2004).

Cultural Diversity: Members with Different Perspectives Increasingly, teams are composed of members from diverse cultures. This is especially true of virtual teams. An extensive survey of 600 employees of multinational corporations who were members of virtual teams, for example, found that in the majority of teams nearly half of the members were located outside of the home country (Solomon, 2010). With member diversity comes a rich array of different, complementary skills and knowledge with the potential for great decision-making and problem-solving creativity (see the Chapter 2 discussion of deep diversity).

Nevertheless, culturally diverse team membership poses significant challenges (Adler, 2002; Barinaga, 2007). Americans, for instance, take pride in decisive decision making. In Japan and China, however, speed is not a high priority. Decision making is a lengthy process of chewing over all possible options before choosing (Adler, 2001).

There are several guidelines for managing membership diversity in teams (Adler, 2002). These closely parallel suggestions offered in Chapter 3 for addressing the challenges of diverse membership in groups generally.

1. Accept diversity as an advantage, not a disadvantage, for the team. With greater challenge can come greater rewards.

2. Choose team members for their complementary skills and knowledge but also for their similarity of attitude. Regardless of cultural background, there is no place for egocentrism or cynicism on teams.

3. Choose a superordinate, transcending goal to bridge differences (more on this in the section on team goals).

4. Be respectful of all team members and avoid cultural bias. The American way of doing things is not always the best way. Be experimental and try different approaches.

5. Keep communication open. Solicit feedback on the decision-making process so that if problems arise, they can be addressed immediately.

Communication Training: Developing Members' Competence Team members often lack necessary communication competence. A study (LaFasto & Larson, 2001) of diverse teams from sports, law, law enforcement, science, education, health care, computing, transportation, and telecommunications, among others, asked the question: "If you could discuss one issue in an open way, involving the team in the discussion, what would that issue be?" Overwhelmingly, team members responded, "the team's communication." Team communication is critical to its effectiveness, and high-performing team members typically exhibit superior communication skills (Curtis et al., 1988).

Training, however, must be an integral part of the team equation for success (Ellis et al., 2005). One study of operating room staff found that those groups trained in effective teamwork had significantly reduced deaths from surgical errors than those groups that did not receive such training (Neily et al., 2010). A college course can provide useful communication training for student team members.

Workplace training, however, is often of dubious quality and efficacy (Goleman, 1998). Frequently, these training programs consist of little more than a weekend "dog and pony show" by an outside consultant followed by "happy sheets" that indicate participants' degree of liking for the training. Liking, however, does not equal learning, and popularity ratings favor slick, cleverly packaged training programs that provide fun and entertainment but are as worthwhile as a sugar donut to a diabetic. Instead of these slick, superficial training sessions, you want training programs that teach team members specific communication knowledge and skills relevant to the team's task (crews flying an airplane; design teams solving problems). Such context-specific team training is effective in enhancing teamwork and team effectiveness (Ellis et al., 2005; Stout et al., 1997).

One such program was piloted in 2007 at Pennsylvania Hospital in Philadelphia. Called the Unit-Based Clinical Leadership (UBCL) program, this program sought to establish doctor–nurse partnerships. UBCL trained participants to improve communication, collaborate, and share responsibility and ownership for patient care, to become members of a team who functioned as a team. "The UBCL pilot not only resulted in breakthrough improvements in quality and patient safety, but also forged better physician–nurse collaboration and job satisfaction as well" (Buckley et al., 2009). Another training program at Maine General Hospital essentially taught the difference between defensive and supportive communication skills addressed in Chapter 4. The results were nothing short of astounding: Team members were 167% more likely to address directly anyone demonstrating poor teamwork behavior and the same percentage were more likely to speak up when a doctor or nurse exhibited disrespectful behavior (Grenny, 2009). Changing the communication changes the system. Communication training works to build teams!

Building Teamwork

Does teamwork improve team performance? The evidence clearly shows that it does (see Stout et al., 1997, for a review). Building teamwork, however, is a complicated process that unfolds over time. In this section, key aspects of building teamwork are discussed.

Focus Questions

1. What kinds of goals work best to build a team?
2. How is a team identity developed?
3. Should team roles be chosen by team members?

▶ Developing Team Goals: The Four Cs

Setting specific goals is an important step in the team-building process (Klein et al., 2009). "As Outward Bound and other team-building programs illustrate, specific objectives have a leveling effect conducive to team behavior. When a small group of people challenge themselves to get over a wall … their respective titles, perks, and other stripes fade into the background" (Katzenbach & Smith, 1993, p. 114). Everyone becomes a team member, not a member of a power structure. Team goals should be *clear, cooperative,* and *challenging,* and team members should be *committed* to team goals.

Clear Goals: Everyone on the Same Page LaFasto and Larson's (2001) study of 600 teams and 6,000 team members found that "With amazing consistency, team members acknowledge the unease that comes with trying to achieve an ambiguous goal" (p. 74). In another study by the same authors, all teams were effective that had clear, identifiable goals that members thoroughly grasped (Larson & LaFasto, 1989). Ambiguous goals, such as "do our best" or "make improvements," offer no clear direction. "Complete the study of parking problems on campus by the end of the term," "raise $350,000 in donations within two years for a campus child care center," or "institute a textbook loan program on campus by the start of spring term" are clear, specific goals. For a group to become an effective team, clearly stated and understood goals are essential (Hoegl & Parboteeah, 2003). This means that terms such as "parking problems," "campus child care center," and "textbook loan program" have to be defined clearly at the very start of a team's effort. Definitional discussions should identify what is and is not included in the team's charge. The **charge** is the task of the team, such as to gather information, to analyze a problem and make recommendations, to make decisions and implement them, or to tackle a specific project from inception to completion. A team can determine that a goal has been clearly articulated when all members can identify how they will know when the charge has been accomplished. For example, is an oral or written report required? Does the team report to a higher authority with its results? Are there statistical measures that indicate completion ($350,000 is raised for the child care center)?

In some cases the goals will be specified by the organization within which teams operate. In other instances, the team will decide through discussion what goals they wish to pursue. In either case, the number of goals should be limited to what can reasonably be accomplished within the specified time period. Romig (1996) found one departmental team in an organization that pursued 60 goals in a single year. None of its goals were achieved, and the team actually threatened the future of the entire organization by losing huge sums of money as it flailed aimlessly in all directions. A few clear goals that each team member can recite from memory are preferable to goals that are too numerous for members to recall.

Cooperative Goals: Interdependent Challenges Cooperative goals require interdependent effort from all team members. It is in every member's self-interest to promote the team goal and help each other achieve team success. Members share information, offer advice, share rewards, and apply their abilities to make every team

Jasper Juinen/Getty Images News /Getty Images

This photo illustrates which of the necessary qualities of team goals?

1. Clear goal
2. Cooperative goal
3. Challenging goal
4. Commitment to goal

Answers are given at the end of the chapter.

member optimally effective. **Research clearly shows that cooperative goals enhance team performance,** while pursuing individual goals within a team structure diminishes team performance (Tjosvold & Yu, 2004; Van Mierlo & Kleingeld, 2010).

A **superordinate goal**, a specific kind of cooperative goal that overrides differences that members may have because it supersedes less important competitive goals, is particularly effective for developing teamwork (Sherif, 1966; Sherif et al., 1988). When a group faces a common predicament that jeopardizes its very existence, for example, survival becomes the superordinate goal that can galvanize members to pull together in common cause.

The story of Fred Beasley illustrates a superordinate goal in action. Fred's father died when he was 12 years old, leaving a wife and nine children to survive on a paltry Social Security income. The superordinate family goal following the loss of Fred's dad was to keep the family intact. No other goal was as important. Achieving this goal was accomplished by sharing labor and resources. Alma Beasley, Fred's mom, got jobs cleaning houses. All nine kids found odd jobs. Whatever income was earned from these jobs was pooled to cover family, not individual, needs. Four boys slept in the same room. Dresser drawers were divided among the kids. Household chores were everybody's responsibility. Alma Beasley explains how the family remained together through difficult times: "It was tough on all of us.... I just did the best I could. I think we all pulled together" (Judge, 1998, p. D8).

Sometimes groups choose a cooperative goal of simply doing the best they can for all members of the team. The first women's team to be invited to climb Mount Kongur in China didn't set as its target getting one team member on top of the mountain. Instead, the team chose a cooperative goal to get as many team members as high up the mountain as possible (Larson & LaFasto, 1989). With a cooperative goal, success is determined by everyone pulling together to produce the best results for every member—no winners or losers.

Challenging Goals: Denting the Universe Accomplishing the mundane motivates no one. Teams need challenging goals to spark members' best efforts. **Members need to feel that they are embarking on a shared mission, with a common vision of how to translate the dream into a team achievement.** The team that built the first successful Macintosh computer had this elevated sense of purpose. Randy Wigginton, a team member, remembers: "We believed we were on a mission from God" (Bennis & Biederman, 1997, p. 83). Steve Jobs, the team leader, promised team members that they were going to develop a computer that would "put a dent in the universe" (p. 80).

Changing the world or setting records, of course, doesn't have to be the team's dream. More down-to-earth visions can easily motivate team members. "Lowering the cost of textbooks by 25%," "doubling the number of effective tutoring programs on campus," or "making the campus safer by replacing old lighting systems with brighter, energy-efficient systems" can be challenging goals for campus teams. Your team may not put a dent in the universe, but it may chip away at a serious local problem.

Commitment to Goals: A Passion to Succeed In a massive study of 1.4 million workers in 66 countries for the Gallup Organization, one key finding was that "trusting that one's coworkers share a commitment to quality is a key to great team performance" (Buckingham & Coffman, 2002). Commitment is a key element of communication competence. It is also essential to team success. "Without it, groups perform as individuals; with it, they become a powerful unit of collective performance" (Katzenbach & Smith, 1993, p. 112).

One key way to create commitment is to have team members share in setting goals for the team (Romig, 1996). Although not always possible, whenever participatory goal setting can be instituted it is advisable to do so. Team members typically respond better to goals that they have had a hand in creating than to those that are foisted upon them by others.

▶ Developing a Team Identity: Unifying Members

A group becomes a team when it establishes its own identity, both to team members and to outsiders. Team identity is an important part of team building. There is no single way to create a team identity; there are a number of possibilities. Certainly, establishing a mission is a key element. Strategies for developing a team identity are developing fantasy themes, creating solidarity symbols, and using team talk.

Symbolic Convergence: Communicating Fantasy Themes Ernest Bormann (1986) developed what he termed **symbolic convergence theory**. Moving beyond an analysis of the individual, Bormann focused on how people communicating with each other develop and share stories that create a "convergence," a group identity that is larger and more coherent than the isolated experiences of individual group members. These stories, or fantasies, create a shared meaning for group members. Bormann defines fantasies without the negative connotation of "delusions" or "flights from reality." **Fantasies**, he says, are the dramatic stories that provide a shared interpretation of events that bind group members and offer them a shared identity. These fantasies will have heroes and villains, a plot, conflict—anything a well-told story would have.

In my own Communication Studies department, composed of between 9 and 12 members over the years, a common **fantasy theme**—a consistent thread that runs through the stories told by departmental members—is the challenge to survive and thrive among many much larger departments with far greater clout. I periodically tell the story of my early days at Cabrillo College when our department was under attack from some members of the administration. I relate the drama over the battle for full-time replacements of two retiring instructors, how this battle got me kicked out of the president's office, and how I waged our departmental campaign before the college board, the faculty senate, and the faculty union. Each new member of the department gets to hear a retelling of this story, embellished somewhat over the years. The story serves to create our team identity as a small but determined, even formidable, department.

More recently, after our department exhibited substantial growth in student demand, I have offered the fantasy theme of empire building. Initially seen as a dubious undertaking, the theme has more recently gained adherents. It permits departmental members to imagine a time when our department will be regarded as a major player on campus. **The fantasy theme serves as a motivation to team members to strive for goals that are not merely ordinary, but rather, extraordinary.** Department members share a common experience, and fantasies provide a shared interpretation of these events. Each member of our department can relate additional stories that play on the fantasy theme, creating **fantasy chains**—a string of connected stories that amplify the theme. In this way, a team creates its own identity.

Solidarity Symbols: Unifying Nonverbally Another way to develop team identity is by creating "solidarity symbols" (Kelley & Littman, 2001). A team name or logo can be a solidarity symbol. The presidential campaign team headed by James Carville that guided Bill Clinton to victory in the 1992 election was dubbed the War Room team. A uniform or style of dress can also serve as a solidarity symbol. The Green Berets uniform or the jeans and T-shirt attire often found at IDEO are examples (Chion, 2013). In fact, T-shirts with individualized inscriptions or sayings—humorous, profound, or just plain whimsical—help establish the loose team climate characteristic of design teams. In other instances, an entire team may wear T-shirts with the same inscription, such as a computer-programming team that wore T-shirts inscribed "Talk Nerdy to Me."

At Urban Prep, a Chicago charter high school started in 2006 by Tim King, the accent is on academic achievement. An all-boys school, Urban Prep is swimming against the tide of young black males dropping out of high school. In Chicago, the drop-out rate is 60% among young African American males, but at Urban Prep, where the focus is on team study groups and high expectations, *all 110 seniors* not only graduated in 2010, but they all were accepted to colleges. In 2013, for the fourth year in a row, all seniors, 167 of them, were accepted at four-year colleges ("Urban Prep Graduates All," 2013). All boys wear blazers and ties and matching wristwatches (to make sure they arrive on time to classes). When a senior receives a letter of acceptance to a college, that letter is posted on a bulletin board as a solidarity symbol of pride. The standard

David Madison/Crush/Corbis

Which solidarity symbols useful for creating team identity are apparent in this photo?

red tie that is part of the uniform, which according to student Israel Wilson "symbolizes that we're here on business," is then traded for one with gold stripes as a symbol of business accomplished (Clark & Meadows, 2010).

Team Talk: The Language of We Team talk is another strategy for creating a team identity and cohesiveness. "A shared language bonds a team together and serves as a visible sign of membership" (Bolman & Deal, 1992, p. 40). Cirque du Soleil refers to auditions as "treasure hunting," intense training sessions as "boot camp," and describes teams as "family" (Quigley & Baghai, 2011). One software team refers to unproductive discussions as *ratholes;* team members spending too much time agreeing with each other are said to be *piling on* (Fisher, 2000, p. 300). At Urban Prep, students recite a creed each day that includes the phrase "I am college bound." Teachers address students as "Mr. Smith" or "Mr. Johnson." As principal King explains, "It's a sign of respect that creates the idea they are special, they are going somewhere" (Clark & Meadows, 2010, p. 134).

Teams establish an identity, a oneness, when they speak in terms of "we" and "our" and "us," not "he/her/they" (Donnellon, 1996). This language of shared identity is especially important for team leaders to use (Platow et al., 2006). Team talk emphasizes interdependence and avoids terminology that emphasizes individuality. The language of individual blame and criticism is avoided. Effective teams speak of collective blame for failure and give collective praise for success. This is the language of team accountability.

Team failure is "our" failure. Team success is also a matter of collective responsibility, and team talk should reflect this. Rafael Aguayo (1990) taught team accountability for success, not individual glory, when he coached a Little League soccer team. Following each game, he asked his players, "Who scored that first goal?" Typically at first, only the player who kicked the ball into the net raised a hand. "No!" Aguayo cried. "We all scored that goal. Every person on a team is responsible for scoring a goal." Then he repeated the question, "Now, who scored that goal?" All team members learned to raise their hands. In four years of Little League soccer, Aguayo's teams lost only a single game.

Language that exhibits power differences also should be avoided. "Think about the difference between 'the boss holds me accountable' and 'we hold ourselves accountable'" (Katzenbach & Smith, 1993, p. 116). "Powerful" and "powerless" language is discussed in detail in Chapter 10.

▶ Designating Clear, Appropriate Roles: Room for One Quarterback

Unlike most informal small groups in which roles emerge from the transactions of members, **teams usually require a formal designation of roles.** You don't want *role ambiguity* that produces confusion and duplication when team members are unsure of the parts they are expected to play (Klein et al., 2009). A football team can't function effectively if individual team members decide which roles they plan to play. You might end up with 15 quarterbacks and no cornerbacks. Remember that formal roles identify a position (goalie, defensive end, project leader, chief surgeon), and a description of the expected behavior is explicitly spelled out (orally or in writing by a coach, supervisor, or team leader).

A team must have every group function covered by a qualified member playing a specific role so there is little or no duplication of effort. A surgical team has clearly designated roles for each member. Nurses aren't supposed to step in and begin performing heart surgery. Every function is critical to the success of the team. If only some roles are played but others are ignored, several important team functions will be sacrificed, sometimes with disastrous results.

In a huge Gallup study of 80,000 managers and 1 million employees (Buckingham & Coffman, 1999), one manager, named Michael, who runs a highly successful restaurant in the Pacific Northwest was singled out. He was asked to tell about his best restaurant team ever. He told of his waitstaff of four individuals: Brad, Gary, Emma, and Susan. According to Michael's description, Brad was a professional waiter who aspired to being the best waiter in town. He could anticipate what customers wanted—more water or coffee, a dessert menu—without needing to be asked. Gary always smiled and was cheerful.

Everyone liked him, especially the customers. He had an optimistic attitude. Emma was the unspoken team builder. She regularly assembled the team and alerted the crew members to potential problems. Finally, there was Susan, who was the greeter. She was lively, energetic, and pleasant. She kept track of customers at lunch who typically needed quick service to return to work. She was attentive. "These four were the backbone of my best team ever. I didn't really need to interfere. They ran the show themselves.... For a good three years they were the restaurant" (Buckingham & Coffman, 1999, p. 14).

Michael noted that each team member had his or her clearly defined role. "Brad is a great waiter, but he would be a terrible manager.... He respects the customers. He is less respectful of some of the new employees" (p. 16). Qualities that made Susan a great greeter wouldn't necessarily translate into being an efficient waitperson. Emma worked well with her team members, but she had a quiet personality not particularly suitable for a greeter. Gary would have been a weak team builder. Michael actually fired him, twice, but hired him back. His joking around went too far and he had to be reined in before he created team friction. Finding the appropriate roles for each team member can be a big challenge. It is vital, however, that each member plays the role suited to his or her abilities. Finding the appropriate team member for each vital role permits full utilization of the team's resources.

The original reason that a person is asked to join a team may make role designation automatic. It is not unusual, however, to find that the roles originally contemplated for

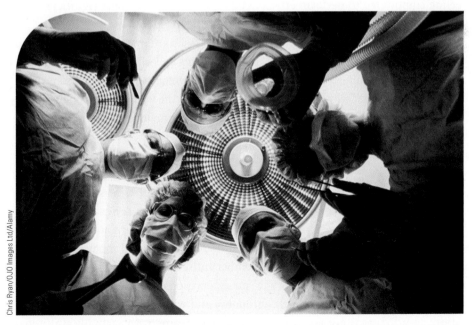

Chris Ryan/OJO Images Ltd/Alamy

Teams usually require a formal designation of roles. Imagine this surgical team functioning efficiently with every member vying for the chief surgeon role.

team members don't work well and must be changed to make the team more effective. **One of the responsibilities of a team leader is to make determinations regarding role designations.**

▶ Structuring Team Empowerment: Enhancing Members' Capabilities

"Highly empowered teams are more effective than less empowered teams" (Jordan et al., 2002). This is true for both face-to-face and virtual teams (Kirkman et al., 2004). A key element of team building is structuring team empowerment.

Definition of Empowerment: Four Dimensions The concept of **empowerment** is the process of enhancing the capabilities and influence of individuals and groups. **There are four dimensions of empowerment: potency, meaningfulness, autonomy, and impact** (Kirkman & Rosen, 1999). **Group potency** is the "shared belief among team members that they can be effective as a team" (Jordan et al., 2002, p. 125). It's a can-do group attitude. There is a strong relationship between group potency and team performance (Gully et al., 2002; Stajkovic et al., 2009). Those teams whose members are confident that their team can perform effectively, not just on a single task but across many different tasks, typically perform effectively, whereas teams with low group potency do not perform as well (Jordan et al., 2002). Feeling empowered to perform effectively as a team can contribute significantly to team success (Kennedy et al., 2009; Kozlowski & Ilgen, 2006).

Meaningfulness is a team's perception that its tasks are important, valuable, and worthwhile (Kirkman & Rosen, 1999). Team members collectively influence this perception of meaningfulness by their communication. Cynicism expressed by some team members can create a "why bother" attitude throughout the team. Optimism expressed by team members can have the reverse effect, convincing members that the team's task is important and worth performing well. When team members view a task as very meaningful, social loafing disappears and they work harder collectively than they would individually (Karau & Elsaid, 2009).

Autonomy is "the degree to which team members experience substantial freedom, independence, and discretion in their work" (Kirkman & Rosen, 1999, p. 59). Choice empowers team members (Chua & Iyengar, 2006). Team autonomy means that important decision making is a shared undertaking by all members. Because of interconnectedness, no single team member entirely runs the show. Nevertheless, autonomy doesn't mean that teams have no supervision or guidance (Dubrin, 2010). Teams with a great deal of member autonomy and with limited supervision (facilitation, coordination) are far more effective than teams with virtually unlimited autonomy (Romig, 1996). IDEO has substantial member autonomy but some supervision by David Kelley and team leaders.

Impact is the degree of significance given by those outside of the team, typically the team's organization, to the work produced by the team (Kirkman & Rosen, 1999). Impact is often manifested by change outside of the team. If a team makes proposals for change in an organization but those proposals are mostly ignored and little change occurs, the message communicated is that the organization is indifferent to the team's suggestions.

▶ Hierarchy of Traditional Organizations

In traditional organizational hierarchies, decision-making power flows from top down to the bottom of the pyramid, and influence from those at the bottom on those at the top levels is difficult. (See Figure 7.1.)

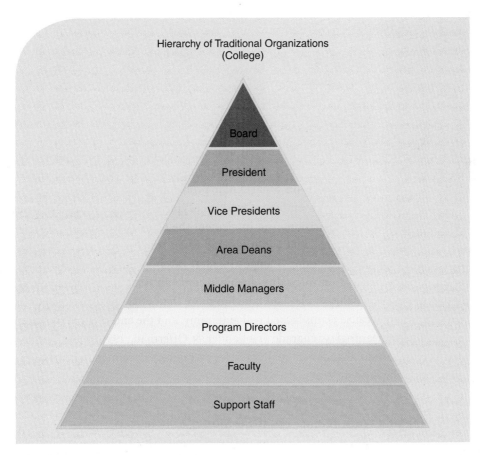

Hierarchy of Traditional Organizations
(College)

Board

President

Vice Presidents

Area Deans

Middle Managers

Program Directors

Faculty

Support Staff

FIGURE 7.1
Hierarchy in traditional organizations with its rigid rules and roles makes empowerment challenging.

Hierarchical Organizations: The Enemy of Empowerment Traditionally, organizations have been hierarchical, meaning that members of the organization are rank ordered in a kind of pyramid of power: CEOs, presidents, and vice presidents are at the top of the pyramid, upper management is next, followed by middle and lower management, and finally the common workers are spread out at the base (see Figure 7.1). Top-down decision making is the rule, with those at the top of the power pyramid issuing edicts to managers, who in turn tell the worker bees what to do. Employees at the bottom of the pyramid mostly check their brains at the door because they won't be asked to participate in decision making and problem solving. Their role is merely the "heavy lifting."

Hierarchy in traditional organizations is the enemy of empowerment (Kelley & Littman, 2001). Although some degree of hierarchy provides necessary structure for organizations, flattening traditional, rigid hierarchy somewhat is desirable. Empowerment flattens the organizational hierarchy by sharing power. The organizational system becomes more open with information and communication flowing in all directions, with few gatekeepers obstructing the flow, and with decision making across the organizational spectrum encouraged.

Quality Circles: Lame First Attempt Motivated by the economic success of Japan in the early 1980s and its successful experience with teams, coupled with anemic economic growth in America, organizations in the United States began attempts to flatten the hierarchy. Initial attempts involved the establishment of **quality circles**—teams composed of employees who volunteered to work on a specific task and attempted to solve a particular problem. Quality circles proved to be a half-hearted attempt to empower workers. Typically, these teams had little autonomy to make final decisions and implement the team's wisdom. Mostly, recommendations were offered that could be, and often were, easily ignored by the higher-ups in the organization. Change (impact) rarely occurred, so the meaningfulness of participation in quality circles became an issue for team members. By the mid-1980s, quality circles had failed in more than 60% of the organizations that tried them because teams lacked real autonomy, and the entire effort too often seemed like a meaningless charade (Hollander & Offerman, 1990; Marks, 1986). Many organizations abandoned quality circles as a failed experiment within a year of initiating them (Dubrin et al., 1989).

Self-Managing Work Teams: The IDEO Model Self-regulating teams that complete an entire task are called **self-managing work teams**. This type of team emerged as a more effective alternative to quality circles. Self-managing work teams embrace empowerment (see Closer Look: "IDEO and Team Empowerment"). After sufficient training and education, team members share responsibility for planning, organizing, setting goals, making decisions, and solving problems (Teubner, 2000). They have a great deal of autonomy because they are self-managed, and since they control a great deal of their own decision making and problem solving, team results seem meaningful to members and have impact on organizations. As self-managing teams manifest success, group potency increases, further reinforcing members' desire to continue with the team.

Impediments to Team Empowerment: No Buy-In There are four primary impediments to team empowerment (Hollander & Offerman, 1990). First, **organizations can sabotage their own teams.** David Kelley's careful structuring of IDEO to foster team empowerment illustrates how important it is that the larger organization doesn't work at cross-purposes with teams working within the organization (LaFasto & Larson, 2001). Teams functioning within organizations are subsystems operating within a larger system. Their interconnectedness requires that every part of the organizational structure embrace empowerment for teams to be successful (Harris & Beyerlein, 2003; Kennedy et al., 2009). IDEO's corporate culture embraces and nurtures empowerment and teamwork. When organizations establish teams but fail to provide sufficient structural support for team empowerment, the organization is merely paying lip service to the concept of empowering teams. Not all organizations, of course, are as dependent on teams as IDEO, nor should they be. In some organizations, **ad hoc teams**—teams that are assembled to solve an immediate problem, then dissolved once the solution has been implemented—are sufficient. Self-managing teams may be too time consuming and irrelevant for simple tasks more easily and efficiently tackled by one or two knowledgeable individuals.

Second, **not everyone embraces empowered teams.** Those accustomed to receiving and following directives from supervisors may not adapt well to new responsibilities and autonomy (Thoms et al., 2002). Some individuals'

CLOSER LOOK

IDEO and Team Empowerment

IDEO, a design firm discussed briefly in Chapter 4, is a prime example of the empowered team approach. In fact, IDEO is considered so effective at team empowerment that for the last several years it has served as a consultant for diverse organizations all over the world (Kelley & Littman, 2001; see also **www.ideo.com**). "IDEO has been on a mission not just to serve business, but to reform it" (Myerson, 2001, p. 8). This effort has been dubbed IDEO University.

IDEO has a flattened hierarchy characterized by few titles and no time clocks or specified vacation schedules (Hyatt, 2010). Employees are free to transfer to overseas offices in London or Tokyo or to transcontinental offices in Chicago or New York, as long as someone from those offices agrees to swap jobs. A team of designers, not "the boss," chooses new team members. At IDEO, employees are treated as equals who set their own schedules (typically 50- to 60-hour workweeks) while meeting demanding standards and strict deadlines. Designers can pick project teams and even occasionally specific projects to tackle. "Its flat multi-disciplinary 'hot team' structure is democratic, engages the client directly in the work, and reflects the idea that 'big ideas come from small teams'" (Myerson, 2001, p. 30).

The pyramid structure and the star system are replaced with team empowerment. Status at IDEO is based on talent, not seniority (Kelley & Littman, 2001). As one designer puts it, "The only way to enhance your reputation in the organization is by earning the respect of your peers" (Myerson, 2001, p. 31). Each of IDEO's studios, with between 25 and 30 designers apiece, has maximum autonomy to shape its work environment. Each studio reflects the personality of the design team residing in the space provided. One studio team hung a $4,000 DC3 airplane wing from the ceiling to create a "cool space."

"Hierarchy is the enemy of cool space" (Kelley & Littman, 2001, p. 136). As founder David Kelley explains, "The general principle with work environments at IDEO is to try stuff and then ask forgiveness, rather than ask for permission first" (Myerson, 2001, p. 30). Traditional organizations assign office space and create a pecking order for the high-status "corner office with a window." Rules forbidding personal items such as family photos, wall posters, and the like are rigidly enforced. Office square footage traditionally is a status symbol in hierarchical organizations. IDEO's director of business development, David Haygood, tells the story of one of his previous employers who assigned workers to dismal, tiny cubicles if they were "grade 19" or lower, while workers given a grade 20 or above got hard-walled offices with an actual door. When reorganization occurred, grade 20 employees engaged in a competitive squabble to seize the offices with the most square footage. When Haygood moved to another company, he had the false ceiling of his office ripped out and overhead fixtures spray-painted black. His office was purposely the worst in the building. When some of his employees complained to him about their inferior offices, Haygood offered to switch with them (Kelley & Littman, 2001). He got no takers. David Kelley's office at IDEO is remarkably similar to the offices of his designers.

QUESTIONS FOR THOUGHT

1. Do you think the IDEO-empowered team approach would work in every organization? What might prevent it from translating well to some organizations?
2. Would an IDEO-type organization appeal to you? Explain. Would you have any reservations about working in an organization structured like IDEO?

attitudes may be antagonistic to empowered teams. If so, they are unlikely to become effective, self-managing team members. This can be true of individuals assigned to teams to act as project leaders. If team leaders are held responsible for team failure when team decisions may contradict the leader's preference, it is not difficult to understand the reluctance of the leader to embrace self-managing teams.

Third, **when participation in decision making is a sham, empowerment is thwarted.** Collaborative effort will disintegrate if group members feel that their participation merely rubber-stamps decisions already made by others with more power. If the team is not trusted to make careful, deliberative decisions, and if the team's choices are not respected, then participative decision making will quickly be perceived as a deceptive game that only creates the illusion of choice.

A review of 47 studies revealed that meaningful participation in decision making increases worker productivity and job satisfaction (Miller & Monge, 1986). When participative decision making fails, it typically fails because participation was minimal, only some individuals were allowed to participate, the decisions teams were allowed to make were relatively inconsequential, or the team's choices were essentially ignored by upper management (Kohn, 1993).

Finally, **when rewards are distributed based on individual effort or ability, not team success, empowerment is impeded.** "These rewards can often inhibit team members' willingness to work together and help one another, even when the success of the team depends on it" (Kozlowski & Ilgen, 2007, p. 57). There are essentially three ways rewards can be distributed in a group: *winner-take-all* based on individual merit, *equitable distribution* (proportional), and *equal distribution*. An equal distribution of rewards to all team members gives the best results for team success; the competitive winner-take-all system gives the poorest results (Deutsch, 1985; Kirkman & Shapiro, 2000). Equal distribution of rewards provides potential motivation for all group members. It also enhances mutual self-esteem and respect, team loyalty, and congenial personal relationships and communication within the group (Deutsch, 1979). A merit system of rewards (winner-take-all) is intrinsically competitive. Designating only some team members as meritorious implicitly brands other members as deficient and unworthy of rewards for team success. Almost all of the 3,000 studies conducted on merit pay show either no positive results or serious disadvantages, such as divisiveness, demoralization, and hostile communication (Charnofsky et al., 1998).

There are also serious drawbacks to equitable reward distribution—proportional reward based on individual effort and influence. "The quest for individual rewards often leads to a great deal of tension when benefits are to be distributed. People disagree if they do not receive as much as expected" (Brislin, 1993, p. 53).

SECOND LOOK

Typical Characteristics of Empowered Teams

1. Teams set their own goals and rules.
2. Team members often set their own work schedules.
3. Teams usually design their own work space.
4. Work space is divided relatively equally among members.
5. Members devise and embrace rules for appropriate member behavior.
6. Teams as a whole are accountable for team performance.
7. Teams determine their membership and remove members who are deemed ineffective or disruptive.
8. Team members are trained to communicate collaboratively and supportively.
9. Decision making is typically democratic, and leadership is participative.
10. Team members don't ask for permission from the team leader to take risks or make changes, but negotiate with the team and strive for consensus.

► Establishing Individual Accountability: Providing Feedback

Team accountability diffuses the blame for failure and spreads the praise for success. Team building, however, also requires **individual accountability**, which establishes a minimum standard of effort and performance for each team member to share the fruits of team success. Team effort is not truly cooperative if some members are slackers who let others do all the work. You must have a mechanism for individual accountability to discourage social loafing (Kozlowski & Ilgen, 2007; Salas et al., 2005). A team needs to catch errors, lapses in judgment, and slip-ups. Establishing a cooperative communication climate for the group is essential to productive individual accountability. Mutual performance monitoring in which all team members take responsibility for catching errors provides descriptive feedback to team members with the emphasis on improvement, not blaming or tearing down someone (see the Chapter 4 discussion on defensive versus supportive communication).

Individual accountability standards should not be set so high that they assure failure. Opportunities for social loafers to redeem themselves should be available. **The focus should be on raising all team members above the minimum standards— way above if possible—not on looking for ways to designate failures** (Druskat &

Wolff, 1999). Minimum standards agreed to in advance by the group might include the following: no more than two missed meetings, no more than two incidents of tardiness or early exits from meetings, work turned in to the group on time, and work of satisfactory quality as determined by peer appraisal.

Individual accountability is not the same as rank ordering of group members' performances or distributing rewards based on merit. **Individual accountability merely provides feedback that establishes a floor below which no one should drop, not a ceiling that only a very few can reach.** A plan to deal with social loafing was discussed in Chapter 3. Implement it.

Competent Team Leadership

Team leadership is a core component of teamwork (Dubrin, 2010; Salas et al., 2005). Teams require leadership even if they are self-managing. Remember that leadership is not a person but a process. A team may have a designated leader (coach, manager, project director), but leadership in teams is a shared responsibility. Teams don't require management from a supervisor, and they don't need to be left leaderless. They do need guidance and facilitation to ensure that goals are being met. In this section, communication strategies that produce competent team leadership are explored.

Focus Questions

1. Which style of leadership, directive or participative, is usually most effective with teams? In all situations?
2. How does fear diminish teamwork and team effectiveness?
3. What are supportive rules and how should they be established in a team?

► Fostering Participative Leadership: Nurturing Empowerment

Team leaders don't act like bosses or supervisors if they hope to be effective. Team leaders are teachers and facilitators—skill builders. They are open to input from team members. The head coach of a football team may make many final decisions, but participative leadership requires consultation with assistant coaches in devising game plans, utilizing personnel effectively, and dealing with the inevitable problems that emerge during the course of a season. Coaches for offensive, defensive, and special teams encourage input from players so that difficulties arising during the game can be discovered, analyzed effectively, and resolved before it's too late. One person cannot be expected to know everything, so participative leadership encourages the sharing of knowledge and wisdom. Encouraging skill building, delegating meaningful responsibility, and sharing decision making and problem solving empowers members (Hollander & Offerman, 1990). Maximum utilization of team resources requires all members, not just the leader, to think for themselves. That's how group potency is fostered. Remember, coaches can't think for the players when they're out on the field playing the game.

As explained in Chapter 6, **a situation (such as military combat) may require directive leadership, but the general leadership pattern for most teams should be participative** (Pearce & Sims, 2002). A cardiac surgery team typically operates under directive leadership during the operation when swift, coordinated action by the entire team is essential, but participative leadership is appropriate when the surgical team considers new operating procedures, ways to improve coordination, and strategies to improve the team's communication. You want to involve team members in decision making and problem solving. Directive leadership typically operates from fear—fear of making a mistake, of looking foolish, and of being criticized. Operating from fear "prevents people from thinking" (Aguayo, 1990, p. 184). A team leader wants to drive away fear. One study by the Positive Employee Practices Institute found that 70% of employees see a problem at work but won't tell anyone because they are afraid to tell management (cited in Romig, 1996). At IDEO, there is a saying, "Fail often to succeed sooner." Those who fear failure can be paralyzed into a play-it-safe stasis. "Failure is the flip side of risk taking, and if you don't risk, odds are you won't succeed" (Kelley & Littman, 2001, p. 232). Team leaders should seek to kill the fear that closes a system and kills thinking, input, innovation, and success.

▶ Insisting on a Cooperative Communication Climate: Jerks Need Not Apply

An effective team leader is a competent communicator capable of using supportive communication and avoiding defensive communication patterns with team members. **Effective team leaders create a climate in which making a mistake is an expected part of learning.** When mistakes are made, members are encouraged to learn from the errors. They aren't criticized, ridiculed, or made to feel stupid, especially in front of other team members. Berating members for making mistakes instills fear of failure.

Effective team leaders also suppress their egos to encourage a cooperative climate (Chemers, 2000). Egocentric leadership is sometimes referred to as **narcissistic leadership**. Such leaders put their own needs ahead of the teams' needs. Not surprisingly, narcissistic leaders make poor team leaders (O'Boyle et al., 2012). Egos create defensiveness and competitiveness.

In 1984, Millard Fuller, founder of Habitat for Humanity, approached former President Jimmy Carter in hopes of getting his help. When Carter expressed an interest to work with Habitat, Fuller drew up a list of 15 possible roles the former president of the United States could play. Fuller expected Carter to agree to one or two roles, and almost everything on the list was a high-profile, prestige activity (speaking through the media, raising money, making a video). Carter agreed to all 15 roles, including working on a building crew. Rather than merely working on a crew for one day, as Fuller envisioned for him, Carter put together his own work crew, traveled by bus to Brooklyn, New York, worked vigorously every day for a week on building a Habitat house, and slept in a local church with the rest of his crew. Jimmy Carter has assembled a building crew and served in similar fashion every year since (Emmons, 2013).

Imagine the result if Carter had demanded special treatment, played prima donna and swung a hammer on a building site only when cameras were rolling, and slept in expensive hotels while crew members slept uncomfortably in a church. Imagine the grumbling and disenchantment such egotism would have engendered. Who would have wanted to work with him, follow his lead, and be inspired by his example? Instead, Carter didn't expect special treatment, even though he was once the most powerful leader in the world. He completely suppressed any ego needs and became just one of the crew. When Tiruwork Leyew was told that the former president was fixing the door to her new home, she responded, "I was so shocked. I cannot believe this. I'm speechless." When an aide summoned Carter to address the media at the home site, he responded, "You can't have me. We're not done yet." It wasn't about him; it was about the work to help the less fortunate (quoted by Emmons, 2013, p. A14).

Finally, **effective team leaders work with team members to develop supportive rules.** Please note: This does not mean that the leader concocts a set of rules and then imposes the rules on the team. It also does not mean that organizational policy rules ("always wear a suit to work" or "file an absence report immediately upon your return to work following an illness") should be followed without question. Supportive rules refer to communication behaviors that empower teams, not to policy rules in organizations.

Supportive rules should emerge from team discussion during the initial meeting of the team. "When the team members set the rules, they follow them" (Romig, 1996, p. 161). All rules should help create a supportive environment and avoid a defensive climate. Some possible rules that the team could embrace might be "no personal attacks," "listen fully and patiently to team members before responding," "treat every member equally," "never bad-mouth a team member behind his or her back," and "always show up on time for meetings." Team members should agree to the rules, they should be posted, and there should be between 5 and 15 rules. Fewer rules likely means something has been left out; more than 15 makes it too difficult for team members to remember the rules (Romig, 1996).

▶ Decision Making and Problem Solving: Using a Plan

Decision making and problem solving without a systematic structured procedure will usually waste huge amounts of time in aimless and unfocused discussion while producing negligible results. Effective teams typically have a systematic, structured procedure for decision making and problem solving; ineffective teams typically do not (LaFasto & Larson, 2001). The point to note here is that **team leaders play an important role in assuring that systematic procedures are established for the team.** This usually involves keeping the team focused on using the Standard Agenda, consensus decision making, and brainstorming procedures. A detailed discussion of these systematic procedures is presented in Chapter 9, not here, because they require substantial explanation and they apply to a much broader spectrum of small groups than just teams.

In summary, teams have a higher level of cooperation, team members have more diverse skills, there is a stronger group identity in teams, and teams usually require greater allocation of time and resources than what is found in most conventional small groups. Developing effective teams begins with assembling effective team members. The best team members eschew egotism, cynicism, and abusive communication practices, and they are experienced and have strong problem-solving abilities, are optimistic, and have received communication training. You build teamwork by developing team goals and team identity, designating clear and appropriate roles for each member, structuring empowerment into the fabric of the team, and having competent leadership. Competent team leadership is a shared process. Team leaders should foster participative leadership, insist on a cooperative team climate, and make sure that team members are guided by a systematic decision-making and problem-solving process. The next two chapters discuss defective and effective decision making and problem solving, also vital considerations for teams as well as small groups in general.

MindTap
Reflect on what you've learned.

In Mixed Company

▶ Online

Now that you've read Chapter 7, access the online resources that accompany *In Mixed Company* at **www.cengagebrain.com**. Your online resources include:

1. Multiple-choice and true-false **chapter practice quizzes** with automatic correction

2. Digital **glossary**

3. **Flashcards**

QUESTIONS FOR CRITICAL THINKERS

1. Can you think of any teams that don't require clear, challenging goals, a team identity, and designated roles?

2. Can a team identity be established that doesn't conform to the team leader's preference?

3. How much say do you think a team member should have when roles are designated? Should this be the exclusive choice of the team leader?

VIDEO *Case Studies*

Gung Ho (1985). Comedy/Drama

An automobile plant in a small town is rescued by Japanese ownership and an imported management team. Analyze this for teamwork and team building in the context of cultural differences. How do individualism and collectivism relate to problems of team building?

Glory Road (2006). Drama; PG

Above-average depiction of a true story. Coach Don Haskins molded a winning team at Texas Western University in the early 1960s, eventually qualifying for the finals of the NCAA basketball tournament. He fielded an all-black starting five against an all-white Kentucky team when racial tensions were heightened nationally. Examine the major elements of team building and teamwork depicted. What specifically did Coach Haskins do to empower his players? How did he develop a team identity?

Invictus (2009). Drama; PG-13

Inspiring account of Nelson Mandela's quest to unify South Africa following the dismantling of apartheid by winning the 1995 World Rugby Cup. Examine the elements of team building and teamwork depicted in the film.

Miracle (2004). Drama; PG

Faithful and involving re-creation of the 1980 "miracle on ice" performed by the U.S. Olympic hockey team when it defeated a far more talented team from the Soviet Union and went on to capture the gold medal. Analyze all elements of teamwork and teambuilding illustrated in this film.

The War Room (1993). Documentary; PG

This documentary about Bill Clinton's 1992 presidential campaign received an Oscar nomination for best documentary. Analyze the film for team building and teamwork. What type of leadership style was used?

We Are Marshall (2008). Feel-Good Drama; PG

A plane crash wiped out most of Marshall University's football team. New coach Jack Lengyel (Matthew McConaughey) rallies surviving players and a grief-stricken community in this somewhat formulaic but poignant depiction of a true story. How does Lengyel build a team from the ashes of disaster?

Answers to Multiple-Choice Questions in Caption

Photo (p. 207): 1, 2, 3, 4.

8 Group Discussion: Defective Group Decision Making and Problem Solving

Theo Wargo/Getty Images Entertainment/ Getty Images

MindTap

Start with a quick warm-up activity.

Irving Janis (1982) relates the story of a tragedy that occurred years ago in the mining town of Pitcher, Oklahoma. The local mining engineer warned the inhabitants that due to an error, the town was in danger of imminent cave-in from undermining. Residents were advised to evacuate immediately. The warnings went unheeded. At a meeting of the local Lion's Club, leading citizens of the town joked about the doom-and-gloom forecast. One club member evoked raucous laughter from the membership when he entered the meeting wearing a parachute on his back in mock preparation for the predicted disaster. Within a few days, several of the club members and their families died when parts of the town caved in, swallowing some of those who spoofed the warnings.

Why would people ignore the threat? We read and hear stories every year of similar collective misjudgments and disasters. On my own campus, for example, how do clear glass windows in a men's restroom get installed to replace opaque windows, when the new windows leave men who stand at the urinals plainly visible to passersby? What gives rise to poor decision making in groups? The terms *decision making* and *problem solving* are sometimes used synonymously. The terms are interconnected but not identical. A **decision** requires a choice between two or more alternatives. Groups make decisions in the process of finding solutions to problems (e.g., where to meet, what process to use in making choices, what is the best solution to the problem, how to implement the solution). **Problem solving** necessitates decision making, but not all decision making involves a problem to be solved.

The principal purpose of this chapter is to explore sources of defective group decision making and problem solving. There are five chapter objectives:

1. To analyze the adverse effects of excessive or insufficient information quantity on group decision making and problem solving,

2. To explain the role of mindsets in defective decision making/problem solving,

3. To explore the contribution of collective inferential error to defective decision making/problem solving,

4. To discuss the troublesome decision-making problem of group polarization,

5. To describe and analyze groupthink as an ineffective group decision-making process.

Put succinctly, **this chapter explores ways in which small groups manifest defective critical thinking,** a major cause of bad decision making and problem solving. **Critical thinking** requires group members to analyze and evaluate ideas and information in order to reach sound judgments and conclusions. Critical thinking, therefore, is central to any discussion of small group decision making and problem solving.

One note of caution, however, is warranted. Russian author Fyodor Dostoyevsky once remarked that "everything seems stupid when it fails." Determining degrees of decision-making and problem-solving effectiveness simply on the basis of outcomes would be misleading and inaccurate. Although suggestive, bad outcomes do not automatically signal defective decision making and problem solving. Bad luck, sabotage, poor implementation by those outside the group, or misinformation may have caused the undesirable result.

Read, highlight, and take notes online.

Information Overload: Too Much Input

Information is the raw material of group decision making and problem solving. Adequate, credible information is essential to effective group decision making and problem solving. With the advent of rapidly proliferating electronic communication technologies, however, information overload has become *the* problem of the new century. **Information overload** occurs when the rate of information flow into a system and/or the complexity of that information exceed the system's processing capacity (Farace et al., 1977). This section will examine the scope and consequences of information overload and ways in which decision-making and problem-solving groups can cope with it.

Focus Questions

1. **What problems are created by information overload?**

2. **What means do groups have of coping with information overload?**

▶ Scope of the Problem: The Information Avalanche

The research firm IDC (International Data Corporation) calculated that the total global digital data available in 2010 was 1.2 million petabytes, an increase of 62% from 2009 (Gantz & Reinsel, 2010). A petabyte is a million gigabytes. So, 1.2 million petabytes is roughly equivalent to "the digital output from a century's worth of constant tweeting by all of Earth's inhabitants" (Wray, 2010). The amount of information available digitally by 2020, however, is estimated to be *50 times greater* than 2010 (Gantz & Reinsel, 2012). The word *staggering* doesn't seem quite sufficient to capture the size of the challenge we face in coming years with information overload.

Consider some prominent examples of exponential growth in digital media. Facebook grew from a few thousand subscribers in 2004 to more than 1.1 billion worldwide in less than a decade ("Facebook Competitors," 2013). Twitter, which started in March 2006, grew to almost 250 million active users worldwide by early 2014 (Smith, 2014). As Thomas Friedman (2013), author of the best-selling book, "The World Is Flat," notes: "When I wrote that book (in 2004), Facebook, Twitter, cloud computing, LinkedIn, 4G wireless, ultra-high-speed bandwidth, big data, Skype, system-on-a-chip (SOC) circuits, iPhones, iPads, and cell-phone apps didn't exist, or were in their infancy" (p. A11).

These electronic communication technologies, considered "critical" by one-fifth of professional employees to their overall success and productivity at work ("Plantronics Study," 2010), produce massive quantities of information, much of it relatively useless. One text analysis of 2,000 randomly selected Twitter tweets, for example, concluded that 41% were "pointless babble" of the "I am eating a sandwich now" variety (Kelly, 2010). Nevertheless, both useless and useful information is expanding at breakneck speed, making the task of separating the two so groups can engage in effective decision making and problem solving, ever more challenging. One study in five countries reported that white-collar employees spend about half of their working hours "receiving and managing information." Almost half of the information is "not important to getting the job done," more than half of the workers say that the quality of their work suffers because they cannot sort through the flood of information fast enough, and half anticipate reaching "a breaking point" where they cannot handle any more information ("International Workplace Productivity Survey," 2010).

Electronic communication technologies contribute enormously to information overload and its consequences.

Clearly, information overload will not diminish in importance but will likely increase in years to come.

▶ Consequences: The Downside of Information

Information overload is not inconsequential (Bodard, 2008). Aside from group members feeling overwhelmed by the avalanche of information, there are three main consequences of information overload relevant to group decision making and problem solving.

Critical Thinking Impairment: Separating Wheat from Chaff Information overload *impairs critical thinking* (Shenk, 1997; Spira, 2011). A glut of information makes it very difficult to distinguish useless from useful information (Bodard, 2008). In fact, **gathering vast quantities of information can increase a group's confidence in its decisions but may actually decrease the accuracy of those decisions** (Hall et al., 2007). It's not the quantity of information, but the quality and relevance of the information that are most important. Consider a riddle that illustrates this point:

Suppose you are a bus driver. On the first stop you pick up six men and two women. At the second stop two men leave and one woman boards the bus. At the third stop one man leaves and two women enter the bus. At the fourth stop three men get on and three women get off. At the fifth stop two men get off, three men get on, one woman gets off, and two women get on. What is the bus driver's name? (Halpern, 1984, p. 201)

Don't reread the riddle! Have you figured it out? The answer, of course, is your name since the riddle begins, "Suppose *you* are a bus driver." All the information about the passengers is irrelevant and merely diverts your attention from the obvious and correct answer.

Immersing ourselves in the vast reservoir of information and snatching bits and pieces here and there impedes comprehension and "deep reading" and prevents quiet contemplation and critical analysis of all this information (Carr, 2010). We have little time to think when information is threatening to drown us in a digital data dump. We become so focused on the quantity of information that we hardly notice if the quality is substandard (Bodard, 2008).

Students working on group projects recognize the problem of information overload. When surrounded by a Mount Everest-size pile of books and articles or a stack of printouts from the Internet related to a group project, you lose sight of the larger picture. How does all this information fit together into a coherent package? Simply sorting through the gigaheaps of information on a subject leaves little time for group members to examine the information critically.

Indecisiveness: Conclusion Irresolution Paradoxically, the technologies that have ushered in the information age speed up almost everything enormously, but a group's ability to make decisions is slowed (see Closer Look: "Technology and the Bias of Speed"). "The psychological reaction to such an overabundance of information … is to simply avoid coming to conclusions" (Shenk, 1997, p. 93). We become overly concerned that some new, instantly available fact or statistic that would invalidate a group decision will be overlooked, making the group appear foolish.

CLOSER LOOK

Technology and the Bias of Speed

"Much time is lost by slow-moving passengers who make no effort to hurry," claimed the president of Otis in a 1953 sales pitch for automated elevators. "They know the attendant will wait for them… . But the impersonal operatorless elevator starts closing the door after permitting you a reasonable time to enter or leave." He noted, "People soon learn to move promptly" (Gleick, 1999, p. 29).

Our technology makes "faster" possible, even necessary. As soon as faster becomes possible, it becomes our expectation. We perceive a "need for speed" whether or not it is required (Bodard, 2008). As psychologist Phillip Zimbardo explains, "Technology makes us impatient for anything that takes more than seconds to achieve. You press a button and you expect instant access" (quoted by Gregoire, 2013). Thus, computer printers of 20 years ago seem painfully slow by today's standard, even though they were viewed as almost miraculously swift in their day. Waiting even a few seconds to log on to our computers produces agitation for many users. When the push-button phone was invented, the rotary dial seemed interminably slow and clunky by comparison, but then came the speed-dial button to shorten the process by a couple of seconds. Federal Express ushered in overnight mail service. Suddenly, regular mail service seemed annoyingly slow. The advent of email initiated speed-of-light transmission of messages. Now regular mail service is "snail mail." Everything compared to email seems like the pace of a slug on tranquilizers, but then comes instant messaging, and texting, and Twitter tweets with their abbreviations and acronyms for quicker message construction to quicken the pace of information access even further. Teenagers especially see email as too slow compared to texting and social networking. As Scott Campbell, coauthor of the Pew Research report on teen media use, observes, "Email doesn't support real-time, flexible contact with others. You have to log in and also be online" (quoted in Murphy, 2010). "Faster is better" has become the modern maxim.

Faster, however, may seem better because we supposedly "save time," yet all these technologies that accelerate the pace of our lives don't actually provide most of us with free time to make careful, deliberate decisions. We now have to "multitask" to keep pace (Gleick, 1999). Harvard economist

Juliet Schor explains, "Technology reduces the amount of time it takes to do any one task, but also leads to the expansion of tasks people are expected to do" (quoted in Shenk, 1997, p. 56). Where once a group might be given a month to finish a report, it now might be expected to finish a professional-looking report in only a few days. Little time is available to reflect, think, analyze, evaluate, or decide. We can become paralyzed into indecisiveness or forced to make rash decisions by the unrelenting pressure to act swiftly.

Group discussion can seem interminably long in a fast-track society. Allowing every group member to express his or her point of view seems like "wasted time." The pressure is to act, not deliberate. We become impatient with searching for creative solutions to complex problems. We feel a need to move quickly to the next problem, not linger on an "old" one. Crises and emergencies proliferate because everything becomes "last minute." Half of American respondents to the LexisNexis survey felt "demoralized" when they couldn't manage all of the information that comes their way at work ("International Workplace Productivity Survey," 2010). The pace of trying to keep up is exhausting. "This is the Information Age, which does not always mean information in our brains. We sometimes feel that it means information whistling by our ears at light speed, too fast to be absorbed" (Gleick, 1999, p. 87). Technology is rapidly eliminating the pauses in our lives, and group decision making is probably not the better for it.

QUESTIONS FOR THOUGHT

1. Have you experienced the difficulties associated with group decision making when faster is perceived to be better? How do you cope with it?

2. Should we try to slow the pace? How could this be done?

3. Is ever-increasing pace an inevitable product of technology, or do some technologies slow the pace?

Inattention: Difficulty Concentrating The mega-mountains of information competing for group members' attention make focusing on any one idea, concept, or problem extremely difficult. As Carr (2010) observes, "We willingly accept the loss of concentration and focus, the division of our attention, and the fragmentation of our thoughts, in return for the wealth of compelling or at least diverting information we receive" (p. 134). Almost 60% of respondents in the LexisNexis survey agreed that electronic communication devices are distracting and can hinder job performance ("International Workplace Productivity Survey," 2010). For example, when cell phones go off repeatedly during group meetings, classes, and the like, everyone is distracted and attention is diverted from decision making and problem solving. It can take a group as much as five minutes to refocus its attention after a 30-second interruption (Spira, 2011).

▶ Coping with Information Overload: Wrestling the Beast

Coping with information overload can't be accomplished by stuffing the technological genie back in the bottle. Instead, you can cope with information overload in several ways.

Screening Information: Separating the Useful from the Useless Screening information, much like you do phone calls, by simply choosing to ignore much of the information is one effective method of coping with information overload. If you find 200 email messages waiting for your attention when you return from a vacation, how do you cope? One way is to use a software program that automatically screens email messages from designated senders. In addition, there are spam filters that automatically screen unsolicited and unwanted messages from strangers and business interests. Emails from virtual group members may be given highest priority. A more low-tech screening method is merely to delete unread messages based on the title and author of the message. Scanning message content is also a means of screening information. In the LexisNexis study, 91% of respondents answered that they scan information regularly at work to cope with information overload ("International Workplace Productivity Survey," 2010). Often a quick glance at message content can determine whether the information is relevant to your needs.

Shutting Off Technology: Hitting the Off Switch A closely related method to screening is shutting off the technology. **Information overload is largely a problem of too much openness in a system.** Don't check emails and text messages until group meetings have ended, and do not text message, update your Facebook page, or

Twitter tweet during a meeting. Some companies have established quiet times when workers stay away from computers altogether and half days in which communication electronically is prohibited to give employees time to think and problem solve, to meet in groups and deliberate, not just gather ever larger quantities of information ("International Workplace Productivity Survey," 2010).

Specializing: Knowing More and More about Less and Less When you specialize you can manage to know a lot about a little. Some specialization is undoubtedly necessary to cope with information overload. No individual or group can possibly manage information sufficiently so that experts on vital subjects will never be required. If group members know little or nothing about the law, for instance, they may be forced to trust the advice of a lawyer counseling the group on some legal issue.

Be cautious, however, about specialization. When a group's knowledge is limited in scope, it becomes more dependent on experts, more vulnerable to their characterizations and perceptions of reality, and more prone to let the experts do the thinking for the group.

Becoming Selective: On a Need-to-Know Basis Another method of coping with information overload is selectivity (Tartakovsky, 2013). Since group members can't attend to all information bombarding them, they should choose selectively on the basis of group priorities and goals. Setting group priorities helps members select which information requires their urgent attention and which can be delayed or ignored entirely. Setting priorities distinguishes what we need to know from what there is to know.

Limiting the Search: When Enough Is Enough The search for information must stop at some point to allow time to reflect and evaluate information (Tartakovsky, 2013). There is a time for searching and a time for thinking and deciding. Setting deadlines for group decisions is critical. Deadlines force a group to bring a search for information to a halt. This means, however, that the search for information should begin early, instead of being postponed until the last minute. Otherwise, with time constraints, the search for relevant information may be far too limited to be effective.

Narrowing the Search: Databases and Patterns Searching the Internet by merely typing a topic into the keyword search window will likely prove to be unproductive. For example, the most recent time that I typed *information overload* into the Google search window, I got a staggering 17.4 million hits. The search

---

SECOND LOOK

Coping with Information Overload

Screening Information—Limit exposure to information.

Shutting Off Technology—Turn off cell phones, pagers, and so on.

Specializing—Know a lot about a little.

Becoming Selective—Attend to information that relates directly to group goals and priorities.

Limiting the Search—Set time for searching and time for deciding.

Narrowing the Search—Use credible databases; find patterns.

---

clearly has to be narrowed. One way to do this is to access high-quality databases. Many academic disciplines provide their own specialized databases that provide credible information, not general information from sources both credible and not so credible.

Pattern recognition is another means of narrowing the search. **Discerning patterns is a group's best defense against information overload.** "Once a pattern is perceived, 90% of information becomes irrelevant" (Klapp, 1978, p. 13). Football teams preparing for a game against an opponent could not possibly perform effectively without a specific game plan (pattern). Only a small number of plays are chosen. The players are instructed by the coaches to concentrate on a few key strategies: establish the running game, contain the opponent's quarterback, double-team the wide receivers. No player can concentrate on more than a few crucial strategies. The plan simplifies the team's approach to the game. It establishes recognizable patterns for players.

Information Underload: Poor Sharing

Although information overload is a far more prevalent and significant problem, information underload can also present problems for groups. **Information underload** refers to an insufficient amount of information (inadequate input) available to a group for decision-making purposes. This information underload often occurs in groups because an individual member sits on critical information and doesn't share it with the group (Greitemeyer et al., 2006), or time pressure impedes information sharing (Bowman & Wittenbaum, 2012).

Many studies show that unshared information in groups leads to poor-quality decision making (Bowman & Wittenbaum, 2012; Galinsky & Kray, 2004; Stasser et al., 2000). The problem of unshared information may even lead to disaster. A study of cockpit crews flying large commercial planes revealed that crews who shared little information did not perform as well as crews who shared a greater quantity of information (Foushee & Manos, 1981). Seventy percent of all civil aviation accidents and near-misses during a five-year period reported by the NASA Safety Reporting System were caused by either improper transmission of information from one crew member to another or by failure to transmit vital information at all (Burrows, 1982). One study of pilot–air traffic controller communication revealed that pilots all too commonly fail to provide necessary information to air-traffic controllers (Howard, 2008). Fewer errors related to mishandling of the engines, hydraulic systems, fuel systems, misreading instruments, and failing to use ice protection were found when sufficient information was communicated to all crew members.

Information underload is usually a problem of too much closedness in a system. The general solution to this problem is greater openness in the lines of communication. All members of the group must have access to the relevant information in order to make quality decisions. Finding the balance between too little and too much information, however, requires critical thinking skills. The competent communicator must acquire sufficient knowledge to recognize within a specific context what information is directly relevant to the task and what is irrelevant or marginal. Increasing the quantity of irrelevant or minimally useful information will confuse rather than assist the group in making effective decisions and solving problems.

Mindsets: Critical Thinking Frozen Solid

Perceptual **mindsets** are psychological and cognitive predispositions to see the world in a particular way (Kitayama, 2013). They interfere with effective group decision making and problem solving. Cognitively, we are prepared to receive only certain messages and ignore others. We are conditioned to view the world narrowly.

Try this demonstration of a mindset on your unsuspecting friends. Have them spell the word *shop* out loud. Now ask them to respond immediately to the question, "What do you do when you come to a green light?" The vast majority will unthinkingly reply "stop." Why? Because spelling the word *shop* narrows our focus to rhyming words even though the correct answer does not rhyme. Our minds are set to view the world in a particular way even if this is inappropriate.

You may be surprised by the power of mindsets. Follow the "shop–stop" demonstration with this version of the same illustration: Spell *joke* out loud. "What do you call the white of an egg?" Most people will be victimized a second time by answering "yolk."

Focus Questions

1. Why does confirmation bias lead to defective decision making/problem solving?

2. Why is dichotomous (either–or) thinking usually false?

► Confirmation Bias: One-Sided Information Searches

Confirmation bias is our strong tendency to seek and attend to information that confirms our beliefs and attitudes and to ignore information that contradicts our currently held beliefs and attitudes. Results of a study conducted by psychologist Drew Westen, presented to the 2006 Conference of the Society for Personality and Social Psychology, showed that Democrats consistently ignored contradictions by John Kerry and Republicans did the same when watching George W. Bush during a 2004 presidential campaign debate, but both partisan groups were keenly aware and strongly critical of contradictions from the opposing candidate ("Political Bias," 2006).

The Problem: Poor Decisions and Solutions "If one were to attempt to identify a single problematic aspect of human reasoning that deserves attention above all others, confirmation bias would have to be among the candidates for consideration" (Nickerson, 1998, p. 175). Confirmation bias is alive and well in small groups (Nickerson, 1998; Tschan et al., 2009). The consequences of confirmation bias to group decision making and problem solving are serious. Looking for the potential weaknesses and disconfirming evidence regarding decisions and solutions is a significant element of effective group decision making and problem solving (Orlitzky & Hirokawa, 2001; Stanovich et al., 2013). Assessing positive qualities or consequences is not nearly as important. Thus, groups that resist confirmation bias and actively search for possible flaws in decisions and solutions usually make better choices than groups that don't.

In one study, confirmation bias was shown to be a key factor in medical misdiagnoses by diagnostic teams (Tschan et al., 2009). In another study, three-member groups evaluated résumés of three candidates who applied for a marketing manager position. Confirmation bias was common. Positive information about a candidate that each subject initially favored was readily shared and discussed with group members; negative information was not. Negative information was shared about disfavored candidates, but positive information was not. Although groups meeting face to face exhibited confirmation bias, online groups reviewing the résumés were *more than twice as likely* to engage in confirmation bias. Almost none of the groups chose the best candidate for the position (Hightower & Sayeed, 1995).

So what happens when disconfirming information is unavoidable and seems indisputable? Groups may still engage in **rationalization of disconfirmation**—the invention of superficial, even glib alternative explanations for information that contradicts a belief. The Heaven's Gate group in San Diego, California, that committed mass suicide exhibited rationalization of disconfirmation. Members purchased a high-powered telescope so a clearer view of the Hale-Bopp comet and the spaceship they steadfastly believed was traveling in its wake—a spacecraft that was to transport Heaven's Gaters to a new cosmic life—could be discerned. The telescope was returned, however, and the owner of the store was politely asked for a refund. When the owner asked what was wrong with the telescope, he was informed, "We found the comet all right, but we can't find the spaceship following it" (quoted in Aronson, 2011, p. 186). The Heaven's Gaters thought the telescope must be defective, not the original belief of a spaceship trailing the comet.

The perpetuation of unwarranted beliefs is the result of confirmation bias and its ally, rationalization of disconfirmation (Nickerson, 1998). False beliefs that pollute the decision-making and problem-solving group process won't be corrected when we aren't open to information that questions our beliefs.

Combating Confirmation Bias: A Plan The competent communicator combats the problem of confirmation bias by taking the following steps:

1. *Seek disconfirming information and evidence.* Since most group members will be predisposed to seek confirming evidence, someone will have to perform an error-correction function for the group. Consider it your personal responsibility to find the disconfirming information and share it. If, after a concerted effort, you find little disconfirming evidence of note, then your decision or solution has an excellent chance of turning out well.

2. *Vigorously present disconfirming evidence to the group.* Be persistent. Members will usually ignore information that disconfirms a strongly held belief unless you assert yourself.

3. *Play devil's advocate.* Develop the habit of challenging the assumptions and claims of those defending a decision or solution in your group. Do it in the spirit of problem orientation—testing group decisions before they are implemented to produce the best group decisions. Clearly indicate your intention to play devil's advocate to avoid any misunderstanding ("Let me play devil's advocate here").

Anyone may play devil's advocate in a group. If groups establish a norm of devil's advocacy, the responsibility won't fall on only one member's shoulders.

4. *Gather allies to help challenge confirmation bias.* Women and ethnic minorities especially profit from developing support with those members of a group who are respected and open-minded.

▶ False Dichotomies: Either–Or Thinking

A **false dichotomy** is the tendency to view the world in terms of only two opposing possibilities when other possibilities are available, and to describe this dichotomy in the language of extremes. Describing objects, events, and people in such extreme polarities as moral–immoral, good–bad, rich–poor, corrupt–honest, intelligent–stupid locks us into a mindset of narrow vision. Most of us don't qualify as either tall or short, fat or skinny, rich or poor; we're someplace in between these dichotomies. Most objects, events, and people are more accurately described in shades of gray, not black or white (pregnancy being a rare exception since it is difficult to be "sort of pregnant"). For instance, when does success turn into failure? When does a small group become a large group, and vice versa? Dichotomous descriptions of events and objects are usually false because most of reality consists of more-to-less, not either–or.

False dichotomies contribute to defective group decision making and problem solving. When group members are predisposed to see problems and solutions only in extremes, the vast middle ground goes largely unexplored. City councils, faced with reduced revenues during a recession, see only layoffs and reductions in public services when they think dichotomously (i.e., tax revenues up—fund services and jobs; tax revenues down—cut services and jobs). They may fail to explore other avenues for raising revenues besides taxes.

Groups locked into the false dichotomy mindset that a decision has to be made may never consider a third alternative besides voting for or against some proposal. Postponing the decision until adequate study of the problem can take place and potential solutions can emerge may be a more viable option.

The competent communicator combats the problem of false dichotomies in small groups as follows:

1. *Be suspicious of absolutes.* When group members argue only two extreme possibilities (e.g., a solution is either all good or all bad), look for a third or even fourth possibility.

2. *Employ the language of provisionalism.* When engaged in group discussion, speak in terms of degrees (i.e., to what extent an argument is true). You'll be using terms such as *sometimes, rarely, occasionally, mostly, usually, unlikely,* and *moderately.* Avoid terms such as *always, never,* or *impossible.*

Collective Inferential Error: Uncritical Thinking

Two American women—a matronly grandmother and her attractive granddaughter—are seated in a railroad compartment with a Romanian officer and a Nazi officer during World War II. As the train passes through a dark tunnel, the sound of a loud kiss and an audible slap shatters the silence. As the train emerges from the tunnel, no words are spoken but a noticeable welt forming on the face of the Nazi officer is observed by all. The grandmother muses to herself, "What a fine granddaughter I have raised. I have no need to worry. She can take care of herself." The granddaughter thinks to herself, "Grandmother packs a powerful wallop for a woman of her years. She sure has spunk." The Nazi officer, none too pleased by the course of events, ruminates to himself, "This Romanian is clever. He steals a kiss and gets me slapped in the process." The Romanian officer chuckles to himself, "Not a bad ploy. I kissed my hand and slapped a Nazi."

This story illustrates the problem of inferential error. **Inferences** are conclusions about the unknown based on what is known. They are guesses varying by degrees from educated to uneducated (depending on the *quantity* and *quality* of information on which the inferences are based). We draw inferences from previous experiences, factual data, and predispositions. The facts of the story are that the sounds of a kiss followed by a slap are heard by all members of the group. Based on what is known, the three individuals who do not know for sure what happened all draw distinctly different and erroneous inferences.

Making inferences is not a problem in itself. The human thinking process is inferential. Our minds "go beyond the information given" (Nisbett & Ross, 1980). We could not function on a daily basis without making inferences. You can't know for certain that your class will convene as scheduled, but you infer it will because it always has in the past weeks. This is a relatively safe inference, but an inference nonetheless because the unusual (the professor is ill) may occur.

Inferences that rely on a quality information base in plentiful supply are educated guesses—not always correct, but probable. Inferences that are drawn from a limited and faulty information base, however, are uneducated guesses—likely to produce inferential errors (Gouran, 1986).

Inferential errors can pose serious problems for group decision making. If we don't exercise our critical thinking abilities by closely examining important inferences central to decision making in groups, bad decisions are highly likely to result.

> ### Focus Questions
>
> 1. What are the primary, general sources of collective, inferential errors?
>
> 2. Should we avoid making inferences?
>
> 3. Why are most correlations noncausal?

▶ Prevalence of the Problem: It's a Group Thing

The centrality of inferences to decision making and problem solving in groups is made apparent by Gouran (1982b) when he explains:

> In virtually every phase of discussion, inferences come into play. Whether you are assessing facts, testing opinions, examining the merits of competing arguments, or exploring which of several alternatives best satisfies a set of decisional criteria, you will have occasion to draw inferences suggested by the information you are examining. How well you reason, therefore, can have as much to do with the effectiveness of a decision-making discussion as any other factor that enters the process. (pp. 96–97)

Individuals are inclined to make inferential errors (see Box 7.1). The problem can be magnified in groups. Gouran calls this *collective inferential error*. Studies have established the prevalence of collective inferential errors (Gouran, 1981, 1982, 1983). As many as half of a group's discussion statements may be inferences. Groups often accept these inferences uncritically. One study (Gouran, 1983) examined student group discussions in which 80 inferences were made regarding questions of policy. Only one inference was challenged. The rest were reinforced or extended, or new inferences were added. Why is this significant? Because ineffective decision-making groups that arrived at faulty decisions displayed more inferential errors in their discussions than did effective groups (Hirokawa & Pace, 1983).

▶ Specific Sources of Inferential Errors

There are several specific sources of inferential errors. Two that are most significant are unrepresentativeness and correlation inferred as causation.

Unrepresentativeness: Distorting the Facts Is a specific example representative of a general category? If the answer is yes, then the inference drawn from the representative example is on solid footing. If the example is unrepresentative,

The vividness effect is illustrated by the crash of Asiana Flight 214 at San Francisco International Airport on July 6, 2013.

however, inferences drawn from it are likely to be erroneous. One study illustrates inferential error among college students resulting from unrepresentativeness. College students indicated their belief that if one member of a group made a particular decision, then all members of the group would make the same decision. This was especially true if the students were observing the decisions of students from other colleges (Quattrone & Jones, 1980). In other words, we stereotype an entire group on the basis of a single individual who may or may not be representative of the group as a whole.

If the unrepresentative example is vivid, then the potential for inferential error is magnified. The grim, grisly, graphic, dramatic event draws our attention and becomes standard fare served up by the mass media hungry to draw viewers. As producer Gary David Goldberg once pointedly observed, "Left to their own devices, the networks would televise live executions. Except Fox—they'd televise live naked executions" ("TV or not TV," 1993, p. 5E). The dramatic event, however, can distort our perception (Sunstein & Zeckhauser, 2009). A single airline disaster can make millions fear boarding a jetliner and induce them to choose driving their automobile instead. Yet the odds of dying in a plane crash are 1 in 11 *million,* whereas the odds of dying in a car crash are 1 in 5 *thousand* (Ropeik, 2008).

BOX 7.1

The Uncritical Inference Test

SELF-ASSESSMENT TEST

Read the following story. For each statement about the story, circle "T" if it can be determined without a doubt from the information provided in the story that the statement is completely true, "F" if the statement directly contradicts information in the story, and "?" if you cannot determine from the information provided in the story whether the statement is either true or false. Read the story once. Do not sneak a peek at the answers until you have finished the test.

The Story

Dr. Chris Cross, who works at St. Luke's Hospital, hurried into room #314 where Yoshi Yamamoto was lying in bed. Pat Sinclair, a registered nurse, was busy fluffing bed pillows when Dr. Cross entered. Dr. Cross said to the nurse in charge, "This bed should have been straightened out long ago." A look of anger came across Nurse Sinclair's face. Dr. Cross promptly turned around and hurried out the door.

1. Chris Cross is a medical doctor who works at St. Luke's Hospital. **T F ?**
2. Dr. Cross is a man in a hurry. **T F ?**
3. Yoshi Yamamoto, who is Japanese, was lying in bed. **T F ?**
4. Pat Sinclair was in room #314 when Dr. Cross entered and found her fluffing bed pillows. **T F ?**
5. Dr. Cross was irritated with Nurse Sinclair because the bed was not straightened out. **T F ?**
6. Yoshi Yamamoto is a patient at St. Luke's Hospital. **T F ?**
7. Nurse Sinclair's face reddened because Dr. Cross was stern with her. **T F ?**
8. When Dr. Cross entered, he became the third person in room #314. **T F ?**
9. This story takes place at St. Luke's Hospital. **T F ?**
10. This story concerns a series of events in which only three persons are referred to: Dr. Cross, Nurse Sinclair, and Yoshi Yamamoto. **T F ?**

Individuals are prone to make inferential errors (Nisbett & Ross, 1980). See if you have such a tendency. I created this version of what Haney (1967) originally devised and called "The Uncritical Inference Test." "?" is the correct answer for all of the statements. Without exception, these statements are based on guesses regarding what is likely but not verifiably true from the information provided. The reasons these statements are uncertain are as follows:

1. Chris Cross is a doctor of some sort but not necessarily a medical doctor (Dr. Cross may be a Ph.D., chiropractor, dentist, etc.).
2. Dr. Cross is not necessarily a man.
3. Yoshi Yamamoto has a Japanese name, but isn't necessarily Japanese (married name, assumed name, adoptive name).
4. Pat Sinclair may be a male, not a "her."
5. This requires an inference that Dr. Cross is irritated and that Nurse Sinclair and "the nurse in charge" are one and the same person, which cannot be ascertained from the information provided.
6. Yoshi Yamamoto may be an orderly taking a break or a visitor resting, not a patient.

7. This requires an inference that a "look of anger" automatically produces a "reddened face." Again, Nurse Sinclair may be male.
8. There may have been four people in room #314 if Nurse Sinclair and the nurse in charge are not the same person.
9. Dr. Cross works at St. Luke's. Nowhere does it say this story occurred there.
10. Again, four people may be in the story: Dr. Cross, Nurse Sinclair, the nurse in charge, and Yoshi Yamamoto.

If we don't even recognize that we've made an inference, then we're not likely to notice when the inference is a bad one. If individually you do poorly on recognizing and critically evaluating inferences, imagine the quality of decision making in a group when most or all of the members are inclined to make inferential errors.

The potential of a single dramatic example sticking in our minds, prompting us to overvalue such an event and undervalue statistical probabilities of such an event occurring, is called the **vividness effect**. The potency of the vividness effect is so real that Stanovich (1992) concludes that it "threatens to undermine the usefulness of any knowledge generated by any of the behavioral sciences" (p. 141).

Correlation Inferred as Causation: Covariation Humans are predisposed to look for causes of events that remain unexplained. When Adam Lanza killed 20 first-graders, 6 adults, and himself in December 2012 at Sandy Hook Elementary School in Newtown, Connecticut, the question that came to mind is "What caused this individual to perform such a dastardly act?" When Malaysia Airlines Flight MH370 on March 8, 2014, abruptly vanished from radar and led to a massive search for the missing plane with 239 passengers and crew on board, everyone wanted to know what caused the disappearance. We want explanations. We seek causes of human behavior.

One such erroneous inference is our tendency to draw causation (X causes Y) from mere correlation (X and Y occur together). A **correlation** is a consistent relationship between two or more variables. There are two kinds of correlations: positive and negative. A positive correlation occurs when X increases and Y also increases (e.g., as you grow older your ears grow larger—nature's practical joke on the elderly). A negative correlation occurs when X increases and Y decreases (e.g., as adults increase in age, their capacity to run long distances decreases).

The main problem with correlations is the strong inclination people have for inferring causation (X causes Y) from a correlation. A large research team collected data in Taiwan to determine which variables best predicted use of contraceptive methods for birth control (Li, 1975). Of all the variables, use of birth control was most strongly correlated with the number of electric appliances (i.e., toasters, ovens, blenders, etc.) found in the home. Birth control usage increased as the number of electric appliances increased (GE doesn't bring good things to life?). So does it make sense to you that a free microwave oven or electric blender for every teenager in high school would decrease teen pregnancy rates? I'm confident that you can see the absurdity of such a suggestion.

The birth control–electric appliances correlation is an obvious case where a correlation, even though a very strong one, is not a causation. The number of electric appliances more than likely is a reflection of socioeconomic status and education levels, which undoubtedly have more to do with the rates of birth control usage than do the number of electric irons and toasters found in the home. Stephen Jay Gould (1981) noted that "the vast majority of correlations in our world are, without doubt, non-causal" (p. 242). Yet, as Gould further notes, "The invalid assumption that correlation implies cause is probably among the two or three most serious and common errors of human reasoning" (p. 242).

I have witnessed the correlation-as-causation inferential error in my own classes. Consider the following discussion that took place in a small group in one of my classes:

J: I think we should choose capital punishment for our topic. I just did a paper on it. We can show that capital punishment works. In a lot of states that have it, murder rates have decreased.

A: Yeah, did you ever see that video where they show executions? Really gross. You know most criminals would think twice about killing someone if they made capital punishment really painful.

B: Well, I heard that when they execute a guy, the murder rate goes up right after. I don't think capital punishment is a very effective solution to murder.

In this brief conversation, group members managed to allege the truth of an asserted causation based only on a correlation, affirm the validity of the inferential error with a little common-sense reasoning, then refute the effectiveness of capital punishment by introducing yet another correlation assumed to be a causation. Correlations are not causations.

▶ Error Correction: Practicing Critical Thinking

For the error-correction function of group discussion to kick in, competent communicators must recognize the sources of inferential errors just discussed. Assertively focusing the group's attention on sources of inferential error can help prevent faulty decision making from occurring. In other words, group members must put their critical thinking abilities into practice if effective decision making is to take place.

Group discussion promotes higher-quality decision making when the following conditions occur:

1. The validity of inferences is carefully examined.

2. Inferences are grounded in valid and plentiful information.

3. At least one member of the group exerts influence to guide the group toward higher-quality decisions (Hirokawa & Pace, 1983).

Notice the last point. A single individual can prevent or minimize inferential error in group decision making because one person can affect the entire system.

Group Polarization: Extremely Uncritical Thinking

Researchers of small group decision making used to believe that group members inevitably influence each other to take greater collective risks than members' initial preferences. This was called the *risky shift phenomenon,* often seen when teenagers goad each other to engage in goofy and dangerous group actions. For example, the National Institute of Child Health and Human Development of the National Institutes of Health released results of a study of teen drivers in 2005 (Bock & Miller, 2005). The study's director, Duane Alexander, noted: "The findings indicate that teen risky driving increases in the presence of teen passengers, particularly male teen passengers." Results of a more recent study parallel these findings (Tefft et al., 2012). We show off for our peers by taking risks.

After hundreds of studies, however, there is ample evidence that groups sometimes have a conservative shift rather than a risky shift (Levine & Moreland, 1990). Thus, group decisions tend to polarize.

Focus Questions

1. **What negative consequences to group decision making emerge from group polarization?**

2. **What produces group polarization?**

▶ Polarization: From Gambling to Guarded

Group polarization is the group tendency to make a decision after discussion that is more extreme, either riskier or more cautious, than the initial preferences of group members. (Group polarization does not mean that disagreement among group members becomes more pronounced.) **Groups tend to polarize decision making if there**

is a clear majority leaning one way (risk) or the other (caution). For example, in one study, 60 participants were assembled into 10 groups, each consisting of 5 to 7 members. Half the groups were from "liberal" Boulder, Colorado, and half were from "conservative" Colorado Springs, Colorado. All groups were instructed to deliberate on three controversial issues: affirmative action, civil unions for gays, and global warming. Groups that initially tended toward liberal positions on these issues took more extreme liberal positions after deliberations; conservative groups became more conservative. Discussion made civil unions, affirmative action, and a global warming treaty more appealing for liberal group members, less appealing for conservative group members (Hastie et al., 2006). This group polarization effect has been shown in hundreds of studies across many cultures (see Sunstein, 2006, for a lengthy discussion).

If most members of a group lean slightly toward risk-taking initially, the group will become more prone to take even greater risks than any individual member might have initially preferred, and if most members of a group lean slightly toward playing it safe, the group will likely become even more cautious than it was initially. It is unlikely that a group will polarize when group members are about evenly split between risk-taking and playing it safe. This is where compromise, or *depolarization,* may result.

Group polarization won't always produce erroneous decision making (Sunstein, 2006), but moving to the extreme can be problematic. Consequences associated with "moving to the fringe," as Myers and Bishop (1970) termed it, can be seen especially on the Internet. Factors that produce group polarization "are present in abundance on the Internet, so we should hardly be surprised when we run into discussion groups whose regular members firmly hold some weird or extreme viewpoints" (Wallace, 1999, p. 80).

The running of the bulls at Pamplona, Spain, reminds us that groups often encourage risk-taking, sometimes to the point of dangerous excess.

Many of these extreme viewpoints encourage high-risk, even reckless political positions (e.g., use of nuclear weapons in the Middle East; killing politicians).

Group polarization and bad decision making, of course, exist outside of the Internet. The 9/11 terrorists were the product of the polarizing influence of mostly in-person deliberations and interactions among the like-minded (Smelser & Mitchell, 2002). Suicide bombers are egged on to commit mass murder by other true believers in their polarized group (Zajonc, 2000).

▶ Why Groups Polarize: Social Comparison and Persuasive Arguments

There are two primary explanations for group polarization (BarNir, 1998). **The first is social comparison (normative influence).** The assumption here is that an individual uses the group norm regarding risk-taking or caution as a point of reference. The individual is inclined to shift after group discussion, to conform more closely to the perceived expectations of the group in this regard. If most group members initially tend toward riskiness, cautious members are inclined to move in the direction of the majority. If most members initially favor caution, all members feel pushed to be cautious.

A second primary explanation for the group polarization effect is persuasive argumentation (informational influence). Individuals in a group will move toward either greater risk or caution when exposed to arguments and information that were not available to members when they made their initial decision. In general, the greater the number of arguments advanced during discussion that support the initial majority group opinion, the more cogent, reasonable, and persuasive they seem to be. Also, the more original or nonredundant the arguments are, the greater will be the group polarization (Smith, 1982). As these arguments get repeated during discussions, they validate the risk-taking or caution predominant in the group (Brauer et al., 1995). Naturally, if the majority is predisposed toward risk-taking (or caution), the number of arguments advanced will usually favor that predisposition.

In addition to social comparison and persuasive arguments explanations for group polarization, research reveals several lesser conditions that can influence risk-taking or caution in groups. Group decisions will likely shift toward risk-taking when groups are large, when members do not know each other well, and when members are knowledgeable and well informed about the problem. Groups will likely shift toward more cautious decision making when the decision is steeped in uncertainty, when the results could be severe, and when the probability of successful risk-taking is questionable (BarNir, 1998). The direction of the group polarization also appears strongly influenced by the preference of the group's informal leader (Pescosolido, 2001). Culture also plays a role. For instance, U.S. groups are more likely to polarize in the direction of risk, whereas Chinese groups are more likely to polarize in the direction of caution (Hong, 1978). Risk could produce disharmony, especially if it turns out badly.

▶ Combating Group Polarization: Necessary Steps

There are a number of steps that can be taken to address the problem of group polarization (see especially Fishkin, 1997; Sunstein, 2000). First, **encourage a wide range of views on issues to be discussed in the group.** Group polarization thrives on uniformity of opinion and the squashing of dissent. Second, if that diversity of viewpoints is not represented by any group member, **provide well-reasoned and researched material in written or oral form to group members for serious discussion and consideration.** This may be the responsibility of a committee chair or designated leader, but any group member can provide such material. Third, a facilitator during group discussions, either appointed or emerging, should strongly encourage group members to consider opposing viewpoints on issues. **Acting as a devil's advocate can improve chances that damaging polarization won't occur.** Finally, when possible, **discuss issues openly before taking a firm position.** Juries, for example, are often counseled by judges to avoid taking an initial poll on guilt or innocence of a defendant before discussing evidence thoroughly. Once a position is publicly declared, it is difficult to back away from it. When a strong majority expresses a clear point of view initially, polarization can occur.

Groupthink: Critical Thinking in Suspended Animation

Sociologist Irving Janis (1982), who extensively analyzed decision-making debacles, argued that Pearl Harbor, the Bay of Pigs fiasco, Watergate, the escalation of the Vietnam War, and other blunders from U.S. history sprang from a defective decision-making process he calls groupthink. Janis defines **groupthink** as "a mode of thinking that people engage in when they are deeply involved in a cohesive in-group, when the members' strivings for unanimity override their motivation to realistically appraise alternative courses of action" (p. 9).

Focus Questions

1. What causes groupthink?
2. Do groups have to display all the symptoms of groupthink to exhibit poor-quality decisions like those that accompany full-blown groupthink?

▶ General Conditions: Excessive Cohesiveness and Concurrence Seeking

Cohesiveness and its companion, concurrence-seeking, are the two general conditions necessary for groupthink to occur. Janis does not argue that all groups that are cohesive and seek agreement among their members exhibit groupthink. These are necessary but not sufficient conditions for groupthink to occur (Mullen et al., 1994). Obviously, a noncohesive group can spend most of its time and energy on social upheaval, diverted from task accomplishment. Also, cohesiveness in a group can be a very positive factor (Miranda, 1994). **Groupthink is rooted in *excessive* cohesiveness and a resulting pressure to present a united front to those outside of the group.** The more cohesive a group is, the greater is the danger of groupthink (Rovio et al., 2009). This is especially true as the size of the group increases (Mullen et al., 1994). Critical thinking and effective decision making are sacrificed when members are *overly concerned* with reaching agreement, avoiding conflict, and preserving friendly relations in the group.

No group member has to squash dissent openly. The concurrence-seeking norm is so firmly established in the group system that critical faculties are often paralyzed seemingly without notice. Frequently, members fail to see issues that should be challenged, positions that should be questioned, and alternatives that should be explored. Even if they do recognize such problems, they choose to go along in order to get along.

Groupthink is not the cause of every decision-making fiasco. Information overload or underload, mindsets, collective inferential error, group polarization, and sometimes the plain stupidity of decision makers may be primarily responsible for blunders. As Janis (1982) argues, however, groupthink often is a contributing cause, and sometimes it is a primary cause. In this next section, some of the evidence that supports the Janis groupthink explanation for abominably bad group decision making is summarized.

▶ Identification of Groupthink: Main Symptoms

Janis lists eight specific symptoms of groupthink, which he then divides into three types. The eight symptoms are discussed within the context of these three types.

Overestimation of the Group's Power and Morality: Arrogance Repeatedly, the main decision makers associated with the Pearl Harbor debacle communicated a sense of invulnerability. Pearl Harbor was thought to be impregnable. The U.S. command in Pearl Harbor ridiculed the idea of a Japanese attack. Torpedo planes were discounted because U.S. torpedoes required a water depth of at least 60 feet to function and Pearl Harbor had a 30-foot depth. Little consideration was given to the possibility that the Japanese had developed a torpedo capable of striking a target in shallow water. The *illusion of invulnerability* exhibited by the fleet command at Pearl Harbor exploded with nightmarish rapidity.

The illusion of invulnerability is a common precursor to major accidents. The BP oil spill in the Gulf of Mexico in 2010 is an example. Reportedly, when a BP operator told a superior on the oil platform that a handful of rubber material seemed to indicate that the rubber seal down in the well had been damaged, the operator's concern was dismissed by his superior with the comment, "No, that can't be" (quoted in Mackin, 2010).

The Fukushima nuclear reactor was designed to withstand an earthquake as powerful as 8.6 in magnitude, in part because some seismologists thought that it was impossible that any earthquake larger than this could occur at this location (Silver, 2012). The plant was also built on the expectation that no tsunami wave from a major earthquake could rise higher than 5.7 meters. On March 11, 2011, however, Japan suffered a 9.0 magnitude earthquake that produced a 15-meter-high tsunami wave that engulfed the reactor and caused a meltdown and severe radiation leak that all-told killed almost 20,000 people (Aldhouse, 2012).

In addition to a sense of invulnerability, groups sometimes overestimate their morality. The U.S. sense of higher moral purpose contributed to the Bay of Pigs

U.S. Coast Guard/Handout/Corbis

The Deepwater Horizon catastrophic oil spill and explosion in the Gulf of Mexico in 2010 is a case of the illusion of invulnerability that led to the disaster. Eleven men were killed and more than 200 million gallons of oil leaked into the sea, enough to drive a Toyota Prius 185,000 times around the world at the equator. Almost 700 miles of coastline were contaminated (Repanich, 2010). Four years later, oil from the spill was still washing on shore.

invasion. The purpose, after all, was to upend a communist dictator (Castro) and free the Cubans. This *unquestioned belief in the inherent morality of the group* is symptomatic of groupthink.

Closed-Mindedness: Clinging to Assumptions Closed-mindedness is manifested by *rationalizations* that discount warnings or negative information that might cause the group to rethink its basic assumptions. The space shuttle *Columbia* disintegrated on its return to Earth because a chunk of foam knocked a hole in the shuttle's wing on takeoff. NASA knew that previous shuttle flights had been hit by foam debris, but shuttle engineers' weak efforts to sound a warning about possible catastrophic consequences from the debris went unheeded by NASA officials (Oberg, 2003; Wald & Schwartz, 2003). The operating assumption was that foam debris did not pose a serious problem to the safety of the shuttle mission.

Another aspect of closed-mindedness leading to groupthink is *negative stereotyped views of the enemy* as weak, stupid, puny, or evil. This characterization helps justify the recklessness of the group. The Japanese were characterized as a "midget nation" by the command at Pearl Harbor. Lyndon Johnson reputedly characterized the North Vietnamese during the Vietnam War in this racist fashion: "Without air power, we'd be at the mercy of every yellow dwarf with a pocketknife" (Lewallen, 1972, p. 37). President Kennedy's advisors considered Castro and his military force to be a joke. The real joke was the invasion plan that sent 1,400 Cuban exiles up against Castro's military force of 200,000. Simple arithmetic should have shot down that idea. The Bush administration also vastly underestimated the difficulty of pacifying Iraq once the military invasion succeeded in 2003.

Pressures toward Uniformity: Presenting a United Front The last type of symptom of groupthink is the pressure to maintain uniformity of opinion and behavior among group members. Sometimes this pressure is indirect and in other cases it is very direct. An indirect form is manifested when group members engage in *self-censorship,* assuming an apparent consensus exists in the group. The importance of doubts and counterarguments is minimized as a result of the perceived uniformity of opinion. Silence is considered assent, which can lead to what some have called "pluralistic ignorance." Other group members have their doubts, but everyone assumes agreement exists and no one wants to rock the boat, so no one questions or raises an objection. Thus, an *illusion of unanimity* is fostered. If even a hint of dissent emerges, *direct pressure on deviants* is applied to squash it. Nonconformity is about as welcome as a thunderstorm at an outdoor wedding. Finally, uniformity is maintained by information control. *Self-appointed mindguards* protect the group from adverse information that might contradict shared illusions. The system closes off to negative influences, protecting uniformity. Once John F. Kennedy had decided to proceed with the ill-fated Bay of Pigs invasion, his brother Robert dissuaded anyone from disturbing the president with any misgivings about the mission. According to George W. Bush's Treasury Secretary Paul O'Neill, Vice President Dick Cheney and his allies created "a praetorian guard that encircled the president" to prevent dissenting views on the 2003 Iraq invasion (Levine, 2004).

A group does not have to display all the symptoms to experience the poor-quality decisions that accompany full-blown groupthink. As Janis (1982) explains, "Even when some symptoms are absent, the others may be so pronounced that we can expect all the unfortunate consequences of groupthink" (p. 175). He argues that "the more frequently a group displays the symptoms, the worse will be the quality of its decisions, on the average" (p. 175).

▶ Preventing Groupthink: Promoting Vigilance

To prevent groupthink, groups must become vigilant decision makers (Tasa & Whyte, 2005). Vigilant decision making requires that several steps be taken (Janis, 1982; Wood et al., 1986). First, and most obvious, **members must recognize the problem of groupthink as it begins to manifest itself.** If even a single member recognizes groupthink developing and points this out energetically to the group, the problem can be avoided.

Second, **the group must minimize status differences.** High-status members exert a disproportionate influence on lower-status group members. High-status leaders who use strongly directive leadership styles are particularly problematic (Street, 1997). The resulting communication pattern is one of deference to the more powerful person (Milgram, 1974). Such deference can produce ludicrous, even disastrous, consequences.

Michael Cohen and Neil Davis (1981), Temple University pharmacy professors and authors of *Medication Errors: Causes and Prevention,* argue that the accuracy of a doctor's prescription is rarely questioned, even when a prescribed treatment makes no sense. Nurses, for example, are used to being told what to do by doctors (directive leadership). They cite one comical instance of blind deference to high-status authority. A physician ordered application of eardrops to a patient's right ear to treat an infection. The physician abbreviated the prescribed treatment to read, "Place in R ear." The duty nurse read the prescription and promptly administered the eardrops where they presumably would do the most good to "cure" the patient's "rectal earache." Neither the nurse nor the patient questioned the doctor's rather unconventional treatment.

On a more serious level, in one study, crews were subjected to flight simulations under conditions of severe weather and poor visibility. Unknown to the crew members, the captains feigned incapacitation, making serious errors that would lead to certain disaster. Airline officials were stunned to learn that 25% of the flights would have crashed because no crew member took corrective action to override the captain's faulty judgment. Weick (1990) claims that this deference to authority contributed to the Tenerife air disaster in 1977, the worst commercial aviation accident in history. Thus, status differences in groups can encourage groupthink, especially when these status differences are magnified by a directive style of leadership that discourages group member participation (Mullen, 1994).

The group leader, as high-status member, has the primary responsibility to minimize the influence of status differences. The leader could withhold his or her point of view from the group until everyone has had an opportunity to express an opinion. As management training consultant Michael Woodruff, speaking of potential employee disagreement with a supervisor, explains, "If I present an idea as something that I am excited about, then my staff has to go against me [if they disagree]. But if I present it neutrally, they will be more likely to speak out if they think it is wrong. Staffers will seldom criticize what the boss has endorsed" (Stern, 1992, p. 104). The high-status group member could also indicate ambivalence on an issue, thereby encouraging the open expression of a variety of viewpoints.

Seeking information that challenges an emerging concurrence is a third way to prevent groupthink. Assessing the negative consequences of choices is a mark of an effective decision-making group (Hirokawa, 1985). Closely related to this, developing a norm in the group that legitimizes disagreement during discussion sessions is a final way to prevent groupthink. Minority dissent stimulates divergent thought in groups and acts to prevent groupthink and improve decision making (Brodbeck et al., 2002; Greitemeyer & Schultz-Hardt, 2003; Schultz-Hardt et al., 2006). This disagreement norm may have to be structured into the group process. **Groupthink is more likely to occur when there is no structured method in place for evaluating alternative ideas during group discussion** (Street, 1997).

There are several ways to accomplish these last two ways of preventing groupthink. First, **assign one or two group members to play devil's advocate.** The primary group presents its proposals and arguments and the devil's advocates critique it. This process can proceed through several rounds of proposals and critiques until the group, including devil's advocates, is satisfied that the best decision has been made. It is a very effective method of overcoming the excessive concurrence-seeking characteristic of groupthink (Stasser & Titus, 1987). However, as Stanford professor Jeffrey Pfeffer (2010) observes, "Unfortunately, devil's advocacy is not practiced very much or institutionalized in many corporate decision-making processes, which may be why so many poor decisions are made."

Second, **institute a dialectical inquiry** (Sims, 1992). This procedure is very similar to devil's advocacy, except that in dialectical inquiry a subgroup develops a counterproposal and defends it side by side with the group's initial proposal. Thus, a debate takes place on two differing proposals. One or the other may be chosen by the group, both may be rejected in favor of further exploration and inquiry before a final decision is made, or a compromise between the two proposals may be hammered out. Both devil's advocacy and dialectical inquiry are effective antidotes to groupthink (Pavitt & Curtis, 1994).

Third, **assign a group member to play the reminder role** (Schultz et al., 1995). This is a formally designated role. The reminder raises questions in a nonaggressive manner regarding collective inferential error, confirmation bias, false dichotomies, and any of the myriad symptoms of groupthink that may arise. The reminder role is an effective method of combating groupthink tendencies (Schultz et al., 1995). Groupthink can be a primary source of poor decision making in groups (Hensley & Griffin, 1986; Herek et al., 1987; Leana, 1985; Moorhead & Montanari, 1986). Recognizing the symptoms of groupthink and taking steps to prevent it from occurring play an important role in any effort to improve the quality of group decisions.

In summary, group members must exercise their critical-thinking abilities. The quality of decision making and problem solving in groups is significantly affected by problems of information quantity, mindsets, inferential errors, group polarization, and

SECOND LOOK

Primary Symptoms

Overestimation of Group's Power and Morality
  Illusion of invulnerability
  Unquestioned belief in the inherent morality of the group

Closed-Mindedness
  Rationalization
  Negative stereotyped views of the enemy

Pressures toward Uniformity
  Self-censorship of contradictory opinion
  Illusion of unanimity
  Direct pressure applied to deviants
  Self-appointed mindguards

Preventing Groupthink
  Recognize groupthink when it first begins
  Minimize status differences
  Develop norm that legitimizes disagreement

groupthink. If groups learn to cope with information overload and underload, recognize and counteract mindsets, avoid or correct collective inferential errors, recognize and respond to group polarization, and avoid groupthink, then decision making and problem solving will be of higher quality.

Reflect on what you've learned.

In Mixed Company

▶ Online

Now that you've read Chapter 8, access the online resources that accompany *In Mixed Company* at **www.cengagebrain.com**. Your online resources include:

1. Multiple-choice and true-false **chapter practice quizzes** with automatic correction
2. Digital **glossary**
3. **Flashcards**

QUESTIONS FOR CRITICAL THINKERS

1. Why is information overload such a problem when we have labor-saving technologies such as personal computers to process huge quantities of data?
2. Why are collective inferential errors more likely when issues are emotionally charged?
3. If cohesiveness is a positive small group attribute, why can it lead to groupthink?

VIDEO *Case Studies*

No End in Sight (2007). Documentary
This is a documentary on the U.S. entry into the Iraq war and its ensuing difficulties. Examine this film's depiction of the war for illustrations of confirmation bias, inferential error, and groupthink.

Thirteen Days (2000). Drama; PG-13
Semi-accurate depiction of the harrowing 13 days of the Cuban Missile Crisis. The Kennedy administration avoided the groupthink mistakes that it made during the Bay of Pigs fiasco. Examine what prevented groupthink during the Cuban Missile Crisis.

Tora! Tora! Tora! (1970). Drama; G
Still the best dramatic depiction of the Japanese attack on Pearl Harbor, providing both sides' perspectives on the worst naval disaster in the United States. Examine events leading up to the attack from the standpoint of groupthink.

9 Group Discussion: Effective Decision Making and Problem Solving

A. Discussion Procedures
1. Phases and Functions: General Considerations
   a. *Multiple Sequence Model: Phases of Decision Making*
   b. *Functional Perspective: Being Systematic*
2. The Standard Agenda: Structuring Group Discussion
   a. *Problem Identification: What's the Question?*
   b. *Problem Analysis: Causes and Effects*

Closer Look: Different Criteria Produce Different Outcomes
   c. *Solution Criteria: Setting Standards*
   d. *Solution Suggestions: Generating Alternatives*
   e. *Solution Evaluation and Selection: Deciding by Criteria*
   f. *Solution Implementation: Follow-Through*

Closer Look: Murphy's Law
3. Group Decision-Making Rules: Majority, Minority, Unanimity
   a. *Majority Rule: Tyrannical or Practical*
   b. *Minority Rule: Several Types*
   c. *Unanimity Rule: Consensus*

B. Participation
1. Cultural Diversity and Participation: Is Silence Golden?

2. Increasing Constructive Participation: Jump-Starting Low Participators

C. Conducting Effective Meetings
1. Group Meetings: The Good, the Bad, and the Ugly
2. Chair's and Members' Responsibilities: Controlling the Meeting Monster

D. Critical Thinking and Effective Decision Making
1. Gathering Information: Accumulating Input
2. Evaluating Information: Applying Criteria
   a. *Credibility: Is It Believable?*
   b. *Currency: Is It Up to Date?*
   c. *Relevance: Looking for Logical Connections*
   d. *Representativeness: Reflecting the Facts*
   e. *Sufficiency: When Enough Really Is Enough*

Closer Look: The Internet: Resource for Information and Misinformation

E. Creative Problem Solving
1. General Overview
2. Specific Creative Techniques
   a. *Brainstorming and Nominal Group Techniques: Generating Lots of Ideas*
   b. *Framing/Reframing: It's All in the Wording*
   c. *Integrative Problem Solving: Satisfying Everyone*

There are approximately 15,000 students who attend Cabrillo College in Santa Cruz County, California, every semester. It is a huge challenge to streamline the registration process to accommodate this many students each term. A few years ago, Cabrillo's new president came to the faculty senate, among other campus bodies, and presented his proposal to consolidate in one building all processes related to registration. The idea was not without merit, but it was badly timed. When quizzed on the cost of such consolidation, the initial estimate was $550,000. Many services on campus would have to be relocated to accommodate any consolidation, creating significant disruption. The campus was in the middle of a $200 million facelift. Adding yet another renovation project would negatively affect the degree, rate, and desirability of change in the campus system.

At the faculty senate meeting on the proposal, the president was repeatedly challenged to show that an urgent problem existed. Construction plans had already been approved for consolidating all on-campus registration procedures to a single location within five years, and almost all students registered online anyway, so they required minimal on-campus contact. The president provided no data to support the need for an urgent consolidation. Nevertheless, the College Board approved the project on the assurances by the president that the consolidation was an urgent need. Shortly after the renovation was completed, it became apparent that the plan was faulty in many respects. A subsequent renovation, at considerable cost, had to be undertaken to correct the president's original unnecessary, slapdash plan.

There is little doubt that had the president established a campus committee to investigate the need for such a project, the conclusion would have been to wait. Delaying the project would have permitted creation of a carefully conceived plan, saved significant money, and it would have avoided unnecessary, substantial disruption on campus.

The Cabrillo College registration project is testament to the importance of implementing effective procedures for group decision making and problem solving. **The primary purpose of this chapter is to explore the process of effective group decision making/problem solving.** Toward this end there are five chapter objectives:

1. To explain procedures for conducting productive group discussions that will result in effective decisions and solutions to problems,

2. To explore ways to encourage productive participation from group members,

3. To describe ways to conduct effective decision-making group meetings,

4. To discuss ways to gather and evaluate information necessary for effective decision making and problem solving,

5. To explain several techniques of creative group problem solving.

Discussion Procedures

Read, highlight, and take notes online.

In this section, guidelines and procedures for conducting effective group discussion are presented. The importance of using a systematic approach during group discussion cannot be underestimated. Special emphasis is given to the Standard Agenda.

Focus Questions

1. How does the Standard Agenda relate to the functional perspective on effective group discussion procedures?

2. What constitutes a true consensus?

3. What are the advantages and disadvantages of various decision-making rules?

▶ Phases and Functions: General Considerations

All decision-making and problem-solving groups exhibit recognizable phases. They follow certain paths to decisions and solutions.

Multiple Sequence Model: Phases of Decision Making The most widely accepted phasic model of group decision making is Poole's (1983) **multiple sequence model** of decision emergence. The multiple sequence model pictures groups moving along three activity tracks: *task, relational,* and *topic.* Groups do not necessarily proceed along these three tracks at the same rate or according to the same pattern. Some groups may devote a significant amount of time to the relational (social) activities of groups before proceeding to a task discussion; other groups may start right in on the task. Groups may also be sidetracked during discussions on task by relational conflicts that need to be addressed.

Groups take three principal paths in reaching decisions (Poole & Roth, 1989a, 1989b). The first path is called the *unitary sequence.* Groups on the unitary sequence path proceed in a rigid, step-by-step fashion toward a decision. The second path is called *complex cyclic.* These groups engage in repeated cycles of focusing on the problem, then the solution, and back again to the problem, and so forth. Finally, the third principal path to decision making is *solution oriented.* Here the group launches into discussion of solutions with little focus on an analysis of the problem. Groups most often choose the complex cyclic path, less often the solution-oriented path, and infrequently the unitary sequence path.

Poole's multiple sequence model of decision development emphasizes that group discussion does not necessarily proceed along a single predictable path. There are several ways that decisions occur in groups. The multiple sequence model mostly *describes* these principal paths that groups often take. The functional perspective, however, *prescribes* procedures for effective decision making and problem solving for groups in general.

Functional Perspective: Being Systematic Discussions that follow some systematic procedure tend to be more productive and result in better decisions than relatively unstructured discussions (LaFasto & Larson, 2001). Structuration theory posits that rules permit group members to understand how the system of decision making works. The drawbacks to unstructured, free-floating group discussion with no clear rules of procedure include: aimless deliberations that are time-consuming and inefficient, premature focus on solutions (the solution-oriented path), inclination to accept the first plausible solution, which may not be the best option, discussion tangents and topic-hopping, domination by the most vociferous group member, and failure to address group conflict (Sunwolf & Seibold, 1999; Sunwolf & Frey, 2005).

There is no single, systematic discussion procedure that guarantees effective decision making and problem solving. *"What happens at each stage and how well necessary functions are executed are the real determinants of success"* (Gouran, 1982, p. 30). Rigidly following a set of prescribed steps, such as the unitary sequence path, can stifle natural discussion and seem robotic. Nevertheless, student and faculty senate meetings, for example, run according to rules of parliamentary procedure and guided by specific detailed agendas, can result in efficient if somewhat stilted meetings.

Steps in any systematic discussion procedure should be looked at as guidelines, not commandments. Some allowance should be made for cycling back to steps previously addressed as group members discuss problems and solutions. The more complex the task being discussed, the more likely the complex-cyclic path will emerge. Flashes of insight don't necessarily follow a preordained sequence of discussion steps. The group may need to backtrack occasionally and address already discussed issues.

Whatever path group decision making and problem solving takes, **variations in the quality of decisions by groups can be accounted for by the relative ability of members to perform systematically five critical decision-making functions** (Orlitzky & Hirokawa, 2001). These *five functions* are problem analysis, establishment of evaluation criteria, generation of alternative solutions, evaluation of positive consequences of solutions, and evaluation of negative consequences of solutions. This functional perspective is reflected in the Standard Agenda discussion procedures.

▶ The Standard Agenda: Structuring Group Discussion

John Dewey (1910) described a process of rational problem solving and decision making that he called **reflective thinking**—a set of logical steps that incorporate the scientific method of defining, analyzing, and solving problems. The Standard Agenda is a direct outgrowth of Dewey's reflective thinking process. It is a highly effective, structured method for decision making and problem solving in groups. The Standard Agenda places the emphasis on the problem initially to counteract premature consideration of solutions (the solution-oriented path), an emphasis that was missing from the Cabrillo College consolidated registration proposal. The Standard Agenda has six steps. This section explains the procedure by using smoking on the Cabrillo College campus as the problem. Note that, unlike the college president's proposal, this was a problem handled effectively through systematic group discussion.

Problem Identification: What's the Question? The problem should be formulated into an open-ended question identifying what type of problem the group must consider. Questions may be phrased as fact, value, or policy. The choice will identify the nature of the problem. A **question of fact** asks whether something is true and to what extent. Objective evidence can be used to determine an answer to the question. "Are there dangers to nonsmokers from secondhand smoke, and, if so, what are these dangers?" is a question of fact. A **question of value** asks for an evaluation of the desirability of an object, idea, event, or person. "Does permitting smoking on campus raise any quality-of-life concerns?" is a question of value. Objective evidence does not lead to any clear answers on questions of values. Quality of life, for example, can't be determined scientifically or statistically. It is a perception based on subjective views of the world. Smokers might find the smell of smoke pleasant, even stimulating, whereas nonsmokers may find it grossly unpleasant. A **question of policy** asks whether a specific course of action should be undertaken to solve a problem. "What changes, if any, should be made regarding the smoking policy on campus?" is a policy question.

Once the problem is phrased as a question of fact, value, or policy, any ambiguous terms should be defined. "Quality of life" would require some further description (no strong odors, freedom from pollutants that might trigger respiratory difficulties, etc.). "Smoking policy on campus" would need to be explained so the group knows exactly what policy is currently in place.

Problem Analysis: Causes and Effects The group researches and gathers information on the problem defined, tries to determine how serious the problem is, what harm or effect the problem produces, and what causes the problem. Smoking on campus was a contentious issue at Cabrillo College for many years. Nonsmoking students complained repeatedly to their student senators about the problem. In an open hearing instituted by the student senate to gather information and help determine the extent of the problem, tempers flared. One student, defending the "rights of smokers," told nonsmokers to "quit school if you don't like our smoking." A student defending nonsmokers' rights vehemently retorted, "Polluters have no rights." Another nonsmoker facetiously suggested "public floggings as a penalty for smoking." The conclusion of the student senate, after much research and debate, was that the smoking policy was too permissive and this was causing numerous hazards and significant unpleasantness for students. One note of caution here: Although analyzing the problem is important and should be undertaken before exploring potential solutions, **analysis paralysis,** or bogging down by analyzing the problem too much, can also thwart effective decision making. It prevents a group from ever getting on with business and making a decision.

Solution Criteria: Setting Standards Standards by which decisions and solutions to problems can be evaluated are called **criteria** (see Closer Look: "Different Criteria Produce Different Outcomes"). In the summer of 2007, the American Film Institute released its list of "100 Best American Movies." *Citizen Kane* topped the list, repeating its previous top spot from a similar 1997 list concocted by AFI ("Citizen Kane," 2007). For most college students of today, this must seem a perplexing choice. *Citizen Kane,* released in 1941, is a black-and-white film, has no real body count, the action is plodding by today's frenetic standards, and the special effects probably seem goofy compared to the blockbuster movies of today. Without knowing the criteria used by the Film Institute to judge the quality of movies, it is very difficult to understand many of the choices that made the 100 Best list and the rankings. Knowing that "influence on future American filmmaking" is a primary criterion helps you understand better why *Citizen Kane* ranked as the top all-time American film. If "entertainment value" were a prime criterion, the top choice may not have fared so well. Even if you knew the criteria used, you may still disagree with the decisions made, but at least you would have a basis for discussion. Criteria help groups determine whether their decisions make sense and are likely to be effective.

CLOSER LOOK

Different Criteria Produce Different Outcomes

Developing appropriate criteria is a critical group function for making effective decisions and solving problems. If you are a member of an interviewing panel whose task is to hire someone for an important job, determining the criteria for hiring helps separate numerous applicants into those who clearly don't qualify (they don't meet even the minimum standards), those who deserve a second look, and those who leap off the page and shout "Look at Me!"

Different criteria, however, can produce wildly different results. On the *U.S. News* list of best universities, the University of Wisconsin, Madison, was ranked *9th* in the nation, but on the *Forbes* list, the same university was ranked *415th* ("America's Best Colleges," 2009; "Best Colleges," 2009). The explanation for the wide difference in rankings lies in the criteria selected by the two magazines. The main criteria for the *U.S. News* list were assessment by administrators at peer institutions, student retention rates, faculty resources, student selectivity, general financial resources, quantity of alumni donations, and graduation rates. The main criteria for the *Forbes* list were student satisfaction, postgraduate success, student debt, graduation rates within four years, and competitive student awards. Although there is some overlap of criteria, there are big differences. In fact, an examination of college

rankings by six different publications (*U.S. News, Forbes, Washington Monthly, Kiplinger, Times Higher Education,* and *Academic Ranking of World Universities*) revealed a total of 30 separate criteria. None of the 30 was used by all six publications and a whopping 22 criteria were used variously by only one of the six publications (Hawley, 2010). Not surprisingly, the rankings of colleges by these six publications differed widely. Thus, choosing appropriate criteria can markedly affect group assessments.

Any list that ranks best colleges or best jobs or best films and the like can change every year, especially when those who formulate the rankings change the criteria for selection. When *Forbes* changed its criteria for college rankings, the University of Wisconsin–Madison vaulted from 415th place in 2009 to 68th in 2013 ("America's Top Colleges," 2013).

Make sure that your group chooses criteria wisely. Discuss carefully what the group agrees are the most important criteria for producing desirable results. If you're hiring a college instructor, do you want the very best teacher or do you want a good teacher who will also likely produce excellent nationally recognized research and publications that bring prestige to the college? There are no perfect criteria fit for all groups. Criteria are debatable issues.

Decide what is your primary group goal (e.g., hire the best teacher possible) and then develop criteria that will likely achieve that goal best from your group's perspective.

Once your group has chosen criteria, determine *appropriate measures* for each criterion. For example, using student evaluations of professors posted on ratemyprofessors.com to measure "quality of instruction" is dubious at best because the sample size is usually very small and the sample is self-selected, not random, and therefore unrepresentative. Vigorous group discussion can usually resolve these issues of appropriate criteria and adequate measures for each criterion.

QUESTIONS FOR THOUGHT

1. What criteria might your student senate use to decide how best to spend funds accumulated by assessing student fees? Which criteria might be most controversial?

2. What criteria do you think are most appropriate for ranking colleges and universities in the United States? Why?

The group should establish criteria for evaluating solutions before solutions are suggested. This may necessitate a vigorous discussion of possible criteria. In some cases the criteria are already dictated by others (e.g., a judge's instructions to a jury to use the legal criterion of "beyond a reasonable doubt" in a murder case). Not all criteria, however, are created equal. The group must consider the relevance and appropriateness of each criterion. Ranking films based on criteria such as "buckets of blood spilled" or "number of sex scenes" would be dubious at best except perhaps for those with extremely narrow (some would say questionable) interests.

Some relevant and appropriate criteria on the smoking question devised by an ad hoc campus committee included: protect the health of nonsmokers, be simple to understand and enforce, avoid alienating either group (smokers or nonsmokers), cost less than $5,000, and maintain a comfortable environment. **The criteria should be ranked in order of priority.** The committee prioritized the criteria on the smoking policy in the order just listed.

Solution Suggestions: Generating Alternatives The group brainstorms possible solutions (see later in this chapter for proper brainstorming technique). Some possibilities on the smoking issue that emerged from the committee deliberations included mandating a total ban on smoking across the campus, designating certain locations outside for smoking, building outside shelters in designated locations around the campus to protect smokers from weather, permitting smoking only in automobiles, and allowing smoking only in parking lots both in cars and outside.

Once a list of ideas has been generated, the group should clarify any ambiguous or confusing ideas. Ideas that overlap should be consolidated into a single idea.

Solution Evaluation and Selection: Deciding by Criteria The story of a military briefing officer asked to devise a method for raising enemy submarines off the ocean floor illustrates the importance of this step. The briefing officer's solution? Heat the ocean to the boiling point. When bewildered Pentagon officials asked him how this could be done, he replied, "I don't know. I decided on the solution; you work out the details." The devil is in the details. **Explore both the merits and demerits (avoid confirmation bias) of suggested solutions.** Devil's advocacy and dialectical inquiry (see Chapter 8) are useful techniques for accomplishing this aspect of the Standard Agenda.

Consider each solution in terms of the criteria established earlier. For instance, protecting the health of faculty, staff, and students was a prime concern of those addressing the smoking policy. Of all the solution suggestions, a total ban on smoking met this criterion best. It didn't avoid alienating smokers on campus, however. Concern was raised that a total ban might alienate student smokers to such an extent that significant enrollment declines would result, costing a great loss of money to the college. Smoking in designated areas seemed to be a promising solution, and was tried on a temporary basis, but smokers had difficulty determining where the designated smoking areas were on campus despite posted maps indicating them. This solution proved to be too complicated and difficult to enforce. Complaints also arose that there weren't shelters in all designated areas so smokers were exposed to some nasty weather. This violated the "maintain a comfortable environment" criterion. Building shelters for smokers to address this complaint proved to be too costly, far exceeding the criterion that set a $5,000 limit on expenses. Relegating smokers to their automobiles proved to be impractical because this would ban smoking for those who chose mass transit or bicycled to campus. Finally, the suggestion that smoking be relegated to parking lots protected the health of nonsmokers; was a simple, easily understood policy; cost less than $5,000 (some concrete ashtrays were distributed in all parking lots at minimal expense); and mostly avoided alienating smokers because smoking was still permitted, although restricted, on campus. Only the maintaining a comfortable environment criterion was not met completely because smokers were still not totally sheltered from the elements. They could, however, smoke in their cars or smoke in the two massive parking structures on campus that provide some shelter, especially from rain.

There are three decision-making methods that are used to make solution choices: majority rule, minority rule, or consensus. A thorough discussion of the merits and demerits of each method appears in the next section of this chapter. The ad hoc campus committee used consensus (unanimity rule); the faculty and student senates and the board of trustees used majority rule. Permitting smoking only in parking lots was the eventual policy adopted by the board of trustees with support from the faculty and student senates. It made Cabrillo College one of the very first colleges in the nation to restrict smoking to this extent. The policy has recently been revisited to discuss a total ban on all smoking on campus, as many campuses have already instituted. Using the same Standard Agenda procedure, it is expected that such a ban will occur in 2015.

Solution Implementation: Follow-through A common failing of decision-making groups is that once they arrive at a decision there is no follow-through. One study found that only 30% of strategic initiatives in businesses are successfully implemented (Davis et al., 2010). **Force field analysis**, suggested by the work of Kurt Lewin (1947), is one method for planning implementation of a group solution or decision. Using force field analysis, groups brainstorm a list of *driving forces*—those that encourage change—and *restraining forces*—those that resist change. Driving forces that encouraged implementation of the new smoking policy at Cabrillo College included multiple complaints from students, stated concerns about the health risks to nonsmokers, and a fear that nonsmokers would stop enrolling at the college. Restraining forces working against implementation of the new smoking policy mostly involve a more general resistance to change itself.

Change does not come easily to most of us. A study by EquaTerra, an independent business and information technology advisory firm, found that the number one barrier to change in business environments is "resistance to change," noted by 82% of respondents ("Survey of CEOs," 2007). A study of business leaders in 80 countries reported that "change is synonymous with downsizing, doing more with less" and this creates resistance. Change fatigue, poor leadership, and "a litany of communication failures" also contribute to this resistance (Anderson, 2012).

There are five ways to reduce resistance to change and consequent restraining forces impeding solution implementation (Tubbs, 1984). They are:

1. As noted previously, **people are more likely to accept change when they have had a part in the planning and decision making.** Imposing change produces psychological reactance (see Chapter 4) and, therefore, increases resistance to change.

2. **Changes are more likely to be accepted if they do not threaten group members.** The larger concern on the smoking issue was whether students would drop out of Cabrillo College because the policy was too permissive, even though some concern was expressed that the more restrictive policy would threaten enrollment declines among smokers.

3. **Changes are more likely to be accepted when the need for change affects individuals directly.** The great majority of students at Cabrillo College are nonsmokers directly affected by a permissive smoking policy.

4. **There will be less resistance to change when the change is open to revision and modification.** The smoking policy revision was presented as a temporary fix, subject to further revision if necessary.

5. **The three factors (degree, rate, and desirability) affecting a group's ability to adapt to change in a system should be considered.** The smoking policy at Cabrillo College addressed excessive degree of change by not banning smoking entirely, addressed too rapid a rate of change by phasing in the policy (designated areas were tried first), and addressed desirability by conducting open hearings on the issue.

A helpful decision-making method that stipulates systematically how to implement small group decisions once resistance to change has been addressed is called **PERT** (Program Evaluation Review Technique). The steps in the PERT method are:

1. Determine what the final step should look like (e.g., restrict smoking to parking lots only).

2. Specify any events that must occur before the final goal is realized (e.g., obtain endorsement from the board of trustees).

3. Put the events in chronological order (e.g., the committee must secure the support of the student and faculty senates, then the college president, before going to the board for endorsement).

4. If necessary, construct a diagram of the process to trace the progress of implementation (useful only if there are numerous steps).

5. Generate a list of activities, resources, and materials that are required between events (e.g., hold a strategy session before making presentations to the student and faculty senates, and again before seeking the president's endorsement).

6. Develop a time line for implementation. Estimate how long each step will take.

7. Match the total time estimate for implementation of the solution with any deadlines (e.g., end of school year approaching). Modify your plan of action as needed (e.g., take any appointment time available with the president that will move the process along).

8. Specify which group members will have which responsibilities.

CLOSER LOOK

Murphy's Law

On March 11, 2011, a 9.0 earthquake off the coast of northeastern Japan produced a gigantic tsunami that swamped the Fukushima Daiichi nuclear power plant and released significant amounts of radiation into the atmosphere, requiring a massive evacuation of citizens. On April 1, ABC News reported that plant operators were "woefully unprepared for the scale of the disaster" (Mark & Willacy, 2011). A team of inspectors from the International Atomic Energy Agency issued a report at the end of May 2011. The report clearly charged that Japan underestimated the danger of tsunamis and did not prepare adequately for such an event (Fackler, 2011).

Murphy's law states that anything that can go wrong likely will go wrong—somewhere, sometime. A common mistake made by groups is failure to plan for Murphy's law to minimize the chance of error or mishap. Human error or simply bad luck must be considered. The more complex the system, the more likely serious errors can and will occur. The 2010 BP oil spill disaster in the Gulf of Mexico is testament to this. Deep-water drilling is enormously complex and full of risks. Those responsible for the disastrous spill were not sufficiently concerned about Murphy's law. As the January 11, 2011, final report from the National Commission on the BP Deepwater Horizon Oil Spill and Offshore Drilling (2011) concluded, "The blowout was not the product of a series of aberrational decisions made by rogue industry or government officials that could not have been anticipated or expected to occur again." Failure to plan for errors or unusual occurrences can be catastrophic. The BP oil disaster killed 11 rig workers and released an estimated 200 million gallons of crude oil into the Gulf of Mexico (Cappiello, 2011).

The enormously successful Mars rover *Sojourner,* mentioned in Chapter 4, was extensively tested prior to its launch. David Gruel, an engineer assigned the task of creating any conceivable problems *Sojourner* might encounter, tested the rover in a "sandbox" that simulated the surface of Mars. The *Sojourner* team needed to know in advance whether the rover could meet any difficulty it might face. Gruel and his team took into account Murphy's law. *Sojourner* passed every test in the sandbox and was a huge success on Mars (Shirley, 1997).

During the solution evaluation and selection phase of discussion, groups should address possible mishaps and mistakes. Backup plans and emergency procedures should be developed. By doing so, likelihood of success, while not guaranteed, is certainly markedly improved. At worst, the consequences of actual mishaps are minimized.

QUESTIONS FOR THOUGHT

1. Can you provide examples of group decision-making errors that could have been avoided or minimized had the group accounted for Murphy's law?

2. Is planning for what might go wrong with a decision or plan the group wants to implement always a good idea? Is this the same as cynicism, the great killer of teamwork?

▶ Group Decision-Making Rules: Majority, Minority, Unanimity

As stated earlier, rules help groups achieve their goals. They foster stability and reduce variability in a system. Majority, minority, and unanimity are the three primary decision-making rules. Any of these decision-making rules can be applied to the Standard Agenda format.

Majority Rule: Tyrannical or Practical No one should be surprised that majority rule is a popular method of decision making in the United States. It has determined winners on *American Idol, Dancing with the Stars, Survivor,* and other media-manufactured contests. The U.S. democratic political system relies on it. Majority rule in groups, however, is not exactly the same as majority rule in our political system. Minorities are protected by the Bill of Rights. Congress is guided by the realization that legislation must not violate constitutional guarantees of individual liberties. Most small groups provide no similar protection for minorities. The quality of the group's decision is a particularly troublesome problem with majority rule. Majorities can sometimes take ludicrous, even dangerous positions. Mob rule is a manifestation of the tyranny of the majority. Racism, sexism, and other bigotry in the United States have been the products of majority rule.

Studies comparing juries using the unanimous decision rule and majority rule (Oregon requires a 10–2 majority and Louisiana a 9–3 split for felony convictions) found several deficiencies in majority rule applicable to most small groups (Abramson, 1994; Hastie et al., 1983). First, **deliberations are significantly shorter and less conscientious.** Deliberations typically end once a requisite majority is reached. Consequently, less error correction takes place, sometimes resulting in faulty decisions (Lee & Paradowski, 2007). Second, **minority factions participate less frequently and are less influential,** thereby underutilizing the group's resources. Third, **jurors' overall satisfaction with the group is lower.** Minorities feel that their point of view is ignored and the style of deliberation is typically more combative, forceful, and bullying.

Despite the disadvantages of majority rule, there are some advantages (Hastie & Kameda, 2005). **When issues are not very important, when decisions must be made relatively quickly, and when commitment of all members to the final decision is unimportant, majority rule can be useful.** Majority rule is efficient and provides quick closure on relatively unimportant issues without necessarily sacrificing decision accuracy. As groups become larger, majority rule may be necessary for democratic decision making to take place because consensus becomes increasingly difficult the larger the group becomes.

Minority Rule: Several Types Majorities don't always make the decisions. Minority rule as a group decision-making method occurs in several forms. First, the *group designates one of its members as an expert* to make the decision. This method relieves group members from devoting time and energy to solving problems. Decision by designated expert, however, is mostly ineffective. Trying to determine who is the clear expert in the group is often difficult, even impossible. Lack of group input also fails to capitalize on synergy.

Second, a *designated authority* (usually from outside the immediate group) makes the decision for the group, either after hearing discussion from group members or without their consultation. Decision by designated authority is popular in business organizations because it reinforces hierarchical power structures, and it is efficient. The Cabrillo College consolidated registration proposal was instituted primarily by the president, despite opposition from student and faculty senates. Sometimes the group acts in an advisory capacity to the designated authority and sometimes not. Since the group has no ultimate authority, this method of decision making has drawbacks. The quality of the designated authority's decision will depend a great deal on how good a listener he or she is. If the group discussion is merely a formality, then none of the benefits of collective deliberations will accrue. Since power is unevenly distributed, group members are likely to vie competitively for attention and seek to impress the authority (Johnson & Johnson, 1988). Members will be tempted to report to the authority what he or she wants to hear, not what should be said. If the authority encourages genuine disagreement and in no way penalizes members for their honesty, he or she can benefit enormously from a dialectical clash of ideas.

Third, in some instances, *executive committees* must be delegated responsibility for making certain decisions because the workload for the group as a whole is overwhelming or the time constraints are prohibitive. The challenge here is to persuade the group to get behind the decision.

Finally, minority rule can take the form of a *forceful faction* making a decision for the group by dominating less forceful members. On rare occasions this may be advisable when the minority faction consists of the most informed, committed members. Too often, however, dominant group members who flex their muscles focus on personal gain more than on what's good for the group (Murnighan, 1978).

Unanimity Rule: Consensus The unanimity rule governs some groups. Juries are the most obvious example. Persuading all members of a group to agree on anything can be daunting. Group consensus is based on the unanimity rule. **Consensus** is "a state of mutual agreement among members of a group where all legitimate concerns of individuals have been addressed to the satisfaction of the group" (Saint & Lawson, 1997). Not all unanimous decisions can be considered a true consensus.

True consensus requires agreement, commitment, and satisfaction (DeStephen & Hirokawa, 1988). All members must agree with the group's final decision, but consensus does not require adoption of every member's personal preference. **Consensus usually requires some give and take.** If all members can agree on an acceptable alternative, even if this alternative is not each member's first choice, then you have come close to achieving a true consensus. Once unanimous agreement has been reached, members must be willing to defend the decision to outsiders, not undermine it by agreeing in the group but disagreeing outside of the group. This shows commitment. Finally, we rarely commit to a group decision when we have little part in formulating it. True consensus requires the opportunity to influence group discussion and choice. Thus, group members must feel satisfied with the decision-making process. Satisfaction is not derived from bullying members into conformity. Satisfaction comes from a cooperative group climate and reasonable opportunities for all members to participate meaningfully in the decision making (Gastil et al., 2007).

Groups that use a consensus approach tend to produce better decisions than groups using other decision rules. This occurs because full discussion of issues is required, every group member must be convinced that the decision is a good one, and minority members are heard (Lee & Paradowski, 2007). Women, who often remain silent during group discussions when outnumbered by men and majority rule is used, are much more vocal when the unanimity rule is in place (Karpowitz et al., 2012). Members feel more confident about the correctness of their decisions with consensus, and they are more satisfied with the group as a whole (Abramson, 1994; Miller, 1989). Group consensus decision making is especially effective when group members have extensive experience using this method (Watson et al., 1991).

Nevertheless, there are two principal limitations to consensus decision making. First, **achieving unanimous agreement from group members is very difficult,** especially when the issues are emotionally charged and time for decision making is limited. Discussions can become contentious and time consuming. Members who resist siding with the majority lengthen the deliberations and increase the frustration level among those looking for a quick decision. Second, **consensus is increasingly unlikely as groups grow larger.** Groups of 15 or 20 rarely achieve a consensus on much of anything. Seeking a consensus, however, even if one is never quite achieved, can produce most of the benefits of true consensus.

Several guidelines can help a group achieve a consensus (Hall & Watson, 1970; Saint & Lawson, 1997):

1. *Follow the Standard Agenda.* Structured group discussion, not aimless conversation, improves the chances of achieving consensus.

2. *Establish a cooperative group climate.* Supportive patterns of communication encourage consensus; defensive patterns discourage consensus.

3. *Identify the pluses and minuses of potential decisions under consideration.* Write these positives and negatives on a chalkboard, whiteboard, large tablet, or type them onto a computer screen projected for all to see. (Avoid confirmation bias.)

4. *Discuss all concerns of group members and attempt to resolve every one.* Try to find alternatives that will satisfy members' concerns. (Avoid groupthink.)

5. *Avoid adversarial, win–lose arguments.* Don't stubbornly argue for a position to achieve a personal victory. Seek ways to break a stalemate. (Avoid the "enemy–friend" competitive false dichotomy.)

6. *Request a "stand aside."* A stand aside means a team member continues to have reservations about the group decision but, when confronted, does not wish to block the group choice. (Avoid the blocker role.)

7. *Avoid conflict-suppressing techniques such as coin flipping and swapping* ("I'll support your position this time if you support mine next time"). The primary objective is to make a high-quality decision, not avoid conflict. Seek differences of opinion. Conflict-suppressing techniques also will not usually produce commitment to the group decision. (Resist groupthink.)

8. *If consensus is impossible despite these guidelines, seek a supermajority (a minimum two-thirds agreement).* A supermajority at least captures the spirit of consensus by requiring substantial, if not total, agreement. Supermajorities, of course, can still lead to stalemate when a small faction steadfastly thwarts the will of the robust majority. Consensus, or something approaching it, is not always achievable.

Participation

The Standard Agenda and decision-making rules used by groups are likely to be effective only if group members are active, effective participants in the process. As important as participation of group members is to group synergy, no one wants to encourage participation from members who are obnoxious or bent on sharing misinformation. Nevertheless, low participation from group members, especially those who are merely shy or reticent to contribute for a variety of reasons, can severely impact group effectiveness. In this section, the challenge of cultural diversity and rates of participation is discussed. Ways to encourage low-participators to become more actively engaged in group discussions are also offered.

SECOND LOOK

Rules	Pros	Cons
Majority Rule	Quick, Efficient	Minorities vulnerable to tyranny of majority
	Expedient in large groups	Quality of decision questionable
		Usually alienates minority
		Underutilization of resources
Minority Rule		
Designated Expert	Saves time	Expertise hard to determine
		No group input
Designated Authority	Clear, Efficient	Members vie for attention
Executive Committee	Divides labor	Weak commitment to decision
Forceful Faction	Faction may be informed/committed	Likely Me-, not We- oriented
Unanimity Rule (Consensus)	Quality decisions	Time-consuming,
	Commitment	Difficult
	Satisfaction	Tension-producing

Focus Questions

1. Should nonminority Americans value silence as much as some ethnic minorities do?

2. Should Americans deemphasize speaking ability?

3. Should you expect ethnic minority group members to become more assertive and outspoken participators in small groups, even though this is not highly valued in their communities?

► Cultural Diversity and Participation: Is Silence Golden?

The year 2009 marked the beginning of Japan's first jury system since World War II. The idea of participating in jury deliberations and deciding court cases does not immediately appeal to Japanese citizens. There is a deep cultural reticence to expressing opinions in public discourse, to arguing different points of view, and to questioning authority (Tabuchi & McDonald, 2009; Onishi, 2007). In keeping with the respect for authority, three-judge panels decide court cases. The new system combines three trained judges and six citizens picked by lottery to make decisions (Tabuchi & McDonald, 2009; Watanabe, 2012). Hundreds of mock trials were held prior to the official start of jury trials in Japan, but despite the training, polls revealed that about 80% of Japanese dread serving on juries (Onishi, 2007). During the mock trial exercises, jurors remained mostly silent, failing to participate in deliberations despite prodding from judges conducting the mock trials. Absence of a jury system is not unusual in Asian countries. South Korea, for example, didn't institute a jury system until 2008 (Young, 2008).

One of the significant challenges facing teachers in an increasingly multicultural educational environment is how to increase the participation level in class of some ethnic minority students. Contributions to group decision making by ethnic minorities are consistently lower than those by nonminorities (Kirchmeyer, 1993). In 76% of the small groups in one study, the member who contributed the least was Asian (Kirchmeyer & Cohen, 1992).

Why is there this difference in verbal participation in small group decision making? First, **the value of verbal participation in decision making is perceived differently from culture to culture.** As already noted, silent individuals are not seriously considered for the role of leader in American culture. Speaking is highly valued in the United States. Talking in an individualist culture is a way of showing one's uniqueness (Samovar & Porter, 2010). In collectivist cultures and co-cultures, by contrast, speaking is not highly prized. Students from collectivist cultural traditions typically see speaking too much in class as a sign of conceit and superficiality (Samovar & Porter, 2010). Among the Cambodians, Chinese, Japanese, Thais, and Vietnamese, emphasis is given to minimal vocal participation. The Chinese have a proverb that states "Those who know do not speak; those who speak do not know" (Lewis, 1996). For the Japanese, "silence is considered a virtue as well as a sign of respectability and trustworthiness" (McDaniel, 1993, p. 19). In business negotiations, Japanese, Chinese, and Koreans are more at ease with long pauses and silences than are Americans. As Andersen (1985) explains, "Cultures reflecting Buddhist tradition hold that knowledge, truth, and wisdom come to those whose quiet silence allows the spirit to enter" (p. 162).

Second, **a relative disadvantage in ability to communicate effectively in groups limits verbal participation of ethnic minorities.** Minorities report considerably less facility for communicating with others in a college setting (Kirchmeyer, 1993). Not only are ethnic minorities at a distinct disadvantage if English is their second language, but they also are at a disadvantage during group discussions dominated by members who are more aggressive and less concerned about other group members' feelings (Kirchmeyer, 1993).

Third, **lackluster participation from ethnic minorities in decision making may result from weak commitment to the group.** Weak commitment may result from group members' failure to indicate that participation from minorities is valued, or cultural differences with members of the dominant culture may make minorities feel less like they belong in the group (Kirchmeyer & Cohen, 1992).

If tapping the resources of cultural diversity is an important group goal, and this would seem to be significant given the synergistic potential inherent in diversity (Gastil et al., 2007; McLeod et al., 1996), then finding ways to boost the verbal participation rates of ethnic minorities in an American culture that values speech is a worthy undertaking. The methods outlined in the next section for encouraging constructive participation from low-contributors in general apply well to ethnic minorities.

▶ Increasing Constructive Participation: Jump-Starting Low Participators

There are several steps that can be taken to promote constructive participation from group members. First, **encourage contributions from low participators.** This is especially important for involving those ethnic minorities whose cultural values discourage assertiveness (Tang & Kirkbride, 1986). Solicit input from reticent members by asking open-ended questions of the group (e.g., "What does everyone think?"). When low participators offer contributions, indicate that their participation is valued by actively listening to what that person has to say, and perhaps thanking them for their contribution.

Second, **make issues and problems for discussion relevant to the interests of low-participators.** When groups work on interesting, involving, or challenging tasks, member contributions increase (Forsyth, 2014).

Third, **give low participators responsibility for certain tasks.** When individuals are designated as responsible for certain important tasks, they are less likely to sit back and wait for someone else to assume the responsibility. If low participators believe that their efforts have an impact on the group's final decision or product, they are less likely to remain uninvolved (Kerr & Bruun, 1983).

Fourth, **establish a cooperative group climate.** This is particularly important for ethnic minorities from collectivist cultures, who are likely to feel more comfortable and committed in such an atmosphere.

Fifth, **encourage devil's advocacy and dialectical inquiry.** These two methods of combating groupthink also encourage constructive participation from all group members. With their emphasis on stimulating a variety of ideas and opinions, fully sharing information, openly addressing differences of opinion, and carefully evaluating alternatives, devil's advocacy and dialectical inquiry substantially increase the participation of ethnic minorities (Kirchmeyer & Cohen, 1992).

Conducting Effective Meetings

Avid baseball fan and conservative columnist George Will, commenting on what he dislikes about football, remarks, "Football combines the two worst features of American life. It is violence punctuated by committee meetings" (Fitzhenry, 1993,

p. 426). Humorist Dave Barry (1991), comparing meetings to funerals, seems to prefer funerals. He claims, "The major difference is that most funerals have a definite purpose. Also, nothing is ever really buried in a meeting" (p. 311). Along this same line, there is this bumper sticker: "Meetings—The practical alternative to work." Paralleling these negative views of meetings is a survey that shows 85% of corporate executives are dissatisfied with the efficiency and effectiveness of company meetings (Mankin, 2004). Despite bad reviews, meetings are an indispensable part of group decision making and problem solving (Blenko et al., 2010; Luong & Rogelberg, 2005). This section discusses ways to master the meeting monster.

Focus Questions

1. Is parliamentary procedure always a useful way to conduct group meetings?

2. What are the main benefits of group meetings?

3. What are the principal drawbacks of group meetings?

4. What are the meeting responsibilities of both chairs and group members?

▶ Group Meetings: The Good, the Bad, and the Ugly

"Meetings are critical venues for groups and teams. Group decision making, problem solving, sense making, and communication come to life in meetings" (Rogelberg et al., 2012, p. 236). Meetings can actually save time and increase productivity of groups. Cecilia Sharpe, who was managing an audit team of six accountants at the time, decided to calculate the effects of eliminating the team's weekly meeting with the understanding that group members would maintain direct communication with each other to coordinate their efforts (Shaffner, 1999). When a proposal to revise work schedules for her auditing team emerged, she discovered that this one decision in the absence of a weekly meeting resulted in a net loss of 18 person-hours in productivity. There were 102 disruptions of team members with phone calls to discuss the proposal, compared to only seven disruptions of any kind during team meetings. The decision was two days late, and no team member was happy with the final decision. Meetings permit face-to-face participation on issues of mutual concern where each member's ideas and arguments can be heard and evaluated simultaneously by all group members.

Group meetings don't have to be a common source of grouphate, but they often are viewed as a hassle and a time waster (Luong & Rogelberg, 2005; Rogelberg et al., 2012). The quality of team meetings is often viewed as poor (Schell, 2010). Business consultant

Mitchell Nash lists **common complaints associated with group meetings:** there is an unclear purpose for the meeting, participants are unprepared, key individuals are absent or late, discussion drifts into irrelevant conversation on unrelated topics, some participants dominate the conversation and stifle discussion, and decisions made at meetings are not implemented (Dressler, 1995). Dysfunctional communication, such as criticizing other group members and complaining without apparent resolution of criticisms and complaints, too much time spent analyzing and describing problems, and getting swamped in minute details also add to the meeting monster perception (Kauffield & Lehmann-Willenbrock, 2012). Effectively addressing these complaints can make meetings highly productive time-savers.

▶ Chair's and Members' Responsibilities: Controlling the Meeting Monster

Whoever chairs a small group meeting has specific responsibilities. Using parliamentary procedure, however, isn't necessarily one of them. **Parliamentary procedure** is a set of hundreds of rules for conducting meetings (see Robert's Rules of Order at *www.robertsrules.com*). **Parliamentary procedure is appropriate for large, formal groups (the U.S. Senate) and even a few smaller groups with formal responsibilities (boards of directors), but for most small groups the rules are too rigid and artificial** (Sunwolf & Frey, 2005). They can stifle productive discussion and squash the creative process. Imagine saying "point of order" or "call the question" when meeting with a project team that is trying to generate creative ideas on a task. Saying "I rise to a point of privilege" or "I move to table the motion" among a small group of close colleagues or friends would likely trigger consternation, even guffaws, from group members. Using an abbreviated version of parliamentary procedure such as skipping the technical terminology but making clearly stated and concise motions, adopting formal votes, and requiring recognition from the chair before speaking is advisable for some small group meetings, especially when the issues discussed are controversial.

Efficient, effective meetings neutralize negative attitudes group members often have about meetings (Rogelberg et al., 2012; Rogelberg et al., 2006). As the chair, there are several ways that you can structure meetings to make them efficient and effective decision-making arenas.

1. *Don't call a meeting unless there is no good alternative.* Don't hold a meeting if your only justification is disseminating information, because you are scheduled to do so every Tuesday afternoon, you are using the meeting as an opportunity to recruit help in researching a topic, or you are hoping to try out new ideas on colleagues. If these objectives can be accomplished without meeting in a group, then don't meet. One of life's little pleasures is the surprise notification, "Meeting has

been canceled." Hold a meeting if an immediate response is required, group participation is essential, participants are prepared to discuss relevant issues, and key players can be present.

2. *Contact every participant.* Indicate in a memo or email what the specific purpose of the meeting is ("to make our final decision on the smoking policy"); where, when, and how long it will be held; and what materials, if any, each participant should bring to the meeting. In the LexisNexis survey of professional workers, 25% noted that they missed a meeting at least once a week because of "scheduling miscommunication" ("International Workplace Productivity Survey," 2010). Schedule meetings clearly so everyone is well informed.

3. *Prepare a clear agenda and distribute it to all participants a few days in advance of the meeting.* Absence of an agenda is a primary cause of failed meetings (Drew, 1994). The agenda should list the topics of discussion (see Box 9.1). If reading materials must accompany the agenda, make certain that they are concise and essential to the discussion.

4. *Use procedural communication to accomplish group goals.* Provide accurate information on all issues, clarify complex issues, correct misconceptions, and especially keep the discussion on track and on point. Such procedural communication improves group decision making (Lehmann-Willenbrock et al., 2013). Aimless discussions are unproductive and they suck the life out of meetings and force captive listeners to endure tedious, brain-killing, sleep-inducing chatter. As Ronald Reagan once quipped, "I have left orders to be awakened at any time in case of national emergency, even if I'm in a cabinet meeting." Designate a specific time allotment for every discussion item. A timekeeper should be assigned at the start of each meeting. When the time on a discussion item has elapsed, the group may decide to extend the time allotment or move to the next item. Time limits establish a crisp pace for the meeting. Keep meetings as short as possible and you'll garner accolades from grateful members.

   Do not allow any participant to be a stagehog and dominate the discussion. "Let's hear from other members" and "Does anyone have a different point of view?" are ways of limiting talkaholics from dominating discussion. If a vote on an issue is appropriate, ask for a "show of hands" or a voice vote to indicate votes for and against a proposal. Call for a vote only after all sides have had an opportunity to express differing points of view.

5. *Reserve a few minutes at the end of the meeting to determine whether the objectives of the meeting were accomplished.* If further work and discussion are deemed necessary, schedule discussion of unfinished business for the next meeting. If the group has made decisions, implementation of those decisions must be monitored. This is usually the chair's responsibility, but all participants have some responsibility for this.

BOX 9.1

Sample Agendas for Group Meetings

AGENDA FOR A BUSINESS MEETING

(Meeting of the student senate)

Date

Boardroom

2:00–3:30 P.M.

Purpose: Biweekly meeting

I. Call meeting to order; introduce any new members

II. Approval of minutes of last meeting (5 minutes)

III. Additions to the agenda (2 minutes)

IV. Committee reports

   A. Student fee committee (5 minutes)

   B. Student activity committee (5 minutes)

   C. Student union committee (5 minutes)

V. Officer's reports

   A. Treasurer's report (5 minutes)

   B. President's report (10 minutes)

VI. Old business

   A. Textbook prices (10 minutes)

   B. Campus parking problems (10 minutes)

   C. Pub on campus (5 minutes)

VII. New business

   A. Computer access on campus (5 minutes)

   B. Safety on campus (20 minutes)

VIII. Building agenda for next business meeting (5 minutes)

IX. Adjournment

AGENDA FOR A DISCUSSION MEETING

(Curriculum task force)

Date

Boardroom

3:00–5:00 P.M.

Purpose: To improve the curriculum change and approval process

I. How does the current curriculum process work?

II. What are the primary problems with present curriculum process?

III. What causes the problems?

IV. What criteria determine an ideal curriculum process?

V. What are some possible improvements in the curriculum process?

VI. Which suggested improvements are the most promising? Why?

VII. Are there any drawbacks to these suggested improvements?

6. *Distribute the minutes of the meeting as soon as possible.* Someone attending the meeting should be delegated the responsibility for taking notes and turning them into meeting minutes. The minutes should indicate what was discussed, who said what, what action was taken, and what remains to be deliberated and decided. Minutes record the gist of a meeting. Don't attempt to provide a transcript of meeting proceedings. Also, do not include confidential information, and keep language neutral and unbiased ("Fred freaked," "Jamie had a meltdown," or "Stephanie begged" lacks neutrality).

The chair has responsibilities to conduct an efficient and effective meeting, but group members also have responsibilities. In their book *We've Got to Start Meeting Like This,* Mosvick and Nelson (1987) offer some important tips for how best to conduct yourself during meetings. They include: be organized when speaking and don't ramble; speak to points made only when your contribution might add light, not just heat; state your arguments clearly and directly, and use evidence to support those arguments whenever possible; and listen carefully to the discussion and state opposing points of view fairly. If a member complains inappropriately, drifts off task, criticizes other members, or dominates discussion, other members should address the troublesome behavior. ("Let's not criticize others; let's describe issues that we can resolve.") Remember that effective leadership is a process involving the entire group, not just one person (Kauffield & Lehmann-Willenbrock, 2012).

Critical Thinking and Effective Decision Making

Group members must exercise their critical reasoning abilities at every stage of the Standard Agenda to maximize the probabilities of effective decisions (Hirokawa, 1992). Consequently, how you go about gathering information and the critical eye you focus on information gathered should be primary concerns.

▶ Gathering Information: Accumulating Input

The output of groups is likely to be no better than the input available to its members. Faulty or insufficient information easily produces collective inferential error (see Chapter 8). **Information gathering is used in all six steps of the Standard Agenda and should be a focused effort by all group members.** The group should divide the labor. Some members may concentrate on certain issues (problem causes and effects), while other members research different ones (potential solutions).

For the most up-to-date information, use the Internet. Learning to use the proper **search engines** and focusing your search take time to master. Consult your librarian for assistance if necessary. Because much of the information on the Internet is irrelevant, erroneous, or plain nutty, virtual libraries were created to provide more selective, higher-quality information. A **virtual library** is a search tool that combines Internet technology and standard library techniques for cataloging and evaluating information.

Virtual libraries are usually associated with colleges, universities, or organizations with credible reputations in information dissemination. Some of the most popular virtual libraries are: Internet Public Library (*http://www.ipl.org*), Social Science Information Gateway (*http://www.sosig.ac.uk*), and WWW Virtual Library (*http://vlib.org*).

To limit information overload, it is critical to narrow your search so that you don't access thousands of websites on a topic. The quickest way to learn how to do this is to locate the "Help," "Frequently Asked Questions," or "Search Tips" button on the Internet search tool's home page. When you click on one of these buttons, instructions will appear on-screen identifying how to use the search engine or virtual library effectively.

Despite the popularity and utility of the Internet, the library is still a useful place to search for information. Libraries have access to many electronic databases such as the general-purpose InfoTrac and EBSCOhost, and education-related ERIC. Libraries also have numerous standard references, such as *Readers' Guide to Periodical Literature, Statistical Abstract of the United States, Facts on File, Information Please Almanac, Vital Statistics of the United States, Psychological Abstracts, and Sociological Abstracts.* Then, of course, there is *Wikipedia.* This online collaborative encyclopedia is the most widely used general reference source on the Internet. By mid-2013, *Wikipedia* had accumulated 27 million articles in 286 languages ("*Wikipedia* Statistics," 2013). As Association for Psychological Science President Mahzarin Banaji (2010) notes, "It is the largest collaboratively produced knowledge repository that has ever existed."

One note of caution about *Wikipedia.* It takes contributions from almost anyone willing to make entries. Information can be unreliable, even wrong. An assessment by the Project on Psychology of 935 articles on *Wikipedia* found only 2% were above "B level" in quality, and many were woefully inadequate, even inaccurate (Banaji, 2010). Duke University English professor Cathy Davidson (2007), however, thinks *Wikipedia* is "the single most impressive collaborative intellectual tool produced at least since the *Oxford English Dictionary*" (p. B20). Anonymous readers from all over the world edit entries, correct grammar, style, and interpretations of fact. She suggests using *Wikipedia* as a "quick and easy reference before heading into more scholarly depths" (p. B20). *Wikipedia* may serve as a useful starting point for research, but it is at present an unsatisfactory primary reference.

Searching for information can be a tedious process. Remaining focused by following the suggestions offered will reduce the tedium and increase group efficiency.

▶ Evaluating Information: Applying Criteria

Knowing where to find appropriate information is helpful, but group members must also know how to evaluate information to avoid basing group decisions on faulty information. There are five criteria for evaluating information.

Credibility: Is It Believable? When the source of your information is *biased* (gains something by taking certain positions), credibility is low. Quoting representatives from BP Oil concerning the effectiveness of cleanup efforts following the disastrous Deepwater Horizon oil spill in the Gulf of Mexico in 2010 would be biased. You want to cite experts who have no profit motive or stake in the outcome. *Authorities quoted outside of their field* of expertise are also not credible. Iben Browning predicted a major earthquake for December 3 and 4, 1990, along the New Madrid Fault located in the Midwest. Schools in several states were dismissed during these two days as a result of his prediction. Browning had a doctorate in physiology and a bachelor's degree in physics and math. He studied climatology in his spare time. Earthquake experts around the country repudiated Browning's predictions. He was not a credible source since earthquake predictions were not in his field of expertise. (As you undoubtedly know, his predictions were wrong. There wasn't a sizable earthquake on this fault until April 17, 2008, and it was considered "moderate" by quake experts.)

Sometimes statistics cited are not credible. For example, the headline "Two Hundred Trillion Text Messages" appears on numerous Internet sites (see especially Gould, 2011). These sites trumpet: "200 trillion text messages are received in America every single day." Elementary arithmetic reveals that for this to be accurate, every person (including infants) in the United States (315 million) would receive, on average, 634,920 text messages each day or more than 440 messages each minute of each day. The statistic is wildly implausible. Please also note that the Internet itself is not a credible source (see Closer Look: "The Internet: Resource for Information and Misinformation"). The Internet is merely a vehicle for finding information. Quoting the Internet as your source is tantamount to quoting television.

CLOSER LOOK

The Internet: Resource for Information and Misinformation

The Internet has become a prime source for student research. A huge national study by UCLA of first-year college students showed that only 41% evaluate the quality and reliability of the information available on the Internet (Pryor et al., 2012).

The Internet is a rich resource of information, but it is also a repository of misinformation. The Internet has spawned hoaxes such as: Kenya erected a sign welcoming travelers to the "birthplace of Barack Obama"; Walmart authorized illegal immigration raids at its stores; and the Olive Garden restaurant chain distributed $500 gift cards to online fans (Stelter, 2010). All of these claims are fabrications debunked by the researchers at *snopes.com. Hoaxbusters.org* also is a good corrective site that lists hundreds of Internet fabrications.

Be extremely cautious about information found on the Internet. Apply the criteria of credibility, currency, relevance, representativeness, and sufficiency (discussed in this section). You can do this by following a few simple steps.

First, consider the source. If no author for the information is provided on the website, be highly skeptical of its validity. If a name is provided but no credentials are offered, again be highly skeptical unless the information can be validated from another source that is reputable (e.g., a national news agency).

Second, attempt to determine if the source is biased. Websites that use a hard sell to promote their ideas, therapies, and products are probably offering misinformation. Search for websites that appear to have no vested interest, no products to sell, and no ideas or conspiracies to peddle. The website address can provide hints; if it contains *.gov* or *.edu,* this means the site is sponsored and maintained by a governmental or educational institution with a reputation to protect. Sites with *.com* or *.org* in their address are commercial ventures, or they are sponsored by reputable and sometimes not-so-reputable organizations. Their credibility varies widely.

Third, determine the currency of the information. Many websites are not regularly updated. You may be accessing a site whose information is 5 to 10 years old. Look for a date when the site was last updated (often at the end of the document). Look for how recent the information in the document is to approximate the date of the original authorship.

Fourth, assess the accuracy of information on the site. Try to verify the accuracy of any information and statistics by comparing them to reputable sources. Do the facts and statistics offered on the site contradict information from reputable sources? For example, population and census statistics can be checked at the U.S. Census Bureau site (*http:// www.census.gov*). Health and medical information can be checked at *http://www.healthcentral.com*, the Centers for Disease Control and Prevention site (*http://www.cdc.gov*), or the health fraud site (*http://www.quackwatch.com*). News events can be checked at reputable news agencies' sites (*http://www.nytimes.com* or *http://www. abcnews.go.com* or *http://www.cnn.com*).

QUESTIONS FOR THOUGHT

1. An anti-Bush website claimed that, when commenting on gains in student achievement since the enactment of his "No Child Left Behind" legislation, George W. Bush produced this blooper in 2007: "As yesterday's positive report card shows, *childrens* do learn when standards are high and results are measured." How would you determine whether the quotation is a hoax or the real thing?

2. A list of a dozen "actual comments" written on students' report cards by teachers in the New York City public schools is circulated on the Internet (a colleague emailed me the list). The list includes statements such as, "I would not allow this student to breed," "Your son is depriving a village somewhere of an idiot," and "If this student were any more stupid, he'd have to be watered twice a week." Is this list a hoax? How would you determine this?

Currency: Is It Up to Date? Information should be as up to date as possible, especially when an event or situation is volatile and likely to change rapidly. What used to be taken as fact may be called into question with new information. Quoting last month's or even last week's stock prices could leave you a pauper if you act on such outdated information. Interest rates on home mortgages can change daily. You must have current rates before you decide to lock in a fixed-rate mortgage on a house you're purchasing.

Relevance: Looking for Logical Connections Information should actually support claims made. Claiming that the public education system in the United States is the world's best because America spends more money in total than any other nation is irrelevant. Total spending doesn't necessarily equate with educational excellence, especially if the money is largely wasted or spent on the wrong priorities.

Representativeness: Reflecting the Facts A single example or statistic may or may not accurately reflect what is true in a particular instance. If a vivid example (e.g., a testimonial from a victim of black lung disease on the health risks of mining coal) illustrates the truth of a claim already supported by solid scientific evidence, then it is representative and provides dramatic impact to the claim. If, however, a claim rests solely on a few testimonials or even many examples, then a real question of representativeness exists. Examples to support a claim may be selectively chosen (confirmation bias), so they may not reflect what is true generally.

There are two principal guidelines for determining whether statistics are representative. First, *the sample size (in polls, surveys, and studies) must be adequate.* This can be determined most easily by the **margin of error,** which is the degree of sampling error accounted for by imperfections in selecting a sample. As the margin of error increases, the representativeness of the statistic decreases. If the margin of error reaches more than plus or minus 3%, the representativeness of the statistic becomes questionable. A study ("Pre-employment," 1990) of 103 California companies testing job applicants for drug use revealed that 17.8% of the applicants tested positive. The margin of error, however, was 7.8%. Thus, the results are questionable since the true level of drug use among the job applicants may have been 25.6% (17.8% *plus* 7.8% margin of error) or 10% (17.8% *minus* 7.8% margin of error). The drug use problem may be substantially overstated or understated by the 17.8% statistic.

A second guideline for assuring representative statistics is that *the sample must be randomly selected, not self-selected.* A *random sample* is a part of the population drawn in such a manner that every member of the entire population has an equal chance of being selected. A *self-selected sample* is one in which the most committed, aroused, or otherwise atypical parts of the population studied are more likely to participate.

For example, The Daily Kos, a liberal blogging site, reported results of an online survey it conducted for the 2012 presidential election using a self-selected sample. Results revealed that 4,268 respondents (94%) favored Barack Obama for president and a paltry 99 respondents (2%) favored Mitt Romney ("Poll," 2012). Obama did not defeat Romney by 92%; he won by 3.9% (Wasserman, 2013).

Sufficiency: When Enough Really Is Enough When do you have enough information to support your claims? There is no magic formula for sufficiency. Determinations of sufficiency are judgment calls. Nevertheless, there are some guidelines for making such a determination.

First, **what type of claim are you making?** Causal relations require more evidence than a single study. In January 2000, results of a study showed that men with significant hair loss on the crown of their heads had a higher risk of heart attack than men with hair loss on the front of their heads. One study is insufficient to establish a causal relationship, so no conclusion can be drawn from this study. Claiming that violence depicted on television "may contribute" to antisocial behavior, however, requires less stringent criteria for sufficiency since only a weak connection is claimed.

Second, **extraordinary claims require extraordinary proof** (Shermer, 2013). When a claim contradicts a considerable body of research and knowledge, extraordinary proof must accompany such a claim. A claim that Earth has been visited by extraterrestrials requires much more evidence than a few alleged sightings. Claims of cancer cures must be rigorously tested. The claims are extraordinary, so they require more than ordinary, commonplace evidence. Ordinary claims such as "flu viruses pose a serious health hazard to the elderly" can be demonstrated sufficiently with one authoritative statistic from the Centers for Disease Control and Prevention. (See Appendix B for additional relevant material on critically examining information and claims.)

Creative Problem Solving

Years ago, a prisoner escaped from a penitentiary in the western United States. He was recaptured after a few weeks. On his return, prison officials grilled him. "How did you cut through the bars?" they demanded. Finally, he confessed. He said he had taken bits of twine from the machine shop, dipped them in glue, then in emery. He smuggled these makeshift "hacksaws" back to his cell. For three months he laboriously sawed through the inch-thick steel bars. Prison officials accepted his story, locked him up, and kept him far away from the machine shop. Is that the end of the story? Not quite. Three-and-a-half years later, he escaped again by cutting through the cell bars. He was never recaptured, but how he escaped became a legend in the underworld. It seems that his original story was a phony. He hadn't fashioned a hacksaw from any materials in the machine shop. Instead, he had used woolen strings from his socks, moistened them with spit, and rubbed them in abrasive dirt from the floor of his cell, then painstakingly sawed through the cell bars (Rossman, 1931). The prisoner had fashioned a creative solution to a challenging problem. Creative problem solving is the focus of this section.

Focus Questions

1. How do imagination and knowledge relate to creative problem solving?
2. What makes the brainstorming technique an effective, creative, problem-solving tool?
3. What is integrative problem solving and reframing?

▶ General Overview

The story of the prisoner's resourceful escape highlights several important points about creativity and problem solving. First, to borrow Thomas Edison's comment on genius, **creativity is more perspiration than inspiration.** We have to work to find creative solutions to problems. This means devoting time and energy to the task, not hoping for imaginative ideas to fall from the sky and clunk us on the head.

Second, **creativity is spurred by challenges.** As the old adage says, "Necessity is the mother of invention." We are creative in response to some felt need, to some problem that requires a solution. The bigger the challenge, the more complex the problem, the greater is the need for creativity.

Third, **creativity flourishes in cooperative, not competitive, environments.** In a competitive atmosphere, thinking "may be used to plan, strategize, and coerce rather than to problem solve and collaborate" (Carnevale & Probst, 1998, p. 1308).

Fourth, **creativity requires sound ideas, not just imaginative ones.** As Vincent Ruggiero (1988) puts it, creative ideas must be more than uncommon; they "must be uncommonly good" (p. 77). Creative solutions are original, but they also must work. I once heard a radio commentator read recipes submitted by children for preparing a Thanksgiving turkey. One child wrote: "Put 10 pounds of butter on the turkey and 5 pounds of salt. Cook it for 20 minutes." M-m-m-m-m good! Creative problem solving and decision making require both imagination and knowledge. Children create foolish things because they don't know any better. Competent communicators create solutions that are workable and effective.

Fifth, **creativity requires many ideas.** Although sheer quantity doesn't guarantee great solutions, the fewer the ideas, the less probable is the discovery of at least one

"Never, ever, think outside the box."

"Thinking outside the box" is often a welcome method for engendering creative decision making, but it has its limits. Some "outside the box" ideas are just plain messy and ineffective. Thus, ideas generated by brainstorming require evaluation after brainstorming by the group to determine which are best to implement.

good idea—that flower among all the thistles. In the pharmaceutical industry, it can take as many as 5,000 ideas before a good one emerges (Lamb et al., 2004). Capital One tested 45,000 credit card ideas; most failed, but some succeeded (Sutton, 2002). IDEO generated more than 4,000 ideas for new toys. Of these, 230 were explored and 12 were eventually produced by clients (Puccio et al., 2007).

Finally, **creativity requires breaking mindsets and thinking "outside the box"** (Puccio et al., 2007). Unless you try adopting different ways of approaching problems, you'll remain stuck in place.

▶ Specific Creative Techniques

As previously noted, group decision making and problem solving are usually more effective when systematic procedures are followed. Systematic procedures apply to group creativity as well (Firestein, 1990). Haphazard, unfocused efforts to induce creativity are often not as productive as more focused efforts.

Brainstorming and Nominal Group Techniques: Generating Lots of Ideas

At IDEO, faced with the problem of an electric car that is so quiet that it would likely cause accidents, a product design team brainstorms solutions to the problem. "How about tire treads that play music?" one team member offers. "How about a little Eric Clapton?" another chimes in, and the ideas begin to fly (O'Brien, 1995).

Alex Osborn introduced the brainstorming technique in 1939. **Brainstorming** is a creative problem-solving technique that promotes plentiful, even zany, ideas in an atmosphere free from criticism and with enthusiastic participation from all group members. Rational approaches to decision making and problem solving run the danger of becoming methodical, stale, and unimaginative. Brainstorming can regenerate a group by opening up a stuffy, plodding, and inhibited group process.

There are several guidelines for using this technique (Kelley & Littman, 2001; Nussbaum, 2004):

1. *Encourage wild ideas.* At IDEO, this is a motto that appears in large print on the walls of each brainstorming room. If edicts such as "It must be practical" or "It can't cost too much" are stated before brainstorming occurs, the group

What needs to occur to implement the most promising suggested improvements? Wild ideas that are not on topic are not helpful. It is the responsibility of the facilitator to keep the group on track. You want focused wild ideas, not just goofy ideas unrelated to the problem.

will go silent. Worry about the practical stuff after ideas have been generated in rapid-fire brainstorming sessions. What appears to be a dumb idea initially can provoke a really good solution to a problem. Bolton (1979) cites the example of a brainstorming session by managers of a major airport who were generating ideas regarding ways to remove snow from the runways. One participant offered the idea that snow could be removed by putting a giant frog on the control tower. The frog could push the snow aside with its enormous tongue. This zany idea provoked a practical solution—a revolving cannon that shoots a jet airstream. Even if zany ideas never trigger effective solutions to problems, they at least encourage a freewheeling, fun climate conducive to creativity.

2. *Don't evaluate ideas while brainstorming.* Critiques will inhibit contributions from group members. Group members need to be self-monitoring. Idea slayers, such as "That will never work" and "It's completely impractical," should be squelched by members. Even a positive evaluation, such as "Great idea," is out of order because group members will quickly interpret absence of positive evaluation as a negative assessment of their ideas.

3. *Don't clarify or seek clarification of an idea.* This will slow down the process (Dugosh et al., 2000). Clarification can come later after a list of ideas has been generated.

4. *Do not engage in task-irrelevant discussion.* Idea generation is significantly diminished when conversation is permitted during brainstorming sessions (Dugosh et al., 2000). With conversation often comes irrelevant chatter. A brainstorming facilitator should invoke this rule whenever talking interrupts idea generation.

5. *Stay focused on the topic.* You want all suggestions to be related to the topic. Wild ideas that are not on topic are not helpful.

6. *Expand on the ideas of other group members.* Halpern (1984) cites the example of a food manufacturer seeking better ways to bag potato chips. Corporate executives were asked to identify the best packaging solution they had ever seen. One brainstormer said that bagging leaves wet was the best method. Dry leaves crumble and use up more air space. Wet leaves pack more easily and require fewer bags. Expanding on this idea, the manufacturer tried packing potato chips wet. When the potato chips dried they became tasteless crumbs. Nevertheless, from this initial failure sprang the popular potato chips in a can, in which a potato mixture is cooked in chip-shaped molds and then stacked in the can. From a bad idea came a good one. **A recent study suggests that this step be delayed until the freewheeling, "wild ideas" step is completed because freewheeling and expansion may be incompatible if done simultaneously** (Goldenberg et al., 2013).

7. *Record all ideas without reference to who contributed the idea.* Do not censor any ideas, no matter how silly they may seem, as long as they are focused on the problem.

8. *Encourage participation from all group members.* The maximum number of ideas requires the maximum effort from every group member.

9. *Evaluate ideas generated once the brainstorming phase is completed* (Sawyer, 2007). The group needs to decide what ideas generated are best to implement.

Brainstorming normally is instituted during the solutions suggestion step of the Standard Agenda. Determining the quality of the ideas generated from brainstorming comes during the solution evaluation and selection step. Ideas are evaluated in terms of solution criteria established earlier in the Standard Agenda process.

A second creative problem-solving method is **nominal group technique** (Delbecq et al., 1975). Individuals work by themselves generating lists of ideas on a problem, then convene in a group where they merely record the ideas generated (usually on a chart, whiteboard, or computer screen for all to see). Interaction occurs only to clarify ideas, not to discuss their merits and demerits. Individuals then select their five favorite ideas, write them on a card, and rank them from most to least favorite. The rankings are averaged and the ideas with the highest averages are the ones selected by the group.

Some research has shown nominal group technique generates more and better ideas than brainstorming (Paulus et al., 1993; Valacich et al., 1994). Mongeau (1993), however, criticizes the research on brainstorming. He notes that "although considerable research has been performed on brainstorming, little of this research is a valid test of Osborn's ideas" (p. 22). Results have been derived from student groups that: have no history together and no future, have no training and experience using the brainstorming technique (aside from a brief explanation of the rules), are provided no opportunity to research the task prior to brainstorming, are given little time to think about the task, are given tasks often unrelated to students' interests, and never actually make choices regarding which ideas are best (Kramer et al., 1997). Also, brainstorming tasks given in laboratory studies are simple enough for an individual to tackle. Highly complex tasks, such as the design challenges faced by IDEO, have not been given to brainstormers to compare the nominal group technique to brainstorming groups (Sawyer, 2007). It's difficult to imagine trained, experienced, and knowledgeable IDEO brainstormers being outperformed by untrained, inexperienced, and poorly informed nominal group brainstormers on complex tasks.

One study of brainstorming at IDEO also found that **idea generation isn't the only value of brainstorming** (Sutton & Hargadon, 1996). Regular brainstorming can reinforce an organizational culture, impress clients, provide opportunities for skill improvement, attract skilled employees to an organization, and improve employee retention. "Brainstorming is the idea engine of IDEO's culture" (Kelley & Littman, 2001). Designers at IDEO refer to brainstorming sessions as "vacations" and note that "brainstorms are a nice change of pace" from other work performed. One designer offered, "Brainstorms are one of the rewards of working here" (Sutton & Hargadon, 1996, p. 701).

Brainstorming, if done properly, can be highly effective (Goldenberg et al., 2013; Isaksen & Gaulin, 2005; Kelley & Littman, 2001). Osborn actually suggested that **the proper brainstorming format should involve first an individual, then a group, followed by an individual brainstorming session** (Isaksen & Gaulin, 2005). Members should be provided with a well-defined problem a few days in advance of the group brainstorming session so members can research it and think of solutions to contribute. Then members meet as a group to share their ideas and generate new ones. After the group session, individuals are given a few days to contemplate further ideas on their own. In addition, members should not be strangers and they should belong to a longstanding (not a zero-history) group. Diverse membership also enhances group creativity, with this caveat: "Group genius can happen only if the brains in the team don't contain all the same stuff" (Sawyer, 2007, p. 72). You want deep diversity where group members have non-overlapping knowledge on a topic. Team members should also receive training and experience in how to use the brainstorming technique. Research shows that training and experience in brainstorming vastly improve idea generation (Baruah & Paulus, 2008; Firestein, 1990). Having a trained facilitator encourages brainstormers to focus on the ideas of others during brainstorming, not simply attend to their own ideas, and vastly improves idea generation significantly beyond that of the nominal group technique (Dugosh et al., 2000; Isaksen & Gaulin, 2005). IDEO uses a trained facilitator for brainstorming sessions (Kelley & Littman, 2005). Research also shows no advantage for the nominal group technique compared to brainstorming in the final evaluation of ideas generated that separates good from bad ideas (Rietzschel et al., 2006).

Electronic brainstorming occurs when group members sit at computer terminals and brainstorm ideas using a computer-based, file-sharing procedure (e.g., Group Decision Support System). This offers an additional method for improving idea generation and creativity. Group members type their contributions, then send the file to a shared pool. Ideas are added and shared with group members. This can be done anonymously if group members fear a critique. Electronic brainstorming has sometimes outperformed nominal groups in idea generation (Dugosh et al., 2000; Valacich et al., 1994), but most studies show that for small groups, electronic brainstorming is not the most effective method for brainstorming (Barki & Pinsonneault, 2001).

Framing/Reframing: It's All in the Wording When MBA students and managers were informed that a particular corporate strategy had a 70% chance of success, most favored it. When it was framed as a 30% chance of failure, however, the majority opposed the strategy (Wolkomir & Wolkomir, 1990). When people were presented with two options for treating lung cancer, 84% chose the surgery option when it was framed in terms of living, while 56% chose the surgery option when it was presented in terms of dying (McNeil et al., 1982). The reason for the difference lies in how the problem is **framed**—the way in which language shapes our perception of choices.

Our frame of reference can lock us into a mindset, making solutions to problems difficult if not impossible to discover. This mental gridlock can block the free flow of creative ideas. Postman (1976) provides an example. You have the number VI. By the addition of a single line, make it into a seven. The answer is simple: VII. Now consider this problem: You have the number IX. By the addition of a single line, make it into a six. The answer is not so obvious because of your frame of reference, which identifies the number as a Roman numeral and all lines as straight. Not until you break away from this frame of reference by reframing the problem—by no longer assuming that the answer must be in terms of a Roman numeral and that all lines are straight—will you solve the problem. Have you found the answer? How about **SIX**?

Frames determine whether people notice problems, how they understand and remember problems, and how they evaluate and act on them (Fairhurst & Sarr, 1996). **Reframing** is the creative process of breaking a mindset by describing the problem from a different frame of reference. For example, a service station proprietor put an out-of-order sign on a soda machine. Customers paid no attention to the sign, lost their money, then complained to the station owner. Frustrated and annoyed, the owner changed the sign to read "$5.00" for a soda. No one made the mistake of putting money in the faulty soda pop dispenser. The problem was reframed. Instead of wondering how to get customers to realize that the machine was on the fritz, the owner changed the frame of reference to one that would make customers not want to put money in the dispenser. Learning to reframe problems by changing language that describes or identifies our choices can significantly influence our perceptions (Deggans, 2012). Reframing can be a highly useful skill for the competent communicator, and it is an essential part of effective leadership in groups (Fairhurst & Sarr, 1996).

When groups become stumped by narrow or rigid frames of reference, interjecting certain open-ended questions can help reframe the problem and the search for solutions. My personal favorite is "What if…?" The group asks, "What if we don't accept this cutback in resources as inevitable?" "What if employees really want to produce quality work but find the work environment tedious?" "What if we tried working together instead of against each other?" Additional reframing questions include: "Why are these the only options?" "What happens if we reject the proposal?" "How could this be turned into a win–win situation for everyone?"

Integrative Problem Solving: Satisfying Everyone Decision making often involves conflicts of interest. **Integrative problem solving** is a creative approach to conflicts of interest; it searches for solutions that benefit everyone. Two forms of integrative problem solving are expanding the pie and bridging (Pruitt & Rubin, 1986).

Expanding the pie refers to increasing the resources as a solution to a problem. When faced with scarce resources, groups often become competitive and experience serious strife, warring over who gets the biggest or best piece of the limited resource pie. Groups, however, sometimes accept the inevitability of scarce resources—what Bazerman and Neale (1983) call the "bias of the fixed pie"—without fully exploring options that might expand the resources. School districts in California, faced with ever-present lean budgets, could issue a collective sigh and proceed to cut programs and teachers. Instead, many districts have found creative ways to increase resources beyond what the state legislature provides. Some districts have established private foundations, raising as much as $435,000 each year in community donations. These foundations throw $125-a-plate dinners, organize black-tie auctions, stage celebrity tennis and golf tournaments, and do car washes. One district foundation purchased a 10-acre vacant school site, developed it, and sold it for a $4-million profit. These efforts to expand the resource pie save teachers' jobs and maintain important educational programs.

Bridging is the second type of integrative solution to conflicts. Bridging offers a new option devised to satisfy all parties on important issues. Bridging was used to solve a conflict of interest over where to eat dinner involving a couple, a friend of the couple's, and the friend's two teenage children. All three adults wished to eat dinner at

Scott Adams, creator of the comic strip, *Dilbert,* enlisted IDEO to brainstorm "Dilbert's Ultimate Cubicle," pictured here. Technological features include devices that alert employees to an approaching boss and can rid the office cubicle of unwanted guests.

a moderately priced restaurant specializing in fresh-fish entrees served with wine. The teenagers wanted burgers, fries, and colas. After a fair amount of wrangling, the pouting and whining began—from the teenagers, not the adults. Frustrated, the mother of the teenagers declared, "I think we'll just take off and eat at home. This isn't working out." A suggestion was made by one of the other adults: "Why don't we send the kids over to that burger joint up the street and have them bring back their meal? We can ask the restaurant if they mind having food brought in by the kids, and, if not, the adults will order dinners with all the trimmings." The restaurant cooperated and both the adults and the teenagers enjoyed their meals.

Competent communicators vigorously explore possible integrative solutions to conflicts of interest. To do this successfully, take the following steps (Pruitt & Rubin, 1986):

1. *Conflicting parties should formulate a clear statement of issues and goals.* If all are to benefit from the integrative solution, what the parties want to accomplish must be apparent. Rausch and his colleagues (1974) discovered that 66% of the conflicts they examined were successfully resolved when the issues were clearly stated; only 18% of the conflicts were effectively resolved when the issues remained vague or unstipulated.

2. *Parties in conflict must determine whether a real conflict of interest exists.* Family members argue over whether to get a dog or not. The two kids say they want a dog very much; the father and mother say they do not. On the surface this looks like a standard conflict of interest. Yet when the issue is discussed, what becomes clear is that the mother doesn't want to take care of the dog and the father dislikes barking. When asked whether a cat would serve as an adequate substitute, the kids enthusiastically agree since they really just want a pet. No conflict really exists since the parents actually like cats, which are low maintenance and mostly quiet, and the kids get their pet.

3. *The parties in disagreement should stick to their goals but remain flexible regarding the means of attaining them.* Both expanding the pie and bridging allow conflicting parties to find flexible, creative means of attaining goals without compromising those goals.

4. *If stalemated, concede on low-priority issues or discard low-priority interests.* The prime goals remain intact. The focus continues to be a solution that satisfies the goals of both parties. You give on minor issues that are relatively unimportant to you but are perhaps more important to the other party.

In summary, there is no dichotomy between rational and creative decision making and problem solving. The two can be complementary paths to effective decisions in groups. The discussion process, however, should be systematic, not haphazard. Consideration of the problem should come before deliberations on solutions. Standard

The Effective Problem-Solving Process

Standard Agenda	Techniques
Problem identification	Form questions of fact, value, or policy
	Define ambiguous terms
Problem analysis	Explore causes of problem (gather information)
	Explore effects (significance) of problem
	Avoid analysis paralysis
	Use framing/reframing
Solution criteria	Establish criteria
	Prioritize criteria
Solution suggestions	Brainstorm solutions
	Clarify ambiguous or confusing ideas
	Consolidate overlapping ideas
	Use integrative problem solving
Solution evaluation/selection	Explore merits/demerits of solutions
	Use devil's advocacy
	Use dialectical inquiry
	Consider solutions in terms of criteria
	Use majority or minority rule, or consensus
Solution implementation	Use force field analysis
	Use PERT

NOTE: Although the consensus technique is used most directly during the solution criteria and solution evaluation/selection steps of the Standard Agenda, consensus rules may operate throughout the problem-solving process. Majority or minority rule may also be inserted at various steps if appropriate conditions exist.

Agenda is the most common and useful set of procedures for rational decision making. Consensus, when applicable, is an effective process for guiding members toward rational decisions. Brainstorming and nominal group technique, framing/reframing, and integrative problem solving all provide systematic techniques for the discovery of creative solutions to problems.

In the next two chapters, the interconnected concepts of power and conflict are discussed. These concepts have already been addressed superficially in earlier chapters. Those brief references, however, were merely the preliminaries. Power and conflict are integral parts of the small group process that are inescapable in any human system.

In Mixed Company

MindTap™
Reflect on what you've learned.

▶ Online

Now that you've read Chapter 9, access the online resources that accompany *In Mixed Company* at **www.cengagebrain.com**. Your online resources include:

1. Multiple-choice and true-false **chapter practice quizzes** with automatic correction
2. Digital **glossary**
3. **Flashcards**

QUESTIONS FOR CRITICAL THINKERS

1. Why is majority rule so popular when consensus decision making, by comparison, is often more advantageous?
2. Since a true consensus requires agreement, commitment, and satisfaction of group members, do you think groups are likely to achieve a true consensus, or is this mostly an ideal?
3. What are some drawbacks to the Standard Agenda approach to decision making? Explain your answer.

VIDEO *Case Studies*

Apollo 13 (1995). Drama; PG
This dramatization of the nearly disastrous Apollo 13 space mission to the moon illustrates creative problem solving. What creative problem-solving techniques are exhibited?

Flight of the Phoenix (2004; 1966). Drama; PG-13
The original 1966 version of this taut drama about a plane crash and efforts of survivors to literally rebuild their damaged plane into a smaller flying machine to escape their plight in the desert is probably superior to the remake. In either case, examine the creative group problem solving required. What methods were used to create the final product? What decision-making rules (unanimity, majority, or minority rule) were used?

O Brother Where Art Thou? (2000). Drama/Comedy; PG-13
Three convicts escape from a Depression-era chain gang. Their problem-solving knowledge and skills are severely deficient. Contrast the problem-solving mistakes of this small group of convicts with advice provided in this chapter on effective problem solving.

The Hobbit. (2012). Adventure/Fantasy; PG-13
Bilbo Baggins, a reluctant hobbit, helps a group of dwarves reclaim their mountain home from the Dragon Smaug. Examine the decision-making and problem-solving methods used by Baggins and the dwarves.

10

Power in Groups: A Central Dynamic

Noam Galai/WireImage/Getty Images

MindTap
Start with a quick warm-up activity.

"Power tends to corrupt, and absolute power corrupts absolutely," Lord Acton reputedly observed. This is a popular view. We are used to thinking of power as illegitimate or unpleasant, unless, perhaps, when we are the person accorded the power. Then, as former Secretary of the Navy John Lehman once quipped, "Power corrupts. Absolute power is kind of neat."

The terms *power politics, seizure of power, power struggles, power hungry, power mad,* and *power play* reflect just some of the negative views most of us associate with this central element of human interaction. How group leaders act when they gain power isn't likely to diminish negative attitudes about power. Research shows that "having power renders many individuals as impulsive and poorly attuned to others as your garden-variety frontal lobe patient, making them prone to act abusively and lose the esteem of their peers. What people want from leaders—social intelligence—is what is damaged by the experience of power" (Keltner, 2007; see also Gonzaga et al., 2008).

Being relatively powerless, however, is not a virtue (Wilmot & Hocker, 2011). Perceptions of powerlessness can induce indifference toward group tasks, diminish task performance, foster member passivity and withdrawal, destroy group cohesiveness, strain personal relationships with group members, erode group members' self-esteem, and trigger destructive group conflict (Keltner et al., 2003; Lee, 1997).

Power is central to group decision making and problem solving, managing conflict, and evoking change. No group can achieve its goals without exercising some power (Canary & Lakey, 2013). As Wilmot and Hocker (2011) explain, "One does not have the option of not using power. We only have options about whether to use power destructively or productively for ourselves and relationships" (p. 115). **The primary purpose of this chapter is to explain how you can use power productively and constructively in the small group arena.** The following are three chapter objectives:

1. To define power, distinguishing its three types,

2. To identify various indicators of power and power resources,

3. To address ways that power imbalances produce negative consequences in groups and how these imbalances can be addressed.

Read, highlight, and take notes online.

Power Defined

Power is *the ability to influence the attainment of goals sought by yourself or others.* This is a general definition. This section explains specifically what power is and, conversely, what it is not.

Focus Questions

1. **What does it mean to say that power is group-centered?**

2. **What are the primary forms of power?**

▶ The Nature of Power: No One Is Powerless

First and foremost, **power is group-centered.** The power that you wield is dependent on the relationships you have with group members (Gilovich & Keltner, 2010). Leaders, for instance, require the support of followers to remain in power. As president of the United States, Richard Nixon wielded immense power. The Watergate scandal, however, soured his relationship with the American public like a quart of milk in a desert sun. He was forced to resign his office in disgrace. Conversely, Bill Clinton weathered the storm of impeachment principally because 70% of the adult population in the United States approved of the job he was doing as president, even though his personal behavior may have disgusted them.

We often speak of powerful or powerless individuals as if the power distribution were all one way or the other. Is a child in a supermarket completely powerless against his or her parents when candy is the target? Have you ever witnessed a child whining, begging, and throwing a fit until exasperated parents capitulate and shove the candy into the child's grasping hands to silence the obnoxious din? "Powerful or powerless" is a false dichotomy. **No group member is completely powerless.** The interconnectedness of components in a system means that all group members have some degree of influence, even if it is to defy or resist the group. Anthony Giddens (1979), the first to develop structuration theory (see Chapter 1), explains that "subordinate positions in social systems are frequently adept at converting whatever resources they possess into some degree of control" (p. 6). If all group members have some degree of power, then the relevant question becomes "How much power does Person A exert relative to other members in that group?" not "Is Person A powerful or powerless?" Rules are established in groups and these rules grant some group members particular forms of power over other members (West & Turner, 2010).

▶ Forms of Power: Competition and Cooperation Revisited

There are three forms of power (Hollander & Offermann, 1990). **Dominance** or *power over* others flows from a hierarchical structure or from differences in status among group members. Dominance is competitive. My gain in power is your loss.

A second form of power is called **prevention** or *power from* the efforts of others to influence (e.g., we defy or resist leader dominance). When someone tries to dominate us, psychological reactance occurs. We try to prevent the dominance. Prevention also is a competitive form of power. Here you're striving not to lose to dominators.

A third form of power is **empowerment**—enhancing the capabilities and influence of individuals and groups. Empowerment is *power to* accomplish your own goals or help others achieve theirs through processes of group potency, meaningfulness, autonomy, and impact (see Chapter 7). Empowerment is cooperative, not competitive. The group as a whole profits from all of its members gaining the ability to succeed together. For example, group members who improve their speaking skills for a class presentation benefit the entire group. One of the positive aspects of the situational leadership model discussed in Chapter 6 is the emphasis on empowerment rather than dominance. The leader role is not geared toward ordering underlings around and keeping followers in their place. Instead, an effective leader actively seeks to increase the readiness levels of followers, thereby empowering them to accomplish tasks without the leader watching their every move.

The three forms of power are substantially different from one another. Those who try to dominate see power as finite. The power pie is only so large and cannot be expanded. Power, therefore, is seen as an *active* struggle between the haves and have-nots. Those who try to prevent domination by fighting back see power as *reactive*. Power is seen in competitive win–lose terms by those who try to dominate and by those who try to prevent the domination. Those group members who try to empower see the power pie as expandable (see Figure 10.1). Resources can be acquired and shared. Integrative problem solving discussed in Chapter 9 is a practical example. Empowerment is *proactive,* meaning each group member takes positive action to assist himself or herself and others to attain goals cooperatively.

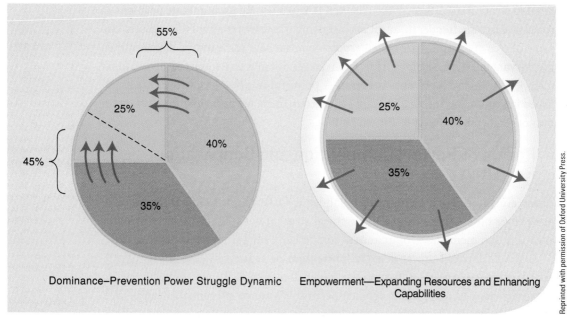

Dominance–Prevention Power Struggle Dynamic

Empowerment—Expanding Resources and Enhancing Capabilities

FIGURE 10.1
Dominance–prevention power struggles are based on seeing the power pie as a fixed, zero-sum contest. The more powerful try to poach power from the less powerful, and the less powerful try to prevent this from occurring. Empowerment is based on seeing the power pie as expandable.

Those who harbor a negative concept of power are usually responding to dominance and its companion form—prevention. This may partly explain why women, historically dominated by men, are more inclined to embrace empowerment than men (Maroda, 2004). Dominance, however, will assuredly remain as the primary form of power in a competitive society. Nevertheless, the dominance–prevention power struggle is a poor model for small groups both ethically and practically. "It is

SECOND LOOK

Forms of Power

Type	Definition	Description
Dominance	Power over	Active
Prevention	Power from	Reactive
Empowerment	Power to	Proactive

not the manipulative, strategic Machiavellian who rises in power. Instead, social science reveals that one's ability to get or maintain power, even in small group situations, depends on one's ability to understand and advance the goals of other group members" (Keltner, 2007). What can be hoped for is that empowerment will gain a wider audience and become more broadly applied.

Indicators of Power

Power indicators are the ways in which relative degrees of power are communicated in groups. If you can spot power indicators, then you will see the presence of power dynamics and appreciate the importance of power in small groups. There are three main categories of power indicators: general, verbal, and nonverbal.

Focus Questions

1. "Those who define others exercise control." What does this mean?
2. In what ways do male and female communication patterns differ in regard to verbal dominance?
3. What are the effects of "powerless" verbal and nonverbal communication patterns?

► General Indicators: Labeling, Following, and Opposing

There are several general indicators of power in groups. First, **those who define others exercise control.** Ordinarily, we define people by attaching a label to them. Teachers define students (e.g., smart, slow learner), physicians define patients (hypochondriac, unhealthy), psychiatrists define clients (schizophrenic), parents define children (sweet, incorrigible), and bosses define employees (good worker, loafer).

Whose decisions are followed is a second general indicator of power in a group. The individual with the position of authority in a group (chair, president) may not be the group member exercising the most power. Another group member respected more by the members may actually be calling the shots, as indicated by whom the group follows.

Who opposes significant change is a third general indicator of power. Those who have been accorded power by the group are usually uncomfortable with change that goes much beyond a little fine-tuning. Substantial change may risk altering the power relationships. The disaffected, who are also relatively powerless, usually clamor for substantial change.

▶ Verbal Indicators: Relatively Powerless and Powerful Speech

Power is reflected in the way we speak. The speech of a subordinate is often flooded with self-doubt, hesitancy, approval seeking, overqualification, and self-disparagement (Mulac & Bradac, 1995). Examples of speech patterns perceived to be relatively powerless include:

Hedges: *"Perhaps* the best way to proceed is…" "I'm a *little* concerned that this might cause problems."

Hesitations: *"Well, um,* the important thing to remember is *ah…"* *"Gosh, ah,* shouldn't we, *ah,* delay the decision?"

Tag Questions: "The meeting will be at noon, *okay?"* "This point seems redundant, *doesn't it?"*

Disclaimers: *"This is probably not very important,* because *I haven't thought it out much,* and *you probably already considered it,* and *you know best* anyway, but…"

Excessive Politeness: *"I'm extremely sorry* to barge in like this, *sir,* but…"

"Powerless speech" suggests uncertainty, indecisiveness, lack of confidence, vacillation, and deference to authority. Speech patterns perceived to be relatively powerful are generally direct, fluent, declarative, commanding, and prone to interrupting or overlapping other group members' speech (Pearson et al., 1991).

In general, group members who use more powerful language patterns are perceived to be more credible, attractive, and persuasive than those using less powerful language. These perceptions are particularly strong for virtual groups primarily because language patterns become more influential when nonverbal cues are restricted (Adkins & Brashers, 1995; Palomares, 2008). The consequences of using powerful or powerless speech can be seen from a study of student impressions of teachers. Teachers created a positive impression by using powerful language that made them seem significantly more dynamic, credible, organized, professional, knowledgeable, and of higher status than teachers using powerless language. It is critical that teachers establish a positive impression in the classroom to enhance learning (Haleta, 1996).

Besides powerful language, verbal dominance is also indicated by competitive interrupting, contradicting, berating, and sheer quantity of speech. Monopolizing a conversation in these ways has obvious power implications. Those who dominate conversations during group meetings are able to get their point presented to members. Those who can't sandwich a word into the conversation are unable to articulate their point of view, and their silence prevents them from being considered a leader.

Powerful speech is not always appropriate (see Focus on Gender/Culture: "Powerful Language Difference"). Abusive and obscene language may be perceived in our culture as powerful speech, but it can offend group members and can destroy the cohesiveness of the group. Sometimes deferential language is a sign of respect and

Focus on Culture
Powerful Language Differences

There are gender differences in verbal indicators of power. Men are typically more verbally dominant. Thus, they are more verbose, more given to long-winded verbal presentation, and more talkative in mixed-sex groups than are women (Crawford & Kaufman, 2006; Leaper & Ayres, 2007). Men are also more verbally aggressive, direct, opinionated, judgmental, and argumentative than women (Brownlow, 2003; Mehl & Pennebaker, 2002). Men are likely to advocate controversial positions during group discussions or to challenge the positions on issues taken by other group members (Stewart et al., 1996). Women are inclined to view verbal aggressiveness and argumentativeness as strategies of dominance and control—a hostile, combative act (Nicotera & Rancer, 1994). Women also use tag questions, disclaimers, and hedges more often than men (Brownlow, 2003). Since men are more likely to seek status and women are more likely to seek connection in conversations (Kwang et al., 2013; Tannen, 2010), these gender differences in verbal indicators of power are not surprising.

The issue of powerless versus powerful speech has interesting cultural complexities (Den Hartog, 2004). Most Asian cultures view our version of powerful speech as immature because it indicates insensitivity to others and is likely to make agreement more difficult (Wetzel, 1988).

In Malagasy society (Madagascar) "women have lower status than men but they use our stereotypical 'powerful' language; they do the confronting and reprimanding and in so doing... their constant violation of societal norms is seen as confirmation of their inferiority" (Smith-Hefner, 1988, p. 536). In Western societies, verbal obscenity and swearing are perceived as powerful language—an aggressive flouting of societal norms. Neither Japanese men nor women, however, use such language except in rare instances (De Klerk, 1991).

When cultures clash over issues of significance, these different views of powerful and powerless speech can pose serious problems. When negotiating teams from Japan and the United States meet, misunderstandings easily arise (Hellweg et al., 1994). The language of Japanese negotiators is rife with indirect language viewed as powerless to American negotiators unfamiliar with cultural differences in perception. Japanese negotiators use such expressions as *I think, perhaps, probably,* and *may be* with great frequency. They will also expect no interruptions while they speak. Americans negotiate in blunt terms, interrupt, and view indirect and qualifying language as signs of weakness and lack of resolve. Misunderstandings of this nature make negotiations difficult and decision making troublesome.

QUESTIONS FOR THOUGHT

1. Do women increase their power by using more powerful language or could there be a backlash to such usage?
2. Do you think there is a relationship between powerful–powerless speech patterns in a culture and the individualism–collectivism focus of the culture? Explain.

not merely powerless speech. Even tag questions can sometimes be used powerfully. If the leader of a small group says, "You'll see that this is done, won't you?" this may be issued more as a directive than a request. In that case, the tag question is authoritative, not weak.

▶ Nonverbal Indicators: Silent Power

There are many nonverbal indicators of power (see especially Hall et al., 2005). In fact, the socioeconomic status of a person can be accurately inferred from a variety of nonverbal indicators of attentiveness to others (e.g., doodling, object manipulations, gazing, head nods, eyebrow raises) (Kraus & Keltner, 2009).

Space is the prerogative of the powerful. Dorothy Parker once noted, "He and I had an office so tiny that an inch smaller and it would have been adultery" (Fitzhenry, 1993, p. 296). The powerful get the best offices with the most space (Durand, 1977). Parents get the master bedroom, while children get stacked vertically in bunk beds in a smaller bedroom. The prime parking spaces are reserved for the higher-status individuals. Lower-status individuals, such as students on college campuses when compared to faculty and administrators, get to park in the next time zone. Space allocation usually follows a pecking order. Private space is the prerogative of the powerful. Those individuals who are regarded as powerful may violate the space of those less powerful, but not vice versa. You must be granted access to the chambers of the privileged.

Posture and gestural communication are also markedly different for superordinates and subordinates. Generally, the powerful exhibit more relaxed, casual posture and gestures (Pavitt & Curtis, 1994). Subordinates can be directed to "sit up straight" or told to "stop slouching" by superordinates. Parents, for example, can tell children how to stand, sit, and move their bodies, but children do not have the same prerogative. Posture that is expansive (i.e., arms outstretched, legs spread apart with feet propped onto a coffee table, or standing tall) is associated with dominance (Hall et al., 2005), and adopting more powerful posture can make you feel more powerful (Carney et al., 2010). Just exhibiting a more powerful posture can make individuals feel powerful even when they may not occupy a powerful position in the group (Huang et al., 2011).

Touch clearly indicates power relationships in groups (Di Biase & Gunnoe, 2004; Henley, 1995). The less powerful often feel required to yield to the touch of their superiors even when the touching triggers a gag reflex. Laws prohibiting sexual harassment have been established in the United States to protect the less powerful from the tactile abuse (among other inappropriate acts) of the more powerful. These statutes recognize that uneven power distribution plays a primary role in most cases of sexual harassment.

Eye contact is yet another nonverbal indicator of relative degrees of power (Henley, 1995). Staring is done more freely by the powerful. The less powerful must monitor their eye contact more carefully. If a superordinate is speaking to a group of subordinates during a meeting, eye contact connotes active listening and deference to authority. Superordinates, however, may feel no obligation to exhibit interest

This cartoon illustrates

1. Nonverbal indicator of power
2. Space as a power indicator
3. Information is power
4. Hedging as a verbal indicator of power

Answers are given at the end of the chapter.

or attentiveness to subordinates by maintaining eye contact. Lowering your eyes and looking down also indicate submissiveness.

Finally, **nonverbal artifacts, or symbols of power, include a wide variety of objects and tangible materials:** large desks, plush carpets, office windows, leather chairs, master keys, company cars, new computers, and the list could go on and on.

One study involving a personal injury lawsuit compared relatively powerful and powerless nonverbal communication (Lee & Ofshe, 1981). When a speaker exhibited powerful nonverbal communication while *arguing for a reduction* in the damage award,

SECOND LOOK

Indicators of Power

General Indicators

Who defines whom

Whose decisions are followed

Who opposes significant change

Verbal Indicators

Powerless/powerful language

Verbal dominance

Nonverbal Indicators

Space

Posture and gestural communication

Touch, eye contact

Artifacts

subjects *reduced* the award by an average of $4,273. When the speaker exhibited power-less nonverbal behaviors, however, subjects *increased* the award an average of $2,843.

Much more could be added here regarding nonverbal indicators of power, but the point has been made. You can discern the relative distribution of power in a group by observing both verbal and nonverbal indicators and noticing a few general communication patterns.

Power Resources

When transacting power in groups, members utilize power resources. A **power resource** is "anything that enables individuals to move toward their own goals or interfere with another's actions" (Folger et al., 1993, p. 100). There are five primary power resources relevant to group situations: information, expertise, punishments and rewards, personal qualities, and legitimate authority. These resources closely parallel French and Raven's (1959) classic types of power in groups.

Focus Questions

1. Information is power, but is all information power?

2. For expertise to serve as a power resource, must the expert always avoid errors?

3. What are the primary drawbacks of punishment and rewards as power resources?

4. How does authority become legitimate?

▶ Information: Restricted or Scarce

Unquestionably, information is power (Sell et al., 2004). Not all information, however, serves as a source of power. **Information assumes value or usefulness when it is perceived to be unavailable.** If information is readily available to everyone, it has no power potential. If you can acquire important information from the Internet, someone in your group offering the same information has no leverage to seek personal benefit.

Information becomes unavailable primarily from *restrictions* and *scarcity* (Brock, 1968). In this era of information overload, restricted or scarce information is the exception, not the rule. Thus, when information is restricted or scarce, whatever is available seems terribly important.

For example, a young woman in my small group communication class told her project group that she could get a highly technical, information-rich report on the subject chosen for the class project. The information from this report, so she claimed, was unavailable anywhere else, but she could get the report from her father, who had access to it because of his high position in a company. Her group members were thrilled. Her prestige and influence in the group immediately soared. Unfortunately, she never produced the report, and two weeks after she offered to obtain the report, she dropped the class. Unavailable information has power potential, but only if it's not too scarce, so you can actually produce it.

The competent communicator can capitalize on information as a power resource as follows:

1. *Provide useful but scarce or restricted information to the group.* Careful, diligent research often produces valuable information relevant to the group task. If this information is unknown to other group members, it then assumes a power potential by increasing your prestige and influence in group decision making.

2. *Be certain information is accurate.* Sharing misinformation could earn you the enmity of group members. Misinformation could easily lead to collective inferential error.

▶ Expertise: Knowing and Showing

Information and expertise are closely related, but not identical (Canary & Lakey, 2013). A group member can possess critical information but be unable to decipher it. Experts not only have valuable and useful information for a group, but they also understand the information and know how to use it to help the group. An expert can give knowledgeable advice (Franz & Larson, 2002).

For expertise to function as a power resource, a minimum of two conditions must be met. First, **the group must be convinced that the person has the requisite skills, abilities, knowledge, and background to function as a real expert.** Experts must demonstrate a mastery of relevant information and exhibit skill using it. Second, **the person must demonstrate trustworthiness.** People the world over are more influenced by experts who stand to gain nothing personally than they are by experts who would gain substantially by lying or offering poor advice (McGuinnies & Ward, 1980).

Assuming that a group member has special knowledge, skills, or abilities useful to the group, he or she could capitalize on the power potential of expertise as follows:

1. *Maintain skills, abilities, and knowledge.* Let your knowledge grow out of date or your skills diminish, and the group will quickly see you as yesteryear's expert—a relic.

2. *Demonstrate trustworthiness and credibility.* Your expertise should be used to benefit the group, not merely bring personal advantages to yourself.

3. *Be certain of your facts before advising the group.* Advice should be based on the best available information. An occasional error may not tarnish your credibility as an expert. Relatively frequent or serious errors will.

4. *Don't assume an air of superiority.* Putting on an air of superiority will trigger defensiveness among group members.

▶ Rewards and Punishments: Carrots and Sticks

Parceling out rewards or meting out punishment can be an important source of power. Salaries, bonuses, work schedules, perks, hirings, and firings are typical job-related rewards and punishments. Money, privacy, car keys, and grounding are a few of the rewards and punishments found in family situations. Social approval or disapproval, performance awards, suspension, and expulsion are a few of the rewards and punishments available to educators when dealing with students.

Punishment is a source of power if it can be and likely will be exercised. If employees are protected from termination by civil service regulations or tenure, threatening to fire them is laughable. Threats of punishment, however, seem to be more effective when we perceive that the chances of punishment are highly probable (Wooton, 1993).

There are serious drawbacks to using punishment to influence group members, however (Kassin, 1998; Uba & Huang, 1999). First, punishment indicates what you *should not do,* but it doesn't teach what you *should do.* Firing a worker doesn't teach that person how to perform better in the future. Second, targets of punishment can become angry and hostile toward their perceived tormenters. If the punishment is perceived to be unfair or excessive, a backlash can easily occur from other group members. Third, punishment can produce a negative ripple effect throughout the group. If the punishment doesn't achieve the desired effect, other group members may be encouraged to engage in similar deviance. Issues of fairness and just cause may surface and escalate into ugly conflicts, spreading tension and creating a competitive group climate. The sign found in workplaces stating that "The beatings will continue until morale improves" expresses ironically the difficulty of using punishment to produce positive results in groups.

Rewards, viewed as the opposite of punishment, seem as though they would produce only positive results for groups. A reward can be an effective power resource, but it should be used carefully. Consider the story of an old man who was besieged daily by a group of 10-year-old boys hurling insults at him as they passed his house on their way home from school. One day, after enduring the boys' abusive remarks about how stupid, bald, and ugly he was, he decided on a plan to deal with the little troublemakers. On the following day, he approached the boys and told them that anyone who came the next day and shouted insults at him would receive a dollar. Dumbfounded, the boys left and returned the next afternoon to scream epithets at the old man. He gave each boy a dollar. He then told them that he would pay each boy 50 cents if they returned the next day and repeated their rude behavior. They returned, shouted insults, and were paid. The old man then said that he would pay them only a dime if they returned the next day and repeated their abusive behavior. At this point, the boys said, "Forget it. It isn't worth it." They never returned.

This story illustrates how **an extrinsic reward can diminish intrinsic motivation to behave in certain ways.** An **extrinsic reward** motivates us to behave or perform by offering us an external inducement such as money, grades, praise, recognition, or prestige. An **intrinsic reward** is enjoying what one does for its own sake (Kohn, 1993). An intrinsic reward motivates us to continue doing what brings us pleasure. The boys initially were intrinsically motivated by perverse pleasure in tormenting the old man. When paid to continue the torment, it became more like a job. Once the pay became minimal, the job seemed pointless and they quit. "Work sucks, but I need the bucks" is a bumper sticker that expresses the common effect an extrinsic reward such as money can have on our interest in and enjoyment of work.

Work teams are likely to perform well when members are intrinsically motivated by commitment to a shared goal, a desire to "change the world," or a keen interest in the task. Teams that are held together only by the extrinsic rewards of money, recognition, or prestige are not as likely to be effective. As a survey of 500 professionals found, "95% agreed that pay and benefits were not the main motivation in their decision whether or not to stay with a job. The key issue was the ability to develop trusting relationships with upper management" (Shilling, 2000). The intrinsic reward derived from good relationships and a trusting group climate outweighs the extrinsic reward of money and benefits.

Does use of extrinsic rewards always produce negative results, as some have argued (Kohn, 1993)? The answer is no. Verbal praise (extrinsic reward), as long as it is not offered as an obvious manipulative strategy to control group members' behavior, can actually *increase* intrinsic motivation (Carton, 1996; Eisenberger & Cameron, 1996). Also, it depends on how recipients perceive the extrinsic reward. If they perceive it as a treat, it can increase intrinsic motivation to perform, but if they perceive it as pressure to perform and be creative, it can decrease their intrinsic interest and motivation to perform (Eisenberger & Armeli, 1997).

Competent communicators use punishment and rewards carefully. Here are some guidelines:

1. *Punishment should be a last resort.* Because punishment can produce serious negative consequences, it should be employed rarely and then only when efforts to change group members' behavior by noncoercive means have failed.

2. *Punishment should be appropriate to the act.* Anemic punishment for seriously flawed, irresponsible performance or severe punishment for relatively inconsequential error is out of proportion to the act. In the former instance, group members will likely ridicule the ineffectual action, and in the latter instance, they will likely rebel against the severity of the sanction.

3. *Punishment should be swift and certain.* The more disconnected punishment becomes from an objectionable act because of delays or uncertainty that punishment will occur, the more ineffectual it becomes. Idle threats are pointless.

4. *Be generous with praise that is warranted.* Praise recognizes accomplishment, nurtures a positive group climate, and can increase intrinsic motivation unless it is obviously manipulative.

5. *Determine what rewards group members value before offering any.* A $1,000 bonus may motivate a poor person, but Bill Gates would likely view it as pocket change. Extrinsic rewards may be effective in circumstances where group members aren't initially motivated intrinsically to accomplish a task if group members value the rewards (Uba & Huang, 1999).

6. *Administer both punishments and rewards equitably and fairly.* Perceived favoritism in receiving rewards creates a competitive group climate.

▶ Personal Qualities and Skills: A Powerful Presence

We all know individuals who exert some influence over us, not because of any of the previous power resources already discussed, but because of attractive personal qualities they seem to possess in abundance. We are more likely to be influenced by those individuals whom we find attractive than by those we don't.

Communication researchers have known for some time that physical attractiveness, expertise, and mastery of certain persuasive and communication skills, dynamism, trustworthiness, reliability, similarity of values and outlook, and identification with the group all contribute to an individual's ability to influence others. There is also substantial research that shows a strong relationship between extraversion and power. Those who exhibit high energy, activity, sociability, and assertiveness (high extraverts) are likely to achieve elevated status in a group (Anderson et al., 2001; Keltner et al., 2008).

Some or all of these personal qualities contribute to charisma. Some people have a great deal of charisma, and others have less charisma than driftwood. Charisma is not determined objectively. Groups decide what is attractive and what is not (Haslam & Reicher, 2012). When Barack Obama first campaigned for president, some in his audiences would faint, others would weep during his speeches. He was greeted like a rock star by adoring fans at campaign rallies. It is unlikely that a similar response to Obama would occur from a group of conservative Republicans. Learning to be charismatic is difficult, perhaps fruitless for some. Nevertheless, charismatic leaders typically exhibit extraordinary communication skills (Hackman & Johnson, 2013). Developing communication competence certainly can improve one's charismatic potential (Antonakis et al., 2010). "As one becomes a more skilled communicator, he or she is more likely to be perceived as 'charismatic' by others" (Riggio, 2010). The more successful groups

Jeff Christensen/AFP/Gettty Images

Who has charisma, Bill Gates or professional wrestler turned actor Dwayne "The Rock" Johnson? On what do you base your answer?

become under the guidance of competent communicators, the more charismatic leaders appear to be in the eyes of group members (Haslam & Reicher, 2012).

▶ Legitimate Authority: You Will Obey

We all play roles, but some of us exercise greater influence in groups because of our acknowledged position or title. Power can be derived from the shared belief that some individuals have a legitimate right to influence us and direct our behavior by virtue of the roles that they play. Society grants parents legitimate authority. In addition to other power resources they have at their disposal, parents are supposed to be accorded respect and deference simply because they are parents. We believe parents have the right to discipline their children and to expect obedience. Similarly, teachers and supervisors at work occupy an authority position considered legitimate by most groups.

Obedience to legitimate authority is intricately woven into the fabric of our society. We learn about the virtues of obedience to authority figures in school, at work, in church, in courtrooms, and in military barracks. American soldiers at Abu Ghraib prison in Iraq tortured Iraqi prisoners, then defended themselves by claiming that they were "just following orders" from superiors (Zernike, 2005; Zimbardo, 2007). (See Closer Look: "The Milgram Studies.")

CLOSER LOOK

The Milgram Studies

An amazing series of studies conducted by Stanley Milgram in the 1960s lends substantial support to the fear that as a society we have thoroughly absorbed the lesson of obedience to legitimate authority. The basic design of the studies by Milgram consisted of a naïve subject who acted as "teacher" and a confederate who acted as "student." The naïve subjects were told that the purpose of the experiment was to determine the effects of punishment on memory and learning. Punishment consisted of electric shocks administered to the student for every wrong answer on a word association test. Shocks began at 15 volts and increased by 15-volt increments to a maximum of 450 volts for each wrong answer from the victim. The experimenter directed the subjects to administer the increasingly intense shocks for every wrong answer even when the subjects objected. The experimenter served as legitimate authority in each of Milgram's experiments.

Almost two-thirds of the subjects progressed to 450 volts and delivered the maximum shock until they were instructed to stop by the experimenter. Subjects continued to administer the shocks even when they could hear the victim's screams of pain and agony. (The victim's anguish was cleverly faked; no electric shocks were delivered, but all except an insignificant few of the subjects thought the punishment was real.) In one of the experiments, the victim complained of a heart condition exacerbated by the shocks. Nevertheless, 26 of the 40 subjects administered the maximum shocks at the direction of the experimenter. In all, Milgram (1974) conducted 19 variations of the obedience to authority study with more than 1,000 subjects of various ages and walks of life.

Replications of Milgram's experiments were conducted in America and abroad with similar results (Blass, 2000). In one dramatic replication, the victim was a cute, fluffy puppy dog, not a human confederate (Sheridan & King, 1972). The subjects actually shocked the helpless puppy. Despite the disbelief commonly expressed by my students that anyone would continue to shock an adorable, helpless puppy held captive in a box whose floor was an electrified grid from which there was no escape, the results of the experiment contradict conventional wisdom. Three-quarters of the subjects, all college students, were obedient to the end (54% of the men and 100% of the women). At the behest of the experimenter, they delivered maximum-intensity shock to the cute puppy dog whose pain they could witness directly. They complained, some female subjects even wept, but they obeyed.

© Liliya Kulianionak/Shutterstock.com

Would you administer 450-volt shocks to this cute puppy? In one experiment, 100% of the women and 54% of the men (all college students) did just that to a puppy.

More recently, a number of television shows have offered various versions of the Milgram studies. Psychologist Jerry Burger at Santa Clara University in 2007 for *ABC Primetime* took extraordinary precautions to protect the psychological well-being of participants, including setting a top level of shock at 150 volts. (Four-fifths of Milgram's subjects proceeded to 450 volts once the 150-volt tipping point was reached.) Nevertheless, at 150 volts, the victim demands to be let out of the experiment and complains about his heart condition. Paralleling previous obedience studies, 70% of participants ignored the victim's pleas and obeyed the authority figure (Burger, 2007). British illusionist Derren Brown conducted a replication for his UK TV program called *The Heist*. More than half of the participants obeyed to the end ("Milgram Experiment, Derren Brown," 2006). Another replication was presented in 2009 on the BBC documentary *How Violent Are You?* Of the 12 participants, 9 were completely obedient ("BBC Two Programmes," 2009). A French documentary film crew recreated the obedience studies in March 2010, but reframed it as a game show called *The Game of Death*. They added the "entertaining" element of live audience participation with calls for "punishment" from the highly vocal crowd and a host that encouraged greater delivery of shocks. Of the 80 subjects on the show, 64 (80%) went to the extreme (Crumley, 2010). None of these television versions of the Milgram studies, with the possible exception of the Burger replication, are completely credible because there is no way of discerning how much editing or fakery occurred to make the programs entertaining to a television audience. Nevertheless, they suggest that nothing much has changed since Milgram conducted his original experiments five decades ago.

Group members, however, do not have to be the pawns of legitimate authority. One study found that when group members discussed their misgivings about what a legitimate authority told them to do, most defied the authority figure (Gamson et al., 1982). Group discussion is a critical factor in defiance. Group members must share concerns about what authorities tell them to do, so individual members realize that they are not alone in their misgivings.

Although results from obedience studies are disturbing, defiance of all authority is as empty-headed as consistent compliance. What kind of society would you live in if few people obeyed police, teachers, parents, judges, bosses, or physicians? The answer to the excessive influence of legitimate authority rests with your ability to discriminate between appropriate and inappropriate use of authority, not the exercise of indiscriminate rebellion against all authority.

QUESTIONS FOR THOUGHT

1. Are the Milgram studies and their replications ethical research? Explain by using the five standards of ethical communication discussed in Chapter 1.
2. Would the results of the Milgram studies have been the same if a woman had been the authority figure? If a woman had been the victim? If a child had been the victim?
3. In Sheridan and King's (puppy dog as victim) replication of the Milgram studies, 100% of the women obeyed, but only 54% of the male subjects. Why the difference in results?

To have power potential, authority must be viewed as legitimate. We are not inclined to comply with directives from those individuals acting authoritatively but who are not deemed legitimate. Group members must grant legitimacy before authority will have any weight. One study revealed that leaders who usurp authority are not granted legitimacy by the group (Read, 1974). Thus, they have less influence than appointed or elected group leaders. The sad, sorry lot of inexperienced substitute teachers illustrates the problem of authority without legitimacy. Teachers are authority figures in a school environment, but substitute teachers must struggle to establish legitimacy in students' eyes. They must combat the strong impression that as a substitute, they are not "real teachers." Even regular teachers aren't automatically granted legitimacy and power in the classroom. "The teacher's influential power resides in students' acceptance of the hierarchical roles of teacher and student and the perception that teachers have the right to direct students in matters related to the course" (Schrodt et al., 2008, p. 182). **The group grants legitimacy.**

Those who aspire to be competent communicators while capitalizing on legitimate authority as a power resource can try the following:

1. *Become an authority figure.* There are two principal sources of authority: appointed (designated) leader and emergent leader (Forsyth, 1990). Becoming either grants you authority. Emergent leader has already been discussed in Chapter 6. Appointed leader occurs because you gain favor of a powerful person, earn the right to be appointed (e.g., by seniority), or are the only group member willing to accept the appointment.

2. *Gain legitimacy.* Legitimacy comes from conforming to accepted principles, rules, and standards of the group. Authority that is imposed on the group (leader appointed from outside the group) usually has problems of legitimacy because the group may resent nonparticipation in making the appointment. Authority that springs from the group (e.g., being voted by membership to represent the group in bargaining talks or earning it by demonstrating competence) has a solid base of legitimacy. When group members respect their team leader, the leader can assert greater influence, especially when conflict arises in the group (Balkundi et al., 2009).

3. *Encourage participative decision making.* Encouraging participative decision making can help maintain the legitimacy of your authority by retaining the goodwill of group members. Keep in mind the qualifiers attached to participative decision making discussed in the preceding chapter.

4. *Act ethically.* The abuses of legitimate authority are the product of unethical practices. Honesty, respect, fairness, choice, and responsibility should guide legitimate authorities whenever they use their power in groups.

In summary, power resources are not properties of individuals. A person does not possess power, but is granted power by the group through transactions with members.

SECOND LOOK

Competent Communicator's Guide to Power Resources

Power Resource	Communication Guidelines
Information Power	Provide the group with scarce but useful information.
	Be certain your information is accurate.
Expertise	Maintain knowledge currency.
	Demonstrate trustworthiness and credibility.
	Be certain of your facts before giving advice.
	Don't assume an air of superiority.
Rewards/Punishments	Punishments should be appropriate to the act.
	Punishment should be swift and certain.
	Be generous with praise that is warranted.
	Determine what rewards group members value before offering any.
	Administer both punishment and reward equitably and fairly.
Personal Qualities	Groups specify qualities that are preferred.
Legitimate Authority	Become an authority figure.
	Gain legitimacy.
	Encourage participative decision making.
	Act ethically.

As such, the group must endorse the resource for it to be influential (Folger et al., 1993). Group endorsement usually depends on whether the resource meets a need of the group.

Effects of Power Imbalances

When power is inequitably distributed in a group and dominance becomes the focus, systemwide power struggles often ensue (Wilmot & Hocker, 2011). With these power struggles come aggression and contempt.

Focus Questions

1. How are power imbalances and violence related?
2. "Dominance breeds conflict." What does this mean?

▶ Physical Violence and Aggression: Waging Power Struggles

Significant power disparities often foster violent or aggressive transactions (Straus, 2007). Gelles and Straus (1988) in their extensive study of family violence conclude: "The greater the inequality, the more one person makes all the decisions and has all the power, the greater the risk of violence. Power, power confrontations, and perceived threats to domination, in fact, are underlying issues in almost all acts of family violence" (p. 82). In families and marriages in which the husband insists on being the dominant decision maker, breakup of the marriage and family or persistent unhappiness experienced by all parties is *four times more likely* than in families in which the husband shares power (Gottman & Silver, 1999).

Violence easily spills beyond the husband–wife relationship and becomes a systemwide problem. "It is not unusual to find a pattern of violence in a home where the husband hits his wife, the wife in turn uses violence toward her children, the older children use violence on the younger children, and the youngest child takes out his or her frustration on the family pet.... At each level the most powerful person is seeking to control the next least powerful person" (Gelles & Straus, 1988, p. 35).

Too often we "settle" our power struggles at work with aggression. According to a report by the U.S. Justice Department, almost 2 million people each year are victims of violence on the job ("DOL Workplace Violence Program," 2014). Workplace bullying is also an increasing problem (WBI Workplace Bullying Research, 2013). **Workplace bullying** "is a persistent form of badgering, abuse, and 'hammering away' at targets" who have less power than their bullies (Lutgen-Sandvik et al., 2005). In the United States, more than a third of workers have experienced workplace bullying ("Results," 2010). "Adult bullying at work is shockingly common and enormously destructive" (Lutgen-Sandvik et al., 2009, p. 41). Although a troublesome problem in the United States, workplace bullying is even worse in other countries. An International Labor Organization survey conducted in 2006 in 32 countries found that workplace bullying is one of the fastest-growing areas of workplace aggression in these countries ("New Forms of Violence at Work," 2006). Dominance breeds violence and aggression.

▶ Verbal and Nonverbal Contempt: Insulting Others

Power struggles in groups do not always end in physical violence. A more likely initial consequence is verbal and nonverbal expressions of contempt. Coaches of teams, for example, may simply tear apart the self-esteem and self-worth of players. Team leaders in the workplace may berate less powerful team members.

Contempt is the expression of insult that emotionally abuses others. Contempt is not merely criticism (Gottman, 1994). It is more destructive because it seeks to humiliate, even destroy, whoever is targeted. Name-calling ("stupid," "fool," "idiot," "incompetent"), cursing, hostile humor (jokes that hurt and ridicule others), vicious sarcasm, and insulting body language (rolling your eyes, curling your upper lip in a sneer, shaking your head side to side while laughing snidely) are types of contempt. Recall the study of doctor–nurse verbal abuse discussed in previous chapters. Almost 98% of the more than 2,100 physicians and nurses who completed the survey said they witnessed acts of verbal contempt, usually by more powerful doctors targeting less powerful nurses (Johnson, 2009).

Power imbalances easily create a climate that encourages physical, verbal, and nonverbal aggression (see Focus on Culture: "Power Distance and Cultural Differences" for a different twist). Both aggressors and victims engage in such negative behavior in a dominance–prevention power struggle. A more equitable sharing of power is a primary preventive of such competitive ugliness in groups.

Focus on Culture
Power Distance and Cultural Differences

In the United States, power imbalances are often the catalyst for aggressive behavior. The responses to power imbalances in some cultures, however, are strikingly different from our own. Cultures vary in their attitudes concerning the appropriateness and acceptance of power imbalances (Hofstede & Hofstede, 2010). These variations are referred to as the **power distance dimension** (hereafter referred to simply as PD).

Countries that are culturally classified as low-PD (relatively weak acceptance of maintaining power differences), such as the United States, Sweden, Denmark, Israel, and Austria, are guided by norms and institutional regulations that minimize power distinctions among group members and between groups. (See Figure 10.2.) Challenging authority (not easy in any culture, as the Milgram studies demonstrate), flattening the organizational hierarchies, and using power legitimately are subscribed to by low-PD cultures. Low-PD cultures do not advocate eliminating power disparities entirely, and in a country such as the United States, power differences obviously exist. The emphasis on maintaining hierarchical

(Continued)

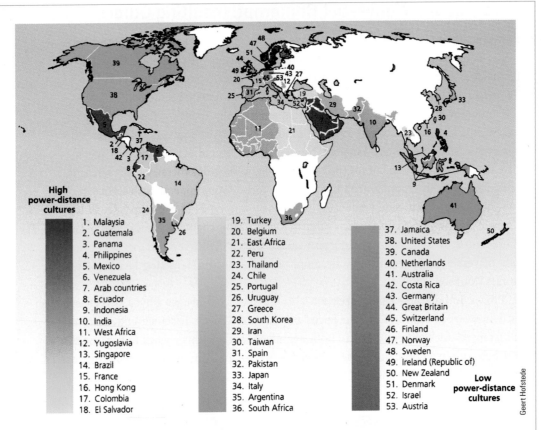

High power-distance cultures

1. Malaysia
2. Guatemala
3. Panama
4. Philippines
5. Mexico
6. Venezuela
7. Arab countries
8. Ecuador
9. Indonesia
10. India
11. West Africa
12. Yugoslavia
13. Singapore
14. Brazil
15. France
16. Hong Kong
17. Colombia
18. El Salvador

19. Turkey
20. Belgium
21. East Africa
22. Peru
23. Thailand
24. Chile
25. Portugal
26. Uruguay
27. Greece
28. South Korea
29. Iran
30. Taiwan
31. Spain
32. Pakistan
33. Japan
34. Italy
35. Argentina
36. South Africa

37. Jamaica
38. United States
39. Canada
40. Netherlands
41. Australia
42. Costa Rica
43. Germany
44. Great Britain
45. Switzerland
46. Finland
47. Norway
48. Sweden
49. Ireland (Republic of)
50. New Zealand
51. Denmark
52. Israel
53. Austria

Low power-distance cultures

Geert Hofstede

FIGURE 10.2

From *In the Company of Others*, Fourth Edition, © 2013 J. Dan Rothwell. Reprinted with permission of Oxford University Press.

boundaries between the relatively powerful and powerless, however, is de-emphasized in low-PD cultures. Workers in low-PD cultures may disagree with their supervisors; in fact, bosses may encourage disagreement. Even socializing outside of the work environment and communication on a first-name basis between workers and bosses is not unusual (Brislin, 1993).

Countries culturally classified as high-PD (relatively strong acceptance of maintaining power differences), such as the Philippines, Mexico, India, Singapore, and Hong Kong, are guided by norms and institutional regulations that accept, even cultivate, power distinctions. The actions

of authorities are rarely challenged, the powerful are thought to have a legitimate right to use their power, and organizational and social hierarchies are encouraged (Hofstede & Hofstede, 2010). Workers normally do not feel comfortable disagreeing with their bosses, and friendships and socializing between the two groups are rare.

The reactions by members to power imbalances in small groups are likely to reflect where a culture falls on the power distance dimension. One study compared people's reactions to insults in a high-PD (Hong Kong) and a low-PD (United States) culture. Subjects from Hong Kong were less upset than those from the United States when they were insulted, as long as the initiator of the insult was a high-status person (Bond et al., 1985). As Brislin (1993) explains, "When people accept status distinctions as normal, they accept the fact that the powerful are different from the less powerful. The powerful can engage in behaviors that the less powerful cannot, in this case insult people and have the insult accepted as part of their rights" (p. 225).

Differences in power distance do not mean that high-PD cultures never experience conflict and aggression in small groups emanating from power imbalances. Members of low-PD cultures, however, are more likely to respond with frustration, outrage, and hostility to power imbalances than members of high-PD cultures because low-PD cultures value power balance even though the experience of everyday life in such cultures may reflect a somewhat different reality. In a low-PD culture, the struggle to achieve the ideal of balanced power in small groups is more compelling, and the denial of power is likely to be perceived as more unjust, even intolerable, than in a high-PD culture where power balance is not viewed from the same vantage point.

QUESTIONS FOR THOUGHT

1. Which leadership style would likely be preferred in high-PD cultures, directive or participative? How about low-PD cultures? Explain.
2. If you were an exchange student in a high-PD culture, how would you react to the "Don't challenge your teachers" norm in that culture?

Addressing Power Imbalances

Transacting power in groups can involve any of five general responses: Compliance, Alliance, Resistance, Defiance, and Significance (**C-A-R-D-S**). The last four alternatives are ways less powerful members attempt to balance power in groups. In this section, the pros and cons of each alternative for balancing power are addressed.

Focus Questions

1. How are obedience and conformity similar to and different from each other?
2. What are the disadvantages of forming alliances?
3. Since resistance strategies rely on deceit and mixed messages, should competent communicators always avoid them?
4. Why are defiant members a threat to the group?
5. In what ways do aggressiveness and assertiveness differ?

▶ Compliance: Group Power

Compliance is the process of consenting to the dictates and desires of others. **Compliance involves both obedience to authority and conformity to group norms.** When compliance is the result of group influence on the individual, it is usually referred to as conformity, since we are expected to comply with norms established by the group. When compliance is the result of a high-power group member (e.g., the leader) influencing lower-power members, it is normally referred to as obedience.

In one study, conformity is pitted against obedience to determine which is most influential (Milgram, 1974). Two confederates administered a test and a naïve subject administered punishment (increasing levels of electric shock) for incorrect answers. At the 150-volt shock level, one of the confederates refused to continue taking part in the experiment. At 210 volts, the second confederate bailed out of the experiment. With two defectors for support, 90% of the naïve subjects refused to comply with the experimenter's command to increase the shocks all the way to 450 volts. Most of the 40 naïve subjects, 60%, stopped at 210 volts or less. Yet in a comparison study where the naïve subject faced the experimenter alone, only 35% refused to comply with the experimenter's command and refusal never occurred before 300 volts. **Conformity to group norms can sometimes prove to be a more powerful tendency than obeying authority.** The defectors created a group norm that opposed shocking victims against their will. Most subjects complied with the norm instead of following the authority figure's insistent directives. This punctuates the power of groups to withstand the unethical or wrong-headed directives of a powerful group leader or member. Gaining allies to defy the orders of a group leader can be effective.

▶ Alliance: Coalition Formation

Alliances are associations in the form of subgroups entered into for mutual benefit or a common objective. When group members form temporary alliances they are called **coalitions**. Power is central to coalition formation (Grusky et al., 1995). Group members form coalitions to increase their power and thus control decisions made in the group when group members don't agree on issues of significance to the group. Coalitions must be negotiated among group members.

Because coalitions can change the distribution of power in a group, coalition formation is typically adversarial, competitive, and contentious. Coalitions are formed not simply to advance the goals of the allied members (e.g., choosing the preferred topic or option for a group project), but also to prevent the attainment of non-coalition members' goals (e.g., choosing an objectionable topic or option for a group topic). Consequently, powerful members often move to stymie formation of coalitions among weaker members. This can be accomplished by forming their own coalitions with weaker parties or by confusing issues and arousing discontent in the ranks of the weak, thus splintering potential allies.

Coalitions may be useful in the political realm and sometimes coalitions help less powerful group members influence group decisions and prevent unethical or disastrous decisions ordered by the group leader, but they can pose problems for groups. In families, parental coalitions may be necessary to present a united front when a dispute with children occurs. Parent–child coalitions (e.g., father–son versus mother–daughter), however, can disrupt the family system (Rosenthal, 1997). Asking children to choose sides in a dispute between parents can risk eroding family solidarity and may threaten the survival of the family system.

Coalitions can also produce intragroup competition between rival coalitions that encourages risky, poorly conceived decisions (Myers & Brashers, 1999). The overall effectiveness of a group might also be diminished by coalitions because communication between the factions often becomes limited and external threats or problems impacting the group are ignored (Myers & Brashers, 1999). Coalitions generally suffer the disadvantages associated with competition by creating a dominance–prevention transaction between group members.

▶ Resistance: Dragging Your Feet

Resistance is normally the choice of the less powerful (Wilmot & Hocker, 2011). **Resistance** is a covert form of communicating noncompliance, and it is often duplicitous and manipulative. Resisters are subtle saboteurs. When faced with a dominant individual (supervisor, parent, or group leader), it is often safer to employ indirect means of noncompliance than direct confrontation or open defiance (Canary & Lakey, 2013). Nevertheless, even high-power individuals on occasion will use resistance strategies. If undercurrents of dissatisfaction are apparent, openly defying the wishes of group members may provoke outright rebellion.

Resistance is the prevention form of power (power from). Done craftily, resistance can be difficult to identify unequivocally for those who are its targets because the sabotage is ambiguous, often communicating a seemingly sincere effort to comply. The target is often left mostly convinced that resistance is taking place, but is unable to make this apparent to the group due to the mixed messages being sent.

In this section, specific communication strategies of resistance, or what Bach and Goldberg (1974) term *"passive aggression,"* are discussed. I have combined their list of strategies with my own (see also Wilmot & Hocker, 2011). Reflect on whether you have used any of these resistance strategies (see Box 10.1).

Strategic Stupidity: Smart Members Acting Dense Your group is working on an important class presentation. Each member has been assigned a topic area to research. At one of your meetings, an inventory is taken regarding information

BOX 10.1

Do You Use Resistance Strategies?

Answer the following questions as honestly as possible.

1. I have purposely acted stupidly to get out of doing some disagreeable task.

   OFTEN   NEVER

   5   4   3   2   1

2. I have purposely acted clumsy or inept to avoid a disagreeable task.

   OFTEN   NEVER

   5   4   3   2   1

3. I have purposely pretended to misunderstand someone who wants me to complete a disagreeable task.

   OFTEN   NEVER

   5   4   3   2   1

4. I find that I am forgetful when I am asked to complete a task I do not wish to perform.

   OFTEN   NEVER

   5   4   3   2   1

5. I'm late to meetings that I am not looking forward to attending.

   OFTEN   NEVER

   5   4   3   2   1

6. I purposely wait until the very last minute to perform tasks I do not want to complete.

   OFTEN   NEVER

   5   4   3   2   1

These six questions correspond to the six resistance strategies (in order): 1. strategic stupidity, 2. loss of motor function, 3. misunderstanding mirage, 4. selective amnesia, 5. tactical tardiness, and 6. purposeful procrastination. Any score above a 2 indicates frequent use of passive aggressive strategies.

collected up to this point on relevant topic areas. When asked for a status report, one of the members of your group whines, "I couldn't find anything on world hunger." Are you faced with a drooling dolt or is this person covertly resisting active involvement in the group project? Bet your money on the latter. When group members do not want to expend energy on a project, especially if the project was not of their choosing, they may feel hesitant to complain directly to the group about their dissension. If they have been outvoted in the group when the proposal for the project was decided, they may resent having little influence on the group decision. They may feign stupidity to penalize the group and to exercise influence, at least in a negative way. When the success of the group presentation depends on all members pulling a load, even one resistant member can create systemwide problems.

Strategic stupidity works exceedingly well when the low-power person claims stupidity, is forced to attempt the task anyway, then purposely performs the task ineptly. Doing a half-baked job of a simple task can frustrate even the most patient person. If group members must spoon-feed their strategically stupid member on where to look on the Internet or in the library for information on world hunger, they may decide in exasperation that this takes too much effort and end up doing the research themselves. If criticized for doing a poor job, the low-power person can always retort, "How was I supposed to know?" or "I told you I didn't know how to do it." The pathetic performance becomes proof that the stupidity was "real." To expect any better performance in the absence of careful and persistent tutelage would be an injustice.

Loss of Motor Function: Attack of the Clumsies This resistance strategy is an effective companion to strategic stupidity. Here the low-power person doesn't pretend to be stupid. The resister just acts incredibly clumsy, often resulting in costly damage. There is a mixed message here. The nonverbal behavior displays resistance, but the verbal statement that often accompanies it feigns a genuine attempt to comply.

Years ago I worked summers at a can factory to pay for college. I was a worker in quality control. In a less-than-admirable effort to avoid the horrid press department, I kept ducking out of sight at the start of the morning shift to avoid the supervisor, who had a habit of selecting some poor college student employee to replace a worker who had quit the press department. The press department was where can lids were stamped out and sent through a machine, coated, and packed in boxes or paper sleeves stacked onto wood pallets.

One day the supervisor spotted me and sent me to the press department to replace someone who had quit. I went reluctantly. The job I was given pitted me against a machine that pumped out can lids in rapid fashion. I had to stack and pack the lids without spilling them onto the floor. I purposely adopted the loss of motor function strategy to get out of the job. By the end of my shift, I had spilled thousands of lids onto the factory floor, shut the machine down four times, incensed the machinist who had to spend 20 minutes starting up the machine each time it was shut down, and forced my supervisor to call in two workers to clean up my mess. I was making the system adapt to my act of sabotage. All the while I insisted in bellicose tones to my upset supervisor that I was trying hard but that the job was impossible to do. The next day I returned to my previous job, pretending not to know that no one ever returned to his previous job in quality control (strategic stupidity). I hid out, watched my supervisor pick another college student to take my press job, and I spent the rest of the summer free from press department duties. I even received a promotion a month later. Ironically, I ended up in the press department the next summer and, with a change of attitude, managed to master the job with little difficulty.

It is the apparent effort exerted that makes this strategy so effective. In my can factory incident I had sweat rolling down my face. I seemed to be making every effort possible to keep up with the diabolical machine. I just couldn't quite stay with it. If the high-power person alleges deliberate sabotage, the low-power person can always become incensed, even incredulous that anyone would even suggest such a thing. It's an awkward position for a high-power person. How does one conclusively prove willfulness? You don't want to look like you're beating up on a less powerful group member. If you make an accusation of willfulness but fail to convince the group, then you may lose power by diminishing your credibility (personal qualities as a power base).

The Misunderstanding Mirage: Feigning Confusion This is the "I thought you meant" or "I could have sworn you said" strategy. The resistance is "expressed behind a cloak of great sincerity" (Bach & Goldberg, 1974, p. 110). I have observed numerous instances of this strategy in my group communication classes. Typically, a student will deliberately miss an important meeting with his or her group and then claim, "Oh, I thought we were going to meet on Thursday. Sorry. I just got confused." I have lost count of the number of times students have used this strategy to excuse their late assignments. "You said it was due Friday, not today, didn't you?" they'll say hopefully. If I respond, "No, your paper is due today," my resistant student often replies, "Well, I thought you said Friday, so can I turn my assignment in then without a penalty?" The implied message attached to this ploy is clear: "Since this is a simple misunderstanding, penalizing me for a late assignment would be unfair."

Again, the high-power person is placed in a seemingly awkward position. The teacher may lose some power (legitimate authority) if the class sees his or her behavior as capricious, unfair, or lacking compassion ("Everyone makes mistakes").

High-power persons sometimes use this strategy of misunderstanding to avoid obligations. Teachers may purposely miss appointments with students or committee meetings on campus because they'd prefer to leave town before the rush-hour traffic. Pretending to have misunderstood when the meeting was scheduled relieves them of having to confront directly their own irresponsibility.

Selective Amnesia: Forgetting the Distasteful Sometimes we get a brain cramp and forget things, but have you ever noticed that certain people are very forgetful, especially about those things that they find distasteful? This amnesia is highly selective when used as a resistance strategy. We rarely forget what is important to us or what we like doing.

The message is again mixed. You manifest no outright signs of noncompliance. You outwardly agree to perform the distasteful task. Appointments, promises, and agreements just slip your mind. If your group insists that you assume a larger share of unpleasant tasks, you can always agree, then forget to do them.

A more sophisticated version of this strategy, however, is truly selective. Take an errand such as purchasing office supplies for your department. Remember to buy all the items except one or two important ones. Hey, you did pretty well. So you forgot cartridges for the laser printers and now the entire office staff is affected. No one's perfect. If your selective amnesia proves to be a recurring problem, that errand gig may shift to someone else.

Tactical Tardiness: Not So Grand an Entrance When you really don't want to go to a meeting, a class, a lecture, or whatever, you can show your contempt by arriving late. If you don't arrive too late, you can still claim that you attended the event, so you're protected from punishment for being absent. Showing up late irritates, frustrates, and even humiliates those who take the meeting seriously. Tactical tardiness is intended to produce these very feelings in those requiring attendance.

Tactical tardiness asserts power in disguised form. The group is faced with a dilemma. The group may wait for your arrival, but this holds the entire group hostage until you appear. Members' plans for the day may be trashed by the delay. The other alternative is to commence without you. This also may prove to be problematic. If you offer reasonable-sounding excuses for your late arrival, the group will feel bound to clue you in on what has already transpired, thereby halting progress until you have been informed. All instances of tardiness are not necessarily tactical. Occasionally, getting to meetings on time is not possible through no fault of your own. Tactical tardiness is a recurrent pattern of resistance, not a rare occurrence.

Tactical tardiness is not the sole province of the less powerful. High-power persons may also use this strategy to reinforce their dominance. Self-important celebrities with egos swelled like puffer fish often arrive late to functions. They hope to underscore their perceived superiority over worshipful fans by making them wait.

Purposeful Procrastination: Intentional Delaying Tactic Most people put off doing that which they dislike. There is nothing purposeful about this. There is no strategy involved. Procrastination, or what someone once called the "hardening of the oughteries," can become a resistance strategy when it is purposefully aimed at a target.

Purposeful procrastinators pretend that they will pursue a task "soon." While promising imminent results, they deliberately refuse to commit to a specific time or date for task accomplishment. Trying to pin down a purposeful procrastinator is like taking a knife and stabbing Jell-O to a wall—it won't stick. They'll make vague promises. When you become exasperated by the ambiguity and noncommittal attitude, the purposeful procrastinator will try to make you the problem. "Relax! You'll stroke out if you're not careful. I said I'd get to it, didn't I?" The implication is clear. You're impatient and unreasonable. The job will get done—not without delay after delay, however. If the task doesn't get accomplished, it is because "something came up unexpectedly." If you express irritation at the delays, you're a nag.

Resistance strategies are generally viewed as negative and unproductive (Bach & Goldberg, 1974). This is true in an ideal sense. Resistance strategies are underhanded, deceitful, and rest on mixed messages. Resistance strategies are not the type of skills a competent communicator needs to learn. Nevertheless, they should not be ruled out unequivocally. Low-power members may have no better tools to resist abuse from dominant group members. Hoping that treatment by dominant group members will improve by itself is too passive. Hope is not a strategy. The essence of the problem, however, doesn't lie in the resistance strategies. The dominance form of power creates a competitive group atmosphere in which resistance strategies are nurtured and encouraged.

From the standpoint of competent communication, however, emphasis must be on how to deal effectively with resistance, since the resistance may not always be noble. There are three principal ways for the competent communicator to deal with resistance strategies in groups:

1. *Confront the strategy directly.* Identify the communication pattern and ferret out the hidden hostility. Once this has been accomplished, efforts must be made to discover alternatives to dominance–submissiveness power patterns. Care should be taken to use the descriptive pattern of communication discussed in Chapter 4.

2. *Don't be an enabler.* We become enablers when we allow ourselves to become ensnared in the resister's net of duplicity. When we continue to wait for the chronically late, we encourage tactical tardiness. If we perform the tasks for those who use loss of motor function to resist, we reward their behavior and guarantee that the behavior will persist. Group members thwart the enabling process by refusing to be a party to the resistance. If a staff member "forgets" an item at the supplies store, guess who gets to make a return visit? If you hear the old refrain, "I can't be expected to remember everything," tell him or her to make a list. If the person is repeatedly late for committee meetings, refuse to interrupt the meeting to fill him or her in on what was missed and encourage the person to come on time. Continued tardiness may necessitate expulsion from the group.

3. *Give clear directions regarding specific tasks.* You want no possibility that confusion or misunderstanding can be used to excuse the poor behavior. Have the group members repeat the directions if resistance is suspected.

Again, **the appropriate focus should not be on how to combat resistance, but instead on why the resistance occurs in the first place.** If the main cause of

---

SECOND LOOK

Resistance Strategies

Strategic Stupidity—smart people acting dumb on purpose; feigned stupidity

Loss of Motor Function—sudden attack of the clumsies

The Misunderstanding Mirage—illusory mistakes

Selective Amnesia—no fear of Alzheimer's; forgetting only the distasteful

Tactical Tardiness—late for reasons within your control

Purposeful Procrastination—promising to do that which you have no intention of doing anytime soon, if ever

---

resistance resides in the dominance form of power, then the focus of attention should be on how to reduce the power imbalance, or at least its perception.

▶ Defiance: Digging in Your Heels

Defiance stands in bold contrast to resistance. **Defiance** is an overt form of communicating noncompliance. It is unmitigated, audacious rebellion against attempts to induce compliance. Defiance, like resistance, is a prevention form of power, but unlike resistance there is no ambiguity or subtlety. No one is left guessing whether an individual supports a specific norm or goal of the group.

When individuals exhibit behaviors that do not conform to group norms, they are called "nonconformists" or "deviants." When this nonconformity is a purposeful, conscious, overtly rebellious act against the wishes of a group leader or the group itself, it becomes defiance. Group members typically turn to defiance when they perceive little or no chance of enhancing their power position through formation of an alliance, resistance strategies seem either inappropriate or ineffective, or they feel like exhibiting independence from group conformity.

Threat of Contagion: Spreading Dissension Defiance can be contagious. In the Asch (1952) study, discussed in Chapter 3, an interesting wrinkle was added. When one of the confederates deviated from the group judgment regarding the correct length of a line, naïve subjects' conformity dropped precipitously to a mere 8%. A single deviant encourages independent decision making, even outright rebellion.

The concern that defiance from even one member could spread throughout the group like a cold virus in a day-care center motivates groups to act quickly to squash it. In Chapter 3, the four strategies to quell nonconformity—reason, seduction, coercion, and ostracism—were discussed. These strategies are what usually await defiant group members. A defiant individual can threaten the power of a group to command compliance from its members.

Variable Group Reaction: Discriminative Defiance All defiance is not created equal. Some instances of noncompliance will produce nary a ripple of concern in the group. Other instances will be perceived as intolerable. Whether a group takes steps to crush noncompliance, adopts a calculated indifference to the defiance, or explores ways to adapt to the challenge posed by the deviant depends in large part on three factors.

First, **some norms are not as important to a group as others,** so the reaction to defiance will vary. For a basketball team, curfews and eating meals together before a game may be considered terribly important, but socializing with team members outside of the basketball environment may be perceived as relatively unimportant.

Second, **the degree of deviation from the norm also affects whether a group discourages noncompliance and, if so, to what extent.** A group may have a norm

AP Images/Jeff Widener

A courageous, unarmed man stops tanks during the Tiananmen Square upheaval in China in 1989. An imbalance of power, starkly evident here, often leads to conflict and defiance. To this day, no one has identified this man publicly or indicated what happened to him.

requiring punctuality. If a member is a few minutes late to a meeting, this deviance is usually ignored. If a member arrives two-thirds of the way through a meeting, however, group members may view this as outright defiance and quite intolerable.

Third, **the deviation from the norm has to be a matter of obvious defiance, not inadvertent noncompliance.** Showing up for a new job dressed inappropriately is rarely an act of defiance. Normally, this show of nonconformity will be interpreted as a clueless blunder, not an act of rebellion. Not all nonconformity is defiance. Deviance must be overt, conscious, and clearly intended to flout group norms to prevent domination by more powerful group members before it becomes defiance. The group reaction to inadvertent deviance will likely be mild compared to unmistakable defiance. We smile indulgently when a small child bangs on the bathroom door and inquires, "Whaddya doin' in there?"

Defiant Member's Influence: Alone against the Group Given the tremendous pressure to conform exerted on those who defy, how do we explain the individual who converts the group to his or her way of thinking, as dramatized in the movie *12 Angry Men?* Admittedly not a frequent occurrence (Meyers & Brashers, 1999), defiance from members does influence groups (Pennington & Hastie, 1990), more often when the minority viewpoint comes from more than one group member (Clark, 2001). For example, a minority view on a jury rarely converts a majority from a guilty to an innocent verdict, but it often convinces the majority of jurors to change their minds on the severity of guilt (from first-degree murder to second-degree murder or manslaughter). Presenting high-quality arguments and effectively refuting majority arguments are primary ways to accomplish such modification of verdicts (Meyers & Brasher, 1999).

If the group cannot reject you (e.g., a juror or an elected official), then the deviant's best chance of converting the group is to remain unalterably and confidently defiant throughout discussions—in other words, defy without cracking (Gebhardt & Meyers, 1995). If, however, the group has the power to exclude the deviant from the group or the deliberations, then the deviant stands a better chance if he or she remains uncompromisingly defiant until the group seems about fed up. At this point, the deviant should indicate a willingness to make some degree of compromise (Wolf, 1979). The group is more likely to modify its position if it sees the deviant as coming around and being more reasonable. Remaining intransigent when the group can reject you is a losing battle. Your consistent defiance will be taken as legitimate justification for your ostracism.

Remaining unalterably defiant will win you no friends. Unwavering deviants are seen as less reasonable, fair, warm, cooperative, liked, admired, and perceptive than other group members (Moscovici & Mugny, 1983). This is not surprising since the deviant creates secondary tension in the group. Although the consistent deviant is not viewed as competent by the group, deviants are perceived to be confident and self-assured, independent, active, and even original.

Consistency may increase the influence of defiant members in groups, especially when there is some ambiguity and indecision among majority members, but it does not necessarily improve group decision making (Gebhardt & Meyers, 1995; Wellen & Neale, 2006). Flexibility is a key to communication competence in groups. Intransigence aimed at winning over the group will likely produce rigidity from the majority of group members. When both the defiant individual and the group members remain rigidly consistent, the majority prevails (Gebhardt & Meyers, 1995).

▶ Significance: Self-Empowerment

When group members grow tired of being dominated by more powerful individuals, they can balance the power in the group more evenly by increasing their value to the group. Becoming more significant to the group can occur in two primary ways: by developing assertiveness and by increasing personal power resources.

Assertiveness: Neither Doormat nor Foot Wiper The terms *assertive* and *aggressive* are often linked, even in scholarly circles. For example, some communication scholars define assertiveness as "a generally constructive aggressive trait" (see especially Infante et al., 1997, p. 129). Distinguishing assertiveness and aggressiveness conceptually does seem important. This is especially true in light of how psychologist David Myers (2003) defines aggression—"any physical or verbal behavior intended to hurt or destroy" (p. 719). This makes "constructive aggression" an oxymoron (I'm trying to destroy you in order to save you?). If assertiveness is associated with aggression, then ethically I could not encourage anyone to learn and use such incompetent communication.

Adler (1977) defines **assertiveness** as the "ability to communicate the full range of your thoughts and emotions with confidence and skill" (p. 6). Assertiveness falls in between the extremes of passivity and aggressiveness and is distinctly different from either. Aggressiveness puts one's own needs first; you wipe your shoes on other people. Passivity underemphasizes one's needs (Lulofs, 1994); you're a doormat in a world of muddy shoes. **Assertiveness takes into account both your needs and the needs of others.**

Assertiveness is perceived by many people to be merely communicating the full range of thoughts and emotions—period. The ability and skill part of the definition is overlooked. So group members sound like arrogant little Nazis in the process of telling the group what they think or feel. Assertiveness is not a "looking out for number one" competitive communication strategy. To be assertive is to be sensitive to others while also looking out and standing up for yourself. You can stand up for yourself without trampling others in the process. Defining assertiveness in terms of empowerment makes this point obvious.

Assertiveness is not a strategy of resistance. As previously explained, resistance tactics are acts of passive aggression. On the surface you seem to be compliant (passive), but under the surface you're sabotaging (aggression). I have not included assertiveness in the section on defiance because it is a primarily empowering form of communication. **We most often use assertive communication not to defy the group, but instead to ensure that our individual needs, rights, and responsibilities or those of other group members are not submerged or ignored by the group.**

There are distinct advantages to learning assertiveness. When a formerly passive member is assertive, the group may view this as a highly constructive change, wholly consistent with the norms of the group, and worthy of encouragement, not ostracism. Self-assertion makes you a more significant person in a group. Your potential influence in group decision making will be enhanced. Passive members become isolates and are easily ignored by the group. Assertive members make their presence felt and express their ideas and feelings to the group for consideration.

Considering previous evidence on compliance rates already cited, it isn't surprising that research shows that **assertiveness is conspicuous by its absence** (Moriarity, 1975). (See Box 10.2.) A group of students in my small group communication class demonstrated this by conducting a field study as a *Candid Camera* project. Three group members formed a line in front of two side-by-side ATMs. Neither cash machine was in use and no "out of order" sign was posted. Within minutes a long line of people wanting to use the ATM formed behind my students. Some individuals seemed agitated at having to wait in line without anyone using the cash machine, but most never said a word. Several people waited 10 to 15 minutes before giving up and leaving in disgust. One woman did ask my students at the head of the line, "Is there something wrong with the ATM?" My students replied, "I don't know." The woman inquired further, "Why are you standing in line?" My students responded again, "I don't know." Did this inspire the woman to move out of line and use the ATM? No, it didn't. She rejoined the line, waited a few more minutes, then left. No one used the ATM the entire time my students stood in line.

Assertiveness seems to be especially challenging for women. In one study, small groups composed of four members met to decide which 12 individuals from a list of 30 were best able to survive on a deserted island. During discussion, a male group member (actually a confederate of the experimenters) utters three sexist remarks ("We definitely need to keep the women in shape"; "One of the women can cook"; "I think we need more women on the island to keep the men satisfied"). Imagine yourself in this situation. Would you speak up and protest? When a comparative group of college students were asked this, only 5% said that they would keep quiet and 48% said that they would be assertive and speak up. When female participants were put to the test,

BOX 10.2

Assertiveness Self-Assessment Questionnaire

Fill out the following Assertiveness Self-Assessment Questionnaire. Be as honest as you can. This is not an assessment of your "ideal self." This should be your "real self." For each situation, indicate how likely you would be to take the action indicated by using the following scale:

5 = Very likely
4 = Likely
3 = Maybe
2 = Unlikely
1 = Very unlikely

_____ 1. You have been invited to a party, but you don't know anyone except the friend who invited you. You see dozens of strangers. You walk up to a group of people and introduce yourself and begin a conversation.

_____ 2. There is a definite undercurrent of tension and conflict in your group. You are feeling that tension as your group begins discussing its project for class. You stop the discussion, indicate that there is unresolved conflict in the group, and request that the group address this issue.

_____ 3. You strongly disagree with your group's choice for a symposium project. Nevertheless, you say nothing and go along with the majority decision.

_____ 4. During class your instructor makes a point that angers you greatly. You raise your hand, are recognized by the instructor, and vehemently challenge your instructor's position, raising your voice to almost a shout.

_____ 5. You're sitting in the back of the class. Two students sitting beside you engage in an audible conversation that is distracting. You can't concentrate on the instructor's lecture. You lean over and calmly ask them to stop talking so you can listen to your instructor.

_____ 6. At a family holiday dinner gathering, your uncle makes a blatant racist remark, then tells a sexist joke. You sit silently.

_____ 7. While on vacation you sign up to receive a group lesson in a new sport (jet skiing, rock climbing). After the instructor has explained the basics, everyone in the group appears to understand perfectly. You, however, are unclear about a couple of instructions. You raise your hand and ask the instructor to repeat the instructions and explain them more fully.

_____ 8. Three individuals representing a religious group knock on your door. When you answer they begin to proselytize, trying to sell you on their religious point of view. You stand there waiting patiently for them to finish, wishing they would go away.

_____ 9. A small group of teenagers talks loudly during a movie you attend at a local theater. You become increasingly annoyed but say nothing to them.

_____ 10. You live in a dorm room with two roommates. Next door loud music is playing, making it impossible for you to study. Your roommates seem not to care, but you are becoming increasingly annoyed by the noise. You walk next door, pound on the door, and when the door is opened you demand that the music be turned way down immediately.

_____ 11. A member of your group couldn't afford to buy the textbook for the class. He asks you if he can borrow your book for "a couple of days." You agree. He has had the book for more than a week and shows no sign of returning it to you. You wait for him to return the book or explain why he hasn't mentioned it.

_____ 12. At work, you are a member of a project team. Every member of the team makes considerably more money than you do, yet your jobs are equivalent. You believe that you deserve a hefty raise. You make an appointment with your boss to ask for a substantial raise.

_____ 13. You receive an email from a team member that has a condescending tone. It angers you that this team member, whom you view as a bit of a screw-up, lectures you on the "right way" to approach your part of the group task. You write back a sarcastic, biting reply.

_____ 14. The coach of your sports team berates players at a team meeting for "lackluster play" and "lackadaisical attitudes." The coach is shouting and abusive. You believe the criticism is mostly unfair and doesn't apply to most of the players. You remain silent, wishing he/she would wind down.

_____ 15. A group member pulls you aside and begins accusing you of "unethical behavior." She is shouting at you, her face is flushed red, and she is wildly gesturing. People are noticing. You shout back at her.

_____ 16. The family next door has a dog that barks all hours of the night. It is disturbing you and your family members. You meet one of the dog owners during a walk through the neighborhood. You stop, begin to talk, and you calmly bring up the barking dog problems.

_____ 17. You are taking an exam. You notice several students cheating on the exam. You're upset because this gives the students an undeserved advantage and may lower your own grade because the instructor grades on a curve. The instructor doesn't notice the cheating. You report the cheating to the instructor after class.

_____ 18. During a group discussion, your point of view clashes with that of another group member. You want very much to convince the group that your viewpoint should be accepted. You interrupt when the member who disagrees with you tries to voice her opinion, you keep talking when she tries to disagree with a point you make, and you insist that she is wrong and you are right.

_____ 19. At work, a member of your project team "steals" your idea and takes credit for work you have done. You angrily denounce him in front of the entire team and insist that he own up to his deception.

_____ 20. One of your team members has extremely bad breath. This is a common problem when you meet. His bad breath bothers you a great deal. Nevertheless, you say nothing and try sitting as far away from him as possible during meetings.

_____ 21. You are waiting in line to be served at a local store. Just as you are about to be waited on, a group of three individuals steps in front of you. You demand that they step aside, insisting that you were in line ahead of them.

Scoring Directions: Total your scores for numbers 4, 10, 13, 15, 18, 19, and 21 (aggressiveness). Now total your scores for numbers 1, 2, 5, 7, 12, 16, and 17 (assertiveness). Finally, total your scores for numbers 3, 6, 8, 9, 11, 14, and 20 (passivity). Enter these raw totals in the appropriate blanks.

_____Aggressiveness ( )
_____Assertiveness ( )
_____Passivity ( )

Now average each raw score by dividing by 7 (e.g., 21 on aggressiveness divided by 7 = 3.0

average). Put the averages in the parentheses provided.

NOTE: Generally speaking, you want to average between 4.0 and 5.0 on assertiveness, and average 2.0 or less on aggressiveness and passivity. This reflects the general desirability of assertiveness and the general undesirability of aggressiveness and passivity. A low score on a specific assertiveness scenario or a high score on a specific aggressiveness or passivity scenario may also mean a need for improvement in these particular situations. Please note, however, that the appropriateness of assertiveness, aggressiveness, and passivity is situational. Assertiveness, although generally a desirable skill, is not always appropriate, especially if harm may come to you by being assertive. Conversely, aggressiveness, although generally an undesirable communication pattern, is not always inappropriate. Likewise, occasionally the appropriate choice is passivity.

however, 55% said nothing and only 16% spoke out against the sexism. The rest mostly asked questions or joked nervously (Swim & Hyers, 1999).

Additional research parallels these results, showing that women are far less assertive than men (Leaper & Ayres, 2007). For example, women are significantly more reticent than men to ask for higher starting salaries (Kay & Shipman, 2014). In one study of students graduating with a master's degree from Carnegie Mellon University, only 7% of the female participants asked for more money, but 57% of the male participants asked for higher starting salaries. Those who requested higher salaries, on average, received $4,053 in additional compensation (Babcock, 2002). Other studies support these findings (Babcock & Laschever, 2007). This additional starting salary compounds over the course of a career to more than *$1 million* (Pinkley & Northcraft, 2000). That's a huge chunk of money lost because no request was made for a higher starting salary. Why don't women typically assert themselves and request more money? Women tend to see negotiation as an unpleasant conflict or contest that may disrupt future interpersonal relations and acceptance into groups (Babcock & Laschever, 2007). In one study, men were two-and-a-half times more likely than women to view a job negotiation as a means to advance their interests (status), while women were two-and-a-half times more likely to see a job negotiation as a means to further their acceptance by others (connection) (Barron, 2003). Women and men have been socialized to view the world in different ways, and this is reflected in their communication in groups (Kwang et al., 2013).

The competent communicator, however, cannot assume that assertiveness is always appropriate. Cultural differences, for example, must be taken into account (Den Hartog, 2004). Assertiveness is not valued in many Asian cultures (Samovar & Porter, 2004). Standing up for yourself and speaking your mind are seen as disruptive and provocative acts likely to create disharmony. One study also discovered that you could be overly persistent in asserting yourself (Schmidt & Kipnis, 1987). Excessive assertiveness can result in less favorable evaluations from supervisors, lower salaries, greater job tension, and greater personal stress than a less vigorous assertion of one's needs and desires.

These results show that **assertiveness is not preferable to passivity or aggressiveness in every circumstance.** The advantages and disadvantages must be weighed within each context. As a general rule, however, assertiveness is empowering, especially in American culture, and more advantageous with far fewer and less severe disadvantages than aggressiveness or passivity.

So how do you become more assertive? Bower and Bower (1976) provide a useful framework for learning assertiveness. They call it DESC Scripting:

Describe: This first step was discussed at length in Chapter 4. Review the language of description.

Express: Here you express how you think and feel about the offending behavior. Again, this is not a verbal assault on the offender. The express step is not an opportunity for finger-pointing (e.g., "You made me feel…"). Instead, you formulate a statement from your perspective (e.g., "I believe," "I feel," "I disagree").

Specify: This step identifies the behavior you would like to see substituted for the bothersome behavior. The request needs to be concrete and spelled out, not vague or merely suggestive. "I think it is only fair that I receive sole credit for this proposal, and in the future I expect to receive credit for my ideas" is better than "I want you to stop plagiarizing my ideas immediately."

Consequences: The consequences of changing behavior or continuing the same behavior patterns should be articulated to the offending party. The emphasis, if possible, should be on rewards, not punishments. "I like working here and expect to continue as long as I'm treated fairly" is better than "If you continue to steal my ideas I'll be forced to quit."

The DESC guidelines for assertiveness will prove to be nothing more than an idealized fantasy cooked up by academics unless "powerless" language and anemic, nonverbal behavior are eliminated from the process. **Expressing your thoughts and feelings must be accomplished with confidence and skill.** This requires direct eye contact, not looks cast downward or side to side. Posture should be erect, not slouched in a cowering whipped-puppy stance. Tone of voice should be modulated so aggression or passivity doesn't emerge. Tag questions, hedges, hesitations, disclaimers, and overly polite references should be minimized or eliminated if possible. If you are interrupted, calmly indicate, "I haven't finished." Everything suggested regarding how to be assertive requires practice. You will find that assertiveness is far easier in some circumstances than in others.

Increasing Personal Power Resources: Mentoring and Networking Since the group confers power on the individual, a person can enhance his or her power by increasing personal resources valued by the group. There are a number of avenues available for personal power enhancement.

Husbands who assume a greater portion of the domestic chores may increase their value in the family. Children whose parents are unemployed or underemployed can exercise greater power if they find a part-time job to supplement family income. Learning certain skills valued by the group can enhance your power position. If you master the skills required to use computers and no one in your group is computer proficient, then your power increases when the group requires such technical expertise.

Finally, the mentoring and networking processes can enhance personal power resources (Feeney & Bozeman, 2008). **Mentors** are knowledgeable individuals who have achieved some success in their profession or jobs and who assist individuals trying to get started in a line of work. Mentors can provide information to the newcomer that prevents mistakes by trial and error. One study showed that women who have mentors move up the corporate ladder much faster than women without mentors. Women also receive promotions more quickly when they are helped by mentors (Kleiman, 1991). Mentors are essential for women trying to advance to the highest levels of corporate leadership (Eagly & Carli, 2007; Hackman & Johnson, 2004).

Networking is a form of group empowerment. Individuals with similar backgrounds, skills, and goals come together on a fairly regular basis and share information that will assist members in pursuing goals. Networks also provide emotional support for members, especially in women's networks (Eagly & Carli, 2007; Stewart et al., 1996).

In summary, power is a central dynamic in all groups. Power is the ability to influence the attainment of goals sought by yourself and others. Power is not a property of any individual. It is the product of transactions between group members. Information, expertise, rewards and punishments, personal qualities, and legitimate authority are primary resources of power. Groups must endorse these resources before they have power potential. The influence that you wield cannot be determined precisely. Nevertheless, you can approximate the distribution of power

SECOND LOOK

Significance (Empowerment)

Assertiveness

Describe the behavior that is troublesome.

Express how you think and feel about the offending behavior.

Specify behavior preferred as a substitute for bothersome behavior.

Consequences of changing behavior or continuing without change should be articulated.

Increasing Personal Power Resources

Personal improvement

Learn valued skills

Mentoring and networking

in groups by observing certain general patterns of communication, plus verbal and nonverbal indicators.

An imbalance of power in groups promotes conflict and power struggles and in some instances can lead to violence. The five ways we transact power in groups, especially when power is unequally distributed, are compliance, alliance, resistance, defiance, and significance. Compliance primarily aims to bring the less powerful in line with the dictates of the more powerful and to discourage deviance, which can be contagious. Alliance, resistance, defiance, and significance are all means used by members to balance the power more equitably in small groups.

In Mixed Company

MindTap™

Reflect on what you've learned.

▶ Online

Now that you've read chapter 10, access the online resources that accompany *In Mixed Company* at **www.cengagebrain.com**. Your online resources include:

1. Multiple-choice and true-false **chapter practice quizzes** with automatic correction

2. Digital **glossary**

3. **Flashcards**

QUESTIONS FOR CRITICAL THINKERS

1. Information is power. Can misinformation also serve as a power resource?
2. If punishment has significant drawbacks, why is it typically used more frequently than rewards by those in power positions?
3. Have you ever used resistance strategies? Did they work? Were they used against dominant individuals?
4. Can you think of instances in your own experience in which assertiveness was inappropriate?

VIDEO *Case Studies*

Crimson Tide (1995). Drama; R
Taut undersea drama that pits the captain of a nuclear submarine (Gene Hackman) against a new executive officer (Denzel Washington). The Washington character must decide whether to obey his superior officer and launch a nuclear "retaliation" against Russian rebels, risking total nuclear war, or to assume command of the submarine by force. All members of the crew must decide where their allegiance and duty lie. Relate this dramatic decision to the Milgram obedience studies and issues of compliance in groups. Consider the ethics of such a decision and how it was implemented.

Lord of the Rings: Fellowship of the Ring (2001). Fantasy/Drama; PG-13
Terrific screen adaptation of the first in a trilogy of the J. R. R. Tolkien fantasy epics. Analyze characters for their power resources. Are there any resistance or defiance strategies evident? Consider the corrupting effects of power.

Morning Glory (2010). Comedy/Drama; PG-13
Workaholic Becky Fuller, played by Rachel McAdams, is the executive producer of a failing early morning network TV show called "Daybreak." Desperate to raise the pathetic ratings of the show, she hires, under protest, egomaniacal news reporter Mike Pomeroy (Harrison Ford) to co-host the show. Pomeroy views the job as distasteful and beneath him. Identify and analyze resistance strategies used by Pomeroy. Analyze the transactional nature of power between the McAdams and Ford characters. What are the power resources of each character?

The Great Debaters (2007). Drama; PG-13
African American poet Mel Tolson (Denzel Washington) forms a debate team at historically black Wiley College in the 1930s. Based on a true story, the Wiley College debate team achieves such distinction that it earns an opportunity to debate powerhouse Harvard University in 1935. Analyze the power dynamics of the debate team with Tolson as its coach. What power resources are used by each character? Are there any defiance or resistance strategies used?

The Hunger Games (2012). Adventure/Sci-Fi; PG-13
Katniss Everdeen volunteers to replace her younger sister in the televised deadly Hunger Games. Examine this film for examples of power resources, instances of defiance or passive aggression, and dominance-prevention transactions. Are there any examples of empowerment present in the film?

Answers to Multiple-Choice Questions in Captions
Cartoon (p. 309): 1, 2.

11 Conflict Management In Groups

A. Definition of Conflict
1. General Definition: Interconnectedness, Incompatibility, and Interference
2. Benefits of Conflict: Dissent Can Be Productive
3. Destructive and Constructive Conflict: It's All in the Communication

B. Styles of Conflict Management
1. Collaborating: Problem Solving
a. Confrontation: Directly Addressing the Problem
b. Integration: Seeking Joint Gains
c. Smoothing: Calming Troubled Waters
2. Accommodating: Yielding
3. Compromising: Halving the Loaf
4. Avoiding: Withdrawing
5. Competing: Power-Forcing
6. Comparing Styles: Likelihood of Success

C. Situational Factors
1. Types of Conflict: Task, Relationship, and Value
a. Task Conflict: Routine or Nonroutine
b. Relationship Conflict: It's Personal
c. Values Conflict: Deeply Felt Struggles

Closer Look: KILL Radio Conflict Case Study
2. Culture and Conflict: Communication Differences

D. Negotiating Strategies
1. Tit for Tat: Do unto Others
2. Reformed Sinner: Spreading Redemption
3. Positional Bargaining: Hard and Soft Negotiating
4. Principled Negotiation: Interest-Based Bargaining
a. The Four Principles: Appropriate Rules
b. Remaining Unconditionally Constructive: Sound Judgment
c. The BATNA: Best Alternative To a Negotiated Agreement

E. Anger Management
1. Constructive and Destructive Anger: Intensity and Duration
2. Managing Your Own Anger: Taking Control
3. Managing the Anger of Others: Communication Jujitsu

MindTap™
Start with a
quick warm-up
activity.

O nce upon a time, there was a quiet little condominium complex composed of 18 units beside a meandering creek in a forest setting. The residents enjoyed seeing the deer wander down in the evening from their habitat above the complex. Wildlife was abundant. A climate of tranquility enveloped this special place.

Then one day, bulldozers and earthmovers of every variety rumbled in unannounced. Peace and quiet were abruptly replaced by ear-splitting noise, incessant vibration from the heavy equipment thundering back and forth across the once-emerald terrain. Families residing in Village Haven were understandably shaken by the realization that 32 additional units were about to be squeezed onto every speck of available space a mere 50 feet across from the original 18 residences.

The situation did not improve once construction of the condos began. Residents were awakened regularly at 6:30 A.M. on weekdays and sometimes on weekends to the sounds of hammering, sawing, and shouting from workers. Cars previously parked along the curb of the one-way road into and out of the complex had to be moved to a small paved area in the center of the development where bulldozers and forklifts whizzed by, showering the autos with dirt and debris. Tires were regularly punctured by nails strewn across the road by careless workers. Huge trucks and construction equipment frequently blocked the single-lane road into and out of the complex, stranding residents in their cars, sometimes for 10 to 15 minutes. Residents occasionally found pathways to their homes dangerous to traverse.

At one point, a signed message from the developer and contractor was taped to the doors of the condos. Residents were instructed to remove their cars from the street so "demolition and reconstruction" could take place. Residents were now ordered to park their cars on a street overlooking the complex about two blocks up a very steep, poorly lighted hill. During the demolition, two residents had stereos stolen out of their cars while parked on this street. The homeowners as a group were not happy!

The inhabitants of Village Haven, working under the auspices of the complex's homeowners association, considered legal action but ran into numerous technical and political roadblocks. The developer and the contractor were asked to begin construction at 8 A.M. instead of 6:30 A.M. Residents were informed that early starts were "the nature of construction" and couldn't be changed. When representatives of the association raised objections to the edict requiring removal of all cars to the street above, they were told that this was an unavoidable inconvenience. Several residents got into shouting matches with the developer and the contractor.

Vandalism started to crop up here and there. The professionally painted sign at the entrance to the complex that read "Village Haven Forest Townhomes" was painted over to read "Village of the Damned." Another sign that read "Welcome to Village Haven" was changed to read "Welcome to Hell." Windows freshly installed in new units were sporadically smashed. Security patrols were increased to thwart the vandals, with little apparent success.

A few days after the message ordering the removal of all cars from paved areas was attached to residents' doors, a tongue-in-cheek message appeared on everyone's doorstep. Attributed to the contractor and developer (real author unknown), but obviously intended as an underground satirical jibe at these two individuals, the message was addressed to Village Haven residents and purported to answer complaints from homeowners. The bogus message was signed under the names of the contractor and developer, with the appellation "The Village Idiots" added.

Frustrated and weary, residents began listing their units for sale, but few potential buyers were interested once they saw the 50 units crammed onto the once beautiful and serene acreage. The project was finally completed; some of the original residents left, but the animosities lingered.

The principal purpose of this chapter is to show you constructive ways to manage a group conflict such as the Village Haven fracas. In previous chapters, several sources of conflict and their corresponding antidotes were discussed at length. Briefly, these include:

Sources	Solutions
Competitive group climate	Structure a cooperative group climate.
Defensive communication patterns	Structure supportive communication.
Self-centered disruptive roles	Adopt strategies for dealing with difficult group members.
Imbalance of power	Balance power among group members.
Conflicts of interest	Use integrative problem solving.

Building on this foundation of previous discussion of conflict, **there are three chapter objectives:**

1. To define conflict, identifying the differences between its constructive and destructive form,

2. To explain the pros and cons of five communication styles of conflict management,

3. To discuss how to transact conflict effectively in small groups.

Definition of Conflict

Read, highlight, and take notes online.

The Village Haven case study (*based on a real situation*) provides us with a means of explaining the general definition of conflict in a group context. In this section, destructive conflict and constructive conflict are also differentiated.

▶ General Definition: Interconnectedness, Incompatibility, and Interference

In general, **conflict** is the expressed struggle of interconnected parties who perceive incompatible goals and interference from each other in attaining those goals (Donohue & Kolt, 1992; Wilmot & Hocker, 2011). You can see all of the elements of this definition in the Village Haven battle.

First, conflict is an *expressed struggle* between parties. If the homeowners of Village Haven had merely sat and stewed over perceived outrages, then no conflict would have existed because the developer and contractor wouldn't have known there was a problem. Often the expression of a struggle is manifested in shouting matches, such as those that occurred between the residents of Village Haven and the developer and contractor. Sometimes it is expressed more indirectly, such as the exchange of written messages placed on residents' doorsteps. Occasionally, the expression is of a nonverbal nature. Vandalism and the reaction to it (beefed-up security) are examples from the Village Haven conflict.

Second, conflict occurs between *interconnected parties* in a group system. This means that for a conflict to exist, the behavior of one or more parties must produce consequences for the other party or parties. The invasion of the bulldozers significantly affected the residents of Village Haven. Likewise, the developer and contractor could not completely ignore residents' angry reactions.

Third, conflict involves *perceived incompatible goals* (Canary & Lakey, 2013). The residents of Village Haven would have preferred an 18-unit instead of a 50-unit complex. The developer and contractor couldn't make any money that way. The goal of the builders to erect 32 additional units collided squarely with the desire of the residents for a quiet, natural, uncrowded setting.

Finally, conflict involves *interference from each other* in attaining desired goals. Unless one party attempts to block the attainment of another party's goal, there is no conflict. You and I may express a disagreement, be interconnected parties, and we may even perceive our goals to be incompatible, yet conflict may not exist even then. You may, in an act of pure selflessness, assist me in the attainment of my goal at the expense of attaining your own goal. There must be an attempt to interfere with another's goal attainment for conflict to exist.

In Village Haven, interference abounded. Builders interfered with residents' tranquility and convenience and transformed the environment from a desirable, low-density development to an undesirable, high-density development. Residents interfered with builders in the form of verbal abuse and vandalism (again assuming the culprits were residents).

▶ Benefits of Conflict: Dissent Can Be Productive

Conflict is not an event that most people welcome, and residents of Village Haven certainly didn't seem thrilled by their battle with developers. Most conflict probably seems destructive (Kerwin et al., 2011), given how poorly conflict is typically managed in groups, and a high level of conflict can be counterproductive for groups because it can interfere with task accomplishment. Low levels or the absence of conflict, however, can lead to complacency and groupthink (Jehn, 1995). **Moderate amounts of conflict can be a constructive force in groups if the conflict is managed competently.** Conflict can instigate positive changes that foster individual and group growth, it can promote creative problem solving (Dovidio et al., 2009; Crano & Seyranian, 2009), it can encourage power balancing, and conflict can even enhance group cohesiveness (Putnam, 2006). Conflict can also prevent groupthink (Jehn, 1995).

Previously, I discussed the value of a devil's advocate in preventing groupthink. A devil's advocate introduces dissent to produce effective decision making and problem solving. In the absence of genuine dissent, a devil's advocate plays an important role for the group. Playing the part of a dissenter for argument's sake and to stimulate processes that can short-circuit groupthink, however, is not genuine dissent and it doesn't have to provoke real conflict. A devil's advocate doesn't have to pursue incompatible goals or interfere with the pursuit of those goals by others. A devil's advocate can introduce disagreement as a role play without personally advocating such disagreement ("for the sake of argument"), and disagreement alone does not constitute conflict (see definition).

Authentic dissent, on the other hand, is genuine disagreement and usually produces an attempt to take the group in a different direction (an expressed struggle).

Thus, authentic dissent can provoke real conflict and make group decision making and problem solving more effective (Nemeth et al., 2001). Those who genuinely disagree with the group tend to have a greater impact on the group's final decisions than a devil's advocate might have. Authentic dissenters are usually more committed to their disagreement with the group and more engaged than someone playing the role of dissenter (devil's advocate). Although this may make for a tougher decision-making process, the benefits of genuine dissent voiced directly for group discussion can be substantial. Encouraging dissenting voices is very useful. How this genuine dissent is communicated, of course, determines whether the conflict will be constructive or destructive.

▶ Destructive and Constructive Conflict: It's All in the Communication

So what distinguishes destructive from constructive conflict? **The principal difference is how competent the communication is when transacting the conflict** (Canary & Lakey, 2013; Olson, 2002). **Destructive conflict** is characterized by dominating, escalating, retaliating, competing, defensive, and inflexible communication patterns (Lulofs, 1994; Wilmot & Hocker, 2011). When conflicts spiral out of control they push conflict to unmanageable levels. Participants lose sight of their initial goals and focus on hurting their adversary.

The Village Haven conflict was essentially a destructive conflict. Escalation, vandalism, threats, shouting, inflexibility on both sides, and expressions of contempt and ridicule occurred. Neither side seemed able to work together to find a mutually satisfactory solution to the conflict.

Recognizing destructive conflict while it is occurring may not always be easy. When it becomes obvious to you that *"Gee, I'm getting stupid,"* you're engaged in destructive conflict (Donohue & Kolt, 1992). When you see yourself engaging in petty, even infantile, tactics to win an argument, you're getting stupid. Becoming physically and verbally aggressive moves the conflict into destructive territory. This doesn't mean that you can never raise your voice, express frustration, or disagree with other group members. **Conflict can remain constructive even when discussion becomes somewhat contentious.** When conflict becomes more emotional than reasonable, when you can't think straight because you are too consumed by anger, then conflict has become destructive (Fisher & Shapiro, 2005; Gottman, 1994).

Constructive conflict is characterized by We-oriented, de-escalating, cooperative, supportive, and flexible communication patterns (Lulofs, 1994; Wilmot & Hocker, 2011). It is competent communication in action. The principal focus is on trying to achieve a solution between struggling parties that is mutually satisfactory to everyone. Even if no mutually satisfactory solution is achieved at the time, the communication process that characterizes constructive conflict allows conflicting parties to maintain cordial relationships while agreeing to disagree. This makes the ultimate emergence of a creative solution that is mutually satisfactory to conflicting parties more likely.

Styles of Conflict Management

Communication is central to conflict in groups. Our communication can signal that conflict exists, it can create conflict, and it can be the means for managing conflict constructively or destructively (Wilmot & Hocker, 2011). Consequently, communication styles have been the center of much research and discussion. A **communication style of conflict management** is an orientation toward conflict. Styles exhibit predispositions or tendencies regarding the way conflict is managed in groups. Individual group members may exhibit a specific style or an entire group may adopt a normative preference for a certain style of conflict management (Kuhn & Poole, 2000). There are five communication styles of conflict management (Blake & Mouton, 1964; Kilmann & Thomas, 1977). I will explain each of the five styles and add some modifications of the original theoretical descriptions.

Let me offer one quick clarification. I have chosen the term conflict "management" instead of "resolution" in most instances because it is more appropriate for a systems perspective. Resolution suggests settling conflict by ending it, as if that is always desirable. **Since conflict can be an essential catalyst for growth in a system, increasing conflict may be required to evoke change** (Johnson & Johnson, 2000). Civil rights demonstrators purposely provoked conflict to challenge racist laws in the South. Women who file sexual harassment lawsuits provoke conflict to end an evil. "Managing conflict" implies no end to the struggle. Although some conflict episodes end within a group and are therefore resolved, conflict overall in a system is a continuous phenomenon that waxes and wanes. Management of conflict also implies no judgment on the goodness or badness of struggles in general.

Focus Questions

1. How do communication styles of conflict management differ on task and social dimensions of small groups?

2. Should group members always use the collaborating style and avoid the competing (power-forcing) style?

▶ Collaborating: Problem Solving

The most complex and potentially productive communication style of conflict management is collaborating, or what some refer to as problem solving. The **collaborating** style is a win–win, cooperative approach to conflict that attempts to satisfy all parties. **Someone employing this style has a high concern for both task and social relationships in groups.** The collaborating style recognizes the interconnection between the task and social components of groups and deals directly with both requirements. A collaborating style has three key components: confrontation, integration, and smoothing.

Confrontation: Directly Addressing the Problem The overt recognition that conflict exists in a group and the direct effort to manage it effectively is called **confrontation**. Although the news media are fond of using the term *confrontation* in a negative sense, as in "There was a violent confrontation between protesters and police," this is not the meaning relevant to this discussion. Confrontation as a conflict-management technique incorporates all the elements already discussed at length regarding assertiveness (describe, express, specify, and identify consequences) and supportive communication patterns (description, problem orientation, etc.). The purpose of confrontation is to manage conflict in a productive way for all parties involved.

Not all issues are worth confronting (De Dreu & Van Vianen, 2001). Members who confront even trivial differences of opinion or can't let a momentary flash of pique go unattended can be like telemarketers at the dinner hour—beyond annoying. Groups have to decide which issues and concerns are priorities and which are tangential. You can overuse confrontation and make yourself a nuisance.

Integration: Seeking Joint Gains A collaborative technique that devises creative solutions that are mutually satisfactory for all parties in conflict is called **integration**. Since integrative solutions to problems were discussed in Chapter 9, they will not be repeated here. Additional examples of how to find integrative alternatives during conflicts, however, are offered later in this chapter.

Integration as a collaborative technique has not been given the attention that it deserves. Negotiators in organizations are typically better at maximizing their own gains (competitive) than they are at maximizing joint gains (integrative) (Brett et al., 1990). Also, negotiators tend to reach agreement on the first satisfactory proposal that comes along rather than looking for a better solution (Pruitt, 1981). Training through lecture, reading, and exercises can vastly improve integrative skills of group members (Neale et al., 1988). Programs that provide extensive training for students on how to negotiate integrative agreements have proved to be highly effective (Johnson & Johnson, 2000).

Smoothing: Calming Troubled Waters   The act of calming the agitated feelings of group members during a conflict episode is called **smoothing**. When tempers ignite and anger morphs into screaming and shedding of tears, no collaboration is possible. Turbulent emotions need to be smoothed. A simple "I'm sorry" is a useful smoothing response. "Let's all calm down. Attacking each other won't help us find a solution everyone can accept" is another example of smoothing. Calming the emotional storm opens the way to confronting conflict and brainstorming integrative solutions.

Since collaborating is such an effective communication style for solving conflicts of interest, why isn't it always used in these situations? There are several reasons. First, **collaborating usually requires a significant investment of time and effort along with greater-than-ordinary communication skills.** Even if you are willing to employ the collaborating techniques of confrontation, integration, and smoothing, collaborating requires mutually agreeable parties. I have witnessed several instances in which an integrative solution was devised, but the group rejected it because the members disliked the person who originated the proposal. Second, **collaboration is built on trust.** If parties are suspicious of each other and worry that one will betray the other by not honoring agreements, then even an integrative solution may be rejected. Third, **parties in a conflict sometimes do not share the same emotional investment in finding an agreeable solution for all involved.** Hypercompetitive group members want a clear "victory," not a mutually satisfactory solution that benefits all parties.

▶ Accommodating: Yielding

The **accommodating** style yields to the concerns and desires of others. Someone using this style shows a high concern for social relationships but low concern for task accomplishment. This style may camouflage deep divisions among group members to maintain the appearance of harmony. If the task can be accomplished without social disruption, fine. If accomplishing the task threatens to jeopardize the harmonious relationships within the group, however, a person using this style will opt for giving members what they want, even though this may sacrifice productivity. Generally, group members with less power are expected to accommodate more often and to a greater degree than more powerful members (Lulofs, 1994).

Although we tend to view accommodating in a negative light, as appeasement with all its negative connotations, this style can be quite positive. A group that has experienced protracted strife may rejoice when one side accommodates, even on an issue of only minor importance. Yielding on issues of incidental concern to your group but of major concern to other parties while holding firm on issues of importance to your group usually achieves mutually advantageous outcomes (Lax & Sebenius, 1986; Mannix et al., 1989).

► Compromising: Halving the Loaf

When **compromising**, we give up something to get something. Some have referred to this as a lose–lose style of conflict management because neither party is ever fully satisfied with the solution. Compromising is choosing a middle ground. **Someone using this style shows a moderate concern for both task and social relationships in groups.** The emphasis is on workable but not necessarily optimal solutions.

Compromise evokes ambivalence—both negative and positive reactions (Jaffe, 2012). We speak disparagingly of those who would "compromise their integrity." On some issues, usually moral or ethical conflicts such as abortion or capital punishment, compromise is thought to be intolerable. Yet despite this negative view of compromise, negotiations of labor–management contracts and political agreements are expected, even encouraged, to end in compromise. Members of task forces, ad hoc groups, and committees of many shapes and sizes often seek a compromise as an admirable goal ("There has to be some give and take").

Half a loaf is better than starvation—not in all circumstances, but certainly in some. **When an integrative solution cannot be achieved, when a temporary settlement is the only feasible alternative, or when the issues involved are not considered critical to the group, compromise can be useful.**

► Avoiding: Withdrawing

Avoiding is a communicating style of withdrawing from potentially contentious and unpleasant struggles. Groups typically change the subject under discussion soon after a period of disagreement among members (Gouran & Baird, 1972). *Flights from fights* may seem constructive at the time because they circumvent unpleasantness. In the long run, however, facing problems proves to be more effective than running from them. **Someone using the avoiding conflict style shows little concern for both task and social relationships in groups.** Avoiders shrink from conflict, even fear it ("I can't deal with this"). By avoiding conflict they hope it will disappear. Group tasks are sacrificed to a preoccupation with dodging trouble. Social relationships within the group have scant possibility of improving when the conflict distorts the behavior of those doing the avoiding. Avoiding may actually increase relationship conflict (Impett et al., 2005).

Avoiding, nevertheless, is sometimes appropriate. If you are a low-power person in a group and the consequences of confrontation are potentially hazardous to you, avoiding might be a reasonable strategy until other alternatives present themselves.

Standing up to a bully may work out well in movies, but confronting antisocial types (workplace bullies) who look like they eat raw meat for breakfast and might eat you for lunch may not be a very bright choice. Staying out of a bully's way, although perhaps ego-deflating, may be the best *temporary option* in a bad situation.

If the advantages of confrontation do not outweigh the disadvantages, avoiding the conflict might be a desirable course of action. In some cases, tempers need to cool. Avoiding contentious issues for a time may prove to be constructive. ("Let's deal with this later when we've had a chance to simmer down a bit, okay? We can think more clearly when we aren't upset.") When passions run high, reason usually trails far behind. We often make foolish, irrational choices when we are highly stressed. In addition, if differences among group members are intractable (e.g., personality clashes), avoiding the differences and focusing on task accomplishment may be a desirable approach (De Dreu & Van Vianen, 2001).

In most cases, avoiding rather than confronting is highly counterproductive. Failure to address conflict early on can lead to destructive conflict later, while addressing conflict effectively early on usually prevents escalation into destructive conflict (Behfar et al., 2008; Greer et al., 2008). From their research on family violence, Gelles and Straus (1988) suggest *confronting the very first incident of even minor violence,* not avoiding the issue while waiting to see if it happens again. They conclude: "Delaying until the violence escalates to a frequency or severity that would generally be considered abusive is too late. A firm, emphatic, and rational approach appears to be the most effective personal strategy a woman can use to prevent future violence" (p. 159). "Don't ever again lay a hand on me in anger—EVER!" makes the point firmly and emphatically.

▶ Competing: Power-Forcing

When we approach conflict as a win–lose contest, we are competing. The **competing** style is communicated in a variety of ways that are likely to produce destructive conflict: threats, criticism, contempt, hostile remarks and jokes, sarcasm, ridicule, intimidation, faultfinding and blaming, and denials of responsibility (Wilmot & Hocker, 2011). The competing style is aggressive, not assertive. It is not confrontation as previously defined; it is an attack. The competing or power-forcing style flows from the dominance perspective on power. Competing and forcing your will on others is a win–lose style. **Someone using a competing or forcing style shows high concern for task but low concern for relationships in groups.** Task comes first. If accomplishing the group task requires a few wounded egos, that is thought to be the unavoidable price of productivity. Someone using the competing/forcing style sees task accomplishment as a means of furthering personal more than group goals (Me-Not-We orientation). Making friends and developing a positive social climate are secondary and expendable.

Tom Cheney/The New Yorker Collection/Cartoon Bank.Com

This cartoon illustrates which of the conflict management styles?
1. Power-forcing
2. Accommodating
3. Compromising
4. Avoiding

Answers are given at the end of the chapter.

One notable aspect of the competing style is the tendency to ascribe blame when groups don't function perfectly. Blame "produces disagreement, denial, and little learning. It evokes fears of punishment. . . . Nobody wants to be blamed, especially unfairly, so our energy goes into defending ourselves" (Stone et al., 1999, pp. 11–12). Blame is about looking backward to judge a group member. "You blew it" or "It's your fault" is blame aimed at assigning responsibility, not on solving the problem.

As with all other styles, the competing style also has its constructive side. If a troublemaker in your group shows no signs of ending disruptions and the seriousness of the situation is clear, then forcing out this difficult member may be the correct choice. Eliminating a troublemaker can revitalize the remaining members and allow progress on the task to proceed unimpeded. If a group is bogged down in bickering and disagreement with no end in sight, the group leader may have to step in and make a final decision for the group. Endless bickering is unproductive.

All five styles of conflict management show different emphases on task and social dimensions of groups. Nevertheless, someone using the competing style may, in some circumstances, manifest genuine concern for social climate. Low concern doesn't mean no concern. An accommodator, on occasion, may regard the task accomplishment as vital. **All of these styles represent tendencies, not unalterably fixed ways of managing conflict in every situation.**

▶ Comparing Styles: Likelihood of Success

As a general rule, research clearly favors some conflict styles over others, even though more than one style may need to be used, perhaps by a single group member, over the course of a conflict (see Closer Look: "KILL Radio Conflict Case Study"). **Collaborating is the most constructive and effective style of conflict management** (DeChurch et al., 2007; Kuhn & Poole, 2000). Impressive field research on a program called Peacemakers, involving students from kindergarten to ninth grade, supports the efficacy of the collaborative method of conflict management. The Peacemaker program specializes in training students in schools throughout North America, Europe, Asia, Central and South America, the Middle East, and Africa to use the collaborative method of conflict management. A review of 17 studies on the Peacemaker program shows that trained students almost always used the method in actual conflict incidents both at school and at home. As a result, student conflicts referred to teachers for resolution were reduced by 80% and referrals to the school principal were reduced to zero. Conflicts between students became less severe and destructive (Johnson & Johnson, 2000).

SECOND LOOK

Communication Styles of Conflict Management

Style	Task–Social Dimension
Collaborating (Problem Solving)	High task, high social
Accommodating (Yielding)	Low task, high social
Compromising (Halving the Loaf)	Moderate task, moderate social
Avoiding (Withdrawing)	Low task, low social
Competing (Power-Forcing)	High task, low social

Overall, the collaborating style in a variety of contexts produces the best decisions and greatest satisfaction from parties in conflict, and the competing/forcing style is least effective. Collaborating encourages constructive conflict; competing tends to promote destructive conflict (Isenhart & Spangle, 2000; Somech et al., 2008).

Despite the clear benefits of the collaborating style, the disadvantages of the competing style, and mixed results for the other three styles, **we seem to use the least effective styles most often to manage conflict in groups.** Students who were not trained to use collaboration in the Peacemakers experiments *never* used integrative negotiations, rarely used accommodation, and most often chose the competing or avoiding styles. Consequently, they left many conflicts to fester, and they experienced mostly negative outcomes (Johnson & Johnson, 2000).

Studies of doctor–nurse abuse found that avoidance was a chief style used by nurses (Johnson, 2009; Maxfield et al., 2005). One study showed that fewer than 7% of nurses confronted abusive doctors (Maxfield et al., 2005). Another study "found countless examples of caregivers who delayed action, withheld feedback, or went along with erroneous diagnoses rather than face potential abuse from a colleague" (Grenny, 2009). In the nursing profession overall, conflict styles are typically used in this order of frequency: compromising, competing, avoiding, accommodating, and finally collaborating (Iglesias & Vallejo, 2012).

In a workplace study, the compromising style was the most widely used across four of six levels within an organization, used less frequently only at the entry and top executive levels (Thomas & Thomas, 2008). In another workplace study, a scant 5% of first-line supervisors, middle managers, and top managers and administrators admitted to actually using the collaborating style in specific conflict situations; 41% selected competing and 26% chose avoiding styles (Gayle, 1991). Both male and female supervisors and managers, according to this study, typically select the least effective styles of conflict management.

Even if the style with the greatest likelihood of success is chosen, when and how it is used must also be figured into the equation. Confrontation used as a collaborative tactic can be highly effective, but it is not effective when used in a hit-and-run fashion (Johnson & Johnson, 1987a). Confronting contentious issues five minutes before the group is due to adjourn or just before you leave for a luncheon date provides no time for another person to respond constructively. Hit-and-run confrontations look like guerrilla tactics, not attempts to communicate competently and work out disputes. Likewise, when to use power-forcing is an important concern. Competing/power-forcing should be a style of last resort, except in times of emergencies in which quick, decisive action must be taken and discussion has no place. If all other approaches to managing conflict produce little result, then competing may be a necessary means of managing the dispute. Power-forcing typically produces psychological reactance. If you try to force, are met with resistance, then attempt to collaborate or accommodate, you may find that this sequence of styles suffers from poor timing. Trying to collaborate after unsuccessfully forcing will be seen as the disingenuous act of a person whose bluff and bluster were challenged. On the other hand, temporarily withdrawing after a protracted feud has stalemated might allow heads to clear and passions to cool. Sometimes we just need a break from the struggle, a chance to think calmly and dispassionately.

Situational Factors

Although some conflict styles have a higher probability of effectiveness than others, the choice of styles always operates within a context. To understand how to transact conflict effectively in a small group context, certain situational factors should be considered, such as the type of conflict and cultural views of conflict-management communication styles.

Focus Questions

1. **How do group members short-circuit conflict spirals?**
2. **Why is principled negotiation superior to other negotiating strategies?**

▶ Types of Conflict: Task, Relationship, and Value

There are several types of conflicts, and we shouldn't attempt to handle them all exactly the same. Communication styles of conflict management have to be adapted to the different types of conflict to be appropriate and effective.

Task Conflict: Routine or Nonroutine Whether conflicts regarding group tasks are beneficial or detrimental depends largely on the type of task, routine or nonroutine, performed by the group. A **routine task** is one in which the group performs processes and procedures that have little variability and little likelihood of change. A **nonroutine task** is one that requires problem solving, has few set procedures, and has a high level of uncertainty. Conflicts about routine tasks often have a negative effect on group performance, while conflicts about nonroutine tasks often have a positive effect (Jehn, 1995). Conflicts regarding routine tasks easily deteriorate into gripe sessions with little opportunity for resolution. As one participant in Jehn's (1995) study noted: "We seem to fight about these things (routine tasks) and they typically can't be changed because that's the way the job has to be done. So the arguments just seem to get in the way of the work" (p. 272). Conflicts about nonroutine tasks, however, promote "critical evaluation of problems and decision options, a process crucial to the performance of nonroutine tasks" (p. 275). These positive results, of course, are predicated on group members choosing a collaborative (problem-solving) style rather than a competing style.

Relationship Conflict: It's Personal Conflicts are not always about task accomplishment; some are about relationships between and among group members. Group members don't always get along well together because of interpersonal incompatibilities. Some of the most frustrating and volatile conflicts are provoked by personality clashes and outright dislike between group members (Varela et al., 2008). Roommate conflicts are a typical instance. A survey of 31,000 first-year college students conducted by the Higher Education Research Institute at UCLA reported that 29% experienced conflicts with roommates (Warters, 2005), and living situations with multiple roommates can increase the complexity of such conflicts. You may simply not like your roommates and this produces tension and disagreements.

Participants in the Jehn (1995) study expressed strong frustration with relationship conflicts of this ilk. One person offered, "Trina and I don't get along. We never will get along. We dislike each other and that's all there is to it" (p. 271). Another participant said, "Personality conflicts, personality conflicts. I can't handle it" (p. 271).

The competing/forcing style tends to provoke relationship conflict when none may have initially existed, while the collaborating style does not (DeChurch et al., 2007). Trying to force your will upon roommates, for example, may trigger dislike among all parties and lead to future discord and recurring battles. Approaching disagreements from a collaborative perspective may prevent relationship conflict from occurring. If not, avoidance may be your next best alternative. Typically, individuals try to avoid each other when personality clashes and outright dislike emerge (Jehn, 1995). They may even redesign their workspace or job to avoid such conflicts. You may avoid much contact with disliked roommates until a more favorable living arrangement emerges.

In actual practice, we do make style choices in terms of our relationships with other parties. Managers typically are accommodating with superiors ("Yes, I will get that report to you by tomorrow") and compromising with peers ("Let's split the workload equally between us") (Rahim, 1985). The reality of power imbalances sometimes makes choosing accommodation a matter of self-preservation. Lower-power group members may want to collaborate. Dominating, high-power group members may see little need to collaborate since they can impose their will on other group members ("Do it because I say so"). Granted, power-forcing may be an unwise choice for the powerful parties in the long run, but it may be an unavoidable reality you have to face if you're the lower-power person in a conflict.

If a relationship is one of trust and cooperation, regardless of the power disparities, then collaborating has real potential. In one study (Tjosvold, 1986), high-power supervisors in cooperative environments actually used their power to assist subordinates ("Let me see what I can do to get that information for you so your report can be completed on time"). This was not so true in environments characterized by a competitive or individualistic climate ("Why should I do your work for you?"). If a relationship is one of mistrust and suspicion, then collaborating will be difficult. Power-forcing is the style of choice among supervisors dealing with subordinates they do not trust (Riccillo & Trenholm, 1983).

In relationships poisoned by mistrust, a collaborative attempt by one party may be seen as a ploy to gain some unforeseen advantage. Accommodating by one party, even as a gesture to change the negative dynamics of the parties in conflict, may be viewed as weakness and a sign that capitulation is likely to occur after a period of waiting.

Recognizing the interconnectedness of task and relationship dimensions of groups can be critical when conflict arises (see Closer Look: "KILL Radio Conflict Case Study"). A conflict initially about task accomplishment can easily morph into mostly a relationship conflict, especially if task accomplishment is affected (Jehn, 1995; Kerwin et al., 2011). Establishing trust among group members is a key component necessary to prevent task conflict from mutating into relationship conflict (Curseu & Schruijer 2010). When working on a group project for class, some group members may exhibit social loafing. Such lackluster effort on a task from some members can trigger relationship conflict. Those members who wish to achieve a high grade may lash out at members who do not produce for the group. They don't trust some group members to fulfill their responsibilities to the group. Anger can erupt, and relationship conflict can escalate into destructive conflict and poor overall group performance on the project. Relationship conflict often diminishes group productivity on tasks (Curseu & Schruijer, 2010; De Dreu & Weingart, 2003). Free expression of conflicting ideas in groups can be constructive and prevent groupthink, but not if such disagreement erupts into personal squabbles and divisive quarrels (Kozlowski & Ilgen, 2006).

Values Conflict: Deeply Felt Struggles   The most difficult disputes to manage are values conflicts (Borisoff & Victor, 1989). **Values** are the most deeply felt views of what is deemed good, worthwhile, or ethically right. We may clash over beliefs and still walk away as friends, especially if the ideas do not touch much on values. **Beliefs** are what we think is true or probable. "Republicans favor big business" or "Democrats are beholden to labor" are beliefs that don't ordinarily degenerate into fistfights or verbal assaults. When disputes about beliefs spill over into value clashes, especially when the values are held passionately, then you have a conflict of a different ilk. Battles over abortion, pornography, flag burning, hate speech, and the like are fundamentally about values such as freedom, right to privacy, and equality. Such conflicts do not lend themselves much

CLOSER LOOK

KILL Radio Conflict Case Study

The situation (*based on a real event*): Open warfare has been raging for almost a year at public radio station K-I-L-L (slogan: "Live radio that'll knock you dead"). The station operates from facilities on the campus of Bayview Community College in Tsunami, California. KILL radio has 1,000 watts of power, enough to reach into the local Tsunami community (population 42,000).

The program director quit after a feud with the general manager (GM). The GM resigned soon after. His reasons for leaving, stated in his letter of resignation, were as follows:

1. The volunteer staff (community members who were not students) inappropriately editorialized while reading news on the air and presented only one side on controversial issues; both are violations of Federal Communications Commission (FCC) regulations for public radio stations.

2. The volunteers were "insubordinate" when they refused to obey his directives concerning substitution of other programs for previously scheduled regular shows.

3. The volunteers threatened him with bodily injury when he ordered them either to implement his directives or terminate their association with the station.

The volunteer staff countered these allegations with its own accusations: the GM showed them little respect and treated them abusively; they were overworked and underappreciated; and the GM never sought their input on programming and scheduling concerns.

The volunteers issued the following demands:

1. Programming should not be determined by one person, but by a consensus of the staff.

2. Program substitution should be made only when prior notice (at least two weeks in advance) has been given so staff members will not prepare material destined to be preempted at the last minute.

3. Volunteers should run the station since they do the lion's share of the work and are the only ones with the necessary technical expertise.

The college supports the station with $85,000 annually, but is seriously considering a drastic cut in the station's budget due to the persistent conflict and because students are not actively involved in the station. The administration wants the station to be a learning laboratory for students interested in pursuing careers in broadcasting.

The volunteer staff has threatened to quit en masse unless their demands are met. The school's board of trustees is getting twitchy because of all the commotion; the faculty in the department of mass communication are in a dither about the conflict because it is disruptive. The local community highly values the station and is upset by the dispute. The college administration named the chair of the mass communication department at Bayview College as the new general manager and temporary program director of the station.

Before reading further, analyze this dispute. How would you manage this conflict if you were the new GM? Which conflict styles would you employ? When? How?

The Analysis: The KILL radio dispute is a power struggle. Competing/forcing has become the primary style of managing the conflict. The previous GM threatened the staff with termination and the staff threatened the GM with bodily injury. So far, the power-forcing style has produced two resignations, the threat of a mass exodus by the staff, several demands from the staff, and a reservoir of ill feeling and disruption. If you, as the new GM, were to continue in this vein by terminating the volunteer staff, you might ignite a conflict spiral. Disgruntled volunteers might vandalize the station in retaliation, and relations between the college and the community would be strained further. The station would have to shut down until qualified staff could be found to replace those individuals terminated. In such an atmosphere, the board and administration just might decide to close the station permanently and cut their losses.

Since the staff has not been actively consulted in the past regarding programming (at least that's the allegation, and perception is the reality you must confront), the climate is one of control, not problem orientation. The staff feels disconfirmed and defensive. The perception exists among them that the previous GM treated them as expendable technicians, not talented employees worthy of respect. A task conflict spilled over into a relationship conflict.

This situation cries out for collaboration. The first step is confrontation. The new GM should immediately meet with the volunteers, probably individually first, to gather information from their perspective. Staff members feel unappreciated and undervalued. Supportive, confirming statements concerning the essential role volunteers play in the functioning of the station should be made to all involved. Smoothing statements (e.g., "We're starting fresh. I want us to work together") should be delivered to the staff. You're seeking a cooperative working relationship with the volunteers.

In keeping with the desire for cooperation, an appeal to the superordinate goal of keeping the station on the air should be delivered. The new GM must impress on the staff that violations of FCC regulations could result in the revocation of the station's operating license. This is not a matter of personal preference but of law. The GM could further state, "Unless we handle our differences constructively, the college may shut down the station. None of us wants this to happen." There should be no threats about firing anyone. The tone and climate should be positive and focused on the central cooperative goal all can agree to—namely, maintaining the station.

Although final say on the programming issue is the GM's responsibility, input from the staff should be sought actively and given serious consideration. After all, the staff has to make the programming work on the air. That's difficult to accomplish if you'd like to play rhythm and blues but are ordered to play country western. The staff could conduct a survey of the community (this is a public radio station) to determine the programming preferences of the station's audience. The GM could then make programming decisions based on data from the survey and not on personal tastes of a single individual or the (possibly narrow) preferences of the staff. One or two experimental programs could be tried as a compromise if community preferences do not match staff preferences in programming. Some compromise may be possible on program substitution (perhaps one week prior notice, not two weeks as demanded).

Integrating the radio station into the college curriculum should be a fairly simple process. Involving students in the actual operation of the station, perhaps as supervised interns earning class credit, would satisfy a primary concern of the administration and board. This would also expand the resources of the station by training additional individuals to help staff members who already feel overworked.

Finally, the demand that the volunteers run the station would have to be denied. More than likely, however, this demand was made without any expectation that it would be accepted. Avoid this issue unless a staff member raises it. Power-forcing would be required if this issue came to a showdown. Handling other issues effectively may reduce this issue to irrelevance. If disruptions or violations of FCC regulations recur, then those responsible should be terminated.

The key to the management of this conflict by a competent communicator is the flexible use of several conflict styles. No single style could effectively manage this complex dispute. The overriding conflict style, however, is collaboration. You begin by confronting central concerns of disputing parties, not competing/forcing. You find integrative solutions where possible. Termination (power-forcing) is a last resort, not a first choice. You compromise only when a better solution cannot be found. You smooth hurt feelings because a supportive environment is essential to the management of conflict. You avoid emotional issues that seem tangential to the real sources of the conflict and are likely to provoke a power struggle and relational conflict.

None of these styles of conflict management, of course, will work unless you think through each step before you take it (act, don't just react). The competent communicator must have knowledge of different conflict styles, the skill to use all the styles, a sensitivity for the requirements of the specific situation and the likely outcomes of each choice made, and a commitment to resolving the dispute as equitably and ethically as possible. Complex conflicts require sufficient time to be resolved. This means patience.

QUESTIONS FOR THOUGHT

1. Before you read the analysis of this case study, what action would you have proposed to resolve the conflict? In what ways were your proposals different from the ones suggested in the analysis?
2. Do you disagree with any suggestions provided in the analysis? Explain.

to compromise (would you compromise your values?). When dichotomous battle lines are drawn—friends versus enemies, saviors versus sinners—power-forcing is often the style required for conflict management. The courts have had to settle these issues by declaring what is permissible, even essential, and what is prohibited.

Values conflicts are especially difficult to manage when members of different cultures clash over divergent worldviews. Rubenstein (1975) presented a hypothetical situation to Arabs and Americans. Suppose that a small boat is occupied by a man and his wife, his mother, and his child when it capsizes. The man is the only occupant who can swim. He can save only one of the three nonswimmers. Which person should he save? All of the Arabs surveyed by Rubenstein would save the mother because a wife and child can be replaced, but not a mother. Sixty of 100 American college freshmen, however, would save the wife, and 40 would save the child.

Saving the mother while sacrificing the wife and child was thought to be laughable. Who has the greatest value among the three is a cultural conundrum. Intercultural values conflicts are probably the most difficult to manage (see the next section for tips on managing intercultural value conflicts).

▶ Culture and Conflict: Communication Differences

Individualist and collectivist cultures exhibit a specific difference in communication patterns. Individualist cultures such as the United States and most Western European countries typically employ what Hall (1981) calls low-context communication, while collectivist countries such as most Latin American and Asian countries use a high-context communication (Griffin, 1994). **Low-context communication** has a message-*content* orientation and **high-context communication** has a message-*context* orientation. "In low-context communication, the listener knows very little and must be told practically everything. In high-context communication, the listener is already 'contexted' and does not need to be given much background information" (Hall & Hall, 1987, p. 183).

The primary difference between the two is exhibited in verbal expression. Low-context communication is verbally precise, direct, literal, and explicit. A legal contract is an example of low-context communication. Instructions given to computers and email addresses are also examples of low-context communication. Computer instructions must be exact for the computer to function as you desire, and email addresses must have every space, number, period, and letter typed exactly.

High-context communication is indirect, imprecise, and implicit. For example, an indirect verbal expression, such as "I'll think about it," may be a face-saving means of saying no in Japan, or it may be assumed that no verbal expression is required to state what should be obvious from the nonverbal context. You are expected to "read between the lines" by recognizing hints and knowing the cultural context and unspoken rules, rituals, and norms.

The difference between the hi- and low-context communication styles is aptly expressed by a Japanese manager working in the United States, "When we say one word, we understand 10, but here you have to say 10 to understand one" (quoted in Kameda, 2003). For example, here is a typical English message written by a Japanese manager: "Our office has moved to Kawasaki. I'm going to buy a Honda." To Americans, this may seem to be two disconnected sentences. To a Japanese, the meaning is obvious: "Our office has moved to Kawasaki. It's too far from the station to walk, so I'll have to buy a car. I'm thinking of getting a Honda" (Kameda, 2003). "If you hear 'one' part of a message you are supposed to understand all the other unsaid 'nine' so that with 'one' part you must understand the whole 'ten' parts" (Kameda, 2007).

Individualist and collectivist values significantly affect the communication styles of conflict management chosen when conflict occurs (Ting-Toomey & Chung, 2005). Individualist, low-context cultures favor direct competitive or compromising styles of conflict management (Cupach & Canary, 1997). Communication during conflict is explicit and direct, sometimes "brutally honest" (Holtgraves, 1997). Americans are inclined to become impatient when members of collectivist cultures "beat around the bush." Allowing a conflict to go unresolved makes most Americans uncomfortable, even agitated. Collectivist, high-context cultures favor avoiding or accommodating styles of conflict management (Chen & Starosta, 1998). Assertive confrontation is

SECOND LOOK

General Conditions for Communication Styles of Conflict Management

	Appropriate	Inappropriate
Collaborating	Complex issues	Trivial issues
	First approach	Last resort (unlikely to work)
	Ample time	
Accommodating	Trivial issues	Complex issues
	Issues significant only to one side	Issues significant to all parties
	Maintaining close relationships (especially collectivist cultures)	Social relationships temporary
	Large power imbalance	Relatively equal power
Compromising	No integrative solution available	Initial goal
	Temporary solution better than no agreement	Giving up too soon on critical issues
Avoiding	Issues are trivial	Issues are significant
	Hazardous to confront	Ignoring disagreements may damage social relationships
	Need temporary break	May increase anger by ignoring issues
Competing	Timely decision required	Time not a constraint
	Last resort	First option
	Disruptive member unresponsive to other approaches	Concern for positive social relations critical (especially collectivist cultures)

See also Rahim (2002).

considered rude and offensive. It is too direct, explicit, and unsettling. For example, avoidance of confrontation is "a core element of Thai culture. Expressions of emotion and excitement are seen as impolite, improper, and threatening" (Knutson & Posirisuk, 2006, p. 211). A Thai avoids conflict and exhibits respect, tactfulness, politeness, modesty, and emotional control (Knutson et al., 2003). Similarly, the collectivist Malaysian culture values harmony, eschews assertiveness, and values face saving. Power-forcing is rarely used because it is perceived to be too aggressive (Rose et al., 2007).

Consider a comparison between typical Chinese and American approaches to conflict. The Chinese culture, for example, considers "harmony as the universal path which we all should pursue" (Chen & Starosta, 1997, p. 6). This philosophy translates into avoiding conflicts that might stir up trouble and disharmony. Conflicts handled ineptly might bring shame on the individual and the entire group. Thus, while Americans tend to focus immediately on task conflicts, Chinese tend to focus on relationship conflicts and avoid task conflicts until the relationships among all disputing parties have had time to build (Jehn & Weldon, 1997). To Americans this may look like stalling to gain advantage.

Conflicts with individuals from other cultures (out-groups), however, are often handled differently in collectivist cultures than are conflicts within the culture (in-group). Although not the initial choice, competing (power-forcing) is not an uncommon way to approach conflict with outsiders, especially if the interests of the opposing parties are highly incompatible. Vicious quarrels, even physical fights, are not uncommon in such circumstances (Chen & Starosta, 1998; Yu, 1998).

Managing intercultural conflicts is challenging where expectations differ on the appropriateness of different communication styles. Remaining flexible by employing a style that is well suited to cultural expectations is a key to effective conflict management in such situations (Knutson et al., 2003). Don't abandon collaborating, but be prepared to accommodate whenever appropriate if group conflict involves members of collectivist cultures. Also recognize that competing/power-forcing is ineffective and inappropriate in most intercultural conflicts.

Negotiating Strategies

Negotiation is "a process by which a joint decision is made by two or more parties" (Pruitt, 1981, p. 1). **Negotiating strategies are the ways we transact these joint decisions when conflicts arise.** In this section, commonly used strategies for negotiating conflict are discussed.

▶ Tit for Tat: Do unto Others

The **tit-for-tat strategy** begins with an act of cooperating, and if the other party or parties in the negotiation follow suit and cooperate, you continue to do the same (you reciprocate). If, however, the other party competes after your initial cooperative offer, then you match them by competing (again you reciprocate).

Those who tout tit for tat (Axelrod, 1984) can make a case for the utility of the strategy when cooperation does occur. Tit for tat will maintain cooperation once it has been initiated because you reciprocate an act of cooperation, thereby encouraging further cooperation from the other party. Tit for tat has been shown to be moderately effective in producing cooperation in some circumstances, particularly when participants are perceived to be firm but fair (Axelrod et al., 2002; Sheldon, 1999). In real situations, however, this strategy runs the risk of provoking **conflict spirals**—the escalating cycle of negative communication that produces destructive conflict. **We tend to adopt those conflict strategies that are used by other parties during a conflict** (Park & Antonioni, 2007). With tit for tat, "once a feud gets started, it can continue indefinitely" (Axelrod, 1984, p. 138). If someone tries to cheat, blackmail, or exploit you in a dispute, should you reciprocate in kind? If another party has a snit fit, should you likewise throw a temper tantrum? If your antagonist demands outrageous concessions from you, should you mindlessly match the demands? Does any of this sound to you like competent communication? As Fisher and Brown (1988) explain, "If you are acting in ways that injure your own competence, there is no reason for me to do the same. *Two heads are better than one, but one is better than none*" (p. 202). Tit for tat predisposes us to stoop to whatever level the other party is willing to sink. Although a common negotiating strategy, it is not recommended.

▶ Reformed Sinner: Spreading Redemption

A second strategy of negotiating is called reformed sinner (Pruitt & Kimmel, 1977). Someone using the **reformed sinner strategy** initially competes or acts tough, then cooperates and relaxes demands. The inducement to cooperate is the demonstrated willingness to compete if necessary. Unlike tit for tat, you try to break a conflict spiral by making the first move toward cooperation.

A rather interesting version of the reformed sinner strategy is Osgood's (1959; 1966) GRIT proposal. **GRIT** stands for **G**raduated and **R**eciprocated **I**nitiatives in **T**ension reduction. Originally offered as a means to de-escalate the international arms race, the strategy has been employed in less-global conflicts. **GRIT tries to break conflict spirals and impasses by initiating a cycle of de-escalation, thus moving from destructive to constructive conflict.** This strategy uses the following sequence of steps (see Folger et al., 1993 and Fells, 2012, for greater detail):

1. Issue a sincere public statement expressing a desire to de-escalate the conflict.

2. Specify the concession to be made, clarifying what, when, and how the action will be undertaken.

3. Follow through and complete the concession, but do not make this contingent on reciprocation by the other parties.

4. Encourage, but do not demand, reciprocation from the other parties.

5. Make no high-risk concessions that leave you vulnerable or in an indefensible position. Don't give away the store.

Someone using this method of promoting cooperation in a competitive conflict situation should consider following the first concession with another concession if no progress is made after a time. Here lies the main weakness of the GRIT strategy—it appears to reward obstinate behavior from the other party (Brett et al., 1998). Thus, don't pile concession onto concession with nothing offered in return. This strategy may take patience and persistence. Offering a minor concession and then withdrawing it when no immediate reciprocation is forthcoming from the other party is not a true GRIT.

▶ Positional Bargaining: Hard and Soft Negotiating

In positional bargaining, parties take positions on contested issues, then they haggle back and forth until concessions are made and an agreement is reached. There are two styles of positional bargaining: hard and soft. **Hard bargainers** (sometimes called tough bargainers) see negotiation as a contest of wills. Hard bargaining is the "negotiate from strength" approach to conflicts of interest, heard so often in foreign affairs deliberations. The focus is on conveying strength and resilience so the other party or parties will yield.

Hard bargaining is a competing/forcing strategy. Hard bargainers can be abusive or sarcastic in an attempt to gain an advantage over the other party. When both sides adopt a hard bargaining style, the battle is joined. Both sides attempt to cut the best deal for themselves (Me-Not-We orientation), instead of finding the most equitable and constructive solution to the conflicts of interest. Opening positions typically are extreme and unreasonable. The more hard bargainers publicly defend these positions, the more hardened the positions tend to become. Egos become identified with positions (task conflict transforms into relationship conflict as well). Concessions easily take on the appearance of "selling out." **Walking out on the negotiations in a huff, refusing to budge even on trivial issues, and issuing ultimatums ("Take it or leave it") are commonplace tactics in hard positional bargaining.** "Getting stupid" is a common hard bargaining tactic.

Consider this example of hard positional bargaining among housemates:

A: I want to have a party here at the house on Saturday.

B: Hey, that's a great idea.

C: Sorry, you can't. I have to study for my law exam, and I sure can't do that with a couple of dozen of your belching, retching friends cranking the music to a decibel level equivalent to a jet airplane taking off. I'd have to lug a truckload of stuff to the library or anywhere else I might choose to study.

A: Who appointed you king? This is our house too. Since when do you dictate what can and can't happen around here?

C: Since I pay a third of the rent and am not about to sacrifice my standing in law school so you can get drunk with your brain-dead friends and act like imbeciles. I'm vetoing your little beer bash.

B: I don't even know why we're bothering to ask for your permission to hold this party. There's no way you can stop us anyway. I say we just go ahead and do it. If you don't like it, sue us.

A: Yeah! Get used to the idea because we're going to have this party and there isn't anything you can do about it.

C: On the contrary, there is a great deal I can do about it. Suing you is actually an option that appeals to me. I could sue you for damages, especially if I do poorly on the exam. I could also argue in small claims court that you violated a verbal contract not to have parties without the consent of all housemates—I have witnesses affirming that you both agreed to such an arrangement. So don't start issuing ultimatums unless you want this party to cost a lot more than the price of beer.

And on and on the silliness escalates, a contest of wills complete with recriminations, threats, name-calling, and anger.

Hard bargaining doesn't have to mean ruthless bargaining and obstinacy, even though it often degenerates into such behavior. A person can achieve positive results by acting tough (Chertkoff & Esser, 1976). Eventually, though, there has to be some give-and-take for a stalemate to be avoided if all parties assume a hard bargaining strategy. The key to making this a constructive conflict strategy is to appear tough but fair.

The main difficulty with this strategy is determining how tough you should be without seeming pigheaded. **As with any competitive strategy, when hard bargainers face off against each other, their moves and countermoves can easily produce an impasse.** Hard bargainers lower the odds of reaching an agreement (Pavitt & Curtis, 1994). The 2005 National Hockey League strike and impasse was a hard bargaining fiasco. By 2011 the NHL had still not recovered its fan base that largely left when the entire season was wiped out by the strike (Segers, 2011).

Soft bargainers, recognizing the high costs of hard bargaining on relationships with people they may have to interact with once the negotiations are concluded, yield to pressure. To soft bargainers, making an agreement and remaining friends is more important than winning a victory. The major drawback to soft bargaining is that the accommodator may give away too much to maintain harmonious relationships during negotiations. Hard bargainers looking to enhance self-interest, not group interests, often exploit those who desire cooperation if a soft bargaining approach is taken (Schei & Rognes, 2005).

"They're willing to throw in their kidneys."

This cartoon illustrates which negotiating strategy?

1. Hard bargaining
2. Principled negotiating
3. Soft bargaining
4. Tit-for-tat

Answers are given at the end of the chapter.

▶ Principled Negotiation: Interest-Based Bargaining

Fisher and his associates (2011) offer a third choice besides hard and soft positional bargaining—**principled negotiation,** or interest-based bargaining. Principled negotiation embodies the essential elements of competent communication.

The Four Principles: Appropriate Rules

All negotiations are conducted according to rules. Principled negotiation changes the rules from competitive (hard bargaining) to cooperative. The four basic elements to this approach with corresponding principles for each element are:

People: Separate the people from the problem.

Interests: Focus on interests, not positions.

Options: Generate a variety of possibilities before deciding what to do.

Criteria: Insist that the result be based on some objective standards.

(Fisher et al., 2011)

Separating the people from the problem reaffirms the importance of support-ive climates (e.g., description, problem orientation, equality, or provisionalism) and the inappropriateness of defensive communication patterns (e.g., evaluation, control, superiority, or certainty) during negotiations. Principled negotiation also focuses on task conflicts and strives to diminish relationship conflicts during negotiations.

When Frank Lorenzo became president of Eastern Airlines, relations between man-agement and labor immediately became tense and personal, and after a year of fruit-less negotiations, Eastern's machinists and pilots went on strike. The machinist union targeted Lorenzo as the issue in negotiations, painting him as an unscrupulous take-over artist. The Airline Pilots Association characterized Lorenzo as a Machiavellian sleazeball whose middle name was Greed. Lorenzo fired back, calling the pilots' role in the strike "suicidal" and akin to the Jonestown cult mass suicide tragedy. Eastern filed for bankruptcy, and thousands lost their jobs because the parties in conflict could not separate the people from the problem.

Negotiating interests first, not arguing positions, is critical. *Positions* (what do you want) differ from *interests* (why do you want it). For instance, a group in my class working on a symposium presentation got into a dispute over topic choice. Two members wanted the group to choose "Global Warming." Two other members pushed for "Capital Punishment." The three remaining group members advocated "Animal Rights." Bickering broke out as each faction chose a hard bargaining approach. Nobody was willing to budge. The focus of the bargaining became the weaknesses of each topic advocated by one faction or the other. Put-downs, snide comments, and abusive remarks were flung back and forth.

When instructed to explore their interests, not the positions of each faction, the group found a mutually satisfactory solution. The capital punishment faction had already done a great deal of research on the topic for other classes. Their primary interest was time management since they had families who wanted them home. They wanted to "double dip" by using research for two classes instead of just one. The global warming faction turned out to have a similar interest. They had done some research on environmental issues. The animal rights faction simply wanted to do a presentation that dealt with an issue of values, not some "dry, scientific report of facts and figures on the environment."

Once the interests of each faction were identified and discussed, the global warm-ing faction realized that the capital punishment faction had already done most of the necessary research for the entire group presentation. This was far more extensive than the research already completed by those urging the environmental topic. The animal rights group agreed that capital punishment was an issue of values as well as "facts and figures," so they settled on capital punishment as the group topic.

Positions are the concrete things one party wants. Interests are the intangible motivations—needs, desires, concerns, fears, aspirations—that lead a party in the conflict to take a position (Ury, 1993). The struggle over which topic best fulfills the assignment is a position, but time management is the interest behind the position in the preceding example. Interest answers the question of why a party takes a position. Focusing on interests instead of positions underlines the importance of structuring cooperation into the deliberations. Positional bargaining structures negotiations as a win–lose game. Negotiating interests structures cooperation into the deliberations because the focus is on the problem and a mutually satisfactory solution, not on the position or the people advocating the position. Focusing on interests, not on positions, is the basis of integrative conflict management.

Generating a variety of options is another aspect of principled negotiation. This involves brainstorming, as already explained in my discussion of problem solving. Integration by expanding the pie or bridging may be discovered in a brainstorming session. The nominal group technique may also prove to be useful here.

Finally, principled negotiation rests on **establishing objective standards** (criteria) for weighing the merits and demerits of any proposal. In the conflict over topic choice just discussed, one primary objective standard that was agreed to was "the least number of hours doing research." An objective standard for "fairness" might be that both parties share equally all risks and financial costs.

Remaining Unconditionally Constructive: Sound Judgment The principled negotiation approach to conflicts of interest must include two additional elements: remaining unconditionally constructive (Fisher & Brown, 1988) and developing a BATNA (**B**est **A**lternative **t**o a **N**egotiated **A**greement) (Fisher & Shapiro, 2005; Fisher & Ury, 1981).

Being unconditionally constructive means you make choices and take only those actions that benefit both you and the other parties in the dispute, regardless of whether the other parties reciprocate. Remaining unconditionally constructive during negotiations short-circuits conflict spirals. If they become abusive, you remain civil. If they purposely misunderstand or confuse issues, you clarify. If they try to bully, you neither yield nor bully back. You try to persuade them on the merits of your proposal. If they try to deceive you, neither trust nor deceive them. You remain trustworthy throughout the negotiations. If they do not listen carefully, you nevertheless listen to them carefully and empathically. This is not a guide to earning your way into heaven. This is a realistic, eyes-wide-open guide to *effective* negotiations. You remain unconditionally constructive because it serves your own best interests to do so (Brett et al., 1998).

A story told (Fadiman, 1985) about Gautama Buddha, an Indian prince who lived in the sixth century B.C. and whose teachings formed the basis of Buddhism, exemplifies the unconditionally constructive attitude necessary for principled negotiations. A man interrupted Buddha's preaching with a torrent of abuse. Buddha waited for the man to finish. He then asked his detractor, "If a man offered a gift to another but the gift was declined, to whom would the gift belong?" The man responded, "To the one who offered it." "Then," said Buddha, "I decline to accept your abuse and request you to keep it for yourself" (p. 84). Reciprocating abuse with abuse only sidetracks negotiations onto unproductive avenues of mutual disparagement. Abuse needs to be neutralized, not encouraged.

What do you do if the other parties insist on hard bargaining, not principled negotiations? You remain unconditionally constructive. If one of your interests is fairness, ask the other parties to explain how their position is fair. Don't assert that the other side offers an unfair proposal. Asking the hard bargainers to justify their position translates positions (e.g., no parties on weekends) into interests (e.g., peace and quiet in order to study). Personal attacks, threats, and bullying tactics can be handled by confronting them openly and immediately. For example, "Threats are not constructive. They won't work. I negotiate only on merit. Can we return to the substantive issues?" Research shows that labeling the hard bargaining tactic as ineffective and refusing to reciprocate bad bargaining behavior effectively refocuses the negotiations on interest-based issues and prevents conflict spirals (Brett et al., 1998). If necessary, redirect the hard bargainers' game plan by forthrightly asking for the rules of the game. For instance, "Before we go any further, I need to know what rules we are following during this bargaining. Does everyone here want to achieve a fair settlement in the quickest amount of time, or are we going to play the hard bargaining game where blind stubbornness wins out?" Make them convince you that their intentions are honorable. In the process they may convince themselves that hard bargaining isn't appropriate. You want to bring hard bargainers to their senses, not to their knees (Ury, 1993).

The BATNA: Best Alternative to a Negotiated Agreement You also need to develop a BATNA as a standard against which any proposal can be measured. Your BATNA tells you what is the best you can do if negotiations fail to produce an agreement. Most important, your BATNA keeps you from accepting an agreement worse than what you could have done without negotiations.

For instance, if you have ever visited towns on the Mexican side of the border with the United States, you have undoubtedly engaged in street negotiations with local merchants on items such as handcrafted rugs, sunglasses, and pottery. Not having a BATNA before entering into negotiations with merchants can lead you to overpay for merchandise. If you have no idea how much comparable items would cost in the United States, then you are likely to make a charitable contribution to the Mexican economy when negotiating with a savvy merchant on what you think is a hot deal. Your BATNA in this instance is a comparable item that sells at a slightly higher price in the United States, a similar item of better quality for more money, or a similar item of lesser quality for less money. You know when you've negotiated a real value if you have such a BATNA. Information is power. A BATNA can save you from making a serious mistake (Fisher et al., 2011).

Anger Management

Conflict often produces anger (Fisher & Shapiro, 2005). Workplace anger, for example, has become widespread and a national concern (Glomb, 2002; Marino, 2000). Although it is not always harmful to dispute resolution in groups, anger can easily trigger a tit-for-tat response of retaliatory anger from others that disrupts constructive negotiations (Friedman et al., 2004). As one study concluded, "Negotiators who felt angry engaged in more competitive and less cooperative behavior" (Liu, 2009, p. 162). The most commonly reported communication behaviors associated with workplace anger include: yelling, swearing, hurling insults, using sarcasm, criticizing, crying, giving dirty looks, making angry gestures, throwing things, and physical assault (Glomb, 2002; Johnson, 2009). Thus, managing anger is an important aspect of constructive conflict management in groups.

▶ Constructive and Destructive Anger: Intensity and Duration

There are numerous ways group members express anger. One study (Domagalski, 1998) reported that women more commonly than men use avoiding, crying, and holding back tears as expressions of anger. Men are more likely than women to express anger outwardly toward others rather than to camouflage or hold in the anger. "Domineering, uncivil behavior by others" is the most common trigger of anger in work situations.

Anger is sometimes justified (e.g., in cases of injustice). **The difference between constructive and destructive anger depends on two conditions: the intensity and the duration of the anger expression** (Adler & Proctor, 2007). The **intensity** of anger can vary from mild irritation to outright rage. The more intense the anger, the more likely it is that outcomes will be negative (Glomb, 2002). Mild to moderate expressions of anger can signal problems that must be addressed in groups. In such circumstances the anger can be constructive. Rage, however, is destructive. It is the antithesis of competent communication because the group member expressing the rage is out of control. In the workplace, rage is not appropriate because it "shows you've lost control—not to mention that it's tough to be articulate if you're having a conniption" (Black, 1990, p. 88).

Temper tantrums, ranting, and screaming fits make you look like a lunatic because you're "getting stupid." When used as a power-forcing strategy during conflict, it will likely provoke counter-rage.

The **duration**, or how long the anger lasts, also determines whether anger is constructive or destructive. The length of an anger episode can vary from momentary to prolonged. Quick flashes of anger may hardly cause group members to notice. Even intense anger, if brief, can underline that you are very upset without causing irreparable damage. Prolonged expressions of anger, even if mild, however, can cause group members to tune out and ignore you. Highly intense anger that is long-lasting is a combustible combination. Venting our anger, despite popular notions to the contrary, merely rehearses our anger and can *increase it* (Bushman, 2002; Tavris, 1989). "Blowing off steam" awakens our anger. It doesn't put it to bed.

▶ Managing Your Own Anger: Taking Control

There are several steps you can take to diffuse your own anger when you sense that it is approaching the destructive stage of intensity and duration.

Bruce Ayres/The Image Bank/Getty Images

Managing the anger of others works best when you

1. remain symmetrical
2. remain asymmetrical
3. assume a problem orientation
4. let others blow off steam to diminish their anger

Answers are given at the end of the chapter.

1. *Reframe self-talk.* Thoughts trigger anger. If you think a group member intentionally sabotaged your work, you feel righteously angry, even vengeful. If you believe that no sabotage was intended and that there was merely a misunderstanding, then anger usually doesn't ignite. As a first step in managing your own anger, try assuming group members did not intend to harm you. View harm as accidental or simply the result of clumsiness unless there is clear evidence to the contrary. Reframing the way we think about events can deflate our anger before it escalates (Baron, 1990; Gottman & Gottman, 2006).

2. *Listen nondefensively.* When group members criticize, blame, or ridicule you, refuse to be defensive. Reframe the criticism or blame as a challenge or problem, not an opportunity for retaliation. Counter defensive communication from others with supportive communication.

3. *Deliberately calm yourself.* Exercise discipline and refuse to vent your anger. When you sense anger boiling to the surface, deliberately slow your breathing. Count to 10 before responding to collect yourself. A cooling-off period often works well to calm your anger (Gottman & Gottman, 2006). Typically, it takes about 20 minutes to recover from a surge of adrenaline that accompanies anger (Goleman, 1995).

4. *Find distractions.* Ruminating, focusing your thoughts on what makes you angry, can bring them to a boiling point (Bushman et al., 2005). Don't rehearse your anger by constantly revisiting past injustices or slights instigated by fellow group members. Distract yourself when old wounds resurface (Bushman, 2002). Read a newspaper, watch television, play with the dog, or take a walk with someone and discuss subjects unrelated to the anger-inducing subject.

Don't attempt to employ all four of these steps at once. Pick one and work on making it an automatic response when your anger wells up, then try a second step, and so on.

▶ Managing the Anger of Others: Communication Jujitsu

Managing conflict constructively means defusing and de-escalating the anger of other group members so you can confront issues without eruptions of verbal or physical aggression. It is usually best to address a group member's anger first before dealing with the substance of the dispute that triggers the anger (Donohue & Kolt, 1992). Try these suggestions for defusing the anger of others:

1. *Be asymmetrical.* When a group member is expressing anger, especially if it turns to rage, it is critical that you not strike back in kind. Be asymmetrical, which means do the opposite. Counter rage with absolute calm. Stay composed.

Hostage negotiators are trained to defuse highly volatile individuals by remaining absolutely calm throughout the interaction. Imagine the outcome if hostage negotiators flew into a rage while talking to hostage takers. Use smoothing techniques to quiet the enraged group member.

2. *Validate the other person.* Validation is a form of the smoothing technique of collaborating. Let the person know that his or her point of view and anger have some validity, even though you may not agree (Fisher & Shapiro, 2005). You can validate another person in several ways. First, you can take responsibility for the other person's anger. "I made you angry, didn't I?" acknowledges your role in provoking anger. Second, you can apologize. "I'm sorry. You have a right to be angry" can be a very powerful validation of the other person. Apologies, of course, should be offered only when truly warranted. Third, actively listening and acknowledging what the other person has said can also be very validating. "I know it upsets you when I don't come to meetings on time" makes the other person feel heard, even if conflict remains.

3. *Probe.* Seek information from an angry group member so you can understand his or her anger (Gottman & Gottman, 2006). When you ask a question of an angry group member, it forces the person to shift from emotional outburst to rational response. Simply asking, "Can we sit down and discuss this calmly so I can understand your point of view?" can momentarily defuse a group member's anger.

4. *Distract.* Shifting the focus of attention when a person is really out of control can sometimes short-circuit rage (Rusting & Nolen-Hoeksema, 1998). A humorous quip, an odd question, a request for help, or pointing to an unrelated event can break a rage cycle.

5. *Assume a problem orientation.* This is supportive communication. This step should occur once you have calmed the angry group member by using previous steps. Approach the anger display as a problem to be solved, not a reason to retaliate. The question "What would you like to see occur?" invites problem solving.

6. *Refuse to be abused.* Even if you are wrong, feel guilty, or deserve another person's anger, do not permit yourself to be verbally battered (McKay et al., 1989). Verbal aggression is unproductive no matter who is at fault in a conflict. "I cannot discuss this with you if you insist on being abusive. I can see you're upset, but verbally assaulting me won't lead to a solution" sets a ground rule on how anger can be expressed.

7. *Disengage.* This is the final step when all else fails to defuse a group member's anger. This step is especially important if the person continues to be enraged and abusive despite your best, most constructive efforts to calm the emotional storm. Firmly state, "This meeting is over. I'm leaving. We'll discuss this another time."

Keeping track of all seven steps to quell the anger of group members, particularly when faced with an enraged person, is too much to expect. **Concentrate on one or two steps until they become almost a reflex reaction, a habit.** Being asymmetrical is the crucial first step, with validation a close second. The remaining steps can gradually become part of your anger-defusing skill package.

Anger is a common companion of group conflict. The constructive management of conflict can occur only when anger is kept under control. This does not mean squelching anger. A group member can feel angry for good reasons. Anger acts as a signal that changes need to occur. Anger should not be used as a weapon, however, to abuse others. We want to learn ways to cope with and express anger constructively, not be devoured by it.

In summary, conflict is a reality of group life. Although most people would prefer that conflict didn't exist, there are both positive and negative aspects to conflict. Constructive management of conflict can turn a dispute into a positive experience for the group. The five primary communication styles of conflict management—collaborating, accommodating, compromising, avoiding, and competing—all have pros and cons, depending on the situation. Nevertheless, collaborating has a higher probability of producing constructive outcomes than does competing. Negotiation is a universal process used to manage conflicts of interests. Principled negotiation is the most productive means of resolving conflicts of interests.

MindTap™
Reflect on what you've learned.

In Mixed Company

▶ Online

Now that you've read Chapter 11, access the online resources that accompany *In Mixed Company* at **www.cengagebrain.com**. Your online resources include:

1. Multiple-choice and true-false **chapter practice quizzes** with automatic correction
2. Digital **glossary**
3. **Flashcards**

QUESTIONS FOR CRITICAL THINKERS

1. If competition has so many disadvantages, why would the competing/forcing style ever be appropriate for a competent communicator?
2. If principled negotiating is so effective, why isn't it used more often?

VIDEO *Case Studies*

The Social Network (2010). Biography/Drama; PG-13
Facebook CEO Mark Zuckerberg's meteoric rise to social networking superstar is presented in this well-made movie. Analyze the communication styles of conflict management used by Zuckerberg and others. What negotiating strategies are used, especially in response to a lawsuit filed against Zuckerberg contesting who came up with the initial idea for Facebook?

The Upside of Anger (2005). Drama; R
Compelling story of a woman (Joan Allen) whose husband appears to have walked out on her and his four daughters and the residual anger that wells up inside of her and others as a result. Kevin Costner plays an ex-baseball player turned radio personality who insinuates himself into the family. Examine anger as destructive or constructive. How do characters handle their anger?

The War of the Roses (1989). Black Comedy; R
This is a very dark comedy depicting all the ways not to manage conflict. Analyze this film for destructive conflict and communication styles of conflict management. Which styles are predominately used by the main characters with what results?

What's Cooking? (2000). Comedy/Drama; PG-13
This is a portrayal of four separate, yet interrelated families (African American, Vietnamese, Mexican American, and Jewish) trying to celebrate Thanksgiving. Identify the communication styles of conflict management used by the characters. Are conflicts mostly task, relationship, or values? How does culture affect conflict management? In what ways is anger managed? Are these ways effective?

Answers to Multiple-Choice Questions in Captions
Cartoon (p. 355): 4; Cartoon (p. 370): 3. Photo (p. 375): 2, 3.

12 Technology and Virtual Groups

Communication technologies permeate our lives daily. The number of Internet users worldwide reached 3 billion in 2014 ("Internet Users," 2014). Cell phone use has almost completely saturated the American and world markets, making those who do not use cell phones a rarity (some would say "dinosaurs"). As reported previously, social networking systems such as Facebook, which claimed more than a billion registered users worldwide in 2014 (Martin, 2014), Twitter, which grew to more than 300 million "monthly users" in the same year ("Top 15," 2014), and LinkedIn, which claimed more than 250 million "unique monthly visitors" ("Top 15," 2014), have become a phenomenon.

To provide some perspective on the rapidity with which electronic communication technologies have grown, in January 2011, a video clip went viral on the Internet and was the subject of great amusement. The clip shows Katie Couric and Bryant Gumbel, hosts of the NBC *Today Show,* in January 1994, discussing Gumbel's question, "What is Internet anyway?" Couric responds, rather uncertainly, "Internet is that massive computer network, the one that's becoming really big now." Gumbel continues, "What do you mean? What do you, write to it, like mail?" "No," Couric responds, "a lot of people use it to communicate." Couric then turns to an unidentified member of the television crew, "Can you explain what Internet is?" (quoted in Pitts, 2011, p. A15). Couric and Gumbel can be forgiven for not knowing exactly what is the Internet back then because the huge majority of the world's population was equally ignorant about this stunning invention that would markedly alter communication everywhere in the world in just a very few years.

MindTap

Start with a quick warm-up activity.

Is this social networking interpersonal or small group communication?

The impact of these electronic technologies on our interpersonal communication is interesting, and I discuss this at length elsewhere (Rothwell, 2013), but such impact is tangential to small group concerns. The more narrow implications of communication technologies on small group communication require a more focused perspective. Although some faculty require or encourage students working on group projects to interact with team members using one of the social networking systems, these networking systems are largely interpersonal in nature. The primary use is to stay in touch with friends or to make new friends (Lenhart, 2007).

Despite the largely interpersonal nature of many communication technologies (cell phone conversations are usually between only two people), these technologies have nevertheless rolled over into the small group arena to some extent. For example, interest groups (such as car nuts) and activist groups (such as feminists or Tea Party activists) form on social networks for members to share ideas and information, debate issues, and promote social action (Preston, 2008). Social media can be a place where group leaders address group members collectively. New questions emerge with social media as well. Should you include your boss or team leader at work as a friend on Facebook? Should you gossip about group members since such messages are more widely available than simple water-cooler small talk? Might issues of confidentiality (contract negotiations between management and workers) be problematic when social networks are so transparent and easy to use (Andersson, 2010)?

Sometimes social network groups remain small by design; most often they are allowed or encouraged to grow large, vastly exceeding the limits of our small group focus. Commenting on these social networks, Scott Kirsner (2007), author of *The Future of Web Video*, observes, "Many of us are obsessed with audience metrics, seeking a tally of how many people we're reaching as something of a touchstone—an indicator of our influence, popularity, or coolness" (p. 6P). These "friends" are often only loosely connected to each other; often not even that. As Daniel Farber, a law professor at the University of California, Berkeley, quips, "I'm a Facebook friend of Bob Dylan, which probably means I have a deeply meaningful relationship with his publicist" (quoted in Ball, 2010). "Friends" and "followers" may wander in and out of contact on the sites, so system interconnectedness (an important element of the definition of a group) is also often dubious.

Virtual groups did not begin in earnest with the advent of computers. The computer revolution was slow to incorporate small groups and teams (Majchrzak et al., 2004). The early mainframe computers were behemoths that facilitated company-wide operations but were largely unavailable to the average worker in an organization. The introduction of the personal computer in the 1970s and 1980s facilitated individual productivity. It wasn't until the late 1990s when the Internet and the World Wide Web were readily available, however, that virtual groups became a staple of most organizations. In 1995, a mere 16 million people worldwide used the Internet (Bazeley, 2005). A billion people worldwide were Internet users 10 years later ("Internet Usage Statistics," 2005). Although rudimentary versions of virtual groups already existed prior to the Internet revolution (e.g., teleconferences), the stratospheric rise in Internet access accelerated the widespread growth of virtual groups.

As noted in Chapter 1, a **virtual group** is a small group whose members interact by means of electronic technologies. **Virtual groups have three primary characteristics that make them different from conventional groups** (Fisher, 2000; Schiller & Mandviwalla, 2007). First, their members are spread across multiple locations and often across multiple time zones. Second, group members often have more diverse backgrounds incorporating members from different cultures speaking multiple languages and harboring varied organizational allegiances. Third, membership tends to be less stable. In short, virtual groups are members "working together apart" (Fisher, 2000).

There are also "degrees of virtuality" when considering what constitutes a virtual group (Connaughton & Shuffler, 2007; Johnson et al., 2009). Highly virtual groups communicate entirely by using electronic technologies. Some virtual groups are **hybrids**—members communicate mostly by electronic means but may occasionally meet face to face. In a study of virtual groups, 46% of the 600 respondents never met with members of their virtual groups, 30% met only once a year, and 24% met two or more times (Solomon, 2010). In addition, members of highly virtual groups are dispersed widely across large geographic areas; less virtual groups may have members in the same building or living in the same city or county.

Although researchers and scholars often make no clear distinction between a virtual group and a virtual team (see Godar & Ferris, 2004; Rad & Levin, 2003), the two are not identical. They have electronic technologies and remote communication in common, but they differ in the same ways that standard face-to-face groups and teams differ: level of cooperation, diversity of skills, group identity, and commitment of members (see Chapter 7). An online class discussion group, for example, is a virtual group but not a virtual team. Electronic technologies make remote communication possible, so class members may never see fellow students face to face. Participants, however, join the virtual discussion to express points of view and share perceptions. A high level of cooperation is not required to participate, members aren't chosen because of diversity of skills, little effort is made to establish a strong group identity (students are merely fulfilling a course requirement), and commitment to the discussion may be lackluster and sporadic.

Given these clarifications and distinctions, **the primary purpose of this chapter is to explore the vast potential of and the new challenges posed by virtual groups.** This chapter focuses on the broader topic of virtual groups, not the narrower virtual teams, although virtual teams qualify as a type of virtual group. The suggestions offered for making virtual groups effective apply well to virtual teams, especially if previous advice on making teams effective is employed. **There are three chapter objectives relevant to the primary purpose:**

1. To describe the many ways technology integrates with small group communication,

2. To discuss the advantages and disadvantages of virtual groups,

3. To offer suggestions regarding how to develop and maintain effective virtual groups.

One cautionary note seems appropriate before addressing these objectives. Despite considerable research that compares virtual groups to face-to-face groups, significant gaps remain in our knowledge about virtual groups (Mortensen at al., 2009; Chiu & Staples, 2013). Our experience with virtual groups is barely beyond its infancy. Nevertheless, that should not prevent sharing what is known, and offering tentative advice based on the available research.

MindTap™
Read, highlight, and take notes online.

Technological Group Options

Multiple electronic communication technologies make virtual groups possible. A **technology** is a tool to accomplish some purpose. A **communication technology** is a tool to achieve a communication purpose. Electronic communication technologies that make virtual groups possible include the Internet, email, phones, video, and voice mail. Any of these technologies, singly or in combinations, create a variety of virtual group opportunities, discussed in this section.

► Text-Messaging: Typing Gone High-Tech

There are several text-based options for virtual groups. Email has become so popular and so taken for granted as part of most of our daily lives that it's difficult to remember when this technological marvel was not readily available. Despite a precipitous drop in email use among teens who prefer social networking sites, **email remains a principal method of communicating in organizations, both within an organization (intranet) and between organizations (Internet), and its importance is not likely to diminish any time soon** (Horn, 2011; "International Workplace Productivity Survey," 2010). The ease with which attached information can be sent by email to any and all group members is potentially a benefit and a drawback simultaneously. The benefit is that a large amount of information is available to the group with minimal effort required, but email attachments can easily produce information overload and can create unreasonable expectations regarding how much information each group member can digest in a short time.

Text-only messaging is not restricted to computer-based email. Text-messaging with cell phones has become a worldwide phenomenon. Although not a prime tool for virtual groups, the potential to text-message team members regularly who are dispersed across the globe is real. Electronic bulletin boards and blogs in which posted messages are available to group members and everyone's responses are available to be read are other options in the text-only toolbox for virtual groups. These are popular options for online college classes.

► Audioconferences: Voice-Only Technology

In-person meetings are what most of us are accustomed to, but as our globe becomes more village-like with the ever-expanding reach of electronic technology, and organizations increasingly conduct business internationally, meeting face to face is often a poor choice. There are several electronic alternatives to the standard in-person format. One of the simplest is the audioconference, commonly referred to as the conference call. The survey of more than 1,800 employees in six countries by Plantronics revealed that 61% of respondents considered audioconferences as critical to their overall success and productivity ("Plantronics Study," 2010). This version of a virtual group allows several individuals to conduct a joint meeting over the telephone or in some instances by a computer-based voice link. Once the exclusive province of corporations, a conference call can now be easily set up by almost anyone (Rodriguez & Solomon, 2007). Most business and many phone services provide conference call capability. Remember that a teleconference is not simply a phone conversation. **Its primary purpose for virtual groups is to conduct meetings.** Most of the guidelines for conducting efficient and effective meetings already discussed in Chapter 8 apply to teleconferences. **The conference call should be necessary, focused, organized, and as short as feasible.**

▶ Videoconferences: Sight and Sound

Videoconferencing has become commonplace in the workplace (Economist Intelligence Unit, 2009). Google jumped into the videoconferencing market in 2014 with its Chromebox for Meetings, designed to make it easier and cheaper to conduct "face-to-face" business meetings even if group members are dispersed in widely varying locations (Liedtke, 2014). The videoconference, similar to the teleconference, is a useful option when participants cannot meet easily in person. It also provides huge savings in travel time and expense when group members are living long distances from each other (Houghton, 2006). Videoconferences provide nonverbal cues, such as facial expressions, gestures, posture, and eye contact, unavailable in teleconferencing. Body language cues help participants assess messages more accurately, and they are instrumental in defining relationships between participants (Thompson & Coovert, 2003).

The technology has become so sophisticated that virtual group members meeting by videoconferencing across several time zones begin to feel that they are all in the same room. Members will offer each other sandwiches or snacks, forgetting they're thousands of miles apart ("Who wants a chocolate? Oops! Forgot. Two of you are in Australia. Oh well, more for us!")

Groups can conduct videoconferencing via Skype rather easily ("Group Video Calling," 2011). Videoconferencing on Skype can accommodate between 3 and 10 members at a time. A smartphone videoconferencing option is also available.

Yet another option is videoconferencing with avatars created using Second Life, an online three-dimensional virtual world (Sherblom et al., 2009). Using avatars created

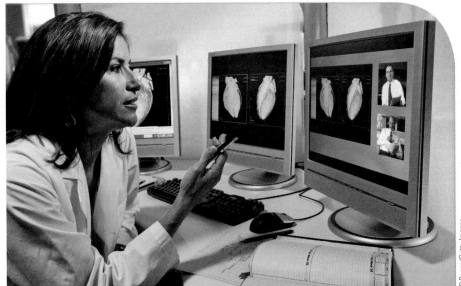

Simple forms of videoconferencing are more readily available than ever before.

by each group member provides a sense of social presence and semi-real interaction during group meetings when actual video of participants is not available. Virtual team building activities can also be conducted using Second Life ("Virtual Team Building in Second Life," 2010). **Videoconferences in any form, as with any meeting, should be necessary, focused, organized, and as short as feasible.**

Benefits and Challenges of Virtual Groups

Virtual groups present a mixed batch of advantages and disadvantages. In this section, several important pros and cons of virtual groups are addressed with the repeated notation that further research will likely modify some of what we "know" about virtual groups.

▶ Time and Space: The Death of Distance

Time and space can be transcended by electronic technologies. Cairncross (1997) coined the phrase "the death of distance" to emphasize, in somewhat overstated fashion, that virtual groups are not restricted by distances separating group members. Group members can communicate with each other at the speed of light over vast distances, even continents. Finding one central meeting place available at a specific time is not an issue for virtual groups. Members can connect at home, at their office, even in airport terminals or restroom stalls—one survey showed that 75% of respondents use a cell phone while answering nature's call (Heaney, 2013). As wireless technology becomes ever more sophisticated and readily available, few limitations on where and when a group member can join discussions and meetings will exist.

Being able to communicate over vast distances, however, removes group members from physical proximity to each other. **Communication competence becomes a significant challenge.** What works well in face-to-face communication may not work well in virtual group communication. Sarcasm, gentle teasing, or harmless joking may be taken as hurtful or insulting in the absence of a glint in the eyes of the sender, a smile, a clarifying gesture, or a subtle facial expression. **The absence of nonverbal cues that we all depend on for helping determine meaning of messages is a substantial limitation of text-only and voice-only virtual groups.** As reported previously, 94% of respondents in one study said that "inability to read nonverbal cues" was the "greatest personal challenge" of virtual groups (Solomon, 2010).

▶ Decision Making: Quality of the Output

"There are no compelling theoretical or empirical reasons for predicting differences in decision quality" (Valacich and Schwenk, 1995, p. 161) when comparing face-to-face and virtual groups (see also Chudoba et al., 2005). This may be true in general when comparing face-to-face communication to all types of virtual groups lumped together. There are exceptions, however. Virtual groups working under time pressure, for example, do not perform as well as face-to-face groups in the same condition (Thompson & Coovert, 2003). This may occur partly because decision making can be slower in virtual groups. A hefty 80% of respondents in the Solomon (2010) study reported that this was a significant concern. Text-only electronic technology, for example, may slow decision making if delays occur because group members haven't checked their email or bulletin board or don't respond immediately, for whatever reason. As one member of a global team explains her experience, "There are delays in response and communication, and in such cases I might lose a day instead of a few hours.... Communication and collaboration can take up a significant chunk of project time" (quoted in Kumar, 2006, p. 25). Students working in teams for online class projects may experience similar challenges.

Presumably, videoconferencing would not produce such delays or consequent frustration from group members pressured to decide, unless technological glitches occur that force delays or require cancellation of the videoconference. One study of 64 virtual groups revealed no significant differences in decision quality when comparing text-only and audio-only technologies, but **the addition of video to the audio-only group produced a significant improvement in decision quality** (Baker, 2002).

The more time-consuming it is for virtual groups to make decisions, the less satisfied members are with final decisions (Thompson & Coovert, 2003). Frustration and annoyance with learning elaborate new technologies, sometimes referred to as *mechanical friction,* may impair the decision-making process, at least until all members feel confident using the technology (Ebrahim at el., 2009; Poole et al., 1993). Mechanical friction may invite human friction—abrasiveness in social relationships—as group members struggle with the frustrations of trying to manage technologies that aren't always user-friendly.

▶ Social Relationships: Developing Personal Connections

Group decision quality can also be significantly affected by social relationships among members (interconnectedness of task and social dimensions). This is no less important in virtual groups than in face-to-face ones. Virtual groups pose unique challenges in this respect. How do you identify with team members you have never met personally or ever seen in many cases? (Some virtual groups, however, attempt to address the invisibility of members by directing participants to Facebook or LinkedIn personal sites for profiles of group members. Those who have not created such a profile are encouraged to develop one.)

Virtual groups seem to require more time than face-to-face groups to develop positive social relationships and cohesiveness (Johnson et al., 2009). Virtual group members tend to rate each other unfavorably early in the development process, but after several weeks of interacting, ratings of members on trust, receptivity, sociability, informality, and relaxation become more positive (Walther & Burgoon, 1992). **Regular and timely feedback is critical to building trust and commitment among virtual group members** (Ebrahim et al., 2009).

One potential benefit of text-only and audio-only group communication is that social bonds between group members can be based on more substantive features such as the quality of conversation, similarities in values and beliefs, and apparent friendliness of members, instead of more superficial physical appearance (McKenna & Green, 2002). Physical features are not readily available in text-only or audio-only group interactions (although members' photographs can be scanned onto social networking sites and email locations). This advantage, however, is more speculative than tested, and to what extent this appearance deficit might be an advantage of virtual groups is not known.

▶ Power Distance: Prominence of Status Cues

Power differences may be less prominent in virtual groups. Rank is less obvious when emailing group members than it is when communicating face to face. This status equalization effect, however, is probably more prominent in text-only group discussion than it is in audioconferences or especially videoconferences.

There are two types of status characteristics that are hidden from text-only communication: (1) physical characteristics such as ethnicity, gender, and age, and (2) communication cues such as rapid speaking rate, fluency of speech (few pauses or disfluencies such as "ums" and "ahs"), emphatic tone of voice, strong eye contact when speaking, and head of the table seating location (Driskell et al., 2003). Email-only communication among group members screens these status markers that are immediately available in face-to-face communication. Audioconferencing screens out some of these status markers, although age, gender, ethnicity, and even physical attributes can often be discerned from voice-only communication (Krauss et al., 2002). Note, however, that this status equalization effect might be only temporary—experienced during the initial development of a virtual group. **More mature groups typically develop status markers even when restricted to text-only communication,** such as waiting a long time to respond to messages from less-powerful group members, answering questions with curt responses, and using "powerful" language (Rocheleau, 2002).

Conversely, grammatical errors and misspellings, especially if they occur often and in numerous messages, may taint a group member as poorly educated, careless, and unconcerned about credibility with other group members (all status-diminishing). Slipping into casual text-messaging acronyms and shorthand may also prove to be inappropriate with more powerful group members who may expect formal communication from others. This is why it is important to proofread text messages for appropriateness (following rules) before sending them to those expecting more professional-looking communication.

▶ Conflict: Constructive and Destructive

As discussed in Chapter 11, not all conflict is counterproductive for groups. Conflict that is competently managed can promote important, positive changes. There are differences, however, between virtual and face-to-face groups in conflict management. Overall, **virtual groups experience more task and relationship conflict than face-to-face groups** (Hinds & Mortensen, 2005). The Solomon (2010) study found that 73% of respondents considered managing conflict to be more challenging in virtual teams than in face-to-face teams, and more challenging than any other virtual group difficulty. When conflict arises, face-to-face groups engage in significantly more constructive conflict management than virtual groups. **Virtual groups are more likely to move in the direction of destructive conflict than are face-to-face groups** (Ebrahim et al., 2009; Zornoza et al., 2002). Overall, face to face is a more suitable medium for constructive conflict management than technological alternatives (Zornoza et al., 2002).

Transactions among virtual group members are more likely to become incendiary than in face-to-face groups (Holahan et al., 2008), especially in text-only formats (Driskell et al., 2003). "Emotional incontinence"—incompetent outbursts of anger, called "flaming"—is more likely (Locke, 1998). The absence of normal constraints on incivility and insults found in face-to-face transactions (such as implicit norms discouraging nasty public displays of rage), coupled with the ease and swiftness of text-only communication, encourage more negative interactions. As Brin (1998) explains:

> Electronic conversations seem especially prone to misinterpretation, suddenly and rapidly escalating hostility between participants, or else triggering episodes of sulking silence. When flame wars erupt, normally docile people can behave like mental patients.... Typing furiously, they send impulsive text messages, blurting out the first vituperation that comes to mind, abandoning the editing process of common courtesy that civilization took millennia to acquire (p. 166).

Communication filters that operate in face-to-face communication to short-circuit emotional incontinence are less apparent when communicating electronically. Nonverbal indicators of disapproval, such as a glance, a frown, or an eye roll, are missing from text-only and audio-only group interactions. What you wouldn't say to a member's face you might say in an email or text message. Research shows that members of virtual groups are more inclined to offer negative, even extreme, evaluations, disapproval, and censure of other members (Walther, 1997). Misunderstandings can be a big problem for virtual teams because perceived slights, insults, or a negative tone in emails may not be quickly cleared up. Members may have to stew over a perceived insult for a day, even a week, if an email response is not accessed right away.

Differences that emerge from virtual group membership representing several diverse cultures can also lead to misunderstandings and perceived insults (Baba et al., 2004; Kayworth & Leidner, 2002). Misunderstanding emerging from cultural and language differences was identified in one survey as the greatest challenge of working in virtual groups (Economist Intelligence Unit, 2009). Establishing group norms can be difficult in virtual groups when cultural differences create clashes about approaches to addressing conflicts, directness of communication, and respect for high-power group members. Cultural differences are often challenging to address in face-to-face groups, but they can be doubly so when text-only or sometimes even audio-only communication is available. The ambiguity of language discussed in Chapter 1 is not easily recognized or clarified when the communication media limit nonverbal contextual cues that help with understanding messages.

Virtual groups, however, don't always have greater difficulty with conflict than face-to-face groups. One study showed that virtual groups have less tendency to transform task conflicts into relationship conflicts than face-to-face groups when conflict is escalated by a member using personal attacks, trivialization of issues, and disagreements about policies (Dorado et al., 2002). Text-only communication in particular may tend to focus members on the task and less on personality clashes and interpersonal hostilities than in-your-face, in-person clashes might ignite.

Text-only communication may also be appropriate when face-to-face communication among members has a history of being awkward or intimidating (Markus, 1994). Sometimes we can be more honest and assertive in an email than in person. Words can also be more carefully chosen, and messages can be edited for tone more judiciously than a group member may be able to do when feeling angry and communicating face to face. How often have you replayed a hostile conversation in your mind and wished you hadn't made certain statements or had cushioned negative comments? In some instances, setting aside an angry email response to a perceived insult or slight by another group member and deciding, upon reflection, to delete it entirely, is a wise choice. Email allows you to edit intemperate messages, but only if you resist firing a flame in the heat of the moment by adopting a standard practice of never responding heatedly to an email until you have had time to reflect, simmer down, and edit offensive remarks.

▶ Member Participation: Motivation to Perform

Motivating group members to participate actively and constructively is one of the common complaints about group work and a frequent reason for grouphate. Virtual groups can enhance participation in some instances and diminish it in others.

Social Anxiety: Reticence to Participate Text-only group discussions encourage low-status members to participate in discussions and to stand their ground more firmly on controversial or contentious issues (Sproull & Kiesler, 1991). In-person discussions can be intimidating, especially if some participants are dominating and aggressive when expressing their points of view. Typing responses on a computer keyboard can embolden reticent group members to be assertive. In one study of social anxiety that compared face-to-face communication to Internet chat room interactions, highly anxious individuals (shy, reticent to communicate) reported feeling extremely uncomfortable in the face-to-face condition; during chat room, text-only communication, however, highly anxious individuals reported feeling almost as comfortable as nonanxious individuals in the face-to-face condition (Green & McKenna, 2002). In addition, these same anxious individuals were perceived by other group members to be confident, likable, and outgoing—exactly the opposite perception group members reported when anxious individuals engaged in face-to-face communication. **There is even some evidence that after two years of active participation in chat room group discussions, socially anxious individuals experience diminished social anxiety in face-to-face interactions** (McKenna et al., 2002). These results suggest that text-only group communication can encourage greater constructive participation from reticent members, thereby potentially enriching the discussions and producing greater overall satisfaction with the group experience, with the added potential bonus of diminished social anxiety in face-to-face interactions.

Videoconferencing, however, may be more intimidating for reticent group members. The surest way to discourage reticent group members from participating is to conduct meetings electronically when members feel intimidated by the hardware and unskilled in the use of software alternatives. Appearing on camera may increase anxiety for reticent members. The mere presence of a camera can cause some individuals to freeze or appear unnatural in their movements, speaking rate, tone of voice, and overall appearance. Looking like a deer in headlights or showing color draining from your face when speaking to a camera doesn't inspire confidence from other virtual group members, and it can be embarrassing for all parties. Gaining experience and skill with videoconferencing will likely diminish such anxiety.

Social Loafing: Virtually Unproductive Although little research has been conducted on social loafing in virtual groups (Piezon & Ferree, 2008), the potential is real for this to be an even more serious problem than it is in face-to-face groups (Driskell et al., 2003; Geister et al., 2006). In the Solomon (2010) study, 75% of respondents reported that social loafing was a significant challenge for virtual teams, and 77% of student respondents at public universities in a study of online learning groups reported social loafing occurred (Piezon & Ferree, 2008).

The nature of virtual groups makes addressing this problem particularly difficult (see Chapter 3 for a detailed discussion of methods to address social loafing). Developing cohesiveness, one method of reducing social loafing, is challenging because strangers are often thrown together in online classes and told by an instructor to magically become a team. Holding members accountable, another method to combat social loafing, is especially challenging because face-to-face appraisal of members' efforts and production is an effective deterrent to social loafing (Druskat & Wolff, 1999). Unless virtual group members meet in person from time to time, however, this option is not available when conducted by email or audioconferences, and delivering a negative appraisal of a virtual group member in a videoconference will likely seem awkward at best. Confronting the loafer about lackluster participation is one promising approach in face-to-face groups, but text-only formats can easily be ignored by loafers when their lethargic effort is addressed directly. Members who don't respond to emails are often assumed to be uncommitted to the group when other factors such as technological problems or emergencies may be the reason for not responding (Panteli, 2004).

The ideal solution to social loafing is to choose virtual group members who find the group task challenging and interesting, and who all seem motivated to excel. This is often the result when virtual teams are formed within organizations. Those most interested in the task and members whose skills are complementary (overlapping but not redundant) are chosen to become part of a team. Nevertheless, because group membership for online courses is usually haphazard (little opportunity is provided to choose members knowledgeably in a virtual environment), social loafing is likely to be a serious problem in most online classes that require group work.

▶ Conversational Documentation: Transactional Transcripts

Reconstructing group conversations is easier and the message fidelity can be better than what is usual in face-to-face group communication when using text-only, computer-mediated communication. When group members communicate by email, there is a transcript of conversations that can be accessed by all team members at any time. Arguments concerning what one member actually said can be settled by consulting previous emailed messages for the exact wording. It's untenable for a group member to insist that he or she said one thing when the email transcript clearly indicates a different message.

This potential advantage of an email transcript, however, could also be a disadvantage in some circumstances. Proving a member wrong by consulting the email record may provoke contentious communication within the group. Settling an issue may stir up hostile, defensive communication patterns. Email communication can also pose potential problems for groups because of its transcript availability (Rocheleau, 2002). Teams operating in organizations could experience a loss of cohesiveness if members forward emails to team leaders or outside supervisors in an attempt to present a member in a negative light. "Ratting" on a team member may bring issues of social loafing or disruption to everyone's attention, but constructively addressing such issues only by email is enormously difficult. Therapy groups offering support and advice to members by email also raise legal issues of confidentiality. Inappropriate jokes, comments, and gossip emailed to group members have a way of leaking beyond the group and igniting legal concerns about sexual harassment (creating a hostile group environment) and bias.

·Caution should also be employed when directing group members to social networking sites for personal profiles used to create group connection and

---

SECOND LOOK

Potential Advantages and Disadvantages of Virtual Groups

Advantages	Disadvantages
Distance not a problem—members connected across many time zones	Learning unfamiliar, complicated technologies
Cost savings on travel, lodging, food	Decision quality jeopardized under time pressure
Initial status equalization	Difficulty developing positive social relations among group members
Greater assertiveness from reticent members	Greater likelihood of destructive conflict
Decreased social anxiety (text-only and audio-only media)	Cultural misunderstandings difficult to address
Settling arguments by consulting text transcripts (email)	Increased social anxiety (videoconferencing—camera-shy)
	Embarrassment from private emails and sites becoming public records

Although MRT isn't an overarching theory of effective media use in virtual groups, it is one explanatory piece of the virtual group puzzle. MRT draws attention to the richness of face-to-face communication and to the challenges posed by leaner technological media. Email, for instance, is often a poor choice for addressing complex conflicts and issues. Its constricted richness, however, makes resolving complex relational conflicts difficult but certainly not impossible.

Media Synchronicity: Extending MRT Media synchronicity theory (MST) extends media richness theory by providing a dynamic, time-changing quality to the richness of each communication medium (Dennis & Valacich, 1999; see also Schiller & Mandviwalla, 2007). MRT suggests that no communication medium can be designated "richest" or "leanest" based on an inherent, unchangeable information transmission capacity. Instead, **the richest media are those that best meet the communication needs of the group.** Sometimes this means using synchronous media and other times asynchronous media. **Synchronous media** are those that permit simultaneous, same-time interactions among group members, modeled after face-to-face meetings. Teleconferences, videoconferences, and chat rooms are examples of synchronous media. **Asynchronous media** are those that permit anytime/anyplace communication among group members without interruption. Messages are posted and read at the convenience of other group members. Standard email, bulletin boards, blogs, and text-messaging are examples.

Media synchronicity theory is appealing and potentially insightful, but little research has been conducted on it. Nevertheless, it offers some help in making media choices for virtual groups. For example, one study of computer-mediated Alcoholics Anonymous (AA) meetings found that "Asynchronous AA groups, in some ways, appear to be the prototypical supportive environment" (VanLear et al., 2005). Asynchronous AA meetings were characterized by highly personal communication, and they were more supportive (exhibited more frequent empathic responses) and less defensive (fewer negative evaluations) than synchronous AA meetings. Asynchronous support groups permit delayed, thoughtful responses, so hair-trigger criticisms may be squelched before they are ever sent (this is probably true more for support groups, given their empathic purpose, than work groups). Individuals too shy to share intensely private revelations during in-person AA meetings are more inclined to share in virtual groups, especially asynchronous bulletin boards. Consider one such bulletin board exchange between a newcomer just joining the virtual group and old-timer AA members (VanLear et al., 2005):

BB: I've gone 12 days [sober].... I'm realizing my incredible shyness is gonna get me drunk. I went to a mtg [meeting] to meet ppl [people] but I left; didn't talk to anyone.... I wish I could force myself not to be shy ... thanks for letting me share.

DD: Glad you're here BB. KCB [Keep coming back].

EE: Thanks BB, I'm shy too. I learned to ask open-ended questions. (p. 23)

BB wasn't able to share her personal revelation about shyness during face-to-face AA meetings, but she shared this almost effortlessly in her new virtual asynchronous group. The impersonal nature of text-only, asynchronous media can permit the communication of highly personal revelations by blunting the awkwardness of face-to-face public disclosure of private information. Text-only asynchronous media may make embarrassing or uncomfortable disclosures less awkward by removing the intimidating and immediate presence of some who might communicate judgment (eye rolling).

▶ Specific Suggestions: Tentative Advice

Any suggestions offered to meet the unique challenge of integrating technologies into the group process are necessarily tentative until much more is learned about virtual groups. Nevertheless, some suggestions can be made that will likely prove helpful should you have an opportunity to participate in a virtual group.

Choosing Media: Richness and Synchronicity Because the use of electronic media is the principal distinction between virtual groups and standard, face-to-face groups, **choosing media wisely is a key consideration.** Groups that choose communication media haphazardly are likely to regret their casual decision. Of course, media choice may be out of your hands. Students doing group projects for online courses are usually told by the instructor to use certain media to accomplish the task (usually what is affordable).

Enriching the virtual group environment is especially important during the initial stages of group development (Thompson & Coovert, 2003). Most virtual teams, recognizing the importance of an enriched media environment during initial group development, tend to rely heavily on face-to-face communication to build cohesiveness (Kerber & Buono, 2004). In-person contact and socializing build trust and improve group success (Creighton & Adams, 1998; Furst et al., 2004). In organizations, this usually involves travel. **The in-person, meet-and-greet process is highly recommended, if possible, during group formation** (Oertig & Buegri, 2006). Online courses often have an initial face-to-face meeting at the beginning of the course, and some (such as public-speaking classes) usually have several interspersed throughout the term. If face-to-face meetings are not feasible, teleconferences or videoconferences are suitable compromises for enriching the online group environment. One respondent in a virtual teams survey reported, "We have created a virtual lunch once a month that co-workers can voluntarily attend … This has helped in building rapport with co-workers" (quoted in Solomon, 2010). Simply socializing via Skype, for instance, can enrich the virtual experience. **As virtual groups mature in development, media richness is not as critical** because members learn to function effectively based on member familiarity and acquired knowledge (McGrath & Hollingshead, 1994).

Nevertheless, as Solomon (2010) suggests, "It is valuable for virtual teams to have periodic face-to-face meetings" (p. 13). Referring to survey findings to support this recommendation, she notes, "Again and again, respondents voiced a desire for more face-to-face meetings among virtual team members" (p. 13). One study found that using computer-mediated communication in groups more than 90% of the time "was detrimental to team outcomes" (Johnson et al., 2009, p. 623). This means that groups that are 100% virtual may have more difficulty remaining effective than virtual groups that mix in at least some face-to-face contact.

As indicated previously, **sometimes virtual groups are more effective using synchronous media and other times asynchronous, depending on the communication needs of the group.** Real-world support for this is provided by a study of 54 highly successful teams whose members represented 26 companies from a wide variety of industries and cultures spread across many time zones (Majchrzak et al., 2004). Detailed reports and interviews from leaders and members of these successful teams noted that when projects require complementary competencies and diverse perspectives and the tasks can be performed using electronic technologies, virtual groups are a better choice than face-to-face groups.

Teams generally had a negative view of asynchronous email and synchronous videoconferences, but they had a positive view of synchronous teleconferences and asynchronous, text-only postings. Emailing in one-to-one exchanges inevitably caused other members to feel left out of the conversational loop, eroding trust and producing dysfunctional behavior. To rectify this, some teams copied all members on every email message. This produced information overload. Members resorted to deleting emails without reading them. This produced confusion. Dissatisfaction with videoconferencing mostly involved poor-quality video production. Teleconferences were easy to conduct (often from home), and they functioned well for discussing disagreements. Text-only postings worked well to prepare members for teleconferences. Successful teams adapted technology to meet their communication needs (see Closer Look: "ComCorp Case Study").

Conducting Virtual Meetings: Special Challenges The specific steps for conducting productive group meetings discussed in Chapter 9 all apply well to virtual groups. Review these steps before your first virtual meeting. There are several additional concerns that you should address as the group leader or meeting chair.

CLOSER LOOK

ComCorp Case Study

For a year and a half, Kerber and Buono (2004) studied the launch and development of a virtual team in the corporate training and development section of a company they refer to as ComCorp. ComCorp is a $3 billion company with about 8,000 employees. The team was composed of 11 members spread across many time zones and four countries (United States, England, Ireland, and Australia). A teleconference, for example, would begin at 1:00 P.M. for some members, 9:00 P.M. for others, and 6:00 A.M. for still other members. The challenge facing this newly developed team was to design training and development solutions that would work well for a large global company experiencing a significant restructuring.

Fostering strong social relations among team members was a challenge for the ComCorp team. The team leader (not identified by name) immediately recognized the need for a rich communication environment. His immediate goal was "to establish, develop, and sustain lavish information flow among all team members, despite their geographic distance and virtual presence" (Kerber & Buono, 2004, p. 12). This was accomplished by using a combination of synchronous communication (such as teleconferences, one-on-one phone calls, and in-person meetings between members who were able) and asynchronous communication media (such as email and voicemail messages). The team leader established a routine to solidify group cohesiveness and build social relationships among members. This routine consisted of exchanging photographs during the formation stage and later updating personal events in members' lives to help cement social

bonds, conducting weekly group teleconferences, having person-to-person phone meetings between the leader and each member every two weeks, engaging in "icebreaker" exercises during teleconferences (such as each member describing his or her most embarrassing experience), and encouraging social conversation during a designated part of the teleconferences. The leader remained accessible to all members.

Team performance was also monitored routinely. Teleconference agendas routinely consisted of open discussions that reviewed the team purpose and relevant results attained by the group at that point, possible modification of objectives, recognition of breaking issues, brainstorming possibilities for achievement, making decisions in a collaborative process, and implementing decisions by assigning members to the implementation process (in other words, the Standard Agenda was mostly followed). Ongoing evaluations of team progress on training projects were conducted during teleconferences. Quarterly reports were issued on team accomplishments. Team members were supported through coaching, frequent feedback, recognition of accomplishments, and an emphasis on personal development. This approach has the effect of reducing social loafing and increasing commitment to the team's challenging goals.

Team leaders must work harder to sustain strong member satisfaction in virtual groups than in face-to-face groups (Hoyt & Blascovich, 2003). Group members reported strong satisfaction with the virtual group experience and the overall team leader and group performance. As one member explained, "Our team leader did an excellent job of leading while respecting the wealth of expertise and experience in the team. We did not feel stifled ... We really worked well as a team, particularly when [the team leader] had us continually focus on our major priorities and strategies" (p. 11). A variety of measures indicated that the ComCorp virtual group was highly successful, due in no small part to the team leader's attention to media richness and synchronicity.

QUESTIONS FOR THOUGHT

1. Is the success of this virtual team the result of unique circumstances or can the results be generalized to all virtual groups?
2. Would videoconferencing have improved the group cohesiveness?

1. *Choose the appropriate technology for the meeting.* Sophisticated technologies are just complicated toys if they are not matched properly with the purposes and objectives of the group. Trial and error will eventually indicate what works best for the group given group goals and restrictions on equipment and facilities.

2. *Limit the size of the group.* It is more difficult to recognize when a group has grown too large for an effective meeting to take place when there are no rooms to get stuffy and no seating capacity concerns. Keep the group size as small as possible so the technology does not complicate the discussion process.

3. *Plan for scheduling difficulties.* If your virtual group is composed of members spread across multiple time zones, don't schedule a meeting at 6:00 P.M. San Francisco time, for example. Members living in London would have to meet at 2:00 A.M. "Time zones presented the greatest general challenge to virtual teams," according to one study (Solomon, 2010).

4. *Check all technological equipment before each meeting to be sure that everything is in top working order.* Technological glitches can disrupt the flow of a meeting, even destroy it. Have someone available at short notice who can correct technological problems during a virtual meeting.

5. *Make certain each group member is well versed in the technology used to conduct the meeting.* Remind members that sensitive microphones may pick up whispers between members during videoconferences. This could cause embarrassment or create cross-talk that interferes with the fidelity of message transmission. Virtual meetings, at first, may seem stilted and difficult to manage, but with practice the technology can almost seem to disappear (Van der Kleij et al., 2009).

This concludes my discussion of communication competence in small groups. One of the central points that I hope has come through loudly and clearly is that one person can make an enormous difference in the quality of the group experience. What you individually do or don't do may be the difference between a successful and a less-than-successful group. Competent communication begins with you. The We-orientation is the core of group effectiveness. Don't look to others to make groups work. Take the knowledge you've garnered from this textbook and the skills that you will develop as you put this knowledge into practice and focus them on improving the group experience.

Reflect on what you've learned.

In Mixed Company

▶ Online

Now that you've read Chapter 12, access the online resources that accompany *In Mixed Company* at **www.cengagebrain.com**. Your online resources include:

1. Multiple-choice and true-false **chapter practice quizzes** with automatic correction.
2. Digital **glossary.**
3. **Flashcards.**

QUESTIONS FOR CRITICAL THINKERS

1. As technology continues to improve, is it likely that virtual groups will ever seem exactly like face-to-face groups?
2. As technology becomes more sophisticated and complicated, which challenges presented by virtual teams might become more problematic? Will any become less so?
3. What challenges and potential benefits might arise from virtual groups comprising older and younger members?

VIDEO *Case Studies*

Citing movies, even recent ones, that involve virtual groups can seem quickly outdated, even quaint, because technology changes so rapidly. Nevertheless, there are movies that can be analyzed and applied to chapter material on technology.

Firewall (2006). Drama, PG-13; Live Free or Die Hard (2007). Drama, PG-13; Tron Legacy (2010). Sci-Fi, PG

Consider these movies. Are there examples of virtual groups? Identify synchronous and asynchronous communication media. How does either affect communication?

Group Oral Presentations

Groups sometimes have public-speaking responsibilities. In some cases the group has been formed to present information orally before an audience of interested people. To assist those with little or no training or experience in public speaking, I am including this brief appendix, which covers some of the basics of oral presentation. I discuss types of group oral presentations, speech anxiety, attention strategies, organization, and use of visual aids.

Typical Types of Group Oral Presentations

There are three main types of oral group presentations. They are panel discussions, symposiums, and forums.

Panel Discussions: Free Exchange of Ideas

Panel discussions assemble a small group of participants, usually experts, to engage in a free exchange of information and ideas on a specific issue or problem before an audience. Purposes of a panel discussion include solving a difficult problem, informing an audience on an issue or topic of interest, or stimulating audience members to think about the pros and cons of a controversial issue.

Panel discussions require a moderator. The moderator usually organizes the group presentation by soliciting panel members who represent different points of view on the topic or issue. Panel members should be informed in advance of the topic to be discussed and major issues that should be addressed by panelists. **The moderator should follow several steps to make the panel discussion successful.**

1. Suitable physical arrangements for the panel discussion should be organized in advance. Usually, the number of panelists should be no fewer than three and no more than seven. Panelists should be seated at a long table in front of the audience, normally on a stage overlooking audience members. When group

discussions involve more than four or five participants, seating panelists at two tables formed in a slight V-shape to the audience helps panelists address each other during discussions without closing off the audience. Name cards placed on the table in front of each speaker will help the audience become familiar with each panelist. If the room where the panel discussion takes place is relatively large, a microphone at the table should be available for each speaker. If panelists request a DVD player and monitor, computer hook-up, Smartboard, easel, whiteboard, or other means of presenting visual aids, provide these if possible and place them in a location where access to them is easy and will not block the audience's view.

2. The moderator usually begins by welcoming the audience, providing a brief background on the topic or issue to be discussed, and introducing each panel member, citing specific background and qualifications of each speaker.

3. Panelists should be encouraged to bring notes, but discouraged from reading a prepared manuscript.

4. Begin the discussion with a question posed to the panel (e.g., "What is the extent of the problem of binge drinking on college campuses?"). The opening question can be posed to the entire panel, or a specific panelist can be asked to begin the discussion. The moderator identifies who has the floor during the discussion.

5. The moderator acts as a discussion guide. If a panelist has been left out of the discussion, the moderator may direct a question to him or her. If a panelist begins to dominate discussion, the moderator should step in and request participation from other panelists. Controversy should be encouraged, but polite conversation should be the norm. It is the responsibility of the moderator to keep the conversation civil. If it begins to turn ugly, the moderator should remind panelists to disagree without being disagreeable. Move the discussion along so that all major issues are discussed in the allotted time (usually about 45 minutes to an hour).

6. The moderator closes discussion by summarizing main points made by panelists and identifying new issues raised during the discussion to be further explored.

Symposium: Structured Group Presentations

A **symposium** is a relatively structured group presentation to an audience. It is composed of several individuals who present uninterrupted speeches with contrasting points of view on a central topic. Unlike a panel discussion, speakers do not engage in a discussion with each other. Each speaker presents a relatively short speech (usually 4–6 minutes apiece) addressing a separate segment of the overall topic.

The primary purpose of a symposium is to enlighten an audience on a controversial issue or to inform audience members on a subject of interest.

A symposium also benefits from having a moderator. **The moderator should follow a few important steps to ensure a successful symposium.**

1. Physical arrangements made for a panel discussion, just discussed, should also be used for a symposium.

2. To avoid redundancy, speakers should be chosen who represent different points of view.

3. The moderator should provide a brief background on the subject, introduce the speakers, and identify the speakers' order of presentation.

Forum Discussion: Audience Participation

A forum discussion allows members of an audience listening to a public speech, panel discussion, symposium, or debate to participate in a discussion of ideas presented. The primary purpose of a forum is to engage the audience in the discussion of issues raised. The moderator's role is critical to the success of a forum discussion. **Some suggestions for the moderator who directs the forum include:**

1. Announce to the audience that an open forum will occur after a panel discussion or symposium has concluded. Audience members can prepare questions or short remarks as they listen to speakers.

2. Rules for forum participation should be clearly articulated before any discussion occurs. Rules may include: raise your hand to be recognized or stand in a line where a microphone has been placed and wait your turn; keep remarks and questions very brief (about 15 to 30 seconds); each person should ask only one follow-up question.

3. Set a time limit for the forum (usually about 30 minutes). Indicate when there is time for only one or two more questions. Accept questions until the deadline has been reached, then conclude the forum by thanking the audience for its participation.

4. Encourage diverse points of view from the audience. A pro and con line might be established. The moderator could move back and forth, recognizing audience members on both sides so a balanced series of questions and comments will be presented.

5. If a question cannot be heard by all members of the audience, the moderator should repeat the question. If a question is confusing, the moderator may ask for a restatement or try to paraphrase the question so panelists or forum speakers can answer.

Speech Anxiety

Virtually everyone experiences some anxiety about having to make a public presentation. In one survey, 85% of the respondents reported that speech anxiety (also referred to by some as stage fright or performance anxiety) was a major and serious fear in their lives (Motley, 1995). This holds true for online speeches presented to remote audiences as well (Campbell & Larson, 2012).

Even college instructors experience speech anxiety. In one study, 87% of psychology instructors confessed that they had experienced speech anxiety associated with some aspect of teaching (Gardner & Leak, 1994). Sixty-five percent of these same subjects rated their most intense case of speech anxiety between "definitely unpleasant" and "severe or extreme." You're not alone if you are anxious about having to make an oral presentation in your class.

You can "cure" speech anxiety with heavy doses of tranquilizers, but, aside from the physiological dangers associated with them (they're potentially addictive), they will make you appear witless in front of an audience because they deaden mental acuity. So if you're concerned about appearing lobotomized in front of groups, avoid using drugs as a cure for anxiety.

Speech anxiety, however, is not necessarily a demon to be exorcised. **The degree of anxiety, not the anxiety itself, requires attention.** A moderate amount of anxiety can enhance performance and energize a speaker. You can present a more dynamic, forceful presentation when energized than when you feel so comfortable that you become almost listless and unchallenged by the speaking experience.

When the intensity of your fear about speaking in front of people gets out of control, however, it becomes debilitative and detracts from your performance. Intense anxiety can be cause for real concern if ignored. It will congest your thought pathways, thereby clogging your free flow of ideas. In such a condition, every speaker's nightmare—going blank—will likely occur. Also, a terror-stricken speaker feels an urge to escape. Consequently, a 7-minute speech is compressed into 3 minutes by a staccato, hyperspeed delivery. The quicker the speech presentation, the quicker the escape.

The causes of speech anxiety are complex and varied. Space does not permit a thorough discussion of these causes. **Generally speaking, the causes of speech anxiety are self-defeating thoughts and situational factors.**

Self-defeating thoughts include negative thoughts that predict failure, desire for complete approval from an audience, and an awareness that audience members will evaluate your speaking performance. *Negative thoughts* about your speaking performance can wildly exaggerate potential problems and thus stoke the furnace of anxiety. Those harboring negative thoughts predict not just momentary lapses of memory, but a complete meltdown of mental functions ("I know I'll forget my entire speech and I'll just stand there like an idiot"). Minor problems of organization are magnified into graphic episodes of total incoherence and nonstop babbling. Perfectionists also anguish over every flaw in their speech and overgeneralize the significance of even minor defects. A flawless public-speaking performance is a desirable goal, but why beat up on yourself when it doesn't happen? Perfectionists make self-defeating statements to themselves such as "I'm such a fool. I mispronounced the name of one of the experts I quoted"; "I must have said 'um' at least a dozen times. I sounded like a moron"; and "My knees were shaking. The audience must have thought I was afflicted with a disorder of my nervous system." Ironically, the imperfections so glaringly noticeable to perfection-ists usually go unnoticed by most people in the audience. This overestimation of the extent to which audience members detect a speaker's nervousness is called the **illusion of transparency** (MacInnis et al., 2010). Even the most talented and experienced public speakers make occasional errors that go unnoticed in otherwise riveting performances.

Another self-defeating thought that triggers speech anxiety is the *desire for complete approval* from your audience, especially from those whose opinion we value. It is irrational thinking, however, to accept nothing less than complete approval from an audience. You cannot please everyone, especially if you take a stand on a controversial issue. When you set standards for success at unreachable heights, you are bound to take a tumble.

The fact that *an audience evaluates you* every time you give a speech, even if no one is formally grading your performance, will usually trigger some anxiety. Human beings are social creatures who dislike, even fear, disapproval from others. Even if you aren't seeking complete approval or adulation from your listeners, you would be a rare individual if you were completely immune to the judgments of others hearing you speak. Public speaking becomes doubly intense when formal grades are given for each speech performance.

There are many situational causes of speech anxiety. Two prominent ones are novel situations and conspicuousness. *Novel situations*—ones that are new to you—create uncertainty, and uncertainty can easily make you tense. For most students, public speaking is a novel situation. Few students have given many speeches in their lifetime, and some have never given a formal public address. Fortunately, as you gain experience speaking in front of audiences, the novelty wears off and your anxiety will diminish.

The *conspicuousness* of the public-speaking situation increases most people's anxi-ety. Most students tell me that speaking to one or two persons is usually not very dif-ficult, but speaking in front of an entire class or an auditorium filled with a thousand people really makes them want to toss their lunch. Here the interaction of conspicuous-ness and approval can be easily seen. Standing alone before a few people and possibly failing is not nearly as big a deal as possibly failing in front of a huge crowd. In the former situation, your potential failure would likely remain an isolated event, but in the latter situation the entire school might be in on your humiliation—so goes the logic.

So how do you manage your speech anxiety, given the variety of causes that induce it? Numerous individuals have suggested to me that picturing your audience nude, or clothed only in underwear or in diapers, can be helpful (assuming you can stifle your laughter when the image pops into your mind). Breathing deeply is also a favorite tidbit of wisdom offered by many as a quick-fix coping strategy for stage fright. These remedies have some merit, especially if they work for you. None of them, however, offers a reliable solution to speech anxiety. There are many more effective methods.

First, there is no substitute for *adequate preparation*. Conducting proper research on your speech topic, organizing your speech clearly and carefully, and practicing it several times are all essential if you hope to manage your anxiety effectively. Adequate preparation also must include physiological preparation, such as ensuring proper nutrition just prior to the speech event. Ignoring your physiological preparation for a speech may cancel out the benefits of other methods used to manage your speech anxiety. Consequently, do not deliver a speech on an empty stomach, but also do not fill your stomach with empty calories. You need high-quality fuel such as complex carbohydrates to sustain you while you're speaking. Simple sugars (doughnuts, Twinkies), caffeine (coffee, colas, chocolate), and nicotine (cigarettes) should be avoided or ingested in very small quantities. Adequate preparation will reduce uncertainty and the fear of failure.

Second, *gain perspective* on your speech situation. Consider the difference between rational and irrational speech anxiety. A colleague of mine, Darrell Beck, worked out a simple formula for determining the difference between the two. **The severity of the feared occurrence times the probability of the feared occurrence** provides a rough approximation of how much anxiety is rational and when you have crossed the line into irrational anxiety. Severity is approximated by imagining what would happen to you if your worst fears came true—you bombed the speech. Would you leave the state? Would you drop out of school? Probably not, since even dreadful speaking performances do not warrant such drastic steps. You might consider dropping the class, but even this is unlikely since fellow students are very understanding when a classmate delivers a poor speech. So even a poor speech does not rationally warrant joining the monastic life or making any significant life changes. The probability that your worst nightmare will come true and you will give a horrible speech, however, is extremely unlikely if you have adequately prepared. Thus, working yourself into a lather over an impending speech lacks proper perspective if you follow the advice given here.

Third, *refocus your attention* on your message and your audience and away from yourself (Motley, 1995). You cannot concentrate on two things at the same time. If you dwell on your nervousness, you will be distracted from presenting your message effectively. Focus on presenting your message clearly and enthusiastically. View the speaking experience as a challenge to keep your audience interested, maybe even an opportunity to change their minds on an issue.

Fourth, *make coping statements* to yourself as you give your speech, especially when you momentarily stumble. When inexperienced speakers make mistakes during a speech, they tend to make negative statements to themselves. You forget a point, momentarily lose your train of thought, or stammer. Immediately, the tendency is for you to say to yourself "I knew I would mess up this speech" or "I told everybody I couldn't give a decent speech." Instead, try making coping statements while you're delivering the speech. When problems arise say "I can do better" or "I'm getting to the good part of my speech." Talk to yourself during your speech in positive ways to counteract self-talk that defeats you. When parts of your speech go well, compliment yourself on a job well done (to yourself, of course, not out loud). This sustains and energizes you as you proceed through the speech.

Gaining and Maintaining Attention

Audience interest doesn't just happen magically. Interest is garnered by carefully planning and utilizing strategies of attention. Although gaining and maintaining attention throughout your speech is an important goal for any speaker, attention strategies should enhance a speech, not detract from it. A disorganized speech gains attention but in a negative way. Frequent verbal and vocal fillers such as "you know," "um," and "ah" draw attention to inarticulateness.

Some attributes of stimuli, by their very nature, attract attention. Consider just a few of these attributes and how they can become attention strategies.

First, *intensity* is a concentrated stimulus that draws attention. Intensity is an extreme degree of emotion, thought, or activity. Relating a story of a woman fleeing for her life from a stalker can be intense, especially for those who fear such an occurrence. Don't be too graphic when describing emotionally charged events, however, or you may offend and alienate your audience.

There are several basic stylistic techniques that promote intensity and rivet an audience's attention. Direct, penetrating eye contact is a useful technique. How does a daydreamer continue to ignore you when you are zeroing in on the daydreamer? **The lack of eye contact so typical of manuscript speeches, in which every word of your speech is written on the paper in front of you, underlines the importance of not reading a speech to an audience because you break connection with your listeners.** Direct eye contact is an attention builder, but lack of eye contact is an attention destroyer.

Variation in vocal volume is a second technique for provoking intensity. A raised voice can be quite intense. It punctuates portions of your speech much as an exclamation point punctuates a written sentence. The use of a raised voice, however, can be a rather shattering experience for an audience. Incessant, unrelenting, bombastic delivery of a message irritates and alienates an audience. Punctuate with a raised voice only those points that are especially significant and deserve closer attention lest your speech sounds like a rant.

Silence can also be intense. A pregnant pause—silence held a bit longer than usual if you were merely taking a breath—interjects drama into your speech and spotlights significant points.

A second stimulus attribute that induces attention is *startling*. You try to stun, surprise, and shake up your audience. A startling statement, fact, or statistic can do this quite effectively. Startling statements such as "AIDS clearly has the potential to decimate the human population," "Calories can kill you," and "You may be living next door to a terrorist" can make an audience sit up and take notice. That it costs more to feed and house a criminal in prison than it does to send him or her to the most expensive university in the country is a startling fact. Of course, you do not want to startle your audience if you can't support your claims with evidence.

Every startling stimulus does not produce constructive attention from an audience. Speakers can startle and offend at the same time. A few examples from my own experience and those of my colleagues make this point. One student (during a speech on food poisoning) gained attention by vomiting scrambled eggs into his handkerchief, raising serious doubts about the speaker's good taste. Another student punched himself so hard in the face that he momentarily staggered (the speech was on violence in America). These examples have one thing in common: the speakers startled their audience but lost credibility in the process. Tasteless jokes, ethnic slurs, and offensive language will also startle an audience and gain attention, but at a substantial cost to the speaker. The general rule applies—**attention strategies should enhance the effectiveness of your speech, not detract from it.**

Making a problem or issue appear *vital* to an audience is a third attention strategy. There are two principal ways to do this. First, the problem must be made vital not in some abstract or general sense, but in a specific, immediate, and meaningful sense. An audience's primary question when told that a problem exists is "How does it affect me?" The problem becomes vital and therefore meaningful when listeners can see how the consequences of inaction directly affect their interests and well-being. "One out of every 10 women in this audience will contract breast cancer and a similar number of men listening to me will contract prostate cancer. Those of you who escape the disease will likely know one or more friends or relatives who will die from these forms of cancer" is an example of how to personalize a problem and make it seem vital to an audience. Be careful, however, not to overstate your case by depicting relatively trivial concerns as vital. For an issue to be accepted as vital, it must have the ring of truth. Credible evidence must substantiate your claim that the problem is vital.

Using *novelty* is a fourth attention strategy. Audiences are naturally drawn to the new and different. Unusual examples, clever quotations, and uncommon stories attract attention because they are new and different. Beginning your speech with a novel introduction is especially important. Do not begin by telling the audience what your topic is. That is very unoriginal and boring. Create interest in your topic with a novel opening—an unusual news event, story, or human interest example related to your subject. For instance, notice how the following introduction grabs attention by using novelty:

> Acting as his own attorney, an Oklahoma City robbery suspect became agitated when a witness identified him in court as the guilty party. "I should have blown your head off," he screamed, adding on quick reflection, "if I'd been the one that was there." The verdict? Guilty. Lesson to be learned? Acting as your own attorney is a foolish idea.

Novelty can be a very effective attention strategy, especially for the introduction to your speech, but also throughout your presentation.

Finally, using *humor* is a superior attention strategy if used adroitly. You should be able to incorporate humorous anecdotes, quotations, and personal stories throughout your speech. **There are several important guidelines, however, for using humor effectively as an attention strategy.** First, don't force humor. If you aren't a particularly funny person and have never told a joke without omitting crucial details or flubbing the punch line, then don't try to be a comedian in front of your audience. Humorous quotations, funny stories, and amusing occurrences can be used without setting them up as jokes. Simply offer them as illustrations of key points, and, if the audience members are amused, they will laugh.

Second, use only relevant humor. Unrelated stories and jokes may be suitable for a comic whose principal purpose is to make an audience laugh, but a formal speech requires you to make important points. Your use of humor needs to make a relevant contribution to the advancement of the speech's purpose.

Third, use good taste. Coarse vulgarities, obscenities, and sick jokes invite anger and hostility. Humor that rests on stereotypes and put-downs may alienate vast sections of your audience. Sexist, racist, and homophobic jokes that denigrate groups exhibit bad taste and poor judgment.

Fourth, don't overuse humor. Don't become enamored with your own wittiness. Telling joke after joke or telling one amusing story after another will likely produce laughter, but the audience will also be dissatisfied if you substitute humor for substance.

Humor can be risky but very satisfying when it works. Using humor is probably the most effective attention strategy when used appropriately and skillfully.

Organizing and Outlining

Presenting a well-organized speech is critical to your success as a speaker. This section, by necessity, will be a cursory treatment of organization and outlining.

Perhaps the easiest way of developing the organization of your speech is to think of your speech as an inverted pyramid. The base of your upside-down pyramid represents the most general part of your speech, namely, the topic. Moving down toward the tip of the pyramid, you fill in the purpose statement, then the main points that flow from the purpose statement, then elaborate on each main point with subpoints and sub-subpoints, and so forth. You begin with the abstract and work toward the concrete and specific.

Let's say that your group has chosen for its symposium topic the problem of violence in America. First, your group must divide this general topic into manageable subtopics so each group member will have about a 4- to 6-minute speech. Subtopics might include violence on television, violence in the movies, guns and violence, gang violence, social and economic causes of violence, and potential solutions to violence (which could be divided even further into specific proposals such as "three strikes and you're out," outlawing handguns, prison reform, and social programs). Each group member would then be given his or her subtopic.

Once you have your subtopic for the symposium, each group member must construct a specific purpose statement. A **purpose statement** is a concise, precise, declarative statement phrased in simple, clear language that provides both the general purpose (to inform or to persuade) and the specific purpose (exactly what you want the audience to understand, believe, feel, or do). A purpose statement ordinarily considers the interests and knowledge level of a particular audience. Your group presentation should always be mindful of audience interest, depth of understanding, and experience of audience members.

TOPIC: Guns and violence
PURPOSE STATEMENT: To inform you that handgun violence is a serious problem in America.

Your purpose statement becomes the blueprint for your entire speech. You determine your main points from your purpose statement.

MAIN POINT I: Death from handguns is a serious problem.
MAIN POINT II: Serious injury from handguns also poses a serious problem for America.

Each main point is then divided into subpoints, sub-subpoints, and so on.

MAIN POINT I: Death from handguns is a serious problem.
    SUBPOINT A: There are more than 16,000 murders from handguns every year in America; Japan has fewer than 100.

SUBPOINT B: More than 1,400 American youths between the ages of 10 and 19 commit suicide with a handgun each year.

Each subpoint is then broken down further with more detail, examples, and supporting evidence.

SUBPOINT A: There are more than 16,000 murders from handguns every year in America; Japan has fewer than 100.

SUB-SUBPOINT 1: Teenage homicide from handguns has almost doubled in the last decade to more than 5,000 annually.

SUB-SUBPOINT 2: The teenage handgun death rate now exceeds the mortality rate for young people from all natural causes combined.

SUB-SUBPOINT 3: Three times more American young men are killed by handguns every 100 hours than were killed during the 100-hour Persian Gulf War.

SUB-SUBPOINT 4: Provide examples of teenagers gunned down in street violence.

SUBPOINT B: More than 1,400 American youths between the ages of 10 and 19 commit suicide with a handgun each year.

SUB-SUBPOINT 1: Nearly two-thirds of suicides are from handguns.

SUB-SUBPOINT 2: Handguns put at risk large numbers of young people who consider suicide.

SUB-SUB-SUBPOINT a: More than one in four high school students seriously contemplate suicide.

SUB-SUB-SUBPOINT b: Sixteen percent of high-schoolers make a specific plan to commit suicide, and half of these actually try to kill themselves.

SUB-SUB-SUBPOINT c: Ready availability of handguns makes teen suicide more likely.

SUB-SUB-SUBPOINT d: Tell the story of 14-year-old Paul Hoffman.

The resulting outline for your first main point would look as follows:

PURPOSE STATEMENT: To inform you that handgun violence is a serious problem in America.

I. Death from handguns is a serious problem.
   A. There are more than 16,000 murders from handguns every year in America; Japan has fewer than 100.
      1. Teenage homicide from handguns has almost doubled in the last decade to more than 5,000 annually.

2. The teenage handgun death rate now exceeds the mortality rate for young people from all natural causes combined.
3. Three times more American young men are killed by handguns in 100 hours than were killed during the 100-hour Persian Gulf War.
4. Provide examples of specific teenagers gunned down in street violence.

B. More than 1,400 American youths between the ages of 10 and 19 commit suicide with a handgun each year.
   1. Nearly two-thirds of suicides are from handguns.
   2. Handguns put at risk large numbers of young people who consider suicide.
      a. More than one in four high school students seriously contemplate suicide.
      b. Sixteen percent of high-schoolers make a specific plan to commit suicide, and half of these actually try to kill themselves.
      c. Ready availability of handguns makes teen suicide more likely.
      d. Tell the story of 14-year-old Paul Hoffman.

You follow the same procedure for outlining your second main point. Note that every subpoint must relate specifically to the main point and likewise every sub-subpoint must relate specifically to the subpoint above it.

The form used in the sample outline follows a standard set of symbols composed of Roman numerals, capital letters, and Arabic numbers. Indent all subdivisions of a more general point. This will help you follow the development of your points as you speak. **Every point that is subdivided has at least two subpoints.**

Preparing the body of your speech is your most difficult and primary organizational task. The introduction, however, creates the all-important first impression with an audience. **Your introduction should satisfy the following objectives, usually in this order:**

1. Gain the attention of the audience.

2. Provide your purpose statement.

3. Relate the topic and purpose statement to the needs and interests of the audience (answering the question "Why should the audience care about your topic and purpose?").

4. Preview the main points of your speech (state them exactly as they appear in your outline).

The conclusion of your speech should strive to accomplish two objectives:

1. Wrap up the speech with a brief summary of your main points.

2. End the speech with an effective attention strategy that brings closure to the speech.

Once you have prepared your speech outline composed of your introduction, body, and conclusion, practice your speech several times. Speaking from an outline instead of a written manuscript is called the **extemporaneous style** of speaking (*extemp*, for short). **When you have prepared your full-sentence outline as already explained, you may want to condense full sentences into terse words or phrases for your actual speaking outline.** Under pressure of performing before an audience, it is usually easier to speak extemporaneously when you do not have to read whole sentences. Glancing at a few words or a phrase to remind you of a point allows you to maintain strong eye contact with your listeners without losing your train of thought.

Finally, as you present your speech, **signpost your primary points. Signposts** indicate exactly where you are in your speech so the audience can follow along easily. Restating your main points as you get to each one is an example of signposting. If you had "three causes of gun violence in America," you would signpost each one as you addressed them in turn, such as "the first cause of gun violence is poverty," "the second cause of gun violence is the ready availability of guns," and "the third cause of gun violence is the breakdown of the criminal justice system." In this way, signposting underscores your important points as you present your speech.

Using Visual Aids

Visual aids can add interest, clarify complex material, make points memorable, and enhance the credibility of the speaker. There are many types of visual aids, and with the advent of computer graphics and technologies still being developed, the possibilities are almost limitless. For inexperienced speakers, however, it is best to keep visual aids simple. Photographs, diagrams, charts, graphs, physical models, video clips, and PowerPoint slides are the standard types of visual aids.

Poorly designed and clumsily used visual aids will detract from your speech. **The following guidelines will assist you in preparing and displaying visual aids effectively:**

1. *Keep visual aids simple.* Visual aids that work well in books, magazines, or newspapers rarely work well in a speech. In printed material a visual aid can be studied carefully. A complicated visual aid used in a speech will distract audience members from listening to the speaker while they try to figure out the complex graph, chart, or diagram.

2. *Visual aids should be large enough to be seen easily.* The general rule of thumb here is that a person in the back of the room should be able to see the visual aid easily.

3. *Visual aids should be neat and attractive.* Sloppy, hastily constructed visual aids are worse than no visual aids at all. Long lists of bulleted points on PowerPoint

slides are boring. Remember, PowerPoint slides are supposed to be *visual* aids. Make slides visually attractive and attention getting.

4. *Display the visual aid where it can be seen easily by all members of the audience.* Audience members should not have to stand up or elongate their necks to see the visual aid. A PowerPoint presentation shown on a small computer screen instead of projected on a large screen is inadequate in almost all group presentations.

5. *Practice with the visual aids.* Remember Murphy's law—whatever can go wrong likely will go wrong. Make certain that any equipment used is in proper working order. Do not attempt to use electronic technology without practicing with it first.

6. *Talk to the audience, not the visual aid.* Don't turn your back on your audience while explaining your visual aid (a common practice even by professional speakers when referring to projected PowerPoint images). Stand facing your audience, point the toes of your feet straight ahead, and imagine that your feet have been nailed to the floor. Stand beside the visual aid when referring to it and use your finger or a laser pointer to guide the audience.

7. *Keep the visual aid out of sight when it is not in use.* Audience members may be distracted by the visual aid when you are talking about an unrelated point. I once had a symposium group, whose topic was surfing, play a surfing movie during all members' speeches. Not surprisingly, the audience was far more attentive to the wave riders than the speakers. If showing a series of PowerPoint slides, insert blank slides in places where you won't be referring to a slide for some time.

8. *Do not circulate a visual aid among the audience members.* Passing around pictures or other visual aids while you're still speaking will distract listeners.

Chapters 8 and 9 have already delved substantially into the process of critical thinking in small group decision making and problem solving. Group members must be able to recognize and deal effectively with problems of information overload and underload, confirmation bias, false dichotomies, collective inferential error, group polarization, and groupthink. In addition, critical thinking is involved in every step of the Standard Agenda, especially when information is gathered and evaluated, criteria for decision making are developed and applied, and final decisions are made by the group.

This bonus appendix is included because in classrooms in some parts of the country, heavier emphasis is placed on reasoning and use of evidence in the small group context than is true of other parts of the country. This appendix is divided into two segments: the structure of arguments and types of fallacies.

The Structure of Arguments

An argument or "train of reasoning" is composed of several constituent parts (Toulmin et al., 1979). These parts are: the **claim**—that which is asserted and remains to be proven; **data**—the grounds (support/evidence) for the claim, such as statistical evidence, expert testimony, documents, objects, exhibits, conclusions from test results, verifiable facts, and conclusions previously established; **warrant**—the reasoning used to link the data to the claim, usually assumed (implied), not stated directly; **backing**—additional evidence and reasoning used to support the inference made in the warrant; **rebuttal**—exceptions or refutation that diminish the force of the claim; and **qualifier**—degree of truth of the claim (such as highly probable, plausible, possible, and so forth).

Consider the following example of all six parts of an argument:

Claim: Jim Davis should be given antibiotics.

Data: Davis suffered severe cuts and injuries on his arms and legs in an auto accident.

Warrant: There is a risk of infection in such injuries.

Backing: Hospital reports and numerous studies indicate that risk of infection is serious and that antibiotics can prevent infection from occurring.

Rebuttal: Overuse of antibiotics can produce superbugs. Antibiotics should be used only when absolutely necessary, or they will eventually be useless to fight disease.

Qualifier: "Probable." This is a strong claim based on solid evidence and reasoning.

Fallacies

Understanding fallacies will help you determine the validity of your claim, the strength of your data, and the solidity of your warrant and backing. The list of fallacies below is not exhaustive. I have chosen only those specific fallacies that seem to occur frequently and that students are likely to encounter almost daily. I am dividing this list of fallacies into three types: **material fallacies**—errors in the process of using supporting materials as proof; **logical fallacies**—errors in the process of reasoning; and **psychological fallacies**—claims that rest on emotional appeal rather than logic and evidence.

Material Fallacies: Misuse of Statistics

There are two primary material fallacies: misuse of statistics and misuse of authority. Misuse of statistics fallacies are numerous. I cover five common ones.

Manufactured or Questionable Statistics: Making Them Up This fallacy consists of statistics that have been fabricated, or statistics whose validity is highly questionable because there is no reasonable method for compiling such statistics, or that which is quantified is too trivial to warrant the time, effort, and resources necessary to compile accurate statistics. Every year the claim is made during the Academy Awards that the presentation of Oscars is viewed by 1 billion people worldwide. Considering that about 40 million viewers in the United States watch it, according to Nielsen ratings surveys (Collins, 2013), and that the Academy Awards is of greater interest to Americans than to other countries because most movies nominated for Oscars are American made, and further considering that the program is aired in English, which is not the language of most other countries, the 1 billion viewers claim is almost certainly a preposterously inflated statistic of pure fabrication (Radosh, 2005).

Irrelevant Statistic: Does Not Apply These are statistics that do not directly prove the implied or stated claim yet they are offered as evidence supporting the claim. For example, "The United States spends a trillion dollars a year on health care, more than any other nation. Clearly, our health care system is the world's best." The amount of money spent doesn't prove money was spent wisely, efficiently, or effectively.

Sample Size Inadequate or Unspecified: Not Nearly Enough This fallacy occurs when the sample size is very small, resulting in a margin of error in excess of plus or minus 3%, or when you are left guessing what the sample size might have been. For example, "Eighty percent of those surveyed support the cable TV legislation." How many were surveyed? Ten people, eight of whom favored the legislation?

Self-Selected Sample: Not Exactly Random Call-in polls by local television stations, and surveys or questionnaires printed in magazines asking readers to respond, are examples. Those who are angry or have a vested interest in the outcome are most likely to participate. MSNBC had an Internet poll that solicited responses on the question of whether George W. Bush should be impeached. Typically, 89% favored impeachment (the poll ran for years). No other major reputable poll using a random sample, not a self-selected sample, showed even a slight majority favoring impeachment.

Dated Statistics: Lack of Currency Statistics should be as up to date as possible, especially if the event, phenomenon, or situation is volatile and likely to change quickly (such as number of unemployed, long-term interest rates on mortgages, murder rates in various cities, and international monetary exchange rates). Some phenomena change very slowly, if at all, over time (such as percentage of U.S. population who call themselves Catholics, Protestants, and other denominations). They require less attention to the recency of statistics. "According to the Department of Housing and Urban Development in a 2000 report to Congress, the median price of a new home in the United States is $120,000" is a statistic that hardly qualifies as current in today's volatile housing market.

Material Fallacies: Misuse of Authority

Testimony of experts and authorities is useful as supporting material for claims because experts draw on a larger data and knowledge base than do nonexperts. Experts are not always correct, but they are more reliable than someone who is uninformed or only marginally knowledgeable, especially about a highly technical subject.

Incomplete Citation: Reference Is Neither Specific nor Complete Minimum requirements for a complete citation include the qualifications of the authority (if not obvious), place of publication, and date of reference. For example, "The

President's Commission on Mental Health, in its January report of this year entitled 'Mental Health, Mental Illness,' concludes, 'The biggest stigma in America is the mental illness label.'" "Research indicates" (unless offered by an expert interpreting the latest results in his or her field), "studies show," and the like are incomplete citations.

Biased Source: Ax Grinders Special-interest groups or individuals who stand to gain money, prestige, power, or influence simply by taking a certain position on an issue, or crusaders for a cause, are all biased even though they may have expertise. An example is quoting R. J. Reynolds Tobacco Company on the safety of cigarette smoking.

Authority Quoted Out of His/Her Field: Expertise Is Not Generic Quote experts in their area of specialization. "Professor of Biology, Dr. Ernhard Bousterhaus, claims that electric cars are impractical and will remain so for at least the next 50 years" is quoting an expert in one field that has little to do with the claim regarding electric cars.

Logical Fallacies: Reasoning Gone Awry

Reasoning is the basis of warrants for arguments. Sometimes our logic is faulty.

Hasty Generalization: Overgeneralizing Drawing conclusions (generalizations) from too few or atypical examples is called a hasty generalization. Testimonials exalting cancer cures, faith healings, and so on are generalizations based on too few and probably atypical experiences of individuals. Audience members at a talk show generalizing on the basis of their individual experiences is another example.

False Analogy: Bogus Comparison A false analogy occurs when two items, events, or phenomena with superficial similarities are viewed as identical, even when a significant point or points of difference exist between the two things compared. "In Turkey, farmers grow poppies (source of heroin) as a cash crop. In the United States, farmers grow corn and soybeans for cash crops. Why outlaw poppies when we don't outlaw corn and soybeans?" This is a false analogy because the poppy crop is not a critical food source capable of feeding the hungry of the world, but corn and soybeans are. Also, poppies are grown as a source of drugs. Although corn can be made into alcohol, that is not its primary purpose.

Correlation Mistaken for Causation: Covariation Fallacy When two phenomena vary at the same time, a causal linkage is often incorrectly asserted. "I ate a lot of chocolate this week and now my face has acne. I guess I'll have to stop eating chocolate so I can get rid of these blasted pimples." This is an example of correlation incorrectly asserted as causation.

Single Cause: Complexity Oversimplified Attributing only one cause to a complex phenomenon with many causes is a single-cause fallacy. "Poor communication is the reason for the alarming increase in the divorce rate" is an example. Poor communication is probably a cause of some divorces, but not necessarily the most important or the only cause.

Psychological Fallacies: Emotion Disguised as Logic

Pretending that an emotional attack is logical steps into fallacious territory. Consider two primary examples: ad hominem and ad populum.

Ad Hominem: Personal Attack Attacking the messenger to divert attention away from the message is an ad hominem fallacy. Not all attacks on a person's credibility, character, and qualifications, however, are fallacious. If character or credibility is the real issue, then it is relevant argumentation (for example, attacking Bill Clinton's integrity during the impeachment proceedings was not a fallacious personal attack). "Why are you always on my back for not studying? Last semester your GPA fell nearly a full point" is an ad hominem fallacy.

Ad Populum: Popular Opinion A claim based on popular opinion rather than reasoning and evidence is an ad populum fallacy. "Go ahead and smoke marijuana. More than a third of all college students do" is an example.

Glossary

A glossary of terms does not substitute for clear understanding of the concepts represented. You can memorize a definition without knowing what it means. Clear understanding requires a context for the terms. By reading the following terms in the context of this book, you will see the interconnections between and among the terms. All terms included in the glossary appear in **boldfaced** type in the body of the text (see the index for location).

A

Accommodating Style of conflict management that yields to the concerns and desires of others.

Active listening Focused listening in which you make a concerted effort to focus your attention on the speaker and his or her message.

Activities groups Groups that engage in specific activities such as chess teams and sports teams.

Ad hoc teams Teams that are assembled to solve an immediate problem, then are dissolved once the solution has been implemented.

Adaptability The adjustment of group boundaries in response to changing environmental conditions.

Aggregation A collection of individuals who do not interact with each other or influence each other to achieve common goals.

Aggression Any physical or verbal behavior intended to hurt or destroy a person.

Alliances Associations in the form of subgroups entered into for mutual benefit or a common objective.

Ambushing Biased listening in which the listener focuses on attacking a speaker's points instead of striving to comprehend them.

Analysis paralysis Bogging down decision making by analyzing a problem too extensively.

Appropriateness Complying with rules and their accompanying expectations.

Argot Private vocabulary peculiar to a specific group.

Artistic groups Groups that form to perform artistic endeavors such as choirs, bands, and quilting circles.

Assertiveness The ability to communicate the full range of your thoughts and emotions with confidence and skill.

Asymmetry Behaving opposite to how others behave, especially when others are angry or enraged.

Asynchronous media Those forms of communicating that permit anytime/anyplace interaction among group members without interruption.

Autocratic style A style of leadership that exerts control over group members.

Autonomy (and empowerment) The degree to which team members experience substantial freedom, independence, and discretion in their work.

Avoiding Style of conflict management in which a group member withdraws from potentially contentious and unpleasant struggles.

B

Backing Additional evidence and reasoning used to support the inference made in the warrant.

BATNA (Best Alternative to a Negotiated Agreement) A fallback position if a negotiated settlement fails to occur.

Beliefs What we think is true or probable.

Boundary control Regulation that determines the amount of access a group has to input and thus influence from outsiders in a system.

Brainstorming A creative problem-solving technique that promotes plentiful, even zany, ideas in an atmosphere free from criticism and encourages enthusiastic participation from all group members.

Bridging An integrative problem-solving technique that offers a new option devised to satisfy all parties on important conflicting issues.

Bypassing When we assume that everyone has the same meaning for a word and fail to check for any differences.

C

Charge The task of a team, such as to gather information, to analyze a problem and make recommendations, to make decisions and implement them, or to tackle a specific project from inception to completion.

Charisma A constellation of personal attributes that people find highly attractive in an individual and strongly influential.

Charismatic leaders All leaders are transformational to some degree, but charismatic leaders are thought to be *highly* transformational.

Claim That which is asserted and remains to be proven.

Cliques Small, narrowly focused subgroups that create a competitive atmosphere.

Coalitions Temporary alliances.

Cohesiveness The degree to which members feel a part of a group, wish to stay in the group, and are committed to each other and to the group's work.

Collaborating Style of conflict management that recognizes the interconnection between the task and social components of groups and deals directly with both requirements; win–win cooperative approach to conflict management.

Collective effort model (CEM) It suggests that group members are strongly motivated to perform well in a group if they are convinced that their individual effort will likely help in attaining valued results.

Commitment The conscious decision to invest time, energy, thought, and feeling to improve oneself or one's relationships with others.

Communication A transactional process of sharing meaning with others.

Communication climate The emotional atmosphere, the enveloping tone that is created by the way we communicate in groups.

Communication competence Communicating effectively and appropriately in a given context.

Communication technology A tool to achieve a communication purpose.

Communication style of conflict management An orientation toward conflict; predisposition or tendency regarding the way conflict is managed in groups.

Competing (power/forcing) Win–lose style of conflict management that attempts to force one's will on another group member.

Competition A mutually exclusive goal attainment process.

Compliance The process of consenting to the dictates and desires of others.

Compromising Style of conflict management that gives up something to get something.

Confirmation bias A strong tendency to seek information that confirms our beliefs and attitudes and to ignore information that contradicts our currently held beliefs and attitudes.

Conflict The expressed struggle of interconnected parties who perceive incompatible goals and interference from each other in attaining those goals.

Conflict spirals The escalating cycle of negative communication that produces destructive conflict.

Conformity The adherence to group norms by group members.

Confrontation A collaborative component of conflict management characterized by the overt recognition that conflict exists in a group and the direct effort to manage it effectively.

Consensus A state of mutual agreement among members of a group in which all legitimate concerns of individuals have been addressed to the satisfaction of the group.

Constructive competition Occurs when competition produces positive, enjoyable experiences and generates increased effort to achieve without jeopardizing positive interpersonal relationships and personal well-being.

Constructive conflict Conflict that is characterized by communication that is We-oriented, cooperative, de-escalating, supportive, and flexible.

Contempt The verbal or nonverbal expression of insult that emotionally abuses others.

Content dimension (of messages) The information transmitted.

Context An environment in which meaning emerges, consisting of who communicates to whom, why the communicator does it, and where, when, and how it is done.

Cooperation A mutually inclusive goal attainment process.

Correlation A consistent relationship between two or more variables.

Credibility A composite of competence (knowledge, skills), trustworthiness (honesty, consistency, character), and dynamism (confidence, assertiveness).

Criteria Standards by which decisions and solutions to problems can be evaluated.

Critical thinking Analyzing and evaluating ideas and information to reach sound judgments and conclusions.

Cyberostracism A form of remote ostracism that occurs in virtual groups.

Cynics They focus on the negative, predicting failure and looking for someone or something to criticize, sapping the energy from a team with their negativity.

D

Data The grounds (support/evidence) for the claim, such as statistical evidence, expert testimony, documents, objects, exhibits, conclusions from test results, verifiable facts, and conclusions previously established as credible.

Decision A choice between two or more alternatives.

Deep diversity Substantial variation among members in task-relevant skills, knowledge, abilities, beliefs, values, perspectives, and problem-solving strategies.

Defensive communication Patterns of communication characterized by evaluation, control, indifference, manipulation, superiority, and certainty.

Defensiveness A reaction to a perceived attack on our self-concept and self-esteem.

Defiance An overt form of communicating noncompliance; unmitigated, audacious rebellion against attempts to induce compliance.

Delegating style (of situational leadership) Nondirective leadership that has low task, low relationship emphasis; lets other group members shoulder the burdens once the leader deems them ready.

Democratic style A style of leadership that encourages participation and responsibility from group members.

Description A first-person report of how an individual feels, what the individual perceives to be true, and what behaviors have been observed in a specific context.

Destructive conflict Conflict that is characterized by domination, escalation, retaliation, competition, defensiveness, and inflexible communication patterns.

Devil's advocate A group role, sometimes assigned to a specific member, that requires the individual "for the sake of argument" to critique and question ideas and proposals that emerge during group discussion.

Dialectical inquiry A subgroup develops a counterproposal and defends it side by side with the group's initial proposal.

Directive style (of leadership) Leadership behavior that puts most of the emphasis on the group task with little concern for the social relationships among members.

Disruptive roles Informal group roles that serve individual needs or goals while impeding attainment of group goals.

Diverse membership Proportional representation by culture, ethnicity, gender, and age.

Dominance A form of power in which individuals attempt to gain power over others.

Duration One of two key indicators that distinguishes constructive and destructive anger; a measure of how long anger lasts.

Dyad Academic term for a two-person transaction.

Dynamic equilibrium A range in which systems can manage change effectively to promote growth and success without pushing the system to disaster.

E

Effectiveness How well we have progressed toward the achievement of goals.

Electronic brainstorming Occurs when group members sit at computer terminals and brainstorm ideas using a computer-based, file-sharing procedure.

Emoticons Typed icons or combinations of punctuation marks meant to indicate emotional tone; a substitute for nonverbal communication in written text messages.

Empathy Thinking and feeling what you perceive another to be thinking and feeling.

Emotional intelligence The ability to perceive, glean information from, and manage one's own and others' emotions

Empowerment The process of enhancing the capabilities and influence of individuals and groups.

Entropy A measure of a system's movement toward disorganization and eventual termination.

Environment The context within which a system operates.

Equifinality Accomplishment of similar or identical goals in highly diverse ways by different groups.

Ethics A set of standards for judging the moral correctness of our behavior.

Ethnocentrism A system for judging the moral correctness of human behavior by weighing that behavior against an agreed upon set of standards of what constitutes right and wrong.

Expanding the pie An integrative problem-solving technique in which creative means of increasing resources as a solution to a problem are generated.

Expert A person who not only has valuable and useful information for a group but also understands the information and knows how to use it to help the group.

Explicit norms Rules in groups that expressly identify acceptable behavior.

Extrinsic reward An external inducement such as money, grades, praise, recognition, or prestige that motivates us to behave or perform.

F

False dichotomy The tendency to view the world in terms of only two opposing possibilities when other possibilities are available, and to describe this dichotomy in the language of extremes.

Fantasies Prime element of symbolic convergence theory; dramatic stories that provide a shared interpretation of events that bind group members and offer them a shared identity.

Fantasy chain A string of connected stories that amplify fantasy; a fantasy theme.

Fantasy theme A consistent thread that runs through the stories that create a shared group identity.

Force field analysis A process for group implementation of decisions by anticipating the driving forces (those that encourage change) and restraining forces (those that resist change).

Formal role A position assigned by an organization or specifically designated by the group leader.

Forum discussion Permits members of an audience listening to a public speech, panel discussion, symposium, or debate to participate in a discussion of ideas presented.

Frame The way in which language shapes our perception of choices.

G

Glass ceiling An invisible barrier of subtle discrimination that excludes women and minorities from top jobs in corporate and professional America.

GRIT (Graduated and Reciprocated Initiatives in Tension reduction) A technique of de-escalating cycles of conflict.

Group A human communication system composed of three or more individuals interacting for the achievement of some common goal(s), who influence and are influenced by each other.

Group climate The emotional atmosphere, the enveloping tone that is created by the way we communicate in groups.

Group endorsement The acceptance by the group of a member's bid to play a specific role.

Grouphate The hostility people harbor from having to work in groups.

Group polarization The group tendency to make a decision after discussion that is more extreme, either riskier or more cautious, than the initial preferences of group members.

Group potency (and empowerment) The shared belief among team members that they can be effective as a team.

Group socialization The communication process in which new and established group members adjust to one another.

Groupthink A mode of thinking that people engage in when they are deeply involved in a cohesive in-group, and members' strivings for unanimity override their motivation to realistically appraise alternative courses of action.

H

Hard bargaining A negotiating from strength approach to conflicts of interest.

Hazing Any humiliating or dangerous activity expected of individuals to join a group, regardless of their willingness to participate in the activity.

Hidden agendas Personal goals of group members that are not revealed openly and that can interfere with group accomplishments.

High-context communication style Cultural tendency to emphasize the cultural context of a message when determining meaning.

Hindsight bias The tendency to overestimate our prior knowledge once we have been told the correct answers.

Hit-and-run confrontations Confronting contentious issues but leaving just enough time to make your point and not enough time for other group members to respond adequately.

Hybrid virtual groups Group members communicate mostly by electronic means but may occasionally meet face to face.

Hypercompetitiveness An excessive emphasis on defeating others to achieve one's goals.

I

Impact (and empowerment) The degree of significance that is given by those outside of the team, typically the team's organization, to the work produced by the team.

Impervious response Failure to acknowledge another person's communication effort either verbally or nonverbally.

Implicit norms Rules in groups that are indirectly indicated by uniformities in the behavior and expressed attitudes of members.

Individual accountability An established minimum standard of effort and performance for each team member to share the fruits of team success.

Individual achievement The attainment of a personal goal without having to defeat another person.

Individualism–collectivism dimension (of cultures) The degree to which cultural values emphasize either the individual or the group as paramount.

Inferences Conclusions about the unknown based on what is known.

Informal role A role that emerges in a group from the group transactions; it emphasizes functions, not positions.

Information overload The rate of information flow into a system and/or the complexity of that information exceeds the system's processing capacity; excessive input.

Information underload The amount of information available to a group for decision-making purposes is insufficient (input is inadequate).

Input Resources that come from outside a system, such as energy (sunlight, electricity), information (Internet, books), and people (a new group member).

Integrative problem solving Creative approach to conflicts of interest that searches for solutions that benefit everyone.

Intensity One of two key variables that distinguishes constructive from destructive anger; an indicator of the magnitude of feelings of anger.

Interdependence When all group members work together to achieve a desirable goal.

Interests The intangible motivations such as needs, desires, concerns, fears, and aspirations that lead a party in a conflict to take a position.

Interpersonal communication Communication between two people (dyads).

Intrinsic reward Enjoying what one does for its own sake; an inner motivation to continue doing what brings us pleasure.

K

Knowledge Learning the rules for and understanding what is required to be appropriate and effective in one's communication.

L

Laissez-faire style A do-nothing style of leadership; no leadership.

Language A structured system of symbols for sharing meaning.

Leader as completer (functional leadership viewpoint) Leaders are thought to perform those essential functions within a group that other members have failed to perform.

Leadership A leader–follower influence process directed toward positive change that reflects mutual purposes of group members and is largely achieved through competent communication.

Learning groups Groups that enhance members' knowledge, such as college seminar groups and class study groups.

Linguistic barriers (for group boundary control) The use of private vocabulary, or argot, peculiar to a specific group to create an in-group/out-group division.

Logical fallacies Errors in the process of reasoning.

Low-context communication style Cultural tendency to emphasize the explicit content of a message when determining meaning.

M

Maintenance roles Informal group roles that focus on social relationships among group members.

Material fallacies Errors in the process of using supporting materials as proof.

Meaningfulness (and empowerment) A team's perception that its tasks are important, valuable, and worthwhile.

Media richness The information-carrying capacity of each form of communication.

Mentors Knowledgeable individuals who have achieved some success in their profession or jobs and who assist individuals trying to get started in a line of work.

Metasearch engines An Internet tool that sends a keyword request to several search engines at once.

Mindsets Psychological and cognitive predispositions to see the world in a particular way, such as biases, preconceptions, and assumptions; they interfere with effective group decision making and problem solving.

Mixed message Positive verbal and negative nonverbal communication, or vice versa; contradictory verbal and nonverbal communication.

Multiple sequence model (of group decision emergence) Groups move along three activity tracks—task, relational, and topic—and take three principal paths to reaching decisions—unitary sequence, complex cyclic, and solution orientation.

Murphy's law Anything that can go wrong likely will go wrong, somewhere, sometime.

Music groups Type of group that provides a creative outlet for members who participate in choirs, bands, and the like.

N

Narcissistic leadership Egocentric leadership; such leaders put their own needs ahead of the team's needs.

Negative climate Group members do not feel valued, supported, and respected; trust is minimal; and members perceive that they are not treated well.

Negative reciprocation A form of retaliation for perceived wrongs from group members.

Negative synergy Group members working together produce a worse result than expected based on perceived individual skills and abilities of members.

Negotiation A process by which a joint decision is made by two or more parties.

Neighborhood groups Groups that provide a sense of community, such as homeowners associations and PTAs.

Network A structured pattern of information flow and personal contact.

Networking A form of group empowerment in which individuals with similar backgrounds, skills, and goals come together on a fairly regular basis and share information that will assist members in pursuing goals.

Nominal group technique Individuals work by themselves generating lists of ideas on a problem, then convene in a group where they merely record the ideas generated and interaction occurs only to clarify ideas. Rankings of each member's five favorite ideas are averaged with the highest average ideas selected by the group.

Nonconformity Violation of a group norm.

Nonroutine task Work to be accomplished that requires problem solving, has few set procedures, and has a high level of uncertainty.

Nonverbal communication Sharing meaning with others without using words.

Norm of group interest A collective prescription that group members should pursue maximum group outcomes (winning at all costs), even if this means acting hypercompetitively against other groups when members may privately not wish to do so.

Norms Rules that regulate behavior in groups.

O

Openness Degree of continuous interchange with the environment outside of a system.

Output The continual results of the group's throughput (the transformation of input), such as decisions made, solutions created, and projects completed.

P

Panel discussion A small group of participants who engage in an exchange of information and ideas on a specific issue or problem before an audience.

Paraphrasing A concise response to a speaker that states the essence of the speaker's content in the listener's own words.

Parliamentary procedure A set of hundreds of rules for conducting meetings.

Participant-observer A self-monitoring process whereby you assume a detached view of yourself communicating in groups.

Participative style (of leadership) Leadership behavior that puts a balanced emphasis on both task and social dimensions of the group.

Pattern recognition A means of coping with information overload; one way to narrow the search for information by noticing patterns that indicate relevant versus irrelevant information.

PERT (Program Evaluation Review Technique) A systematic process for group implementation of decisions.

Physical barriers (of group boundary control) Includes walls, locked doors, an inconvenient location in a building, and partitions and cubicles in offices to restrict input.

Positions Concrete things that one party wants in a negotiation.

Positive climate Group members perceive that they are valued, supported, and treated well.

Power The ability to influence the attainment of goals sought by yourself or others.

Power distance dimension (of cultures) Degree to which different cultures vary in their attitudes concerning the appropriateness of power imbalances.

Power indicators Ways in which relative degrees of power are communicated in groups.

Power resource Anything that enables individuals to move toward their own goals or to interfere with another's actions.

Prevention A form of power in which group members resist or defy attempts to dominate them by other group members.

Primary groups Groups that provide a sense of belonging and affection such as family and friends.

Primary tension The initial jitters and uneasiness felt by individuals when they first join a group.

Principled negotiation Interest-based bargaining process that uses a collaborative approach to negotiating conflicts of interest, focusing on merits of arguments, not on hard bargaining strategies.

Probing Seeking additional information from a speaker by asking questions.

Problem solving Process whereby groups decide on solutions to problems.

Productivity The result of the efficient and effective accomplishment of a group task.

Project groups Groups that work on specific tasks such as self-managing work teams and task forces.

Provisionalism Qualifying statements and avoiding absolute claims.

Pseudo-teams Small groups that only half-heartedly exhibit the several criteria that constitute a true team. They give the appearance of being teams and of engaging in teamwork without exhibiting the substance of teams.

Psychological barriers (for group boundary control) Anything that makes an individual feel that he or she is not a true member of a group.

Psychological fallacies Claims that rest on emotional appeal rather than logic and evidence.

Psychological reactance The more someone tries to control us by telling us what to do, the more we are inclined to resist such efforts, even to do the opposite.

Psychopath Someone who has no conscience and feels no remorse or empathy.

Public speaking Communication in a formal setting between a clearly identified speaker and an audience of listeners.

Purpose statement A concise, precise, declarative statement phrased in simple, clear language that provides both the general purpose (to inform or persuade) and the specific purpose (exactly what you want the audience to understand, believe, feel, or do).

Q

Qualifier Degree of truth of the claim (such as highly probable, plausible, possible, and so forth).

Quality circles Teams composed of workers who volunteer to work on a similar task and attempt to solve a particular problem.

Question of fact Asks whether something is true and to what extent.

Question of policy Asks whether a specific course of action should be undertaken to solve a problem.

Question of value Asks for an evaluation of the desirability of an object, idea, event, or person.

R

Rationalization of disconfirmation Inventing superficial, glib alternative explanations for information that contradicts beliefs.

Readiness How ready a person is to perform a particular task; determined by ability and willingness of the person.

Reciprocal pattern A tit-for-tat interaction between rivals during a conflict negotiation.

Reflective thinking A set of logical steps that incorporate the scientific method of defining, analyzing, and solving problems.

Reformed sinner strategy Negotiating strategy in which one party initially competes or acts tough, then cooperates and relaxes demands.

Reframing A creative process of breaking a mindset by placing the problem in a different frame of reference.

Relationship dimension (of messages) How messages define or redefine the relationship between group members.

Reminder role A formally designated role in which the individual assigned the role raises questions in a nonaggressive manner regarding collective inferential error, confirmation bias, false dichotomies, and any of the myriad symptoms of groupthink that may arise during group discussions.

Reservations Exceptions or rebuttals that diminish the force of the claim.

Resistance A covert form of communicating noncompliance, often duplicitous and manipulative.

Ripple effect A chain reaction that begins in one part of a system and spreads across an entire system.

Role A pattern of expected behavior associated with parts that members play in groups.

Role conflict When group members play roles in different groups that contradict each other.

Role fixation The acting out of a specific role, and only that role, no matter what the situation might require.

Role flexibility The capacity to recognize the current requirements of the group and then enact the role-specific behaviors most appropriate in the given context.

Role reversal Stepping into a role distinctly different from or opposite of a role one usually plays.

Role specialization When an individual group member settles into his or her primary role.

Role status The relative importance, prestige, or power accorded a particular role.

Routine task Work to be accomplished in which the group performs processes and procedures that have little variability and little likelihood of change.

Rule Prescription that indicates what you should or shouldn't do in specific contexts.

Rule of seven Each member added to a group of seven reduces decision-making effectiveness by about 10%.

S

Search engine An Internet tool that computer-generates indexes of web pages that match, or link with, keywords typed in a search window.

Secondary tension The stress and strain that occurs within a group when disagreements and conflicts emerge and decisions must be made.

Self-help groups Groups that provide social support.

Self-justification Providing excuses that absolve us of blame.

Self-managing work teams Teams that complete an entire task under self-regulation.

Selling style (of situational leadership) Directive leadership that is high task, high relationship in emphasis.

Sensitivity Receptive accuracy whereby you can detect, decode, and comprehend signals sent in groups.

Servant leadership A perspective on leadership that places the emphasis on the needs of followers and helps them to become more knowledgeable, freer, more autonomous.

Service groups Groups that provide social service to others, such as fraternities and sororities and Rotary and Lions clubs.

Shift response An attention-getting initiative by listeners in which the listeners attempt to shift the focus of attention from others to themselves by changing the topic of discussion.

Signposts A speech organizational technique that indicates exactly where you are in your speech so the audience can follow along easily.

Skill (in communicating) The successful performance of a communication behavior and the ability to repeat such a behavior.

Smoothing Collaborative component of conflict management characterized by acting to calm agitated feelings during a conflict episode.

Social compensation A group member's increased motivation to work harder on a group task to counterbalance the lackluster performance of other members.

Social dimension (of groups) The relationships that form among members in a group and their impact on the group as a whole.

Social groups Groups that provide social connections and whose goal is to help others.

Social loafing The tendency of a group member to exert less effort on a task when working in a group than when working individually.

Social networks Groups that communicate via Facebook, Twitter, and other social networking sites.

Soft bargaining Negotiating strategy that typically yields to pressure from hard bargainers.

Stand aside A team member continues to have reservations about the group decision but, when confronted, does not wish to block the group consensus.

Structuration theory Explains that systems, such as groups, establish structures for discussion and problem solving by creating rules, roles, norms, and power distribution to permit the system to function effectively and sustain itself.

Structure The systematic interrelation of all parts to the whole, providing form and shape.

Style shift A flexible adaptation of one's communication to the changes in a system.

Superordinate goals A specific kind of cooperative goal that overrides differences that members may have because the goal supersedes less important competitive goals.

Support groups Groups that provide social support to address life problems.

Supportive communication Patterns of communication characterized by description, problem orientation, empathy, assertiveness, equality, and provisionalism.

Support response An attention-giving process in which listeners focus their attention on another group member, not on themselves, during discussion.

Symbolic convergence theory Focuses on how group members communicating with each other develop and share stories (fantasies) to create a convergence or group identity that is larger and more coherent than the isolated experiences of individual group members.

Symbols Representations of referents (whatever the symbol refers to).

Symposium A relatively structured group presentation to an audience composed of several individuals who present uninterrupted speeches with contrasting points of view on a central topic.

Synchronous media Those forms of communicating that permit simultaneous interactions among group members modeled after face-to-face meetings.

Synergy Group performance from joint action of members exceeds expectations based on perceived abilities and skills of individual group members.

System A set of interconnected parts working together to form a whole in the context of a changing environment.

T

Task dimension (of groups) The work to be performed by a group.

Task roles Informal group roles that move the group toward attainment of its goals.

Team A small number of people with complementary skills who act as an interdependent unit, are equally committed to a common mission, subscribe to a cooperative approach to accomplish that mission, and hold themselves accountable for team performance.

Team accountability The team, rather than individual members, assumes responsibility for success and failure.

Technology A tool to accomplish some purpose.

Telling style (of situational leadership) Directive leadership that is high task, low relationship in emphasis.

Throughput The process of transforming input into output to keep a system functioning.

Tit-for-tat strategy Negotiating strategy in which one either cooperates or competes with rivals, depending on what the other party does; you give back what you receive.

Traits Relatively enduring characteristics of an individual that highlight differences between people and that are displayed in most situations.

Transaction A process in which each person communicating is both a sender and a receiver simultaneously, not merely a sender or receiver, and all parties influence each other.

Transactional leadership Leadership often associated with management that typically strives to maintain the status quo efficiently.

Transformational leadership Leadership often associated with changing the status quo; frequently linked to charisma.

Twenty percent rule The minimum standard to combat gender and ethnic bias in groups; when no less than 20 percent of group members are composed of women and minorities, discrimination against these groups drops substantially.

V

Values The most deeply felt views of what is deemed good, worthwhile, or ethically right.

Verbal dominance A verbal form of dominance characterized by competitive interrupting, contradicting, berating, and high quantity of speech.

Virtual group/team A small group whose members rarely interact face to face and who mostly communicate by means of electronic technologies.

Virtual library A search tool that combines Internet technology and standard library techniques for cataloging and evaluating information.

Vital functions (functional leadership viewpoint) Sees leaders performing a list of vital group functions different in kind and/or degree from other members.

Vividness effect A graphic, outrageous, shocking, controversial, dramatic event draws our attention and sticks in our minds, prompting us to overvalue such events and undervalue statistical information that shows patterns and trends that often contradict the sensational event.

W

Warrant The reasoning used to link the data to the claim; usually assumed, not stated directly.

Wikipedia Online encyclopedia that allows almost anyone to contribute.

Workplace bullying A persistent form of badgering, abuse, and "hammering away" at targets who have less power than their bullies.

References

Abrams, D., Weick, M., Thomas, D., Colbe, H., & Franklin, K. M. (2010). On-line ostracism affects children differently from adolescents and adults. *British Journal of Developmental Psychology* 29, 110–123.

Abramson, J. (1994). *We, the jury*. New York: Basic Books.

Abril, P. S. (2008). A (My)Space of one's own: On privacy and online social networks. *Northwestern Journal of Technology and Intellectual Property*. [Online]. Available: http://www.law.north western.edu/journals/njtip/v6/n1/4

Acuff, F. L. (1997). *How to negotiate anything with anyone anywhere around the world*. New York: American Management Association.

Adkins, M., & Brashers, D. E. (1995). The power of language in computer-mediated groups. *Management Communication Quarterly*, 8, 289–322.

Adler, N. J. (2001). *From Boston to Beijing: Managing with a world view*. Cincinnati, OH: South-Western.

Adler, N. J. (2002). *International dimensions of organizational behavior*. Cincinnati, OH: South-Western.

Adler, R. (1977). *Confidence in communication: A guide to assertive and social skills*. New York: Holt, Rinehart & Winston.

Adler, R. B., Elmhorst, J. M., & Lucas, K. (2013). *Communicating at work: Principles and practices for business and the professions*. New York: McGraw-Hill.

Adler, R. B., & Proctor, R. F. (2013). *Looking out/looking in*. Belmont, CA: Thomson Wadsworth.

Aglionby, J. (2002, November 2). Singapore's fine culture keeps people in line. *Guardian Unlimited*. [Online]. Available: http://www.guardian.co.uk/ crime/article/0,2763,824569,00.html

Aguayo, R. (1990). *Dr. Deming: The American who taught the Japanese about quality*. New York: Simon & Schuster.

Aldhous, P. (2012, March 9). Fukushima's fate inspires nuclear safety rethink. *New Scientist*. [Online]. Available: http://www.newscientist .com/article/dn21556-fukushimas-fate-inspired-nuclear-safety-rethink.html

Alge, B. J., Wietfhoff, C., & Klien, H. J. (2003). When does medium matter? Knowledge-building experiences and opportunities in decision-making teams. *Organizational Behavior and Human Decision Processes*, 91, 26–37.

Allan, E. J., & Madden, M. (2008, March 11) Hazing in view: College students at risk; initial findings from the National Study of Student Hazing. *The University of Maine*. [Online]. Available: http://www.umaine.edu/ hazingstudy/hazinginview1.htm

Allen, T. D., McManus, S. E., & Russell, J. E. A. (1999). Newcomer socialization and stress: Formal peer relationships as a source of support. *Journal of Vocational Behavior*, 54, 453–470.

AMA 2010 critical skills survey. (2010). *American Management Association*. [Online]. Available: http://www.p21.org/documents/critical%20 Skills%20Survey%20Executive%20Summary .pdf

America's best colleges. (2009, August 5). *Forbes .com*. [Online]. Available: http://www.forbes .com/lists/2009/94/colleges-09_University-of-Wisconsin-Madison_94518.html

America's best colleges. (2010, August 11). *Forbes*. [Online]. Available: http://www.forbes.com/ lists/2010/94/best-colleges-10_Americas-Best-Colleges_Rank.html

America's Top Colleges. (2013, July 24). *Forbes*. [Online]. Available: http://www.forbes.com/ top-colleges/list/

Andersen, J. (1988). Communication competency in the small group. In R. Cathcart & L. Samovar (Eds.), *Small group communication: A reader*. Dubuque, IA: Wm. C. Brown & Company.

Andersen, P. (1999). *Nonverbal communication: Forms and functions.* Mountain View, CA: Mayfield.

Andersen, P. A. (2006). The evolution of biological sex differences in communication. In K. Dindia & D. J. Canary (Eds.), *Sex differences and similarities in communication.* Mahwah, NJ: Lawrence Erlbaum.

Anderson, C. M., Riddle, B. L., & Martin, M. M. (1999). Socialization processes in groups. In L. R. Frey (Ed.), *Handbook of group communication theory & research.* Thousand Oaks, CA: Sage.

Anderson, C., John, O. P., Keltner, D., & Kring, A. M. (2001). Who attains social status: Effects of personality and physical attractiveness in social groups. *Journal of Personality and Social Psychology*, 81, 116–132.

Anderson, K., & Leaper, C. (1998). Meta-analyses of gender effects on conversational interruption: Who, what, when, where, and how. *Sex Roles*, 39, 225–252.

Anderson, N. (2012, March 15). Why do people resist change? Leadership survey findings (1072 managers, 510 CEOs, 80 countries). *The Crispian Advantage.* [Online]. Available: http://thecrispianadvantage.com/2012/03/15/top-reasons-for-resistance-to-change-1072-managers-15-counries/

Andersson, L. L. (2010). Leadership 2.0 through Web 2.0. *International Leadership Association Conference.* [Online]. Available: http://www.ila-net.org/conferences/Program3.asp?ProgramDBID=96

Anti-hazing law and jail terms in Fla. may spur other states, expert says. (2007, January 31). *Chronicle of Higher Education News Blog.* [Online]. Available: http://chronicle.com/news/article/1587/anti-hazing-law-and-jail-terms-in-fla-may-supr-other-states-expert-says

Antonakis, J., Fenley, M, & Liechti, S. (2011). Can charisma be taught? Tests of two interventions. *Academy of Management Learning & Education*, 10, 374–396.

Appleby, J., & Davis, R. (2001, March 1). Teamwork used to be a money saver, now it's a lifesaver. *USA Today*, pp. 1B–2B.

Are six heads as good as twelve? (2004, May 28). *American Psychological Association.* [Online]. Available: http://www.apa.org/research/action/jury.aspx

Aronson, E. (2012). *The social animal.* New York: Worth.

Aronson, E., Wilson, T. D., & Akert, R. M. (2013). *Social psychology.* New York: Pearson.

Arrow, H., & Crosson, S. (2003). Musical chairs: Membership dynamics in self-organized group formation. *Small Group Research*, 34, 523–556.

Asch, S. E. (1955). Opinions and social pressure. *Scientific American*, 19, 31–35.

Aube, C., Rousseau, V., & Tremblay, S. (2011). Team size and quality of group experience: The more the merrier? *Group Dynamics: Theory, Research, and Practice*, 15, 357–375.

Avolio, B. J. (2007). Promoting more integrative strategies for leadership theory-building. *American Psychologist*, 62, 25–33.

Axelrod, R. (1984). *The evolution of cooperation.* New York: Basic Books.

Axelrod, R., Riolo, R., & Cohen, M. (2002). Beyond geography: Cooperation with persistent links in the absence of clustered neighborhoods. *Personality and Social Psychology*, 4, 341–346.

Baba, M. L., Gluesing, J., Ratner, H., & Wagner, K. H. (2004). The contexts of knowing: Natural history of a globally distributed team. *Journal of Organizational Behavior*, 25, 547–587.

Babcock, L. (2002). *Do graduate students negotiate their job offers?* Carnegie Mellon University. Unpublished manuscript.

Babcock, L., & Laschever, S. (2007). *Women don't ask: The high cost of avoiding negotiation—and positive strategies for change.* New York: Bantam.

Babiak, P., & Hare, R. D. (2006). *Snakes in suits: When psychopaths go to work.* New York: HarperCollins.

Bach, G., & Goldberg, H. (1974). *Creative aggression.* New York: Avon.

Baghai, M., & Quigley, J. (2011). *As one: Individual action, collective power.* New York: Portfolio.

Baker, G. (2002). The effects of synchronous collaborative technologies on decision making:

A study of virtual teams. *Information Resources Management Journal*, 15, 79–93.

Balkundi, P., Barsness, Z., & Michael, J. H. (2009). Unlocking the influence of leadership network structures on team conflict and viability. *Small Group Research*, 40, 301–322.

Ball, A. L. (2010, May 28). Are 5,001 Facebook friends one too many? *The New York Times*. [Online]. Available: http://www.nytimes.com/2010/05/30 fashion/30FACEBOOK.html?pagewanted=print

Banaji, M. R. (2010, December). Presidential column: Wikipedia is the encyclopedia that anybody can edit. But have you? *Observer*. [Online]. Available: http://www.psychologicalscience .org/index.php/publications/observer/2010/ december-10/anyone-can-edit-wikipedia-have-you.html

Barge, J., & Hirokawa, R. (1989). Toward a communication competency model of group leadership. *Small Group Behavior*, 20, 167–189.

Barinaga, E. (2007). "Cultural diversity" at work: "National culture" as a discourse organizing an international project group. *Human Relations*, 60, 315–340.

Barker, V. E., Abrams, J. R., Tiyaamornwong, V., Seibold, D. R., Duggan, A., Park, H. S., & Sebastian, M. (2000). New contexts for relational communication in groups. *Small Group Research*, 31, 470–503.

Barki, H., & Pinsonneault, A. (2001). Small group brainstorming and idea quality: Is electronic brainstorming the most effective approach? *Small Group Research*, 32, 158–205.

Barnes, S. B. (2003). *Computer-mediated communication*. New York: Allyn & Bacon.

BarNir, A. (1998). Can group- and issue-related factors predict choice shift? *Small Group Research*, 29, 308–338.

Baron, R. (1988). Negative effects of destructive criticism: Impact on conflict self-efficacy and task performance. *Journal of Applied Psychology*, 73, 199–207.

Baron, R. (1990). Countering the effects of destructive criticism: The relative efficacy of four interventions. *Journal of Applied Psychology*, 75, 235–243.

Barron, L. A. (2003). Ask and you shall receive: Gender differences in negotiators' beliefs about requests for a higher salary. *Human Relations*, 56, 635–662.

Barry, D. (1991). *Dave Barry's guide to life*. New York: Wings Books.

Baruah, J., & Paulus, P. B. (2008). Effects of training on idea generation in groups. *Small Group Research*, 39, 523–541.

Bass, B. M., & Bass, R. (2008). *The Bass handbook of leadership: Theory, research, and managerial applications*. New York: Free Press.

Bass, M. (1960). *Leadership, psychology and organizational behavior*. Westport, CT: Greenwood Press.

Baumeister, R. F., & Leary, M. R. (1995). The need to belong: Desire for interpersonal attachments as a fundamental human motivation. *Psychological Bulletin*, 117, 497–529.

Bazeley, M. (2005, August 7). Brave new Web. *San Jose Mercury News*, pp. 1A, 26A.

Bazerman, M., & Neale, M. (1983). Heuristics in negotiation: Limitations to dispute resolution effectiveness. In M. Bazerman & R. Lewicki (Eds.), *Negotiating in organizations*. Beverly Hills, CA: Sage.

BBC Two Programmes — How Violent Are You? (2009). [Online]. Available: http://www.bbc.co .uk/programmes/b00kk4bz

Beal, D. J., Cohen, R. R., Burke, M. J., & McLendon, C. I. (2003). Cohesion and performance in groups: A meta-analytic clarification of construct relations. *Journal of Applied Psychology*, 88, 989–1004.

Bechler, C., & Johnson, S. (1995). Leadership and listening: A study of member perceptions. *Small Group Research*, 26, 77–85.

Becker, J. A. H., Halbesleben, J. R. B., & O'Hair, H. D. (2005). Defensive communication and burnout in the workplace: The mediating role of leader-member exchange. *Communication Research Reports*, 22, 143–150.

Behfar, K., Peterson, R., Mannix, E. A., & Trochim, W. (2008). The critical role of conflict resolution in teams: A close look at the links between conflict type, conflict management strategies, and team outcomes. *Journal of Applied Psychology*, 93, 170–180.

Belbin, R. (1996). *Team roles at work*. London: Butterworth-Heinemann.

Bell, M. (1974). The effects of substantive and affective conflict in problem-solving discussions. *Speech Monographs*, 41, 19–23.

Benenson, J. F., Gordon, A. J., & Roy, R. (2000). Children's evaluative appraisals of competition in tetrads versus dyads. *Small Group Research*, 31, 635–652.

Benenson, J. F., Nicolson, C., Waite, A., Roy, R., & Simpson, A. (2001). The influence of group size on children's competitive behavior. *Child Development*, 72, 921–934.

Benenson, J. F., Roy, R., Waite, A., Goldbaum, S., Linders, L., & Simpson, A. (2002). Greater discomfort as a proximate cause of sex differences in competition. *Merrill-Palmer Quarterly*, 48, 225–248.

Benne, K., & Sheats, P. (1948). Functional roles of group members. *Journal of Social Issues*, 4, 41–49.

Bennis, W. (1976). *The unconscious conspiracy: Why leaders can't lead*. New York: AMACOM.

Bennis, W. (2007). The challenges of leadership in the modern world. *American Psychologist*, 62, 2–5.

Bennis, W., & Biederman, P. (1997). *Organizing genius: The secrets of creative collaboration*. New York: Addison-Wesley.

Bennis, W., & Nanus, B. (1985). *Leaders: The strategies for taking charge*. New York: Harper & Row.

Bernieri, F. J. (2001). Toward a taxonomy of interpersonal sensitivity. In J. A. Hall & F. J. Bernieri (Eds.), *Interpersonal sensitivity: Theory and measurement*. Mahwah, NJ: Lawrence Erlbaum.

Berscheid, E., & Reis, H. T. (1998). Attraction and close relationships. In D. T. Gilbert, S. T. Fiske, & G. Lindzey (Eds.), *The handbook of social psychology* (Vol. 2). New York: McGraw-Hill.

Best colleges: Top public schools: National universities. (2009, August 19). *U.S. News and World Report*. [Online]. Available: http://www.usnews.com/articles/education/best-colleges/2009/08/19/how-we-calculate-the-college-rankins_print.htm

Bettinghaus, E., & Cody, M. (1987). *Persuasive communication*. New York: Holt, Rinehart & Winston.

Binge drinking statistics. (2013). *The Century Council*. [Online]. Available: http://www.centurycouncil.org/binge-drinking/statistics

Black, K. (1990, March). Can getting mad get the job done? *Working Woman*, pp. 86–90.

Black enterprise publishes exclusive registry of African Americans on corporate boards. (2013, September 6). *Black Enterprise Media Kit*. [Online]. Available: http://www.blackenterprise.com/mediakit/2013/09/06/black-enterprise-publishes-exclusive-registry-of-african-americans-on-corporate-boards/

Blake, R., & Mouton, J. (1964). *The managerial grid*. Houston: Gulf Publishing.

Blass, T. (2000). *Obedience to authority: Current perspectives on the Milgram paradigm*. Mahwah, NJ: Lawrence Erlbaum.

Blenko, M. W., Mankins, M. C., & Rogers, P. (2010). *Decide & deliver: 5 steps to breakthrough performance in your organization*. Boston: Harvard Business Review Press.

Bock, R., & Miller, M. G. (2005, August 24). Teens' driving riskier with male passenger. *NIH News*. [Online]. Available: http://www.nih.gov/news/pr/aug2005/nichd-24a.htm

Bodard, G. (2008, January 20). Information behaviour of the researcher of the future (report). *The Stoa Consortium*. [Online]. Available: http://www.stoa.org?p=767

Bok, S. (1978). *Lying: Moral choice in public and private life*. New York: Random House.

Bolman, L. G., & Deal, T. E. (1992). What makes a team work? *Organizational Dynamics*, 21, 34–44.

Bolton, R. (1979). *People skills: How to assert yourself, listen to others and resolve conflicts*. New York: Simon & Schuster.

Bond, M., Wang, K., Leung, K., & Giacalone, R. (1985). How are responses to verbal insults related to cultural collectivism and power distances? *Journal of Cross-Cultural Psychology*, 16, 111–127.

Bond, R., & Smith, P. B. (1996). Culture and conformity: A meta-analysis of studies using Asch's line judgment task. *Psychological-Bulletin*, 119, 111–137.

Borisoff, D., & Victor, D. (1989). *Conflict management: A communication skills approach*. Englewood Cliffs, NJ: Prentice Hall.

Bormann, E. G. (1986). Symbolic convergence theory and group decision making. In R. Y. Hirokawa

& M. S. Poole (Eds.), *Communication and group decision making.* Beverly Hills, CA: Sage.

Bormann, E. G. (1990). *Small group communication: Theory and practice.* New York: Harper & Row.

Bormann, E. G., & Bormann, N. (1988). *Effective small group communication.* Edina, MN: Burgess Publishing.

Bostrom, R. (1970). Patterns of communicative interaction in small groups. *Speech Monographs,* 37, 257–263.

Boudreau, J. (2007, August 12). Beijing brushes up on its English skills. *San Jose Mercury News,* p. 17A.

Boudreau, J. (2011, January 4). Facebook's value: $50 billion. *San Jose Mercury News,* p. D1, D2.

Bower, S., & Bower, G. (1976). *Asserting yourself.* Reading, MA: Addison-Wesley.

Bowman, J. M., & Wittenbaum, G. M. (2012). Time pressure affects process and performance in hidden-profile groups. *Small Group Research,* 43, 295–314.

Boyd, R. (1996, June 9). Survival of the most cooperative? New insights into Darwin's theory. *San Jose Mercury News,* p. 1C.

Brannigan, M. (1997, May 30). Why Delta Air Lines decided it was time for CEO to take off. *Wall Street Journal,* pp. A1, A8.

Brauer, M., Judd, C. M., & Gliner, M. D. (1995). The effects of repeated expressions on attitude polarization during group discussion. *Journal of Personality and Social Psychology,* 68, 1014–1029.

Brehm, J. (1972). *Responses to loss of freedom: A theory of psychological resistance.* Morristown, NJ: General Learning Press.

Brescoll, V. L., Dawson, E., & Uhlmann, E. L. (2011). Hard won and easily lost: The fragile status of leaders in gender-stereotype—incongruent occupations. *Psychological Science,* 21.

Brett, J. (1990). Designing systems for resolving disputes in organizations. *American Psychologist,* 45, 162–170.

Brett, J. M., Shapiro, D. L., & Lytle, A. L. (1998). Breaking the bonds of reciprocity in negotiations. *Academy of Management Journal,* 41, 410–425.

Brewer, C. S., Kovner, C. T., Obeidat, R. F., & Budin, W. C. (2013). Positive work environments of early-career registered nurses and the correlation with physician verbal abuse. *Nursing Outlook,* 61, 408–416.

Brin, D. (1998). *The transparent society: Will technology force us to choose between privacy and freedom?* Reading, MA: Addison-Wesley.

Brislin, R. (1993). *Understanding culture's influence on behavior.* Fort Worth, TX: Harcourt Brace Jovanovich.

Brock, T. (1968). Implications of commodity theory for value change. In A. Greenwald, T. Brock, & T. Ostrom (Eds.), *Psychological foundations of attitudes.* New York: Academic Press.

Brodbeck, F. C., Kerschreiter, R., Mojzisch, A., Frey, D., & Schultz-Hardt, S. (2002). The dissemination of critical, unshared information in decision-making groups: The effects of prediscussion dissent. *European Journal of Social Psychology,* 32, 35–56.

Bronson, P., & Merryman, A. (2011). *Nurtureshock: New thinking about children.* New York: Twelve.

Brown, D. (2013, December 29). Living in a digital minefield. *San Jose Mercury News,* pp. A1 & A16.

Brown, H. (2010, January 22). Business schools sweeten lures for women. *WeNews.* [Online]. Available: http://womensenews.org/story/business/100121/business-schools-sweeten-lures-women

Brownlow, S. (2003). Gender-linked linguistic behavior in television interviews. *Sex Roles: A Journal of Research.* [Online]. Available: http://www.findarticles.com/

Bruess, C. J., & Pearson, J. C. (1996). Gendered patterns in family communication. In J. Wood (Ed.), *Gendered relationships.* Newbury Park, CA: Sage.

Bryant, M., & Higgins, V. (2010). Self-confessed troublemakers: An interactionist view of deviance during organizational change. *Human Relations,* 63, 249–277.

Buckingham, M., & Coffman, C. (1999). *First, break all the rules: What the world's greatest managers do differently.* New York: Simon & Schuster.

Buckingham, M., & Coffman, C. W. (2002a, Spring). Item 9: Doing quality work. *Gallup*

Management Journal. [Online]. Available: http://www.gallupjournal.com/q12Center/articles/19990517.asp

Buckingham, M., & Coffman, C. W. (2002b, Spring). Recognition or praise. *Gallup Management Journal.* [Online]. Available: http://www.gallupjournal.com/q12Center/articles/19990412.asp

Buckley, M., Laursen, J., & Otarola, V. (2009). Strengthening physician-nurse partnerships to improve quality and patient safety. *Physician Executive Journal*, 35, 24–28.

Burfeind, M., & Witkemper, T. (2010, July 14). TeleNav-commisioned survey suggests both genders have similar views on abiding by and breaking the rules of the road. *TeleNav.* [Online]. Available: http://www.telenav.com/about/driving-behavior/

Burger, J. (2007, December). Replicating Milgram. *APS Observer.* [Online]. Available: http://www.psychologicalscience.org/observer/getArticle.cfm?id=2264

Burggraf, C., & Sillars, A. (1987). A critical examination of sex differences in marital communication. *Communication Monographs*, 54, 276–294.

Burke, M., Kraut, R., & Joyce, E. (2010). Membership claims and requests: Conversation level newcomer socialization strategies in online groups. *Small Group Research*, 41, 4–40.

Burnett, A., & Badzinski, D. M (2005). Judge nonverbal communication on trial: Do mock trial jurors notice? *Journal of Communication*, 55, 209–224.

Burns, C., Barton, K., & Kerby, S. (2012, July 12). The state of diversity in today's workforce. *American Progress.* [Online]. Available: http://www.americanprogress.org/issues/labor/report/2012/07/12/11938/the-state-of-diversity-in-todays-workforce/

Burns, J. (1978). *Leadership.* New York: Harper & Row.

Bushman, B. J. (2002). Does venting anger feed or extinguish the flame? Catharsis, rumination, distraction, anger, and aggressive responding. *Personality and Social Psychology Bulletin*, 28, 724–731.

Bushman, B. J., Bonacci, A. M., Pedersen, W. C., Vasquez, E. A., & Miller, N. (2005). Chewing on it can chew you up: Effects of rumination on triggered displaced anger. *Journal of Personality and Social Psychology*, 88, 969–983.

Buzaglo, G., & Wheelan, S. (1999). Facilitating work team effectiveness: Case studies from Central America. *Small Group Research*, 30, 108–129.

Byrne, J. (1999). *Chainsaw: The notorious career of Al Dunlap in the era of profit-at-any-price.* New York: HarperBusiness.

Cairncross, F. (1997). *The death of distance: The trendspotter's guide to new communications.* Boston: Harvard Business School Press.

Callahan, D. (2004). *The cheating culture: Why more Americans are doing wrong to get ahead.* New York: Harcourt.

Campbell, S., & Larson, J. (2012). Pubic speaking anxiety: Comparing face-to-face and web-based speeches. *Journal of Instructional Pedagogies.* [Online]. Available: http://www.aabi.com/manuscripts/121343.pdf

Canary, D. J., & Lakey, S. (2013). *Strategic conflict.* New York: Routledge.

Cappiello, D. (2011, January 11). Gulf oil spill commission report: Increased regulation, more liability needed. *Huffington Post.* [Online]. Available: http://www.huffingtonpost.com/2011/01/11/gulf-oil-spill-commission_n_807353.html

Carey, H. R., & Laughlin, P. R. (2012). Groups perform better than the best individuals on letters-to-numbers problems: Effects of induced strategies. *Group Processes and Intergroup Relations*, 15, 231–242.

Carletta, J., Garrod, S., & Fraser-Krauss, H. (1998). Placement of authority and communication patterns in workplace groups: The consequences for innovation. *Small Group Research*, 29, 531–559.

Carnevale, P., & Probst, T. (1998). Social values and social conflict in creative problem solving. *Journal of Personality and Social Psychology*, 74, 1300–1309.

Carney, D. R., Cuddy, A. J. C., & Yap, A. J. (2010). Power posing: Brief nonverbal displays affect neuroendocrine levels and risk tolerance. *Psychological Science*, 21, 1363–1368.

Carr, A. (2010, May 18). The most important leadership quality for CEOs? Creativity. *Fast Company*. [Online]. Available: http://www.fastcompany.com/1648943/most-important-leadership-quality-ceos-creativity

Carr, N. (2010). *The Shallows: What the Internet Is Doing to Our Brains*. New York: W. W. Norton & Company.

Carreon, C. (2005, March 1). Internet sites caught up in gangs' wars of words. *San Jose Mercury News*, pp. 1A, 9A.

Carron, A., & Spink, K. (1995). The group size-cohesion relationship in minimal groups. *Small Group Research*, 26, 86–105.

Carter, S., & West, M. (1998). Reflexivity, effectiveness, and mental health in BBC-TV production teams. *Small Group Research*, 29, 583–601.

Carton, J. (1996). The differential effects of tangible rewards and praise on intrinsic motivation: A comparison of cognitive evaluation theory and operant theory. *Behavior Analyst*, 19, 237–255.

Caruso, E. M., Epley, N., & Bazerman, M. H. (2006). The costs and benefits of undoing egocentric responsibility assessments in groups. *Journal of Personality and Social Psychology*, 91, 857–871.

Catalyst 2013 census of Fortune 500: Still no progress after years of no progress. (2013, December 10). *Catalyst*. [Online]. Available: http://www.catalyst.org/media/catalyst-2013-census-fortune-500-still-no-progress-after-years-no-progress

Catchpole, K., Mishra, A., Handa, A., & McCullough, P. (2008). Teamwork and error in the operating room: Analysis of skills and roles. *Annals of Surgery*, 247, 699–706.

Caulderwood, K. (2013, October 8). Delta Airlines (DAL) CEO Richard Anderson charts independent course: Buying a refinery, half of a rival, and avoiding gas guzzlers. *International Business Times*. [Online]. Available: http://www.ibtimes.com/delta-air-lines-dal-ceo-richard-anderson-charts-independent-course-buying-refinery-half-rival

Chamberlin, J. (2010, October). Study reveals startling abuse of teachers by students, even parents. *Upfront*. [Online]. Available: http://www.apa.org/monitor/2010/10/teachers.aspx

Chang, A., Duck, J., & Bordia, P. (2006). Understanding the multidimensionality of group development. *Small Group Research*, 37, 327–350.

Chao, G. T., & Moon, H. (2005). The cultural mosaic: A metatheory for understanding the complexity of culture. *Journal of Applied Psychology*, 90, 1128–1140.

Charnofsky, H., Cherny, R., DuFault, D., Kegley, J., & Whitney, D. (1998, December 16). *Final report of Merit Pay Task Force, CSU Academic Senate*. [Online]. Available: http://www.academicsenate.cc.ca.us

Chatman, J., & Barsade, S. (1995). Personality, organizational culture, and cooperation: Evidence from a business simulation. *Administrative Science Quarterly*, 40, 423–443.

Chemers, M. M. (2000). Leadership research and theory: A functional integration. *Group Dynamics: Theory, Research, and Practice*, 4, 27–43.

Chen, G., & Starosta, W. (1997). Chinese conflict management and resolution. Overview and implications. *Intercultural Communication Studies*, 7, 1–16.

Chen, G., & Starosta, W. (1998). *Foundations of Intercultural Communication*. Boston: Allyn & Bacon.

Chen, S., Geluykens, R., & Chong, J. C. (2006). The importance of language in global teams: A linguistic perspective. *Management International Review*, 46, 679–695.

Chertkoff, J., & Esser, J. (1976). A review of experiments in explicit bargaining. *Journal of Experimental Social Psychology*, 12, 464–486.

Chidambaram, L., & Tung, L. L. (2005). Is out of sight, out of mind? An empirical study of social loafing in technology-supported groups. *Information Systems Research*, 16, 149–160.

Chin, P. (2000, January 24). The buddy system. *People*, 98–105.

Chiocchio, F., & Essiembre, H. (2009). Cohesion and performance: A meta-analytic review of disparities between project teams, production teams, and service teams. *Small Group Research*, 40, 382–420.

Chion, J. (2013, October 24). What it's like to work at IDEO. *Leadership Journal*. [Online]. Available: https://medium.com/leadership-journal/6ca2c961aae4

Chiu, Yi-Te, & Staples, S. S. (2013). Reducing faultlines in geographically dispersed teams: Self-disclosure and task elaboration. *Small Group Research*, 44, 498–553.

Choo, T. S. (2010, April 19). Need for a M'sian Ajay Banga. *Sun2Surf*. [Online]. Available: http://www.sun2surf.com/articlePrint.cfm?id=45703

Chua, R. Y.-J., & Iyengar, S. (2006). Empowerment through choice? A critical analysis of the effects of choice in organizations. In B. M. Staw (Ed.), *Research in organizational behavior: An annual series of analytical essays and critical reviews*. New York: Elsevier.

Cirque du Soleil on teamwork and creativity. (2011, June 28). *Business Banter*. [Online]. Available: http://businessbanter.wordpress.com/2011/06/28/cirque-du-soleil-on-teamwork-and-creativity/

Citizen Kane holds its spot as AFI's top American film. (2007, June 21). *San Jose Mercury News*, p. 2A.

Clark, C., & Meadows, B. (2010, June 21). Mr. King's class goes to college. *People*, 131–134.

Clark, R. D. (2001). Effects of majority defection and multiple minority sources on minority influence. *Group Dynamics: Theory, Research, and Practice*, 5, 57–62.

Coates, J. (1993). *Women, men, and language*. New York: Longman.

Cohen, M., & Davis, N. (1981). *Medication errors: Causes and prevention*. Philadelphia: G. F. Stickley.

Collins, S. (2013, February 25). Oscar 2013: TV ratings rise with Seth MacFarland as host. *L.A. Times*. [Online]. Available: http://articles.latimes.com/2013/feb/25/entertainment/la-et-st-oscars-2013-tv-ratings-rise-with-seth-macfarland-as-host-20130225

Colvin, G. (2014, April 7). The world's 50 greatest leaders. *Fortune*.

Connaughton, S. L., & Shuffler, M. (2007). Multinational and multicultural distributed teams: A review and future agenda. *Small Group Research*, 38, 387–412.

Conquergood, D. (1994). Homeboys and hoods: Gang communication and cultural space. In L. Frey (Ed.), *Group communication in context: Studies of natural groups*. Hillsdale, NJ: Lawrence Erlbaum.

Coutu, D. (2009, May). Why teams don't work: An Interview with J. Richard Hackman. *Harvard Business Review*. [Online]. Available: http://hbr.org/2009/05/why-teams-dont-work

Cox, T., Lobel, S., & McLeod, P. (1991). Effects of ethnic groups' cultural differences on cooperative and competitive behavior on a group task. *Academy of Management Journal*, 34, 827–847.

Crano, W. D., & Seyranian, V. (2009). How minorities prevail: The context/comparison–leniency contract model. *Journal of Social Issues*, 65, 335–363.

Crawford, M., & Kaufman, M. R. (2006). Sex differences versus social processes in the construction of gender. In K. Dindia & D. J. Canary (Eds.), *Sex differences and similarities in communication*. Mahwah, NJ: Lawrence Erlbaum.

Creighton, J. L., & Adams, W. R. (1998). The cyber meeting's about to begin. *Management Review*, 87, 29–31.

Critical listening skills. (2014, March). *The Ken Blanchard Companies*. [Online]. Available: http://www.kenblanchard.com/img/pub/pdf_critical_leadership_skills.pdf

Crown, D. F. (2007). The use of group and group-centric individual goals for culturally heterogeneous and homogeneous task groups: An assessment of European work teams. *Small Group Research*, 38, 489–508.

Crumley, B. (2010, March 17). The Game of Death: France's shocking TV experiment. *Time*. [Online]. Available: http://www.time.com/time/printout/0,8816,1972981,00.html

Crystal, D. (1997). *English as a global language*. Cambridge, UK: Cambridge University Press.

Cupach, W. R., & Canary, D. J. (1997). *Competence in interpersonal conflict*. Prospect Heights, IL: Waveland Press.

Curseu, P. L., & Schruijer, S. G. L. (2010). Does conflict shatter trust or does trust obliterate conflict? Revisiting the relationships between team diversity, conflict, and trust. *Group Dynamics: Theory, Research, and Practice*, 14, 66–79.

Curtis, B., Krasner, H., & Iscoe, N. (1988). A field study of the software design process for large systems. *Communications of the ACM*, 31, 1268–1287.

Daft, R. L., & Lengel, R. H. (1986). Organizational informational requirements, media richness, and structural design. *Management Science*, 32, 554–571.

Dann, C. (2013, June 3). College Republicans latest to issue warnings for party's future. *NBC News*. [Online]. Available: http://nbcpolitics.nbcnews .com/_news/2013/06/03/18725854-college-republicans-latest-to-issue-warnings-for-par-tys-future?lite

Darling, A. L., & Dannels, D. P. (2003). Practicing engineers talk about the importance of talk: A report on the role of oral communication in the workplace. *Communication Education*, 52, 1–16.

Davidson, C. (2007, March 19). We can't ignore the influence of digital technologies. *Chronicle of Higher Education*, p. B20.

Davidson, J. (1996). The shortcomings of the information age. *Vital Speeches*, 495–503.

Davis, J. H., Au, W. T., Hulbert, L., Chen, X., & Zarnoth, P. (1997). Effects of group size and procedural influence on consensual judgments of quantity: The example of damage awards and mock civil juries. *Journal of Personality and Social Psychology*, 73, 703–718.

Davis, J., Frechette, H. M., & Boswell, E. H. (2010). *Strategic speed: Mobilize people, accelerate execution*. Boston, MA: Harvard Business Press.

De Cremer, D., & Leonardelli, G. J. (2003). Individual differences in the need to belong and cooperation in social dilemmas: The moderating effect of group size. *Group Dynamics: Theory, Research, and Practice*, 7, 168–174.

De Dreu, C. K. W., & Van Vianen, A. E. M. (2001). Responses to relationship conflict and team effectiveness. *Journal of Organizational Behavior*, 22, 309–328.

De Dreu, C. K. W., & West, M. A. (2001). Minority dissent and team innovation: The importance of participation in decision making. *Journal of Applied Psychology*, 86, 1191–1201.

De Dreu, C. K., & Weingart, L. R. (2003). Task versus relationship conflict, team performance, and team member satisfaction: A meta-analysis. *Journal of Applied Psychology*, 88, 741–749.

De Klerk, V. (1991). Expletives: Men only? *Communication Monographs*, 58, 156–169.

De Souza, G., & Kline, H. (1995). Emergent leadership in the group goal-setting process. *Small Group Research*, 26, 475–496.

De Waal, F. (2010). *The age of empathy: Nature's lessons for a kinder society*. New York: Three Rivers Press.

Deal, J. J. (2000). Gender differences in the intentional use of information in competitive negotiations. *Small Group Research*, 31, 702–723.

Dean, C. (2005, February 1). For some girls, the problem with math is that they're good at it. *New York Times*, p. F3.

Dean, J. (2009). How newcomers can influence established groups. *Psyblog*. [Onine]. Available: http://www.spring.org.uk/2009/07/how-newcomers-can-influence-established-groups.php

DeChurch, L. A., Hamilton, K. L., & Haas, C. (2007). Effects of conflict management strategies on perceptions of intragroup conflict. *Group Dynamics: Theory, Research, and Practice*, 11, 66–78.

Deggans, E. (2012). *Race-baiter: How the media wields dangerous words to divide a nation*. New York: Palgrave Macmillan.

Delbecq, A., et al. (1975). *Group techniques for program planning*. Glenview, IL: Scott, Foresman.

Delton, A. W., & Cimino, A. (2010). Exploring the evolved concept of newcomer: Experimental tests of a cognitive model. *Evolutionary Psychology*, 8, 317–335.

Den Hartog, D. N. (2004). Assertiveness. In R. J. House, P. J. Hanges, M. Javidan, P. W. Dorfman, & V. Gupta (Eds.), *Culture, leadership, and organizations: The GLOBE study of 62 societies*. Thousand Oaks, CA: Sage.

Denison, D., & Sutton, R. (1990). Operating room nurses. In J. Hackman (Ed.), *Groups that work (and those that don't)*. San Francisco: Jossey-Bass.

Dennis, A. R., & Kinney, S. T. (1998). Testing media richness theory in the new media: The effects of cues, feedback and task equivocality. *Information Systems Research*, 9, 256–274.

Dennis, A. R., & Valacich, J. S. (1999). *Rethinking media richness: Towards a theory of media synchronicity*. In Proceedings of the 32nd Hawaii International Conference on System Sciences, Maui, Hawaii.

Derber, C. (1979). *The pursuit of attention: Power and individualism in everyday life*. New York: Oxford University Press.

Derber, C. (2009). *The Wilding of America*. New York: Worth.

DeStephen, R., & Hirokawa, R. (1988). Small group consensus: Stability of group support of the decision, task process, and group relationships. *Small Group Behavior*, 19, 227–239.

Deutsch, M. (1979). Education and distributive justice: Some reflections on grading systems. *American Psychologist*, 34, 391–401.

Deutsch, M. (1985). *Distributive justice: A social-psychological perspective*. New Haven, CT: Yale University Press.

Dewey, J. (1910). *How we think*. Lexington, MA: D. C. Heath.

Dezenhall, E. (2010, June 9th). Why BP didn't plan for this crisis. *The Daily Beast*. [Online]. Available: http://www.the dailybeast.com/blogs-and-stories/2010-06-09/bp-pr-eric-dezenhall-on-oil-spill-crisis-management/2/

Di Biase, R., & Gunnoe, J. (2004). Gender and cultural differences in touching behavior. *Journal of Social Psychology*, 144, 49.

Dindia, K. (2006). Men are from North Dakota, women are from South Dakota. In K. Dindia and D. J. Canary (Eds.), *Sex differences and similarities in communication*. Mahwah, NJ: Lawrence Erlbaum.

DOL workplace violence program. (2014). *United States Department of Labor*. [Online]. Available: http://www.dol.gov/oasam/hrc/policies/dol-workplace-violence-program.htm

Domagalski, T. (1998). *Experienced and expressed anger in the workplace*. Unpublished doctoral dissertation, University of South Florida.

Donnellon, A. (1996). *Team talk*. Boston: Harvard Business School Press.

Donohue, W., & Kolt, R. (1992). *Managing interpersonal conflict*. Newbury Park, CA: Sage.

Dorado, M. A., Medina, F. J., Munduate, L., Cisneros, I. F. J., & Euwema, M. (2002). Computer mediated negotiations of an escalated conflict. *Small Group Research*, 33, 509–524.

Dorfman, P. W. (2004). International and cross-cultural leadership research. In B. J. Punnett & O. Shenkar (Eds.), *Handbook for international management research*. Ann Arbor: University of Michigan Press.

Dorfman, P. W., Hanges, P. J., & Brodbeck, F. C. (2004). Leadership and cultural variation: The identification of culturally endorsed leadership profiles. In R. J. House, P. J. Hanges, M. Javidan, P. W. Dorfman, & V. Gupta (Eds.), *Culture, leadership, and organizations: The GLOBE study of 62 societies*. Thousand Oaks, CA: Sage.

Dotan-Eliaz, O., Sommer, K. L., & Rubin, Y. S. (2009). Multilingual groups: Effects of linguistic ostracism on felt rejection and anger, coworker attraction, perceived team potency, and creative performance. *Basic and Applied Social Psychology*, 31, 363–375.

Dovidio, J. F., Saguy, T., & Shnabel, N. (2009). Cooperation and conflict within groups: Bridging intragroup and intergroup processes. *Journal of Social Issues*, 65, 429–449.

Dowd, E. T., Hughes, S., Brockbank, L., Halpain, D., Seibel, C., & Seibel, P. (1988). Compliance-based and defiance-based intervention strategies and psychological reactance in the treatment of free and unfree behavior. *Journal of Counseling Psychology*, 35, 363–369.

Drecksel, G. (1984). *Interaction characteristics of emergent leadership*. Unpublished doctoral dissertation, University of Utah.

Dressler, C. (1995, December 31). Please! End this meeting madness! *Santa Cruz Sentinel*, p. ID.

Drew, J. (1994). *Mastering meetings: Discovering the hidden potential of effective business meetings*. New York: McGraw-Hill.

Driskell, J., & Salas, E. (1992, June). Collective behavior and team performance. *Human Factors*, 34, 277–288.

Driskell, J., Radtke, P., & Salas, E. (2003). Virtual teams: Effects of technological mediation on team performance. *Group Dynamics: Theory, Research, and Practice*, 7, 297–323.

Druskat, V. U., & Wolff, S. B. (1999). Effects and timing of developmental peer appraisals in self-managing work groups. *Journal of Applied Psychology*, 84, 58–74.

Dubrin, A. J. (2010). *Leadership: Research findings, practice, and skills*. Mason, OH: South-Western Cengage Learning.

Dubrin, A. J., Ireland, R. D., & Williams, J. C. (1989). *Management and organization*. Cincinnati, OH: South-Western.

Dugosh, K. L., Paulus, P. B., Roland, E. J., & Yang, H. (2000). Cognitive stimulation in brainstorming. *Journal of Personality and Social Psychology*, 79, 722–735.

Dunlap, A. (1997). *Mean business: How I save bad companies and make good companies great*. New York: Simon & Schuster.

Dunning, K. (2003). Why people fail to recognize their own incompetence. *Current Directions in Psychological Science*, 22, 77–87.

Durand, D. (1977). Power as a function of office space and physiognomy: Two studies of influence. *Psychological Reports*, 40, 755–760.

Eagly, A. H. (1995). The science and politics of comparing women and men. *American Psychologist*, 50, 145–158.

Eagly, A. H. (2007). Female leadership advantage and disadvantage: Resolving the contradictions. *Psychology of Women Quarterly*, 31, 1–12.

Eagly, A. H., & Carli, L. L. (2007). *Through the labyrinth: The truth about how women become leaders*. Boston: Harvard Business School Press.

Eagly, A. H., & Karau, S. J. (2002). Role congruity theory of prejudice toward female leaders. *Psychological Review*, 109, 573–598.

Eagly, A. H., Johannesen-Schmidt, M. C., & Van Engen, M. L. (2003). Transformational, transactional, and laissez-faire leadership styles: A meta-analysis comparing women and men. *Psychological Bulletin*, 129, 569–591.

Early, C. (1989). Social loafing and collectivism: A comparison of the United States and the People's Republic of China. *Administrative Science Quarterly*, 34, 555–581.

Ebrahim, N. A., Ahmed, S., & Taha, Z. (2009). Virtual teams: A literature review. *Australian Journal of Basic and Applied Sciences*, 3, 2653–2669.

Economist Intelligence Unit. (2009). Managing virtual teams. *The Economist*. [Online]. Available: http://graphics.eiu.com/upload/eb/NEC_Managing_virtual_teams_WEB.pdf

Eisenberger, R., & Armeli, S. (1997). Can salient reward increase creative performance without reducing intrinsic creative interest? *Journal of Personality and Social Psychology*, 72, 652–663.

Eisenberger, R., & Cameron, J. (1996). Detrimental effects of reward: Reality or myth? *American Psychologist*, 51, 1153–1166.

Ellingson, L. L. (2008). Interdisciplinary health care. In L. C. Lederman (Ed.), *Beyond these walls: Readings in health communication*. New York: Oxford University Press.

Ellis, A. P. J., Bell, B. S., Ployhart, R. E., Hollenbeck, J. R., & Ilgen, D. R. (2005). An evaluation of generic teamwork skill training with action teams: Effects on cognitive and skill-based outcomes. *Personnel Psychology*, 58, 641–672.

Ellison, S. (2009). *Taking the war out of our words*. Deadwood, OR: Wyatt-MacKenzie Publishing.

Emery, C., Danilowski, K., & Hamby, A. (2011). The reciprocal effects of self-view as a leader and leadership emergence. *Small Group Research*, 42, 199–224.

Emmons, M. (2005, April 10). Scholarship pressure changes youth sports. *San Jose Mercury News*, pp. 1A, 12A–13A.

Emmons, M. (2013, October 9). Ex-president helps build East San Jose home. *San Jose Mercury News*, p. A14.

Employers rank communication skills first among job candidate skills and qualities. (2010). *National Association of Colleges and Employees*. [Online]. Available: http://www.naceweb.org/Press/Releases/Employers_Rank_Communication_...ob_Candidate_Skills_and_Qualities.aspx?referal=pressroom&menuid=104

En-Lai, Y. (2003, July 13). Singapore loosens up to shed its dull image. *San Jose Mercury News*, p. 18A.

Epley, N., Caruso, E. M., & Bazerman, M. H. (2006). When perspective taking increases taking: Reactive egotism in social interaction. *Journal of Personality and Social Psychology*, 91, 872–889.

Epstein, R. (2010, January/February). How science can help you fall in love. *Scientific American Mind*, 26–33.

Evans, C. R., & Dion, K. L. (2012). Group cohesion and performance: A meta-analysis. *Small Group Research*, 43, 690–701.

Excessive individualism threatens our children, say experts. (2009, February 2). *The Children's Society*. [Online]. Available: http://www.childrenssociety.org.uk/news-views/press-release/excessive-individualism-threatens-our-children-say-experts

Fackler, M. (2011, June 1). Report finds Japan underestimated tsunami danger. *The New York Times*. [Online]. Available at: http://www.-nytimes.com/2011/06/02/world/asia/02japan.html?ref5world

Fadiman, C. (Ed.). (1985). *The Little, Brown book of anecdotes*. Boston: Little, Brown & Company.

Fairhurst, G., & Sarr, R. (1996). *The art of framing: Managing the language of leadership*. San Francisco: Jossey-Bass.

Fandt, P. (1991). The relationship of accountability and interdependent behavior to enhancing team consequences. *Group and Organization Studies*, 16, 300–312.

Farace, R., Monge, P. R., & Russell, H. M. (1977). *Communicating and organizing*. Reading, MA: Addison-Wesley.

Fastenberg, D. (2010, October 18). Top 10 worst bosses. *Time*. [Online]. Available: http://content.time.com/time/specials/packages/article/0,28804,2025898_2025900_2026107,00.html

Feeney, M. K., & Bozeman, B. (2008). Mentoring and network ties. *Human Relations*, 61, 1651–1676.

Fells, R. (2012). *Effective negotiation: From research to results*. New York: Cambridge University Press.

Felps, W., Mitchell, T. R., & Byington, E. (2006). How, when, and why bad apples spoil the barrel: Negative group members and dysfunctional groups. *Research in Organizational Behavior*, 27, 175–222.

Fenton, B. (2005, June 5). "Chainsaw" to the rescue? Think again! *Fenton Report*. [Online]. Available: http://www.fentonreport.com/wealth_articles/news/chainsaw_al_dunlap.htm

Fernald, L. (1987). Of windmills and rope dancing: The instructional value of narrative structures. *Teaching Psychology*, 14, 214–216.

Fernet, C., Gagne, M., & Austin, S. (2010). When does quality of relationships with coworkers predict burnout over time? The moderating role of work motivation. *Journal of Organizational Behavior*, 31, 1163–1180.

Fiechtner, S. S., & Davis, E. A. (1992). Why some groups fail: A survey of students' experiences with learning groups. In A. S. Goodsell, M. R. Maher, & V. Tinto (Eds.), *Collaborative learning: A sourcebook for higher education*. Syracuse, NY: National Center on Postsecondary Teaching, Learning, & Assessment at Syracuse University.

Fiedler, F. (1967). *A theory of leadership effectiveness*. New York: McGraw-Hill.

Fiedler, F., & House, R. (1988). Leadership theory and research: A report of progress. In C. Cooper & I. Robertson (Eds.), *International review of industrial and organizational psychology*. New York: John Wiley & Sons.

Finkelstein, K. E. (2001, August 3). Tempers seem to be growing shorter in many jury rooms. *New York Times*. [Online]. Available: http://www.nytimes.com/2001/08/03/nyregion/03JURY.html?ex_997841696&

Firestein, R. (1990). Effects of creative problem solving training on communication behaviors in small groups. *Small Group Research*, 21, 507–521.

Fisher, B. A. (1986). Leadership: When does the difference make a difference? In R. Hirokawa & M. S. Poole (Eds.), *Communication and group decision-making*. Beverly Hills, CA: Sage.

Fisher, B. A., & Ellis, D. (1990). *Small group decision making: Communication and the group process*. New York: McGraw-Hill.

Fisher, C., & Gitelson, R. (1983). A meta-analysis of the correlates of role conflict and ambiguity. *Journal of Applied Psychology*, 68, 320–333.

Fisher, K. (2000). *Leading self-directed work teams: A guide to developing new team leadership skills*. New York: McGraw-Hill.

Fisher, R., & Brown, S. (1988). *Getting together: Building a relationship that gets to yes.* Boston: Houghton Mifflin.

Fisher, R., & Shapiro, D. (2005). *Beyond reason: Using emotions as you negotiate.* New York: Penguin Books.

Fisher, R., Ury, W. L., & Patton, B. (2011). *Getting to yes: Negotiating agreement without giving in.* New York: Penguin Books.

Fishkin, J. S. (1997). *The voice of the people: Public opinion and democracy.* New Haven, CT: Yale University Press.

Fiske, S. T. (1993). Social cognition and social perception. *Annual Review of Psychology, 44,* 155–194.

Fitzhenry, R. (Ed.). (1993). *The Harper book of quotations.* New York: HarperPerennial.

Flauto, F. J. (1999). Walking the talking: The relationship between leadership and communication competence. *Journal of Leadership Studies,* 6, 86–97.

Flinn, R. (2010, November 23). Silicon Valley design firm IDEO aims to rethink books, cars. *Bloomberg.* [Online]. Available: http://www.bloomberg.com/news/print/2010-11-23/silicon-valley-design-firm-ideo-s-employees-aim-to-rethink-books-cars.html

Florida jury convicts 2 fraternity members in first test of state's anti-hazing law. (2006, December 18). *Chronicle of Higher Education News Blog.* [Online]. Available: http://chronicle.com/article/Florida-Jury-Convicts-2/37987

Flory, J. A., Leibbrandt, A., & List, J. A. (2010, November). Do competitive workplaces deter female workers? A large-scale natural field experiment on gender differences in job-entry decisions. *National Bureau of Economic Research.* [Online]. Available: http://www.nber.org/papers/w16546

Foderaro, L. W. (2003, September 15). Death in frat's hazing ritual shakes a SUNY campus. *New York Times.* [Online]. Available: http://www.nytimes.com/2003/09/15/nyregion.15HAZI.html?th

Folger, J., Poole, M., & Stutman, R. (1993). *Working through conflict: A communication perspective.* Glenview, IL: Scott, Foresman.

Ford, H. (2003). *My life and work.* Whitefish, MT: Kessinger Publishing.

Forsyth, D. (2014). *Group dynamics.* Belmont, CA: Wadsworth, Cengage Learning.

Forsyth, D. (2013, February 23). The costs of hazing. *Group Dynamics.* [Online]. Available: http://donforsythgroups.wordpress.com/2013/02/23/the-costs-of-hazing/

Forsyth, D., Heiney, M., & Wright, S. (1997). Biases in appraisals of women leaders. *Group Dynamics: Theory, Research, and Practice,* 1, 98–103.

Foushee, H., & Manos, K. (1981). Information transfer within the cockpit: Problems in intra-cockpit communications. In C. Billings & E. Cheaney (Eds.), *Information transfer problems in the aviation system (NASA Report No. TP-1875).* Moffett Field, CA: NASA-Ames Research Center.

Foust, D. (2009, May 14). How Delta climbed out of bankruptcy. *Bloomberg Businessweek.* [Online]. Available: http://www.businessweek.com/print/magazine/content/09_21_b4132036798289.htm

Franz, T. M., & Larson, J. R. (2000). The impact of experts on information sharing during group discussion. *Small Group Research,* 33, 383–411.

Freed, A. (1992). We understand perfectly: A critique of Tannen's view. In K. Hall, M. Bucholtz, & B. Moonwomon (Eds.), *Locating power.* Berkeley: Berkeley Women and Language Group, University of California.

French, J., & Raven, B. (1959). The bases of social power. In D. Cartwright (Ed.), *Studies in social power* (pp. 150–167). Ann Arbor, MI: Institute for Social Research.

Friedman, R., Anderson, C., Brett, J., Olekalns, M., Goates, N., & Lisco, C. C. (2004). The positive and negative effects of anger in dispute resolution: Evidence from electronically mediated disputes. *Journal of Applied Psychology,* 89, 369–376.

Friedman, T. L. (2013, January 31). Passion, curiosity will outweigh IQ. *San Jose Mercury News,* p. A11.

Frings, D., Hopthrow, T., Abrams, D., Hulbert, L., & Gutierrez, R. (2008). Groupdrink: The effects of alcohol and group process on vigilance errors. *Group Dynamics: Theory, Research, and Practice,* 12, 179–190.

Fullinwider, R. K. (2006, February). Sports, youth and character: A critical survey. *The Center for Information & Research on Civic Learning & Engagement*. [Online]. Available: http://www.civicyouth.org/PopUps/WorkingPapers/WP44Fullinwider.pdf

Furst, S. A., Reeves, M., Rosen, B., & Blackburn, R. S. (2004). Managing the life cycle of virtual teams. *Academy of Management Executives*, 18, 6–12.

Gabrenya, W., Wang, Y., & Latane, B. (1985). Social loafing on an optimizing task: Cross-cultural differences among Chinese and Americans. *Journal of Cross-Cultural Psychology*, 16, 223–242.

Galanter, M. (1999). *Cults: Faith, healing, and coercion*. New York: Oxford University Press.

Galinsky, A. D., & Kray, L. J. (2004). From thinking about what might have been to sharing what we know: The effects of counterfactual mind-sets on information sharing in groups. *Journal of Experimental Social Psychology*, 40, 606–618.

Gammage, K. L., Carron, A. V., & Estabrooks, P. A. (2001). Team cohesion and individual productivity: The influence of the norm for productivity and the identifiability of individual effort. *Small Group Research*, 32, 3–18.

Gamson, W., Fireman, B., & Rytia, S. (1982). *Encounters with unjust authority*. Homewood, IL: Dorsey.

Gantz, J., & Reinsel, D. (2010, May). The digital universe—are you ready? *IDC*. [Online]. Available: http://idcdocserv.com/925

Gantz, J., & Reinsel, D. (2012, December). The digital universe in 2020: Big data, bigger digital shadows, and biggest growth in the Far East. *International Data Corporation*. [Online]. Available: http://idcdocserv.com/1414

Gardner, L., & Leak, G. (1994). Characteristics and correlates of teacher anxiety among college psychology teachers. *Teaching of Psychology*, 21, 28–32.

Garrett, L. (1994). *The coming plague: Newly emerging diseases in a world out of balance*. New York: Penguin Books.

Gastil, J. (1994). A meta-analytic review of the productivity and satisfaction of democratic and autocratic leadership. *Small Group Research*, 25, 384–410.

Gastil, J., Black, L. W., Deess, E. P., & Leighter, J. (2008). From group member to democratic citizen: How deliberating with fellow jurors reshapes civic attitudes. *Human Communication Research*, 34, 137–169.

Gastil, J., Burkhalter, S., & Black, L. W. (2007). Do juries deliberate? A study of deliberation, individual difference, and group member satisfaction at a municipal courthouse. *Small Group Research*, 38, 337–359.

Gayle, B. (1991). Sex equity in workplace conflict management. *Journal of Applied Communication Research*, 19, 152–169.

Gebhardt, L., & Meyers, R. (1995). Subgroup influence in decision-making groups: Examining consistency from a communication perspective. *Small Group Research*, 26, 147–168.

Geis, F., et al. (1984). Sex vs. status in sex-associated stereotypes. *Sex Roles*, 11, 771–786.

Geister, S., Konradt, U., & Hertel, G. (2006). Effects of process feedback on motivation, satisfaction, and performance in virtual teams. *Small Group Research*, 37, 459–489.

Gelles, R., & Straus, M. (1988). *Intimate violence: The causes and consequences of abuse in the American family*. New York: Simon & Schuster.

Gerard, H. B., & Mathewson, G. C. (1966). The effects of severity of initiation on liking for a group: A replication. *Journal of Experimental Social Psychology*, 2, 278–287.

Gerrig, R. J. (2013). *Psychology and life*. Upper Saddle River, NJ: Pearson.

Getter, H., & Nowinski, J. (1981). A free response test of interpersonal effectiveness. *Journal of Personality Assessment*, 45, 301–308.

Gibb, J. (1961). Defensive communication. *Journal of Communication*, 11, 141–148.

Giles, H., & LePoire, B. A. (2006). The ubiquity and social meaningfulness of nonverbal communication. In V. Manusov & M. L. Patterson (Eds.), *The Sage handbook of nonverbal communication*. Thousand Oaks, CA: Sage.

Gilovich, T., & Keltner, D. (2010). *Social psychology*. New York: W. W. Norton & Company.

Glasner, B. (1999). *The culture of fear*. New York: Basic Books.

Glassman, J. K. (1998, May 29). Put shootings in proper perspective. *San Jose Mercury News*, p. B7.

Glovin, D. (2013, July 24). Mother of golf prodigy in hazing death defied by FratPAC. *Bloomberg Politics*. [Online]. Available: http://www .bloomberg.com/news/2013-07-24/mother-of-golf-prodigy-in-hazing-death-defied-by-fratpac.htm

Gleick, J. (1999). *Faster: The acceleration of just about everything*. New York: Pantheon Books.

Glomb, T. M. (2002). Workplace anger and aggression: Informing conceptual models with data from specific encounters. *Journal of Occupational Health Psychology*, 7, 20–36.

Godar, S. H., & Ferris, S. P. (2004). *Virtual and collaborative teams: Process, technologies and practice*. London: Idea Group Publishing.

Goethals, G., & Darley, J. (1987). Social comparison theory: Self-evaluation and group life. In B. Mullen & G. Goethals (Eds.), *Theories of group behavior*. New York: Springer-Verlag.

Goktepe, J., & Schneier, C. (1989). Role of sex and gender roles, and attraction in predicting emergent leaders. *Journal of Applied Psychology*, 74, 165–167.

Goldenberg, O., Larson, J. R., & Wiley, J. (2013). Goal instructions, response formats, and idea generation in groups. *Small Group Research*, 44, 227–256.

Goldhaber, G. (1990). *Organizational communication*. Dubuque, IA: Wm. C. Brown & Company.

Goldman, T. (2014, February 3). Young athletes risk back injury by playing too much. Shots: *Health News from NPR*. [Online]. Available: http://www.npr.org/blogs/health/2014/02/03/269521744/young-athletes-risk-back-injury-by-playing-too-much-too-soon

Goleman, D. (1995). *Emotional intelligence: Why it can matter more than I.Q.* New York: Bantam Books.

Goleman, (2013). *Focus: The hidden driver of excellence*. New York: HarperCollins.

Goleman, D. (1998). *Working with emotional intelligence*. New York: Bantam Books.

Goleman, D., Boyatzis, R., & McKee, A. (2002). *Primal leadership: Realizing the power of emotional intelligence*. Boston: Harvard Business School Press.

Gonchar, M. (2012, September 20). Would you ever go through hazing to be part of a group? *The New York Times*. [Online]. Available: http://learning.blogs.nytimes.com/2012/09/20/would-you-ever-go-through-hazing-to-be-part-of-a-group/

Gonsalkorale, K., & Williams, K. D. (2007). The KKK won't let me play: Ostracism even by a despised outgroup hurts. *European Journal of Social Psychology*, 37, 1176–1186.

Gonzaga, G. C., Keltner, D., & Ward, D. (2008). Power in mixed-sex stranger interactions. *Cognition and Emotion*, 22, 1555–1568.

Goodwin, E. (2010, February 21). Primary reasons why kids drop out of community sports programs. *Youth Sports Quality Institute*. [Online]. Available: http://ysqi4ed.wordpress .com/2010/02/

Gottman, J. (1994). *What predicts divorce? The relationship between marital processes and marital outcomes*. Hillsdale, NJ: Lawrence Erlbaum.

Gottman, J. M., & DeClaire, J. (2001). *The relationship cure: A five-step guide for building better connections with family, friends, and lovers*. New York: Crown Books.

Gottman, J. M., & Gottman, J. S. (2006). *10 lessons to transform your marriage*. New York: Crown.

Gottman, J., & Silver, N. (1999). *The seven principles for making marriage work*. New York: Crown.

Goudreau, J. (2010, April 26). What men and women are doing on Facebook. *Forbes*. [Online]. Available: http://www.forbes.com/2010/04/26/popular-social-networking-sites-forbes-woman-time-facebook-twitter_print.html

Gould, D. (2011, February 3). Two hundred trillion text messages [infographic]. *PSFK*. [Online]. Available: http://www.psfk.com/2011/02/two-hundred-trillion-text-messages-infographic.html

Gould, S. (1981). *The mismeasure of man*. New York: W. W. Norton.

Gouran, D. (1981). Cognitive sources of inferential error and the contributing influence of interaction characteristics in decision-making groups. In G. Ziegelmueller & J. Rhodes (Eds.), *Dimensions of argument: Proceedings of the Second Annual Summer Conference on Argumentation*. Annandale, VA: Speech Communication Association.

Gouran, D. (1982a, April). A theoretical foundation for the study of inferential error in decision-making groups. Paper presented at the Conference on Small Group Research, Pennsylvania State University.

Gouran, D. (1982b). *Making decisions in groups: Choices and consequences*. Glenview, IL: Scott, Foresman.

Gouran, D. (1983). Communicative influences on inferential judgments in decision-making groups: A descriptive analysis. In D. Zarefsky et al. (Eds.), *Argument in transition: Proceedings of the Third Summer Conference on Argumentation*. Annandale, VA: Speech Communication Association.

Gouran, D. (1986). Inferential errors, interaction, and group decision-making. In R. Hirokawa & M. Poole (Eds.), *Communication and group decision-making*. Beverly Hills, CA: Sage.

Gouran, D. (1988). Principles of counteractive influence in decision-making and problem-solving groups. In R. Cathcart & L. Samovar (Eds.), *Small group communication: A reader*. Dubuque, IA: Wm. C. Brown & Company.

Gouran, D., & Baird, J. (1972). An analysis of distributional and sequential structure in problem solving and informal group discussions, *Speech Monographs, 39*, 16–22.

Grady, D. (2010, November 25). Study: Hospitals still not very safe. *San Jose Mercury News*, p. A6.

Grasz, J. (2014, January 16). Employers share most memorable interview blunders. *CareerBuilder* [Online]. Available: http://www.careerbuilder.com/share/aboutus/pressreleasesdetail.aspx?sd=1/16/2014&id=pr798&ed=12/31/2014

Green, A. S., & McKenna, K. Y. A. (2002). *The Internet attenuates the effects of social anxiety*. Manuscript submitted for publication, New York University.

Greengross, G., & Miller, G. F. (2008). Dissing oneself versus dissing rivals: Effects of status, personality, and sex on the short-term and long-term attractiveness of self-deprecating and other-deprecating humor. *Evolutionary Psychology Journal, 6*, 393–408.

Greenleaf, R. K. (1977). *Servant leadership: A journey into the nature of legitimate power and greatness*. New York: Paulist.

Greer, L. L., Jehn, K. A., & Manniz, E. A. (2008). Conflict transformation: A longitudinal investigation of the relationship between different types of intragroup conflict and the moderating role of conflict resolution. *Small Group Research, 39*, 278–302.

Gregoire, C. (2013, December 6). How technology speeds up time (and how to slow it down again). *Huffington Post*. [Online]. Available: http://www.huffingtonpost.com/2013/12/06/technology-time-perception_n_4378010.html

Greitemeyer, T., & Schultz-Hardt, S. (2003). Preference-consistent evaluation of information in the hidden profile paradigm: Beyond group-level explanations for the dominance of shared information in group decisions. *Journal of Personality & Social Psychology, 84*, 322–339.

Greitemeyer, T., Schultz-Hardt, S., Brodbeck, F. C., & Frey, D. (2006). Information sampling and group decision making: The effects of an advocacy decision procedure and task experience. *Journal of Experimental Psychology: Applied, 12*, 31–42.

Grenny, J. (2009). Crucial conversations: The most potent force for eliminating disruptive behavior. *Physician Executive Journal, 35*, 30–33.

Griffin, E. (1994). *A first look at communication theory*. New York: McGraw-Hill.

Grondahl, P. (2013). One of last Shakers talks about "the life" *Timesunion*. [Online]. Available: http://www.timesunion.com/local/article/One-of-last-Shakers-talks-about-the-life-4298710.php

Group video calling. (2011). *Skype*. [Online]. Available: http://www.skype.com/intl/en-us/features/allfeatures/group-video-calls/

Grusky, O., Bonacich, P., & Webster, C. (1995). The coalition structure of the four-person family. *Current Research in Social Psychology*, 2, 16–28.

Gully, S. M., Incalcaterra, K. A., Johi, A., & Beaubien, J. M. (2002). A meta-analysis of team efficacy, potency and performance: Interdependence and level of analysis as moderators of observed relationships. *Journal of Applied Psychology*, 87, 819–832.

Gully, S., Devine, D., & Whitney, D. (2012). A meta-analysis of cohesion and performance: Effects of level of analysis and task interdependence. *Small Group Research*, 43, 702–725.

Gurrie, C. (2013, November 20). Group work: A Millennial myth? Improving group communication in traditional undergraduate settings. Paper presented at the National Communication Association convention, Washington, D.C.

Guzzo, R. A., & Dickson, M. W. (1996). Teams in organizations: Recent research on performance effectiveness. *Annual Review of Psychology*, 47, 307–338.

Habitat for Humanity raises walls on its 800,00th milestone home. (2013, November 6). *Habitat for Humanity*. [Online]. Available: http://www.habitat.org/newsroom/2013archive/11_06_2013_800k_milestone

Hackman, J. R. (2003). Learning more by crossing levels: Evidence from airplanes, hospitals, and orchestras. *Journal of Organizational Behavior*, 24, 905–922.

Hackman, M., & Johnson, C. (2004). *Leadership: A communication perspective*. Prospect Heights, IL: Waveland Press.

Haleta, L. L. (1996). Student perceptions of teachers' use of language: The effects of powerful and powerless language on impression formation and uncertainty. *Communication Education*, 45, 16–28.

Hall, C. C., Ariss, L., & Todorov, A. (2007). The illusion of knowledge: When more information reduces accuracy and increases confidence. *Organizational Behavior and Human Decision Processes*, 103, 277–290.

Hall, E. (1981). *Beyond culture*. New York: Doubleday.

Hall, E., & Hall, M. (1987). *Understanding cultural difference*. Yarmouth, ME: Intercultural Press.

Hall, J. A. (2006). How big are nonverbal sex differences? The case of smiling and nonverbal sensitivity. In K. Dindia & D. J. Canary (Eds.), *Sex differences and similarities in communication*. Mahwah, NJ: Lawrence Erlbaum.

Hall, J. A., & Bernieri, F. J. (2001). *Interpersonal sensitivity: Theory and measurement*. Mahwah, NJ: Lawrence Erlbaum.

Hall, J. A., Coats, E. J., & LeBeau, L. S. (2005). Nonverbal behavior and the vertical dimension of social relations: A meta-analysis. *Psychological Bulletin*, 131, 898–924.

Hall, J., & Watson, W. (1970). The effects of a normative intervention on group decision-making. *Human Relations*, 23, 299–317.

Hall, M. (2014, April 15). PayWatch: CEO pay hits "insane level." *AFL-CIO*. [Online]. Available: http://www.aflcio.org/Blog/Corporate-Greed/PayWatch-CEO-Pay-Hits-Insane-Level

Halpern, D. (1984). *Thought and knowledge: An introduction to critical thinking*. Hillsdale, NJ: Lawrence Erlbaum.

Haney, W. (1967). *Communication and organizational behavior*. Homewood, IL: Irwin.

Hansen, R. S., & Hansen, K. (2005). What do employers really want? Top skills and values employers seek from job-seekers. *Quintessential Careers* [Online]. Available: http://www.quintcareers.com/job_skills_values.html

Hardy, J., Eys, M. A., & Carron, A. V. (2005). Exploring the potential disadvantages of high cohesion in sports teams. *Small Group Research*, 36, 166–187.

Hare, A. (1994). Types of roles in small groups: A bit of history and a current perspective. *Small Group Research*, 25, 433–448.

Harlan, D. (2001). The Shakers. [Online]. Available: http://religiousmovements.lib.virginia.edu/nrms/Shakers.html

Harris, C. L., & Beyerlein, M. M. (2003). Team-based organization: Creating an environment for team success. In M. A. West, D. Tjosvold, & K. G. Smith (Eds.), *International handbook of organizational teamwork and cooperative working*. New York: John Wiley & Sons.

Harrison, D. A., Price, K. H., Gavin, J. H., & Florey, A. T. (2002). Time, teams, and task performance: Changing attitudes of surface and deep-level diversity on group functioning. *Academy of Management Journal*, 445, 1029–1045.

Hart, J. W., Bridgett, D. J., & Karau, S. J. (2001). Coworker ability and effort as determinants of individual effort on a collective task. *Group Dynamics: Theory, Research, and Practice*, 5, 181–190.

Haslam, S. A., Reicher, S. D., & Platow, M. J. (2011). *The new psychology of leadership: Identity, influence and power*. New York: Psychology Press.

Haslam, S. A., & Reicher, S. D. (2012, July/August). In search of charisma. *Scientific American Mind*, 42–49.

Haslett, B. B., & Ruebush, J. (1999). What differences do individual differences in groups make? The effects of individuals, culture, and group composition. In L. R. Frey, D. S. Gouran, & M. S. Poole (Eds.), *The handbook of group communication theory and research*. Thousand Oaks, CA: Sage.

Hastie, R., & Kameda, T. (2005). The robust beauty of majority rules in group decision. *Psychological Review*, 112, 494–508.

Hastie, R., Schkade, D., & Sunstein, C. R. (2006). What really happened on deliberation day? Unpublished manuscript, University of Chicago Law School.

Hawkins, K. (1995). Effects of gender and communication content on leadership emergence in small task-oriented groups. *Small Group Research*, 26, 234–249.

Hawley, J. (2010, September 7). School rankings: What's really important? *HigherEdMorning.com*. [Online]. Available: http://www.higheredmorning.com/school-rankings-whats-really-important

Heaney, K. (2013, June 11). Everyone is using their smartphones on the toilet. *BuzzFeed*. [Online]. Available: http://www.buzzfeed.com/katie heaney/everyone-is-using-their-smartphones-on-the-toilet

Heilman, M. E., Wallen, A. S., Fuchs, D., & Tamkins, M. M. (2004). Penalties for success: Reactions to women who succeed at male gender-typed tasks. *Journal of Applied Psychology*, 89, 416–427.

Hellweg, S., Samovar, L., & Skow, L. (1994). Cultural variations in negotiation styles. In L. Samovar & R. Porter (Eds.), *Intercultural communication: A reader*. Belmont, CA: Wadsworth.

Henley, N. (1995). Body politics revisited: What do we know today? In P. Kalbfleisch & M. Cody (Eds.), *Gender, power, and communication in human relationships*. Hillsdale, NJ: Lawrence Erlbaum.

Henningsen, D. D., Cruz, M. G., & Miller, M. L. (2000). Role of social loafing in predeliberation decision making. *Group Dynamics: Theory, Research, and Practice*, 4, 168–175.

Henry, J. (1963). *Culture against man*. New York: Random House.

Hensley, T., & Griffin, G. (1986). Victims of groupthink: The Kent State University Board of Trustees and the 1977 gymnasium controversy. *Journal of Conflict Resolution*, 30, 497–531.

Hersey, P., Blanchard, K. H., & Johnson, D. E. (2001). *Management of organizational behavior: Leading human resources*. Upper Saddle River, NJ: Prentice Hall.

Hickson, M., & Stacks, D. (1989). *Nonverbal communication: Studies and applications*. Dubuque, IA: Wm. C. Brown & Company.

Hightower, R. T., & Sayeed, L. (1995). The impact of computer mediated communication systems on biased group discussion. *Computers in Human Behavior*, 11, 33–44.

Hill, C. A. (2009). Affiliation motivation. In M. R. Leary & R. H. Hoyle (Eds.), *Handbook of individual differences in social behavior*. New York: Guilford Press.

Hinds, P. J., & Mortensen, M. (2005). Understanding conflict in geographically distributed teams: The moderating effects of shared identity, shared context, and spontaneous communication. *Organization Science*, 16, 290–307.

Hingson, R. W., Zha, W., & Weitzman, E. E. (2009). Magnitude of and trends in alcohol-related mortality and morbidity among U.S. college students ages 18–24, 1998-2005. *Journal of Studies on Alcohol and Drugs*, 16, 12–20.

Hirokawa, R. (1985). Discussion procedures and decision-making performance: A test of a functional perspective. *Human Communication Research*, 12, 203–224.

Hirokawa, R. (1987). Why informed groups make faulty decisions: An investigation of possible interaction-based explanations. *Small Group Behavior*, 18, 3–29.

Hirokawa, R. (1992). Communication and group decision-making efficacy. In R. Cathcart & L. Samovar (Eds.), *Small group communication: A reader*. Dubuque, IA: Wm. C. Brown & Company.

Hirokawa, R., & Pace, R. (1983). A descriptive investigation of the possible communication-based reasons for effective and ineffective group decision-making. *Communication Monographs*, 50, 363–379.

Hirokawa, R., & Scheerhorn, D. (1986). Communication in faulty group decision-making. In R. Hirokawa & M. Poole (Eds.), *Communication and group decision-making*. Beverly Hills, CA: Sage.

Hitlan, R. T., Kelly, K. M., Schepman, S., Schneider, K. T., & Zarate, M. A. (2006). Language exclusion and the consequences of perceived ostracism in the workplace. *Group Dynamics: Theory, Research, and Practice*, 10, 56–70.

Hoegl, M., & Parboteeah, K. P. (2003). Goal setting and team performance in innovative projects: On the moderating role of teamwork quality. *Small Group Research*, 34, 3–19.

Hofstede, G., & Hofstede, G. J. (2010). *Cultures and organizations: Software of the mind*. New York: McGraw-Hill.

Hogan, R., Curphy, G. J., & Hogan, J. (1994). What we know about leadership: Effectiveness and personality. *American Psychologist*, 49, 493–504.

Hoigaard, R., & Ommundsen, Y. (2007). Perceived social loafing and anticipated effort reduction among young football (soccer) players: An achievement goal perspective. *Psychological Reports*, 100, 857–875.

Hoigaard, R., Safvenbom, R., & Tonnessen, F. E. (2006). The relationship between group cohesion, group norms, and perceived social loafing in soccer teams. *Small Group Research*, 37, 217–232.

Holahan, P., Mooney, A., Mayer, R. C., & Paul, L. F. (2008, Fall). *Current Issues in Technology Management*, 12, 1–4.

Hollander, E. (1978). *Leadership dynamics*. New York: Free Press.

Hollander, E. (1985). Leadership and power. In G. Lindzey & E. Aronson (Eds.), *Handbook of social psychology* (pp. 485–537). New York: Random House.

Hollander, E., & Offerman, L. (1990, February). Power and leadership in organizations. *American Psychologist*, 179–189.

Hollenbeck, J. R., DeRue, D. S., & Guzzo, R. (2004). Bridging the gap between I/O research and HR practice: Improving team composition, team training and team task design. *Human Resource Management*, 43, 353–366.

Hollingshead, A. (1998). Group and individual training: The impact of practice on performance. *Small Group Research*, 29, 254–280.

Holtgraves, T. (1997). Styles of language use: Individual and cultural variability in conversational indirectness. *Journal of Personality and Social Psychology*, 73, 624–637.

Homan, A. C., Greer, L. L., Jehn, K. A., & Koning, L. (2010). Believing shapes seeing: The impact of diversity beliefs on the construal of group composition. *Group Processes & Intergroup Relations*, 13, 477–493.

Homan, A. C., van Knippenberg, D., van Kleef, G. A., & de Dreu, C. K. W. (2007). Interacting dimensions of diversity: Cross-categorization and the functioning of diverse work groups. *Group Dynamics: Theory, Research, and Practice*, 11, 79–94.

Hong, L. (1978). Risky shift and cautious shift: Same direct evidence on the cultural-value theory. *Social Psychology*, 41, 342–346.

Horn, L. (2011, Februry 8). Social network use up, e-mail down, especially among teens. *PCMag .com*. [Online]. Available: http://www .pcmag .com/article2/0,2817,2379677,00asp

Hornsey, M. J., Grice, T., Jetten, J., Paulsen, N., & Callan, V. (2007). Group-directed criticisms and recommendations for change: Why newcomers arouse more defensiveness than old-timers. *Personality and Social Psychology Bulletin*, 33, 1036–1048.

Hornsey, M. J., Robson, E., Smith, J., Esposo, S., & Sutton, R. M. (2008). Sugaring the pill: Assessing rhetorical strategies designed to minimize defensive reactions to group criticism. *Human Communication Research*, 34, 70–98.

Hornsey, M. J., Trembath, M., & Gunthorpe, S. (2004). "You can criticize because you care": Identity attachment, constructiveness, and the intergroup sensitivity effect. *European Journal of Social Psychology*, 34, 499–518.

Houghton, M. (2006). Videoconferencing your way to cost savings. *Enterprise IT Planet*. [Online]. Available: http://www.enterpriseitplanet.com/networking/features/article.php/3594756

House, R. J. (2004). Illustrative examples of GLOBE findings. In R. J. House, P. J. Hanges, M. Javidan, P. W. Dorfman, & V. Gupta (Eds.), *Culture, leadership, and organizations: The GLOBE study of 62 societies*. Thousand Oaks, CA: Sage.

House, R. J., & Aditya, R. N. (1997). The social scientific study of leadership: Quo vadis? *Journal of Management*, 23, 409–473.

House, R. J., & Javidan, M. (2004). Overview of GLOBE. In R. J. House, P. J. Hanges, M. Javidan, P. W. Dorfman, & V. Gupta (Eds.), *Culture, leadership, and organizations: The GLOBE study of 62 societies*. Thousand Oaks, CA: Sage.

Howard, J. W. (2008). "Tower, am I cleared to land?": Problematic communication in aviation discourse. *Human Communication Research*, 34, 370–391.

Howell, W. S. (1982). *The empathic communicator*. Belmont, CA: Wadsworth.

Hoyt, C. L. (2012). Women, men, and leadership: Exploring the gender gap at the top. *Social and Personality Psychology Compass*, 4, 484–498.

Hoyt, C. L., & Blascovich, J. (2003). Transformational and transactional leadership in virtual and physical environments. *Small Group Research*, 34, 678–715.

Huang, L., Galinsky, A. D., Gruenfeld, D. H., & Guillory, L. E. (2011). Powerful postures versus powerful roles: Which is the proximate correlate of thought and behavior? *Psychological Science*, 22, 95–102.

Huguet, P., Charbonnier, E., & Monteil, J.-M. (1999). Productivity loss in performance groups: People who see themselves as average do not engage in social loafing. *Group Dynamics: Theory, Research, and Practice*, 3, 118–131.

Hui, C. H., & Triandis, H. C. (1986). Individualism-collectivism: A study of cross-cultural researchers. *Journal of Cross-Cultural Psychology*, 17, 225–248.

Husband, R. (1992). Leading in organizational groups. In R. Cathcart & L. Samovar (Eds.), *Small group communication* (pp. 464–476). Dubuque, IA: Wm. C. Brown & Company.

Hunt, R. (2013, July 24). Forty-three percent of workers say their office has cliques, finds CareerBuilder survey. *Careeer Builder*. [Online]. Available: http://www.careerbuilder.com/share/aboutus/pressreleasesdetail.aspx?sd=7%2F24%2F2013&id=pr773&ed=12%2F31%2F2013

Hyatt, J. (2010, May 21). Smarter, by design. *Newsweek*. [Online]. Available: http://www.newsweek.com/2010/05/21/smarter-by-design.print.html

Hyde, J. S. (2005). The gender similarities hypothesis. *American Psychologist*, 60, 581–592.

Hyman, M. (2009). *Until it hurts: America's obsession with youth sports and how it harms our kids*. Boston: Beacon Press.

Iglesias, M. E. L., & Vallejo, R. B. (2012). Conflict resolution styles in nursing profession. *Contemporary Nurse*, 43, 73–80.

Impett, E. A., Gable, S. L., & Peplau, L. A. (2005). Giving up and giving in: The costs and benefits of daily sacrifice in intimate relationships. *Journal of Personality and Social Psychology*, 89, 327–344.

Infante, D., Rancer, A., & Womack, D. (1997). *Building communication theory*. Prospect Heights, IL: Waveland Press.

International workplace productivity survey: White collar highlights. (2010, October). *LexisNexis*. [Online]. Available: http://www.multivu.com/players/English/46619-LexisNexis-International-Workplace-Productivity-Survey/flexSwf/

Internet users (2014). *Internet Live Stats*. [Online]. Available: http://www.internetlivestats.com/internet-users/

Internet world users by language. (2014, January 10). *Internet World Stats*. [Online]. Available: http://www.internetworldstats.com/stats7.htm

Interview: Clifford Nass. (2010, February 2). *Frontline*. [Online]. Available: http://www.pbs.org/wgbh/pages/frontline/digitalnation/interviews/nass.html

Isaksen, S. G. (1988). Innovative problem solving in groups. In Y. Ijiri & R. I. Kuhn (Eds.), *New directions in creative and innovative management: Bridging theory and practice*. Cambridge, MA: Ballinger.

Isaksen, S. G., & Gaulin, J. P. (2005). A reexamination of brainstorming research: Implications for research and practice. *Gifted Child Quarterly*, 49, 315–329.

Isenhart, M. W., & Spangle, M. (2000). *Collaborative approaches to resolving conflict*. Thousand Oaks, CA: Sage.

Is your team too big? Too small? What's the right number? *Wharton: University of Pennsylvania*. [Online]. Available: http://knowledge.wharton.upenn.edu/article/is-your-team-too-big-too-small-whats-the-right-number-2/

Jaffe, E. (2012). Give and take: Empirical strategies for compromise. *Observer*, 25, 9–11.

Jaksa, J., & Pritchard, M. (1994). *Communication ethics: Methods of analysis*. Belmont, CA: Wadsworth.

James, D., & Clarke, S. (1993). Women, men, and interruptions: A critical review. In D. Tannen (Ed.), *Gender and conversational interaction*. New York: Oxford University Press.

James, D., & Drakich, J. (1993). Understanding gender differences in amount of talk: A critical review of research. In D. Tannen (Ed.), *Gender and conversational interaction*. New York: Oxford University Press.

James, J. (2013). A new, evidence-based estimate of patient harm associated with hospital care. *Journal of Patient Safety*, 9, 122–128.

Janis, I. (1982). *Groupthink: Psychological studies of policy decisions and fiascoes*. Boston: Houghton Mifflin.

Jarc, R. (2012, October 31). The ethics of American youth: 2012. *Josephson Institute Center for Youth Ethics*. [Online]. Available: http://charactercounts.org/programs/reportcard/2012/installment_report-card_bullying-youth-violence.html

Jayanthi, N., Pinkham, C., Dugas, L., Patrick, B., & LaBella, C. (2012). Sports specialization in young athletes: Evidence-based recommendations. *Sports Health*. [Online]. Available: www.ncbi.nlm.nih.gov/pubmed/24427397

Jean-Arsenault, E., & Conseil, D. (2007). Circus arts in Quebec and in Canada. *Circus Conservatory of America*. [Online]. Available: http://enpiste.qc.ca/files/publications/state_of_affairs_shedding_light_on_a_paradox.pdf

Jehn, K. A. (1995). A multimethod examination of the benefits and detriments of intragroup conflict. *Administrative Science Quarterly*, 40, 256–282.

Jehn, K. A., & Weldon, E. (1997). Managerial attitudes toward conflict: Cross-cultural differences in resolution styles. *Journal of International Management*, 3, 291–321.

Jetten, J., Spears, R., & Manstead, A. S. R. (1996). Intergroup norms and intergroup discrimination: Distinctive self-categorization and social identity effects. *Journal of Personality and Social Psychology*, 71, 1222–1233.

Johnson, C. (2009). Bad blood: Doctor-nurse behavior problems impact patient care. *Physician Executive Journal*, 35, 6–10.

Johnson, D. W. (2003). Social interdependence: Interrelationships among theory, research, and practice. *American Psychologist*, 58, 934–945.

Johnson, D. W., & Johnson, R. T. (1987). *Cooperation and competition*. Hillsdale, NJ: Lawrence Erlbaum.

Johnson, D. W., & Johnson, R. T. (2000, June). Teaching students to be peacemakers; Results of twelve years of research. [Online]. Available: http://www.coolearn.org/pages/peacemeta.html

Johnson, D. W., & Johnson, R. T. (2003). Field testing integrative negotiations. *Peace and Conflict: Journal of Peace Psychology*, 9, 39–68.

Johnson, D. W., & Johnson, R. T. (2005). Learning groups. In S. A. Wheelan (Ed.), *The handbook of group research and practice*. Thousand Oaks, CA: Sage.

Johnson, D. W., & Johnson, R. T. (2009). An educational psychology success story: Social interdependence theory and cooperative learning. *Educational Researcher*, 38, 365–379.

Johnson, S. K., Bettenhausen, K., & Gibbons, E. (2009). Realities of working in virtual teams: Affective and attitudinal outcomes of using computer-mediated communication. *Small Group Research*, 40, 623–649.

Johnson, S., & Bechler, C. (1998). Examining the relationship between listening effectiveness and leadership emergence: Perceptions, behaviors, and recall. *Small Group Research*, 29, 452–471.

Jones, A. P., Rozelle, R. M., & Chang, W. C. (1990). Perceived punishment and reward values of supervisor actions in a Chinese sample. *Psychological Studies*, 35, 1–10.

Jones, E. E., & Kelly, J. R. (2007). Contributions to a group discussion and perceptions of leadership: Does quantity always count more than quality? *Group Dynamics: Theory, Research, and Practice*, 11, 15–30.

Jordan, M. H., Field, H. S., & Armenakis, A. A. (2002). The relationships of group process variables and team performance. *Small Group Research*, 33, 121–150.

Josephson, M. (2002). *Making ethical decisions*. Los Angeles: Josephson Institute of Ethics.

Judge, C. (1998, July 31). Rookie's father would be proud. *San Jose Mercury News*, p. D8.

Judge, T. A., & Piccolo, R. F. (2004). Transformational and transactional leadership: A meta-analytic test of their relative validity. *Journal of Applied Psychology*, 89, 755–768.

"Jurors" body language: Why we look, what to notice and what to ignore. (2013). *DecisionQuest*. [Online]. Available: http://www.decisionquest.com/utility/showArticle/?objectID=302

Kalbfleisch, P. J., & Herold, A. L. (2006). Sex, power, and communication. In K. Dindia & D. J. Canary (Eds.), *Sex differences and similarities in communication*. Mahwah, NJ: Lawrence Erlbaum.

Kameda, N. (2003). Miscommunication factors in Japanese-US trade relationships. [Online]. Available: http://www.rcwob.doshisha.ac.jp/review/5_2/5_2_011.pdf

Kameda, N. (2007). Communicative challenges for Japanese companies: Strategies in the global marketplace. Proceedings of the Association for Business Communication 7th Asia-Pacific Conference.

Karakowsky, L., & Siegel, J. P. (1999a). The effects of proportional representation and gender orientation of the task on emergent leadership behavior in mixed-gender work groups. *Journal of Applied Psychology*, 84, 620–631.

Karakowsky, L., & Siegel, J. P. (1999b). The effects of proportional representation on intragroup behavior in mixed-race decision-making groups. *Small Group Research*, 30, 259–279.

Karau, S. J., & Elsaid, A. M. M. K. (2009). Individual differences in beliefs about groups. *Group Dynamics: Theory, Research, and Practice*, 13, 1–13.

Karau, S. J., & Hart, J. W. (1998). Group cohesiveness and social loafing: Effects of a social interaction manipulation on individual motivation within groups. *Group Dynamics: Theory, Research, and Practice*, 2, 185–191.

Karau, S. J., & Williams, K. D. (2001). Understanding individual motivation in groups: The collective effort model. In M. E. Turner (Ed.), *Groups at work: Theory and research*. Mahwah, NJ: Erlbaum.

Karpowitz, C. F., Mendelberg, T., & Shaker (2012). Gender inequality in deliberative participation. *American Political Science Review*, 106, 533–547.

Kassin, S. (1998). *Psychology*. Upper Saddle River, NJ: Prentice Hall.

Katz, D. (1982). The effects of group longevity on project communication. *Administrative Science*, 27, 81–104.

Katz, D., & Kahn, R. (1978). *The social psychology of organizations*. New York: John Wiley & Sons.

Katzenbach, J. R., & Smith, D. K. (1993, March–April). The discipline of teams. *Harvard Business Review*, 111–120.

Kauffeld, S., & Lehmann-Willenbrock, N. (2012). Meetings matter: Effects of team meetings on team and organizational success. *Small Group Research*, 43, 30–58.

Kay, K., & Shipman, C. (2014, April 14). The confidence gap. *The Atlantic*. [Online]. Available: http://www.theatlantic.com/features/archive/2014/04/the-confidence-gap/359815/

Kayne, E. (2013, June 13). Census: White majority in U.S. gone by 2043. *NBC News.* [Online]. Available: http://usnews.nbcnews.com/_news/2013/06/13/18934111-census-white-majority-in-us-gone-by-2043?lite

Kayworth, T. R., & Leidner, D. E. (2002). Leadership effectiveness in global virtual teams. *Journal of Management Information Systems,* 18, 7–40.

Keating, C. F., Pomerantz, J., Pommer, S. D., Ritt, S. J. H., Miller, L. M., & McCormick, J. (2005). Going to college and unpacking hazing: A functional approach to decrypting initiation practices among undergraduates. *Group Dynamics: Theory, Research, and Practice,* 9, 104–126.

Kellett, J. B., Humphrey, R. H., & Sleeth, R. G. (2006). Empathy and the emergence of task and relations leaders. *Leadership Quarterly,* 17, 146–162.

Kelley, T., & Littman, J. (2001). *The art of innovation.* New York: Doubleday.

Kelley, T., & Littman, J. (2005). *The ten faces of innovation.* New York: Doubleday.

Kelly, R. (2010, May). Twitter study—August 2009. *PearAnalytics.* [Online]. Available: http://www.pearanalytics.com/blog/wp-content/2010/05/Twitter-Study-August-2009.pdf

Keltner, D. (2007). The power paradox. *Greatergood.* [Online]. Available: http://greatergood.berkeley.edu/article/item/power_paradox/

Keltner, D., Gruenfeld, D. H., & Anderson, C. (2003). Power, approach, and inhibition. *Psychological Review,* 110, 265–284.

Keltner, D., Van Kleef, G. A., Chen, S., & Kraus, M. W. (2008). A reciprocal influence model of social power: Emerging principles and lines of inquiries. In M. Zanna (Ed.), *Advances in experimental social psychology.* Amsterdam: Elsevier.

Kennedy, F. A., Loughry, M. L., Klammer, T. P., & Beyerlein, M. M. (2009). Effects of organizational support on potency in work teams. *Small Group Research,* 40, 72–93.

Kerber, K. W., & Buono, A. F. (2004). Leadership challenges in global virtual teams: Lessons from the field. *SAM Advanced Management Journal,* 69, 4–11.

Kerr, N., & Bruun, S. (1983). Dispensability of member effort and group motivation losses: Free-rider effects. *Journal of Personality and Social Psychology,* 44, 78–94.

Kerwin, S., Doherty, A., & Harman, A. (2011). "It's not conflict, it's differences of opinion": An in-depth examination of conflict in nonprofit boards. *Small Group Research,* 42, 562–594.

Ketrow, S. M. (1999). Nonverbal aspects of group communication. In L. R. Frey, D. S. Gouran, & M. S. Poole (Eds.), *The handbook of group communication theory and research.* Thousand Oaks, CA: Sage.

Kets de Vries, M. F. R. (2014, January 7). Is your boss a psychopath? *HBR Blog Network.* [Online]. Available: http://blogs.hbr.org/2014/01/is-your-boss-a-psychopath/

Key news audiences now blend online and traditional sources. (2008, August 17). *The Pew Research Center for the People & the Press.* [Online]. Available: http://people-press.org/report/?pageid=13538

Keyton, J., & Beck, S. J. (2010). Examining laughter functionality in jury deliberations. *Small Group Research,* 41, 386–407.

Kichuk, S. L., & Wiesner, W. H. (1998). Work teams: Selecting members for optimal performance. *Canadian Psychology,* 39, 23–32.

Kidder, R. M, Mirk, P., & Loges, W. E. (2002). Maricopa values & ethics survey. *The Institute for Global Ethics.* [Online]. Available: https://www.maricopa.edu/gvbd/vei/Values%20&%20Ethics%20Survey.pdf

Killion, A. (2004, August 16). Yet another "wake-up call" won't rouse this U.S. team. *San Jose Mercury News,* pp. 1D, 3D.

Kilmann, R., & Thomas, K. (1977). Developing a force-choice measure of conflict-handling behavior: The MODE instrument. *Educational and Psychological Measurement,* 37, 309–325.

Kinard, B., & Webster, C. (2010). The effects of advertising, social influences, and self-efficacy on adolescence tobacco use and alcohol consumption. *The Journal of Consumer Affairs,* 44, 24–43.

King, E. B., Hebl, M. R., & Beal, D. J. (2009). Conflict and cooperation in diverse workgroups. *Journal of Social Issues,* 65, 261–285.

Kirchmeyer, C. (1993). Multicultural task groups: An account of the low contribution level of minorities. *Small Group Research*, 24, 127–148.

Kirchmeyer, C., & Cohen, A. (1992). Multicultural groups: Their performance and reactions with constructive conflict. *Group and Organization Management*, 17, 153–170.

Kirka, D. (2009, July 19). Henry Allingham, world's oldest man. *San Jose Mercury News*, p. B8.

Kirkman, B. L., & Shapiro, D. L. (2000). Understanding why team members won't share: An examination of factors related to employee receptivity to team-based rewards. *Small Group Research*, 31, 175–209.

Kirkman, B., & Rosen, B. (1999). Beyond self-management: Antecedents and consequences of team empowerment. *Academy of Management Journal*, 42, 58–74.

Kirkman, B. L., Rosen, B., Tesluk, P. E., & Gibson, C. B. (2004). Team empowerment on virtual team performance: The moderating role of face-to-face interaction. *Academy of Management Journal*, 47, 175–192.

Kirn, W. (1997, October 3). Drinking to belong. *New York Times*, p. A11.

Kirsner, S. (2007, May 27). On the Web, audience size matters. *San Jose Mercury News*, pp. 1P, 6P.

Kitayama, S. (2013). Mapping mindsets: The world of cultural neuroscience. *Observor*, 26, 21–23.

Kjerulf, A. (2012, September 12). The top 5 ways not to praise people at work. *The Chief Happiness Officer*. [Online]. Available: http://positivesharing.com/2012/09/the-top-5-ways-not-to-praise-people-at-work/

Klapp, O. (1978). *Opening and closing: Strategies of information adaptation in society*. New York: Cambridge University Press.

Kleiman, C. (1991, July 28). A boost up the corporate ladder. *San Jose Mercury News*, p. 1PC.

Klein, C., DiazGranados, D., Salas, E., Le, H., Burke, C. S., & Goodwin, G. F. (2009). Does team building work? *Small Group Research*, 40, 181–222.

Klein, S. (1996). Work pressure as a determinant of work group behavior. *Small Group Research*, 27, 299–315.

Kluger, J. (2009, March 2). Why bosses tend to be blowhards. *Time*, 48.

Knutson, T. J., & Posirisuk, S. (2006). Thai relational development and rhetorical sensitivity as potential contributors to intercultural communication effectiveness. Jai Yen Yen. *Journal of Intercultural Communication Research*, 35, 205–217.

Knutson, T. J., Komolsevin, R., Chatiketu, P., & Smith, V. R. (2003). A cross-cultural comparison of Thai and U.S. American rhetorical sensitivity: Implications for intercultural communication effectiveness. *International Journal of Relations*, 27, 63–78.

Koenig, A. M., Eagly, A. H., Mitchell, A. A., & Ristikari, T. (2011). Are leader stereotypes masculine? A meta-analysis of three research paradigms. *Psychological Bulletin*, 137, 616–642.

Kohn, A. (1992). *No contest: The case against competition*. Boston: Houghton Mifflin.

Kohn, A. (1993). *Punished by rewards*. New York: Houghton Mifflin.

Kolata, G. (1999). *Flu: The story of the Great Influenza Pandemic of 1918 and the search for the virus that caused it*. New York: Farrar, Straus, & Giroux.

Kolb, J. (1997). Are we still stereotyping leadership? *Small Group Research*, 28, 370–393.

Kotter, J. P. (1990). *A force for change: How leadership differs from management*. New York: Free Press.

Kouzes, J. M., & Posner, B. Z. (2003). *Credibility: How leaders gain and lose; why people demand it*. San Francisco: Jossey-Bass.

Kozlowski, W. J., & Ilgen, D. R. (2006). Enhancing the effectiveness of work groups and teams. *Psychological Science in the Public Interest*, 7, 77–124.

Kozlowski, W. J., & Ilgen, D. R. (2007, June/July). The science of team success. *Scientific American Mind*, 54–61.

Kramer, M. W., Kuo, C. L., & Dailey, J. C. (1997). The impact of brainstorming techniques on subsequent group processes: Beyond generating ideas. *Small Group Research*, 28, 218–242.

Kraul, C. (2006, December 20). Renowned for longevity, Ecuadoran town changing. *San Jose Mercury News*, p. 16A.

Kraus, M. W., & Keltner, D. (2009). Signs of socioeconomic status. *Psychological Science*, 20, 99–106.

Krause, S., James, R., Faria, J.J., Ruxton, G. D., & Krause, J. (2011). Swarm intelligence in humans: Diversity can trump ability. *Animal Behavior*, 81, 941–948.

Krauss, R. M., Freyberg, R., & Morsella, E. (2002). Inferring speakers' physical attributes from their voices. *Journal of Experimental Social Psychology*, 38, 618–625.

Krieger, L. M. (2007, October 31). Stanford lures Harvard economist. *San Jose Mercury News*, pp. 1B, 2B.

Kruger, J., & Dunning, D. (1999). Unskilled and unaware of it: How difficulties in recognizing one's own competence lead to inflated self-assessments. *Journal of Personality and Social Psychology*, 77, 1121–1134.

Kuhn, T., & Poole, M. S. (2000). Do conflict management styles affect group decision making? Evidence from a longitudinal field study. *Human Communication Research*, 26, 558–590.

Kumar, J. (2006). Working as a designer in a global team. *Interactions*, 13, 25–26.

Kunkel, A. W., & Burleson, B. R. (2006). Revisiting the different cultures thesis: An assessment of sex differences and similarities in supportive communication. In K. Dindia & D. J. Canary (Eds.), *Sex differences and similarities in communication*. Mahwah, NJ: Lawrence Erlbaum.

Kwang, T., Crockett, E. E., Sanchez, D. T., & Swann, W. B. (2013). Men seek social standing, women seek companionship: Sex differences in deriving self-worth from relationships. *Psychological Science*, 24, 1142–1150.

LaFasto, F., & Larson, C. (2001). *When teams work best: 6,000 team members and leaders tell what it takes to succeed*. Thousand Oaks, CA: Sage.

Lamb, C. W., Hair, J. F., & McDaniel, C. (2004). *Marketing*. Mason, OH: South-Western.

Landers, A. (1995, February 25). Low income families need fire protection too. *Santa Cruz Sentinel*, p. D5.

Landrum, R. E., & Harrold, R. (2003). What employers want from psychology graduates. *Teaching of Psychology*, 30, 131–133.

Langfred, C. (1998). Is group cohesiveness a double-edged sword? *Small Group Research*, 29, 124–143.

Langlois, J. H., Kalakanis, L., Rubenstein, A. J., Larson, A., Hallam, M., & Smoot, M. (2000). Maxims and myths of beauty? A meta-analytic and theoretical review. *Psychological Review*, 126, 390–423.

Lardner, G. (1998, July 27). Violent crime stalks the workplace: A study by the Justice Department shows that there are 2 million victims each year. *The Morning Call*. [Online]. Available: http://articles.mcall.com/1998-07-27/news/3215264_1_national-crime-victimization-survey-workplace-violence-violent-crime/2

Larson, C., & LaFasto, F. (1989). *Teamwork: What must go right, what can go wrong*. Newbury Park, CA: Sage.

Larson, J. R. (2007). Deep diversity and strong synergy: Modeling the impact of variability in members' problem-solving strategies on group problem-solving performance. *Small Group Research*, 38, 413–436.

Laughlin, P. R., Hatch, E. C., Silver, J. S., & Boh, L. (2006). Groups perform better than the best individuals on letter-to-numbers problems: Effects of group size. *Journal of Personality and Social Psychology*, 90, 644–650.

Lax, D. A., & Sebenius, J. K. (1986). *The manager as negotiator: Bargaining for cooperation and competitive gain*. New York: Free Press.

Le, P. (1995, October 23). Foundations give schools a growing shot in the arm. *San Jose Mercury News*, p. 1A.

Leaders CEOs most admire. (2014). *PWC*. [Online]. Available: http://www.pwc.com/gx/en/ceo-survey/2013/key-findings/admired-leaders-leadership-attributes.jhtml

Leana, C. (1985). A partial test of Janis's groupthink model: Effects of group cohesiveness and leader behavior on defective decision making. *Journal of Management*, 11, 5–17.

Leaper, C., & Ayres, M. M. (2007). A meta-analytic review of gender variations in adults' language use: Talkativeness, affiliative speech, and assertive speech. *Personality and Social Psychology Review*, 11, 328–363.

Leavitt, H. (1964). *Managerial psychology*. Chicago: University of Chicago Press.

Lederer, R. (1990). *Crazy English: The ultimate joy ride through our language*. New York: Pocket Books.

Lee, B. (1997). *The power principle: Influence with honor*. New York: Simon & Schuster.

Lee, M. D., & Paradowski, M. J. (2007). Group decision-making on an optimal stopping problem. *The Journal of Problem Solving*, 1, 53–73.

Lee, M., & Ofshe, R. (1981). The impact of behavioral style and status characteristics on influence: A test of two competing models. *Social Psychology Quarterly*, 44, 73–82.

Legal professions: The status of women and men (2014, March 5). *Center for Research on Gender in the Professions*. [Online]. Available: http://crgp.ucsd.edu/documents/ GenderinLegalProfessionsCaseStudy.pdf

Lehmann-Willenbrock, N., Allen, J. A., & Kauffield, S. (2013). A sequential analysis of procedural meeting communication: How teams facilitate their meetings. *Journal of Applied Communication Research*, 41, 365–388.

Lenaghan, J. A., & Sengupta, K. (2007). Conflict, role balance and affect: A model of well-being of the working student. *Institute of Behavioral and Applied Management*. [Online]. Available: http://www.ibam.com/pubs/jbam/articles/ vol9/no1/JBAM_9_1_5.pdf

Lenhart, A. (2007, January 7). Social networking websites and teens. *Pew Research Center Publications*. [Online]. Available: http:// pewresearch.org/pubs/118/social-networking- websites-and-teens

Leonhardt, D. (2012, June 22). Old vs. young. *The New York Times*. [Online]. Available: http://www.nytimes.com/2012/06/24/opinion/ sunday/the-generation-gap-is-back.html? pagewanted=all&_r=0

Levin, M. (2010, July 13). It's hard out here for a snitch. *Mother Jones*. [Online]. Available: http://motherjones.com/politics/2010/07/ osha-whistleblowers-protection-retaliation

Levine, D. I. (2004, February 5). The wheels of Washington: Groupthink and Iraq. *SFGate*. [Online]. Available: http://www.sfgate.com/ cgi-bin/article.cgi?file=/c/a/2004/02/ 05EDGV34OCEP1.DTL

Levine, J., & Moreland, R. (1990). Progress in small group research. *Annual Review of Psychology*, 41, 585–634.

Levine, K., Muenchen, R., & Brooks, A. (2010). Measuring transformational and charismatic leadership: Why isn't charisma measured? *Communication Monographs*, 77, 576–586.

Levine, S. (1984, August). Radical departures. *Psychology Today*, 20–27.

Lewallen, J. (1972, April). Ecocide: Clawmarks on the yellow face. *Earth*, 36–43.

Lewin, K. (1947). Frontiers in group dynamics. *Human Relations*, 1, 5–42.

Lewin, K. (1953). Studies in group decision. In D. Cartwright & A. Zander (Eds.), *Group-Dynamics*. Evanston, IL: Row, Peterson.

Lewin, K., Lippitt, R., & White, R. (1939). Patterns of aggressive behavior in experimentally created social climates. *Journal of Social Psychology*, 10, 271–299.

Lewis, R. (1996). *When Cultures Collide: Managing Successfully Across Cultures*. London: Nicholas Brealey.

Liberto, J. (2013, April 15). CEOs earn 354 times more than average worker. *CNN Money*. [Online]. Available: http://money.cnn .com/2013/04/15/news/economy/ceo-pay- worker/

Liedtke, M. (2014, February 7). Google jumps into viedoeconferencing. *San Jose Mercury News*, p. B8.

Lipman-Blumen, J., & Leavitt, H. J. (1999). *Hot groups*. New York: Oxford University Press.

Lipman, V. (2013, June 13). New employee study shows recognition matters more than money. *Psychology Today*. [Online]. Available: http:// www.psychologytoday.com/blog/mind-the- manager/201306/new-employee-study-shows- recognition-matters-more-money

Lipnack, J., & Stamps, J. (1997). *Virtual teams: Reaching across space, time, and organizations with technology*. New York: John Wiley & Sons.

Lippincott, S. M. (1999). *Meetings: Do's, don'ts, and donuts*. Pittsburgh, PA: Lighthouse Point Press.

Liptak, K., & Acosta, J. (2013, October 22). Fmr. Obama innovation expert: HealthCare.gov created by "sloppy" contractors. *CNNPolitics*. [Online]. Avaialble: http://politicalticker.blogs. cnn.com/2013/10/22/fmr-obama-innovation- expert-healthcare-gov-created-by-sloppy- contractors/

Littlejohn, S. W., & Foss, K. A. (2011). *Theories of human communication*. Long Grove, ILL: Waveland Press.

Liu, M. (2009). The intrapersonal and interpersonal effects of anger on negotiation strategies: A cross-cultural investigation. *Human Communication Research*, 35, 148–169.

Locke, J. (1998). *The de-voicing of society: Why we don't talk to each other anymore*. New York: Simon & Schuster.

Lodewijkx, H. F., van Zomeren, M., & Syroit, J. E. M. M. (2005). The anticipation of a severe initiation: Gender differences in effects on affiliation tendency and group attraction. *Small Group Research*, 36, 237–262.

Lopez-Zafra, E., Garcia-Retamero, R., & Landa, J. M. A. (2008). The role of tranformational leadership, emotional intelligence, and group cohesiveness on leadership emergence. *Journal of Leadership Studies*, 2, 37–49.

Lowry, P. B., Roberts, T. L., Romano, N. C., Cheney, P. D., & Hightower, R. T. (2006). The impact of group size and social presence on small-group communication: Does computer-mediated communication make a difference? *Small Group Research*, 37, 631–661.

Lubman, S. (1999, October 13). Nation's response to crisis belies its devotion to detail. *San Jose Mercury News*, p. 21A.

Lulofs, R. (1994). *Conflict: From theory to action*. Scottsdale, AZ: Gorsuch Scarisbrick.

Lumsden, G., & Lumsden, D. (1993). *Communicating in groups and teams: Sharing leadership*. Belmont, CA: Wadsworth.

Luong, A., & Rogelberg, S. G. (2005). Meetings and more meetings: The relationship between meeting load and the daily well-being of employees. *Group Dynamics: Theory, Research, and Practice*, 9, 58–67.

Lurey, J. S., & Raisinghani, M. S. (2001). An empirical study of best practices in virtual teams. *Information & Management*, 38, 523–544.

Lustig, M., & Koester, J. (2003). *Intercultural competence: Interpersonal communication across cultures*. New York: Longman.

Lutgen-Sandvik, P., Tracy, S., & Alberts, J. K. (2005, February). Burned by bullying in the American workplace: A first time study of U.S. prevalence and delineation of bullying "degree." Paper presented at Western States Communication Association, San Francisco.

Lutgen-Sandvik, P., & Sypher, B. D. (2009). Workplace bullying: Causes, consequences, and corrections. In P. Lutgen-Sandvik & B. D. Sypher (Eds.), *Destructive organizational communication*. New York: Routledge.

Lykken, D. T. (1997). The American crime factory. *Psychological Inquiry*, 8, 261–270.

Lynch, J. J. (2000). *A cry unheard: New insights into the medical consequences of loneliness*. Baltimore: Bancroft Press.

MacDonald, L. (2014). What is a self-managed team? *Chron*. [Online]. Available: http://smallbusiness.chron.com/selfmanaged-team-18236.html

MacInnis, C.C., MacKinnon, S. P., & MacIntyre, P. D. (2010). The illusion of transparency and normative beliefs about anxiety during public speaking. *Current Research in Social Psychology*. [Online]. Available: http://www.uiowa.edu/~grpproc/crisp/crisp15_4.pdf

Mackin, D. (2010, June 10th). BP oil spill, the Challenger and Columbia explosions, and the deaths on Mt. Everest: Key decisions making tragedies and what we can learn from them. *New Directions* [Online]. Available: http://www.newdirectionsconsulting.com/wordpress/2010/06/bp-oil-spl..est-key-decision-making-tragedies-and-what-we-can-learn-from-them/

MacLean, P. (2011, April). Jurors gone wild. *California Lawyer*. [Online]. Available: http://www.callawyer.com/Clstory.cfm?eid=914907&wteid=914907_Jurors_Gone_Wild

MacNeil, M., & Sherif, M. (1976). Norm change over subject generations as a function of arbitrariness of prescribed norm. *Journal of Personality and Social Psychology*, 34, 762–773.

Majchrzak, A., Malhotra, A., Stamps, J., & Lipnack, J. (2004, May). Can absence make a team grow stronger? *Harvard Business Review*, pp. 131–137.

Managing virtual teams: Taking a more strategic approach. (2009). *Economist Intelligence Unit*. [Online]. Available: http://graphics.eiu.com/upload/eb/NEC_Managing_virtual_teams_WEB.pdf

Mandel, J. (2010). Social life in middle and high school: Dealing with cliques and bullies. *NYU*

Child Study Center. [Online]. Available: http://www.education.com/print/bullying-in-middle-and-high-school/

Mankins, M. (2004, September). Stop wasting valuable time. *Harvard Business Review*.

Mannix, E. A., Thompson, L. L., & Bazerman, M. H. (1989). Negotiation in small groups. *Journal of Applied Psychology*, 74, 508–517.

Mannix, E., & Neale, M. A. (2005). What differences make a difference: The promise and reality of diverse teams in organizations. *Psychological Science in the Public Interest*, 6, 31–55.

Manusov, V., & Patterson, M. L. (Eds.). (2006). *The Sage handbook of nonverbal communication*. Thousand Oaks, CA: Sage.

Marcus-Newhall, A., Miller, N., Holtz, R., & Brewer, M. B. (1993). Cross-cutting category membership in role assignment: A means of reducing intergroup bias. *British Journal of Social Psychology*, 32, 125–145.

Mariah "quote" spreads. (1999, February 21). *San Jose Mercury News* P.2A

Marino, V. (2000, November 12). It's all the rage at work, too. *Ne*, p. 2A. *New York Times*, Money & Business section, p. 2A.

Mark, D., & Willacy, M. (2011, April 1). Crews "facing 100-year battle" at Fukushima. *ABC News*. [Online]. Available at: http://www.abc.net.au/news/stories/2011/04/01/3179487.htm

Markkula, P. (2009, June 2). Decision making in inter-corporate projects: A qualitative and quantitative study of project workers in automobile research and pre-development projects in Japan and Germany. [Online]. Available: http://www.essays.se/essay/a838b1e678/

Marks, M. (1986, March). The question of quality circles. *Psychology Today*, 36–46.

Marks, M. A., Sabella, M. J., Burke, C. S., & Zaccaro, S. J. (2002). The impact of cross training on team effectiveness. *Journal of Applied Psychology*, 87, 3–13.

Markus, M. L. (1994). Finding a happy medium: Explaining the negative effects of electronic communication on social life at work. *ACM Transactions on Information Systems*, 12, 119–149.

Maroda, K. J. (2004). A relational perspective on women and power. *Psychoanalytic Psychology*, 21, 428–435.

Martell, R. F., Lane, D. M., & Emrich, C. (1996). Male-female differences: A computer simulation. *American Psychologist*, 51, 157–158.

Martin, J., & Nakayama, T. (2008). *Experiencing intercultural communication: An introduction*. New York: McGraw-Hill.

Martin, S. (2014, February 3). Status update: 10 years in, Facebook still a force. *USA Today*. [Online]. Available: http://www.usatoday.com/story/tech/2014/02/03/facebook-juggernaut/4849409/

Matsui, T., Kakuyama, T., & Onglatco, M. L. U. (1987). Effects of goals and feedback on performance on groups. *Journal of Applied Psychology*, 72, 407–415.

Maxfield, D., Grenny, J., McMillan, R., Patterson, K., & Switzler, A. (2005). Silence kills: The seven crucial conversations in healthcare. *VitalSmarts*. [Online]. Available: http://www.silencekills.com/UPDL/SilenceKillsExecSummary.pdf

Maxwell, J. C. (2001). *The 17 indisputable laws of teamwork: Embrace them and empower your team*. Nashville, TN: Thomas Nelson.

May, M. (2005, February 3). Pledge dies in hazing at Chico fraternity: House was kicked off CSU campus in 2002 for infraction. *San Francisco Chronicle*. [Online]. Available: http://sfgate.com/cgi-bin/article.cgi?f5/c/a2005/02/03/BAGIGB497T1.DTL

May, P. (2007, May 26). Governor salutes rapid repair of Maze. *San Jose Mercury News*, pp. 1B, 6B.

Mayk, V. (2010, November 29). Wilkes University professors examine use of text messaging in the college classroom. *Latest Wilkes News Archives*. [Online]. Available: http://www.wilkes.edu/pages/194.asp?item=61477

McCrae, R. R., Martin, T. A., Hrebickove, M. Urbanek, T. Willemsen, G. & Costa, P. T. (2008). Personality trait similarity between spouses in four cultures. *Journal of Personality*, 76, 1137–1163.

McDaniel, E. (1993, November). *Japanese nonverbal communication: A review and critique of literature*. Paper presented at the Annual Convention of the Speech Communication Association, Miami Beach, FL.

McEldowney, R. P., Bobrowski, P., & Gramberg, A. (2009). Factors affecting the next generation of women leaders: Mapping the challenges, antecedents, and consequences of effective leadership. *Journal of Leadership Studies*, 3, 24–30.

McFadden, C., & Whitman, J. (2014, March 10). Sheryl Sandberg launches "Ban Bossy" campaign to empower girls to lead. *ABC News*. [Online]. Available: http://abcnews.go.com/US/sheryl-sandberg-launches-ban-bossy-campaign-empower-girls/story?id=22819181

McGrath, J. E., & Hollingshead, A. B. (1994). *Groups interacting with technology: Ideas, evidence, issues, and an agenda*. Thousand Oaks, CA: Sage.

McGuinnies, E., & Ward, C. (1980). Better liked than right: Trustworthiness and expertise as factors in credibility. *Personality and Social Psychology Bulletin*, 6, 467–472.

McGuire, P. A. (1998, August). Historic conference focusing on creating a new discipline. *APA Monitor*, 29, 1–15.

McKay, M., Rogers, P., & McKay, J. (1989). *When anger hurts: Quieting the storm within*. Oakland, CA: New Harbinger.

McKenna, K. Y. A., & Green, A. S. (2002). Virtual group dynamics. *Group Dynamics: Theory, Research, and Practice*, 6, 116–127.

McKenna, K. Y. A., Green, A. S., & Gleason, M. (2002). Relationship formation on the Internet: What's the big attraction? *Journal of Social Issues*, 58, 9–31.

McLaughlin, K. (2004, December 24). Couple fulfill wish for a family many times over. *San Jose Mercury News*, pp. 1A, 19A.

McLeod, H., & Cooper, J. (1996, July 31). Politically unplugged. *San Jose Mercury News*, p. 7B.

McLeod, P. L., Lobel, S. A., & Cox, T. H. (1996). Ethnic diversity and creativity in small groups. *Small Group Research*, 27, 248–264.

McNeil, B. J., Pauker, S. G., Sox, H. C., & Tversky, A. (1982). On the elicitation of preferences for alternative therapies. *New England Journal of Medicine*, 306, 1259–1262.

McNutt, P. (1997, October/November). When strategic decisions are ignored. *Fast Company*, 17–22.

Mead, M. (1961). *Cooperation and competition among primitive peoples*. Boston: Beacon.

Medical mistakes. (2003, January 5). *San Jose Mercury News*, p. 4C.

Mehl, M., & Pennebaker, J. (2002). Mapping students' natural language use in everyday conversations. Paper presented at the third annual meeting of the Society for Personality and Social Psychology, Savannah, GA.

Melton, J. G. (1992). *Religious bodies in the United States: A directory*. New York: Garland Press.

Member FAQs. (2011). *Office of the Clerk, U.S. House of Representatives*. [Online]. Available: http://clerk.house.gov/member_info/member-faq.html

Mennecke, B. E., Valacich, J. S., & Wheeler, B. C. (2000). The effects of media and task on user performance: A test of the task-media fit hypothesis. *Group Decisions and Negotiation*, 9, 507–529.

Miceli, M. P., & Near, J. P. (1992). *Blowing the whistle: The organizational and legal implications on companies and employees*. New York: Lexington.

Michaelson, L., et al. (1989). A realistic test of individual versus group consensus decision making. *Journal of Applied Psychology*, 74, 834–839.

Milgram, S. (1974). *Obedience to authority*. New York: Harper & Row.

Miller, C. (1989). The social psychological effects of group decision rules. In P. Paulus (Ed.), *Psychology of group influence*. Hillsdale, NJ: Lawrence Erlbaum.

Miller, K., & Monge, P. (1986). Participation, satisfaction, and productivity: A meta-analytic review. *Academy of Management Journal*, 29, 727–753.

Memoli, M. A. (2014, January 24). Boehner on "Tonight Show": Shutdown was a "predictable disaster." *Los Angeles Times*. [Online]. Available: http://articles.latimes.com/2014/jan/24/news/la-pn-john-boehner-tonight-show-20140123

Missing pieces: Women and minorities on Fortune 500 boards. (2014). *Alliance for Board Diversity*. [Online]. Available: http://theabd.org/ABD_Fact_Sheet_Final.pdf

Mitchell, T. R., & Lee, T. W. (2001). The unfolding model of voluntary turnover and job embeddedness: Foundations for a comprehensive theory of attachment. In B. M. Staw & R. I. Sutton (Eds.), *Research in Organizational Behavior*. Greenwich, CT: JAI Press.

Mongeau, P. (1993, February 15). The brainstorming myth. Paper presented at the Western States Communication Association Conference, Albuquerque, NM.

Moore, D. W. (2002, May 10). Americans more accepting of female bosses than ever. *Gallup Poll News Service*. [Online]. Available: http://www.gallup.com/login/?URL_/poll/releases/pr970829a.asp

Moorhead, G., & Montanari, J. (1986). An empirical investigation of the groupthink phenomenon. *Human Relations*, 39, 399–410.

Moreland, R. L. (2010). Are dyads really groups? *Small Group Research*, 41, 251–267.

Moreland, R., & Levine, J. (1987). Group dynamics over time: Development and socialization in small groups. In J. McGrath (Ed.), *The social psychology of time*. Beverly Hills, CA: Sage.

Morello, C., & Mellnik, T. (2012, May 17). Census: Minority babies are now majority in United States. *The Washington Post*. [Online]. Available: http://www.washingtonpost.com/local/census-minority-babies-are-now-majority-in-united-states/2012/05/16/gIQA1WY8UU_story.html

Moriarty, T. (1975, April). A nation of willing victims. *Psychology Today*, 43–50.

Mortensen, M., Caya, O., & Pinsonneault, A. (2009). Virtual teams demystified: An integrative framework for understanding virtual teams and a synthesis of research. *MIT Sloan Research Paper No. 4738-09*. [Online]. Available: http://ssrn.com/abstract=1282095

Moscovici, S., & Mugny, G. (1983). Minority influence. In P. Paulus (Ed.), *Basic group processes*. New York: Springer-Verlag.

Mosvick, R. K., & Nelson, R. B. (1987). *We've got to start meeting like this!* Glenview, IL: Scott, Foresman.

Motley, M. (1995). *Overcoming your fear of public speaking: A proven method*. New York: McGraw-Hill.

Moving forward, but still behind. (1999, June 7). *Newsweek*, 32–33.

Mudrack, P., & Farrell, G. (1995). An examination of functional role behavior and its consequences for individuals in group settings. *Small Group Research*, 26, 542–571.

Mulac, A. (2006). The gender-linked language effects: Do language differences really make a difference? In K. Dindia & D. J. Canary (Eds.), *Sex differences and similarities in communication*. Mahwah, NJ: Lawrence Erlbaum.

Mulac, A., & Bradac, J. (1995). Women's style in problem solving interaction: Powerless, or simply feminine? In P. Kalbfleisch & M. Cody (Eds.), *Gender, power, and communication in human relationships*. Hillsdale, NJ: Lawrence Erlbaum.

Mullen, B., Anthony, T, Salas, E., & Driskell, J. E. (1994). Group cohesiveness and quality of decision making. *Small Group Research*, 25, 189–204.

Murnighan, J. (1978). Models of coalition formation: Game theoretic, social psychological, and political perspectives. *Psychological Bulletin*, 85, 1130–1135.

Murphy, D. (2010, October 31). Twitter: On-track for 200 million users by year's end. *PCMag.com*. [Online]. Available: http://www.pcmag.com/article2/0,2817,2371826,oo.asp

Murphy, S. (2010, August 5). Teens lead the way in shift away from email. *Tech News Daily*. [Online]. Available: http://www.technewsdaily.com/teens-lead-the-way-in-shift-away-from-email-0983/

Murphy, W. (2013, September 4). Prosecutor: "Disrespect" led to gang killings. *Long Island Newsday*. [Online]. Available: http://www.newsday.com/long-island/suffolk/prosecutor-disrespect-led-to-gang-killings-1.6013382

Muskal, M. (2013, December 13). Fraternity hazing death of New York student being investigated in Pa. *Los Angeles Times*. [Online]. Available: http://articles.latimes.com/2013/dec/13/nation/la-na-nn-fraternity-hazing-death-2013121

Mydans, S. (2008, May 11). In Singapore, a gadfly's return. *San Jose Mercury News*, p. 17A.

Myers, D. G. (2002). *Intuition: Its power and perils*. New Haven, CT: Yale University Press.

Myers, D. G. (2003). *Psychology*. New York: Worth.

Myers, D. G., & Bishop, G. D. (1970). Discussion effects on racial attitudes, *Science*, 169, 278–334.

Myers, R. A., & Brashers, D. E. (1999). Influence processes in group interaction. In L. R. Frey, D. S. Gouran, & M. S. Poole (Eds.), *The handbook of group communication theory and research*. Thousand Oaks, CA: Sage.

Myers, S. A., & Goodboy, A. K. (2005). A study of grouphate in a course on small group communication. *Psychological Reports*, 97, 381–386.

Myerson, J. (2001). *IDEO: Masters of innovation.* New York: teNeues Publishing.

Nagourney, E. (2006, May 9). Behavior: Surgical teams found lacking, in teamwork. *The New York Times*. [Online]. Available: http://www.nytimes.com/2006/05/09/health/09beha.html?_r=0

Narcisco, J., & Burkett, T. (1975). *Declare yourself.* Englewood Cliffs, NJ: Prentice Hall.

National Center for Education Statistics. (2010). *Fast Facts.* [Online]. Available: http://nces.ed.gov/fastfacts/display.asp?id=372

National Commission on the BP Deepwater Horizon Oil Spill and Offshore Drilling. (2011, January 11). Deep water: The Gulf oil disaster and the future of offshore drilling. [Online]. Available: http://www.oilspillcommission.gov/

National Geographic-Roper Public Affairs Geographic Literacy Study (2006, May). *Final Report.* [Online]. Available: http://www.nationalgeographic.com/foundation/pdf/NGSRoper2006Report.pdf

Naus, F., van Iterson, A., & Roe, R. (2007). Organizational cynicism: Extending the exit, voice, loyalty, and neglect model of employees' responses to adverse conditions in the workplace. *Human Relations*, 60, 683–718.

Neale, M., et al. (1988). *Joint effects of goal setting and expertise on negotiator behavior.* Unpublished manuscript, Northwestern University, Evanston, IL.

Neily, J., Mills, P. D., et al. (2010). Association between implementation of a medical team training program and surgical mortality, *Journal of the American Medical Association*, 304, 1693–1700.

Nelson, M. (1998). *Embracing victory: Life lessons in competition and compassion.* New York: William Morrow & Company.

Nemeth, C., Brown, K., & Rogers, J. (2001). Devil's advocate versus authentic dissent: Stimulating quantity and quality. *European Journal of Social Psychology*, 31, 707–720.

Neuliep, J. W. (2014). *Intercultural communication: A contextual approach.* Thousand Oaks, CA: Sage.

New forms of violence at work on the rise worldwide, says the ILO (2006, June 14). *Workplace Bullying Institute*. [Online]. Available: http://www.bullyinginstitute.org/bbstudies/iloepidemic.html

Newport, F., & Wilke, J. (2013, November 11). Americans still prefer a male boss. *Gallup Economy*. [Online]. Available: http://www.gallup.com/poll/165791/americans-prefer-male-boss.aspx

New survey finds doctors and nurses behaving badly. (2009, November 3). *E-releases*. [Online]. Available: http://www.ereleases.com/pr/survey-finds-doctors-nurses-behaving-badly-27864

Nezlek, J. B., Wesselmann, E. D., Wheeler, L., & Williams, K. D. (2012). Ostracism in everyday life. *Group Dynamics: Theory, Research, and Practice*, 16, 91–104.

Nickerson, R. S. (1998). Confirmation bias: A ubiquitous phenomenon in many guises. *Review of General Psychology*, 2, 175–220.

Nicotera, A. M. (1995). *Conflict and organizations: Communicative processes.* Albany: State University of New York Press.

Nicotera, A., & Rancer, A. (1994). The influence of sex on self-perception and social stereotyping of aggressive communication predispositions. *Western Journal of Communication*, 58, 283–307.

Nisbett, R., & Ross, L. (1980). *Human inference: Strategies and shortcomings of social judgment.* Englewood Cliffs, NJ: Prentice Hall.

Noller, P. (1993). Gender and emotional communication in marriage: Different cultures or differential social power? *Journal of Language and Social Psychology*, 12, 132–152.

Northouse, P. (2007). *Leadership: Theory and practice.* Thousand Oaks, CA: Sage.

Notarius, C., & Markman, H. (1993). *We can work it out: Making sense of marital conflict.* New York: G. P. Putnam's Sons.

Nurok, M., Sundt, T. M., & Frankel, A. (2011). Teamwork and communication in the operating room: Relationship to discrete outcomes and research challenges. *Anesthesiology Clinics*, 29, 1–11.

Nussbaum, B. (2004, May 17). The power of design. *Business Week*, pp. 86–94.

Nye, J. L. (2002). The eye of the follower: Information processing effects on attributions regarding leaders of small groups. *Small Group Research*, 33, 337–360.

O'Boyle, F. H., Forsyth, D. R., Banks, G. C., & McDaniel, M. A. (2012). A meta-analysis of the dark triad and work behavior: A social exchange perspective. *Journal of Applied Psychology*, 97, 557–579.

O'Brien, T. (1995, November 5). No jerks allowed. *West*, pp. 8–26.

O'Leary, K., Curley, A., & Clark, C. (1985). Assertion training for abused wives: A potentially hazardous treatment. *Journal of Marital and Family Therapy*, 11, 319–322.

Oates, J., & Cullen, D. (2005, February 9). Carly Fiorina quits. *Register*, p. 13.

Obama approval inches up, tied with Putin as leader, Quinnipiac University national poll finds. (2014, April 2). *Quinnipiac University*. [Online]. Available: http://www.quinnipiac .edu/news-and-events/quinnipiac-university-poll/national/release-detail?ReleaseID=2027

Oberg, A. (2003, August 26). From Challenger to Columbia. *San Jose Mercury News*, p. 7B.

Oertig, M., & Buegri, T. (2006). The challenges of managing cross-cultural virtual project teams. *Team Performance Management*, 12, 23–30.

Oglensky, B. D. (2008). The ambivalent dynamics of loyalty in mentorship. *Human Relations*, 61, 419–448.

Olson, L. N. (2002). "As ugly and painful as it was, it was effective": Individuals' unique assessment of communication competence during aggressive conflict episodes. *Communication Studies*, 53, 171–189.

Olympic basketball/2008 Olympics. (2008). *InsideHoops.com*. [Online]. Available: http:// www.insidehoops.com/olympics.shtml

Onishi, N. (2007, July 16). Japanese wary as they prepare to join juries. *San Jose Mercury News*, p. 8A.

Orlick, T. (1978). *Winning through cooperation: Competitive insanity, cooperative alternatives.* Washington, DC: Acropolis Books.

Orlitzky, M., & Hirokawa, R. Y. (2001). To err is human, to correct for it divine: A meta-analysis of research testing the functional theory of group decision-making effectiveness. *Small Group Research*, 32, 313–341.

Osgood, C. (1959). Suggestions for winning the real war with communism. *Journal of Conflict Resolution*, 3, 295–325.

Osgood, C. (1966). *Perspective in foreign policy.* Palo Alto, CA: Pacific Books.

Out of "Internet time." (2005, February 12). *San Jose Mercury News*, p. 6B.

Oyserman, D., Coon, H. M., & Kemmelmeier, M. (2002). Rethinking individualism and collectivism: Evaluation of theoretical assumptions and meta-analyses. *Psychological Bulletin*, 128, 3–72.

Palomares, N. A. (2008). Explaining gender-based language use: Effects of gender identity salience on references to emotion and tentative language in intra-and intergroup contexts. *Human Communication Research*, 34, 263–286.

Panteli, N. (2004). Discursive articulation of presence in virtual organizing. *Information and Organization*, 14, 59–81.

Park, H., & Antonioni, D. (2007). Personality, reciprocity, and strength of conflict resolution strategy. *Journal of Research in Personality*, 41, 110–125.

Parks, C., & Vu, A. (1994). Social dilemma of individuals from highly individualist and collectivist cultures. *Journal of Conflict Resolution*, 3, 708–718.

Pauleen, D. J., & Young, P. (2001). Relationship building and the use of ICT in boundary-crossing virtual teams: A facilitator's perspective. *Journal of Information Technology*, 16, 205–220.

Paulus, P., Dzindolet, M., Poletes, G., & Camacho, M. L. (1993). Perceptions of performance in group brainstorming: The illusion of group productivity. *Personality and Social Psychology Bulletin*, 19, 78–89.

Pavitt, C. (1999). Theorizing about the group communication-leadership relationship. In L. R. Frey, D. S. Gouran, & M. S. Poole (Eds.), *The handbook of group communication theory and research.* Thousand Oaks, CA: Sage.

Pavitt, C., & Curtis, E. (1994). *Small group discussion.* Scottsdale, AZ: Gorsuch Scarisbrick.

Pearce, C. L., & Sims, H. P. (2002). Vertical versus shared leadership as predictors of the effectiveness of change management teams: An examination of aversive, directive, transactional, transformational, and empowering leader behaviors. *Group Dynamics: Theory, Research, and Practice*, 6, 172–197.

Pearson, C. M., Andersson, L. M., & Porath, C. L. (2000). Assessing and attacking workplace incivility. *Organizational Dynamics*, 29, 123–137.

Pennington, N., & Hastie, R. (1990). Practical implications of psychological research on juror and jury decision making. *Personality and Social Psychology Bulletin*, 16, 90–115.

Perman, C. (2011, September 2). Think your boss is a psychopath? That may be true. *CNBC*. [Online]. Available: http://www.cnbc.com//id/44376401

Perrewe, P. L., Zellars, K. L., Ferris, G. R., Rossi, A. M., Kacmar, C. J., & Ralston, D. A. (2004). Neutralizing job stressors: Political skills as an antidote to the dysfunctional consequences of role conflict. *Academy of Management Journal*, 47, 141–152.

Perry, M. J. (2013, January 29). Staggering college degree gap favoring women, who have earned 9 million more college degrees than men since 1982. *AEIdeas*. [Online]. Available: http://www.aei-ideas.org/2013/01/staggering-college-degree-gap-favoring-women-who-have-earned-9-million-more-college-degrees-than-men-since-1982/

Pescosolido, A. T. (2001). Informal leaders and the development of group efficacy. *Small Group Research*, 32, 74–93.

Pettigrew, T., & Martin, J. (1987). Shaping the organizational context for black American inclusion. *Journal of Social Issues*, 43, 41–78.

Pew Research Center. (2009, June 29). Growing old in America: Expectations vs. reality. [Online]. Available: http://www.pewsocialtrends.org/files/2010/10/Getting-Old-in-America.pdf

Pfeffer, J. (2010, July 16). Why predicting organizational disasters doesn't prevent them. *BNET*. [Online]. Available: http://www.bnet.com/blog/business-psychology/why-predicting-organizational-disasters-doesn-8217t-prevent-them/201

Phillips, K. W., Liljenquist, K. A., & Neale, M. A. (2009). Is the pain worth the gain? The advantages and liabilities of agreeing with socially distinct newcomers. *Personality and Social Psychology Bulletin*, 35, 336–350.

Pickler, N. (2014, February 13). Federal guide offers tips to fend off cyberattacks. *San Jose Mercury News*, p. B8.

Piezon, S. L., & Ferree, W. D. (2008). Perceptions of social loafing in online learning groups: A study of public university and U.S. Naval War College students. *The International Review of Research in Open and Distance Learning*, 9. [Online]. Available: http://www.irrodl.org/index.php/irrodl/article/view/484/1034

Pinkley, R. L., & Northcraft, G. B. (2000). *Get paid what you're worth*. New York: St. Martin's Press.

Pitts, L. (2011, February 6). What is this thing called the Internet? *San Jose Mercury News*, p. A15.

PlaneBusiness Ron Allen airline management award. (2008, February). *PlaneBusiness*. [Online]. Available: http://www.planebusiness.com/ronallen.shtml

Plantronics study reveals how global professionals utilize new and traditional communication technologies to succeed at work. (2010, September 30). *Plantronics*. [Online]. Available: http://press.plantronics.com/us/plantronics-study-reveals-how-global-professionals-utilize-new-and-traditional-communication-technologies-to-succeed-at-work/

Platow, M. J., van Knippenberg, D., Haslam, S. A., van Knippenberg, B., & Spears, R. (2006). A special gift we bestow on you for being representative of us: Considering leader charisma from a self-categorization perspective. *British Journal of Social Psychology*, 45, 303–320.

Playing havoc with hormones. (1996, June 7). *San Jose Mercury News*, p. 14A.

Plotz, D. (1997, August 30). Al Dunlap: The chainsaw capitalist. [Online]. Available: http://www.slate.com/Assessment/97-08-30/Assessment.asp

Poliakoff, A. R. (2006, January). Closing the gap: An overview. *ASCD*. [Online]. Available: http://www.ascd.org/publications/newsletters/infobrief/jan06/num44/toc.aspx

Political bias affects brain activity, study finds. (2006, January 24). *MSNBC*. [Online]. Available: http://www.msnbc.msn.com/id/11009379/

Poll: College students feel pressure to drink. (2000, June 20). *San Jose Mercury News*, p. 9A.

Poole, M. S. (1983). Decision development in small groups III: A multiple sequence model of group decision making. *Communication Monographs*, 50, 321–341.

Poole, M. S., & Roth, J. (1989a). Decision development in small groups IV: A typology of group decision paths. *Human Communication Research*, 15, 323–356.

Poole, M. S., & Roth, J. (1989b). Decision development in small groups V: Test of a contingency model. *Human Communication Research*, 15, 549–589.

Poole, M. S., Holmes, M., Watson, R., & DeSanctic, G. (1993). Group decision support systems and group communication: A comparison of decision making in computer-supported and non-supported groups. *Communication Research*, 20, 176–213.

Poole, M. S., Seibold, D. R., & McPhee, R. D. (1996). The structuration of group decisions. In R. Hirokawa & M. S. Poole (Eds.), *Communication and group decision making*. Thousand Oaks, CA. Sage.

Postman, N. (1976). *Crazy talk, stupid talk*. New York: Dell.

Poto, J. (2010, November 7). The world of hypercompetitive graduate scholarships. *The Stanford Review*. [Online]. Available: http://stanfordreview.org/article/the-world-of-hypercompetitive-graduate-scholarships

Powell, G. N., & Graves, L. M. (2006). Gender and leadership: Perceptions and realities. In K. Dindia & D. J. Canary (Eds.), *Sex differences and similarities in communication*. Mahwah, NJ: Lawrence Erlbaum.

Prapavessis, H., & Carron, A. V. (1997). Sacrifice, cohesion, and conformity to norms in sports teams. *Group Dynamics: Theory, Research, and Practice*, 1, 231–240.

Pratkanis, A., & Aronson, E. (2001). *The age of propaganda*. New York: W. H. Freeman & Company.

Pre-employment drug tests ground almost 20% in state. (1990, May 24). *San Jose Mercury News*, p. 1A.

Preston, L. (2008). A space of our own: MySpace and feminist activism in the classroom. *Radical Teacher*, 81, 14–19.

Prothrow-Stith, D. (1991). *Deadly consequences*. New York: HarperCollins.

Provonost, P. J., & Freischlag, J. A. (2010). Improving teamwork to reduce surgical mortality. *Journal of the American Medical Association*, 304, 1721–1722.

Pruitt, D. (1981). *Negotiation behavior*. New York: Academic Press.

Pruitt, D., & Kimmel, M. (1977). Twenty years of experimental gaming: Critique, synthesis, and suggestions for the future. *Annual Review of Psychology*, 28, 363–392.

Pruitt, D., & Rubin, J. (1986). *Social conflict: Escalation, stalemate, and settlement*. New York: Random House.

Puccio, G. J., Murdock, M. C., & Mance, M. (2007). *Creative leadership: Skills that drive change*. Thousand Oaks, CA: Sage.

Put enjoyment ahead of achievement. (1994, February 20). *Santa Cruz Sentinel*, p. D2.

Putnam, L. L., (2006). Definitions and approaches to conflict and communication. In J. G. Oetzel & S. Ting-Toomey (Eds.), *The Sage handbook of conflict communication: Integrating theory, research, and practice*. Thousand Oaks, CA: Sage.

Quattrone, G., & Jones, E. (1980). The perception of variability within in-groups and out-groups: Implications for the law of small numbers. *Journal of Personality and Social Psychology*, 38, 141–152.

Raban, J. (1997, November 24). What the nanny trial tells us about transatlantic body language. *New York Times*, p. 55.

Rabbie, J. (1993). Determinants of ingroup cohesion and outgroup hostility. *International Journal of Group Tensions*, 23, 309–328.

Rad, P. F., & Levin, G. (2003). *Achieving project management success using virtual teams*. Boca Raton, FL: J. Ross Publishing.

Radosh, D. (2005, February 28). The pictures: One billion. *New Yorker*, 32.

Raghubir, P., & Valenzuela, A. (2010). Male-female dynamics in groups: A field study of The Weakest Link. *Small Group Research*, 41, 41–70.

Rahim, M. (1985). Referent role and styles of handling interpersonal conflict. *Journal of Social Psychology*, 12, 731–745.

Rahim, M. A. (2002). Toward a theory of managing organizational conflict. *International Journal of Conflict Management*, 13, 206–235.

Rains, S. A., & Turner, M. (2007). Psychological reactance and persuasive health communication: A test and extension of the intertwined model. *Human Communication Research*, 33, 241–269.

Rains, S. A., & Young, V. (2009). A meta-analysis of research on formal computer-mediated support groups: Examining group characteristics and health outcomes. *Human Communication Research*, 35, 309–336.

Rampton, S., & Stauber, J. (2001). *Trust us, we're experts*. New York: Jeremy Tarcher/Putnam.

Rasters, G., Vissers, G., & Dankbaar, B. (2002). An inside look: Rich communication through lean media in a virtual research team. *Small Group Research*, 33, 718–754.

Read, P. (1974). Source of authority and the legitimation of leadership in small groups. *Sociometry*, 37, 189–204.

Reicher, S. D., Haslam, S. A., & Platow, M. J. (2007, August/September). The new psychology of leadership. *Scientific American Mind*, 22–29.

Repanich, J. (2010, August 10). The Deepwater Horizon spill by the numbers. *Popular Mechanics*. [Online]. Available: http://www.popularmechanics.com/science/energy/coal-oil-gas/bp-oil-spill-statistics

Results of the 2010 WBI U.S. workplace bullying survey. (2010). *Workplace Bullying Institute*. [Online]. Available at: http://www.workplacebullying.org/research/WBI-NatlSurvey2010.html

Riccillo, S., & Trenholm, S. (1983). Predicting managers' choice of influence mode: The effects of interpersonal trust and worker attributions on managerial tactics in a simulated organizational setting. *Western Journal of Speech*, 47, 323–339.

Ridgeway, C. L. (1982). Status in groups: The importance of motivation. *American Sociological Review*, 47, 76–88

Rietzschel, E. F., Nijstad, B. A., & Strobe, W. (2006). Productivity is not enough: A comparison of interactive and nominal brainstorming groups on idea generation and selection. *Journal of Experimental Social Psychology*, 42, 244–251.

Rifkin, J. (2009). *The empathic civilization: The race to global consciousness in a world in crisis*. New York: Jeremy P. Tarcher/Penguin.

Riggio, R. E. (2006). Nonverbal skills and abilities. In V. Manusov & M. L. Patterson (Eds.), *The Sage handbook on nonverbal communication*. Thousand Oaks, CA: Sage.

Riggio, R. E. (2009, March 18). Leaders: Born or made? *Psychology Today*. [Online]. Available: http://www.psychologytoday.com/blog/cutting-edge-leadership/200903/leaders-born-or-made

Riggio, R. E. (2010, June 10). Are charismatic leaders born or made? *Psychology Today*. [Online]. Available: http://www.psychologytoday.com/blog/cutting-edge-leadership/201006/are-charismatic-leaders-born-or-made

Riggio, R. E., Riggio, H. R., Salinas, C., & Cole, E. J. (2003). The role of social and emotional communication skills in leader emergence and effectiveness. *Group Dynamics: Theory, Research, and Practice*, 7, 83–103.

Riley, P. (1994). *The winner within*. New York: Berkley Publishing Group.

Rinerip, M. (2005, December 14). How one suburb's black students gain. *New York Times*. [Online]. Available: http://www.nytimes.com/2005/12/14/education/14education.html.

Robbins, M. S., Alexander, J. F., & Turner, C. W. (2000). Disrupting defensive family interactions in family therapy with delinquent adolescents. *Journal of Family Psychology*, 14, 688–701.

Rocheleau, B. (2002). E-mail: Does it need to be managed? Can it be managed? *Public Administration & Management: An Interactive Journal*, 7, 83–116.

Rodriguez, D., & Solomon, D. (2005). Leadership and innovation in a networked world. *Innovations: Technology/Governance/Globalization*, 2, 3–14.

Rodriguez, R. O., Green, M. T., & Ree, M. J. (2003). Leading Generation X: Do the old rules apply? *Journal of Leadership & Organizational Studies, 9*, 67–76.

Roese, N. J., & Vohs, K. D. (2012). Hindsight bias. *Perspectives on Psychological Science, 7*, 411–426.

Rogelberg, S. G., Leach, D. J., Warr, P. B., & Burnfield, J. L. (2006). "Not another meeting!" Are meeting time demands related to employee well-being? *Journal of Applied Psychology, 91*, 83–96.

Rogelberg, S. G., Shanock, L. R., & Scott, C. W. (2012). Wasted time and money in meetings: Increasing return on investment. *Small Group Research, 43*, 236–245.

Roland, N., & Mathewson, J. (2002, September 4). Sunbeam ex-CEO "Chainsaw Al" Dunlap settles SEC case. *Bloomberg News*, p. 1.

Romero, E., & Pescosolido, A. (2008). Humor and group effectiveness. *Human Relations, 61*, 395–418.

Romig, D. (1996). *Breakthrough teamwork: Outstanding results using structured teamwork.* Chicago: Irwin Professional Publishing.

Ropeik, D. (2008, April 13). How risky is flying? *NOVA*. [Online]. Available: http://www.pbs .org/wgbh/nova/planecrash/risky.html

Rose, R. C., Suppiah, W. R. R. V, Uli, J., & Othman, J. (2007). A face concern approach to conflict management from a Malaysian perspective. *Journal of Social Sciences, 2*, 121–126.

Rosenfeld, L. (1983). Communication climate and coping mechanisms in the college classroom. *Communication Education, 32*, 169–174.

Rosenthal, N. (1997, July 15). How to prevent that "us vs. them" feeling within the family. *San Jose Mercury News*, p. 4E.

Rosin, H. (2010, July/August). The end of men. *The Atlantic*, 56–72.

Ross, L., Amabile, T., & Steinmetz, J. (1977). Social roles, social control and biases in the social perception process. *Journal of Personality and Social Psychology, 37*, 485–494.

Rossman, J. (1931). *The psychology of the inventor.* Washington, DC: Inventors' Publishing Company.

Rost, J. C. (1991). *Leadership for the twenty-first century.* New York: Praeger.

Rothwell, J. D. (2013). *In the company of others: An introduction to communication.* New York: Oxford University Press.

Rovio, E., Eskola, J., Kozub, S. A., Duda, J. L., & Lintunen, T. (2009). Can high group cohesion be harmful? A case study of a junior ice-hockey team. *Small Group Research, 40*, 421–435.

Rubenstein, M. (1975). *Patterns of problem solving.* Englewood Cliffs, NJ: Prentice Hall.

Ruggiero, V. R. (1988). *The art of thinking: A guide to critical and creative thought.* New York: Harper & Row.

Ruining it for the rest of us. (2008, December 19). *This American Life.* [Online]. Available: http:www.thisamericanlife.org/radio-archives/ episode/370/ruining-it-for-the-rest-of-us

Rusting, C. L., & Nolen-Hoeksema (1998). Regulating responses to anger: Effects of rumination and distraction on angry mood. *Journal of Personality and Social Psychology, 74*, 790–803.

Rutkowski, A-F, Saunders, C., Vogel, D., & van Genuchten, M. (2007). "Is it already 4 a.m. in your time zone?" Focus immersion and temporal dissociation in virtual teams. *Small Group Research, 38*, 98–129.

Ruvolo, C. M., Petersen, S. A., & LeBoeuf, J. N. G. (2004). Leaders are made, not born: The critical role of a developmental framework to facilitate an organizational culture of development. *Consulting Psychology Journal: Practice and Research, 56*, 10–19.

Saint, S., & Lawson, J. (1997). *Rules for reaching consensus.* San Diego: Pfeiffer.

Salas, E., Sims, D. E., & Burke, C. S. (2005). Is there a "Big Five" in teamwork? *Small Group Research, 36*, 555–599.

Salazar, A. (1995). Understanding the synergistic effects of communication in small groups. *Small Group Research, 26*, 169–199.

Samovar, L., & Porter, R. (2010). *Communication between cultures.* Belmont, CA: Wadsworth, Cengage Learning.

Sawyer, K. (2007). *Group genius: The creative power of collaboration.* New York: Basic Books.

Scandura, R. A., Von Glinow, M. A., & Lowe, K. B. (1999). When East meets West: Leadership "best practices" in the United States and the

Middle East. In W. Mobley, M. J. Gessner, & V. Arnold (Eds.), *Advances in global leadership*. Greenwich, CT: JAI.

Schachter, S. (1951). Deviation, rejection, and communication. *Journal of Abnormal and Social Psychology, 46*, 190–207.

Schei, V., & Rognes, J. K. (2005). Small group negotiation: When members differ in motivational orientation. *Small Group Research, 36*, 289–320.

Schell, A. (2010). *European business meeting culture: As ad-hoc survey of employees and managers who regularly participate in business meetings*. Munich, Germany: Schell Marketing Consulting.

Schiller, S. Z., & Mandviwalla, M. (2007). Virtual team research: An analysis of theory use and a framework for theory appropriation. *Small Group Research, 38*, 12–59.

Schimmack, U., Oishi, S., & Ciener, E. (2005). Individualism: A valid and important dimension of cultural differences between nations. *Personality and Social Psychology Review, 9*, 17–31.

Schmidt, S., & Kipnis, D. (1987, November). The perils of persistence. *Psychology Today*, 32–34.

Schrodt, P., Witt, P. L., Myers, S. A., et al. (2008). Learner empowerment and teacher evaluations as functions of teacher power use in the college classroom. *Communication Education, 57*, 180–200.

Schultz, B., Ketrow, S., & Urban, D. (1995). Improving decision quality in the small group: The reminder role. *Small Group Research, 26*, 521–541.

Schultz-Hardt, S., Brodbeck, F. C., Mojzisch, A., Kerschreiter, R., & Frey, D. (2006). Group decision making in hidden profile situations: Dissent as a facilitator for decision quality. *Journal of Personality & Social Psychology, 80*, 918–930.

Schwartz, J. (2009, March 18). As jurors turn to Web, mistrials are popping up. *The New York Times*. [Online]. Available: http://www.nytimes.com/2009/03/18/us/18juries.html?_r=1&hp=&pagewanted=print

Schwartz, S. (1990). Individualism–collectivism: Critique and proposed refinements. *Journal of Cross-Cultural Psychology, 21*, 139–157.

Seeding innovation in the water sector. (2010). *Ripple Effect*. [Online]. Available: http://www.rippleeffectglobal.com/

Segers, D. (2011, April 1). The five longest work stoppages in professional sports history. *YahooSports*. [Online]. Available at: http://sports.yahoo.com/nhl/news?slug5ycn-8170603

Sell, J., Lovaglia, M. J., Mannix, E. A., Samuelson, C. D., & Wilson, R. K. (2004). Investigating conflict, power, and status within and among groups. *Small Group Research, 35*, 44–72.

Shaffner, G. (1999). *The arithmetic of life and death*. New York: Ballantine Books.

Sharpe, R. (2000, November 20). As leaders, women rule. *Business Week*, 75–84.

Shaw, M. (1981). *Group dynamics: The psychology of small group behavior*. New York: McGraw-Hill.

Sheehy, K. (2013, January 3). Online course enrollment climbs for 10th straight year. *U.S. News & World Report*. [Online]. Available: http://www.usnews.com/education/online-education/articles/2013/01/08/online-course-enrollment-climbs-for-10th-straight-year.

Sheldon, K. M. (1999). Learning the lessons of tit-for-tat: Even competitors can get the message. *Journal of Personality and Social Psychology, 77*, 1245–1253.

Shenk, D. (1997). *Data smog: Surviving the information glut*. New York: HarperCollins.

Sherblom, J. C., Withers, L. A., & Leonard, L. G. (2009). Communication challenges and opportunities for educators using Second Life. In J. Kingsley & C. Wankel (Eds.), *Higher education in virtual worlds: Teaching and learning in Second Life*. Bingley, UK: Emerald.

Sheridan, C., & King, R. (1972). Obedience to authority with an authentic victim. *Proceedings of the 80th Annual Convention, American Psychological Association, 7*, 165–166.

Sherif, M. (1966). *In common predicament*. New York: Houghton Mifflin.

Sherif, M., et al. (1988). *The Robbers Cave Experiment*. Middletown, CT: Wesleyan University Press.

Shermer, M. (2008, February/March). Don't be evil: Enron, Google and the evolutionary psychology of corporate environments. *Scientific American Minds*, 59–65.

Shermer, M. (2013, February 1). What is skepticism, anyway? *Huffington Post*. [Online]. Available: http://www.huffingtonpost.com/michael-shermer/what-is-skepticism-anyway_b_2581917.html

Shih, C. (2010). *The Facebook era: Tapping online social networks to market, sell, and innovate.* Upper Saddle River, NJ: Prentice-Hall.

Shilling, D. (2000, September). How to find and keep top talent in today's tight labor market. *Medical Marketing & Media*, 35, 125.

Shimanoff, S. (1992). Group interaction via communication rules. In R. Cathcart & L. Samovar (Eds.), *Small group communication: A Reader.* Dubuque, IA: Wm. C. Brown & Company.

Shimanoff, S. (1980). *Communication rule: Theory and research.* Beverly Hills, CA: Sage.

Shimanoff, S., & Jenkins, M. (2003). Leadership and gender: Challenging assumptions and recognizing resources. In R. Cathcart, L. Samovar, & L. Henman (Eds.), *Small group communication: Theory and practice.* Los Angeles: Roxbury.

Shirley, D. (1997). Managing creativity: Inventing, developing, and producing innovative products. *Managing Creativity* [Online]. Available: http://www.managingcreativity.com

Shollen, S. L. (2010). The value of collaborative leadership: Leadership approach and leader emergence in virtual work groups. *International Leadership Association Conference.* [Online]. Available: http://www.ila-net.org/conferences/Program3.asp?ProgramDBID=96

Sieburg, E., & Larson, C. (1971). Dimensions of interpersonal response. Paper presented to the International Communication Association, Phoenix, AZ.

Silver, N. (2012). *The signal and the noise: Why so many predictions fail–but some don't.* New York: The Penguin Press.

Simonsen, L., Spreeuwenberg, P., Lustig, R., Taylor, R.J., et al. (2013). Global mortality estimates for the 2009 influenza pandemic from the GlaMOR Project: A modeling study. *PLOS Medicine.* [Online]. Available: http://www.plosmedicine.org/article/info%3Adoi%2F10.1371%2Fjournal.pmed.1001558

Simons, L., & Zielenziger, M. (1996, March 3). Culture clash dims U.S. future in Asia. *San Jose Mercury News*, p. 1A.

Simpson, G. G. (1994). *Alternative medicine: Expanding medical horizons; A report to the National Institutes of Health on Alternative Medical Systems.* Washington, DC: U.S. Government Printing Office.

Sims, R. (1992). Linking groupthink to unethical behavior in organizations. *Journal of Business Ethics*, 11, 651–662.

Sirota, T. (2007). Nurse/physician relationships: Improving or not? *Nursing 2007, 37*, 52–56.

Smelser, N. J., & Mitchell, F. (Eds.) (2002). *Terrorism: Perspectives from the behavioral and social sciences.* Washington, DC: National Research Council, National Academies Press.

Smith, A., & Williams, K. D. (2004). R U there? Ostracism by cell phone text messages. *Group Dynamics: Theory, Research, and Practice, 8*, 291–301.

Smith, C. (2014, February 5). (February 2014) By the numbers: 116 amazing Twitter statistics. *Digital Marketing Ramblings*. [Online]. Available: http://expandedramblings.com/index.php/march-2013-by-the-numbers-a-few-amazing-twitter-stats/

Smith-Hefner, N. (1988). Women and politeness: The Javenese example. *Language in Society*, 17, 535–554.

Smith, M. (1982). *Persuasion and human interaction: A review and critique of social influence theories.* Belmont, CA: Wadsworth.

Smith, P. (1990). *Killing the spirit: Higher education in America.* New York: Viking.

Solomon, C. (2010). The challenge of working in virtual teams: Virtual teams survey report 2010. *RW3 Culture Wizard.* [Online]. Available: http://rw3.com/VTSReportsv7.pdf

Somech, A., Desivilya, H. S, & Lidogoster, H. (2008). Team conflict management and team effectiveness: The effects of task interdependence and team identification. *Journal of Organizational Behavior*, 30, 359–378.

Sommers, S. R. (2006). On racial diversity and group decision making: Identifying multiple efffects of racial composition on jury deliberations. *Journal of Personality and Social Psychology*, 90, 597–612.

Sorensen, S. (1981, May). *Grouphate*. Paper presented at the International Communication Association, Minneapolis, MN.

Spears, L.C. (2010). Servant leadership and Robert K. Greenleaf's legacy. In D. van Dierendonck & K. Patterson (Eds.), *Servant leadership: Developments in theory and research*. New York: Palgrave Macmillan.

Spira, J. B. (2011). *Overload: How too much information is hazardous to your organization*. Hoboken, NJ: Wiley.

Spitzberg, B. H. (2000). A model of intercultural communication competence. In L. A. Samovar & R. E. Porter (Eds.), *Intercultural communication: A reader*. Belmont, CA: Wadsworth.

Spitzberg, B., & Cupach, W. (1989). *Handbook of interpersonal competence research*. New York: Springer-Verlag.

Spitzberg, B., & Hecht, M. (1984). A component model of relational competence. *Human Communication Research*, 10, 575–599.

St. Eve, A. J., & Zuckerman, M. A. (2012). Ensuring an impartial jury in the age of social media. *Duke Law & Technology Review*, 11, 1–29.

Stahel, P. F., Sabel, A. L., Victoroff, M. S., et al. (2010). Wrong-site and wrong-patient procedures in the universal protocol era: Analysis of a prospective database of physician self-reported occurrences. *Archives of Surgery*, 145, 978–984.

Stahelski, A., & Tsukada, R. (1990). Predictors of cooperation in health care teams. *Small Group Research*, 21, 220–233.

Stahl, G. K., Maznevski, M. L., Voight, A., & Jonsen, K. (2010). Unraveling the effects of cultural diversity in teams: A meta-analysis of research on multicultural work groups. *Journal of International Business Studies*, 41, 690–709.

Stajkovic, A. D., Lee, D., & Nyberg, A. J. (2009). Collective efficacy, group potency, and group performance: Meta-analysis of their relationships, and test of a mediation model. *Journal of Applied Psychology*, 94, 814–828.

Stamoulis, D., & Mannion, E. (2014). Making it to the top: Nine attributes that differentiate CEOs. *Russell Reynolds Associates*. [Online]. Available: http://www.russellreynolds.com/content/making-it-top-nine-attributes-differentiate-ceos

Stanne, M. B., Johnson, D. W., & Johnson, R. T. (1999). Does competition enhance or inhibit motor performance: A meta-analysis. *Psychological Bulletin*, 125, 133–154.

Stanovich, K. (1992). *How to think straight about psychology*. New York: HarperCollins.

Stanovich, K. E., West, R. F., & Toplak, M. E. (2013). Myside bias, rational thinking, and intelligence. *Current Directions in Psychological Science*, 22, 259–264.

Stasser, G., & Titus, W. (1987). Effects of information load and percentage of shared information during group discussion. *Journal of Personality and Social Psychology*, 53, 81–93.

Stasser, G., Vaughan, S. I., & Stewart, D. D. (2000). Pooling unshared information: The benefits of knowing how access to information is distributed among group members. *Organizational Behavior and Human Decision Processes*, 82, 102–116.

Stasson, M., & Bradshaw, S. (1995). Explanations of individual-group performance differences: What sort of bonus can be gained through group interaction? *Small Group Research*, 26, 296–308.

State anti-hazing laws. (2005, February 3). *StopHazing.org*. [Online]. Available: http://www.stophazing.org/laws.html

State anti-hazing laws. (2010). *StopHazing.org*. [Online]. Available:www.stophazing.org/laws.html

Steffens, N. K., Haslam, S. A., Ryan, M. K., & Kessler, T. (2013). Leader performance and prototypicality: The inter-relationship and impact on leaders' identity entrepreneurship. *European Journal of Social Psychology*, 10.

Stelter, B. (2010, April 4). Debunkers of fictions sift the Net. *The New York Times*. [Online]. Available: http://www.nytimes.com/2010/04/05/technology/05snopes.html?pagewanted=print

Stephens, K. K., Houser, M. L., & Cowan, R. L. (2009). R U able to meat me: The impact of students' overly casual email messages to instructors. *Communication Education*, 58, 303–326.

Stern, A. (1992, May). Why good managers approve bad ideas. *Working women*, 104.

Stewart, G. L., Courtright, S. H., & Barrick, M. R. (2012). Peer-based control in self-managing teams: Linking rational and normative influence with individual and group performance. *Journal of Applied Psychology*, 97, 435–447.

Stevens trial jurors warned after "violent outbursts." (2008, October 24). *San Jose Mercury News*, p. 3A.

Stewart, L., Cooper, P. J., Stewart, A. D., & Friedley, S. (1996). *Communication and gender*. Scottsdale, AZ: Gorsuch Scarisbrick.

Stewart, M. (2009). *The management myth: Debunking modern business philosophy*. New York: W. W. Norton & Company.

Stogdill, R. M. (1948). Personal factors associated with leadership: A survey of the literature. *Journal of Psychology*, 25, 35–71.

Stogdill, R. M. (1972). Group productivity, drive, and cohesiveness. *Organizational Behavior and Human Performance*, 8, 26–43.

Stogdill, R. M. (1974). *Handbook of leadership*. New York: Free Press.

Stone, B. (2003, October 27). Reinventing everyday life. *Newsweek*, 90–92.

Stone, D., Patton, B., & Heen, S. (1999). *Difficult conversations: How to discuss what matters most*. New York: Viking Press.

Stone, F. (1997, February). We've got to stop meeting like this. *Getting Results... for the Hands-on Manager*, 42, 5.

Stout, R. J., Salas, E., & Fowlkes, J. E. (1997). Enhancing teamwork in complex environments through team training. *Group Dynamics: Theory, Research, and Practice*, 1, 169–182.

Straub, D., & Karahanna, E. (1998). Knowledge worker communications and recipient availability: Toward a task closure explanation of media choice. *Organizational Science*, 9, 160–175.

Straus, M. A. (2007). Dominance and symmetry in partner violence by male and female university students in 32 nations. *Children & Youth Services Review*, 30, 252–275.

Straus, W., & Howe, N. (2006). *Millennials and the pop culture*. Great Falls, VA: Lifecourse Associates.

Street, M. (1997). Groupthink: An examination of theoretical issues, implications, and future research suggestions. *Small Group Research*, 28, 72–93.

Striking numbers. (2008, February 13). *Newsweek*. [Online]. Available: http://www.newsweek.com/id/110892/

Sulek, J. P. (2004a, November 8). A nod means "I agree"... or does it? *San Jose Mercury News*, pp. 1A, 9A.

Sulek, J. P. (2004b, December 14). Peterson verdict: Death. *San Jose Mercury News*, pp. 1A, 16A.

Sundell, W. (1972). *The operation of confirming and disconfirming verbal behavior in selected teacher–student interactions*. Doctoral dissertation, University of Denver.

Sundstrom, E., et al. (1990, February). Work teams: Applications and effectiveness. *American Psychologist*, 120–133.

Sunstein, C. R. (2000). Deliberative trouble? Why groups go to extremes. *Yale Law Journal*, 110, 71–119.

Sunstein, C. R. (2006). *Infotopia: How many minds produce knowledge*. New York: Oxford University Press.

Sunstein, C., & Zeckhauser, R. (2009). Overreaction to fearsome risks. In E. Michel-Kerjan and P. Slovic (Eds.), *The irrational economist: Future directions in behavioral economics and risk management*, Washington, DC: Public Affairs Press.

Sunwolf, D. R., & Frey, L. R. (2005). Facilitating group communication. In S. A. Wheelan (Ed.), *The handbook of group research and practice*. Thousand Oaks, CA: Sage.

Sunwolf, D. R., & Seibold, D. R. (1999). The impact of formal procedures on group processes, members, and task outcomes. In L. Frey (Ed.), *The handbook of group communication theory and research*. Thousand Oaks, CA: Sage.

Superhuman heroes. (1998, June 6). *Economist*, 10–12.

Surowiecki, J. (2005). *The wisdom of crowds: Why the many are smarter than the few and how collective wisdom shapes business, economics, and nations*. New York: Anchor.

Survey shows value of personal praise. (2012, November 23). *NIH Record*. [Online].

Available: http://nihrecord.od.nih.gov/newsletters/2012/11_23_2012/story5.htm

Sutton, R. (2011, October 24). A few troublesome employees can outweigh the good. *The Wall Street Journal.* [Online]. Available: http://online.wsj.com/news/articles/SB100014240529 702034997045766225503253233260

Sutton, R. I. (2002). *Weird ideas that work: Eleven-and-one-half practices for promoting, managing, and sustaining innovation.* New York: The Free Press.

Sutton, R. I., & Hargadon, A. (1996). Brainstorming groups in context: Effectiveness in a product design firm. *Administrative Science Quarterly,* 41, 685–718.

Sutton, R. M., Elder, T. J., & Douglas, K. M. (2006). Reactions to internal and external criticisms of outgroups: Social convention in the intergroup sensitivity effect. *Personality and Social Psychology Bulletin,* 32, 563–575.

Survey of CEOs regarding business transformation: Barriers to success. (2007). *EquaTerra.* [Online]. Available at: http://www.cisco.com/en/US/services/ps2961/ps2664/ent_social_software_whitepaper_services.pdf

Swift, J. S., & Huang, Y. (2004). The changing nature of international business relationships and foreign language competence. *International Journal of Management Practice,* 1, 21.

Swim, J. K., & Hyers, L. L. (1999). "Excuse me—what did you just say?": Women's public and private reactions to sexist remarks. *Journal of Experimental Social Psychology,* 35, 68–88.

Tabuchi, H., & McDonald, M. (2009, August 7). In first return to Japan court, jurors convict and sentence. *The New York Times.* [Online]. Available: http://www.nytimes.com/2009/08/07/world/asia/07japan.html?_r=1&pagewanted=print

Tang, S., & Kirkbride, P. (1986). Developing conflict management skills in Hong Kong: An analysis of some cross-cultural implications. *Management Education and Development,* 17, 287–301.

Tannen, D. (1990). *You just don't understand: Women and men in conversation.* New York: Ballantine Books.

Tannen, D. (2010, May/June). He said, she said. *Scientific American Mind,* 55–59.

Tapscott, D., & Williams, A. D. (2006). *Wikinomics: How mass collaboration changes everything.* New York: Portfolio.

Tartakovsky, M. (2013). Overcoming information overload. *Psych Central.* [Online]. Available: http://psychcentral.com/blog/archives/2013/01/21/overcoming-information-overload/

Tasa, K., & Whyte, G. (2005). Collective efficacy and vigilant problem solving in group decision making: A non-linear model. *Organizational Behavior and Human Decision Processes,* 96, 119–129.

Tauer, J. M., & Harackiewicz, J. M. (2004). The effects of cooperation and competition on intrinsic motivation and performance. *Journal of Personality and Social Psychology,* 86, 849–861.

Tavris, C. (1989). *Anger: The misunderstood emotion.* New York: Simon & Schuster.

Tavris, C. (1992). *The mismeasure of women.* New York: Simon & Schuster.

Tavris, C., & Aronson, E. (2007). *Mistakes were made (but not by me).* New York: Harcourt.

Taylor, S. (2002). *The tending instinct: How nurturing is essential for who we are and how we live.* New York: Times Books.

Teamwork characterizes surgical teams that are faster learners of new procedures. (2002, October 22). *Healthcare Review,* 15, 5.

Tefft, B. C., Williams, A. F., & Grabowski, J. G. (2012, May). Teen driver risk in relation to age and number of passengers. *AAA Foundation for Traffic Safety.* [Online]. Available: https://www.aaafoundation.org/sites/default/files/research_reports/2012TeenDriverRiskAgePassengers.pdf

Teubner, G. (2000, November 9). The emergence of control in the flattened organizational structure: Toward a theory of the spiral of control following organizational change. Paper presented at the National Communication Association conference, Seattle, WA.

The MAC scholars program: Students leading students to greater success. (2014). *Shaker Heights Schools.* [Online]. Available: http://www.shaker.org/macscholars1.aspx

The Milgram experiment (Derren Brown). 2006. *YouTube.* [Online]. Available: http://uk.youtube.com/watch?v=y6GxIuljT3w

Thomas, K. W., & Thomas, G. F. (2008). Conflict styles of men and women at six organizational levels. *International Journal of Conflict Management, 14,* 1–38.

Thomma, S. (2004, June 11). Shock jock aids demos. *San Jose Mercury News,* pp. 3A, 4A.

Thompson, L. F., & Coovert, M. D. (2003). Teamwork online: The effects of computer conferencing on perceived confusion, satisfaction, and postdiscussion accuracy. *Group Dynamics: Theory, Research, and Practice, 7,* 135–151.

Thoms, P., Pinto, J. K., Parente, D. H., & Druskat, V. U. (2002). Adaptation to self-managing work teams. *Small Group Research, 33,* 3–31.

Timmerman, C. E., & Scott, C. R. (2006). Virtually working: Communicative and structural predictors of media use and key outcomes in virtual work teams. *Communication Monographs, 73,* 108–136.

Timmerman, T. A. (2000). Racial diversity, age diversity, interdependence, and team performance. *Small Group Research, 31,* 592–606.

Ting-Toomey, S., & Chung, L. C. (2005). *Understanding intercultural communication.* Los Angeles: Roxbury.

Tjosvold, D. (1986). *Working together to get things done.* Lexington, MA: Lexington Books.

Tjosvold, D., & Yu, Z. (2004). Goal interdependence and applying abilities for team in-role and extra-role performance in China. *Group Dynamics: Theory, Research, and Practice, 8,* 98–111.

Tjosvold, D., Johnson, D. W., Johnson, R. T., & Sun, H. (2003). Can interpersonal competition be constructive within organizations? *Journal of Psychology, 137,* 63–84.

Tjosvold, D., Johnson, D. W., Johnson, R. T., & Sun, H. (2006). Competitive motives and strategies: Understanding constructive competition. *Group Dynamics: Theory, Research, and Practice, 10,* 87–99.

Tomasello, M. (2009). *Why we cooperate.* Cambridge, MA: MIT Press.

Tomasello, M., Melis, A. P., Tennie, C., Wyman, E., & Herrmann, E. (2012). Two key steps in the evolution of human cooperation: The interdependence hypothesis. *Current Anthropology, 53,* 673–692.

Top 10 skills for job candidates. (2013, April 3). *National Association of Colleges and Employers.* [Online]. Available: https://www.naceweb.org/s04032013/top-10-job-skills.aspx

Top 15 most popular social networking sites. (2014, May). *eBiz/MBA.* [Online]. Available: http://www.ebizmba.com/articles/social-networking-websites

Toulmin, S., Rieker, R., & Janik, A. (1979). *An introduction to reasoning.* New York: Macmillan.

Townsend, P. (1999b, May 23). Some students watch the "in crowd" from afar. *Santa Cruz Sentinel,* pp. A1, A8–A9.

Traffic. (2011, January 24). *Quantcast.* [Online]. Available: http://www.quantcast.com/linkedin.com#traffic

Triandis, H. C. (1995). *Individualism and collectivism.* Boulder, CO: Westview Press.

Trompenaars, F. (1994). *Riding the waves of cultures,* Burr Ridge, IL: Irwin.

Tschan, F., Semmer, N. K., Gurtner, A., Bizzari, L., Spychiger, M., Breuer, M., & Marsch, S. U. (2009). Explicit reasoning, confirmation bias, and illusory transactive memory: A simulation study of group medical decision making. *Small Group Research, 40,* 271–300.

Tubbs, S. (1984). *A systems approach to small group interaction.* Reading, MA: Addison-Wesley.

Tuckman, B. (1965). Developmental sequences in small groups. *Psychological Bulletin, 63,* 384–399.

Turman, P. D. (2003). Athletic coaching from an instructional communication perspective: The influence of coach experience on high school wrestlers' preferences and perceptions of coaching behaviors across a season. *Communication Education, 52,* 73–86.

Tutzauer, F., & Roloff, M. (1988). Communication processes leading to integrative agreements: Three paths to joint benefits. *Communication Research, 5,* 360–380.

TV or not TV. (1993, April 19). *San Jose Mercury News,* p. 5E.

Tversky, A., & Kahneman, D. (1981, June 30). The framing of decisions and the psychology of choice. *Science,* 453–458.

Tweets and threats: Gangs find new home on the Net. *The Gainesville Sun.* [Online]. Available: http://www.gainesville.com/article/20140111/WIRE/140119927?p=1&tc=pg

U.S. women in business. (2010, August 9). *Catalyst*. [Online]. Available: http://www.catalyst.org/publications/132/us-women-in-business

Uba, L., & Huang, K. (1999). *Psychology*. New York: Longman.

Unger, N. C. (2007, January 11). Pioneering women in Congress aren't guaranteed success. *San Jose Mercury News*, p. 16A.

Urban prep graduates all college-bound for fourth year in a row. (2013, March 29). *Huffington Post*. [Online]. Available: http://www.huffingtonpost.com/2013/03/29/urban-prep-graduates-all-_n_2981203.html

Ury, W. (1993). *Getting past no: Negotiating your way from confrontation to cooperation*. New York: Bantam Books.

Valacich, J. S., & Schwenk, C. (1995). Devil's advocacy and dialectical inquiry effects on face-to-face and computer-mediated group decision making. *Organizational Behavior and Human Decision Processes*, 63, 158–173.

Valacich, J., Dennis, A. R., & Connolly, T. (1994). Idea generation in computer-based groups: A new ending to an old story. *Organizational Behavior and Human Decisions Processes*, 57, 448–467.

Van de Vliert, E., Euwema, M. C., & Huismans, S. E. (1995). Managing conflict with a subordinate or a superior: Effectiveness of conglomerated behavior. *Journal of Applied Psychology*, 80, 271–281.

Van der Kleij, R., Schraagen, J. M., Werkhoven, P., & De Dreu, C. K. W. (2009). How conversations change over time in face-to-face and video-mediated communication. *Small Group Research*, 40, 355–381.

Van Engen, M. L. R., & Willemsen, T. M. (2004). Sex and leadership styles: A meta-analysis of research published in the 1990s. *Psychological Reports*, 94, 3–18.

Van Kleef, G. A. (2010). On angry leaders and agreeable followers: How leaders' emotions and followers' personalities shape motivation and team performance. *Psychological Science*, 21, 1827–1834.

Van Mierlo, H., & Kleingeld, A. (2010). Goals, strategies, and group performance: Some limits of goal setting in groups. *Small Group Research*, 41, 524–555.

Van Oostrum, J., & Rabbie, J. (1995). Intergroup competition and cooperation within autocratic and democratic management regimes. *Small Group Research*, 26, 269–295.

Van Quaquebeke, N., & Eckloff, T. (2010). Defining respectful leadership: What it is, how it can be measured, and another glimpse at what it is related to. *Journal of Business Ethics*, 91, 343–358.

Vandello, J. A., & Cohen, D. (1999). Patterns of individualism and collectivism across the United States. *Journal of Personality and Social Psychology*, 77, 279–292.

Vangelisti, A., Knapp, M., & Daly, J. (1990). Conversational narcissism. *Communication Monographs*, 57, 251–274.

VanLear, C. A., Sheehan, M., Withers, L. A., & Walker, R. A. (2005). AA online: The enactment of supportive computer mediated communication. *Western Journal of Communication*, 69, 5–27.

Varela, O. E., Burke, M. J., & Landis, R. S. (2008). A model of emergence and dysfunctional effects of emotional conflict in groups. *Group Dynamics: Theory, Research, and Practice*, 12, 112–126.

Vasilogambros, M. (2009, November 10). Two students charged with hazing. *The Times-Delphic*. [Online]. Available: http://www.timesdelphic.com/2009/11/10/two-students-charged-with-hazing

Vecchio, R. P., Bullis, R. C., & Brazil, D. M. (2006). The utility of situational leadership theory. *Small Group Research*, 37, 407–424.

Vergano, D. (2014, January 23). 1918 flu pandemic that killed 50 million originated in China, historians say. *National Geographic Daily News*. [Online]. Available: http://news.nationalgeographic.com/news/2014/01/140123-spanish-flu-1918-china-origins-pandemic-science-health/

Victor, D. A. (2007, March 27–31). What is the language of business? Affecting business outcome before you say a word. Proceedings of the Association for Business Communication, 7th Asia-Pacific Conference, City University of Hong Kong.

Virtual team building in Second Life. (2010). *PossibiliTeams*. [Online]. Available: http://www.possibiliteams.com/virtual_world_team_building.html

Vroom, V. H., & Jago, A. G. (2007). The role of the situation in leadership. *American Psychologist*, 62, 17–24.

Wald, M. L., & Schwartz, J. (2003, July 12). Shuttle probe blames managers, foam equally. *San Jose Mercury News*, p. 8A.

Wallace, P. (1999). *The psychology of the Internet*. New York: Cambridge University Press.

Walther, J. B. (1997). Group and interpersonal effects in international computer-mediated collaboration. *Human Communication Research*, 23, 342–369.

Walther, J. B., & Burgoon, J. K. (1992). Relational communication in computer-mediated communication. *Human Communication Research*, 19, 50–83.

Walumbwa, F. O., Hartnell, C. A., & Oke, A. (2010). Servant leadership, procedural justice climate, service climate, employee attitudes, and organizational citizenship: A cross-level investigation. *Journal of Applied Psychology*, 95, 517–529.

Wanous, J. (1980). *Organizational entry: Recruitment, selection, and socialization of newcomers*. Reading, MA: Addison-Wesley.

Warters, B. (2005, November). Changing patterns of roommate conflict fueled by the Net. *Conflict Management in Higher Education Report*. [Online]. Available: http://www.campus-adr.org/CMHER/ReportEvents/Edition6_1/roommates.html

Washington, J. (2009). Barriers slow black women's progress. *San Jose Mercury News*, p. 4C.

Wasserman, D. (2013). 2012 national popular vote tracker. [Online]. Available: https://docs.google.com/spreadsheet/lv?key=0AjYj9mXElO_QdHpla01oWE1jOFZRbnhJZkZpVFNKeVE&toomany=true

Watanabe, A. (2012, June 3). Japan's "lay judge" system to be revised. *Asian Correspondent*. [Online]. Available: http://asiancorrespondent.com/83631/japans-lay-judge-system-to-be-revised/

Watson, W., Michaelsen, L. K., & Sharp, W. (1991). Member competence, group interaction, and group decision making: A longitudinal study. *Journal of Applied Psychology*, 76, 803–809.

Watzlawick, P., Beavin, J. H., & Jackson, D. D. (1967). *Pragmatics of human communication*. New York: W. W. Norton.

WBI workplace bullying research—List of 33 studies by topic. (2013, February 21). *Workplace Bullying Institute*. [Online]. Available: http://www.workplacebullying.org/2013/02/21/wbi-33/

Wech, B., Mossholder, K., Streel, R., & Bennett, N. (1998). Does work group cohesiveness afflict individuals' performance and organizational commitment? *Small Group Research*, 29, 472–494.

Wechsler, H., & Wuethrich, B. (2003). *Dying to drink: Confronting binge drinking on college campuses*. New York: Rodale Books.

Wechsler, H., & Nelson, T. F. (2008). What we have learned from the Harvard School of Public Health College Alcohol Study: Focusing attention on college student alcohol consumption and the environmental conditions that promote it. *Journal of Studies on Alcohol and Drugs*, 73, 1–10.

Weick, K. (1990). The vulnerable system: An analysis of the Tenerife air disaster. *Journal of Management*, 16, 571–593.

Weingart, L. R., & Todorova, G. (2010). Jury tensions: Applying communication theories and methods to study group dynamics. *Small Group Research*, 41, 495–502.

Weisser, D. (2013, March). 2013 trends report: The state of employee engagement. *Quantum Workplace*. [Online]. Available: http://www.quantumworkplace.com/wp-content/uploads/2013/03/Resources-Whitepapers-2013-Employee-Engagement-Trends-Report.pdf

Weiss, T. (2011). The blurring border between the police and the military: A debate without foundation. *Cooperation and Conflict*, 46, 396–405.

Wellen, J. M., & Neale, M. (2006). Deviance, self-typicality, and group cohesion: The corrosive effects of the bad apples on the barrel. *Small Group Research*, 37, 165–186.

West, R., & Turner, L. H. (2014). *Introducing communication theory: Analysis and application*. New York: McGraw-Hill.

Wetzel, P. (1988). Are powerless communication strategies the Japanese norm? *Language in Society*, 17, 555–564.

Wheelan, S. A. (2009). Group size, group development, and group productivity. *Small Group Research*, 40, 247–262.

Wheelan, S. A., Davidson, B., & Tilin, F. (2003). Group development across time: Reality or illusion? *Small Group Research*, 34, 223–245.

White, A. E., Kenrick, D. T., & Neuberg, S. L. (2013). Beauty at the ballot box. *Psychological Science* [Online]. Available: http://pss.sagepub.com/content/early/2013/10/11/0956797613493642.abstract

Wikipedia statistics. (2013, June). *Wikipedia* [Online]. Available: http://stats/wikimedia.org/EN/Table/ArticlesTotal.htm

Wildschut, T., Insko, C. A., & Gaertner, L. (2002). Intragroup social influence and intergroup competition. *Journal of Personality and Social Psychology*, 82, 975–992.

Wildschut, T., Pinter, B., Vevea, J. L., Insko, C. A., & Schopler, J. (2003). Beyond the group mind: A quantitative review of the interindividual-intergroup discontinuity effect. *Psychological Bulletin*, 129, 698–722.

Williams, K. D. (2007). Ostracism: The kiss of social death. *Social and Personality Psychology Compass*, 1, 236–247.

Williams, K. D. (2011, January/February). The pain of exclusion. *Scientific American Mind*, 30–37.

Williams, K. D., & Karau, S. J. (1991). Social loafing and social compensation: The effects expectations of co-worker performance. *Journal of Personality and Social Psychology*, 61, 570–581.

Williams, K. D., & Sommer, K. L. (1997). Social ostracism by coworkers: Does rejection lead to social loafing or compensation? *Personality & Social Psychology Bulletin*, 23, 693–706.

Williams, K. D., Cheung, C. K. T., & Choi, W. (2000). Cyberostracism: Effects of being ignored over the Internet. *Journal of Personality and Social Psychology*, 79, 748–762.

Wilmot, W., & Hocker, J. (2011). *Interpersonal conflict*. New York: McGraw-Hill.

Wilson, G., & Hanna, M. (1990). *Groups in context*. New York: Random House.

Wolf, S. (1979). Behavioral style and group cohesiveness as sources of minority influence. *European Journal of Social Psychology*, 9, 381–395.

Wolkomir, R., & Wolkomir, J. (1990, February). How to make smart choices. *Reader's Digest*, 27–32.

Women CEOs of the Fortune 1000. (2014, January 15). *Catalyst*. [Online]. Available: http://www.catalyst.org/knowledge/women-ceos-fortune-1000

Women in government. (2010, October). *Catalyst*. [Online]. Available: http://www.catalyst.org/publication/244/women-in-government

Women in the Senate. (2011). *Senate.gov*. [Online]. Available: http://www.senate.gov/artandhistory/common/briefing/women_senators.htm

Women in state legislatures 2014. (2014). *Center for American Women and Politics*. [Online]. Available: http://www.cawp.rutgers.edu/fast_facts/levels_of_office/documents/stleg.pdf

Women in statewide elective executive office 2014. (2014). *Center for American Women and Politics*. [Online]. Available: http://www.cawp.rutgers.edu/fast_facts/levels_of_office/Statewide-Current.php

Women in U.S. management and labor force. (2013, December 10). *Catalyst*. [Online]. Available: http://www.catalyst.org/knowledge/women-us-management-and-labor-force

Women serving in the 113th Congress 2013-2015. (2014). *Center for American Women and Politics*. [Online]. Available: http://www.cawp.rutgers.edu/fast_facts/levels_of_office/Congress-Current.php

Wood, J. T. (2004). *Communication theories in action: An introduction*. Belmont, CA: Thomson Wadsworth.

Wood, J. T. (2015). *Gendered lives: Communication, gender, and culture*. Stamford, CT: Cengage Learning.

Wood, J., Phillips, G. M., & Pedersen, D. J. (2006). *Group discussion: A practical guide to participation and leadership*. Long Grove, ILL: Waveland Press.

Woolley, A. W., Chabris, C. F., Pentland, A., Hashmi, N., & Malone, T. W. (2010). Evidence for a collective intelligence factor in the performance of human groups. *Science*, 330, 686–688.

Wray, R. (2010, May 3). Goodbye petabytes, hello zettabytes. *Guardian.co.uk.* [Online]. Available: http://www.guardian.co.uk/technology/2010/may/03/humanity-digital-output-zettabyte/print

Wright, N. S., & Drewery, G. P. (2006). Forming cohesion in culturally heterogeneous teams: Differences in Japanese, Pacific Islander and Anglo experiences. *Cross Cultural Management, 13,* 43–53.

Wurman, R. (1989). *Information anxiety.* New York: Doubleday.

Yang, J. L. (2006, June 12). The power of number 4.6. *Fortune,* 122.

Yardley, J., Rodcriguez, M. D., Bates, S. C., & Nelson, J. (2009). True confessions? Alumni's retrospective reports on undergraduate cheating behaviors. *Ethics & Behavior, 19,* 1–14.

Young, F. (1965). *Initiation ceremonies.* New York: Bobbs-Merrill.

Young, L. J. (2008, April 9). South Korea adopts jury system. *UPI Asia Online.* [Online]. Available: http://www.upiasia.com/Society_Culture/2008/04/09/south_korea_adopts_jury_system/1409/?view=print

Yu, X. (1998). The Chinese "native" perspective on Mao-dun (conflict) and Mao-dun resolution strategies: A qualitative investigation. *Intercultural Communication Studies, 7,* 63–82.

Yukl, G. (2006). *Leadership in organizations.* Upper Saddle River, NJ: Prentice Hall.

Yurkiw, J. (2013, May 8th). Benchbook for U.S. District Court judges adds a section on e-discovery and jury instructions for jurors' use of social media and electronic devices. *Technology Law Source.* [Online]. Available: http://www.technologylawsource.com/2013/05/articles/information-technology/benchbook-for-us-district-court-judges-adds-new-section-on-ediscovery-and-jury-instructions-for-jurors-use-of-social-media-and-electronic-devices/

Zajonc, R. B. (2000). *Massacres: Mass murders in the name of moral imperatives.* Unpublished manuscript, Stanford University.

Zander, A. (1982). The psychology of removing group members and recruiting new ones. *Human Relations, 29,* 1–8.

Zenger, J., & Folkman, J. (2012, March 15). Are women better leaders than men? *Harvard Business Review Blog Network.* [Online]. Available: http://blogs.hbr.org/2012/03/a-study-in-leadership-women-do/

Zerrnike, K. (2005, January 16). Army guard gets 10 years in prison. *San Jose Mercury News,* p. 4A.

Zimbardo, P. (2007). *The Lucifer effect: Understanding how good people turn evil.* New York: Random House.

Zornoza, A., Ripoll, P., & Peiro, J. M. (2002). Conflict management in groups that work in two different communication contexts: Face-to-face and computer-mediated communication. *Small Group Research, 33,* 481–508.

Subject Index

A

Abusive behavior, 138-139, 140-141,
    155-157, 171, 202, 224, 306-307,
    321, 357, 374, 377, 390-391
Accommodation in conflict manage-
    ment, 352-353, 357-358, 365
Accountability
    individual, 94, 220-221
    leadership, 174, 178
    team, 212
Adaptability, to changing environ-
    ment, 49-60
Ad hoc groups, 217
Agendas, meeting, 280
Aggregation vs. group, 33, 34
Aggression, 320, 334, 339, 349, 353
Agreeableness, and leadership, 166
Alliances, power relationships, 324-325
Ambushing, conversational, 131-132
Analysis, and decision making, 263
Anger management, 374-378
Anxiety, 392, 406-409
Appropriateness in communication.
    See Communication Competence
Arguments, structure of, 417-418
Assertiveness, 7, 125, 176, 334-340,
    351, 353, 365-366
Asynchronous communication, 397-399
Attention, gaining and maintaining,
    409-411
Attraction, and joining groups, 74-75
Autocratic leadership style, 182, 190, 222
Autonomy as empowerment,
    214-215, 303
Avoidance of conflict, 353-354, 357.
    See Conflict Management

B

Bad apples, *See* Difficult group members
Bargaining, *See* Negotiating
BATNA (best alternative to a negoti-
    ated agreement), 373-374
Beliefs, 361

Belonging, need to, 74, 90
Bias of the fixed pie, 294
Binge drinking, 84-85
Blame, 120, 354, 355
Boundary control. *See* systems
Brainstorming, 224, 289-293
Bridging, method for integrative prob-
    lem solving, 294-296
Bullying, 320
Bypassing, 13

C

Certainty vs. provisionalism, 120, 127
Change, 11, 52, 350
    and adaptability, 52
    resistance to, 77, 267-268, 305
Charge, 206
Charisma,
Cheating, 28, 111
Cirque du Soleil, 195, 198
Claims, 286
Climate, *See* Communication climate
Cliques, 62, 73, 87-88
Closed-mindedness, 58, 252
Closedness, in systems, 56-60, 236
Coalition formation, 324-325
Coercion, 89, 90
Cohesiveness, group, 71-72, 199
    building, 72-73, 95
    and communication climate, 71-72,
        75, 77, 114-115, 116
    and conformity, 88, 157
    and groupthink, 250
Collaboration, 351-352, 356-357, 362
Collaborative interdependence, 196-198
Collective effort model, 93
Collective inferential errors, 240-246
Collectivist cultures. *See* Culture
Commitment to group, 27-28, 272
Common agreement, and meaning, 12
Communication
    context, 17, 23
    definition, 9-17
    environment, 17

myths about, 6-7; 9
as process, 11
as sharing meaning, 11-17
as transactional, 9-10, 33
See also Communication com-
    petence; Competitive climate;
    Cooperative climate;
    Defensive and Supportive com-
    munication; Verbal and nonverbal
    communication
Communication climate, 62, 72,
    105-132, 147, 222, 360
Communication Competence, 5, 7-9,
    17-32
    appropriateness, 19-20, 23-24, 31,
        306, 307, 312-313, 317, 330-331,
        339, 353-354, 358-360, 365-366,
        370-372, 391
    commitment, 27-28, 272
    and competitiveness, 113, 118-132
    definition, 9-17
    effectiveness, 7, 18-19, 31, 43,
        179-192, 195-196, 203, 204,
        205-209, 259-297, 311-312,
        356-360, 372-374, 388, 395-402
    ethics, 28-29, 32, 156, 190-191, 319
    and gender, 29-32
    and grouphate, 4
    knowledge, 7, 24-25, 26, 31, 96, 203
    and leadership, 168-169
    sensitivity, 26-27
    skill, 7, 26, 110, 168, 198, 199,
        203, 221-222, 303, 311
Competition, 10, 13, 77, 107, 108,
    303, 325, 354-355, 374. *See also*
    Constructive competition
Competitive climate, 52, 321. See also
    Defensive climate
    in conflict management, 81
    creativity and, 287
    definitions, 106, 107
    hypercompetitiveness, 106
    and group productivity, 113-114
    and group cohesiveness, 114-115
    ineffectiveness of, 273, 360
    and teams, 116